Dalits in the New Millennium

Dalits in the New Millennium interrogates the major aspects of Dalit experience in multiple spheres and traces how Dalit politics is no longer merely content with desire for social justice but has become more assertive and aspirational in its demands.

The volume represents the individual voices of the editors and contributors, who are eminent academics and activists, and situates Dalit life amidst all the major changes that have occurred over the last three decades. It aims to provide a more holistic approach to studying the community's socio-economic and political life in the new millennium and adds to the existing literature on Dalit politics, focusing especially on the changes that are taking place in the realm of electoral politics, popular culture, political economy, ideological worldview, and representation, among others.

Sudha Pai is former Professor, Centre for Political Studies, Jawaharlal Nehru University, New Delhi, and former Rector of the same university. She was National Fellow at the Indian Council of Social Science Research, New Delhi (2016–17) and Senior Fellow at the Nehru Memorial Museum and Library, New Delhi (2006–09).

D. Shyam Babu is Senior Fellow, Centre for Policy Research, New Delhi. A former journalist, he now focuses on how economic changes in India have been shaping social change and transformation for the benefit of marginalized sections, especially Dalits.

Rahul Verma is Fellow, Centre for Policy Research, New Delhi, and Visiting Assistant Professor, Department of Political Science, Ashoka University, Sonepat. He has a PhD in Political Science from the University of California, Berkeley. He is a regular columnist for various news platforms and has published papers in many academic journals.

W0018919

Dalits in the New Millennium

Edited by

Sudha Pai

D. Shyam Babu

Rahul Verma

CAMBRIDGE
UNIVERSITY PRESS

Shaftesbury Road, Cambridge CB2 8EA, United Kingdom

One Liberty Plaza, 20th Floor, New York, NY 10006, USA

477 Williamstown Road, Port Melbourne, VIC 3207, Australia

314–321, 3rd Floor, Plot 3, Splendor Forum, Jasola District Centre, New Delhi – 110025, India

103 Penang Road, #05–06/07, Visioncrest Commercial, Singapore 238467

Cambridge University Press is part of Cambridge University Press & Assessment, a department of the University of Cambridge.

We share the University's mission to contribute to society through the pursuit of education, learning and research at the highest international levels of excellence.

www.cambridge.org
Information on this title: www.cambridge.org/9781009231206

First published 2023

Printed in India by Avantika Printers Pvt. Ltd.

A catalogue record for this publication is available from the British Library

ISBN 978-1-009-23120-6 Hardback
ISBN 978-1-009-44160-5 Paperback

Contents

List of Figures		ix
List of Tables		xi
Acknowledgements		xiii

1. Introduction: Dalit Discourse in the New Millennium   1
   Sudha Pai, D. Shyam Babu, and Rahul Verma

Part I Shifting Patterns of Electoral Politics

2. Voting Patterns among Dalits since the 1990s   25
   Rahul Verma and Pranav Gupta

3. On the Peculiar Absence of Dalit Politics: Punjab and West Bengal   45
   Dwaipayan Sen

4. Decline of the Bahujan Samaj Party: Dalit Politics under
   Right-Wing Hegemony   59
   Sudha Pai

5. A Democratic Dilemma: Dalit Parties, Campaign Finance, and
   Coalition Politics   78
   Michael A. Collins

6. Why Are More Dalits Voting for the Bharatiya Janata Party since 2014?   95
   Abhinav Prakash Singh

Part II Popular Culture, Discourse, and Protest

7. Music as the Language of the Bahujan Movement: Locating the Social
   History of the Dalit Shoshit Samaj Sangharsh Samiti   115
   K. Kalyani and Satnam Singh

8. Anti-Caste Music and Cinema   133
    Prashant Ingole

9. Portrayal of Dalits in the Media: A Study of Select Newspapers from
    Uttar Pradesh   150
    Swadesh Singh

10. Hierarchy in Protest: A Comparison of Dalit and Upper-Caste
    Agitations   166
    Amit Ahuja and Rajkamal Singh

Part III   Transformations in Ideology and Identity

11. Annihilation, Identity, Representation: Kanshi Ram and the
    Conundrums of Dalit Political Agency   193
    Surinder S. Jodhka

12. Reading Caste and Class Together: A Dalit–Bahujan–Left Alliance?   210
    Dwaipayan Bhattacharyya

13. Towards Radical Democracy: The Dalit–Bahujan Claim for Political Power   232
    Harish S. Wankhede

14. Liberation Panthers and the Dalit Challenge to Hindutva in Tamil Nadu   247
    Meena Kandasamy and Hugo Gorringe

15. Dalit–Bahujan Politics: Crisis and Future   267
    Badri Narayan

Part IV   Aspirations and Anxieties

16. Technology in the Lives of Young Dalits   285
    Snigdha Poonam and Samarth Bansal

17. Dalit Middle Class: Aspirations, Networks, and Social Capital   302
    Gurram Srinivas

18. The Persisting Developmental Gap: A Case for Restitution and Reparations   316
    Amit Thorat

19. Dalit Capitalism: Adversity, Opportunity, and Agency   340
    D. Shyam Babu

Part V   Discrimination and Representation

20. Do Scheduled Caste Reservations for Political Office Improve the Lives
    of Dalits?   357
    Simon Chauchard and Francesca R. Jensenius

21. Are Dalit Legislators Performing Their Oversight Role? Evidence from
     the Question Hour in the Lok Sabha and Select State Legislatures   374
     Kaushiki Sanyal

22. Why Are Some Backward Castes Demanding Scheduled Caste
     Reservation?   394
     Arvind Kumar

23. Measuring Caste-Based Discrimination   414
     Victoire Girard, Cléo Chassonnery-Zaïgouche, and Peter Mayer

24. Dalit Suicides in India   433
     Vikas Arya, Andrew Page, Gregory Armstrong, and Peter Mayer

About the Contributors   448
Index   455

Figures

2.1 Percentage of Dalit votes for the Indian National Congress, the
Bharatiya Janata Party (BJP), and the Bahujan Samaj Party (BSP),
1996–2019   27

2.2 Bahujan Samaj Party's (BSP) vote share in Uttar Pradesh since 1989   32

2.3 Mayawati's popularity among Dalits and across social groups, 2009
and 2014   33

2.4 Profile of support for the Bharatiya Janata Party (BJP) and its allies in
the Lok Sabha elections, 2014 and 2019   35

2.5 Preference for prime minister among different caste groups, 2019   37

2.6 Caste-wise responses on benefitting from central government
schemes, 2019   38

7A.1 Poonam Bala singing during a Bahujan Samaj Party (BSP) rally   126

7A.2 Poonam Bala and Harnam Singh Bahelpuri's album *Jang Jaari Hai*   127

7A.3 Poonam Bala and Harnam Singh Behalpuri's album *Qaum Nu
Bachaun Walia*, popular during the Dalit Shoshit Samaj Sangharsh
Samiti (DS4), with Mayawati featured on the cover   127

7A.4 Albums of Harnam Singh Bahelpuri (*clockwise from top*): *Jagan da Vella*,
Dalita de Rahbar, *Kafan Chahida*, and *Damdar Shahida di Yaad*   128

7A.5 Kanshi Ram releasing an album of Harnam Singh Bahelpuri in Punjab   128

7A.6 Harnam Singh Bahelpuri playing the *tumbi*; artist on the right playing
the *algoza* (as locally known in Punjab), and artist on the left playing
the *bugatu*, a ring-like instrument with attached bells   129

7A.7 Singer and activist Ashok Kumar with Kanshi Ram in Punjab   129

7A.8 Mohan Bangar during one of his performances   130

10.1 Total number of Scheduled Caste (SC) and upper-caste (UC) protests
      and applications at Jantar Mantar, New Delhi, between January 2016
      and August 2019   174

21.1 Frequency of participation in the Question Hour by Scheduled Caste
      (SC) legislators and non-SC legislators   381

21.2 Frequency of participation in the Question Hour by gender of
      Scheduled Caste (SC) legislators and non-SC legislators   381

21.3 Frequency of participation in the Question Hour by age of Scheduled
      Caste (SC) legislators and non-SC legislators   382

21.4 Frequency of participation in the Question Hour by education level of
      Scheduled Caste (SC) legislators and non-SC legislators   382

21.5 Frequency of participation in the Question Hour by experience among
      Scheduled Caste (SC) legislators and non-SC legislators   383

23.1 Murders of members of the Scheduled Castes (SCs) and atrocity cases,
      2012   422

23.2 Untouchability practice and victims, 2012   423

23.3 Dalit murder rate in Bihar, 1977–2019   426

24.1 Dalit suicide rates in India, 2014–15   435

Tables

2.1 Dalit voting patterns in states, 2014 and 2019   28

2.2 Reserved constituencies in India and their electoral record since 2009   30

2.3 Performance of the Bahujan Samaj Party (BSP) in the Lok Sabha elections since 1989   31

2.4 The Bahujan Samaj Party's (BSP) eroding base in the Uttar Pradesh assembly elections   33

2.5 Ideological leanings of Dalit voters   40

2.6 Views across caste groups on issues raised by the Bharatiya Janata Party (BJP)   40

4.1 Budget expenditure in selected sectors by the Bahujan Samaj Party (BSP) government, 2007–12   64

9.1 News and editorials covering Dalit issues in three newspapers of Lucknow, 2016–17   156

10.1 Number and proportion of permitted protests across caste groups at Jantar Mantar, New Delhi, between January 2016 and August 2019   175

18.1 Distribution of households, land area, and average land size in India, 2003 and 2013   322

18.2 Distribution of households across land-size classifications by socio-religious groups in India, 2013   323

18.3 Gross enrolment ratio in higher education in India, 1956–2018   325

18.4 Dropout rate in education in India, 2017–18   325

18.5 Childhood morality rate by social groups in India, 2015–16 (per 1000)   326

18.6 Stunting and underweight rates for children under five years by social groups in India, 2015   326

18.7 Headcount poverty rates by social groups in India, 2004–05 and 2011–12   327

18.8 Percentage distribution of workers (UPSS) by social groups and work status in India, 2004–05 and 2017–18   329

19.1 Occupational diversity and mobility of Dalits in Uttar Pradesh, 1990 and 2007   344

21.1 Snapshot of Lok Sabha data (84 out of 545 seats reserved for Scheduled Castes [SCs]), 2018–19   377

21.2 Snapshot of Uttar Pradesh legislative assembly data (84 out of 404 seats reserved for Scheduled Castes [SCs]), 2019–20   377

21.3 Top five ministries to whom questions are targeted in the Question Hour   384

22.1 Sub-categorization of the Other Backward Classes (OBCs) by the Hukum Singh Committee   400

22.2 Traditional occupations and social status of the Most Backward Classes (MBCs)   401

22.3 Overview of the interview questionnaire   403

23.1 Correlation between police statistics and household survey answers (Pearson pairwise correlation matrix)   424

24.1 State-wise Dalit suicide rates and Dalit population percentage, 2014–15   436

24.2 Dalit suicides and social discrimination   438

24.3 Dalit suicides and human development   440

Acknowledgements

Perhaps more books have been written on Dalits than on any other social group in India, and yet our understanding of how Dalits are engaging with and in turn getting shaped by the new socio-economic and political forces remains rather vague. Dalits are unique in three aspects among the persecuted minority groups in the world: First, the social and economic subordination of Dalits goes far back into antiquity. Second, together with the tribal communities and Muslims, Dalits not only form more than 40 per cent of India's population but are found at the bottom on most development indices. Third, the sheer size of the Dalit population in India, now roughly standing at 240 million, makes it difficult for any political or policy platform to ignore the community.

In this volume, we make an attempt to document the shift in Dalit experience by focusing on the complexity (hundreds of endogamous sub-castes who speak many languages are clubbed into one group) which further accentuates multiple uncertainties regarding social and economic life that Dalits confront. These two factors – complexity and uncertainty – we suggest shape the community's social cognition in the sense of how Dalits, like any other social group, internalize certain aspects of political culture and confront them simultaneously. No community is static, and Dalits too are moving with times. Their work-participation profile, food habits, lifestyle, and modes of social and political assertion, among others, are changing. Still, so much seems to be frozen in time: celebrations over their upward mobility are marked by humiliation, and political assertions are often punctuated by everyday discrimination, humiliation, heinous cases of sexual assault, physical violence sometimes culminating in cold-blooded murder, and social boycott of the community members, among others.

The volume situates Dalit reality in the new millennium in the most holistic manner possible, broadening our horizons to interrogate the major aspects of Dalit life: political economy, popular culture, ideology and identity, public sphere, and electoral politics. All these aspects, in our opinion, are linked together in complex ways, and such an integrated approach would be immeasurably more helpful than the hitherto preferred isolationist approaches. A central argument that runs through the volume is that in the backdrop of the Bharatiya Janata Party's (BJP) ascendance to power at the national level, the Dalit movement has entered a new phase. We believe that this volume builds up on the work done in the past and advances our understanding in many ways. It has acquired a more complex character and thus necessitates revisiting many scholarly formulations theorized earlier.

To take stock of the developments since the 1990s insofar as they are concerned with Dalits, the Centre for Policy Research (CPR), New Delhi, hosted a round table of more than two dozen scholars, journalists, and activists to discuss 'the future of Dalit politics in India' in November 2019. The day-long round table was an eye-opener for many of us, and everyone echoed during the concluding session that the research agenda on this subject needs a revisit. In the backdrop of the COVID-19 pandemic, we, the editors of this volume, met on several occasions to conceptualize the research agenda and agreed to compile a comprehensive volume that situates Dalit life amidst all the major changes that have occurred over the past three decades.

We have accumulated multiple debts in the process of completing the volume. Our foremost gratitude goes to the CPR for becoming the institutional home of this project. Yamini Aiyar, the CPR president, was generous in accommodating our various request related to this project.

We also greatly value the partnership of the Rosa Luxemburg Stiftung (RLS) (Rosa Luxemburg Foundation), South Asia, for supporting this research endeavour. Stefan Mentschel and Pragya Khanna of the RLS were supportive at every stage of this project. The research grant provided by the RLS helped in hosting the round table in November 2019 at the CPR and the virtual paper-presentation workshop in December 2020.

In many ways the participants of the CPR round table in 2019 and the contributors form the intellectual backbone of this project. We sincerely thank the contributors, who weathered several personal hardships induced by the pandemic in the past two years and yet responded to our messages and queries related to this project at each stage with great urgency. Not only did these contributions make our task easier in compiling the volume, but we also hope that collectively the arguments presented here raise several sets of new inquiries.

We would also like to thank Ankita Barthwal in helping us with the logistical arrangements during the paper-presentation workshop and to Tript Kaur for editorial assistance on the first draft of the manuscript that was submitted to Cambridge University Press for peer review. This volume in many ways is better organized thanks to the suggestions and helpful reflections offered by the three reviewers.

We extend our heartfelt gratitude to Anwesha Rana at the Press for her stewardship and patience. Anwesha's regular email reminders were extremely helpful in keeping us on our toes. This volume is what it is now thanks to the tremendous effort put in by Priyanka Das and the editorial team at the Press.

Last but not least, we would like to thank everyone who shared their insights and helped shape the volume as it stands now, though they may not share all the views expressed and agree with all the arguments made here. Errors, if any, are our own.

14 April 2023   Sudha Pai
New Delhi   D. Shyam Babu
                                                                                          Rahul Verma

1

Introduction

Dalit Discourse in the New Millennium

Sudha Pai, D. Shyam Babu, and Rahul Verma

The rapid economic and political shifts that have taken place in India in the last three decades have brought about considerable change in the lives of Dalit citizens. This is not to suggest that the social pyramid has been turned upside down as Dalits continue to face discrimination on everyday basis. Some level of progress across domains, however, is amply visible. The political assertion of the 1990s has brought about change in self-perception and renewed self-confidence. Similarly, some degree of economic mobility has made at least a section of Dalits better off than they were a generation ago. There has also been a spate of academic writings on Dalit movements and politics in the recent past, which has brought 'Dalit Studies' to the mainstream. Yet the academic lens to study Dalit social and political reality has largely remained the same, rooted in the static axes of oppression and the oppressed. Through the chapters in this volume, we present a much more nuanced picture of key changes and contemporary challenges in Dalit politics beyond existing frameworks. While the immediate post-independence period has not been ignored, our focus is on the dawn of the new millennium, which not only constitutes a defining phase in Indian politics, but also in the cultural, social, and political life of Dalits. The central argument that binds this volume is that in the backdrop of the Bharatiya Janata Party's (BJP) ascendance to power at the national level, Dalit politics has acquired a more complex character which necessitates revisiting many scholarly formulations theorized earlier. We are witnessing the emergence of a new political economy; there is a need to make sense of what this means for the Dalit movement and political parties, and how they have reacted to it.

The rise of the BJP under Narendra Modi has received some serious scholarly attention. For example, Chatterji, Hansen, and Jaffrelot's (2019) edited volume addresses the construction of Hindu nationalism, the 'deep' majoritarian state, right-wing hegemony, and their impact on disadvantaged sections and minorities.

Similarly, a collection of essays edited by Vaishnav (2019) analyses the BJP's 2014 victory, its core ideological beliefs, economic policy, and impact on secularism. Scholars have also reflected on the changes in the national party system following the rise of the BJP and tried to make sense of the new India that has emerged – a good example of which being Niraja Gopal Jayal's (2019) edited volume on the 're-forming' of the nation, which has a section on Dalit politics. However, we argue that despite this proliferating literature, there has been little sustained and comprehensive effort to trace the new directions in the economic, political, and cultural life of Dalits in the new millennium. We suggest that new forms of aspirations, everyday anxieties, and occasional protests signify this multifaceted churn: rising aspirations for faster economic and sociocultural mobility, and anxiety not only against atrocities, but also frustration and disillusionment over lack of employment and opportunities, in the new polity and economy.

In the 1990s, issues of identity, social justice, dignity, and self-respect drove both mass and electoral Dalit politics. In contrast, we argue that Dalit thinking on self-identity and ideology, aspirations and mobility, discourse and protest, and their reflection and translation into politics, in the new millennium, is undergoing a fundamental change. Two significant developments underpin the transformations in Dalit politics: globalization and cultural changes. While earlier the notion of identity was central to the functioning of Dalit politics, we are witnessing a move from the desire for social justice to material advancement. The former has not disappeared, as it retains immense value for Dalits, but the latter has presently come to occupy greater centrality. Simultaneously, cultural changes amongst sections of Dalits may be linked to their desire for inclusion within the saffron fold of the BJP. While some may argue that this is merely an electoral move, the possibility of deeper underlying ideological changes needs greater exploration. These developments have created a division between a small, but influential, better-off, educated, upwardly mobile middle class, and the poorer and marginalized sections of Dalits. This class division overlaps with, and accentuates, traditional sub-caste divisions and demands for power within the community and movement or party and competition for state-provided reservation, employment, and welfare.

These identity-related and ideological shifts among Dalits, the decline of Dalit parties, and the divisions these changes have produced are reflected in politics. They have created internal fractures in the Dalit movement, leading to feelings of uncertainty and ambiguity over both ideology and political action. A shift towards the BJP is also simultaneously mirrored by strident protests against the party, providing greater evidence of these fractures. In the vacuum created by the decline of older Dalit parties, new Dalit organizations have emerged to protest against the the myriad atrocities and discrimination – the Bhim Army in Uttar Pradesh (UP) led by Chandrashekhar Azad, the Vanchit Bahujan Aghadi (VBA) in Maharashtra led by Prakash Ambedkar, and the Una Dalit Atyachar Samiti in Gujarat led by Jignesh Mevani, among others. Do these organizations represent the crisis facing Dalit politics today or do they embody new forms of regeneration following the eclipse of the older Dalit parties? Whether these leaders have the capacity to carry their mobilization forward and create a strong movement or political parties remains to be seen.

This new churn has also created greater awareness of sub-caste identities among Dalits. However, there is no pan-Indian Dalit discourse. And therefore generalization across the subcontinent is unwarranted. Dalit politics in the Hindi heartland states of UP and Bihar is different from that of Tamil Nadu, Kerala, Andhra Pradesh, or West Bengal. There have been historically marked differences between these regions in terms of ideology and movements, though Ambedkarism as a form of resistance has come to occupy centre stage across India. Such an iconic status for B. R. Ambedkar has not come overnight. He is unique in his accomplishments and continues to be a role model for many. The desecration of Ambedkar's statue anywhere is a good enough reason for the community to march together. Ambedkar has acquired a god-like status among Dalits – millions observe his birth and death anniversaries. Ambedkar's role as a champion of the community, and his advocacy that led to the creation of a 'schedule' of untouchable castes under the Government of India Act of 1935, continue to be significant pillars in a pan-India creation of a Dalit identity. Thus, even though Dalits remain divided on the basis of various regional, social, economic, and political factors, Ambedkar, having created a community, has naturally become its totem.

Drawing on the chapters in this volume about multifaceted aspects of Dalit social, economic, and political experiences, we suggest that the hallmark of Dalit politics arising out of the crisis in the new millennium is along two axes: *aspirations* and *anxieties*. These refer to rising aspirations for faster economic and sociocultural mobility, and anxieties translated through a discourse of protest not only against atrocities, but also against frustration due to joblessness and lack of improvement in material conditions. Using this frame, the chapters in this volume grapple with transformation and change in Dalit reality on multiple fronts in the new millennium - electoral politics, political economy, popular culture, ideology and identity, representation, and discrimination. The attempt is to explore Dalit reality in the new millennium in the most holistic manner possible, broadening our horizons to interrogate major aspects of Dalit experience. All these aspects, in our opinion, are linked together in complex ways, and such an integrated approach would be immeasurably more helpful than the hitherto preferred isolationist approaches.

Shifting Patterns of Electoral Politics

A central feature in the new millennium has been a marked shift in Dalit electoral politics and voting preferences. The 1990s witnessed the emergence of the Bahujan Samaj Party (BSP) in the Hindi heartland (especially in UP and adjoining border districts in other states) that was able to consolidate and gain the support of a sizeable section of Dalits. In recent years, we are witnessing the collapse of strong Dalit parties such as the BSP as a considerable section of Dalits is moving towards the BJP. But the pattern of Dalit electoral preference is not the same across the country. Although Dalits form a substantial portion of the population in Punjab, they have not moved towards the BJP and instead divided their support among the Indian National Congress (hereafter Congress), the Aam Aadmi Party (AAP), and the Akali Dal. The rise of the BJP in West Bengal, however, relies on a Dalit support base to a large extent (Verma, 2021).

It is in the Hindi heartland, particularly in UP, that a substantial section of Dalits in search of a political alternative has shifted towards the BJP since 2014, mostly from the smaller and poorer non-Jatav sub-castes. This substantial contribution of Dalit support helped the party obtain an absolute majority in 2014 and 2019 at the centre as well as in the 2017 and 2022 assembly elections in UP. There is now good evidence to suggest that a significant portion of BSP's Jatav voters have too shifted towards BJP in the 2022 assembly elections. In Rajasthan and Madhya Pradesh, following the decline of the BSP, the Congress gained a modicum of the Dalit vote. On the other hand, in states such as Andhra Pradesh and Telangana, where Dalit assertion has historically been important, it is the regional parties that have retained the support of the Dalit population. These patterns suggest that no single party can claim to have the support of Dalits.

The question of why Dalit electoral behaviour has undergone a remarkable change remains controversial. Some scholars have argued that during the campaign for the 2014 general elections, the BJP under the leadership of Modi deftly combined communal polarization, which provided the party a Hindu vote bank, and promises of rapid economic development, which attracted a large segment of the population across caste groups. Also, the use of social media to create the image of Modi as an ordinary tea seller who climbed the ladder of his political career with hard work to become the prime minister, the messiah of the poor and disadvantaged, may have attracted a segment of voters towards the BJP (Pai and Kumar, 2015). Added to this was the use of nationalism plank emanating from increased tensions with Pakistan on terrorism-related incidents as well as India's military response. These national security issues dominated the 2019 election campaign.

Another viewpoint is that while polarizing Hindutva and muscular nationalism are important, what enables Modi and the BJP to win are the pro-poor policies of the government, and the ability to identify the basic amenities that are required by needy voters, formulate appropriate schemes such as the Pradhan Mantri Awas Yojana, Saubhagya Yojana, Ujjwala, Ayushman Bharat, Jan Dhan Yojana, and more, and ensure last-mile delivery. This has been accompanied by the able marketing of these schemes, as being part of a massive welfare state (Aiyar, 2019), just before the elections. Introduced in and widely implemented after 2014, information on these schemes was disseminated through huge digital and personal outreach by BJP workers. Prior to the 2019 elections, the BJP's campaign made efforts to reach out to almost 22 crore (220 million) poor beneficiaries, including Dalits, using socio-economic census and the Aadhaar[1] database (Mehrotra, 2019). The BJP's campaign team made sure to remind these beneficiaries that the central government, headed by prime minister Modi, should be credited for these schemes.

A further explanation is that the BJP laboured for more than two decades to make itself acceptable to the community. Its 'conversion' process started slowly with embracing Ambedkar and even defending reservations (Narayan, 2021). Therefore, one may argue that before Dalits turned pro-BJP, the BJP turned pro-Ambedkar, at least in rhetoric. By using such strategies, the BJP has been attempting to spread its footprint from the Hindi heartland to the rest of the country. This aim was visible in electoral campaigns by BJP leaders including the prime minister, most notably in the 2021 elections in West Bengal, which has a substantial proportion of Dalit population. Only the future can tell how this process will unfold. Having embraced Ambedkar, will the BJP remain unaffected by his transformative ideas and philosophy? The successes of the BJP, and its strategies, aims, and ambitions in different states, are discussed by the contributions in this part.

Rahul Verma and **Pranav Gupta** use electoral and survey data to examine the reasons underlying the increasing preference for the BJP, particularly among smaller Dalit groups. Their study shows that in the 2014 and 2019 general elections, the BJP gained nearly one-fourth and one-third of Dalit votes, respectively, mostly from the upwardly mobile, urban, educated middle classes. While Verma and Gupta point out that the steep decline of the BSP, the loss of popularity of BSP leader Mayawati, and emergence of new Dalit organizations have provided room for the BJP's growing popularity, they also point out how, together with the personal popularity of Modi, it is the increasing ideological alignment between the BJP's ethno-political majoritarianism and the views of the BJP's Dalit supporters that has increased preference for the BJP among Dalit voters. Nevertheless, they acknowledge that Dalit politics is under considerable stress, throwing up assimilative and challenging tendencies; any one of these could prevail and determine the future of Dalit politics.

Based on a reading of the scholarly literature on Punjab and West Bengal, **Dwaipayan Sen** addresses an interesting puzzle: why, despite containing some of the largest Dalit populations among the states in India, has neither region given rise to explicit Dalit political assertion? The reasons suggested are multiple fissures of political–ideological preferences, lack of capable Dalit leadership; absence of an ideology that would appeal to all sections; hegemonic dominance of non-Dalit groups, and class, occupation, and caste differences. While the BSP has a modest presence in Punjab, no political formation has developed among the Namasudras or Rajbanshis, the two largest Dalit castes, in West Bengal. Yet both states have experienced different forms of cultural assertion by Dalits. Sen concludes that the presence of a large number of Dalits does not necessarily mean its translation into the political arena, but as there are shared socio-economic and political exclusions, the possibility of formation of wider, counter-hegemonic solidarities continues to exist.

Sudha Pai analyses the decline of the BSP and its impact on Dalit politics during a period of right-wing hegemony, in the context of changes in UP after 2012. These shifts are explained by using the lens of a new relationship between caste, development, and electoral politics, which has effected a move from identity politics towards material aspiration. But it has also created fragmentation: large-scale, protests against atrocities, and yet increasing electoral support by the non-Jatavs for the BJP. Arguing that a *normative and political* crisis is facing the Dalit movement, Pai holds that while older norms lack credibility, Dalits have not been able to organize resources for renewed action.

While much has been written on the rise of a Dalit middle class, aspirations for upward mobility, and entering the democratic process, there is little exploration of how Dalit parties raise funds for elections. **Michael A. Collins** attempts to fill this gap by examining the obstacles that recently launched Dalit-led parties face in mobilizing resources, organizing election campaigns, and representing Dalit interests, and shows how these challenges impact their representative capacity. Using the tools of interviews and ethnography, Collins analyses the campaign finance experiences of the Viduthalai Chiruthaigal Katchi (VCK) in Tamil Nadu and shows how first-generation Dalit politicians negotiate the dilemmas of democratic politics.

Taking these arguments forward, **Abhinav Prakash Singh** explores the factors behind the shift in Dalits' electoral preferences in favour of the BJP in the Hindi heartland. Some of the long-term reasons are the decline of Nehruvian secularism and reassertion of India's essentially Hindu character with the rise of the BJP.

The Rashtriya Swayamsevak Sangh (RSS) and its affiliate organisations in the past, too, have made efforts to attract Dalits by promising greater access to mobility, cultural capital, and political power. Yet Prakash points out that this politico-cultural relationship remains tenuous; the larger, influential, and assertive Dalit sub-castes have not come into the fold of the pro-BJP sections among the Dalit population. The sustainability and furtherance of the subaltern Hindutva project depends on providing faster economic advancement and greater political representation to larger numbers of Dalits.

Popular Culture, Discourse, and Protest

Popular culture, both historically and in present times, has played a key role in the social and political life of Dalit communities across the country. Beginning in the colonial period, when consciousness of low-caste identity arose, the discourse based on Dalit popular culture took numerous forms: songs, music, dramas, and then the celebration of Ambedkar's birthday. Over the past few decades, this culture has been increasingly expressed through the symbolization of Ambedkar beyond his role as a community leader, and more as a representation of Dalit-ness. Therefore, it is very common for educated Dalits to buy and read his writings and speeches. In fact, at most Dalit gatherings his books are on sale, and they do sell. His impeccable dress code and liberal outlook towards life make him an evergreen role model for the community. Today, the rise of social media has provided a new platform to spread his ideas to a much larger audience. Films, art, and Dalit writings have also provided an avenue of self-expression, an alternative to upper-caste thinking and beliefs. The aim of these forms of popular culture over the years is twofold: to spread the message of Ambedkar and other Dalit leaders, and to emerge as a form of protest against upper-caste domination.

In north India, particularly in UP, Dalit popular culture has spread through a process of Ambedkarization – that is, growth in the political and cultural consciousness among Dalits, particularly Chamar–Jatavs, of their low-caste status and in knowledge about the teachings of Babasaheb Ambedkar (Singh, 1998). This took one of the earliest forms during the late colonial period through the celebration of Ambedkar's birthday by the Chamar–Jatavs of Agra, who prospered due to the leather industry (Lynch, 1969). Kanshi Ram gave this form new life through his cultural organization, the Dalit Shoshit Samaj Sangharsh Samiti (DS4), using cycle rallies and *yatra* songs as a form of political-cum-cultural protest against upper-caste rule (Joshi, 1986). And Mayawati later used iconography, when she became the chief minister of UP, installing 15,000 statues of Ambedkar all over the state.

In Tamil Nadu, until the 1980s, Periyar was the only major icon among Dalits. However, there has been a growing recognition of Ambedkar as a leader and symbol. Statues, posters, and nameplates bearing Ambedkar's image have proliferated in *cheris*, schools, and colleges; Dalit organizations have fought for public space to put up cultural symbols such as flags and posters and carry out processions (Gorringe, 2005). The emergence of vibrant Dalit literature, which portrays a new feeling of confidence and fresh thinking on questions of nation, democracy, citizenship, and development, has been equally important (Satyanarayana and Tharu, 2011). Similarly, in Punjab, the Dera movement has generated new programmes and literature similar to the process of Ambedkarization in UP (Jodhka, 2010).

Of late we are witnessing the rise of a separate Dalit media to express feelings and desires – for instance, Dalit Dastak, Dalitsong.com, and Dalit Camera capture narratives, public meetings, songs, talks, and discussions on Dalit issues 'through untouchable eyes'. A rich debate has also emerged on how Dalits are, and should be, represented in Indian cinema, and more so in Bollywood where few films have depicted Dalit struggle for dignity and self-respect. However, over the last two decades, and particularly with the rise of the Dalit public sphere, cinema is being used to express Dalit cultural identity and as an agency of protest. This is truer of regional language films, a good example of which being Telugu cinema following the atrocities at Karamchedu and Chundur in the 1980s–90s (Misrah-Barak, Satyanarayana, and Thiara 2020).

Along with popular cultural expression, *protest* is also part of the Dalit discourse and requires analysis. The 1980s and 1990s witnessed mainly social protest against atrocities, driven by social conflicts when upper and backward castes found that Dalits had improved their economic position, evident in better housing and ownership of white goods, and attempted to assert dominance through arson, murder, and violence. More recently, we are witnessing increasing frequencies of protest by the community, not only against atrocities but also arising out of frustration due to joblessness and lack of improvement in material conditions. Ironically, established Dalit parties are on the margins of these protests, while new Dalit organizations are at the centre.

Arguing that music has been an important component in bringing about sociocultural–political consciousness and change among the Dalit masses, **K. Kalyani** and **Satnam Singh** throw light on the role played by the DS4 and evaluate the role of cultural resistance in the success of the early BSP movement. Discussing the musical practices, instruments, and singers of the DS4, it provides interesting ethnographic accounts, particularly of the active agency of little-known women Bahujan singers, their motivations, and their lifeworld.

Moving to popular cinema, **Prashant Ingole** shows how the re-energization of anti-caste cultural politics is introducing change in India's largest 'cultural industry'. Discussing the portrayal of the caste question, Ingole argues that mainstream cinema largely falls in the category of castelessness, while the cinema of the oppressed follows the anti-caste perspective. He points out that anti-caste political resistance is now represented through music and cinematic articulation. Juxtaposing mainstream music and cinema with alternative music and cinema by Dalits or Bahujans, he offers critical insights into the capacity of anti-caste music and cinema to create counter-cultural spaces and articulate resistance.

In the 1990s, globalization created aspirations for better jobs and salaries in the private sector among educated Dalit youth, who had so far looked to government employment alone. **Swadesh Singh** examines the process of representation of Dalits in the private sector, especially in new media. He explores the impact of such representation based on content analysis of three Hindi newspapers (Lucknow edition) and through interviews and discussions with journalists.

From varied forms of cultural assertion, we move to analysing Dalit protest, which **Amit Ahuja** and **Rajkamal Singh** argue is pure 'protest politics'. Using an event-based dataset of protest activity at Jantar Mantar in Delhi, India's most prominent designated protest site, between 2016 and 2019, they demonstrate that Dalit protest activity differs sharply from that of upper castes. Dalits are far more likely to organize caste-based protests and ally with other caste groups with their demands more likely to be hierarchy contesting, whereas upper-caste protest activity is more likely to be hierarchy preserving. Their findings suggest that caste-based protest activity is reflective of the effects of caste hierarchy; caste disparity, and not caste difference, still informs Dalit politics.

Transformations in Identity and Ideology

Identity and ideology have occupied centre stage in the consciousness of Dalits, from the colonial period and beyond. In post-independence India, the Republican Party of India (RPI) and the Dalit Panthers in the 1960s, particularly in Maharashtra, popularized the ideology of Ambedkar – drawing on Ambedkar's symbolizing of the transformative power of modern secular education and a visionary leader who understood India well. It was only in the 1990s, in the Hindi heartland, that the BSP, both as a Bahujan movement and as a party, created a new and radical identity and counter-ideology to the *varna* system, one of 'Dalit' and 'Ambedkarism', respectively (Pai, 2002).

But as studies have shown, identities are in constant flux and are being re-fashioned, with consequences for democratic politics (Hobsbawm and Ranger, 1983). Analysis of Kanshi Ram's legacy and movement suggests that Bahujan identity and consciousness did not penetrate into all sub-castes. Consequently, following the decline of the BSP in the decade of the 2010s, the break-up of the constructed identity of 'Dalit' has once again brought to the forefront the dominance of the better-off and leading section of the Jatavs, with smaller sub-castes emphasizing their separate social and cultural identities. While not completely setting aside their Dalit self-identity and ideology, large sections of the smaller sub-castes now aspire to be part of the larger Hindu identity. One of the chief instruments employed by the Hindu right in attracting these groups has been that of providing them greater cultural space within the larger Hindu identity, religion, and society and appropriating Dalit historical icons, myths, and leaders (Narayan, 2008).

The weakening of the larger identity of 'Dalit' has created ideological divisions among the community, splitting them into the Ambedkarites and the Hindutvawadis, groups close to the BSP and the BJP, respectively. The Ambedkarites are further divided on the ground, with some in western UP are looking for other options with the decline of the BSP, such as the Azad Samaj Party of Chandrashekar Azad, formed in 2015. Yet the ideas and writings of Ambedkar remain at the centre of Dalit identity and ideology as all groups claim his legacy, attempt to shape his ideas in their own conception, and ideologically appropriate him for their own political and cultural mobilization, among others. The appointment of Ram Nath Kovind, a Dalit from the smaller Kori sub-caste, as the president of India in 2015 also aided the party's efforts to make further electoral gains within the community.

In this backdrop, there are also several cases of historical divergences in ideological formulations of Dalit identity in many parts of the country. For example, a number of Dalit organizations, some of them radical in outlook, espousing both Marxism and Ambedkarism, emerged in Tamil Nadu following clashes with backward castes in parts of the state.

These ideological shifts by Dalit organizations or parties raise some seminal questions. Why do some Dalit groups perceive Hindutva as an unyielding agent of oppression, while others perceive it as a vehicle of social and economic progress? How deep is the internal fragmentation within the Dalit community over Ambedkarism and Hindutva? The contributions in this part make an attempt to capture the nuances and complexities of different dimensions of contemporary Dalit ideology.

Surinder S. Jhodka revisits the legacy of Kanshi Ram, the founder of the All India Backward and Minority Communities Employees Federation (BAMCEF) and the BSP, who visualized himself as taking Ambedkar's work forward. Jodhka argues that Ram had been the most creative and influential leader in the post-Ambedkar Dalit movement. Examining Ram's best-known work, the *Chamcha Age*, Jhodka holds that Ram disagreed with Ambedkar on foregrounding the agenda of the *Annihilation of Caste*. His idea of the *bahujan samaj* was to bring together Dalits, Other Backward Classes (OBCs), and Muslims, but it did not work on the ground. For this reason, he chose the path of *hissedari*, or power sharing, through a Bahujan identity.

Dwaipayan Bhattacharyya examines the challenges arising out of the political context in which the Dalit movement is placed, with the rise of Hindu majoritarianism. A counter-hegemonic movement is required, he argues, to bring the solidarities along caste and class lines – which in themselves and in relation to the other have been weakened – together, and to imagine a new popular force. Bhattacharyya seeks a way out of this impasse by attempting to think of a new popular solidarity, simultaneously through class and caste by bringing Marx and Marxists in dialogue with Ambedkar and Ambedkarites and exploring the immense possibilities inherent in these two ideational traditions.

Harish S. Wankhede provides insights into the ideological bases of contemporary Dalit politics by evaluating the performance of Dalit parties through the lens of liberal democracy. While Ambedkar identified Dalits as a crucial political community in the discourse of democracy, later discussions critically examine them for their failures in electoral battles or relegate them to being poor state subjects or passive claimants of social welfare. Little attempt has been made to visualize them as vanguards of radical democracy, who could govern the nation state under the Dalit–Bahujan ideology. Today, the rise of Hindutva politics has added a new challenge. Based on his analysis, Wankhede suggests that Dalits, Bahujans, and Vanchit in UP and Maharashtra, are distinct conceptual categories put forward by the deprived communities. Hoping to escape social domination and emerge as the new ruling class, they suffer from the 'trust deficit' syndrome. The political ideologies of social elites are more trusted, but similar capacity demonstrated by Dalit–Bahujan counterparts is not trusted or supported.

Arguing that much attention has been given to the emergence of Jignesh Mevani and Chandrashekhar Azad in Gujarat and UP, respectively, as exemplars of a 'new' Dalit politics, **Meena Kandasamy** and **Hugo Gorringe** point to Gail Omvedt's injunction to 'look south' as Tamil Nadu offers important lessons for Dalit politics. Accordingly, Kandsamy and Gorringe focus on the VCK, or Liberation Panther Party, and its resistance to the Hindutva project, to demonstrate that political engagement need not entail co-optation. They examine the VCK's strategies and attempts by the BJP to provide a counter to its leader, Thirumavalavan, such as organizational restructuring and appointing a Dalit as the state BJP President. In this context, they opine that the VCK has reframed current Indian politics as the struggle between right-wing forces and Ambedkarites.

Badri Narayan traces the evolution of Dalit politics and movements, beginning with Ambedkar, moving to Kanshi Ram and Mayawati's leadership of the BSP, and then to the rise of new leaders like Jignesh Mevani and Chandrashekhar Azad. Against this backdrop, he critically evaluates Dalit politics and the Dalit movement in north India – their forms and content, language and epistemology, issues, agendas, and the mobilizational politics followed by it.

Aspirations and Anxieties

While studies in recent years have focused on the rise of an Indian middle class in the context of globalization (Fernandes, 2007; Harriss, 2007; Varma, 2007), little attention has been paid to the emergence of a small but influential, educated, upwardly mobile, and politically conscious Dalit middle class. A product of state policies of protective discrimination and democratization leading to high levels of political consciousness, this new class reached a 'critical mass' precisely when the Indian polity experienced globalization moving towards a market-oriented economy.

At the same time, the impact of the rapid growth of the economy in the early 2000s has been differential. The vast majority of Dalits are poor and marginalized, remain landless, face unemployment, or relegated to working in the informal sector of the economy, and are unable to access reservations in education or employment. The census of 2011 points to considerable improvement among Dalits in areas such as literacy, urbanization, and employment among the key indicators of socio-economic progress; though rates remain well below the general population, the gap has begun to close. Even amongst this new Dalit middle class, there has been an overall stagnation in their experiences of upward mobility due to the general slowdown of the economy, as well as a barrier to entry in government jobs due to the shrinking of the government itself. This, along with the rise and accessibility of the internet as a tool for mobilization – starting with the Dalit middle class and extending more and more through local networks – has led to the Dalit experience in this new order being one of both aspiration and anxiety. While the former reflects new ways of thinking about the relationships of Dalits with the state and the economy and has sought to create

Dalit entrepreneurs, the latter has been experienced, explained, and disseminated through online spaces – with the important awareness of the challenges and opportunities offered by the internet as a 'neutral' entity.

While Dalit movements and parties like the BSP have mobilized on issues of sociopolitical empowerment such as identity, dignity, and self-respect, this new class emphasizes on the need for economic empowerment through a variety of means, such as increased reservations in higher education and equality of business opportunity through government support, amongst others. Their ideas are best reflected in the 'Dalit Agenda' formulated at the Bhopal Conference in 2002, which witnessed a debate on the effectiveness of traditional policies of reservation and state welfarism and new types of required preferential policies so that Dalits can reap the benefits of globalization, and where they forcefully argued for 'democratization' of control over 'capital' and the need for a strong Dalit business or industrial class, which could equally participate in the national economy (Babu, 2003; Pai, 2010).

The new millennium has also witnessed the establishment of the Dalit Chamber of Commerce in Mumbai in 2005 and the rise of a few Dalit millionaire industrialists and businessmen, but the latter constitute a minute fraction of the Dalit population. A study shows that as much as 40 per cent of Dalits in 2006–07, unable to obtain employment, had taken to small-scale or micro businesses in the informal sector, a form of self-employment using largely family labour, established out of necessity and being survival-driven (Deshpande and Sharma 2013). Abhijit Banerjee and Esther Dufflo (2011), in fact, describe them as *reluctant entrepreneurs*. Furthermore, the rapid decline of the economy in 2020 due to the Covid-19 pandemic, after a period of growth in the early 2000s, has hurt Dalits disproportionately (Mondal and Karmakar, 2021).

The contributions in this part analyse how Dalits have adapted to and been shaped by two fundamental forces transforming India over the past three decades: liberalization and the rise of the internet. They attempt to unpack the role of the Dalit middle class in the social, economic, and political life of the community, and in doing so they provide important insights into Dalit aspirations beyond just this class. This part also investigates whether 'Dalit capitalism' represents a mere statistically insignificant number of entrepreneurs or is a phenomenon indicative of radical transformation amongst the community.

Snigdha Poonam and **Samarth Bansal** examine how the internet has introduced tremendous change in the lives of young Dalits in the new millennium. While a majority of India's 200 million Dalits have limited access to mainstream technologies, these are increasingly central to the lives of those who do. Young Dalits are using the internet in greater numbers every day: asserting identities, expressing views, finding communities, organizing protests, and so on. These are usual online activities for internet users belonging to any caste. But for young Dalits, many of them are often fraught with tensions, risks, and threats that define their physical worlds; the freedoms offered to them by the internet can be conditional. Asserting caste pride online can result in real-life vengeance, trying to find love can be frustrating, the support mobilized for a cause can be fleeting, and many voices remain unheard. The inequalities are not limited to the internet alone. Dalits continue to face discrimination in tech education and jobs in India as well as abroad.

Against rising aspirations in the new millennium, **Gurram Srinivas** traces the transition from 'Dalits in the middle class' to a 'Dalit middle class', which he conceptualizes as a distinct segment within the larger Indian middle class and the Dalit population. Its miniscule size points to limited socio-economic transformation and slow mobility among Dalits. But over the last two decades, this class has spread into smaller towns and across marginalized sub-castes. Limited educational and employment opportunities are pushing them towards opportunities in the private sector and into entrepreneurship. Surveying extant scholarship on the aspirations, networking, and social capital this class carries, Srinivas suggests that while it undergoes marginalization during mobility, it is a source of inspiration and leadership to the community.

Amit Thorat takes a historic and data-driven view to analyse the reduced yet persisting gap between Dalits and the general category. Using this lens, Thorat examines existing evidence about the conditions of the ex-untouchables as *enslaved* in the ancient, medieval, and colonial period; measures the quantum and nature of the gap that persist between Dalits and others in various spheres of well-being today; and considers evidence of people's mindsets and prejudices that reflect continuing belief in the inherent inequality of human beings, arising out of the caste system. In conclusion, Thorat calls for reparations through acceptance of the practice of enslavement and untouchability, an unconditional apology for the same, and a reparation commission to find ways of correcting historic denials.

D. Shyam Babu analyses the Dalit quest for upward mobility through the path of 'Dalit capitalism', tracing its roots to the Bhopal Conference, which broached it *as an addition to* reservations, in an emerging market economy. Using Thomas Marshall's three-dimensional concept of citizenship – civil, political, and social – Babu argues that, in India, Dalit social citizenship, which for Ambedkar was 'fraternity', remains the weakest. While civil and political aspects of the citizenship can be obtained through the state's fiat, social citizenship requires recognition by non-Dalits. As Dalit labour is devalued, and jobs through reservations discredited as meritless, can a few thousand Dalit entrepreneurs, who made it big without any props, play a positive role in transforming societal attitudes and encourage fellow Dalits to adopt entrepreneurship as another pathway for mobility and empowerment?

Discrimination and Representation

We move to issues of reservation, discrimination, and atrocities that are of seminal importance for Dalits. While the context has undergone change, representation and reservation for Dalits are under strain and discrimination persists. The new millennium has witnessed the reopening of old debates such as whether reserved constituencies have provided adequate representation to Dalits, whether Dalits elected on reserved seats participate in legislative debates and policymaking, and about increasing demands for expanding reservations to more lower-caste groups, who feel left out, entering into the mainstream. Another issue that deserves greater attention is the growing instances of suicides among Dalits. With rising aspirations and new demands by upwardly mobile groups, these are difficult challenges before the state.

In one of the first assessments of the working of reserved seats, Marc Galanter (1979) observed that Scheduled Caste (SC) representatives had, quietly yet effectively, helped shape policies in committees, resulting in the adoption of several developmental policies to benefit the community; subsequent decades have also witnessed the revamping of the Untouchability Offence Act, 1955, into the Protection of Civil Rights Act, 1955, as well as the enactment of the Scheduled Castes and Scheduled Tribes (Prevention of Atrocities) Act, 1989. A recent study by Francesca Jensenius (2017) also shows that reservation has helped create a new, Dalit political elite class, which is integrated with the rest of society, and has helped reduce caste bias over the long run.

At the same time, recent policies by the BJP government have 'transformed' the reservation system, impacting Dalits. The decline in public-sector employment has resulted in a steady decrease in the number of jobs reserved for SCs; the creation of lateral entry in the Indian administration has diluted the quota system; and the introduction of a 10 per cent quota in 2019 for economically weaker sections (EWS) has altered the standard definition of backwardness as the upper castes too have been granted educational and job quotas. How the EWS quota may adversely affect Dalits or the OBCs remain understudied though.

With increasing pressure on reservations, we are also witnessing increasing demands by lower OBCs for inclusion into the SC category, particularly from UP, Rajasthan, Jharkhand, and West Bengal. Such demands represent the emergence of a strong desire for upward mobility and improvement in economic status, through education, employment, and welfare, on the part of the smaller OBC groups.

Despite the Scheduled Castes and Scheduled Tribes (Prevention of Atrocities) Act, 1989, discrimination and atrocities have increased in the past few years, taking new forms such as lynching due to cow vigilantism, and the rape and murder of Dalit women. In the last decade, crimes against Dalits have risen (Sadanandan, 2018), while conviction rates remain abysmally low. Similarly, crimes against Dalit women, including incidents of horrific gang rapes in recent years, have gone up. Infamous examples include the Hathras, Balrampur, Mahoba, and Unnao incidents, in which most women were teenagers and were killed in many cases.

A related issue which gained prominence with Rohith Vemula's case in the University of Hyderabad in 2016 is that of suicide by Dalit students, but it still remains an under-researched area. Suicides in the general population in India have been steadily rising, with the 2014 National Crime Records Bureau (NCRB) data indicating that Scheduled Tribes (STs) and Dalits make up the highest percentages of suicides (Tiwary, 2017). A perusal of media reports suggests that reasons for suicide by Dalit students are harassment and ill-treatment by peers and administrators, as in the case of Payal Tadvi in 2019, or due to high standards set for them by teachers and administrators that are often measured against their suggested entry through reservations (Patel and Kumar, 2021).

The contributions in this part also shed light on the effect of SC politicians both in the realms of policymaking and community empowerment. As most SC politicians get elected from seats reserved for the community, it becomes pertinent to investigate the effect of these reservation policies, especially in the light of newer groups demanding inclusion in the SC category. Despite the positive changes highlighted in many chapters in this volume, Dalits continue to bear the brunt of their lower status in the caste hierarchy.

Francesca Jensenius and **Simon Chauchard** provide an overview of what we know about the effects of SC reservations in the Indian parliament, state legislatures, and local-level elected bodies to date. They detail the literature on this subject and look at four types of outcomes that have been studied empirically in the Indian context in recent years: (*a*) political and electoral outcomes, (*b*) material or developmental outcomes such as the provision of public goods, (*c*) state–citizen relations such as access to bureaucracy and police, and (*d*) Dalits' relations with non-Dalits. Overall, recent empirical research on SC quotas paints a nuanced picture: reservations have played an important – though perhaps disappointingly limited – role in improving the lives of Dalits.

How effective are Dalit legislators in their oversight role? **Kaushiki Sanyal** sheds light on this question by analysing Question Hour data from the Lok Sabha and the UP Legislative Assembly, quantitatively and qualitatively.

The investigation finds that SC legislators, especially those who are young, female, and less experienced, do lag behind their non-SC counterparts in their frequency of participation. However, they do ask questions that are hard-hitting as well as span a wide variety of ministries, showing that their interests have broadened into other areas, thus partly fulfilling one of the purposes of reservation – that is, the mainstreaming of Dalits.

Arvind Kumar examines the reasons for increasing requests among the most backward castes (MBCs) for SC reservation. Kumar begins by analysing the stigma associated with untouchability, lists castes and *jatis* belonging to the MBC communities, discusses how the MBC category came into existence, focuses on the MBC *jatis* in UP, and then shows the causative factors behind these demands. He then argues that the MBCs' demand rests on the expectation of material advancement and political empowerment, and that inclusion or exclusion from the SC list has multiple, contextual, and historical determining factors.

How can we best measure inter-caste tension and discrimination in India? **Victoire Girard**, **Cléo Chassonnery-Zaïgouche**, and **Peter Mayer** highlight that Dalit murders, or household survey responses regarding untouchability practices, provide consistent proxies of inter-group tensions across Indian states. A case study of Bihar allows the scholars to show that historically Dalit murder rates reflect the experience of Dalits at moments of mobilization for asserting their rights. In contrast, they highlight the limitations of using statistics compiled under the Scheduled Castes and Scheduled Tribes (Prevention of Atrocities) and the Protection of Civil Rights Acts, which aim at combating caste-based discrimination but are affected by both the discrimination and empowerment of Dalits.

On the incidence of Dalit suicides in India, **Vikas Arya**, **Andrew Page**, **Gregory Armstrong**, and **Peter Mayer** reflect on how there is a severe lack of caste- and religion-segregated suicide data, and the relationship between caste and suicides has received little attention. Further, they argue that more research needs to be conducted on the phenomenon of 'copy-cat suicides' in the country, while showing how higher educational levels among Dalits lead to higher suicide rates. Finally, they argue for more social, policy, and media sensitivity in preventing Dalit suicides, a complex phenomenon shaped by psychological, socio-economic, and cultural factors.

Concluding Observations

The chapters in this volume have addressed the transformations that have taken place in the socio-economic and political life of Dalits in the new millennium. Politics is the arena where change is most ostensible and visible following the decline of Dalit parties, the weakening of the Dalit movement, and the rise of the BJP. As many of our contributions illustrate, this has altered the context in which Dalit politics has operated over the last few decades. Its manifestations are evident in other arenas as well – in debates on historical legacies and present-day changes in identity and ideology, which are shaping Dalit thinking, ideas, and activism. The discourse on caste distinctions and hierarchy gets reflected in everyday practices, literature, and arts to condition people to think and act in a predictable manner. It is ironical that in the post-Ambedkar era, the cognitive link has been ignored and Ambedkar's stress on education has been reduced to a mere slogan, as in 'educate, organize, and agitate'. If the identity of Dalits as (former) untouchables is the source of their perceived inferior status, the same identity is used as the basis for emancipating them. A part of the trouble is unavoidable insofar as the government's policies and programmes are concerned. But India's approaches to ending untouchability and discrimination have not even been informed by the cognitive burden of identity. At the same time, liberalization and the rise of a private sector have created an aspirational class among the educated youth seeking employment and opportunities in the economy. The chapters also illustrate how the lives of the younger generation of Dalits are being shaped through access to information technology, the use of social media, music and cinema of cultural resistance, and the discourse of protest politics. There remain troubling areas of concern such as discrimination, atrocities, demands for reservation and better representation, and, in more recent years, suicides among Dalit youth.

These rapid changes in the past two decades have created an urgency to adopt a new approach and enter into new areas of research. The chapters presented in this volume are born out of an effort to make sense of this evolving reality. An expansive volume like ours carries many differing individual voices reflecting diverse backgrounds of our contributors. Nevertheless, the one common inquiry that animates this discussion is the space available for Dalit identity in the new millennium. While no single characterization of this identity is possible, experiences of liminality and deprivation exert a powerful influence in shaping it. With this volume, we have attempted to provide a blueprint for those who would wish to study this shifting paradigm.

Note

1. Each resident of India and non-resident Indian passport holder is given a 12-digit unique identification number (UID) called 'Aadhaar' (which, in Hindi, means 'foundation', 'basis', or 'proof') by the government in the context of the Aadhaar (Targeted Delivery of Financial and Other Subsidies, Benefits, and Services) Act, 2016. However, it has transformed into a national identification and authentication system.

Bibliography

Aiyar, Y. 2019. 'Modi Consolidates Power: Leveraging Welfare Politics'. *Journal of Democracy* 30(4): 78–88.

Ambedkar, B. R. 1936. *Annihilation of Caste*. Bombay: Self-published.

Babu, D. S. 2003. 'Dalits and the New Economic Order: Some Prognostications and Prescriptions from the Bhopal Conference'. RGICS Working Paper Series 44, October, Rajiv Gandhi Institute for Contemporary Studies, New Delhi.

Banerjee, A., and E. Dufflo. 2011. *Poor Economics: Rethinking Poverty & the Ways to End It*. New Delhi: Penguin.

Chatterji, A. P., T. B. Hansen, and C. Jaffrelot (eds.). 2019. 'Majoritarian State: How Hindu Nationalism Is Changing India'. London. Hurst Publishers.

Deshpande, A., and S. Sharma. 2013. 'Can Dalit Capitalism Be a Vehicle for Social Mobility in India?' *Mint*, 23 September. http://www.livemint.com/Opinion/DwEs4I3fddUBwBViuxMNZI/Can-Dalit-capitalism-be-a-vehicle-for-social-mobility-in-Ind.html. Accessed on 11 October 2022.

Fernandes, L. 2007. *India's New Middle Class: Democratic Politics in an Era of Economic Reform*. New Delhi: Oxford University Press.

Galanter, M. 1979. 'Compensatory Discrimination in Political Representation: A Preliminary Assessment of India's Thirty-Year Experience with Reserved Seats in Legislatures'. *Economic and Political Weekly* 14 (7–8): 437–54.

Gorringe, H. 2005. *Untouchable Citizens*. New Delhi: SAGE Publications.

Harriss, J. 2007. 'The Onward March of the New "Great Indian Middle Class"'. *The Hindu*, 15 August.

Hobsbawm, E., and T. Ranger. 1983. *The Invention of Tradition*. Cambridge and New York: Cambridge University Press.

Jayal, N. G. (ed.). 2019. 'Re-Forming India: The Nation Today'. New Delhi: Penguin Books.

Jaffrelot, C. 2021. 'The Return of Upper Caste Politics'. *Indian Express*, 10 February.

Jensenius, F. 2017. *Social Justice through Inclusion: Consequences of Electoral Quotas in India*. New York: Oxford University Press.

Jodhka, S. 2010. 'Engaging with Caste: Academic Discourses, Identity Politics and State Policy'. IIDS and UNICEF Working Paper Series, 2(2). New Delhi: Indian Institute of Dalit Studies and United Nations Children's Fund (UNICEF).

Joshi, B. (ed.) 1986. *Untouchable! Voices of the Dalit Liberation Movement*. London: Zed Books.

Kalaiyarasan, A. 2020 'A Black Spring'. *The India Forum*, 26 June. https://www.theindiaforum.in/article/black-spring. Accessed on 11 October 2022.

Kapur, D., C. B. Prasad, L. Pritchett, and D. S. Babu. 2010. 'Rethinking Inequality: Dalits in Uttar Pradesh in the Market Reform Era'. *Economic and Political Weekly* 45(35): 39–49.

Lynch, O. 1969. *The Politics of Untouchability*. New York: Columbia University Press.

Mehrotra, K. 2019. 'How BJP Marketed to a New Voting Bloc: The 22 Crore Beneficiaries'. *Indian Express*, 23 May.

Misrah-Barak, J., K. Satyanarayana, and N. Thiara (eds.). 2020. *Dalit Text: Aesthetics and Politics Re-imagined*. London and New York: Routledge.

Mondal, S., and R. Karmakar. 2021. 'Caste in the Time of the COVID-19 Pandemic'. *Contemporary Voice of Dalit* (August). DOI: 10.1177/2455328X211036338.

Narayan, B. 2008. 'Demarginalisation and History: Dalit Re-invention of the Past'. *South Asia Research* 28(2): 169–84.

———. 2021. *Republic of Hindutva: How the Sangh Is Reshaping Indian Democracy*. New Delhi: Penguin Books.

Pai, S. 2002. *Dalit Assertion and the Unfinished Democratic Revolution: The Bahujan Samaj Party in Uttar Pradesh*. New Delhi: SAGE Publications.

———. 2005. 'Quest for Identity through Politics: The Scheduled Castes in Uttar Pradesh'. In *Electoral Reservation, Political Representation and Social Change in India*, edited by S. T. L. Rewal, 21–52. New Delhi: Manohar.

———. 2010. *Developmental State and the Dalit Question in Madhya Pradesh: Congress Response*. New Delhi: Routledge.

———. 2013. *Dalit Assertion*. Oxford India, Short Introduction. New Delhi: Oxford University Press.

Pai, S., and A. Kumar. 2015. 'Understanding the BJP's Victory in Uttar Pradesh'. In *India's 2014 Elections: A Modi-Led BJP Sweep*, edited by P. Wallace, 119–38. New Delhi: SAGE Publications.

Pandian, M. S. S. 2000. 'Dalit Assertion in Tamil Nadu: An Explanatory Note'. *Journal of Indian School of Political Economy* 12 (3–4): 501–17.

Patel, A. B., and S. Kumar. 2021. 'Dalit Suicide an Emerging Social Problem in India'. In *Suicide*, edited by R. W. Motta. IntechOpen. https://doi.org/10.5772/intechopen.99320. Accessed on 11 October 2022.

Ram, K. 1982: *The Chamcha Age: An Era of Stooges*. Delhi: DS4 Office.

Sadanandan, A. 2018. 'What Lies beneath the Alarming Rise in Violence against Dalits?' *The Wire*, 15 June. https://thewire.in/caste/rise-in-violence-against-dalits. Accessed on 10 December 2022.

Satyanarayana, K., and S. Tharu (eds.). 2011. *No Alphabet in Sight: New Dalit Writing from South India*, dossier 1: *Tamil and Malayalam*. New Delhi: Penguin.

Singh, J. 1998. 'Ambedkarisation and Assertion of Dalit Identity: Socio-Cultural Protest in Meerut District of Western Uttar Pradesh'. *Economic and Political Weekly* 33(40): 2611–18.

Still, C. 2014. *Dalits in Neoliberal India: Mobility or Marginalisation?* New Delhi: Routledge.

Thorat, S. K. 2018. 'Social Discrimination and Socioeconomic Realities Add to Disadvantages Faced by Scheduled Castes in the Labour Market'. *Hindustan Times*, 7 September.

Tiwary, D. 2017. 'Second Year in Row, Data on Suicide by Caste and Religion Is Not Disclosed'. *Indian Express*, 14 February. https://indianexpress.com/article/india/ncrb-second-year-in-row-data-on-suicide-by-caste-and-religion-is-not-disclosed-4523505/ (Accessed on 11 October 2022).

Vaishnav, M. 2019. 'The BJP in Power: Indian Democracy and Religious Nationalism.' Washington, DC: Carnegie Endowment for International Peace. https://carnegieendowment.org/files/BJP_In_Power_final.pdf. Accessed on 18 June 2022.

Varma, P. 2007. *The Great Indian Middle Class*. New Delhi: Penguin Books.

Verma, R. 2021. 'Explained: What Is Driving the Dalit–Muslim Divide in West Bengal?' *India Today*, 9 March. https://www.indiatoday.in/elections/west-bengal-assembly-polls-2021/story/explained-what-driving-dalit-muslim-divide-west-bengal-1777285-2021-03-09. Accessed on 11 October 2022.

Part I

Shifting Patterns of Electoral Politics

2

Voting Patterns among Dalits since the 1990s

Rahul Verma and Pranav Gupta

In the past, Dalits have been successfully mobilized by various political parties across the country (Chandra, 2004). The monopoly of the Indian National Congress (hereafter Congress) over Dalit votes declined considerably after the emergence of an effective opposition in many states in the post-emergency period.[1] This period also witnessed the arrival of the Bahujan Samaj Party (BSP) as a major claimant of Dalit votes in north India (Pai, 2002). The 2014 Lok Sabha elections marked a significant shift in Dalit voting patterns, with the Bharatiya Janata Party (BJP) winning nearly one-fourth of Dalit votes. While support for the BJP among Dalits in 2014 largely comprised upwardly mobile segments – urban, educated, middle class, with high media exposure (Kumar and Gupta, 2018)[2] – our analysis of the results of the 2019 Lok Sabha elections as well as the 2022 Uttar Pradesh (UP) assembly elections suggests that the party now enjoys broad-based support among Dalit communities. The party managed to secure one-third of Dalit votes in the 2019 Lok Sabha elections, which was nearly three times that of the BSP.[3]

While the Congress witnessed a secular decline in votes across caste groups in 2014, why Dalits also deserted the BSP in North India remains unclear. Furthermore, many observers expressed doubts over the BJP's ability to retain its support base among Dalits in the 2019 elections. During prime minister Narendra Modi's first term, the apparent dissatisfaction owing to incidents of flogging of Dalit youth and protests against proposed changes to the Scheduled Castes and Scheduled Tribes (Prevention of Atrocities) Act, 1989, among others, had led many observers to express doubts over the BJP's ability to retain its support base among the Dalits in the 2019 elections. How did the BJP then manage to remain as the pre-eminent choice of Dalit voters in many parts of the country in 2019? More importantly, what explains the shifts in Dalit voting patterns since the 1990s?

We begin with a broad overview of voting patterns among Dalits since the 1990s. We extensively draw on National Election Studies (NES) data to provide evidence of how the BJP has fared among Dalit voters in various states in the past two national elections. We also show that the BJP's share of seats reserved for Dalits has grown over time. Next, we find that the BSP's dominance among Dalits, especially non-Jatavs, is being seriously challenged by the BJP. The BSP now faces an existential crisis and continues to decline across the country, including in UP. The party has barely 3 per cent of the votes in any state outside UP and, at best, can just hope to remain an important player in the state. Finally, while we show that the recent shift among Dalits towards the BJP is both due to Modi's popularity and the receipt (or expectation) of welfare benefits, we find evidence that indicates that this shift is also associated with high resonance for the party's ideological agenda. In that sense, the conventional wisdom that Dalit politics is at odds with Hindutva politics, at least in the current electoral battlefield, needs serious introspection (see Narayan, 2009).

Broad Overview of Voting Patterns among Dalits

Data from the NES post-poll surveys conducted by Lokniti, Centre for the Study of Developing Societies (CSDS),[4] New Delhi, show that nationally, between 1996 and 2009, the Congress always managed to get at least a quarter of Dalit votes, the BSP was a close second, and the BJP was a distant third. The 2014 Lok Sabha elections marked a distinct phase in Dalit politics in the country (Kumar and Gupta, 2018). For the first time ever, a plurality of Dalits voted for the BJP, and the party surpassed both the Congress and the BSP. In the 2014 elections, almost one-fourth (24 per cent) of Dalit voters voted for the BJP. The trend continued in the 2019 elections as well, and the BJP was successful in making further inroads into the community (see Figure 2.1).

A detailed analysis of Dalit voting patterns in the 2009 Lok Sabha elections clearly showed that the community did not vote *en bloc* for any particular party; instead, their vote choice was rooted in the nature and dynamics of the state party system (Verma, 2009). This has stayed true for the major state and national elections held after 2014. What has changed, however, is the regional dynamics of inter-party competition, which has created favourable conditions for the BJP to gain a stronger footing among Dalit voters (see Table 2.1).

The BJP made tremendous gains among Dalits in the 2014 Lok Sabha elections. The BSP lost a substantial segment of its Dalit vote base to the BJP in UP, Haryana, Delhi, Madhya Pradesh, and Maharashtra. The Aam Aadmi

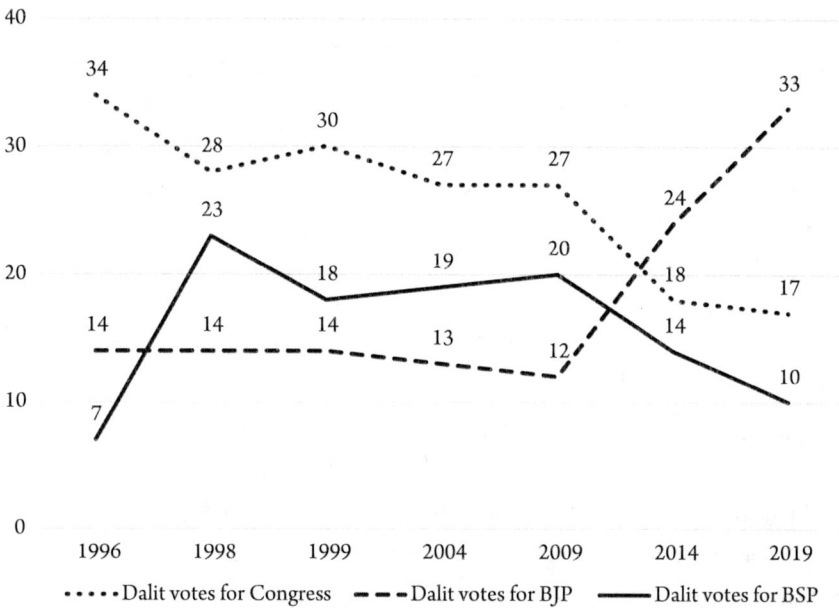

Figure 2.1   Percentage of Dalit votes for the Indian National Congress, the Bharatiya Janata Party (BJP), and the Bahujan Samaj Party (BSP), 1996–2019

Source: Time-series National Election Studies (NES) data 1996–2019, Lokniti, Centre for the Study of Developing Societies (CSDS), New Delhi.

Party (AAP) became the principal beneficiary of the shift of Dalit voters away from the Congress and the BSP in Delhi and Punjab. The BSP's support base beyond UP largely comprises Dalit voters. The party failed to win even a single seat in the 2014 Lok Sabha elections, and its national vote share declined from 6.2 per cent in 2009 to 4.1 per cent in 2014. This was chiefly due to the drubbing it received in UP, where its vote share declined from 27.4 per cent in 2009 to 19.6 per cent in 2014. In two-party competition states (Himachal Pradesh, Uttarakhand, Rajasthan, and Gujarat), the Congress lost a substantial share of its Dalit vote to the BJP. In states where regional parties continued to dominate and successfully resisted the rise of the BJP, these parties also dominated among Dalits. For instance, the All India Trinamool Congress (TMC) in West Bengal, the Biju Janta Dal (BJD) in Odisha, and the Dravida Munnetra Kazgham (DMK) in Tamil Nadu received a substantial portion of the Dalit vote. The Left Front in West Bengal received a major electoral setback, and its Dalit vote base shifted towards the TMC. The BJD in Odisha gained a share of Dalit votes from the Congress. Similarly, the Congress lost a substantial

Table 2.1   Dalit voting patterns in states, 2014 and 2019

State	Dalit population (per cent)	Who did Dalits vote for in 2014 and 2019?
Punjab	31.9	Congress gets a larger share; marginal presence of BSP.
Himachal Pradesh	25.2	BJP gets a larger share.
West Bengal	23.5	BJP makes serious inroads.
Uttar Pradesh	20.7	BJP wins a large chunk; significant presence of BSP.
Haryana	20.2	BJP gets a larger share.
Tamil Nadu	20.0	DMK gets a larger share; marginal presence of the Viduthalai Chiruthaigal Katchi (VCK).
Uttarakhand	18.8	Divided between Congress and BJP.
Rajasthan	17.8	Divided between Congress and BJP.
Tripura	17.8	BJP makes serious inroads.
Odisha	17.1	BJD gets a larger share than BJP.
Karnataka	17.1	Congress gets a larger share.
Delhi	16.8	Split between BJP, Congress, and AAP.
Andhra Pradesh	16.2	Split between TDP and YSR Congress.
Bihar	15.7	Votes are divided between major parties, LJP, and Hindustani Awam Morcha (Secular) (HAM-S).
Pondicherry	15.7	DMK gets a larger share.
Madhya Pradesh	15.6	Congress gets a larger share than BJP, with marginal presence of BSP.
Chhattisgarh	12.8	BJP gets a larger share than Congress, with marginal presence of BSP.
Jharkhand	12.1	Votes are divided between major parties.
Maharashtra	11.8	Votes are divided between major parties; VBA emerges.
Kerala	9.1	Votes are divided between Congress and Left.
Assam	6.9	BJP gets a larger share than Congress.
Gujarat	6.7	Congress gets a larger share than BJP.

Source: Authors' analysis based on National Election Studies (NES) data.

Note: Only states with more than 5 per cent Dalit population have been considered for the analysis.

share of Dalit votes to the Telangana Rashtra Samithi (TRS) in Telangana and to the BJP's ally, the Telegu Desam Party (TDP), and the Yuvajana Shramika Rythu (YSR) Congress Party in Andhra Pradesh.

In 2014, the BJP also gained from strategic alliances with Dalit parties in a few states. In Bihar, Ram Vilas Paswan's Lok Janshakti Party (LJP) joined the National Democratic Alliance (NDA), which ensured that the NDA led among Dalits in the state. In Maharashtra, the inclusion of Ramdas Athawale's Republican Party of India (Athawale) (RPI[A]) helped in building the perception that it was serious about mobilizing Dalit voters. Evidence from the survey data suggest that Modi's popularity cuts across caste lines. Modi and his party became symbolic vehicles representing dissatisfaction with the Congress-led United Progressive Alliance (UPA) government.

The voting pattern among Dalits in the 2019 elections largely followed the same trend, with minor changes in a few states. The two-party states in northern and western India largely remained with the BJP, and the Congress was unable to make any significant comeback. In southern India, a different set of state-level parties performed well this time among Dalit communities: the YSR Congress in Andhra Pradesh and the Dravida Munnetra Kazhagam (DMK) alliance in Tamil Nadu.

The biggest change took place in India's eastern and north-eastern states, where the BJP managed to make significant inroads into West Bengal, Assam, Tripura, and many other states for the first time, helped in no small measure by the party receiving greater support among Dalit communities. For example, in West Bengal, the party, in fact, received greater support from Dalits than from any other caste group (61 per cent [Lokniti 2019 poll]). The party has also been locked in a battle over Namasudra votes with its chief rival, the TMC. The BJP has made it a point to reach out to smaller Dalit groups, such as the Matuas, a community of Dalit migrants from Bangladesh, through their inclusion under the Citizenship Amendment Act (CAA) (Daniyal, 2019). In Assam, the BJP and its allies together secured two-thirds of Dalit votes.

The party's growing clout among Dalit communities is further reflected in the BJP's ability to win more reserved seats. There were 84 reserved seats in the country in 2019, out of which 46 were won by the BJP, with its average vote share in such seats being 35 per cent (see Table 2.2). Winning a reserved seat does not necessarily foreground the party's position as a Dalit party, as voters from non-Dalit castes are likely to play a crucial role in deciding the results in these constituencies. It is nevertheless still important to recognize that for political parties, these constituencies also act as a signalling device influencing the perception of Dalit voters in general.

Table 2.2 Reserved constituencies in India and their electoral record since 2009

Year	Bharatiya Janata Party (BJP)		Indian National Congress		Bahujan Samaj Party (BSP)	
	Seats won	Vote share (per cent)	Seats won	Vote share (per cent)	Seats won	Vote share (per cent)
2019	46	35.3	6	16.7	2	9.4
2014	40	27.6	7	17.6	0	5.9
2009	12	15.7	30	26.4	2	7.8

Source: Authors' analysis of Election Commission of India (ECI) data.
Note: In 2019, Congress allies won six seats, and BJP allies won eight seats. In 2014, Congress allies won zero seats, and BJP allies won nine seats. In 2009, Congress allies won eight seats, and BJP allies won eight seats.

The Decline of the BSP in North India

The BSP has been a riddle wrapped in an enigma for political analysts. It has survived amidst numerous predictions of terminal decline in the past and bounced back with greater vigour in times of crisis (see Table 2.3). However, if the assembly elections in various states since the 2009 Lok Sabha elections are an indicator, prospects of the BSP's revival look extremely grim.[5] The BSP's ambition of becoming a pan-India party has undeniably hit a dead end. Similarly, its chances of re-emerging as an important player in UP do not look bright, especially after the party's poor performance in the 2022 assembly elections in the state.

The party successfully managed to increase its vote share in UP in successive elections due to favourable social arithmetic and increasing party competition. In the initial phase which lasted from 1989 to 1992 assembly elections, the BSP's support was limited to its Dalit voter base and remained below double-digit figures. The BSP contested the 1993 elections in alliance with the Samajwadi Party (SP) and managed to win 67 seats. Samajwadi Party leader Mulayam Singh Yadav became the chief minister with support from the BSP and other parties. Kanshi Ram and Mayawati tried to expand their party's social base by slowly nurturing the Other Backward Classes' (OBCs) leadership within their rank and file. This helped the BSP in making gains among the most backward classes (MBCs), who resented the dominance of upper OBCs like Yadavs and Lodhs.

The electoral decline of the BJP in UP, over the course of a decade beginning in 2002, coincided with the BSP establishing itself as the primary alternative to the SP. After the 2004 Lok Sabha elections, Mayawati played a masterstroke by

Table 2.3   Performance of the Bahujan Samaj Party (BSP) in the Lok Sabha elections since 1989

Lok Sabha election	Seats contested	Seats deposit lost	Vote share (per cent)	Total seats won
1989	245	221	2.07	3
1991	243	217	2.20	3
1996	210	138	4.02	11
1998	251	176	4.67	5
1999	225	154	4.16	14
2004	435	358	5.33	19
2009	500	410	6.17	21
2014	503	447	4.19	0
2019	383	345	3.67	10

Source: Authors' analysis of Election Commission of India (ECI) data.

transforming her party's message from 'Bahujan hitay, bahujan sukhay' to 'Sarvajan hitay, sarvajan sukhay'. The social engineering experiment of bringing together Dalits, MBCs, and upper castes helped the BSP secure a majority on its own. The party's vote share in UP crossed the 25 per cent threshold in the 2007 state elections, and its footprint expanded across various regions of the state. Many have argued that BSP candidates in the decade of the 2000s were almost assured of mobilizing the party's Dalit base. The party leadership capitalized on this and welcomed politicians who were willing to give funds to contest as its nominees. The BSP slowly transformed itself from a movement-based party to a group of individual politicians who had defected from other parties for purely pragmatic reasons.

The data presented in Figure 2.2 show the rise and decline of the BSP in UP. In the 2014 Lok Sabha elections, the party faced severe erosion in its vote share as it dipped below 20 per cent largely due to the shift of a section of Dalit voters towards the BJP. The substantial decline in the BSP's vote share between the 2017 and 2022 assembly elections shows that the party is standing on thin ice in state politics. The unlikely gambit of forming an alliance with the SP in the 2019 Lok Sabha elections in UP did not reap significant electoral dividends. Despite the alliance, the BJP remained the pre-eminent political player in the state. The BSP had polled close to half the non-Jatav Dalit votes in the 2007 and 2012 assembly

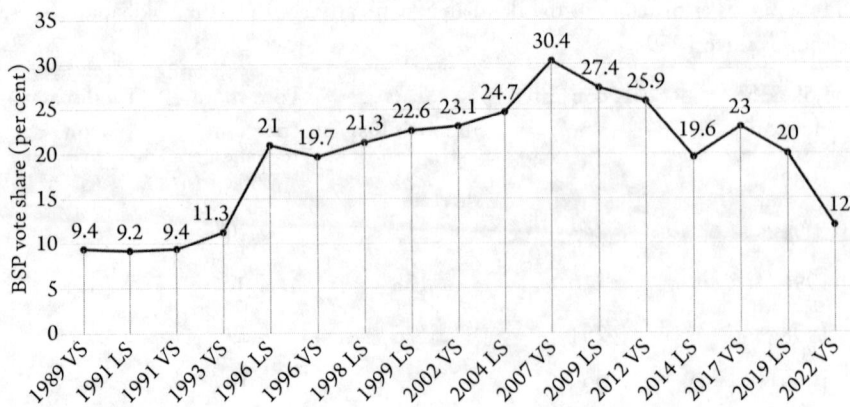

Figure 2.2   Bahujan Samaj Party's (BSP) vote share in Uttar Pradesh since 1989

Source: Authors' analysis of Election Commission of India (ECI) data.

Note: VS stands for Vidhan Sabha, or state legislative assembly; LS stands for Lok Sabha.

elections, which came down to less than one-third (30 per cent) in the 2014 Lok Sabha elections. It was not able to arrest this decline in time for the 2017 assembly or 2019 Lok Sabha elections and lost much ground in this segment to the BJP (Ghildiyal, 2017). Also, the party has gradually lost support among multiple other groups, which was carefully cultivated by Kanshi Ram. Many backward castes such as Kurmis, Koeris, Rajbhars, Nishads, and so on, and lower castes among Muslims had turned out for the BSP in large numbers in previous elections. Since the 2014 Lok Sabha elections, however, the BSP has performed poorly among these voters.

Furthermore, the party's ability to win seats has been dented since the 2017 assembly elections. For instance, in 2007, the party had either won or was a runner up in 310 seats, which marginally declined to 289 seats in 2012. This picture changed drastically in the 2017 elections, where it won just 19 seats and stood second in only 119. An analysis of constituency-level vote swings between the 2012 and 2017 assembly elections reveals the scale of the BSP's electoral defeat. Overall, the party's vote share declined in 295 constituencies, as compared to 2012, and increased in only 108 constituencies. In 163 constituencies, it faced an adverse vote swing of more than 5 percentage points. The 2022 assembly elections in the state signalled the eroding support for the party even among its core base of Dalits. The party barely managed to win just one seat (and came second in merely 18 seats) and 12 per cent of the total votes. It lost its deposit or won less than one-sixth of the total votes polled in 290 seats – that is, in almost three of every four seats, it no longer had a substantial voter base (see Table 2.4). The post-poll survey data indicate that less than half of the Dalits in the state voted for the party.

Table 2.4   The Bahujan Samaj Party's (BSP) eroding base in the Uttar Pradesh assembly elections

Assembly elections	Seats the party was runner-up for	Seats where the party forfeited deposit
2012	209	51
2017	119	83
2022	18	290

Source: Authors' analysis of Election Commission of India (ECI) data.

A quarter of Jatav and almost half of non-Jatav Dalits voted for the BJP instead. The party's dismal performance indicates that it will have to achieve a substantial vote share increase to return as even a contender for power in the state.

The survey data collected by Lokniti also help in underscoring the declining popularity of the BSP leader, Mayawati. In the 2009 Lok Sabha elections, the BSP and Mayawati were aiming for the high office in Delhi after securing a majority in UP in 2007, but this opportunity quickly faded away. The data presented in Figure 2.3 clearly show that the preference for Mayawati as a prime minister has declined tremendously since 2009.

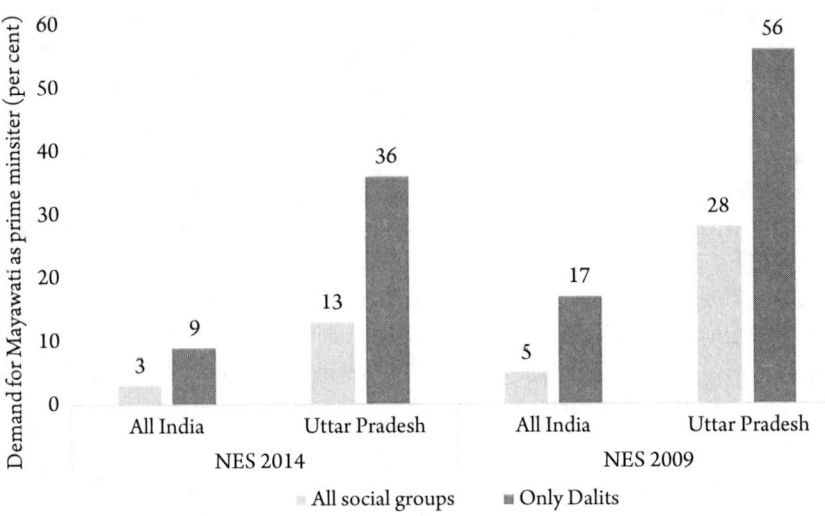

Figure 2.3   Mayawati's popularity among Dalits and across social groups, 2009 and 2014

Source: National Election Studies (NES) data, Lokniti, Centre for the Study of Developing Societies (CSDS), New Delhi.

Mayawati's earlier style of political campaigning, which solely focused on building an assertive narrative around caste identity, has lost its resonance among the Dalit electorate for two reasons. First, a new social constituency has emerged among Dalits in the past few years, which is upwardly mobile and aspirational. This group identifies more with Modi's style of politics, who, while claiming pride in his backward caste identity, talks of economic transformation. Second, her own image of being an able administrator and transformative leader has been tarnished due to corruption scandals, centralization of authority, and dilution of the BSP's ideological message. Furthermore, she has not made any serious effort to reinvent her organizational machinery, encourage the second line of leadership, or develop a credible political message.

Increasing Popularity of the BJP among Dalit Voters

The BJP's Dalit mobilization in the 2014 and 2019 Lok Sabha elections should be viewed as distinct phases. Between both elections, not only did the BJP expand support among Dalits but even the profile of support within the community changed. Who voted for the BJP among Dalits in the 2014 and 2019 Lok Sabha elections? Did various segments among Dalits vote differently in 2014 and 2019? A disaggregated analysis of voting patterns since 2014 reveals convergence between various sub-groups within Dalits. While inter-caste differences in vote choice, much lower than that in earlier elections, still persist – that is, Dalits are relatively less likely to vote for the BJP as compared to upper castes, OBCs, and tribals – support for the party within the community transcends various boundaries.

In 2014, the BJP had relatively higher support among core segments like urban, middle- and upper-class, and educated Dalit voters. In the 2014 Lok Sabha elections, support for the BJP was much higher among urban Dalits. While 22 per cent rural Dalits voted for the BJP, more than one-fourth (27 per cent) urban Dalits had supported the party. By 2019, the party not only managed to cement these gains but also broadened its appeal among a cross-section of Dalit voters. It also managed to reverse the rural–urban gap, where the support for the party among rural Dalits was almost five percentage points higher. There were negligible class-based differences in support for the BJP among Dalits in 2019. We find that slightly more than one-fifth (22 per cent) of lower-class Dalits voted for the BJP in 2014 as compared to more than one-fourth (27 per cent) middle- and upper-middle-class Dalits. In the 2019 elections, class ceased to be a factor in understanding the Dalit vote, as a similar proportion of the rich and the poor supported the BJP. Further, education-based differences also disappeared: in 2014, the BJP had lower support among less-educated Dalits. Though a plurality of non-literate and primary-school educated Dalits had voted for the BJP, the magnitude of support was much lower than high-school- and college-educated voters. In 2019, support for the BJP did not differ much based on education levels.

We conducted multivariate analysis to understand the similarities and differences in the profile of Dalit support for the BJP between the 2014 and 2019 Lok Sabha elections (Figure 2.4). In 2014, economic class, residence in urban areas, and religiosity were positively associated with support for the BJP

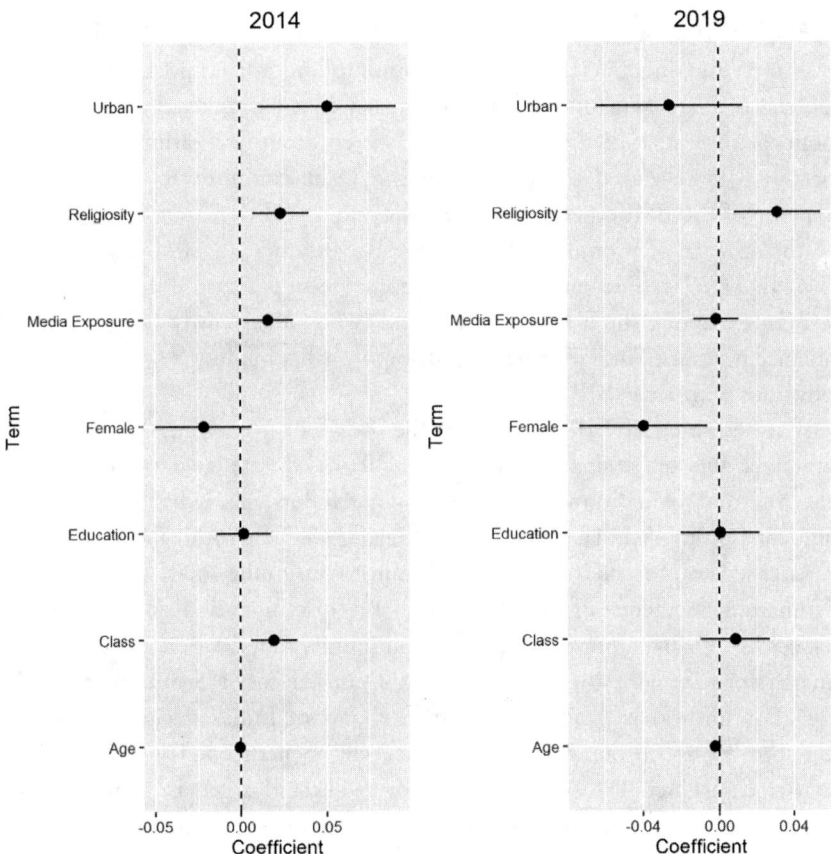

Figure 2.4   Profile of support for the Bharatiya Janata Party (BJP) and its allies in the Lok Sabha elections, 2014 and 2019

Source: National Election Studies (NES) data, Lokniti, Centre for the Study of Developing Societies (CSDS), New Delhi.

and its allies. The coefficients for these variables were positive and statistically significant. However, the profile of BJP support among Dalits changed in the 2019 Lok Sabha elections. In the model for the 2019 elections, only religiosity remains statistically significant. None of the other individual attributes seem to be associated with support for the BJP among Dalits. The results clearly demonstrate that there was convergence in political preference among Dalits. While the 2014 elections suggest Dalit support for the BJP to be a phenomenon limited to the elites of the community, the 2019 elections made this a broad-based reality.

What Explains the Dalit Shift towards the BJP?

While Dalit disenchantment with the Congress has been steadily developing over the years, it is unclear why the community did not support the BSP. After all, the BSP is an unambiguously Dalit party that has enjoyed unprecedented political success since the 1990s. What is even more fascinating is that much of the BJP's electoral success among the Dalit communities comes at the expense of the BSP, especially in the politically significant state of UP, in spite of the absence of prominent Dalit faces. For instance, in 2018, two-thirds of the NDA's 27 cabinet ministers were from the upper castes. There were five OBCs (excluding the prime minister) and two Dalits, mostly from the party's alliance partners. Similarly, the proportion of Dalits holding key organizational positions within the BJP remains low.

Furthermore, the BJP has been on the back foot over rising discontentment among Dalits on several occasions since 2014. Educated Dalit youth were at the forefront of nationwide student protests following Hyderabad University student Rohith Vemula's suicide. The flogging of Dalit youth in Gujarat's Una district led to protests in many states against continuing social discrimination. Numerous incidents of caste violence and discrimination in Western UP, especially in Saharanpur district, led to community mobilization and culminated in the formation of the Bhim Army, a Dalit-led social organization headed by Chandrashekhar Azad. The Supreme Court of India's decision to weaken the provisions of the Scheduled Castes and Scheduled Tribes (Prevention of Atrocities) Act, 1989, was followed by rallies and a general strike by Dalit organizations. Even a few Dalit members of parliament of the BJP had openly expressed concerns over support for the party among the community due to these developments. In fact, the Mood of the Nation (MotN) survey, 2018, conducted by Lokniti showed that a majority of Dalits were dissatisfied with the Modi government's attitude towards atrocities, crimes, and violence against vulnerable and marginalized sections. Similarly, a substantial proportion of Dalit respondents indicated that under no circumstances should the Scheduled Castes and Scheduled Tribes (Prevention of Atrocities) Act be changed.[6] Despite no significant increase in the number of Dalit representatives within the BJP (Suri and Verma, 2017), the party not only managed to quell resistance arising due to various incidents of community mobilization, but also increased its Dalit vote share in the 2019 elections.

What explains this apparent puzzle? Scholars have mulled over this question primarily through the lens of leadership or provision of welfare benefits. As regards the former, some have argued that it is the prime minister's personal popularity and his messianic image that have brought erstwhile indifferent Dalit groups to the BJP's fold (Poonam, Jyoti, and Prakash, 2019). This is also closely linked to the concerted efforts of outreach aimed towards the community by the BJP's ideological parent, the Rashtriya Swayamsevak Sangh (RSS) (Narayan, 2009). Two aspects of this have been particularly significant: outreach through targeted welfarist expansion of schemes and services (Thachil and Herring, 2008) and cultural outreach through careful social engineering and reworking of Dalit symbols within the broader Hindutva nationalistic fold (Gorringe and Waghmore, 2019; Narayan, 2009).

Our analysis shows that both Modi's leadership and the delivery of welfare benefits are clearly correlated with Dalits voting for the BJP. Figure 2.5 shows

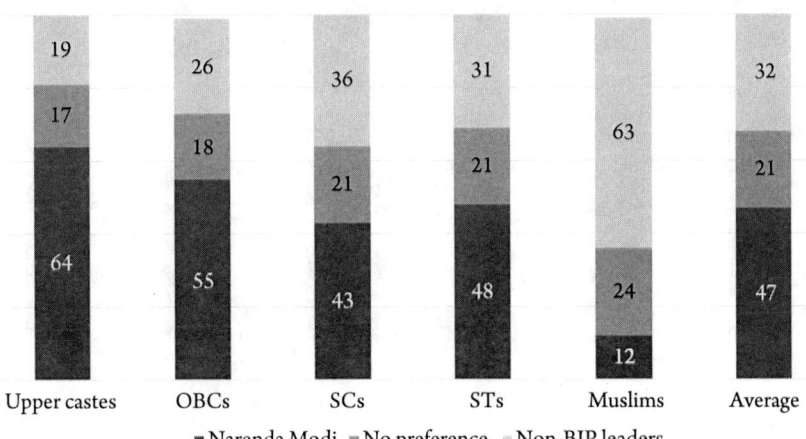

■ Narenda Modi ■ No preference ▪ Non-BJP leaders

Figure 2.5 Preference for prime minister among different caste groups, 2019

Source: National Election Studies (NES) 2019 data, Lokniti, Centre for the Study of Developing Societies (CSDS), New Delhi.

Note: OBCs, SCs, and STs stand for Other Backward Classes, Scheduled Castes, and Scheduled Tribes, respectively.

the caste-wise distribution of preference for Narendra Modi as the prime minister in the 2019 elections. It is evident that Modi was the foremost choice across all communities among the Hindus. Similar to the voting pattern, preference for Modi as the prime minister was far less among Dalits than among upper-caste voters, who have been the traditional support base of the BJP. We also find that Dalit respondents seem to have benefitted from government schemes in a like proportion to other communities (Figure 2.6). While welfare benefits may have increased support for the BJP in the 2019 Lok Sabha elections, they are unlikely to adequately explain the party's significant inroads as a challenger in 2014.

The BJP's social engineering strategy of driving a wedge between Dalit *jatis* seems to have paid the party a rich dividend since 2014 (Jaffrelot, 2019). The party mobilized non-dominant Dalit *jatis* and cultivated a segment among the community which is more inclined towards it. For instance, in UP, the BJP repeatedly claimed that the BSP prioritizes the interests of Jatavs over other Dalit groups. It maintained that benefits for Dalits under the BSP were not equitably distributed and disproportionately accrued to the Jatavs. The party used a similar strategy in Karnataka where Dalits are divided into two groups: the 'Left Dalits' (the Madigas) and the 'Right Dalits' (the Holeyas). The BJP tried to expand

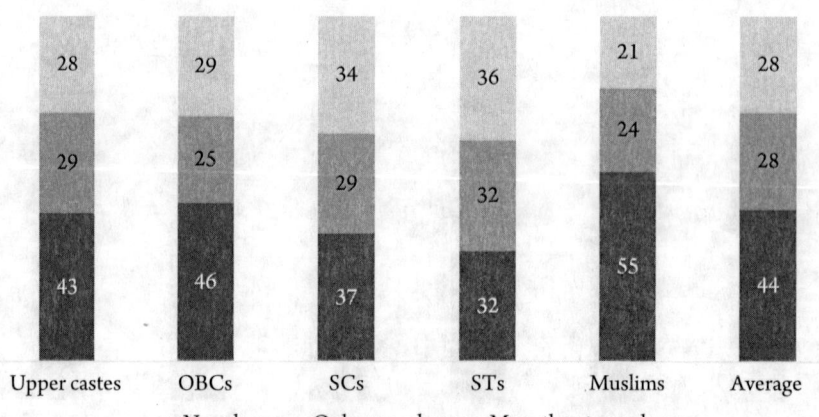

■ No scheme ■ Only one scheme ■ More than two schemes

Figure 2.6 Caste-wise responses on benefitting from central government schemes, 2019

Source: National Election Studies (NES) 2019 data, Lokniti, Centre for the Study of Developing Societies (CSDS), New Delhi.

Note: OBCs, SCs, and STs stand for Other Backward Classes, Scheduled Castes, and Scheduled Tribes, respectively.

support among Dalits by backing the former's demand for implementation of the Sadashiva commission's report on internal reservation.

The party's cultural outreach has been further strengthened by the numerous symbolic acts undertaken by Modi. On several occasions, Modi has described himself as a follower of B. R. Ambedkar. The central government has promised to develop five places associated with the Dalit icon as *panchteerth* (five holy places). These include Ambedkar's birthplace in Mhow in the Indore district in Madhya Pradesh, the apartment in London where he stayed during his student days, 'Deeksha Bhoomi' in Nagpur, 'Mahaparinirvan Sthal' in Delhi, and 'Chaitya Bhoomi' in Mumbai. The government's widely used unified payments interface (UPI) platform, BHIM (Bharat Interface for Money), has also been named after him. Furthermore, Modi chose 5 April, the birth anniversary of Babu Jagjivan Ram, another Dalit leader of national prominence, to unveil the 'Stand-up India' scheme. The BJP proposed Shri Ram Nath Kovind, a Koli Dalit from UP, as the NDA's presidential nominee in 2017. These steps may not have led to direct electoral mobilization but may have collectively helped the BJP get into good graces of Dalits.

Electoral support can be rarely explained by a single factor. The BJP's increased support among Dalits should thus be understood as a culmination of several factors. While there has been recognition of this increased electoral support among Dalits, whether this is also accompanied by an ideological acceptance of the BJP's position has not been fully explored. We argue that, contrary to the prevailing belief, the data suggest greater ideological assimilation of Dalits into the larger Hindutva ideology of cultural nationalism. We measure the index of ethno-political majoritarianism and Hindu nationalism as used by Chhibber and Verma (2019) and find strong evidence of ideological congruence: Dalit voters who vote for the BJP have a far higher score on the ethno-political majoritarian index than those who vote for other parties (Table 2.5). A higher score here implies a greater acceptance of majoritarian ideas, most of which fall squarely under the ideological narrative and goals of the BJP.[7] Another measure that suggests greater ideological congruence is the community's views on Hindu nationalism. Here too we find evidence that suggests that Dalits do not think differently on the issue as compared to other communities.

Since its election in 2014, the BJP has consistently raised issues of aggressive nationalism, seeking to delegitimize its opponents, whether on the basis of their religious or food habits or simply their failure to engage in outward nationalistic posturing. A survey among voters in numerous states and union territories across the country found limited divergence between the views of Dalits and upper castes on some dimensions of religious conservatism and nationalistic

Table 2.5   Ideological leanings of Dalit voters

Ideological views	Indian National Congress	Bharatiya Janata Party (BJP)	Other parties	Average
Ethno-political majoritarianism	−0.22	0.18	0.05	0.04
Hindu nationalism	0.08	0.17	0.06	0.09

Source: Chhibber and Verma (2019).
Note: This analysis has been conducted among Dalit respondents only. The data presented here are the average score on the two indices.

Table 2.6   Views across caste groups on issues raised by the Bharatiya Janata Party (BJP)

	Support punishment for …			
	… not saying 'Bharat Mata ki jai' in a public function	… not standing during the national anthem at public places	… consumption of beef	… engaging in religious conversion
Upper castes	56	64	64	54
Peasant castes	58	61	50	50
Upper OBCs	61	66	56	50
Lower OBCs	47	60	47	45
Dalits	56	62	59	51
STs	30	46	41	51

Source: Kumar and Gupta (2020).
Note: OBCs and STs stand for Other Backward Classes and Scheduled Tribes, respectively. On each of these four questions, 15–20 per cent respondents expressed no opinion. The no-opinion rate was slightly lower than average among upper castes, at par among Dalits, and higher among STs.

expression (see Table 2.6). For instance, the proportion of Dalits who supported punishment for consumption of beef and religious conversion was similar to those belonging to other castes and communities. Similarly, Dalits are almost as likely as upper castes to enforce nationalistic expression like standing during the national anthem (Kumar and Gupta, 2020).[8]

The Future of Dalit Politics in India

In this chapter, we have seen that despite the emergence of the BSP in the 1980s, the Congress continued to garner the maximum share of Dalit votes. This changed in 2014 with the BJP winning one in every four Dalit votes. Since then Dalit politics has remained in flux. While on the one hand, the BJP under Modi has left no stone unturned in its efforts to mobilize Dalit voters, on the other, ending systematic persecution of Dalits in many parts of the country, including violent attacks by members of upper castes, continues to remain a serious challenge for any government.

The analysis presented in this chapter indicates that the interplay of three factors is likely to shape the future of Dalit politics in the country. First, the BJP has made successful inroads into support from Dalit voters (especially among non-Jatavs), associated with a resonance with the party's ideological message. Gupta (2022) finds that there are limited inter-caste differences in a few domains like nationalism, social conservatism, and religious conservatism. The analysis suggests that limited differences in mass attitudes are not merely a post-Modi development as mass attitudes on numerous domains were fairly similar even earlier. The increasing resonance of the BJP's ideological agenda with Dalits indicates that the electoral shift among Dalits may not be contingent on merely the personal popularity of Modi or a transactional relationship with the incumbent government. There is a realistic possibility of greater ideological cohesion.

Second, the BSP now faces an existential crisis and continues to decline across the country, including in UP. This is further reinforced by Mayawati's increasing marginalization in the discourse, while new political formations such as the Azad Samaj Party (ASP) and the Vanchit Bahujan Aghadi (VBA) have emerged at the forefront of this new churn in Dalit politics. The leadership vacuum has led to the emergence of new political entrepreneurs like Jignesh Mevani and Chandrashekhar Azad. While these parties and figures may remain marginal players in the short run, their ability to challenge the BJP's base among Dalits in their respective states cannot be completely ruled out.

Third, the absence of prominent Dalit leadership within the BJP has not proven detrimental for the party because other parties have also failed to develop effective Dalit leadership. Even the Congress and most regional parties have not made any real effort to promote Dalit leadership within their ranks. The election of Mallikarjun Kharge, a prominent Dalit face, as the party president is unlikely to do much to change the Congress' prospects among Dalits. This is a matter of concern for major Dalit parties like the BSP, the LJP, and the RPI(A) as well, which remain dependent on their main leader or founder. This leadership vacuum among Dalits has meant that co-ethnic representation has ceased to become a differentiating factor between parties, and it has also provided the BJP enough room to use symbolic gestures to mobilize Dalits.

While the 2019 verdict may conceal the churn within Dalit politics, it is bound to bounce back as the BJP-led party system has two opposing tendencies vis-à-vis Dalit politics – at times accommodative; at others, dominative. How long can these two tendencies coexist? The answer will determine the direction of Dalit politics in the future.

Notes

1. A section of Dalits had voted for the Republican Party of India (RPI) even in the late 1960s in areas where the party was strong.
2. Analysis of National Election Studies (NES) 2014 data suggests that support for the party was around 6 percentage points higher among younger Dalits.
3. The ratio was even higher if one accounts for the National Democratic Alliance (NDA) coalition.
4. The NES are post-poll surveys conducted after Lok Sabha elections by the Lokniti programme of the CSDS. The surveys are conducted among a randomly selected representative sample of voters.
5. Pradeep Chhibber and Rahul Verma (2019) show that the BSP has declined in every state.
6. See the MoTN survey (Lokniti, 2018: 22–23).
7. The ethno-political majoritarianism index captures the sentiment that the will of the majority should prevail, minorities should adopt the custom of the majority, and that the government should treat both groups equally. We use two questions to measure Hindu nationalism: whether India is primarily a land of Hindus, and whether a respondent is more likely to consider Hindus as more nationalist than Muslims.
8. Scheduled Tribe (ST) respondents expressed much lower support for punishment for all activities except religious conversion. This was mainly due to the lack of any response to many questions. More than four out of ten ST respondents did not answer some of these questions.

Bibliography

Ahuja, A. 2019. *Mobilizing the Marginalised: Ethnic Parties Without Ethnic Movements.* New York: Oxford University Press.

Chandra, K. 2004. *Why Ethnic Parties Succeed: Patronage and Ethnic Head Counts in India.* Cambridge, UK: Cambridge University Press.

Chauchard, S. 2017. *Why Representation Matters: The Meaning of Ethnic Quotas in Rural India.* Cambridge: Cambridge University Press.

Chhibber, P. K., and R. Verma. 2019. 'The Rise of the Second Dominant Party System in India: BJP's New Social Coalition in 2019'. *Studies in Indian Politics* 7(2): 131–48.

Daniyal, S. 2019. 'Communalism, Vanishing Communists and WhatsApp: Why the BJP's Star Is Rising Fast in Bengal'. *Scroll.in*, 13 May. https://scroll.in/article/922292/communalism-vanishing-communists-and-whatsapp-why-the-bjp-s-star-is-rising-fast-in-bengal. Accessed on 15 February 2021.

Dhara, T. 2020. 'BJP Makes Further Inroads into Telangana with the Dubbak By-election Win'. *Caravan*, 24 November. https://caravanmagazine.in/politics/bjp-dubbak-by-election-win. Accessed on 15 February 2021.

Ghildiyal, S. 2017. 'Non-Jatav Votes Helped BJP, Yet Again'. *Times of India*, 12 March. https://timesofindia.indiatimes.com/elections/assembly-elections/uttar-pradesh/news/non-jatav-votes-helped-bjp-yet-again/articleshow/57603406.cms. Accessed on 15 February 2021.

Gorringe, H., and S. Waghmore. 2019. '"Go Write on the Walls That You Are the Rulers of This Nation": Dalit Mobilisation and the BJP'. *Indian Politics and Policy* 2(1–2): 31–52.

Gupta, P. 2022. 'Partisan Differences in Mass Attitudes in India'. Mimeo.

Jaffrelot, C. 2003. *India's Silent Revolution: The Rise of the Low Castes in North Indian Politics.* Delhi: Permanent Black.

———. 2019. 'Class and Caste in the 2019 Indian Election: Why Have So Many Poor Started Voting for Modi?' *Studies in Indian Politics* 7(2): 149–60.

Jensenius, F. 2017: *Social Justice Through Inclusion: The Consequences of Electoral Quotas in India.* New York: Oxford University Press.

Kumar, S., and P. Gupta. 2018. 'Why Retaining the Dalit Vote Is a Tough Challenge for the BJP'. *Mint*, 26 April. https://www.livemint.com/Politics/wdH2vukWm2rycBnmU2LPYL/Why-retaining-the-Dalit-vote-is-a-tough-challenge-for-the-BJ.html. Accessed on 2 November 2022.

———. 2020. 'BJP's Ideological Hegemony: Combining Religious Conservatism and Nationalism'. *Studies in Indian Politics* 8(2): 203–13.

Kumar, V. 2006. *India's Roaring Revolution: Dalit Assertion and New Horizons.* New Delhi: Gagandeep Publications.

Lokniti (2018). *Mood of the Nation Survey, Round 3 (May 2018).* https://www.lokniti.org/media/upload_files/Lokniti-ABP-News-Mood-of-the-Nation-Survey-Round-3-May-2018.pdf. Accessed on 15 February 2021.

Narayan, B. 2006. *Women Heroes and Dalit Assertion in North India.* New Delhi: SAGE Publications.

———. 2009. *Fascinating Hindutva: Saffron Politics and Dalit Mobilisation.* New Delhi: SAGE Publications.

Pai, S. 2002. *Dalit Assertion and the Unfinished Democratic Revolution: The Bahujan Samaj Party in Uttar Pradesh*. New Delhi: SAGE Publications.

Palshikar, S. 2007. 'Dalit Politics in the Nineties: Electoral Politics and Predicament Before an Underprivileged Community'. *Indian Journal of Social Work* 68(1): 101–29.

Poonam, S., D. Jyoti, and G. Prakash. 2019. 'Why Dalits Voted for the BJP'. *Seminar* 720 (August). https://www.india-seminar.com/2019/720/720_snigdha_dhrubo_guru.htm. Accessed in September 2022.

Pushpendra. 1999. 'Dalit Assertion Through Electoral Politics'. *Economic and Political Weekly* 34(36): 2609–18.

Suri, K. C., and R. Verma. 2017. 'Democratizing the BJP'. *Seminar* 699 (November). https://www.india-seminar.com/2017/699/699_k_c_suri-rahul_verma.htm. Accessed in September 2022.

Thachil T., and R. Herring. 2008 'Poor Choices: De-alignment, Development and Dalit/Adivasi Voting Patterns in Indian States'. *Contemporary South Asia* 16(4): 441–64.

Verma, R. 2009. 'Dalit Voting Patterns'. *Economic and Political Weekly* 44(34): 95–98.
———. 2014. 'The Story of Dalit Vote: Between the BJP and the BSP'. *The Hindu*, 6 June. https://www.thehindu.com/opinion/op-ed/the-story-of-dalit-vote-between-the-bjp-and-the-bsp/article6090744.ece. Accessed on 15 February 2021.

3

On the Peculiar Absence of Dalit Politics

Punjab and West Bengal

Dwaipayan Sen

Despite being home to some of the largest proportions of Dalit population across states in India, neither Punjab nor West Bengal has given rise to the robust presence of radical Dalit political assertion, particularly of the Ambedkarite variety, in the formal institutions of the government. What explains this puzzling absence? Indeed, this is a question that has been raised with respect to both states, even if in their distinct regional contexts. While demographics alone may not be the surest indicator of political dynamics, the sheer size of the Dalit population in both regions invites closer inspection. As per the data available from the 2001 census of India, Punjab's Dalits accounted for 28.9 per cent of its total population, or just over seven million people. The comparable figure for West Bengal was 23 per cent, or nearly 18.5 million people. Uttar Pradesh (UP), arguably the most important site for the articulation of radical Dalit political assertion, lagged behind both states at just over 21 per cent, even if the actual number of individuals concerned was substantially higher (Census of India, 2011).

The high proportion of Dalits in the respective populations of the two states is not the only factor that invites comparison between them. Another obvious source of comparison would be the fact that both states were carved out of the only two provinces that were divided during the partition of British India. Furthermore, and of course related to this historical predicament, was the presence of a degree of religious heterogeneity observable in a relatively few other provinces of late-colonial India. In addition, both regions are situated at the geographical margins, historically speaking, of what is commonly supposed to be the heartland of Brahminical supremacy. Both, for a variety of complex reasons, have been subject to the mythology that 'caste does not matter'. There are thus a number of reasons to undertake comparison between these two otherwise distinctive states with specific regard to Dalit political assertion or its relative failures.

This chapter surveys some of the available literature that speaks, directly or indirectly, to the question framing this comparative investigation from the partition of India onwards. It argues that a wide range of factors, both internal and external to Dalit communities themselves, can help explain the puzzling absence of Dalit politics in the formal institutions of both states. While there are similarities in the kinds of explanations that have been offered, there also exist reasons unique to both states. Common to both regions are the kinds of challenges facing Dalit consolidation and political unity across caste lines and within major Dalit communities. The differences stem from the historical and sociopolitical contexts particular to each state.

Punjab

Despite the overall dominance of Punjab in partition historiography, the Dalit political history of this region and period remains an area requiring further elaboration. Mark Juergensmeyer's pioneering study of the Ad Dharm movement, the most significant instance of Dalit assertion in the colonial era, suggested a significant shift in the 1940s, marked by the emergence of what he called 'the Ambedkar alternative'. Ad Dharm leaders were increasingly drawn to B. R. Ambedkar's All India Scheduled Castes Federation, the rising popularity of which spelled the demise of the Ad Dharm and the leadership's increasing preoccupation with questions of political representation. In a rather schematic sketch of the last two decades of British rule, however, Juergensmeyer (1982: 164) asserted: 'During the final struggle for independence and the trauma involved in the partitioning of the Punjab, issues regarding the lower castes were all but forgotten in the chaos of migration and resettlement.' Independence from British colonial rule thus coincided with a subsidence of radical Dalit political activity. As Neeru Sharma (2012: 31) has observed, the early years of the republic witnessed the failure of the Republican Party of India (RPI; the party that was formed out of Ambedkar's All India Scheduled Castes Federation) to mobilize Dalit groups due to the lack of a strong leadership and divisions amongst them over the strategies to be pursued.

Even if there appears to be a relative paucity of studies dealing with the first several decades of the post-colonial period with respect to the possibilities of emergence of radical Dalit politics in Punjab, the focus has resumed in the latter decades of the century and thereafter. Pritam Singh (2017) has recently attributed what he terms 'Punjab's story of failed Dalit mobilization' to the 'fractured nature of Dalit identity and consolidation' in the state. While he concedes that there are differences amongst Dalits in Maharashtra and UP as well, they are 'nowhere close to the depth and scale of these internal cleavages among Punjabi Dalits' (Singh, 2017). Dalits in Punjab have been differentiated along religious, occupational, caste, and class lines that have, to varying degrees, prevented an amalgamation of their overall population. Differential access to reservations, as between the Ravidassias and Balmikis, for instance, has contributed to these differences even further. Singh also takes note of what he calls the accommodation mechanism of the ruling parties – the Indian National Congress (hereafter Congress) and the Shiromani Akali Dal (SAD) – towards the leaders of the major subaltern castes in the state, which has worked to exacerbate fissiparous tendencies. As he puts it: 'One can only hope that the new generations of educated Dalits in Punjab are able to liberate themselves from the patronising accommodation that is tantalisingly thrown at them by the upper-caste leadership of mainstream political parties' (Singh, 2017).

I. P. Singh (2019) confirms this sense of rupture within the Dalit population in Punjab. In an article in the *Times of India*, he asserts:

SCs [Scheduled Castes] may be one third of the population, but they are far from being a homogenous entity. Two biggest SC communities – Adhi-dharmi/Ravidassia and Valmiki/Mazhabis – remain sharply divided not just socially but also politically. Their presence is estimated to be one fourth of the state population. With every election it becomes clearer: Their politics remain as divided as their caste[s].

Singh goes on to show how differences along caste lines arose amongst Dalit leaders in the Congress with respect to the party's announcement of which candidates it would support. A similar situation transpired several years earlier in 2014, but this time in connection with the SAD. Singh subsequently notes that even the Bahujan Samaj Party (BSP), despite its ideological strengths, has largely remained confined to Ravidassias. The party's founder, Kanshi Ram, attempted to bring both communities onto the same political platform but met with little success.[1]

The rise and subsequent decline of the BSP in Punjab over the last two decades of the twentieth century constitutes arguably the most significant phase in the possibilities for radical Dalit politics in the state. Born of Ad Dharmi resentment with their lack of representation in extant political parties, the BSP seems to have initially enjoyed modest success in articulating the concerns of Dalit groups, before turning to a series of alliances over the course of the 1990s. These evidently failed to materialize and led to the demise of the party's fortunes.

Providing further ballast to claims of Dalit political disunity, Neeru Sharma (2012: 37) has argued:

> This decline of [the] BSP could be attributed to the continuing deep divisions and splits within the party over issues of power sharing and alliances with the main parties … The failure of the leadership to find a genuine ally in the social and political spheres led to great disillusionment among both the Ad-Dharmis and the Mazhabhis of Punjab, as their newly formed identity and stirring political consciousness could enable them to move away from the groups that dominated them earlier. Despite initial successes in the early years of its initiation, the BSP leadership in Punjab could not evolve an integrated ideology that could unite the different [D]alit castes in the state under one umbrella.

Sharma avers that the unevenness in the literacy rates of the SCs, with Ad Dharmis and Chamars being the most educated, meant that office positions came to be largely dominated by them, and this failed to mobilize the poorest of the SC groups such as the Mazhabhis. As a consequence, the Mazhabhis and Balmikis felt threatened by the increasing influence of the Ad Dharmis. In addition, the BSP failed to grasp the regional, cultural, and economic specificities of Punjab. The purity–pollution issue and Manuvad, which are the BSP's main ideological planks in UP, did not find expression in the sociocultural domain of Punjab. The failure of the BSP to capitalize on the most important Talhan caste-conflict issue in Punjab at the time (in June 2003), and its non-intervention in cases involving caste conflicts, led to the gradual withdrawal of Ad Dharmi support to the party (Sharma, 2012: 38).

Such a view of the limitations of the BSP in Punjab finds confirmation in Nirmal Singh's study of the party's attempt to mobilize Dalits in the state. Singh links the failure of the party to capture Dalit political sentiments to its organizational and strategic shortcomings. Of particular note is the factionalism within the party, the ability of *deras* to address only some of the concerns of the Dalit population, an emphasis on the politics of identity compared to class-based demands, the relatively authoritarian nature of the power structure within the party, and the failure of what Singh calls the 'Bahujan' strategy for securing political power. Singh (2019: 31–32) also observes that the party does not seem to have had a social and political programme:

> The most distinctive trait is that in Punjab, the BSP and its leaders have displayed their reluctance to be involved in mass agitation. Strangely, despite the BSP's aggressive agenda representing the cause of deprived and oppressed Dalits, lower castes and minorities against the upper-caste

establishment, party leaders and activists have stayed away from protests and demonstrations. They have, instead, devoted all their organization energies towards promotional activities projecting the party and its leaders mostly in preparation for the next elections.

Prerna Trehan's study of the 2017 Punjab elections offers further insight into the shortcomings of the BSP in particular and Dalit politics more generally. Trehan asserts that the party has been unable to develop an adequate leadership, in part because its more prominent leaders have shifted their allegiances to the Aam Aadmi Party (AAP). The BSP has 'failed to wage a movement against casteism in Punjab or produce an indigenous leader to mobilize Dalits across religious and regional divides' (Trehan, 2018: 79). Trehan notes that while Punjabi Dalits have sought out avenues of assertion within sociocultural domains, such independence of mind is yet to translate into the political-electoral domain. Like other commentators considered previously, she observes: 'Foundations for a political transformation require a social change wherein the various sub-groups of [the] SC population of Punjab are able to empathize with concerns of one another, thereby creating a consolidated Dalit base aimed at political assertion and representation' (Trehan, 2018: 81).

Yet another explanation for the relative failure of an autonomous Dalit politics in Punjab has been probed by Santosh K. Singh, who has proposed that the key may lie in the critical role that multiple religious traditions play within the Dalit community, thereby inhibiting a broader consolidation. Singh's ethnographic study of Buddhist–Ambedkarite, Ravidassia–Ambedkarite, and Sikh–Ambedkarite activists, in turn, reveals the substantial differences amongst them in terms of their respective theological preferences and how these translate into the question of political praxis. Singh (2018: 35) asserts: 'It is amply evident that religion plays a critical role in the region as it creates multiple axes of alliance as also divisions along regional and class-based dimensions.' Despite these differences however, Singh perceives a possibility and source of optimism in Ambedkar as a 'grand constant'. Ambedkar's omnipresence across sites of otherwise divided loyalties holds out the prospect of a future consolidated Dalit political presence in the state.

The scholarship surveyed thus points to the many sources of fracture within the Punjabi Dalit population as a whole as the reason for why their politics are yet to build a substantial independent and autonomous presence within the state. While particular scholars have placed different degrees of emphasis on a variety of factors, the consensus, such as it exists, seems to rest on the fact of the multifarious cleavages that prevent the consolidation of a unified Dalit political voice.

While some have expressed the hope that such a development comes to pass, others appear less convinced that such possibilities may be imminent given the present state of affairs.[2]

West Bengal

Undivided Bengal was home to one of the most active and politicized Dalit movements in late colonial India. Such was its power that Ambedkar turned to his associates in the Bengal branch of the All India Scheduled Castes Federation to seek his election to the Constituent Assembly of India, which he was able to secure. The Federation, however, bucked the dominant trend over the course of the last decade of colonial rule – namely a shift from alienation to integration with the dominant strands of Indian nationalism due to the persuasive tendencies of the latter (Bandyopadhyay, 2011). This shift helps explain, in part, the subsidence of demands for Dalit political autonomy. The drastic consequences of partition and its aftermath, however, resulted in the complete and utter destabilization of the movement (Bandyopadhyay and Chaudhury, 2014). After the transfer of power, the Namasudras, who constituted the caste that anchored Dalit mobilization in the region, found themselves in hostile territory in Muslim-majority East Pakistan and gradually made their way to West Bengal in fits and starts. They subsequently came to form the bulwark of the refugee movements that characterized the political life of the state from the mid-1950s to the late 1960s. Sekhar Bandyopadhyay (2009) has thus compellingly argued that the effect of partition on Dalit mobilization was to produce ruptures in the movement, with several key leaders pursuing diverging paths to deal with the fallout of that cataclysmic event on Dalit life and existence.

It goes without saying that West Bengal is a state that has long fostered a political culture hostile to and dissuasive of even a limited form of radical Dalit political mobilization. Arguably, the last time one might have observed such developments was in the mid-to-late 1960s, when the Ambedkarite Namasudra politician Jogendranath Mandal was attempting to propagate the RPI within the state. Yet his story offers a salutary lesson about the fate of Dalit political desire in West Bengal. The first two decades of independent rule in West Bengal gave rise to political forces in which Mandal was refused any meaningful participation time and again. After his death in 1968, upper-caste leadership, which was predominant in the state, promised the rehabilitation of all Dalit migrants from East Bengal in West Bengal in the politically necessary context of partition and ended up forcibly removing thousands of Dalit refugees from the state.

This was a leadership whose assurances of social justice with respect to the constitutional rights of Dalits in West Bengal went singularly unfulfilled in Mandal's lifetime, even if he was aware that modest changes were underway in some arenas; it was a leadership that seemed adamant on refusing him even the slightest semblance of political power. His trajectory illuminates a central complex of reasons why a political formation structured by questions of caste inequality did not, rather could not, emerge in post-colonial West Bengal. This was not for any lack of his trying.

The materials I have consulted over the years suggest that of critical importance in this regard was that neither Indian nationalist and Hindu nationalist nor communist parties, which were all led by upper-caste men, could countenance the notion that the Dalits of Bengal evolve an independent political presence. This negative and dissuasive political sentiment – their misrecognition – was rooted in the logic of their own political desires and mobilizations which grasped this particular community (thus determining the terms of their engagement) as a historical agent of ideologies in which considerations of caste played little role; they were mobilized as Indian citizens, Hindus, refugees, and peasants, but never primarily as Dalits. They would have much preferred the effacing of the entire manner of seeing required of the latter's categorial logic. The failure of Mandal's repeated efforts to secure political power in West Bengal thus constitutes an especially apt instantiation of this upper-caste refusal.[3]

Tethered to such an anti-Dalit ethos have been the cumulative effects of what the political scientist Dwaipayan Bhattacharya has termed the 'party-society' of West Bengal, which can be observed in the operations of governance under both the Left and, with certain qualifications, its successor, the All India Trinamool Congress (TMC). To put it simply, politics in Bengal did not revolve around solidarities based on caste, religion, language, or ethnicity. It instead lay in the political party in power, which mediated everything you did in your personal and work life, 'often transgressing the lines of separation between private and public, civic and political, social and familial' (Biswas, 2011). Needless to say, it has proved immensely challenging, under such conditions, to raise, much less articulate, specifically Dalit political concerns.

A related feature of West Bengal's political culture concerns the hegemony that the upper castes have exercised on the grammar of politics in the state, which has worked to forestall the emergence of caste-subaltern assertion. In Partha Chatterjee's reading (2016: 99), upper-caste hegemony has been sustained because of the elite's ability to 'present itself as a universal class standing above all cultural and local particularities and, moreover, as one that was open to entry by those who acquire the necessary cultural accomplishments'. As he goes on to argue:

> In short, the upper-caste elite culture became hegemonic precisely because it was not exclusively about caste. Its persuasive power came from its ability to create and defend larger social consolidations. Had it been only about caste dominance – a hypocritical attempt to cling on to age-old privileges – it would have been easily unmasked. Consequently, the question of resistance – or lack of resistance – to this dominance has to be answered in terms of the possibilities of counter-hegemonic struggle. (Chatterjee, 2016: 100)

Turning to some of the reasons internal to the Dalit communities of the state, one of the overriding factors that acts as a hindrance to the formulation of explicitly Dalit political mobilization is the overwhelming poverty of these communities and the economic pressures of basic survival on them. Politics, after all, is an expensive business, beyond the slate of possibilities available to the common person in West Bengal. In conversations with Dalit community activists, the author has learned that an active assertion within the electoral politics of the state is a luxury few can afford.

Next, one might point to the relative lack of community consciousness, solidarity, and unity either amongst Dalits as a whole or within particular SCs. There is little that binds, for instance, the three most numerically significant SCs in the state – the Rajbanshis, Namasudras, and Bagdis – and such lack of affinity prevents the articulation of a Dalit consciousness. Furthermore, rather than a shared sense of identity amongst these caste groups, there exists a fairly substantial sense of caste difference, in addition to a not inconsiderable degree of class and occupational differentiation within them. As Chatterjee (2016: 100) puts it: 'There is little common cause shared between these groups.' He notes the variations amongst the four largest Dalit castes in West Bengal: the Namasudras were, for much of the first couple of decades since independence, preoccupied with questions of relief and rehabilitation following their migration from East Pakistan; the Rajbanshis are internally differentiated into Jotdars and Adhiars; the Bagdis remain mostly landless and amongst the poorest groups of rural society; and the Paundra have entered the urban informal economy of Calcutta and its suburbs. Chatterjee (2016: 100) thus asks, albeit rhetorically: 'Where is the ground for a common mobilization against the dominance of the upper castes?' He also points to suggestive evidence of elements of social mobility amongst certain Dalit castes, which may have led some of them to no longer wish to be identified as such.

Further, one may consider the question of Dalit political leadership. A quick glance at the West Bengal legislative assembly reveals that the vast majority of Dalit members of the legislative assembly (MLAs) are from the TMC. Not a single one belongs to the BSP or any other party traditionally associated with specifically Dalit mobilization. Indeed, the BSP does not command a single seat within West Bengal's legislative assembly. Furthermore, there are no signs that this leadership as a whole is driven by a particularly Ambedkarite ideology. Amongst relatively radicalized segments of the Dalit community, there remains an abiding sense that their political leadership, as it is currently constituted, is not especially concerned with the needs and requirements of Dalits per se; it is rather far more motivated by the quest to feather their own nests. Relatedly, there is the question of the political form of the leadership which is yet to coalesce around the authority of a single politician who has won the confidence of competitors and claimants to power and the wider community at large. The emergence of a singular and exceptional leader who has tended to accompany Dalit politics in states where it has made its presence felt, in both the past and the present, is yet to occur in West Bengal.

The author's conversations with Dalit community activists reveal yet another reason for the relative absence of explicitly Dalit political demands within the political grammar of the state. Although this may be an inconvenient, if not uncomfortable, truth to confront, this concerns the relative quiescence, self-satisfaction, or indifference to communitarian initiatives displayed by those who have benefitted from the reservation policy in a variety of state institutions. The complaint seems to be that individuals who have been fortunate to receive such benefits are not especially inclined to share them with others or to agitate for the extension of the same to a wider circle of recipients.

Although this may have been overestimated in some circles, yet another factor militating against the formulation of a Dalit politics in West Bengal is the much-commented-on rise of the Bharatiya Janata Party (BJP) and its affiliated organizations in the state. There is no doubt that certain segments of Dalits have displayed a receptivity to the varied overtures of that party towards their community. Recent reports (see Das, 2017) indicate, for instance, that since 2012 the Rashtriya Swayamsevak Sangh (RSS) has made great inroads by establishing numerous *shakha*s, schools, and other community outreach initiatives in the northern districts of Alipurduar, Jalpaiguri, Cooch Behar, and Uttar Dinajpur. Here, RSS workers have predominantly targeted Adivasi, Dalit, and Other Backward Classes (OBC) groups. Furthermore, in the 2016 assembly elections, the BJP had given party tickets for various assembly seats to Dalit and Adivasi candidates, even in seats that were unreserved.

Arguably, the most significant demonstration of intent by the BJP to the Dalit voters in the state was through the polarizing Citizenship Amendment Act (CAA), 2019. In the border areas of Malda, Nadia, and Murshidabad districts, the BJP has attempted to mobilize support amongst Dalit refugee groups, particularly those belonging to the Namasudra community, where many individuals since 1971 have till date not been granted citizenship or received attendant rights. Prime minister Narendra Modi's visit in 2018 to 'Boro Ma', the matriarch of the Matua Mahasangha, an influential social and religious organization of the Namasudra Dalits, gave a personal touch to the BJP's outreach. While the TMC has initiated a variety of programmes in response to the BJP's attempt to wrest control of Dalit political loyalties, the overall landscape reinforces the impression that Dalits, far from being the originators of primary political agendas and ideologies, have become one of the battlegrounds on which the dominant contending parties (that continue, despite important transformations and adjustments, to perpetuate an upper-caste hegemony) will seek to establish their political supremacy.

So, in sum, the prospects for the emergence of a Dalit politics genuinely committed to the welfare and well-being of those communities and the critique of upper-caste dominance are difficult to discern at the present conjuncture. The reasons, as I have suggested, are numerous, and they certainly interact in complex ways. This is not to imply, however, that nothing has changed or that there are no domains of Dalit activism beyond the scope of formal electoral politics that can potentially contribute to the gradual formation of a radical consciousness and eventually, formal politics. One might consider the substantial growth of non-governmental organizations (NGOs) – in particular Ambedkar Missions – working towards the educational development of Dalit communities. In the literary domain, one may take note of the relatively recent burgeoning of the field of Dalit literature and its analysis, the outcome of organizations like the Dalit Sahitya Sanstha, and the publication house Chaturthha Duniya. The award-winning work of authors like Manoranjan Byapari, among several others, for instance, has gone a considerable way towards raising both Bengali and national awareness of the vicissitudes of Dalit experience and has contributed to a growing interest in Bengali Dalit lifeworlds. In the year 2000, the foundation of the Dalit Sahitya Academy at the behest of the ruling party constitutes another avenue whereby specifically Dalit concerns may find address. Despite such welcome developments, however, it is hard to see how they necessarily translate into the assertion and demonstration of political power.

What then are the potentialities for the growth and development of Dalit politics in West Bengal in the years to come? Historians are not especially well-equipped at hazarding such predictions, but one (perhaps distant) possibility may include the emergence of an autonomous Dalit political platform born of the dialectics of betrayal by and alienation from both the major contenders for power in the state: the TMC and the BJP. While there is not much to suggest the plausibility of such an emergence at present, the speculation concerns the likelihood of fractures and polarizations born of crises yet to fully blossom in the fragile alliances and balances of power that characterize West Bengal's political scene. There is no doubt that the political leadership of the state has over the course of several decades become far more representative of the true ethnic diversity of its population, even if incrementally so. Should this trajectory continue, and the historic upper-caste stranglehold on the levers of political power be further loosened in the years to come, it may open up room for opportunities inconceivable at present.

Comparisons and Contrasts

This survey of the limited available literature on why Dalit politics has remained constrained in both Punjab and West Bengal thus points to a number of similarities as well as areas of difference. Among the features that seem in common with and most germane to the present investigation are undoubtedly the multiple fractures that exist within the Dalit populations of both states. Indeed, it is an open question whether the concept of 'community', with its suggestion of solidarity and unity, is applicable in either of these cases. Dalits in Punjab and Bengal appear different by fissures of political–ideological preferences, class, occupation, and caste difference. Taken together, the extant scholarship suggests that such substantial differences within Dalit identities and social locations present the greatest challenge to the understandable and, depending on one's perspective, desirable objective of Dalit consolidation. Other features that appear to exist in both states are the various shortcomings of the Dalit political leadership. Neither set of leaders seem to have been able to evolve a political ideology that has had significant appeal for Dalits as a whole; nor have Dalit political representatives attempted to develop unity amongst themselves. Rather, the dissensions apparent amongst the Dalit populations of both states have been reflected in their political representatives who are subject to the vagaries of contention between the dominant political parties. Finally, one may take note of the fact that both states have witnessed a hegemonic social and political dominance of elite and non-Dalit groups within the politics, society, and culture of each region. Within such a context, it has proved challenging to mount an effective counter to caste-elite dominance.[4]

Alongside the analogous reasons for the limitations on Dalit politics in Punjab and West Bengal, there are also those quite distinct to each state. Whereas Punjab has witnessed the emergence, albeit modest, of the BSP within the politics of the state, West Bengal has not produced a similar formation from within either the Namasudras or the Rajbanshis, the two largest Dalit castes in the region. Furthermore, whereas the majority of, if not all, Dalit castes are classified as Hindus in West Bengal, Dalits in Punjab straddle the Hindu and Sikh populations, lending an added layer of complexity to their collective predicament.

While a wide range of factors have inhibited the formation of a radical Dalit political consciousness that has translated into electoral dividends, there is also the issue of the different forms that Dalit assertion, even if not explicitly political, has indeed taken in both states. Both states have witnessed the outgrowth of cultural expression of various kinds that, while standing outside the purview of electoral politics, nonetheless holds out the promise of contributing to growing awareness of shared socio-economic and political-cultural exclusions. It remains to be seen whether such cultures of dissent will translate into the formation of wider and, ultimately, counter-hegemonic solidarities.

Perhaps the lesson to be drawn from this brief survey is that the assumption underlying the question framing this examination is a flawed one. Punjab and West Bengal may indeed be home to two of the largest populations of Dalits in India, but it does not necessarily follow that such numerical strength can easily translate into the political arena. The prospect for the growth of Dalit political formations, however, ought not to be ruled out for in the final analysis, there can be no gainsaying the truth that the Indian democratic experiment is deepened and enriched by the fuller participation of those groups who have been traditionally excluded from the exercise of political power. One can only hope such an eventuality arrives in both Punjab and West Bengal, sooner than later.

Notes

1. See Surinder S. Jodhka's chapter in this volume (Chapter 11) for an account of the challenges that Ram encountered.
2. While the election of Charanjit Singh Channi as the first Dalit chief minister of the state in 2022 is a major development in this regard, it remains to be seen whether this consolidates Dalits in Punjab or not.
3. See the author's study, Sen (2018), for further details.
4. As such, the evidence surveyed here resonates with the findings of several other contributions to this volume, in particular, the chapter by Badri Narayan (see Chapter 15 in this volume).

Bibliography

Bandyopadhyay, S. 2009. 'Partition and the Ruptures in Dalit Identity Politics in Bengal'. *Asian Studies Review* 33(4): 455–67.

————. 2011. *Caste, Protest and Identity in Colonial India: The Namasudras of Bengal, 1872–1947*. New Delhi: Oxford University Press.

Bandyopadhyay, S., and A. B. R. Chaudhury. 2014. 'In Search of Space: The Scheduled Caste Movement in West Bengal after Partition'. *Policies and Practices* 59 (February): 1–22. Kolkata: Mahanirban Calcutta Research Group.

Biswas, S. 2011. 'Is Communism Dead in India?' British Broadcasting Corporation (BBC), 14 May. https://www.bbc.com/news/world-south-asia-13395074. Accessed on 26 December 2022.

Census of India (2011). 'T 00-005: Total Population, Population of Scheduled Castes and Scheduled Tribes and Their Proportions to the Total Population'. New Delhi: Office of the Registrar General and Census Commissioner, Ministry of Home Affairs, Government of India. https://censusindia.gov.in/Tables_Published/A-Series/A-Series_links/t_00_005.aspx. Accessed 26 November 2020.

Chatterjee, P. 2016. 'Partition and the Mysterious Disappearance of Caste in Bengal'. In *The Politics of Caste in West Bengal*, edited by U. Chandra, G. Heierstad, and K. B. Nielsen, 83–102. New York: Routledge.

Das, Soumya. 2017. 'RSS-Affiliated Schools Bloom across Bengal'. *Hindu*, 25 February, https://www.thehindu.com/news/national/other-states/rssaffiliated-schools-bloom-across-bengal/article17368168.ece. Accessed on 26 December 2022.

Juergensmeyer, M. 1982. *Religion as Social Vision: The Movement against Untouchability in 20th-Century Punjab*. Berkeley: University of California Press.

Sen, D. 2018. *The Decline of the Caste Question: Jogendranath Mandal and the Defeat of Dalit Politics in Bengal*. Cambridge: Cambridge University Press.

Sharma, N. 2012. 'Caste in Punjab: Political Marginalization and Cultural Assertion of Scheduled Castes in Punjab'. *Journal of Punjab Studies* 19(1): 27–47. https://punjab.global.ucsb.edu/sites/default/files/sitefiles/journals/volume19/no1/2-NeeruSharma19_1.pdf. Accessed 26 November 2020.

Singh, I. P. 2019. 'Why Dalits in Punjab Couldn't Dominate Politically'. *Times of India*, 22 April. https://timesofindia.indiatimes.com/city/chandigarh/why-dalits-in-punjab-couldnt-dominate-politically/articleshow/68982830.cms. Accessed on 26 November 2020.

Singh, N. 2019. 'Dalits, Their Support Base and the Bahujan Samaj Party: A Case Study of the Doaba Region'. *Contemporary Voice of Dalit* 11(1): 44–54.

Singh, P. 2017. 'Punjab's Dalits and the Politics of Patronage'. *Alternatives*, 1 January. https://www.alterinter.org/?Punjab-s-Dalits-and-Politics-of-Patronage. Accessed on 22 September 2022.

Singh, S. K. 2018. 'Dalit Politics and Its Fragments in Punjab: Does Religion Hold the Key?' *Economic and Political Weekly* 43(35): 32–36.

Trehan, P. 2018. 'Understanding Obstacles to Dalit Mobilization and Political Assertion During the 2017 Punjab Elections'. *Journal of Punjab Studies* 25(1): 61–89.

4

Decline of the Bahujan Samaj Party

Dalit Politics under Right-Wing Hegemony

Sudha Pai

The Dalit movement in the country is at a turning point today. Dalit parties are in electoral decline, with a substantial section of Dalits having moved towards non-Dalit parties, particularly the Bharatiya Janata Party (BJP). Uttar Pradesh (UP) provides an important site for the study of this phenomenon as it is a key state where Dalit assertion led to the formation of a strong Dalit party, the Bahujan Samaj Party (BSP), which has shaped national politics over the last few decades. Also, UP is the state from where two strong leaders – Mayawati and Narendra Modi – have influenced Dalit politics in the Hindi heartland in the new millennium.

In the 1990s, the success of the BSP under the leadership of Mayawati lay in harnessing the desire for self-respect and dignity among Dalits into a strong party. By the mid-1990s, she was able to consolidate the various sub-castes, insofar as voting was concerned, behind the BSP and emerge as a notable Dalit leader. These developments enabled Mayawati to move beyond her core constituency and form the Sarvajan alliance in 2007, which helped her gain a majority in the assembly elections. But the success of the BSP proved to be short-lived. Defeated in the 2012 assembly elections, it has experienced swift decline, following the revival of the BJP in UP. The BSP failed *to win even a single seat* in the Lok Sabha elections in 2014, won 19 seats in the 2017 assembly elections, and 10 seats in the 2019 Lok Sabha elections, though it managed to gain around 20 per cent of the votes each time (Election Commission of India [ECI], 2014, 2017, 2019). In the 2022 assembly elections, the party obtained only one seat in the Rasara constituency in Ballia district of eastern UP. It obtained just 12.9 per cent of the vote, which was its lowest since 1989, when it gained 9.46 percent of the vote but had managed to gain 13 seats.

Following the BSP's defeat in 2012, when Dalits began to actively search for an alternative, Modi was able to take advantage of these shifts and attract a section of Dalits in the 2014 national elections. This chapter analyses, first, why a considerable segment of Dalits today has rejected the BSP and prefers the BJP, once decried as *manuvadi*, and, second, the nature of the crisis facing the Dalit movement following the collapse of the BSP. Regarding the former, I argue that significant longer-term developments in the political arena of the Hindi heartland underlie these seminal shifts. Beginning in the late 1990s and continuing into the 2000s, a new relationship between *caste*, *development*, and *electoral politics* emerged, which helps explain both the decline of the BSP and the BJP's co-option of Dalits in a new form of inclusionary politics. Caste, and identity alignments based on it, had been weakening since the late 1990s, and caste alone was no longer a 'predictor of vote choice' and was 'probably at its weakest for thirty years in 2012' (Heath and Kumar, 2012: 6).

Within this larger shift, the waning of identity politics since the early 2000s in UP produced a rising aspiration for advancement among Dalits, impacted by globalization and cultural modernization (Pai, 2019). In UP, compared to states in southern and western India, economic reform did not lead to higher growth, as short-lived, unstable regimes, including those led by the BSP, in the 1990s and early 2000s, were unable to put forth effective policies for development. These circumstances created a growing economic divide between an educated, rising middle- and lower-middle class mainly from the better-off, dominant Jatavs, and the smaller, poorer, marginalized sections, such as the Balmikis and Pasis.[1] In the 1990s, Mayawati (2001: 15) had argued that 'self-respect is more important to Dalits than material gains' and 'what we are fighting for is dignity and self-respect'. But, by the 2000s, Dalits began to question whether self-respect alone is enough, amidst growing disappointment over Mayawati not having put forward an agenda to provide economic advancement.

This study shows that the immediate reason for the BSP's defeat in 2012 was the perception among Dalits that the Sarvajan agenda followed by Mayawati's government had not improved their material conditions. Also, considerable funds were spent on building memorials and statues of Dalits icons, while their villages lacked roads, drinking water, healthcare, and so on. A trickle from the BSP had begun earlier, from 1996 to 2000, when the Indian National Congress (hereafter Congress) had gained at least a quarter of Dalit votes, with the BSP coming a close second (Bhuyan, 2017). But it was disillusionment with the Sarvajan policy that led to an exodus – first towards the Samajwadi Party (SP) in 2012, and later the BJP, though the Jatavs have largely remained with Mayawati. Taking advantage of these conditions, Modi packaged rapid economic development for Dalits as something the BSP had failed to deliver, attracting a considerable number of the non-Jatav sub-castes in the 2014 elections. Simultaneously, the BJP catered to their cultural aspirations by promising inclusion within the 'Hindu' identity, employing a redefined, *subaltern Hindutva*. This success was carried forward by Modi through well-crafted, inclusionary strategies in the 2017 assembly, 2019 general, and the recent 2022 assembly elections.

Despite the success of the BJP, Dalit politics has exhibited both *preference and protest* from 2015 onwards. As this study shows, on the one hand, large-scale, violent protests against atrocities on Dalits in UP and elsewhere committed by upper and backward castes emboldened by the victory of the BJP took place; yet, on the other, electoral support by non-Jatav, smaller sub-castes increased for the BJP in the 2017 and 2019 elections. In the 2022 assembly elections, the BJP made significant gains among both the Jatavs and the non-Jatavs. It won over two-fifth of the support of non-Jatavs, as opposed to one-third in the 2017 assembly elections. More importantly, it made, for the first time, some of its most impressive inroads among the Jatavs, a community that has supported Mayawati in the past, securing nearly a fifth of their votes, more than double of 2017. The BSP's vote share among the Jatavs came down drastically from 87 per cent to just 65per cent. Among the non-Jatavs, too, who had already started moving away from the party since the last few elections, the BSP's vote share reduced considerably (Lokniti–Centre for the Study of Developing Societies [CSDS], 2022). Internally, this reflects insecurity, coming together against atrocities, and yet rivalry and division in elections between the Jatavs and non-Jatavs. The increasing support for the BJP in the UP elections also raises the question of whether this signifies an ideological shift into the Hindutva fold by a section of Dalits, or it is the result of a variety of highly successful mobilizational strategies – including the use of social media by the BJP, along with the charismatic personality of Modi, viewed as a 'messiah' of the poor and a provider of welfare and good governance.

As a consequence of these significant developments, I argue that the growing crisis in Dalit politics in the Hindi heartland is both *normative and political*. It is normative as Dalits reject partially or review earlier norms and ideas, which held the Dalit movement together and provided moral meaning to their existence and identity. It is political as sub-caste divisions have regained importance following the collapse of the BSP, and class divisions have assumed significance due to the desire for upward mobility; overlying them is another major political divide – namely between the Ambedkarites and the Hindutvawadis, both of whom are further fractured on the ground. The older norms and discourse now lack credibility, but Dalits facing a right-wing hegemonic party have not been able to marshal the resources needed to replace them for renewed action.

Sarvajan: Challenge of Inclusive Development

Mayawati's Sarvajan strategy was based on the idea of creating an umbrella party, like the erstwhile Congress but with a Dalit core. On assuming office, the BSP faced the challenge of taking care of the specific needs of Dalits and fulfilling the expectations of the upper castes who believed they had contributed to its victory. During the campaign, Mayawati was able to convince her Dalit followers that the BSP remained 'their' party; it was not easy to do the same while in power. As Sukhdev Singh Rajbhar declared when Mayawati assumed office, it was understood that Dalit aspirations should not manifest themselves as demands immediately. Any considerable improvement in their position would necessarily take time (Ramakrishnan, 2007: 7). But this was not a feeling shared by the large majority whose expectations had been roused.

On assuming power, Mayawati announced that her government's focus would be on the welfare of all, not only the Dalit–Bahujans.[2] Her economic agenda was radically different from the BSP's past programme of retributive social justice.[3] On 20 July 2007, when she sought a special economic package of INR 80,000 crores for the Eleventh Plan period from the centre, the 'priority areas' announced were 'rural development, agriculture, social development and infrastructure, [and] making the state conducive for attracting investment' (*Indian Express*, 2007). She requested the prime minister for a 'Special Area Incentive Package' of INR 9,400 crores and INR 4,700 crores separately for developing Purvanchal and Bundelkhand. She also sought INR 22,000 crores for the development of agriculture and allied sectors, INR 6,500 crore for rural development, and INR 13,300 crores for the integrated development of the state. Mayawati emphasized that her government had set a target of 10 per cent growth and reducing the number of people living below the poverty line (BPL) by half during the Eleventh Plan (*Indian Express*, 2007).

After months of negotiation, Mayawati was able to obtain INR 80,000 crores despite the Planning Commission's caution that the funds provided would need 'major increase in the absorptive capacity, improvement in governance structures and major reform of the delivery system' and were 'clearly beyond the capacity of the state to spend' (*Indian Express*, 2008). It was a political settlement, with the BSP providing support to the Congress-led United Progressive Alliance (UPA) government. But her pronouncements provided her the support of senior bureaucrats and created 'cautious optimism' among retired Indian Administrative Service (IAS) officers, voiced in a seminar in 2009, that Mayawati would provide better governance as she had full majority (Ramakrishnan, 2009).[4]

Table 4.1, which provides the budget expenditure by the BSP government from 2007 to 2012 in selected sectors, shows that the largest amount was spent on education; welfare of Scheduled Castes (SCs), Scheduled Tribes (STs), and minorities and the Scheduled Caste Special Component Plan; women and child welfare; health; and urban development. These were programmes meant for the poorer sections within all caste groups.[5] During its tenure, the government spent on three major areas: social welfare, infrastructure, and governance. In the area of social welfare, some important schemes were the Uttar Pradesh Mukhyamantri Mahamaya Garib Aarthik Madad Yojana, the Mahamaya Garib Balika Ashirvad Yojana, and an Anganwadi programme for children. Under the Savitri Bai Phule Balika Shiksha Madad Yojana, 10 lakh bicycles were distributed to Muslim and poor schoolgirls from 2008 to 2011. But a study points out that in areas, such as health and education, government response was not satisfactory; mostly old schemes were renamed, and a few new centrally funded ones were implemented (Singh, 2010).

Some important rural infrastructural programmes undertaken were the Bhimrao Ambedkar Rural Integrated Development Programme (*The Hindu*, 2007), which included revamping of the Ambedkar Village Programme for upliftment of the entire village community and provision of funds to *gram panchayat*s (village councils) for brick laying, covering drains, village roads, drinking water, toilets for schools, and so on; the Jawahar Rozgar Yojana (JRY); the Mahatma Gandhi National Rural Employment Guarantee Scheme (MNREGS); the Indira Awas Yojana (IAY); and so on. In 2008, three housing security schemes were launched: (*a*) the Kanshi Ram Sahari Gareeb Awaas Yojana (KSGAY) for the urban poor in the general category in which the OBCs and the SCs received 23 per cent and 27 per cent of total benefits, respectively; (*b*) for city dwellers 1.01 lakh houses were to be built, and in three years 96,418 houses were constructed; and (*c*) for the rural poor, two new schemes were started: the Mahamaya Awas Yojana (MAY) exclusively for the SCs and the STs, under which 3.06 lakh SC and ST families benefitted at a cost of INR 949 crore, and the Mahamaya Sarva Awas Yojana (MSAY) for the non-SC and the non-ST poor under which 50,000 families benefitted at a cost of INR 180 crore. Key towns were to be provided housing, roads, drinking water, sewage, cleanliness, and employment, spending INR 3,000 crores over five years (*Times of India*, 2007). For the rural poor, the IAY and the MAY were exclusively meant for SC and ST communities in which 3.06 lakh SC and ST families benefitted at a cost of INR 949 crores; the MSAY for the non-SC and non-ST poor was also implemented (Singh, 2010).

Numerous infrastructure projects were initiated: the Ganga and Yamuna expressways to connect parts of UP to Delhi and Noida were proposed or

Table 4.1 Budget expenditure in selected sectors by the Bahujan Samaj Party (BSP) government, 2007–12

Sectors	2007–08	2008–09	2009–10	2010–11	2011–12
			(in thousands)		
Housing	87,30,748	1,57,34,396	1,03,53,409	1,35,86,474	1,16,34,862
Industry (all types)	63,19,354	47,39,849	54,65,687	78,20,729	58,57,314
Sugarcane	55,62,464	73,96,294	71,31,019	19,84,077	55,06,732
Energy	7,28,63,146	7,66,89,276	7,57,54,466	7,66,02,938	8,22,34,678
Agriculture	5,78,36,787	6,96,29,976	7,74,45,597	9,72,90,854	3,53,70,306
Health	3,96,65,341	4,52,05,569	5,56,57,775	6,61,91,366	6,96,46,313
Urban development	1,23,70,203	3,04,44,330	1,16,33,629	2,34,24,310	3,20,80,187
Public works department (only buildings)	5,26,72,935	6,20,06,894	6,06,29,861	6,68,52,160	9,20,000
Education	12,42,947	10,81,620	4,42,836	6,09,376	NA
	12,27,99,210	13,35,39,835	16,83,06,968	22,36,61,611	28,27,07,408

(Contd)

Table 4.1 (*Contd*)

Social welfare	7,50,69,709	10,67,38,126	11,80,62,292	14,10,46,230	1,51,29,361
Disabled persons and backward class welfare	1,03,44,465	1,49,02,021	1,53,72,244	1,51,86,599	NA
Scheduled Class welfare	1,76,30,962	2,38,07,459	2,72,75,323	3,17,27,598	3,45,78,143
Scheduled Tribe welfare	2,26,298	2,79,009	3,10,547	8,15,072	10,96,227
Scheduled Caste Special Component Plan	4,68,67,984	6,77,49,637	7,51,04,178	9,33,16,961	11,61,29,857
Minority welfare	26,40,406	48,08,170	55,99,802	1,22,10,192	1,11,44,823
Women and child welfare	1,79,94,482	2,06,07,549	2,97,23,087	3,50,59,473	4,01,91767

Source: Data for 2007–11 provided by the Chief Minister's Secretariat, Lucknow, on 10 August 2011, during fieldwork conducted to obtain the figures; data for 2011–12 provided at a later date by the Secretariat.

constructed (*Economic Times*, 2012), the Noida Metro was inaugurated by Mayawati in November 2009 (Rawat, 2009), and new multispecialty hospitals were built in Lucknow and Noida (One India, 2007; *Times of India*, 2013). Solar power plants were set up, and the first 5 megawatt plant at Naini, Prayagraj district, began functioning in March 2012, with more powerhouses to be built by the National Thermal Power Corporation (NTPC) (*Business Standard*, 2007). A new airport was proposed at Jewar near Noida. However, the media described many of these projects, built under public–private partnership (PPP), as corruption-ridden (see Tripathi, 2012). On the governance front, there was improvement in law and order and administrative functioning. The UP Anti-terrorism Act, 2007, helped remove land mafia, professional killers, liquor and drug mafia, kidnappers, and extortionists, and the organized crime rate fell. To ensure confidence in the police, 23 per cent of all *thana* heads appointed were from SC or ST backgrounds, 27 per cent from backward categories including minorities, and 50 per cent from other caste groups. Attempts were made to remove corruption in many government departments (*Times of India*, 2007).

Media reports, despite the criticism about spending on statues, pointed out that vital parameters of the economy had changed for the better in UP (Tripathi, 2011). The Human Development Index report of 2010 showed that its net state domestic product (NSDP) grew by 76 per cent between 2007 and 2011, almost at par with Gujarat. The planning ministry revealed that UP was among the five states which had higher growth rates than their Eleventh Plan (2007–12) targets; the gross domestic product (GDP) grew at 7.28 per cent as against a target of 6.10 per cent. It was also awarded 'best performing state in agriculture' by the UPA. Mayawati, it was argued, had, in her five-year tenure, pumped over INR 1,00,000 crores into various schemes, particularly for Dalits and the marginalized (Tripathi, 2011).

Return to the Dalit Agenda

Yet within a few months into her regime, Mayawati faced the inherent contradiction of providing development to all, versus satisfying her core constituency. There were rumblings of discontent, particularly among the powerful Jatavs, who felt there was increasing emphasis on Brahmins, while their needs were neglected. A return to the symbolic politics of building memorials to Dalit leaders such as the Manyawar Shri Kanshiram Ji Green Eco Garden, one of the biggest ecological parks in the world with 500 artificial animals made of bronze, 10 bronze fountains with water bodies and a pathway of about 13 kilometres surrounding it, which opened on 3 March 2011 (*Times of India*, 2011). Increase in the budget for Dalit welfare every year, for 2007–12, as Table 4.1 shows, failed to assuage feelings. Despite the expenditure to improve their position, the vast difference between Dalits, who constitute the poorest sections, and the upper castes, which have long formed the elite and controlled the commanding heights of the economy, could not be bridged within a short time.

By the 2009 Lok Sabha elections, there were reports of Dalits complaining that their villages lacked water, roads, and schools, while Mayawati was spending on memorials to Dalit icons. In the 2009 elections, the Congress gained 21 seats in UP, one more than the BSP. As UPA-II was neither willing nor able to provide funds due to the economic slowdown, recourse was made to organizational change: Brahmin leader S. C. Mishra was marginalized, and renewed importance was given to old timers such as Other Backward Classes (OBC) leader Babu Singh Kushwaha and minority leader Naseemuddin Siddiqui; 100 chairmen and vice presidents of various local boards were replaced; reshuffling of top bureaucrats to induct lower-caste officers was undertaken; and hints of a possible ministerial reshuffle and a Dalit mega rally in Lucknow in March 2010 came up (Singh, 2010).

Electoral Defeat: Loss of Core Support

Despite the unhappiness voiced, the BSP won the three assembly and two Lok Sabha seats in the by-elections in April 2008 (Ghildiyal, 2008) and virtually swept the *panchayat* polls in October 2010 (Verma, 2010). However, it suffered a crushing defeat in the 2012 assembly elections, obtaining 80 seats and 25.91 per cent of the votes compared to 206 seats and 30 per cent of the votes in 2007, despite obtaining *more* votes from Brahmins, Rajputs, Vaishyas, and other upper castes than in 2007. Most importantly, it lost support from Mayawati's core group, the Jatavs, from a high of 86 per cent in 2007 to 62 per cent in the 2012 assembly elections. There was also a drop among Balmikis from 71 per cent to 42 per cent, among Pasis from 57 per cent to 53 per cent, and among other SCs from 58 per cent to 45 per cent; the bulk of these votes shifted to the SP (*Economic and Political Weekly*, 2012). The results indicated *a seminal shift in the pattern of electoral support to the BSP*. For over two decades, the BSP's success had rested on a strategy of securing the votes of the vast majority of the state's 35 million Dalits, who make up 21 per cent of the electorate, and topping it up with a scattering of votes from the backward sections of other communities (Heath and Kumar, 2012). This pattern disappeared and has not reappeared again.

A post-poll survey reveals the desire among a section of Dalits for expenditure on *development* rather than *identity* (Heath and Kumar, 2012). Not all were happy with the construction of memorials commemorating Dalit leaders or icons: 73 per cent of Jatavs supported the construction of statues and voted for the BSP, but only 57 per cent of Dalits who 'somewhat supported' did so, and this fell further to less than 50 per cent among those who 'did not support' (Heath and Kumar, 2012). Regarding development, less than 50 per cent of Jatavs and less than 40 per cent from other sub-castes thought there was improvement, particularly among those with college education and high incomes (Heath and Kumar, 2012: 47). In sum, expenditure on monuments, lack of development, perception of corruption, and failure in public policies such as those pertaining to land acquisition, road construction, and education underlay the rejection of the BSP.

The BJP's Politics of Dalit Inclusion

The shift of a significant section of Dalits, unlike the backward castes, towards the BJP, witnessed in the 2014 general elections, is largely a recent phenomenon. It primarily emerged after the defeat of the BSP in 2012 but has been quite rapid since. However, much before the rise of Modi, an early phase of quiet mobilization at the grassroots of Dalits and backward castes had begun from the late 1990s and early 2000s onwards to revive the party's Hindu base, which the BJP–RSS felt had declined under the leadership of Atal Behari Vajpayee (Pai and Kumar, 2018). Consequently, the BJP's Dalit vote share in 2014 was twice that in 2009, partly achieved by co-opting Dalit leaders (a large number just prior to the 2014 elections), and partly through Modi's mobilizational strategies (Bhuyan, 2017).

Modi's achievement lay in taking forward this early mobilization during the long 2014 electoral campaign, together with social engineering. He realized that for the lower castes, rather than identity, economic advancement had become important; also winning seats in UP required the BJP, an upper-caste party, to shift downwards and gain the support of the backward castes and Dalits, who together constitute almost half the state population. Employing a twofold agenda – developmental and cultural – Modi evoked the 'Gujarat model' (Mathew, 2014), which he claimed underlay the growth of 10 per cent over 10 years in Gujarat, promising *achhe din* (good times) through rapid economic development and employment for the lower castes in UP (Pai and Kumar, 2015). In sum, he focused on arousing the frustrations and aspirations of the poor, smaller sub-castes, and unemployed Dalits.

Simultaneously, building on the earlier quiet grassroots mobilization, the BJP catered to the cultural aspirations of the smaller and poorer non-Jatav sub-castes, promising inclusion within the 'Hindu' identity by employing a redefined ideology of *non-Brahminical Hindutva* and creating a new social-electoral coalition of the upper castes, sections of backward castes, and Dalits, prior to the 2014 elections (Pai and Kumar, 2018). This was possible as local BJP–RSS leaders, since the early 2000s, had wooed the highly fragmented and competitive individual sub-castes, unearthing local heroes, histories, and myths to link Dalits to Hindutva – for example, the linking of three Dalit communities, numerous in eastern UP, with the Ramayana: the Pasis, Musahars, and Nishads (Narayan, 2009: 10, 30). Once in power, since 2014, the BJP–RSS has attempted to take this cultural mobilization further by providing greater space within the Hindu identity and community to these smaller Dalit groups, acknowledging their specific sub-caste identity and right to practice local rituals, building small temples to their local deities, and thereby according them dignity and respect. A good example is the Mata Shabari temple in the prime minister's adopted village of Jayapur in Varanasi district, in Musahar Basti of the village (Narayan, 2017).

This strategy proved electorally successful in 2014 and to a greater extent in 2019, creating fragmentation among Dalits into pro-BSP and pro-BJP sections. Having recently entered the democratic arena, the smaller sub-castes had begun undergoing a process of modernization in the 2000s that often tends to proceed unevenly, benefiting some sections more than others, leading to conflict and competition for economic benefits and social status among social groups, both within and among different ethnic categories[6] – in this case, between the dominant and better-off Jatav and the poorer non-Jatav sub-castes. Also, since the mid-1990s, with its preoccupation with power, the BSP under Mayawati has not been a democratizing force as earlier, when it moved downwards to mobilize and recognize these smaller sub-castes, particularly in eastern UP. Therefore, these smaller sub-castes have felt neglected and view the BSP as a Jatav party. Rather than identity, which was important for defining and cementing sociopolitical relations among various Dalit groups earlier, social jealousies, cultural aspirations, and economic anxieties are the driving forces today.

Preference and Protest

The BJP performed well in UP in the 2014 election, gaining 71 seats and 42.3 per cent of the votes. More importantly, it gained 18 per cent of the Jatav votes but 45 per cent of the non-Jatav votes, while the BSP gained 68 per cent of the Jatav votes and 29 per cent of the non-Jatav votes (Beg, Pandey, and Kare, 2019). Once in power at the centre in 2014, the new government under Modi took numerous steps to consolidate its Dalit base, particularly through attempts to appropriate Dalit icon Ambedkar.

However, the BJP's 2014 victory encouraged the upper and backward castes, leading to rising atrocities against Dalits. Consequently, the post-2014 period has been marked by recurrent patterns of *preference and protest*: protest against atrocities by dominant groups such as the Jatavs and smaller ones coming together, and feelings of competition, rivalry, and antagonism resurfacing between them during elections at the same time. The protests are not led by the BSP or other Dalit parties but have links with new Dalit organizations in many parts of the country – for instance, the Bhim Army in UP (Pai, 2020).

Rising atrocities and the lack of any remedial steps led to violent protests[7] by Dalits: against the suicide of Dalit student Rohit Vemula at Hyderabad University in 2016; the Una cow-vigilantism incident in Gujarat in July 2016; the clashes in Saharanpur district in 2017; the attacks on Dalits at Bhima-Koregaon, a village close to Pune in Maharashtra, on 1 January 2018; and the apparent reluctance and delay by the central government in filing a review petition in the Supreme Court against its 20 March order that called for changes in the Scheduled Castes and Scheduled Tribes (Prevention of Atrocities) Act, 1989, leaving 11 dead and many injured, which forced the central government to pass legislation to overcome the Supreme Court order.

Yet, in the 2017 UP assembly elections, the BJP gained a majority with 312 seats and 39.7 per cent votes; it gained just 9.4 per cent of Jatav votes but 38.9 per cent of non-Jatav votes (Lokniti–CSDS, 2017). The victory of the alliance between the SP, the BSP, and the Rashtriya Lok Dal (RLD) in the Lok Sabha by-polls in Gorakhpur and Phulpur, and again in Kairana in March 2018 and June 2018 in eastern and western UP respectively – particularly the victory by high margins in the prestigious seats vacated by chief minister Yogi Adityanath and deputy chief minister Keshav Prasad Maurya, just a year after the formation of the new government – was widely viewed as revival of the social justice parties.[8] But in the 2019 general elections, the BJP once again performed well, gaining an absolute majority at the centre, and 18 per cent of Jatav votes but 48.9 per cent of non-Jatav votes in UP (Beg, Pandey, and Kare, 2019). Support for the BJP in the 2019 election has been followed by atrocities and protests, the most important example of which being the September 2020 Hathras rape case, in which the victim was from the Valmiki sub-caste, but there were protests from all sections of Dalits (*Indian Express*, 2020). These repeated shifts between preference and protest, rivalry and unison, reflect feelings of uncertainty and anxiety among Dalits.

Ideological or Electoral Shift

The expansion of the BJP's support base among smaller Dalit sub-castes between the 2014 and 2019 elections raises the question of whether it merely signifies electoral support or acceptance of the party's ideology. Pradeep Chhibber and Rahul Verma (2019), in their study, suggest a 'profound ideological shift' and a consensus around 'ethno-political majoritarianism' delinked from religious nationalism as the reason for increasing identification with the BJP by the 'new voters', including Dalits, in 2019. However, the study does not explore if the support by Dalits is limited to the electoral arena or has entered their social consciousness.

Our analysis suggests that a gradual but partial process of cultural inclusion is taking place, as the constant shift between protest and preference described earlier shows, but largely among the smaller non-Jatav sub-castes. The Jatavs have remained with Mayawati or joined the Bhim Army in western UP. The Mahagathbandan (Grand Alliance) formed by the SP and the BSP prior to the 2019 elections, consisting mainly of the dominant Yadavs and Jatavs, led to a counter-mobilization of the much larger non-Yadav, non-Jatav, non-Muslim voters around the BJP (Pai and Kumar, 2020). The BJP cashed in on the strong resentment of the smaller *jatis* against the sociopolitical dominance of the Jatavs; also, the BJP's success was due to meticulous selection of the right *jati* candidate from among the non-Jatavs (Jaffrelot, 2019).

The shift of the smaller sub-castes between 2014 and 2019 towards the BJP is also due to the well-crafted mobilizational strategies of the party that appeal to the poor and disadvantaged – for instance, the highly personalized and plebiscitary-like campaign in 2019 through social media and Modi's charismatic, almost demagogic speeches to construct a 'brand' image of a *chaiwallah* (tea seller) risen from a humble background. Another example is the use of hyper-nationalism, a few weeks before the election, based on the Pulwama and Balakot incidents[9] in a state in which lower castes contribute to the army in large numbers. Such strategies deflected attention from the rapidly declining economic growth and rising unemployment that had badly affected large sections of Dalits (Pai and Kumar, 2020). Even amidst the crisis of migration during the COVID-19 pandemic, with many poorer migrants being Dalits, the Mood of the Nation (MoTN) survey showed that Modi remained popular (*India Today*, 2020).[10]

Another significant factor is the 'New Welfarism of the Right' (Anand, Dimble, and Subramanian, 2020) employed by the Modi government, which represents a politics and policy approach of redistribution and inclusion. Rather than attempting to deliver intangible traditional forms of redistribution, such as health and education, the BJP used a distinctive approach based on the 'political calculation' that there is a 'rich electoral opportunity' in providing tangible goods and services that are easier to deliver and monitor and which can be delivered in the political present, as opposed to intangibles, such as education, which will deliver benefits in the distant future. The policy provided subsidized public provision of essential goods and services, normally provided by the private sector, such as bank accounts, cooking gas, toilets, electricity, housing, and more recently water and also plain cash (Anand, Dimble, and Subramanian, 2020). Though it started in 2014, the government ably marketed, prior to the 2019 elections, the populist image of a massive welfare state and of Modi as a strong leader and provider of good governance and welfare using beneficiary schemes like the Pradhan Mantri Ujjwala Yojana and the Pradhan Mantri Awas Yojana, distributed through huge personal and digital outreach, which connected it to, as claimed by Amit Shah, almost 22 crore beneficiaries (Mehrotra, 2019). Those who had not received these goods were assured by BJP workers that their names were on the beneficiary list and that they should give Modi another chance. Hence, what we are witnessing in UP is 'politically induced cultural change', the process by which political elites select some aspects of a group's culture, attach new value and meaning to them, and use them as symbols to mobilize the group (Brass, 1991: 75).

Conclusion

The 2000s have witnessed two fundamental changes in UP that have impacted Dalit politics: an existential crisis of the BSP and a revival of the BJP, thus creating a period of right-wing hegemony. The 1990s were a decade when primordial identities and desire for social justice drove Dalit politics under the BSP. Today, following the desire for material and cultural advancement among Dalits, there is a shift from social to economic justice, in which development, cultural aspiration, greater participation, and improved governance occupy centre stage. Caste remains important, but a new relationship has grown between caste and development, in which greater priority is accorded to the latter. Consequently, neither Mayawati's attempt to use the Sarvajan agenda for development of all castes nor her brief return to symbolic politics could satisfy Dalits who felt it was the upper castes that benefitted the most. Mayawati's efforts, in fact, heightened aspirations that could not be satisfied within five years. The defeat of the BSP in the 2012 assembly elections points to the limits of the older caste politics in the 2000s in UP.

Having achieved a modicum of self-respect and dignity in the 1990s, Dalits began a search for a political alternative. The gradual shift from the BSP, which started first towards the Congress in 2009 and then towards the SP in 2012, finally led a sizeable section to the BJP. In the 2014 elections, Modi was able to attract the smaller and marginalized sub-castes through assurance of economic betterment and cultural inclusion. Despite economic decline, rising unemployment, atrocities by upper and backward castes, and the failure to provide development, the BJP, by 2019, could successfully attract a larger number of the smaller Dalit groups. The reasons lie in a series of well-planned, mobilizational strategies such as hyper-nationalism, welfarism, and deft opinion management through social media. But also, provision of greater room and self-esteem within the Hindu community under the BJP–RSS for these smaller Dalit groups – compared to their feeling of neglect by Mayawati who was seen as having favoured the Jatavs – has helped their gradual incorporation into the Hindu fold. Yet, at the same time, the post-2015 period has been marked by both preference for and protests against the BJP, which points to fragmentation, resulting in both unison and rivalry among Dalit groups.

But, as this study also suggests, this does not mean that the smaller Dalit sub-castes fully share the desire to be part of the 'Hindu Rashtra' (Hindu Nation). Rather, the BJP has attempted cultural inclusion through political means, using various strategies that have appealed to these groups. The process of incorporation of Dalits into the saffron fold is in a transitory phase today. However, the Dalit movement in UP and elsewhere is riven by fragmentation, uncertainty, aspirations, anxieties, and lack of direction. While many Dalits feel that the actions of the BJP, once in power, despite its promises, have been *anti-Dalit*, considerable sections have joined the saffron fold. In this situation, in spite of the existence of strong assertion on the ground evident in the rise of the Bhim Army, the Dalit movement has reached an impasse. There is no political alternative to turn to, following disillusionment with the BSP. No new leadership has yet emerged, which can unite all sections of Dalits. While Chandrashekhar Azad commands respect and a following, he is not viewed as an electoral option, being limited to western UP and a small organization. Moreover, the political arena within which Dalit politics operated earlier has significantly altered in the country. Dalits are facing the onslaught of a right-wing, Hindu majoritarian party supported by a conservative upper-caste society, an authoritarian government, and rising atrocities. In this situation, the space for revival of older Dalit parties or for new organizations to build a new movement seems severely limited and challenging. If the new sociopolitical coalition of upper and backward and lower castes formed by Modi continues for as long as the dominant ruling dispensation, more sections of Dalits being absorbed and incorporated into the envisaged Hindu Rashtra remains a possibility.

Notes

1. Dalits, or the Scheduled Castes (SCs), in UP consist of 63 sub-castes. Kanshi Ram's attempt to create *bahujan* consciousness in the 1990s mainly influenced the numerically preponderant and dominant Jatavs and did not extend to the smaller sub-castes, who retained their specific historical and local identities. See Gail Omvedt (1994).
2. See the interview of Mayawati in Venkitesh Ramakrishnan (2007: 8).
3. In keeping with this agenda, Mayawati's ministry had eight Dalits, four Brahmins, four from Other Backward Classes (OBC), and one each from the Muslim, Bania, Thakur, and Bhumihar (landholding) communities. See Rai (2007).
4. In 2009, retired senior bureaucrats V. Ravi Shankar and Anand Swarup pointed to changes introduced by the new government like improvement in the fiscal position, public–private partnerships (PPPs), improvement in the investment climate, introduction of value added tax (VAT), and so on, which they felt would improve the economy of UP. This was at a seminar at the Observer Research Foundation, New Delhi, on 23 and 24 May 2008. The papers presented have been published in Ramakrishnan (2009).
5. A study by Shyam Singh (2010) of some key policies of the BSP government in its first three years in office enables us to evaluate its performance. See also *The Hindu* (2010).
6. On this, see Paul Brass (1991).
7. For detailed description of the protests listed, see Anand Teltumbde (2020: 142–81).
8. For details, see Pai (2018).
9. On 14 February 2019, a Pakistan-backed terrorist killed 46 Indian soldiers in Pulwama in Jammu and Kashmir. The attack sparked off a series of events, including India's surgical strikes on a terrorist training camp in Balakot in Pakistan, culminating in the capture and subsequent release of an Indian fighter pilot from Pakistani custody. This incident was used by Modi in his campaign speeches to create a nationalist fervour which contributed to the victory of the BJP-led National Democratic Alliance (NDA) in the 2019 general elections as it deflected attention from the poor condition of the Indian economy (see Shah, 2021).
10. It shows that Modi's popularity remained high among lower castes marginally more than among upper castes: 3.08 per cent of OBCs and MBCs, 3.01 per cent of SCs and STs, and 2.99 per cent of upper castes.

Bibliography

Anand, A., V. Dimble, and A. Subramanian. 2020. 'New Welfarism of India's Right'. *Indian Express*, 22 December.

Beg, M. A., S. Pandey, and S. Kare. 2019. 'Post-Poll Survey: Why Uttar Pradesh's Mahagathbandhan Failed'. *The Hindu*, 26 May.

Bhuyan, R. 2017. 'The Political Battle for Dalit Votes'. *The Mint*, 2 November. https://www.livemint.com/Politics/olG5xKe8zJnKS3pyFmzdNP/The-political-battle-for-Dalit-votes.html. Accessed on 5 June 2021.

Brass, P. R. 1991. *Ethnicity and Nationalism: Theory and Comparison*. New Delhi: SAGE Publications.

Buncombe, A. 2008. 'Mayawati Kumari: Untouchable and Unstoppable'. *The Independent*, 4 February.

Business Standard. 2007. 'NTPC, UP Ink MoU for 1,320-MW Plant'. 23 November.

Chhibber, P., and R. Verma. 2019. 'The Rise of the Second Dominant Party System in India: BJP's New Social Coalition in 2019'. *Studies in Indian Politics* 7(2): 131–48.

Economic and Political Weekly. 2012. 'Special Statistics: Sixteenth Assembly Elections in UP'. *Economic and Political Weekly* 47(14): 80–86.

Economic Times. 2012. 'Yamuna Expressway to Become Operational This Month'. 7 April.

Election Commission of India (ECI). 2014. 'State-Wise Seat Won and Valid Votes Polled by Political Party'. https://eci.gov.in/files/file/2824-state-wise-seat-won-and-valid-votes-polled-by-political-party. Accessed in September 2022.

———. 2017. 'Uttar Pradesh General Legislative Election 2017'. https://eci.gov.in/files/file/3471-uttar-pradesh-general-legislative-election-2017/. Accessed in September 2022.

———. 2019. 'State-Wise Seat Won and Valid Votes Polled by Political Party'. https://eci.gov.in/files/file/2824-state-wise-seat-won-and-valid-votes-polled-by-political-party/. Accessed in September 2022.

Ghildiyal, S. 2008. 'Maya Has Opp on Mat as BSP Sweeps UP Bypolls'. *Times of India*, 17 April.

Heath, O., and S. Kumar. 2012. 'Why Did Dalits Desert the BSP in UP'. *Economic and Political Weekly* 47(28): 41–49.

Indian Express. 2007. 'Mayawati Wants Rs. 80,000 Crore to Change the Face of UP'. 21 July.

———. 2008. 'Maya Gets Her Way, PM Clears Rs. 80,000 Crore'. 19 February.

———. 2020. 'Impunity in Hathras'. 1 October.

India Today. 2020. 'Mood of the Nation Survey'. August. https://www.indiatoday.in/mood-of-the-nation. Accessed on 6 June 2021.

Jaffrelot, C. 2019. 'Class and Caste in the 2019 Indian Election: Why Have So Many Poor Started Voting for Modi?' *Studies in Indian Politics* 7(2): 1–19. DOI: 10.1177/2321023019874890.

Lokniti–Centre for the Study of Developing Societies (CSDS). 2017. 'ABP News–CSDS Lokniti–Uttar Pradesh Postpoll 2017 Survey Findings'. https://www.lokniti.org/media/PDF-upload/1536304136_23631500_download_report.pdf. Accessed in December 2022.

———. 2022. 'Post Poll Analysis 2022'. https://www.lokniti.org/POST-POLL-ANALYSIS-2022. Accessed in December 2022.

Mathew, J. 2014. 'India Elections 2014: Can Narendra Modi Make His Gujarat Model Work?' *International Business Times*, 16 May.

Mayawati. 2001. *Bahujan Samaj aur Uski Rajniti* (English version). Delhi: n.p.

Mehrotra, K. 2019. 'How BJP Marketed to a New Voting Bloc: The 22 Crore Beneficiaries'. *Indian Express*, 23 May.

Narayan, B. 2009. *Fascinating Hindutva: Saffron Politics and Dalit Mobilization*. New Delhi: SAGE Publications.

———. 2017. 'In Narendra Modi's Model Village, Development Has a Caste'. Catch News, 13 February. http://www.catchnews.com/india-news/in-narendra-modi-s-model-village-development-has-a-caste-1445878063.html. Accessed on 10 June 2021.

Omvedt, G. 1994. 'Kanshi Ram and the BSP'. In *Caste and Class in India*, edited by K. L. Sharma, 153–77. Jaipur: Rawat.

One India. 2007. 'Super Specialty Hospital for Poor in Kanshi Ram's Memory'. 29 September. https://www.oneindia.com/2007/09/27/super-speciality-hospital-for-poor-in-kanshi-rams-memory-1191039668.html. Accessed in September 2022.

Pai, S. 2015. 'Building Caste–Class Alliances: The BSP Experiment in Uttar Pradesh'. Workshop on 'Political Economy of Caste–Class Alliances in India', Jawaharlal Nehru University, New Delhi.

———. 2018. 'The BJP Is Losing Dalit Support in the Hindi Heartland'. *The Wire*, 4 April. https://thewire.in/caste/the-bjp-is-losing-the-support-of-dalits-in-the-hindi-heartland. Accessed in September 2022.

———. 2019. 'Changing Political Preferences among Dalits in Uttar Pradesh in the 2000s: Shift from Social Justice to Aspiration'. *Journal of Social Inclusion Studies* 5(1): 33–43.

———. 2020. 'Future of Dalit Politics Swings between Decline and Regeneration'. *The Wire*, 25 March. https://thewire.in/politics/dalit-politics-chandra-shekhar-aazad. Accessed on 12 June 2021.

Pai, S., and A. Kumar. 2015. 'Understanding the BJP's Victory in Uttar Pradesh'. In *India's 2014 Elections: A Modi-Led BJP Sweep*, edited by P. Wallace, 119–38. New Delhi: SAGE Publications.

Pai, S., and S. Kumar. 2018. *Everyday Communalism: Riots in Contemporary Uttar Pradesh*. New Delhi: Oxford University Press.

————. 2020. 'War of Perception, Brand Modi and Voters' Choice'. In *India's 2019 Elections: The Hindutva Wave and Indian Nationalism*, edited by P. Wallace, 119–37. New Delhi: SAGE Publications.

Rai, Man Mohan. 2007. 'Maya, 49 Ministers Sworn In'. *Economic Times*, 14 May. https://economictimes.indiatimes.com/news/politics-and-nation/maya-49-ministers-sworn-in/articleshow/2042080.cms?from=mdr. Accessed in December 2022.

Ramakrishnan, V. 2007. 'Dalit Power'. *Frontline*, 1 June.

————. (ed.). 2009. *Uttar Pradesh: The Road Ahead*. New Delhi: Academic Foundation.

Rawat, V. S. 2009. 'Mayawati Launches Noida Metro'. *Business Standard*, 13 November.

Singh, S. 2010. 'Three Years of BSP Government in UP'. *Economic and Political Weekly* 45(38): 77–81.

Shah, K. M. 2021. 'Looking Back: Two Years since the Pulwama Attack and the Balakot Strikes'. Observer Research Foundation, 9 March. https://www.orfonline.org/expert-speak/looking-back-two-years-since-pulwama-attack-balakot-strikes/. Accessed in December 2022.

Teltumbde, A. 2020 'Dalits under the Hindu Rashtra in the Making'. In *Dalits: Past, Present and Future*, 142–81. New Delhi: Routledge.

The Hindu. 2007. 'Mayawati to Develop Gram Sabhas'. 14 September.

————. 2010. 'Mayawati Launches Welfare Scheme for Poor'. https://www.thehindu.com/news/national/other-states/Mayawati-launches-welfare-scheme-for-poor/article15672368.ece. 2 November. Accessed in December 2022.

Times of India. 2007. 'Mayawati ki Sarkar ke Che Mah ki Uplabhdiya Iss Bath ki Sakshi Hai'. Advertisement, Information and Publicity Department, Government of UP, Lucknow.

————. 2011. '"Eco-friendly" Mayawati gifts Rs 834 Cr Park'. 4 March. https://timesofindia.indiatimes.com/city/lucknow/eco-friendly-mayawati-gifts-rs-834-cr-park/articleshow/7623582.cms. Accessed in December 2022.

————. 2013. 'OPD at Kanshiram Hospital in Greater Noida Starts'. 3 April.

Tripathi, A. 2011. 'How Dalits Have Actually Fared in Uttar Pradesh'. *Economic Times*, 1 November.

————. 2012. 'CAG Reports Tabled in UP Assembly Reveal Financial Irregular'. *Times of India*, 30 May. https://timesofindia.indiatimes.com/india/cag-reports-tabled-in-up-assembly-reveal-financial-irregularities-of-over-rs-10000-crore-in-mayawaitis-rule/articleshow/13676599.cms. Accessed in December 2022.

Verma, A. 2010. 'UP BSP Wins the Panchayat Polls'. *Deccan Chronicle*, 1 November.

5

A Democratic Dilemma

Dalit Parties, Campaign Finance, and Coalition Politics

Michael A. Collins

In recent decades, India has experienced what numerous analysts christened a 'democratic revolution', referring to the surge in electoral participation among socially underrepresented groups (Yadav, 2002). This broadening social profile of democratic practice has, in turn, spurred the creation of new political parties representing historically disadvantaged communities (Hasan, 2002; Chhibber, 2001). In a study of how these developments altered the demographics of state legislatures and the national parliament, Christophe Jaffrelot (2003) proclaimed a 'silent revolution', referring to a mostly non-violent transfer of power whereby 'plebeians' gradually dislodged a once entrenched political elite from elected office. While these scholars documented how traditional caste and class barriers to elected representation had begun to yield to a wide range of new actors, their findings pertained foremost to intermediate caste groups, traditional non-elites that converted their numerical preponderance and rising economic status into electoral clout.[1] Such accounts are not representative of the experience of most Dalit-led parties, which have typically foundered in the electoral arena.[2]

Penned on the heels of this great churning in Indian democracy, some early works overstated the ameliorative effects of formal democratic integration for marginalized groups and underestimated the systemic hurdles they would face upon entering elections. While ample ink has been spilled on this transition *into* democratic politics and the changing social profile of elected representatives, noticeably less scrutiny has considered its afterlife. This raises important questions that warrant further examination: how do recently launched Dalit parties navigate the complex landscape of democratic politics?[3] What obstacles do they encounter in mobilizing resources, organizing campaigns, and promoting minority interests? And, importantly, how do these challenges reconfigure the character of Dalit representation? Combining ethnography and interviews, this chapter investigates democratic integration in retrospect, drawing on the experiences and perspectives of first-generation Dalit politicians who steered a radical social movement into electoral politics more than two decades earlier.

To explore these questions, the chapter presents field research conducted with members of the Viduthalai Chiruthaigal Katchi (VCK; Liberation Panthers Party), which is among the most prominent Dalit parties in India today. Established in Madurai, Tamil Nadu, in 1982, as a state-unit of the Dalit Panthers of India, the movement borrowed its name and early inspiration from the Black Panthers of America (Collins, 2017). As it built a strong grassroots presence across the 1990s, the VCK developed into a radical movement reputed for its militant disposition and contentious street politics (Gorringe, 2005). Engineering an array of disruptive protests including road, rail, and airport *roko*s (obstructions), movement activists demanded that Dalits receive equal treatment under the law and equitable access to education and other means of socio-economic development. Confronting stringent police measures that crippled their operations and a growing chorus of state authorities that called for their movement to be banned, VCK leaders waded into electoral politics in 1999, seeking to use elections as a platform to demand justice, advocate for civil rights, and promote their community's development. Since then the party has enjoyed some, albeit limited, electoral success, winning seven seats in the state legislature and another three in the parliament over two decades (1999–2021).[4]

This chapter examines the dilemmas of democratic incorporation ethnographically with attention to the intertwined challenges that campaign finance and coalition politics create for Dalit parties. Until now scholars have typically sidestepped questions related to election finance, its uneven effects in the democratic arena, and the unique difficulties that it creates for Dalit parties. Although elections present a minefield for all new entrants, these obstacles are particularly acute for Dalit party candidates who most often lack the independent wealth, political pedigree, and social capital characteristic of India's political classes. It is significant that India's much-heralded 'democratic revolution' occurred alongside the liberalization of its economy and a disquieting growth in campaign expenditure. This ushered these new politicians into a democratic system whose financial playing field tilted heavily in favour of better-resourced parties. The chapter opens with an overview of campaign expenditure, providing a snapshot of the sheer depth of election spending and its exponential growth in recent decades. Next, it explores the dynamics of campaign finance between coalition partners and its implications for Dalit-led parties. Finally, the chapter documents how these arrangements and their constitutive compromises set the terms of electoral participation and may contribute to deficits in minority representation today.

Cash, Candidates, and Campaigns

By now it is well established that India is among the world's most expensive democracies (Vaishnav and Kapur, 2018b). According to the Centre for Media Studies (CMS) (2019), aggregate election spending has not simply grown in recent years but proliferated. The CMS estimates that gross expenditure in the 2019 Lok Sabha elections may have even reached INR 60,000 crores – a hefty price tag of nearly USD 8 billion and a twofold increase over the prior 2014 polls. Of course, most of this money is undeclared and in direct violation of election codes, which increases the already formidable responsibility of the Election Commission of India (ECI) to curb the flow of illicit cash and gifts during campaigns.[5] The introduction of 'electoral bonds' in 2018, which were proposed under a pretence of transparency, has further fuelled the salience of money in the democratic process by removing limits on party contributions and offering a cloak of anonymity to corporate donors. At the same time, campaign expenditure on digital media platforms such as Google, Facebook, and WhatsApp – which are far more difficult to monitor than conventional media – is thought to have increased twenty-fold, skyrocketing from INR 250 crores in 2014 to a staggering INR 5,000 crores in 2019 (Chaudhary and Rodrigues, 2019). On average, the CMS projects that INR 100 crores were spent per parliamentary constituency and, while this figure is specific to the recent national elections, the costs of campaigns are rising across the board, including in state assembly and local-body polls.[6]

In India, elections are an extravagant affair. Campaigns openly flout expenditure limits, which, in 2019, were fixed between INR 50–70 lakhs for a parliamentary constituency and INR 20–28 lakhs per assembly segment. Money pours into campaigns in staggered phases and from multiple sources. While spending begins well before the notification period, it intensifies once the campaign kicks off. Fleets of vehicles are commissioned to ferry candidates and their entourages throughout the constituency to canvass votes. Mega rallies costing crores of rupees are held to drum up support and popular attention. Candidates organize feasts with food and liquor. Campaign workers blanket entire constituencies with lakhs of political flyers and party merchandise. Then, as the election day nears, party operatives distribute cash directly to voters, typically on the eve of polling, whether slyly tucked in the morning newspaper, included with daily milk sachets, or distributed through direct bank transfers in the name of particular government schemes (CMS, 2019).[7] In addition to cash, politicians lavish voters with various kinds of inducement, from manifesto promises to 'freebies' that run the gamut from computers and cookware to clothing and cattle.

Political parties have acclimated to the escalating costs of elections by fielding more *crorepati* candidates who are expected – wholly or in part – to self-finance their campaign and contribute to the party coffer (Gowda and Sridharan, 2012). While aggregate spending does not single-handedly determine electoral outcomes, it demonstrably boosts overall performance (Sircar, 2018). In fact, it is telling that, as reported by the Association for Democratic Reforms (ADR, 2019), 88 per cent of winning candidates in 2019 were *crorepati*s, as were 83 per cent of candidates fielded by the Indian National Congress (hereafter Congress) and the Bharatiya Janata Party (BJP). By way of comparison, the Bahujan Samaj Party (BSP) – the most prominent Dalit party in India – fielded 33 per cent *crorepati*s, while most Dalit parties, including the VCK, struggle to field even a single *crorepati* candidate. In addition to their independent wealth, candidates appeal to well-heeled patrons in corporate boardrooms, real estate, mining, construction, and other industries to offset polling costs, which results in a *quid pro quo* exchange of political favours for campaign finance (Vaishnav and Kapur, 2018a). Further, parties remain primary conduits of election spending even as their candidates assume a larger share of expenditure.[8] A recent survey by Jennifer Bussell (2018) found that 60 per cent of candidates in state and national elections received party funds. In all likelihood, this trend will continue following the creation of 'electoral bonds', which, within two years, had already transferred more than INR 6,000 crores to political parties – primarily the BJP – which are exempt from limits on campaign spending (see ADR, 2020; Patel, 2019).

Today, it is well-recognized that the trifecta of personal wealth, corporate patronage, and party funds fuels democratic politics; yet remarkably little attention has scrutinized its socially differentiated effects in India. Although the rising tide of campaign expenditure complicates the arrival of all new entrants into electoral politics, it presents unique challenges to Dalit parties whose candidates lack the social and economic capital available to most other politicians. In light of this, how do Dalit parties and their candidates, most of whom are relative upstarts in the democratic arena, mobilize resources to finance their campaigns? And how do such fiscal constraints structure the terms of electoral participation? To offer insights into these questions, the next section examines the inner workings of campaign finance in Tamil Nadu, where expenditure norms – widely pegged to be among the highest in India – corral Dalit parties into alliances with their erstwhile adversaries. As we will see, the coalition-leading party administers and finances allied campaigns but, as the final section illustrates, this support comes with significant strings attached.

Navigating Fiscal Constraints

For the VCK – the largest Dalit party in Tamil Nadu and among the most prominent in India – the implications of 'money power' in elections are particularly acute. Of the party's original leadership, most are first-generation politicians from landless families (or those with meagre landholdings) who were the first in their households to access higher education. Many of them resigned from public-sector jobs, thereby forfeiting the security of government employment, to enter democratic politics in 1999. This contrasts sharply with the backgrounds of elite new politicians in Tamil Nadu (and across India) who tapped family connections or capitalized on successful business ventures to enter elected office.[9] Although the economic resources available to VCK leaders have certainly grown through two decades of participation, they remain at a stark comparative disadvantage in terms of their access to the wealth and corporate connections necessary to finance competitive election campaigns. This dearth of what party insiders glossed over in our discussions as 'candidate capacity' prompts them to forge alliances with established parties to access the infrastructure, capital networks, and technical expertise required for electoral competition.[10]

Tamil Nadu has a competitive, bipolar political system where no party can win with Dalit votes alone. Lacking party members with access to sufficient wealth and corporate patrons, the VCK has foremost relied on political coalitions with the state's dominant Dravidian parties – the Dravida Munnetra Kazhagam (DMK) and the All India Anna Dravida Munnetra Kazhagam (AIADMK) – to organize and finance election campaigns. In exchange for electoral support from allied partners (such as the VCK), the Dravidian financier shoulders the lion's share of campaign expenditure and undertakes costs related to political propaganda, print and digital advertising, vehicle and equipment hire, political rallies, food, transportation, daily *bhatta* (informal wages) for cadres, and miscellaneous day-to-day expenses incurred on campaign activity. Moreover, the Dravidian patron administers allied campaigns, marshalling its party infrastructure and canvassing expertise in support of allied candidates. While Dravidian benefactors may earmark crores of rupees to finance their campaigns, their allies are still expected to remunerate their own cadre and cover party-specific expenses. In effect, the Dravidian sponsor underwrites and administers the campaigns of allied parties, providing time-tested experience in electioneering, extensive party networks and infrastructure, and legions of cadres for vote canvassing. Wherever possible, lucrative election contracts are awarded to businesses owned by or affiliated with party members, their families, and close supporters.

In conversations over the years, former VCK candidates shared their experience with election finance, recognizing the importance of external support while also being aware of the compromises folded into these arrangements.[11] For example, a former VCK candidate recounted his failed assembly bid:

> In 2001, the DMK supplied INR 1 crore to support each of our assembly campaigns. In 2006, the AIADMK supported us during assembly elections and then, in 2011, we contested alongside the DMK. In 2011, the DMK allocated INR 2 crores for my campaign, but the DMK office bearers alone managed my election expenses. Every day they would disburse some INR 5,000 directly to me for my canvassing activities or to cover fuel, posters, and other expenses, but they themselves administered the election fund. On a daily basis, they would circulate some INR 10 lakhs among their cadres for vehicles, fuel, food, propaganda, *bhatta*, and other expenses.

With a wry grin, the candidate stressed the irony that even with strong financial backing, he accrued substantial personal debt. He quipped: 'Despite having INR 2 crores allocated to finance my campaign, I had to sell my personal vehicle to raise funds to cover my expenses!'

Far from being an isolated case, this personal anecdote resonates with the experience of other party candidates. For instance, another former candidate related how the AIADMK allocated a hefty sum to finance his 2006 assembly campaign. He similarly acknowledged that its office bearers managed the expenses, disbursing 'his' funds through a combination of personal and party networks, with the party's district secretary acting as the primary supervisor. He recalled: 'In 2006, the AIADMK spent money through its own party infrastructure. AIADMK office-bearers handled all the expenditure. Although their party provided substantial support to allies such as myself, AIADMK leaders managed the money themselves, and, as allied partners, we still bore many of our own expenses.' To supplement AIADMK support, the candidate mobilized an additional INR 17 lakh through a combination of party funds, private donations, and personal sources; yet he found himself saddled with post-poll debts. Poking fun at the ineptitude of campaign finance regulations, he noted that even his personal spending, which amounted to a fraction of that of his AIADMK financier, exceeded the ECI expenditure limit.

Despite receiving crores of rupees from allied parties, VCK leaders profess that financial concerns are among the 'important criteria' they must consider when selecting candidates. They candidly expressed a preference for what they call 'economically developed candidates'. 'Can this person spend for their campaign?'

one organizer asks rhetorically, before adding: 'If so, he will have an edge in a close race.' 'When we select candidates', another party leader asserts, 'we ideally seek individuals with their own financial means; those who own a car and can spend on their own without expecting party money.'[12] As election costs have continued to skyrocket in recent years, it has further incentivized the selection of candidates with access to credit and liquid assets, who are able (and willing) to offset campaign costs. This was a recurrent theme in my conversations with former VCK candidates, who told stories about selling off modest plots of land and assets to pay off campaign-incurred debt. However, while some party leaders rationalize their preference for affluent candidates as a pragmatic accommodation of 'money power', it has generated resentment among the party's rank and file who, after decades of committed activism, feel shunted aside when party leaders pass over their applications for wealthier aspirants.[13]

Financial constraints not only pressure VCK organizers to nominate 'economically developed candidates', but also undercut their leverage in coalition negotiations where they are routinely pressed to accept unfavourable terms with allied parties. Electoral coalitions are not reducible to an aggregation of 'vote banks'. They entail fraught negotiations among the competing, if not antagonistic, interests of bitter rivals. 'Money power', as it is popularly known, vests more powerful parties with substantial influence over virtually all aspects of coalition politics, including but not limited to seat allocation, candidate selection, and election symbols. In the recent past, dominant parties have placed their own supporters on allied tickets. For instance, in the 2009 Lok Sabha elections, the VCK nominated a non-party member with ties to DMK leaders as its second candidate, reportedly in exchange for additional campaign support. More recently, financial leverage has been employed to pressure VCK candidates to contest with the election symbol of the coalition leader. This undercuts the VCK's attempt to secure ECI recognition and subjects its candidates, if elected, to the authority of another party's whip, thereby curbing their latitude to serve as autonomous Dalit representatives. In sum, election finance not only affects the performance of Dalit parties but also structures the terms of their participation, including who can face election and under what conditions.[14]

In Tamil Nadu, the increasing costs of elections have not so much kept Dalit parties out of the electoral arena as they have further entrenched the dominant Dravidian parties as the twin gatekeepers of state politics, as the chief custodians of the coffers, cadres, and infrastructure required for an election campaign. As described previously, financial constraints corral VCK politicians into pre-poll alliances with their Dravidian patrons, which provide the financial resources, infrastructure, and expertise necessary to administer competitive campaigns.

Moreover, these arrangements enable allied parties to piggyback in other areas of campaign expenditure such as print and televised media, state-wide political marketing, and digital canvassing efforts.[15] While it is easy to marvel at the sheer scale of campaign spending, its consequences exceed the sum of all expenditure. As the next section shows, the proliferating costs of elections and exigencies of coalition politics not only impact the performance of Dalit parties, but also constrict Dalit representation.

An Intractable Balance

VCK leaders recognize the irony of their present impasse. As activists who had earlier declared 'elections are the paths of thieves' and cut their teeth exposing caste bias in the state bureaucracy and political establishment, they now ally with the same parties and politicians they had once vehemently opposed. One prominent VCK leader nostalgically recalled how, before entering electoral politics, the movement had exhorted Dalit communities 'to rise up and hit back' in the face of oppression without concerning themselves with the official posts or professional titles their opponents held:

> Before entering electoral politics, we would proclaim: 'Where is [name omitted] the MLA? We demand to speak with him immediately!' At that time, even though he was a powerful minister, we nonetheless pressured him: 'You must not act against Dalits. If you continue to do so, we will not allow you to walk peacefully in the streets of Tamil Nadu!' In such a manner, we won the people's support behind our movement.

But, after entering democratic politics, electoral calculations generated friction with this early programme. Upon entering elections, he admits: 'We were required to collaborate with the same individuals against whom we were previously opposed ... Suddenly, the local union president, the town secretary, the very individuals we had earlier identified as "caste fanatics" had now become our "allies".'

These alliances are not simply a marriage of convenience in which rival parties consolidate vote banks to 'capture power' but asymmetric mergers that may contribute to democratic deficits and undermine minority representation. In conversations over the past decade, former VCK candidates described instances where coalition politics wrought troubling compromises. For example, a former candidate recounted how the district secretary of the coalition leader – the person responsible for administering his election campaign and managing 'his' finances – pressured him to not pursue cases that he had previously filed under the Scheduled Castes and Scheduled Tribes (Prevention of Atrocities) Act, 1989 – a law designed to protect Dalits from atrocities and hate crimes.[16] Although he withheld his response to this pressure, he spoke about the proposition in general terms, insinuating that it was not an isolated occurrence:

> When VCK members are given a seat on a coalition ticket, they are expected to compromise their positions. If they had previously filed cases under the SC–ST Act, they are now expected to compromise those cases to gain entry to upper-caste settlements for electioneering work.[17] Otherwise, the caste Hindus will declare: 'Hey, you are the man who lodged complaints against us and pressured the police to take action! It was at your insistence that the police filed cases against our people. With these cases underway, they will not vote for you!'

Elaborating further, he expressed his frustration at the implications of this trade-off and how a dilution of Dalit advocacy – in this instance, recourse to litigation – was presented to him as a precondition to canvass votes with coalition allies, knowing his response would impact his access to political resources.

These compromises, which VCK leaders described in terms of 'moral corruption', are integral to the electoral process, even in reserved constituencies where elected Dalit candidates are widely expected to act as representatives of their community. Ethnography of Dalit representatives casts light on the constraints under which they operate, *if* and *when* elected, and echoes the observations of Oliver Mendelsohn and Maria Vi.ziany (1998: 256) who found that Dalit representatives were often discouraged from 'taking too active a political interest in issues of greatest relevance to their own people'. While Mendelsohn and Vicziany's study focused on Dalits in the Congress, I noticed similar tensions among coalition allies in Tamil Nadu. Compromises that may dilute Dalit representation are not confined to the halls of the parliament and backrooms of state legislatures; they occur among allies and routinely begin before the first vote is cast. On the campaign trail, Dravidian politicians carefully stage-managed the presence of VCK cadres and curated policy issues that they viewed as 'pro-Dalit', wary of their potential to ignite caste tensions that endanger non-Dalit support. This reveals a structural problem that Dalit politicians contend with in elections: their access to campaign resources reinforces their dependence on allies for whom Dalit advocacy is frequently regarded as an electoral liability rather than a political asset.

Anticipating these challenges, B. R. Ambedkar was a staunch advocate of separate electorates – at-large constituencies in which Dalit voters would elect their own representatives. Wary that reserved seats in joint electorates would render elected Dalit representatives as 'bondsmen' of upper-caste majorities,

Ambedkar advocated for separate electorates, not as a permanent solution but as a stopgap until Dalits were better assimilated within the body politic. His position displayed a perceptive awareness of how the institutional design of elections affects the character of minority representation, adamant that Dalit representatives should be elected by Dalit voters to ensure they are accountable to the community and enjoy sufficient latitude to act as autonomous representatives. While his writings on minority representation and electoral systems are widely known, Ambedkar was equally suspicious of the rising salience of money in Indian politics. In a caustic critique of M. K. Gandhi and M. A. Jinnah, Ambedkar (2014 [1979]: 227) noted: 'In establishing their supremacy they have taken the aid of "big business" and money magnates. For the first time in our country money is taking the field as an organized power'. Though Ambedkar anticipated that reserved seats in joint electorates would undercut minority representation by 'bonding' their representatives to an upper-caste majority, he did not fully discern how campaign finance would, in due time, expand upon and further cement different yet similarly restrictive bonds.

Recently, Hugo Gorringe (2017) observed growing criticism among VCK cadres who are unable to palate their leaders' obsequious behaviour to dominant parties and their predominantly upper-caste leaders. During fieldwork, I noted similar critiques, though shared more discreetly, among the highest tiers of VCK leadership. For example, a district leader, who left the movement when it entered elections but continues to support the party, conjured a poignant metaphor to describe the aftermath of its democratic transformation:

> Earlier, we chanted *adanga maru*, declaring that we would not yield, but upon entering electoral politics we felt compelled to join a major coalition. Then – regardless of which coalition – the question naturally arose: 'How many seats will they allocate?' In earlier days, our people begged for bread; now we are begging for seats! ... We never imagined that we would yield, but this is submission; electoral politics is a form of submission.

While long-time party organizers and prior members alike are often critical of what they see as a dilution of the movement's once radical promise, their criticism is rarely directed at the party president. Instead, they point to the exigencies of an electoral system that calls for such compromises in the first place.

VCK leaders are aware of these compromises. However, contrary to what some pundits might suggest, they do not believe that they have been 'co-opted by the system'. In our interviews, they shared perceptive insights into their predicament and did not shy away from self-critique. Their commentary on elections reveals a belief that they must strike an intractable balance to 'win' in an electoral system where their interests are often bracketed from those of the general public, and Dalit representation is regarded as a political liability by their allies. Over the years, I noted a growing consensus among party organizers that a contradiction is hardwired into the democratic system. Although they emphasized that surviving in politics requires winning elections, they also recognized that any election in a bipolar, winner-take-all political system is prone to become a majoritarian instrument. In order to promote their popular 'acceptance' and 'enter the mainstream', Dalit politicians are incentivized, as one VCK leader hesitantly admitted, to 'cut soft corners' on caste issues. This presents a dilemma: should they adapt to the electoral system to improve their performance? Or, alternatively, should they seek to transform it, likely to the detriment of their electoral viability and access to critical resources?

Conclusion

In recent decades, there has been much fanfare surrounding the salience of caste to democratic politics in modern India. Scholars have analysed the broadening social demographics of electoral participation, indicating that underprivileged citizens now exercise their franchise at an unprecedented rate. Further, recent studies have captured the changing caste profile of electoral representation, which better reflects the general population. Taken collectively, this scholarship coined a new – and ostensibly optimistic – lexicon to describe India's political present, declaring a 'democratic upsurge' and 'silent revolution'. While these studies chronicled the integration of historically underrepresented groups into the democratic process, significantly less attention has considered its afterlife. Today, the formation of Dalit parties is often interpreted uncritically as an index of India's democratization, a feat of Dalit assertion, or evidence of greater political equity. However, popular commentaries on elections fail to take into account that elections rarely transform society. More often, they reflect it. Ethnography of Dalit party leadership offers novel insights into the distinctive challenges that these individuals face in elections. Moreover, it illustrates how democratic incorporation opened up new space for their political advancement while also reconfiguring Dalit representation in some democratically troubling ways.[18]

The rising costs of elections pose a recurring predicament for Dalit parties. While a chorus of academics, civil society activists, and policymakers have long criticized the deluge of cash in elections by emphasizing well-documented consequences of rampant campaign spending on the integrity of the democratic process, remarkably little scrutiny has evaluated the socially differentiated and unevenly distributed effects of these 'costs of democracy'. Throughout the country, Dalit parties often require pre-poll alliances to access the political resources required to conduct competitive campaigns. In Tamil Nadu, this has pressed the VCK to enter coalitions with their erstwhile foes – the Dravidian parties – in order to face elections. Yet, as this chapter shows, coalitions are not a mere marriage of convenience, a temporary merger of partisan rivals each jockeying to consolidate their respective 'vote banks' ahead of elections. Rather, these arrangements entail contentious negotiations in which less-resourced parties are pressured to accept compromises that set the terms of democratic participation and may contribute to deficits in minority representation. In recent years, these negotiations have influenced the candidate selection of Dalit parties, restricted the channels through which they pursue justice, and resulted in their policy preferences being overridden by the agendas of dominant parties.

An analysis of Dalit parties calls attention to how long-standing social and material inequalities structure the electoral field, and the barriers to entry and capital constraints under which their leaders operate, *if* and *when* elected. The VCK has achieved some success in the electoral arena. The party's leaders have used elections as a platform to lobby for reform in policing, education, and environmental policy, and draw attention to caste violence and discrimination. Specifically, the leaders point to their role in a DMK housing programme that replaced mud-and-thatched huts with concrete structures.[19] Moreover, in the past two decades, the party has gained greater visibility in the Tamil public sphere and recognition as a legitimate player in state politics. However, there is reason to interpret such progress as resulting from its stance on non-caste-specific matters (such as Tamil nationalism and opposition to ethno-religious majoritarianism) instead of ushering Dalit interests into the 'political mainstream'. Still, the formation of Dalit parties like the VCK has helped reshape political discourse and pressured dominant parties to promote more Dalits to leadership positions and integrate their issues – even if only nominally – into their election manifestos and policy programmes.[20] But the pursuit of a broader social and economic transformation that inspired a generation of Dalit activists to enter politics two decades earlier remains muddled in the democratic field, where they struggle to reconcile the demands of Dalit representation with the exigencies of elections. In the eyes of some activists, these achievements have come at a steep cost.

Notes

1. The social category of 'plebeians' or 'lower castes' in India is highly differentiated. While manifestly non-elite and composed of groups that were largely excluded from previous political regimes, they are socially dominant communities in

rural India. Although the rising political stature of these castes – termed Other Backward Classes (OBCs) in legal parlance – has been hailed as a 'silent revolution' and example of 'lower-caste empowerment', these political and electoral gains are concentrated among intermediate castes and have rarely extended to Dalits. Moreover, OBC parties are frequently at loggerheads with Dalit parties.

2. With the exception of the Bahujan Samaj Party (BSP) in Uttar Pradesh (UP), Dalit parties have experienced limited electoral success and, in recent years, the BSP has struggled to replicate its earlier performance. For Dalit politics, the BSP is an anomaly that emerged in a unique social and historical context. Jatavs, the party's primary Dalit support base, are the single largest caste in UP. Further, UP elections tend to feature multiple (often four) coalitions pitted against each other, thereby lowering the vote share required to win an election. Additionally, the BSP was founded after its leaders had spent decades organizing grassroots support (that is, the Dalit Shoshit Samaj Sangharsh Samiti [DS4], and the All India Backward and Minority Communities Employees Federation [BAMCEF]). In contrast, Tamil Nadu has a bipolar party system where locally dominant, better organized intermediate castes outnumber Dalits in most constituencies, and the state's largest Dalit party, the Viduthalai Chiruthaigal Katchi (VCK) had been a mass movement for only a few years when state police began to ban its meetings and corralled the movement into elections. Although the BSP is often taken today as a paradigm of Dalit politics, its historical development and prior electoral success are an anomaly among Dalit parties.

3. The phrase 'Dalit party' is often used without precision and is prone to misinterpretation. Dalit-led parties often feel constricted by this label and seek recognition as a 'common party'. The VCK had done this by installing non-Dalits in key leadership posts, actively soliciting non-Dalit support, and advancing a broad policy agenda beyond caste-specific issues. For consistency, I use the phrase 'Dalit party' while acknowledging that the VCK and many other Dalit-led parties contain diverse membership and address a wide breadth of non-caste-specific issues.

4. In the 2019 Lok Sabha elections, two leading VCK figures were elected to the parliament: president Thirumavalavan and general secretary D. Ravikumar. Yet, as part of its coalition agreement with the DMK, Ravikumar contested and won his seat under the DMK's 'rising sun' election symbol. Thus, while technically a DMK member of parliament (MP), Ravikumar is popularly recognized as a VCK MP. I have included him in my count of VCK MPs.

5. Of the estimated INR 12,000–15,000 crores distributed directly to voters in 2019, the ECI confiscated nearly INR 3,500 crores, or roughly USD 500 million.

6. For an investigative account of money in the 2016 Tamil Nadu assembly polls, see, Subramanian (2019).

7. Money does not flow indiscriminately to voters. An early CMS study found that cash handouts targeted below-poverty-line (BPL) voters, especially in southern states where BPL voters were two to three times more likely to receive election money than non-BPL voters (CMS, 2014).

8. According to CMS (2019), candidate expenditure (40 per cent) is believed to have surpassed party expenditure (35 per cent) in the share of aggregate campaign spending.

9. For a study of the symbiosis of politics and business, see Sinha and Wyatt (2019) and Harriss and Wyatt (2016).

10. In Tamil Nadu, upstart parties among intermediate castes (such as, the Pattali Makkal Katchi [PMK], Desiya Murpukku Dravida Kazhagam [DMDK], and Marumalarchi Dravida Munnetra Kazhagam [MDMK]) bolstered their bargaining power by first contesting elections independently and, thereby, demonstrating their support base prior to entering pre-poll coalitions with Dravidian parties. This strategy requires economic resources and a pool of wealthy candidates. The relative economic disparity separating the VCK from these OBC-led parties and the exorbitant costs of elections has rendered the VCK more reliant on dominant parties from the start.

11. Due to the sensitive nature of my conversations with VCK leaders and activists, I have protected their anonymity when appropriate.

12. Hugo Gorringe notes instances of VCK cadres criticizing the high fees that are now attached to applications for party posts and running on the party ticket. See Gorringe (2017: 117).

13. Many of the VCK's *nouveau riche* joined after the party dissolved its organizational structure in 2007 and conducted a fresh membership drive to attract non-Dalits and religious minorities by extending plum leadership posts. This effort sought to broaden its social base, eschew the stigma associated with being a 'Dalit party', and lend credence to its self-designation as a party of 'democratic forces'. See Gorringe (2013a, 2013b).

14. Additionally, VCK leaders have protested against their allies' reluctance to allocate seats beyond the state's northern districts where their predominant base of Dalit-Paraiyars is concentrated. Dravidian parties are disinclined to allot these seats as it may facilitate the VCK's growth into new regions and signal recognition that the VCK is more than just a sub-regional, sub-caste party. Seat allocations are used to keep their party's presence in check and confine them to particular regions and demographics.

15. In the 2016 Tamil Nadu assembly elections, the AIADMK reportedly amassed a team of nearly 82,000 'IT warriors' to conduct targeted digital canvassing. See *The Hindu* (2016).

16. As Grace Carswell and Geert De Neve demonstrate, recourse to litigation and, in particular, the Scheduled Castes and Scheduled Tribes (Prevention of Atrocities)

Act, 1989, has provided a valuable – even if not always litigiously effective – tool for assertion. See Carswell and De Neve (2015).

17. The geographic segregation of the Tamil countryside into *ur* (caste settlements) and *ceri* (Dalit colonies) structures electioneering practices. Entry into upper-caste areas often requires support from non-Dalit allies. See Collins (2018).

18. In his analysis of post-revolutionary Guatemala, Nicholas Copeland (2019) similarly observes how programmes designed to develop a 'capacity for democracy' among indigenous communities provided a means for political advancement while also reconfiguring the nature of their politics.

19. This scheme was formally announced in the DMK's 2009 Lok Sabha election manifesto; yet its conceptualization began when then DMK chairman Muthuvel Karunanidhi participated in the VCK's Conference on Land Rights (17 June 2007). The plan pledged to support the construction of 21 lakh houses, but by the time the DMK lost the 2011 assembly elections, only five lakh houses had been completed. In subsequent elections, VCK politicians have reiterated their commitment to complete the project (personal communication, D. Ravikumar, 9 September 2020).

20. For example, the formation of Dalit parties is reputed to have spurred Communist parties in Tamil Nadu (the Communist Party of India [CPI] and the Communist Party of India-Marxist [CPI-M]) to establish new wings focusing on Dalit issues. Additionally, the DMK amended its rules to accommodate a Dalit at all levels of party posts. Yet such changes may be more cosmetic than transformative (personal communication, D. Ravikumar, 9 September 2020).

Bibliography

Ambedkar, B. R. 2014 [1979]. 'Ranade, Gandhi and Jinnah'. In *Dr. Babasaheb Ambedkar: Writings and Speeches*, vol. 1, compiled by V. Moon, 205–40. New Delhi: Dr Ambedkar Foundation.

Association for Democratic Reforms (ADR). 2019. 'Analysis of Assets Comparison of Re-Contesting MPs in the 2019 Lok Sabha Elections'. https://adrindia.org/content/analysis-assets-comparison-re-contesting-mps-2019-lok-sabha-elections. Accessed on 7 October 2022.

———. 2020. *Analysis of Electoral Bonds Sold and Redeemed during the Thirteen Phases (March 2018–January 2020)*. New Delhi: Association for Democratic Reforms.

Bussell, J. 2018. 'Whose Money, Whose Influence? Multilevel Politics and Campaign Finance in India'. In *Costs of Democracy: Political Finance in India*, edited by M. Vaishnav and D. Kapur, 232–72. New Delhi: Oxford University Press.

Carswell, G., and G. De Neve. 2015. 'Litigation against Political Organization? The Politics of Dalit Mobilization in Tamil Nadu, India'. *Development and Change* 46(5): 1106–32.

Chaudhary, A., and J. Rodrigues. 2019. 'Why India's Election Is Among the World's Most Expensive'. *Economic Times*, 12 March. https://economictimes.indiatimes. com/news/elections/lok-sabha/india/why-indias-election-is-among-the-worlds-most-expensive/articleshow/68367262.cms. Accessed on 7 August 2020.

Chhibber, P. 2001. *Democracy without Associations: Transformation of the Party System and Social Cleavages in India*. Ann Arbor: University of Michigan.

Centre for Media Studies (CMS). 2014. 'Alarming Trend of Note-for-Vote'. CMS India Blog, 14 May. https://cmsindiablog.wordpress.com/2014/05/14/alarming-trend-of-note-for-vote. Accessed on 7 October 2022.

———. 2019. *A CMS Report: Poll Expenditure, the 2019 Elections*. New Delhi: CMS Research House.

Collins, M. 2017. 'Writing Dalit Assertion: Early Dalit Panther Politics and Legal Advocacy in 1980s Tamil Nadu'. *Contemporary South Asia* 25(3): 238–54.

———. 2018. 'Navigating Fiscal Constraints: Dalit Parties and Electoral Politics in Tamil Nadu, India'. In *Costs of Democracy: Political Finance in India*, edited by M. Vaishnav and D. Kapur, 119–52. New Delhi: Oxford University Press.

Copeland, N. 2019. *The Democracy Development Machine: Neoliberalism, Radical Pessimism, and Authoritarian Populism in Mayan Guatemala*. Ithaca, NY: Cornell University Press.

Gorringe, H. 2005. *Untouchable Citizens: Dalit Movements and Democratisation in Tamil Nadu*. New Delhi: SAGE Publications.

———. 2013a. 'From Untouchable to Dalit and Beyond: New Directions in South Indian Dalit Politics'. *South Asianist* 2(1): 40–56.

———. 2013b. 'Interview with Gowthama Sannah, Propaganda Secretary of the VCK'. *South Asianist* 2(1): 57–91.

———. 2017. *Panthers in Parliament: Dalits, Caste, and Political Power in South India*. New Delhi: Oxford University Press.

Gowda, M. V. R., and E. Sridharan. 2012. 'Reforming India's Party Financing and Election Expenditure Laws'. *Election Law Journal* 11(2): 226–40.

Harriss, J., and A. Wyatt. 2016. 'Business and Politics in Tamil Nadu'. Simons Papers in Security and Development, No. 50/2016, School for International Studies, Simon Fraser University, Vancouver.

Hasan, Z. 2002. *Parties and Party Politics in India*. New Delhi: Oxford University Press.

Jaffrelot, C. 2003. *India's Silent Revolution: The Rise of the Lower Castes*. New York: Columbia University Press.

Mendelsohn, O., and M. Vicziany. 1998. *The Untouchables: Subordination, Poverty and the State in Modern India*. Cambridge: Cambridge University Press.

Patel, A. 2019. 'BJP Benefits Most from Modi Govt's Electoral Bonds: Data'. *India Today*, 4 April. https://www.indiatoday.in/elections/lok-sabha-2019/story/bjp-benefits-most-from-modi-govt-s-electoral-bonds-data-1494014-2019-04-04. Accessed on 4 September 2020.

Sinha, A., and A. Wyatt. 2019. 'The Spectral Presence of Business in India's 2019 Election'. *Studies in Indian Politics* 7(2): 247–61.

Sircar, N. 2018. 'Money in Elections: The Role of Personal Wealth in Election Outcomes'. In *Costs of Democracy: Political Finance in India*, edited by M. Vaishnav and D. Kapur, 36–73. New Delhi: Oxford University Press.

Subramanian, L. 2019. 'AIADMK Spent Rs 641 Crores in 2016 to Bribe Its Way Back to Power'. *The Week*, 13 April. https://www.theweek.in/theweek/statescan/2019/04/12/aiadmk-spent-rs-641-crores-in-2016-to-bribe-its-way-back-to-power.html. Accessed on 26 August 2020.

The Hindu. 2016. 'Poll Diary: May 15, 2016'. 15 May.

Vaishnav, M., and D. Kapur. 2018a. 'Builders, Politicians, and Election Finance'. In *Costs of Democracy: Political Finance in India*, edited by M. Vaishnav and D. Kapur, 74–118. New Delhi: Oxford University Press.

——— (eds.). 2018b. *Costs of Democracy: Political Finance in India*. New Delhi: Oxford University Press.

Yadav, Y. 2002. 'Understanding the Second Democratic Upsurge: Trends of Bahujan Participation in Electoral Politics in the 1990s'. In *Transforming India: Social and Political Dynamics of Democracy*, edited by F. Frankel, Z. Hasan, R. Bhargava, and B. Arora, 120–45. Delhi: Oxford University Press.

6

Why Are More Dalits Voting for the Bharatiya Janata Party since 2014?

Abhinav Prakash Singh

One of the most noticeable and intriguing phenomena of the last decade is the increasing attraction of the Bharatiya Janata Party (BJP) as a political alternative for the Dalit castes. The massive mandate won by the BJP in 2014 and 2019 represents political realignment and a significant shift in society. One of the critical factors behind the continuing electoral dominance of the BJP is the successful inroads it has made among the Dalit castes (Kumar and Gupta, 2019). This chapter argues that the shift of Dalit voters towards the BJP is due to several long-term and short-term factors. One way to look at this phenomenon is to see the BJP as the beneficiary of a long-term fundamental shift in underlying socio-economic conditions. Another angle is to investigate the churning within the Dalit community. The chapter also looks at the strategy and tactics deployed by the BJP to attract voters from the Dalit castes.

Further, we must question if the present trend is sustainable. Will these long-term trends ultimately pull the party and Dalits apart, or are the BJP strategy and policies themselves creating instability in this relationship? In this chapter, we will explore the dynamics between Dalits and the BJP through the prism of these issues. Since it is not possible to do an overall analysis of Dalit politics for India due to the sheer diversity of the Dalit community and politics, the vantage point adopted is that of the Gangetic belt. The study is based on (*a*) secondary surveys and reporting and (*b*) interviews and interaction with BJP leaders and members, Dalit activists, and Dalit youth. For this purpose, several BJP parliamentarians, general secretaries, and other office-bearers were interviewed along with activists from the Dalit castes. While some of them are quoted in the chapter, most preferred not to be directly quoted.

Long-Term Changes

In the twenty-first century, India is undergoing several significant churns that will have a long-term impact on its future trajectory (Singh, 2019b). India is the most diverse country in the world with thousands of castes, tribes, and communities with different concerns and aspirations; therefore, the task of delineating all meta-trends is impossible. Nevertheless, in this chapter, we try to pick up those that are most relevant to the changing nature of Dalit society and politics.

First is the collapse of Nehruvian secularism and reassertion of India's Hindu character (Chandra, 2018). Despite its secular pretence, India's freedom movement was effectively a Hindu movement in its vision, language, symbolism, and mass mobilization; and despite self-denial, the post-colonial state was essentially a Hindu polity. The misleading secular–communal debate obscured the obvious – that the Republic of India is a Hindu reformist state. The Indian state is the first state in the subcontinent's history to legally abolish caste-based discrimination and take a stand favouring the Dalit castes and their upliftment. Its policies integrated and Sanskritized Dalits and large sections of tribals, codified Hindu social laws, patronized folk art, and replaced Urdu–Persian with Hindi and native languages. It controls Hindu temples, has introduced uniformity in temple laws, and continues to intervene in Hindu social and religious matters with popular legitimacy. The Indian state created fertile ground for the strengthening of Hindu nationalism, or Hindutva, via its homogenization policies for Hindus, apart from increasingly drawing Dalits into the Hindu mainstream.

Contrary to the popular academic discourse, the allure of Hindutva and promise of a common Hindu identity have always been strong for Dalits and those belonging to the Other Backward Classes (OBCs). Hindutva promises to supersede the narrower identity of weaker castes and make them members of the broader and powerful 'Hindu community' (Singh, 2019a). This is especially true for the non-dominant Dalit and OBC castes. Due to smaller demographics and weaker socio-economic and cultural capital, these castes find that this gives them more straightforward access to social mobility, inclusion, and political power. They find it easier to push back against caste discrimination and exclusion under the political umbrella of Hindu identity rather than creating an independent political outfit like the numerically stronger Dalit castes.

The strengthening of the Hindutva discourse and the penetration of the Dalit castes by the BJP have gone together with the Ram Janmabhoomi (Birthplace of Ram) movement, which created a stronger Hindu identity than before (Nandy, 1996). In India, in order to succeed, a political party must be able to 'aggregate' the diverse population of the country. And so far only the Indian National Congress (hereafter Congress) was able to do so under the umbrella of secularism and socialism. However, now Hindutva enables the BJP to upend the Congress and emerge as the new aggregator in the Indian polity. The rise of Narendra Modi led the BJP to aggressively push the social engineering project of weaving a massive alliance of Hindu castes known as the 'United Spectrum of Hindu Votes', or USHV (Patil, 2015). The most determined push was among the Dalit castes who have not been the traditional voters of the BJP. Creating micro-alliances with smaller Dalit castes, often limited to one or two districts, coupled with aggressive posturing and rhetoric by Modi on Dalit symbolism, signalled to Dalits that the party is now more open and accommodating of Dalits concerns.

Second, the neglected process of Sanskritization and Hinduization of Dalits over the past century is an important factor. By 'Hinduization' here, I do not mean the process of non-Hindus being drawn into the Hindu fold, but the growth of the consciousness of 'Hindu identity and unity' in the modern sense. Hinduism itself is a synthesis of several indigenous traditions, including those of Dalits and tribals. However, Hinduism is seen as synonymous to Brahmanism in the academic and activist discourse. This flawed understanding and politics of rhetoric built on it blinded its practitioners from realizing that Sanskritization was among the most potent forces sweeping the country.

The politics of anti-Hinduism with attacks on Hinduism and deconstruction of myths were major components of the old Dalit politics and mobilization. The Gotra and Puranic identity, adopted during the Hindu revivalist movements of the nineteenth and twentieth centuries, was sought to be discarded (Jaffrelot, 2000). There were attempts to rewrite history to locate Dalit castes in the historical narrative and resurrect Dalit personalities and heroes. There were attempts to replace Hinduism with Buddhism though these hardly succeeded beyond some castes like the Mahars in Maharashtra. Most Dalits never gave up their Hindu beliefs, rituals, and festivals rooted in folk traditions. However, these developments led to the decline of the ritual and social power of the upper castes, especially the legitimacy of the Brahmanical social order.

More and more Dalits moved outside the older narratives of identity and social order, creating their own identity and self-image within the larger Hindu fold (Narayan, 2009). An example would be of many Dalits mentioning their *vamsa* (clan name) or sub-caste during *sankalpa* (where one is supposed to speak aloud his name and lineage) while performing *puja* (worship or religious rituals) in temples instead of *gotra* (male lineage from mostly Brahmin ancient *rishi*s [Hindu sages or saints]) and being accepted as such by the mostly Brahmin priests. Therefore, the anti-Hindu stance of old Dalit politics had the opposite of the intended effect. This process was complemented by several Hindu organizations working towards temple entry, training Dalit priests, and performing *yagna* (a ritual sacrifice with a specific objective) and other *samskara*s (ceremonies or rites marking a major event in one's life) for Dalits.

Third, the revival of the economy in the post-independence era after two centuries of stagnation has been fundamentally reshaping society. In the West, industrialization and modern economic growth created conditions for the rise of nations by breaking down the old agrarian–feudal social order and creating a shared common culture in the new urban centres where people uprooted from their parochial identities found themselves. The progressive industrialization, urbanization, and growth of India's capitalist economy is causing dissolution of the economic underpinnings of the caste system and migration of Dalits from villages to cities. This process has accelerated after the economic reforms of 1991.

Modern economic growth undermines the feudal caste order, and urbanization creates a new socio-economic reality of the middle and lower-middle urban classes where people of different castes increasingly share the same space (Kapur et al., 2010). Unlike the deeply entrenched segregation in villages, Dalits are part of this new urban landscape. This has led to the emergence of a 'new class of Hindu castes' (Singh, 2019c) that increasingly shares similar experiences and aspirations. Dissolution of old parochial identities leads to the consolidation of Hindu identity in urban centres as the common denominator among people from different social backgrounds undergoing a slow process of homogenization. This has enabled the Hindutva politics of the BJP to grow among these urban classes – Dalits included.

Together, the aforementioned three factors have consolidated the phenomenon of 'subaltern Hindutva', with more and more Dalit castes finding themselves attracted towards the Hindu political identity and searching for mobility within the Hindu fold as against the radical politics of the earlier era.

Fourth, there is an intensifying conflict between the old urban class and the new. The old urban elites, beneficiaries of the Nehruvian patronage system, were mostly drawn from socially and economically privileged sections. The new urban class is the product of economic reforms and recent rural-to-urban migration across all castes. It is rooted in local concerns and aspirations and sharply differs from the old urban class in its conception of religion, nationalism, and democracy. The clash for political supremacy between the two was inevitable. The BJP emerged as the point of convergence of the neo–middle class as against the old urban class identified with the Congress. Dalits, newly inducted into the ranks of the neo–middle class, or aspirational class, find themselves on the side of the BJP.

Upheaval within Dalit Politics

The characteristics of Dalit society and the composition of the Dalit political landscape are undergoing a noticeable change. Several factors stand out.

The first is the emergence of a Dalit middle and neo-middle class (Srinivas, 2016). Over the years, the breakdown of the *jajmani* system,[1] the decline in the disabilities imposed upon Dalits, and the reservation policy, which provided an avenue of socio-economic mobility, have enabled the creation of a strong Dalit middle class. Now new generation Dalits are increasingly diversifying out of the government sector into the private sector and business. Even though this is a smaller class, it is steadily growing and becoming a strong supporter of good governance and economic reforms. It has given birth to the new discourse of 'Dalit capitalism' which advocates 'Market vs Manu' (Prasad, 2008). It champions entrepreneurship and access to markets as the route to socio-economic mobility and emancipation rather than the old policies of government jobs and reservations. And as such, it has a natural tilt towards the BJP which is seen as a pro-business, pro-reform, and pro-growth party.

The second factor is the percolation of democracy and increasing assertion of the heterogeneity of Dalit politics and aspirations. Earlier, Dalit discourse and politics were decided from the prism of the numerically stronger castes who were the first movers in modern education, jobs, and, subsequently, politics. Today, more and more Dalit castes are mobilizing to become visible to the state and claim their share in the politics of social justice, power structures, and state resources (Narayan, 2016). This has created confusion in the broader Dalit discourse and politics where the old Ambedkarite and neo-Buddhist narratives are facing pressure from the heterogeneity of Dalit aspirations.

Moreover, as the competition (Mendelsohn and Vicziany, 1998) between Dalit castes for political representation and political power intensifies, several Dalit castes are increasingly looking beyond traditional boundaries and willing to join hands with political parties outside the Ambedkarite fold. This development has complemented the efforts of the BJP to make inroads into the Dalit community (Mendelsohn and Vicziany 1998). It has successfully garnered substantial Dalit votes with deft alliances and smart ticket distribution.

The third is a deterioration in the discourse of Dalit social and political movements (Singh, 2019d). Increasing radicalism, based on racist theories like *moolnivasi* that preach permanent conflict with the non-Dalit castes and neo-Buddhist puritanism, has detached the Dalit discourse from the everyday concerns of the masses (Singh, 2016). More and more people are getting alienated due to a failed cultural war to de-Hinduize Dalits. Dalit parties and organizations are unable to decide whether they are a religious missionary group, a social reform movement, or a political party. Moreover, given the vital role that Dalit discourse and intellectual classes play in political mobilization, mass disenchantment has affected Dalit political parties.[2]

Fourth, there is the emergence of class differentiation within the Dalit community. Dalit politics and leadership have mostly arisen from the educated class and beneficiaries of reservations. This has led to the neglect of the concerns and issues of poor Dalits. Dalits in villages and those with no stake in government jobs find it increasingly difficult to identify with the Dalit parties and organizations who have neglected them beyond tokenism and symbolism. This has left the field wide open for any political party which can promise immediate improvement in their day-to-day lives (Lal, 2021). As we shall see, the BJP was quick to capitalize on these gaps via its massive pitch on welfare schemes and pro-poor rhetoric.

What Did the BJP Do?

We have seen that long-term churnings favoured the BJP and its ideological agenda. Furthermore, the weakening of Dalit politics due to its internal upheavals provided an opportunity to make inroads into the Dalit castes. However, the BJP's success ultimately depended on its ability to identify and capitalize on these changes. Here, the new-BJP, under the leadership of Modi and Amit Shah, surpassed all other political parties.

As suggested by interviews with top-ranking leadership in the party organization,[3] the BJP sees this as a lengthy process made possible due to persistent effort. The party had to overcome both the Dalit community's scepticism and resistance from within. In the party's view, even though caste discrimination and untouchability are real problems, Nehruvian approaches are responsible for exacerbating the caste fault-lines in politics. The party's self-image is that of being part of the reform movement that seeks to unite Hindus across caste and regional divides. Its organizational leadership accepts that the Brahmin–Baniya tag took a heavy toll on the party and inhibited its expansion; overcoming it has been an uphill task. It was branded a Brahmin party in some states, and a Baniya party in others, while being called a north-Indian Hindi party in the states in the south. It has been making a consistent effort to counter this image by restructuring itself organizationally and modifying the political language it deploys to appeal to a more extensive base (Mehta, 2022). The party claims that overturning the Supreme Court decisions on the Scheduled Castes and Scheduled Tribes (Prevention of Atrocities) Act, 1989, and in the university reservation case (*Indian Express*, 2019), despite upper-caste opposition, helped allay distrust among Dalits.

Party leaders view the Ram Janmabhoomi movement as the pivotal moment[4] in its history of outreach to non-traditional constituencies, including Dalits. The movement provided the party's first opportunity to expand among the Dalit castes based on the religious plank. It is often forgotten that Ram is a central deity in the anti-caste Bhakti movement of medieval India in both *nirgun* and *sagun* bhakti (schools of the Bhakti tradition in Hindu philosophy). Furthermore, the academic debates around the Ram of the Bhakti movement and the Ram of the Ramayana have little resonance in the beliefs of the masses. For the first time, Ram Janmabhoomi opened the possibility of the USHV that the party would capitalize on two decades later.

Another factor that stands out in their view is the aggressive expansion of party membership under Shah in 2015. The party claims that it enrolled 11 crore new members[5] and leveraged this database in organizational planning and electoral politics (Mehta, 2022). This enabled BJP activists to reach every section of society and popularize the party's ideology and programmes. The second membership drive of 2019 also saw some three crore new members with massive growth in Uttar Pradesh (UP) and West Bengal.

This made the erstwhile upper-caste, urban-based party a household name in the countryside and helped create a groundswell in the elections that followed. Massive electoral machinery and innovations like booth-level officials and *panna pramukhs*[6] also enabled the party to include more people from the Dalit castes in its functioning. The BJP could bypass the intense lobbying for party posts and accommodate more Dalits without antagonizing its traditional upper-caste voter base. For instance, in Bihar, the BJP has introduced a new organizational innovation called 'Shakti Kendra'. It consists of five–six polling booths and is a separate team beyond the formal party structure. This has allowed the party to engage with Dalits at the local level by involving them in election work and bestowing responsibilities upon them.[7]

The party leadership credits its focus on *antyodaya* (welfare of people at the bottom of the socio-economic pyramid) and last-mile delivery of public goods for increasing its popularity among Dalits and other weaker castes. According to the party, ideology is a marginal factor in the rural belt where everyday realities of caste, corruption, and access to the government dominate the discourse.[8] This view demonstrates the pragmatism of a party often accused of harbouring a narrow ideological vision. A crucial way caste works in the Indian polity is via clientelism and patronage, favouring the dominant castes in a region. The weaker castes, especially Dalits, are excluded from access to state resources and welfare schemes. Government policies and programmes are mediated through local power configurations shaped by social structures with caste at their centre. This leads to the exclusion and marginalization of Dalit castes and is one of the primary reasons for the failure of government welfare programmes on the ground.

The Modi-led government transformed the mechanism of public service delivery and welfare schemes. The delivery of public goods and public provision of private goods like electricity, gas cylinders, housing, insurance, banking, and so on to remote corners and marginalized sections of society was actualized through the unprecedented use of technology like Aadhaar (a unique identification number provided by the government to its citizens) and direct benefit transfers. This ensured that benefits reached intended recipients while bypassing the old patronage networks. It reduced arbitration and corruption as the benefits were directly transferred, and selection criteria were based on the Socio-Economic Caste Census, 2011. Under the old patronage system, a person would benefit if he belonged to a caste which supported local politicians and the party in power. This had created a 'politics of unfreedom' for the weaker Dalit castes who had to rely upon the goodwill of local dominant castes. By the universal and direct provision of goods and services based on clearly defined criteria, the BJP government caused significant social and political disruption by freeing Dalit castes from the tutelage of dominant castes. Around 22 crore families benefited from the direct provision of goods and services, and a significant number of them accessed these for the first time. This has consolidated the party's appeal among voters, and the results were seen during the 2019 Lok Sabha and 2022 assembly elections (Kishore, 2022).

Several BJP leaders claim that the younger generation of Dalits is more concerned with the issues of governance and service delivery and appreciates the BJP for performing better. It has generated goodwill among new-age voters, which the party can mobilize during elections. According to Tejasvi Surya,[9] the Modi-led BJP has best understood the aspirational factor among the youth from the Dalit castes. It has tried to mobilize them by superseding the old status-quo politics and offering them economic empowerment via support to Dalit entrepreneurship through schemes like the Pradhan Mantri Mudra Yojana (PMMY). Another factor is social engineering undertaken by the party, which goes far beyond what other political parties have ever attempted. Sanjay Paswan[10] says that the Rashtriya Swayamsewak Sangh (RSS) is the forerunner of the BJP on Dalit outreach and social engineering. In the run-up to the assembly elections in five states in 2022, the BJP launched a unique campaign named 'Samajik Samvad'[11] for outreach to the middle and upper-middle classes of Dalits and promptly responded to the issues and concerns raised by them.

According to Paswan, as well as other leaders from the Dalit castes who do not wish to be quoted, the party is now more comfortable discussing caste and Dalit issues at party forums and tries to address the concerns of Dalits. He narrates the discussion generated during his presidentship when he put pictures of Babu

Jagjivan Ram and Kanshi Ram in his office and how this was well-received despite murmurs from some quarters. He was invited by the Dalits of Kanshi Ram's village in Punjab, and more than 5,000 members of the Dalit community attended the meeting. This convinced the party leadership that adopting Dalit icons and symbolism from across the political divide can generate long-term dividends. However, it was the student wing of the RSS, the Akhil Bharatiya Vidhyarthi Parishad (ABVP), which first started incorporating Ambedkar in its discourse and symbolism in its attempts to make inroads into the Dalit student community (Ambekar, 2019). This was then taken up by the RSS and later the BJP, especially under Modi.

The BJP has consciously adopted two strategies from the past and scaled them up to reap unprecedented rewards. First, the party under Modi and Amit Shah has extended the *Shekhawat doctrine* (Singh, 2019c), which originally envisioned the expansion of its social base beyond the traditional urban 'Brahmin–Baniya' constituency and advocated the localization of Hindutva. The Hindutva narrative was initially adapted according to the regional and caste-specific imagination of Rajputs in Rajasthan. It has been redesigned to incorporate the narratives of Dalits and OBCs. Their desire to be visible in history, and their icons, oral traditions, and histories, contemptuously dismissed by secular and left-wing history-writing, were mainstreamed into the Hindutva fold by the BJP–RSS and deployed for political mobilization as seen in the case of the Pasi–Bhar king, Maharaja Suheldev in UP (Rashid, 2018).

Second, the *Karpoori Thakur formula* (Gupta, 2017) helped mobilize the lower OBCs, or Extremely Backward Classes (EBCs). These castes, somewhere between the upper OBCs and Dalits, are individually small in their numbers but form a significant chunk of the population if taken together. The BJP has not only mobilized them but also replicated the model within the Dalit community to rally the numerically smaller castes and negate the weight of the numerically larger Dalit castes with their autonomous politics. In the 2019 elections, the BJP, and its ally Apna Dal, gave representation to nine Dalit castes on the 17 reserved seats in UP. On the other hand, the main Dalit party, the Bahujan Samaj Party (BSP), fielded nine candidates from Mayawati's caste on the 10 reserved seats it got in the alliance between the Samajwadi Party (SP) and the BSP.

However, non-BJP Dalit activists[12] differ, claiming that it is not the BJP that is winning but the opposition that is losing. The BJP has deftly outcompeted the opposition parties in caste politics by exploiting the differences between the Dalit castes. It has benefitted from the resentment of the smaller Dalit castes against the dominance of the numerically stronger Dalit castes in the politics of social justice and political power by pitting them against each other. The caste-based social justice parties have been converted into family-run enterprises and lack any clear social and economic agenda.[13] This has caused mass disenchantment with the traditional social justice parties. They lack leadership and are now cut off from the Dalit masses. Several Dalit activists pointed out that the link between Dalit social and cultural movements and Dalit political parties has weakened over the past decade, thus sapping the energy out of the political parties.

The absence of a positive and forward-looking discourse and the rise of fanaticism and neo-Buddhist puritanism were repeatedly pointed out as significant reasons for the fading appeal of Dalit social and cultural movements. Dalit activists from UP and Bihar also flagged the increasing distance between the Dalit educated class and government employees, who drive Dalit discourse and politics, and those outside its ambit.[14] It is becoming more difficult to mobilize the masses on the traditional plank of 'saving reservations' as was evident during the crisis created by the judiciary on the university recruitment roster. Dalit activists are blamed for acting as a one-person army with the tendency of fragmentation even within an organization. This tendency flows from the insistence on ideological purity of the Ambedkarite discourse and the differences between Dalit castes.

On the other hand, the BJP has been able to woo the Dalit masses with its pro-poor stance and persistent efforts to engage with them, mostly spearheaded by the RSS cadres. The BJP's media and social media lead to push its message across the country is unrivalled and seen as a significant factor by Dalit activists. They blame 'brainwashing' by the media on Hindu–Muslim issues and nationalism for the shift of Dalit votes to the BJP. They repeatedly point out that the upper castes in the villages still play the role of influencers and shape the pro-BJP discourse via continuous propaganda. However, they could not explain how this works or what the exact propaganda was, except for some statements by politicians and some news channels.

A young post-holder[15] in the BJP from a Dalit caste pointed out that the Dalit masses do not have sharp pro-BJP or anti-BJP views and that all the narrative of resentment we hear is only coming from those with political aspirations or strong ideological views.[16] It is not easy to bracket Dalit political behaviour into neat categories on the ground. However, he also pointed out that there is no substantial shift of Dalits in favour of the BJP, and votes are mostly for the leadership of Modi or a negative vote against opposition parties. Many Dalits relate to Modi, a person who comes from a deprived background like them. Moreover, Modi too has consciously cultivated this relationship with his speeches and symbolism. Another Dalit caste activist pointed out that Modi's visit and symbolism at Kedarnath and reconstruction of Kashi Vishwanath Dham were instantly relatable to the Dalits in the countryside, who form a significant proportion of those undertaking the annual Kanwar *yatra* (journey). There is a revival of popular religiosity aided by mass media and social media, and the BJP has been quick to identify with the trend.

The Future

Despite the success of the BJP in gaining a foothold within the Dalit community, this relationship remains fragile. As Paswan puts it: 'Dalits are detained votes of the BJP due to lack of alternative; the challenge is to convert them into retained votes.' According to Devi Dayal Gautam, assistant principal secretary to the former union social justice minister, the politics of both the Congress and the BJP are based on what is called *sadhe satiya*, or 7.5 per cent votes, representing peripheral Dalit castes, and this is unsustainable in the long run. This is an important point. Dalit castes can be divided into two broad groups: peripheral, or *sevadar* castes, and non-peripheral castes. Peripheral castes are those that had settled near villages as they provided essential services to *savarnas* (upper castes); these include castes like Kamhar, Sonkar, Dhobi, and so on.

In contrast, non-peripheral castes are the outcasts in the real sense, apart from being numerically more significant like the Jatavs, Mahars, and Pasis. Peripheral castes were included in the Dalit category due to their socio-economic plight. They did not suffer the full extent of untouchability and, despite their lower social status, were part of regular village life. The non-peripheral castes suffered extreme deprivation, exclusion, and untouchability, and were the first to engage in anti-caste movements that emerged during the colonial period. Due to their social position and demographics, these castes emerged as the 'political castes' among Dalits with strong political mobilization and Ambedkarite consciousness (Narayan, 2011).

However, after the experience of the Congress with Babu Jagjivan Ram,[17] who threatened the social hierarchy by staking claim to the prime minister's post, political parties adopted the policy of sidelining the more numerous non-peripheral castes by promoting the smaller peripheral castes to meet the quota of Dalit representation. This started from the 1984 elections, with the Congress allotting most tickets on reserved seats to the peripheral castes. Such marginalization later played an essential role in the emergence of independent Dalit political parties, most noticeably the BSP in UP (Pai, 2002). The formula has been adopted even by the BJP. However, this is an unsustainable trajectory as the demographic and political weight of these castes is bound to impact the party and the country's political future.

Since the formation of BJP government at the centre in 2014, all the major crises on the Dalit front have emerged from these castes, be it the Bhima Koregaon violence, the protests against dilution of the Scheduled Castes and Scheduled Tribes (Prevention of Atrocities) Act by the Supreme Court, or Rohith Vemula's case. What is important to note is the ability of these castes to spontaneously mobilize and act as a pressure group irrespective of their leaders in mainstream politics.[18] The intensity of these movements was impossible for the BJP to ignore, but it found itself in a fix. It had no faces from these castes who could act as mediators or pacify the crowds and had no backchannel to talk and negotiate at the local level. Although they fall under the SC category, the leadership of the peripheral castes does not have much social intercourse with the non-peripheral or political castes. This means that the direct heat of such movements reaches the top levels of the party and the government itself, forcing responses under pressure with unintended consequences. For instance, the party's attempt to resolve the Dalit unrest over dilution of the Scheduled Castes and Scheduled Tribes (Prevention of Atrocities) Act by the judiciary evoked a sharp reaction from the upper castes which imposed a political cost on several seats during the Madhya Pradesh and Rajasthan elections (Upreti, 2018).

While the overall votes of the Dalit castes for the BJP have increased, this is truer of the smaller or peripheral Dalit castes than of the larger or political Dalit castes. BJP Dalit activists and political leaders accept that resistance is high among the larger Dalit castes, and it has proven to be difficult to make inroads despite some gains in recent years. The members of these castes have more Ambedkarite consciousness and raise issues like jobs, reservations and privatization, judiciary, and market discrimination which party cadres find challenging to answer. But the BJP has continued to make efforts to gain popularity among non-peripheral castes by increasing representation in the organization and ticket distribution during elections. It has been able to reap some successes like among Jatavs during the 2022 UP elections (Beg, Pandey, and Sardesai, 2022). Attempts to further expand into the Dalit castes will necessitate several concessions like representation in the private sector and judiciary which may antagonize the upper castes. It is often remarked that 'Sabka Saath, Sabka Vikas', the popular slogan that swung BJP to power in 2014, has become 'Sabka Saath, Sabka Vivad'. It is far easier to create a social coalition of Hindu castes than to sustain it (Singh, 2018).

A significant reason behind the success of the BJP is the consolidation of Hindutva due to long-term trends reshaping Indian society. However, the sustainability of Hindutva as a political construct depends on, first, the rapid socio-economic mobility of the subaltern, and, second, ensuring representation and a share in power for the subaltern castes. Here, the subaltern component of Hindutva differs from the dogmatic ideological construct because of the emphasis on material and instrumental values, as opposed to purely ideological ones. Moreover, the socio-economic mobility of Dalit castes mainly depends on two factors: access to government jobs and migration from villages to cities in search of better economic opportunities. However, what we see today is a significant shrinking of both these routes (Thorat, 2018). The persistent economic slowdown and the pandemic have caused massive unemployment and collapse of jobs in urban centres. Job losses among Dalits have been almost three times those among non-Dalit castes (Deshpande and Ramachandran, 2020). Reverse migration is also a reversal of social mobility. Government jobs, too, are declining due to privatization, contractualization, and an undeclared freeze on recruitments across the centre and states. There were some 7,00,000 vacancies in the centre alone (Press Trust of India, 2019). Public employment in India is already among the lowest globally and needs a substantial increase. However, the image of the BJP is of a party hostile to government jobs, and the undeclared freeze on millions of government jobs is increasing discontent across all castes, including Dalits. The closing doors for socio-economic mobility due to the adverse economic situation can potentially unravel the entire Hindutva project and reverse the gains made by the BJP.

The shift of Dalit castes towards the BJP was also due to the promise of better representation and share in power. However, that promise has not materialized in the government and appointments to decision-making bodies. While the BJP today is the most inclusive Hindu party, the rising representation in the organization has not translated into power-sharing. Several Dalit leaders and activists pointed out that decision-making is still highly concentrated, and they hardly have any say in the process. There is sparse representation of Dalits in the cabinet, bureaucratic appointments, commissions and boards, the judiciary, co-operatives, and even as vice chancellors of universities. This is already causing disillusionment among the politically engaged section of the Dalit youth that recently shifted towards the party. However, the party is quietly trying to broaden representation at several levels like having general secretaries (ETV Bharat, 2020), not only in the national team but also in state units, and state-unit presidents like in Tamil Nadu and Punjab (Mohan, 2016). The party is now proactively recommending names from backward and Dalits castes for various committees and commissions as an internal process and is more tactful in representation in the government (Pandey, 2022).

The economic downturn and question of representation and power distribution along with the sidelining of the larger Dalit castes are potentially the most serious threats to the sustainability of the party's efforts to woo Dalit castes.

But the BJP has repeatedly demonstrated its ability to identify its weak spots, read emerging trends, and evolve a long-term response due to its organizational capabilities. And the BJP leadership looks at the recent significant shift of Dalit votes towards the party as an initial phase of the long-term restructuring of the Indian polity.

Notes

1. The *jajmani* system refers to a patron–provider system where landholding patrons (*jajamans*) are linked through exchanges of food for services with providers (*kamans*), such as brahmin priests, artisans, agricultural labourers, and so on.
2. This issue was flagged by several non-political Dalit activists.
3. The concerned individuals asked not to be quoted due to the nature of the organizational posts they hold, requiring delicate balancing of competing claims of different castes and communities.
4. Author's interview with BJP leader Ram Madhav. This factor was pointed out by almost every senior BJP leader.
5. It was argued that expansion among Dalits was also a by-product of this development. It gave the party an important database to strategize during elections.
6. *Panna Pramukh*s are typically BJP- or RSS-affiliated members in charge of one page of the electoral roll of a specific constituency. They maintain regular communication with these voters and mobilise them during elections.
7. Author's interview with Guru Prakash, the national spokesperson of the BJP.
8. Author's interview with a senior BJP leader in an important organizational role, who did not wish to be quoted.
9. Author's interview with Tejasvi Surya, the president of the BJP youth wing and a member of parliament (MP), South Bengaluru.
10. Author's interview with Sanjay Paswan, a member of the legislative council (MLC) of Bihar and the former president of the BJP Scheduled Castes (SC) wing.
11. I am part of the core committee of 'Samajik Samvad' and have extensively travelled on the ground during elections, holding small closed-door meetings with the target audience. The campaign will run till the 2024 Lok Sabha elections.
12. Author's interview with several activists in the academia and local caste organizations who are not members of any political party. All of them refused to be quoted.
13. Author's interview with Arvind Kumar, a research scholar at Royal Holloway, University of London.

14. The experience of the failure to mobilize Dalit masses against the Supreme Court order on the roster system, which effectively killed reservation in universities and colleges, was invoked repeatedly.
15. The concerned individual wished to remain anonymous.
16. This is also the reason why the author avoided interviewing Dalits who are active members of opposition parties.
17. There is a lot of ambivalence regarding Jagjivan Ram. One the one hand, he is criticized for opposing Ambedkar; on the other, he is mentioned as a pivotal leader by several Dalit activists.
18. Author's interview with academics from Dalit castes who refused to be quoted.

Bibliography

Ambekar, S. 2019. *The RSS: Roadmaps for the 21st Century*. New Delhi: Rupa Publications.

Beg, M. A., S. Pandey, and S. Sardesai. 2022. 'The BJP'S Rock Solid Social Coalition'. *The Hindu*, 12 March.

Chandra, K. 2018. 'The Triumph of Hindu Majoritarianism'. *Foreign Affairs*, 23 November. https://www.foreignaffairs.com/articles/india/2018-11-23/triumph-hindu-majoritarianism. Accessed on 21 December 2022.

Deshpande, A., and R. Ramachandran. 2020. 'Differential Impact of COVID-19 and the Lockdown'. *The Hindu*, 22 August.

ETV Bharat. 2020. 'BJP's New Appointment Shows Party's Focus on Punjab's Dalit Vote Bank'. EVT Bharat, 17 November. https://react.etvbharat.com/english/national/state/punjab/special-bjps-new-appointment-of-punjab-shows-partys-focus-on-dalit-votebank/na20201117200616649. Accessed on 21 December 2022.

Gupta, S. 2017. 'Following the Karpoori Thakur Model, OBC Sub-Categorisation Could Be Icing on BJP's Cake'. *The Print*, 4 October. https://theprint.in/opinion/following-karpoori-thakur-model-obc-sub-categorisation-icing-bjps-cake/11509/.

Hindustan Times. 2020. 'Hathras Gang-Rape: BJP Stares at the Return of Dalit Unrest'. 30 September. https://www.hindustantimes.com/india-news/hathras-gang-rape-bjp-stares-at-the-return-of-dalit-unrest/story-tCHwxyoaMqQNOg9dxlYGLN.html. Accessed on 26 December 2022.

Indian Express. 2019. 'Explained: Why Govt Has Moved to Overturn SC's Quota-in-University-Jobs Order'. *Indian Express*, 7 March.

Jaffrelot, C. 2000. 'Sanskritization vs. Ethnicization in India: Changing Identities and Caste Politics Before Mandal'. *Asian Survey* 40(5): 756–66.

Kapur, D., C. B. Prasad, L. Pritchett, and D. Babu. 2010. 'Rethinking Inequality: Dalits in Uttar Pradesh in the Market Reform Era'. *Economic and Political Weekly* 45(35): 39–49.

Kishore, R. 2022. 'Number Theory: Did Women and Welfare Sweep UP for the BJP?' *Hindustan Times*, 12 March.

Kumar, S., and P. Gupta. 2019. 'Where Did the BJP Get Its Votes from in 2019?' *Mint*, 3 June. https://www.livemint.com/politics/news/where-did-the-bjp-get-its-votes-from-in-2019-1559547933995.html. Accessed on 21 December 2022.

Lal, S. 2021. *Crisis of Dalit Leadership*. Jaipur: Rawat Publications.

Mehta, N. 2022. *The New BJP: Modi and the Making of the World's Largest Political Party*. Chennai: Westland Books.

Mendelsohn, O., and M. Vicziany. 1998. *The Untouchables: Subordination, Poverty, and the State in Modern India*. Cambridge: Cambridge University Press.

Mohan, A. 2016. 'BJP Picks OBC, Dalit Leaders to Head Key State Units'. *Business Stnadard*, 8 April.

Nandy, A. 1996. *Creating a Nationality: The Ramjanmabhumi Movement and Fear of the Self*. New Delhi: Oxford University Press.

Narayan, B. 2009. *Fascinating Hindutva: Saffron Politics and Dalit Mobilisation*. New Delhi: SAGE Publications. DOI: 10.4135/9788132101055.

———. 2011. *The Making of the Dalit Public in North India: Uttar Pradesh, 1950–Present*. New Delhi: Oxford University Press.

———. 2016. *Fractured Tales: Invisibles in Indian Democracy*. New Delhi: Oxford University Press.

New Indian Express. 2020. 'Devyani Khobragade Appointed India's Next Ambassador to Cambodia'. 1 October. https://www.newindianexpress.com/nation/2020/oct/01/devyani-khobragade-appointed-indias-next-ambassador-to-cambodia-2204447.html. Accessed on 26 December 2022.

Pai, S. 2002. *Dalit Assertion and the Unfinished Democratic Revolution: The Bahujan Samaj Party in Uttar Pradesh*. New Delhi: SAGE Publications.

Pandey, M. C. 2022. 'Yogi Adityanath Cabinet 2.0: BJP Looks to Strike Regional and Caste Balance'. *Hindustan Times*, 26 March.

Patil, P. 2015. 'A Fight Outside the Caste Silos'. *The Hindu*, 27 June.

Prasad, C. B. 2008. 'Markets and Manu: Economic Reforms and Its Impact on Caste in India'. CASI Working Paper 08-01, Center for the Advanced Study of India, University of Pennsylvania, Philadelphia. https://casi.sas.upenn.edu/content/markets-and-manu-economic-reforms-and-its-impact-caste-india-chandra-bhan-prasad. Accessed on 21 December 2022.

Press Trust of India. 2019. 'Nearly Seven Lakh Vacant Posts in Central Government Departments: Minister'. *Times of India*, 21 November.

Rashid, O. 2018. 'Modi to Release Stamp on Suheldev'. *The Hindu*, 28 December.

Singh, A. P. 2016. 'Dalit Religious Discourse Is Not Homogenous, Let Its Plurality Assert Itself'. *Swarjaya*, 27 October. https://swarjyamag.com/culture/dalit-religious-discourse-is-not-homogenous-let-its-plurality-assert-itself. Accessed on 26 December 2022.

———. 2018. 'What Lotus Needs to Do to Bloom Again in UP'. *Economics Times*, 18 March.

———. 2019a. 'A Common Hindu Identity Has Always Appealed to OBC and Dalit Castes'. *Hindustan Times*, 18 July. https://www.hindustantimes.com/columns/a-common-hindu-identity-has-always-appealed-to-obc-and-dalit-castes/story-n8CXPw1CKTx0V27Zk8VTSJ.html. Accessed on 23 December 2022.

———. 2019b. 'New Socio-Political Churn Reshaping India?' Observer Research Foundation. https://www.orfonline.org/expert-speak/new-socio-political-churn-reshaping-india-51126/. Accessed on 23 December 2022.

———. 2019c. 'Subaltern Hindutva, How India Voted'. *Seminar* 720. https://www.india-seminar.com/2019/720/702_abhinav_prakash_singh.htm. Accessed on 21 December 2022.

———. 2019d. 'The Twin Crisis of Dalit Politics and Dalit Discourse'. *Hindustan Times*, 27 December.

Srinivas, G. 2016. *Dalit Middle Class: Mobility, Identity, and Politics of Caste*. Jaipur: Rawat Publications.

Thorat, S. 2018. 'Scheduled Castes among Worst Sufferers of India's Job Problem'. *Hindustan Times*, 7 September.

Upreti, D. K. 2018. 'Dismayed at SC/ST Act, Upper Castes Opt NOTA'. *The Pioneer*, 14 December. https://www.dailypioneer.com/2018/page1/dismayed-at-sc-st-act--upper-castes-opt-nota.html. Accessed on 21 December 2022.

Part II

Popular Culture, Discourse, and Protest

7

Music as the Language of the Bahujan Movement

Locating the Social History of the Dalit Shoshit Samaj Sangharsh Samiti

K. Kalyani and Satnam Singh

Popular culture is an important parameter for understanding contested spaces within society. Stuart Hall (1996: 4) argues that identities are formed and contested within 'specific historical and institutional sites within specific discursive formations and practices'. He further argues that cultural studies are not just an 'umbrella' term for knowing anything and everything; it is rather about understanding the new popular culture in the context of 'the larger historical or political project that now confronts the humanities' (Hall, 1990: 23). This chapter contextualizes the emergence of the Dalit Shoshit Samaj Sangharsh Samiti (DS4) in Dalit–Bahujan sociopolitical history, by engaging with the musical tradition and practices of the 'Bahujan mission'.[1]

Music is an important aspect of this popular culture. Within the sociopolitical movement of the Bahujan, led by Kanshi Ram, musical practices and performances have played a significant role in raising anti-caste consciousness. It is relevant to mention here that the relationship between popular cultural practices and political movements cannot be compartmentalized neatly, because they are not mutually exclusive. There has been constant overlap between what is popular culture and how the political sphere uses elements of the 'popular' from time to time.

When one investigates the 'practice' of music, every form of music has its history and is associated with an ethnic group (Bohlman, 1991: 266–67). Music is a shared consciousness through which cultural history is reiterated and retold. This shared consciousness and culture are reflected through the song's dialect, the materiality used, the lyrics of the song, and so on. Thus, every form of musical practice has its context and history. However, music has the potential to transcend the essentialized identity within which it is conventionally embedded as well. Simon Firth (1996) has argued that while the social context of music is relevant, it is also important to understand how music has the potential to travel beyond conventional boundaries of identity. Within popular culture, music can be seen as a cultural aspect that creates a contested space with the existing popular culture, both by appropriation and denunciation of aspects that exist in mainstream popular culture.

Dalit–Bahujan musical practices have their sociopolitical–cultural rootedness as well. This chapter tries to explore the musical practices that had emerged during the rise of the DS4, a sociocultural wing formed by Kanshi Ram in 1981, before the formation of the Bahujan Samaj Party (BSP). While the history of Dalit–Bahujan music is much older and goes back to the Bhakti tradition, the music developed during the 1980s under the DS4 had a unique sense of assertion for the Bahujan in particular. This uniqueness can be recounted in terms of icons used, ideology, leadership, and the very 'practice' of music. The contested cultural space created through the DS4 was also important for creating a political space and giving the Dalit–Bahujan a sense of belongingness and dignified identity. Through an ethnographic engagement with the singers of the DS4 the chapter explores the cultural facets that the songs of resistance represented.

The DS4: Its History and Emergence

The beginning of the DS4 can be particularly traced back to the region of Punjab, where a large number of singers began to emerge, many of whom volunteered in the organization in 1981 (Kalyani, 2022: 12). This new cultural-wing was an offshoot of the All India Backward and Minority Communities Employees Federation (BAMCEF).[2] The DS4 was formally founded on 6 December 1981, the death anniversary of B. R. Ambedkar. The organization was subsumed within the BSP later but was never formally dissolved (Jaffrelot, 2003: 395). From Punjab, the cultural movement further spread to Jammu, Himachal Pradesh, Haryana, and other regions.

The emergence of the DS4 was an important cultural shift, particularly in pockets of north India. It involved local singers from the Dalit–Bahujan community. The presence of women in the DS4 was also very striking. Many of the singers who got involved with the DS4 were already popular locally and used to perform Ravidassia music.[3] With the emergence of the DS4, new genres of music also began to emerge. For instance, in Punjab and Himachal Pradesh, the 'Jago' form of music became popular. These songs are widely sung during different cultural events, wedding ceremonies, and the involvement of women in their performance is particularly important. The changing patterns of musical genres also reflected the changes that were occurring in how the culture was imagined. While previously wedding songs used images of Hindu gods, the songs used Dalit–Bahujan icons and constantly evoked anti-caste sentiments after the emergence of the DS4. One such 'Jago' song was worded as follows:

Dalita jag bhai, hun 'Jago' aayia.

My Dalit brothers, get up for the anti-caste struggle; the 'Jago' has arrived.

During its emergence, the DS4 engaged with cultural production in different forms. These included the production of booklets, popular literature, posters, and so on. However, among the many forms of cultural engagement under the DS4, the performance of songs was the most popular and gained acceptance among the masses. Music can create a sense of cultural association. Steven Feld (2012) in his study, *Sound and Sentiment*, has argued that music has the potential to evoke emotions in an individual. Through his ethnographic study of Kaluli,[4] he maintained that the sonic world can give unique experiences. The experience of music gives a specific sense of association and can connect with feelings and thoughts (Finnegan, 2012: 358).

It is important to discuss what music means and what it does to a community. Ruth Finnegan (2012) argues that understanding musical experience through ethnographic specificities can give a more realistic perception of what music means for a community or a group. Tia DeNora (2004) has discussed the significance of music in everyday life and the affect it generates. Popular music studies show how people experience music and how this music is embodied in their everyday social life. The songs of resistance by the Dalit–Bahujans, too, have gradually become a part of the everyday life of people who have stood for anti-caste consciousness.

It is important to mention that songs of resistance were already prevalent in different areas of Punjab in the form of Ravidassia music, among others. Furthermore, the Punjabi language was well known in parts of Haryana and Himachal Pradesh, which in some ways better connected people from these regions to the 'Mission Geet'.[5] The Akashvani Kendra, Jalandhar, and the Doordarshan Kendra, Jalandhar, played a great role in spreading the Punjabi language to Haryana and Himachal Pradesh. Acquaintance with the language helped the initial spread and popularity of the Punjabi DS4 songs. Later, when the DS4 gained popularity in other regions, local versions of the songs began to emerge as well.

The DS4 had emerged as a sociocultural organization to reclaim cultural space through assertion. However, Kanshi Ram also realized the importance of capturing the political space. Christophe Jaffrelot has argued that because of the Indian National Congress' attitude of giving space only to 'sycophant Schedule Caste members', Kanshi Ram felt the need to bring in 'genuine fighters' for the Bahujan cause. For this reason, the DS4 proposed 46 candidates for the assembly elections in Haryana (Jaffrelot, 2003: 395). Even though it failed to get political success, the sociocultural consciousness it created was indeed a foreground for the BSP in the making.

DS4 Musical Traditions

The emergence of the DS4 witnessed the advent of a large number of singers from different regions of north India. This cultural wing can be considered a pioneer in creating songs of resistance and in generating anti-caste consciousness. Singers like Ashok Kumar and Saroj Kumari, who were siblings, were quite popular in Punjab, with their popularity extending even beyond the state, to Himachal Pradesh. Their songs of resistance discussed the inhumane condition of Dalits and their aspiration to rise above their stigmatized caste position in society. The songs also included political critiques of the then incumbent party (the Congress). They reflected a constant shift from pain to resistance. One of their songs was worded as follows.

> *Agg lag jave iss Indira de raj nu.*
> *Paithi saal ho gaye, pani khua de paroundi nu.*

> May this Indira-led government be set fire to.
> We have been fetching water from far off places for 35 years; we despise this now.

Similarly, another song by Saroj reads:

> *Sadak te rorhi kut rahiya mutiyaran nu dekho*
> *Mahli rang mana rahiya auna nara nu dekho.*

> Watch a Dalit woman who is breaking stones by the side of the road.
> Also, see how her lifeworld is different from an upper-caste woman who has all the luxury of a palace.

The aforementioned song discusses a Dalit woman who is breaking stones by the side of a road. This imagery of Dalit women is then contrasted with the image of an upper-caste woman who has access to all aspects of a good, comfortable life. Such songs of resistance were one of the early interventions by Dalit women for not only accessing the public sphere, but also for questioning the double marginalization[6] that Dalit women undergo. It is interesting to see how the songs of resistance in the DS4 captured the double marginalization of Dalit women even before academic debates (Rege, 2000; Chakravarti, 1993), which raised some of these issues only in the late 1980s and the 1990s.

Further, it is significant to mention that women were active participants in DS4 events. Besides singing, they were also involved in collecting party funds through smaller contributions made by people. For women, this sociocultural participation was emancipating as it allowed them access to the public sphere. The position of women in DS4 songs was quite egalitarian. One of the songs discusses a sister insisting on her brother including her in the Bahujan *andolan* (agitation). It is worded:

> *Bahain nu bana le jaytheband ve.*
> *Meri qaum diya virna.*

> Include your sister in your Bahujan group.
> I want to stand for my community.

The DS4 singers were from impecunious backgrounds and would often participate in the movement only after having worked all day. In our conversation with Poonam Bala, one of the foremost singers of the DS4, she said that she would compromise on her children's care to take part in the movement.[7] Many of the activists were involved on the ground and spread anti-caste consciousness from village to village. The 'bicycle' used by these activists and singers to travel became an important symbol for the Bahujan movement that was led by Kanshi Ram.

The use of songs for generating anti-caste consciousness was an important cultural shift. The songs and their performance not only allowed for the development of the anti-caste narrative, but also gave people a sense of association with the Bahujan community. Most of the Punjabi songs included the word *qaum*, which the DS4 used extensively to mean the caste community. The sense of belonging and shared history of pain were important for generating a long-term association of people with Kanshi Ram's Bahujan struggle. Such association with Kanshi Ram and his struggle was so deeply entrenched in people's memory that during our interaction, they would often get emotional while remembering him and the movement. The Bahujan movement for the activists and singers was not just a political goal but also a sociocultural struggle to reclaim the public sphere with a sense of dignity. It will not be an exaggeration to consider the DS4 as an organization that developed an emotional cohesiveness, something which was strongly needed for conceptualizing the idea of the 'Bahujan'.

With the spread of the songs of resistance beyond Punjab, the songs also began to diversify into different languages and dialects. These included Haryanvi, Dogri, and Pahari, to name a few. Local singers from different regions also started emerging. For instance, in Himachal Pradesh, there was a famous singer called Sangli Ram whom we came to know about through interactions with another DS4 singer named Usha Devi. Usha Devi said that she, along with Sangli Ram, had written many DS4 songs. In our interaction with her, she sang one such song:[8]

> *Horna ne munnu padhi afsar bane*
> *Tijo me Dr Ambedkar banana.*
> *Ho sutya Dalit jagana*
> *Wo nindra chari deya munnuna.*

(In this song, a father is conveying to his son that while others become officers after their education, he has to be more than that. 'After your education, you have to be like Dr Ambedkar, who has uplifted the conditions of Dalits. You have to quit your comfort and sleep, for the cause of society.')

Another prominent name among DS4 singers was Mohan Bangar. He had compiled several music albums, which were popular in Jammu, Himachal Pradesh, Punjab, and Haryana. Satnam Singh, a Bahujan activist, recalls that Bangar would often carry a *tumbi* (a traditional one-stringed instrument from the Punjab region) in his hand, and would give spontaneous performances of his songs on public demand. It is significant to mention that most of the singers from the DS4 were identified with the *tumbi*. The *tumbi* is a lightweight instrument and is easy to carry. Other musical instruments used were the *algoza*, *bugatu*, *chimta*, and so on (see Figure 7A.6).

Mohan Bangar belonged to the initial generation of the DS4. His songs, like those of many other singers, can be recalled only through the memories of early-generation Bahujan activists. One of his popular songs was as follows.

> *Uth sutiye qaume jaag tere.*
> *Jagan da vela aya hai.*

Hey, sleeping society, you need to wake up now.
Now the time has arrived for us to be awake.

Others included Kewal Sambara, a singer from Baharwal village, Shahid Bhagat Singh Nagar, Punjab. Amrit Kaur, a doctor at Chandigarh Hospital, was also associated with the DS4. Many of these names find mention in the *Bahujan Sanghatak*, which was edited by Kanshi Ram himself. From Uttar Pradesh (UP), Kishor Kumar 'Pagla' was one of the most well-known singers. Some of his popular albums were *Saheb ka Sandesh Desh ko, Saheb ko Sat-Sat Pranam*, and so on.

Ethnographic Accounts of DS4 Singers

Ethnography is a powerful tool for in-depth understanding of culture. Feld (2012) has argued that ethnographic writing is much more than a writing convention or intellectual fad. It is about accounting for unique experiences in a dialogic manner. For women respondents, ethnography has worked differently. Women often open up to conversation only after they have comfortably established rapport with the researcher. A closed-ended questionnaire might restrict them from candidly discussing their lived experiences. Ethnography has thus been an effective tool for understanding the lived experiences of DS4 singers, particularly women.

Our interaction with Dalit–Bahujan singers from the DS4 focused on those who were active during the 1980s and 1990s, in particular. At the time, technology was limited; hence, access to their recordings is either through available cassettes or through their memories of those songs. Further, a narrative analysis of their memories and recounting of the past was an important method for our inquiry. While the list of such singers is extensive, the account here is of some popular DS4 singers.

Access to these singers was gained through the snowballing method[9] and by interacting with a series of activists, particularly from the early phase of the Bahujan movement. The research involved engagement with the singers over some time, and much of the information was gathered through a process of constant interaction.

Poonam Bala

Poonam Bala is a singer by profession, who has had a long-standing association with the DS4 and the Bahujan movement. She is from Nawanshahr in Shaheed Bhagat Singh Nagar district, Punjab, and has been singing for over 35 years. Her association with the Bahujan movement started with the BAMCEF, which she joined in 1979. During our interaction, she revealed the long and sustained struggle she had undertaken ever since she was 30 years old. During her activism and singing, she would often have to leave her children and travel to distant places. She said: 'I was so deeply attached to Manyawar's struggle that I would travel to far-off places to meet him and perform for the cause of the Bahujan struggle that he had taken up.' She also mentioned that being a woman, she felt the need to include other women in the movement too. She said:

> I became active in the Bahujan struggle for social justice before Mayawati *ji* had even started. Mayawati *ji* also often used to visit us. Being a woman, I was married early and had many familial responsibilities. The main reason that I started and strongly got attached to the Bahujan struggle was due to Kanshi Ram. He would treat us like his children. During the movement, he would ensure that we had sufficient food to eat and a place to stay.

She recalled her travels with the DS4 team to Ropar and other places. She has sung many songs together with Harnam Singh Behalpuri in Punjab, Haryana, and Himachal Pradesh.

Poonam said that she has been associated with singing since her childhood. Her grandfather, Shahad Das, was also a singer from Jalandhar, Punjab. For her, the DS4 was a different platform altogether as it gave her public visibility. She said: 'I used to not only sing but also establish a sense of communication with my fellow sisters, which would have otherwise not been possible within the domestic space.' Professionally, she was associated with Prasar Bharti as a folk singer from Jalandhar. She had performed at several schools and colleges. Some of her older albums are *Tujh Bin Kaun Kare*, *Qaum Nu Bachaun Walia*, *Jang Jaari Hai*, and *Dharti te Rab Aa Gaya* (see Figures 7A.2 and 7A.3). She sang one of her most popular songs for us:

> *Raj pandhra karde ne*
> *Oo tussi sau de vichon pachassi*
> *Mangte ban firde oo*
> *Tussi desh de mulnivasi*
> *Zara parh ithihas dekho*
> *Tuhada daya ithihas chupya*
> *Eka karlo dalito cheti*
> *Raj tusanda aya*

Fifteen per cent of people are ruling you when your number is 85 per cent
You are begging for your rights even though you are Mulnivasi.[10]
You need to read history; your history has been hidden.
Hey, Dalit friends, show your solidarity; your political power awaits.

For Poonam, DS4 was an entirely new space to which she gave her best. As a woman singer, her experience of accessing the public sphere was novel. Many women did not have such access. Poonam said:

> As a woman singer, I ensured that I had other women, too, along with me, who understood what 'Bahujan' means. My husband, Mahendra Pal Singh, was also a dedicated DS4 member; he encouraged me in the movement. If he would not have supported me, who would have listened to us women?

This statement reflected the comradeship that existed among people active in the movement, irrespective of their gender.

Harnam Singh Behalpuri

Harnam Singh Behalpuri was a dedicated DS4 singer from Hoshiarpur, Punjab. He said he has been singing since 1974, and his songs were initially dedicated to Guru Ravidas. He got associated with songs of resistance after he joined the BAMCEF in Chandigarh. He was active in various states in north and central India including Punjab, Haryana, Jammu and Kashmir, Delhi, UP, Rajasthan, Madhya Pradesh, Maharashtra, and Himachal Pradesh. Behalpuri first met Kanshi Ram in Ambala, Haryana, during elections. He had gone there as a singer for a DS4 programme. Thereafter, he met him at several places and eventually got fully associated with the Bahujan movement of north India.

His association with the anti-caste struggle and the 'Bahujan mission' has never weakened. He says: '[The Bahujan] mission never gets old, and it will keep going on till our dream of a casteless society has been achieved.' He had several cassettes that he had recorded and that were quite popular in Punjab, in particular. These included *Kanshi Ram da Danka, Jang Jari Hai, Jagan da Vella, Dalita de Rahabar, Kafan Chahida*, and so on. One of his very popular songs sung in the DS4 was worded as follows.

Ve gal sun le meriya chana
Teri har ek gal mai mana
Tere agee hath me bana
Sachi das bol
Tinda vich kahde ja bajaunda dhol ve

Pind pind meetinga jaa karwa
Babasaheb de mission chalawa
DS4 ware samjana
Sutte Dalita tain jagawa

This song is a dialogue between a husband and wife. In the first stanza, the wife is enquiring about her husband's visit to different villages. She says that she has been a dedicated wife and listens to whatever he says. She requests him to tell her the truth about his visit to different villages and the songs that he sings while travelling. Her husband replies that he goes from one village to another to conduct different meetings and to ensure that Babasaheb's mission goes on. 'I sing to make people understand about DS4 and what it means. Through my songs I want my Dalit brothers to become aware of their rights.'

This song reflects how songs of resistance were intertwined with the everyday lived reality of singers and activists. Further, these songs often blurred the lines between the public and the private spaces, which allowed people to wholeheartedly connect with the Bahujan movement.

Behalpuri's association with the DS4 and its cultural programmes reflected his desire for a casteless society. He had inducted many other people to the DS4, including many women singers. Among them were Ravidassia singers, who had begun to recognize Bahujan icons and shifted to songs of resistance, popularly known as 'Mission Geet'. While many singers continued to associate with the movement over time, those like Behalpuri were some of the earliest in the Bahujan movement and were nurtured through platforms like the DS4.

Kasturi Gautam

Kasturi Gautam is a popular singer from Saharanpur, UP. She was associated with the DS4 since 1982 and part of the BSP till 2003. Currently (2022), she serves as a Mandal chairperson in the Azad Samaj Party. She is a popular singer in Western UP and has recorded several cassettes and CDs. Most of these songs were election songs sung during rallies. However, while she was part of the DS4, her songs were more about making people aware of their history and culture.

During our interaction, she recalled the struggles that she faced when participating in the Bahujan movement. She would often perform in rallies led by Kanshi Ram. She said: 'I have worked together with Bahen *ji* [referring to Mayawati]. We used to work the whole day with the DS4 organization. Even at night, when we used to return to our homes completely tired, we ensured that we made a few collections for the organization.' When part of the DS4 movement, the activist often collected coupons instead of cash. This coupon money would range from INR 2 to INR 5. She was also active in the first Lok Sabha elections fought by the BSP from Saharanpur.

She said that the emergence of the DS4 and the BSP was a particularly enabling experience for her as it gave her a sense of dignity and self-worth. However, the cultural assertion by the DS4 was not an easy path. She recalled:

> We would often have to face the anger of upper-caste people. They never wanted that we should reclaim our dignity, and thus they created hurdles in our path. I remember the *mukhiya* [village headman] would often insist that everyone should vote for him. But after the DS4 and the Bahujan movement, we knew our history and struggle better. We resisted them. They would often get our activists beaten up, and even the police would stand by their side. They used abusive language against us; like, they said the DS4 meant 'Maa tumhari baap chaar' [a colloquial way of using derogatory language against Dalit women, calling them prostitutes and sexually promiscuous women]. But at last, through our struggle, we ensured that we gained a position of power. For us, the Bahujan movement was like a dream. Manyawar Kanshi Ram and his untiring commitment were always sources of inspiration for us.

Even though Gautam did not have older recordings from the DS4, she did share some popular songs from the time. One of them was:

Kar kar Baba ko yaad kyu tu nir bhahata hai?
Wo samay hath se nikal gaya, jisko tu pachtata hai.
Jis samay azadi thi azadi Hindustan me,
Sab lage hue the apni apni khanja tanne.
Lekin Babasaheb lage the kalyan me.

Those good times are gone when Babasaheb was there for us.
Why do you cry and miss those times, remembering our icon, Babasaheb?
When India got independence, everyone was only interested in their selfish needs, while Babasaheb stood for social justice and the well-being of others.

Many of her songs during her time in DS4 were about revering Bahujan icons and also about questioning myths that dehumanized and celebrated the killing of Dalits. For instance, in one of her songs, she questions the killing of Bahujan figures like Shambhuk Muni and Bali by Ram in the Ramayana as something unacceptable. Gautam said that when the DS4 began, very few people knew about Bahujan history, and DS4 singing was a powerful medium through which these histories were told to Bahujan people.

Conclusion

It is interesting to see how the Bahujan movement that had started with the BAMCEF was expanded to the DS4 and eventually integrated into a political party, the BSP. Each of these stages had its uniqueness, and Bahujans from across the spectrum in north India were associated with this consistent anti-caste struggle. The engagement with music gave an entirely new dimension to the DS4 struggle. Jacques Attali (2009: 4) has argued that music is a mirror of society and thus needs to be looked at beyond just economic categories. While music is fetishized as a commodity, it also has a social context in which it is produced. This social context determines the words, theme, ideology, as well as materiality of the song.

Thus, the DS4 can be marked as one of the initial phases of a cultural movement in northern India, which played an important role in the Bahujan movement. It was significant in reclaiming the Dalit–Bahujan space and a sense of dignity, particularly for women. The songs of resistance, or 'Mission Geet', were vital components of the cultural movement, keeping it alive and eventually giving political mileage to Dalit–Bahujan politics as well. This chapter is situated in contextualizing the social history of the DS4, particularly by looking into different components of musical practices that prevailed at the time.

In the contemporary context, most of these songs are part of collective memory. While many singers have continued to show their allegiance to current-day BSP politics, others have been forgotten and live in a state of penury (Asianet News, 2020). State support to the singers is minimal, and anti-caste songs, too, see little encouragement from state-led initiatives. With the gradual political decline of the BSP since 2012 and, especially, the substantial decrease in vote percentage in the recent 2022 UP assembly elections, political support for the cultural movement has taken a back seat. Emotional attachment to the movement, however, continues. The emergence of new political spaces like the Azad Samaj Party led by Chandrashekhar Azad Ravan, particularly in north India, has been a new ray of hope for many to search for remnants of the Bahujan movement that was envisioned under the leadership of Kanshi Ram. However, the remaking of the Bahujan movement needs a lot more work than is visible in the contemporary scenario. Nevertheless, DS4 music remains an important moment in history in which anti-caste sentiments were witnessed, and it has become part of the cultural memory of the Bahujan community.

Appendix 7A

Figure 7A.1   Poonam Bala singing during a Bahujan Samaj Party (BSP) rally
Source: Poonam Bala's personal archive.

Figure 7A.2 Poonam Bala and Harnam Singh Bahelpuri's album *Jang Jaari Hai*

Source: Poonam Bala's personal archive.

Figure 7A.3 Poonam Bala and Harnam Singh Behalpuri's album *Qaum Nu Bachaun Walia*, popular during the Dalit Shoshit Samaj Sangharsh Samiti (DS4), with Mayawati featured on the cover

Source: Poonam Bala's personal archive.

Figure 7A.4 Albums of Harnam Singh Bahelpuri (*clockwise from top*): *Jagan da Vella*, *Dalita de Rahbar*, *Kafan Chahida*, and *Damdar Shahida di Yaad*

Source: Harnam Singh Bahelpuri's personal archive.

Figure 7A.5 Kanshi Ram releasing an album of Harnam Singh Bahelpuri in Punjab

Source: Harnam Singh Bahelpuri's personal archive.

Figure 7A.6 Harnam Singh Bahelpuri playing the *tumbi*; artist on the right playing the *algoza* (as locally known in Punjab), and artist on the left playing the *bugatu*, a ring-like instrument with attached bells

Source: Harnam Singh Bahelpuri's personal archive.

Figure 7A.7 Singer and activist Ashok Kumar with Kanshi Ram in Punjab

Source: Harnam Singh Bahelpuri's personal archive.

Figure 7A.8   Mohan Bangar during one of his performances
Source: Satnam Singh's personal archive.

Notes

1. Kanshi Ram, a Bahujan leader and the founding president of the Bahujan Samaj
    Party (BSP), referred to the anti-caste consciousness of the 1980s as a 'mission'
    led by the 'Bahujan'. The term 'Bahujan' was used by him to refer to the roughly
    85 per cent of the population consisting of the Scheduled Castes (SCs), Scheduled
    Tribes (STs), Other Backward Classes (OBCs), minorities, and women. Within
    popular imagination, Kanshi Ram's idea of the 'Bahujan' is often captured through
    his image of holding a pen, in which he said: 'Political activity has become a game
    wherein "rich men's notes manipulate poor men's votes". This way, with every
    election, the well-entrenched higher castes secure the right not only to govern
    but also to oppress and exploit the lower castes of India who constitute about
    85% of India's total population' (Kanshi Ram, quoted in Velivada, 2018). Kumar
    (2013) has discussed Kanshi Ram as an 'organic leader' who connected with the
    masses through political as well as non-political participation.

2. The BAMCEF was formed by Kanshi Ram with the aim of organizing the elites and educated employees from SC, ST, and OBC communities. According to Christophe Jaffrelot (2003), the organization began as an association on 14 October 1971. In 1973, this association became a federation. By 1978, the BAMCEF had expanded to 150 districts across the country. It was aimed at organizing a 'Bahujan Samaj' through meetings and conferences.

3. Ravidassia music refers to songs composed by and/or dedicated to the Bhakti saint and poet Ravidas. Forty of Ravidas's verses are part of the holy text, the Sri Guru Granth Sahib. He promoted rationality of thought and criticized blind faith and superstition. This is reflected in one of his verses, 'Anubhav Pad Lahije', which translates to 'believing something only if it stands firm on the grounds of rationality and experience'. Ravidassia music is mostly centered around singing verses written by Ravidas. Some more recent forms of Ravidassia music involve singing the biography of Ravidas.

4. Kaluli is a form of music from the regions of Papua New Guinea.

5. In Jammu and lower Himachal, Dogri, Kangari, Chambyali, Kulluvi, and so on are the local languages that are widely spoken. These are all dialects of Punjabi. There are also similarities between Haryanvi and Punjabi. The access and connect with language facilitated the widespread popularity of DS4 music.

6. 'Double marginalization' of Dalit women was a concept used by Sharmila Rege (2000) to understand the positionality of Dalit women vis-à-vis upper-caste women. Unlike an upper-caste woman, a Dalit woman is rendered vulnerable not just because of her gender location in society but also because of her caste location.

7. A telephonic interview with Poonam Bala was conducted on 21 October 2020. We have had a previous informal conversation with her as well.

8. We had a conversation with Usha Devi on 21 September 2020.

9. Snowballing is a research technique in which the research participants help the researcher to gather other potential information that will be helpful to the research. For this research the technique was helpful as it was exploratory in nature.

10. 'Mulnivasi' is a term used in the Bahujan movement to refer to SCs, STs, OBCs, and other minorities. The term was popularized through slogans like 'Bol pichasi, jai Mulnivasi' (We, 85 per cent, are the Mulnivasi).

Bibliography

Asianet News. 2020. 'After Covid-19 Pandemic, Bahujan Samaj Soldiers of Kanshi Ram's Mission Kishor Kumar Pagala in Worst Condition'. 14 August. https://hindi.asianetnews.com/uttar-pradesh/after- covid-19-pandemic-bahujan-samaj-soldiers-of-kanshiram-s-mission-kishor-kumar-pagala-in-worst-condition-kpm-qf1v9j. Accessed on 21 December 2021.

Attali, J. 2009. *Noise: The Political Economy of Music*. London: University of Minnesota Press.

Bhabha, H. K. 1996. 'Culture's In-Between'. In *Questions of Cultural Identity*, edited by S. Hall and P. Du Gay. London: SAGE Publications.

Bohlman, P. V. 1991. 'Of Yekkes and Chamber Music in Israel: Ethnomusicological Meaning in Western Music History'. In *Ethnomusicology and Modern Music History*, edited by S. Blum, P. V. Bohlman, and D. M. Neuman, 254–67. Urbana and Chicago: University of Illinois Press.

Chakravarti, U. 1993. 'Conceptualising Brahmanical Patriarchy in early India: Gender, Caste, Class and State'. *Economic and Political Weekly* 28(14): 579–85.

DeNora, T. 2004. *Music in Everyday Life*. Cambridge: Cambridge University Press.

Feld, S. 2012. *Sound and Sentiment: Birds, Weeping, Poetics, and Song in Kaluli Expression*, 3rd edition. Durham, NC: Duke University Press.

Finnegan, R. 2012. 'Music, Experience and Anthropology of Emotions'. In *The Cultural Study of Music: A Critical Introduction*, 2nd edition, edited by M. Clayton, T. Herbert, and R. Middleton, 181–92. New York: Routledge.

Firth, S. 1996. 'Music and Identity'. In *Questions of Cultural Identity*, edited by S. Hall and P. Du Gay, 108–27. London: SAGE Publications.

Hall, S. 1990. 'The Emergence of Cultural Studies and the Crisis of the Humanities'. *The Humanities of Social Technology* 53 (Summer): 11–23.

———. 1996. 'Introduction: Who Needs "Identity"?' In *Questions of Cultural Identity*, edited by S. Hall and P. Du Gay, 1–17. London: SAGE Publications.

Jaffrelot, C. 2003. *India's Silent Revolution: The Rise of the Low Castes in North Indian Politics*. Ranikhet: Permanent Black.

Jaoul, N. 2007. 'Political and "Non-Political" Means in the Dalit Movement'. In *Political Process in Uttar Pradesh: Identity, Economic Reforms and Governance*, edited by S. Pai, 191–220. New Delhi: Pearson Education.

Kalyani, K. 2022. 'Emergence of Dalit Art Entrepreneurs: Exploring Anti-Caste Songs as the New-Creative Industry in North India.' *Local Development and Society*: 1–15.

Kumar, V. 2013. 'Dynamics of Kanshi Ram's Movement'. CounterCurrents.org, https://www.researchgate.net/publication/344928476. Accessed on 21 December 2021.

Pai, S. 2002. *Dalit Assertion and the Unfinished Democratic Revolution: The Bahujan Samaj Party in Uttar Pradesh*. New Delhi: SAGE Publications.

Rege, Sharmila. 2000. '"Real Feminism" and Dalit Women: Scripts of Denial and Accusation'. *Economic and Political Weekly* (5 February). https://www.epw.in/system/files/pdf/2000_35/06/Real_Feminism_and_Dalit_Women.pdf. Accessed on 1 November 2022.

Velivada. 2018. 'From the Pen of Saheb Kanshi Ram: A Part of Editorial from "The Oppressed Indian" Magazine'. https://velivada.com/2018/03/16/from-the-pen-of-saheb-kanshi-ram-a-part-of-editorial-from-the-oppressed-indian-magazine. Accessed on 2 February 2023.

8

Anti-Caste Music and Cinema

Prashant Ingole

> We understand struggle and resistance, nowadays, rather better than we do reform and transformation … Popular culture is neither, in a 'pure' sense, the popular traditions of resistance to these processes; [nor] it is the forms which are superimposed on and over them. It is the ground on which the transformations are worked.
>
> —Stuart Hall (1998: 443)

> The work of generating anti-caste consciousness was being done by Babasaheb himself and his colleagues through various mediums such as large gatherings, conferences, delivering speeches, leading satyagraha, writing in newspapers etc, but there was a need to tell this to the Dalit masses – who were illiterate, uneducated and superstitious – in a simpler, easier, entertaining manner and especially in their mother tongue.
>
> —quoted in Yogesh Maitreya (2019: 71)

Introduction

The coming of 'social media' and 'new media' has opened up multiple possibilities for anti-caste scholars to unite and speak against the fictitious representation of Dalits (ex-untouchables). Historically speaking, to deconstruct upper-caste–class narratives about the Dalit world, Dalit themselves, through *bhajan*s, poetry, and autobiographical writings, have been telling stories of struggle and assertion against caste society. No matter what kind of social and infrastructural progress has been made, the notion of caste cannot be erased from India's cultural industry. In this relation, if we look at mainstream music and cinema that plays an important role in generating consciousness among the public in general, they largely depict upper-caste–class elite culture, and thereby the anti-caste projection of an egalitarian society remains excluded. However, as a result of the re-energization of anti-caste cultural politics, the picture of the Indian 'culture industry'[1] has started to change in the recent past, specifically after the 1990s. Drawing from casteless and anti-caste understandings, the present chapter offers an extended meaning of anti-caste resistance through new forms of expression. It evaluates the past and present scenarios and how caste-imposed forms of expression that are represented through music and cinematic articulation have become a tool for anti-caste political resistance. The chapter looks at contemporary cinematic politics to understand why (or why not) these mediums are relevant in order to talk about 'cultural' change. In addition, it considers how anti-caste symbols and images are depicted in music and cinema, affecting the dynamics of caste at large. By foregrounding the dialogue on the way anti-caste music and cinema centres around culturally erased anti-caste history, the chapter highlights the manner in which the subjugated masses have altered the historically imposed casteist labour as a reverse mechanism to fight against the problem of caste. It underlines the capacity of anti-caste narratives to create a counter-cultural space to articulate resistance.

Following Jyotirao and Savitribai Phule's fight against caste and patriarchal society, Babasaheb Ambedkar unlocked the anti-caste struggle for the rights of the downtrodden masses. He directed his struggle towards instilling egalitarian and humanitarian values and discarding the graded hierarchical order called caste. Through critical analysis of Indian social structure, he paved the way to raise untouchable communities to a new stature and instil a sense of hope and confidence among them. In the larger vision of annihilating caste, he ensured constitutional protection, and by showing the path of the Buddha, he created an environment by which Dalits can achieve dignity and self-respect. In its historicity, the anti-caste movement in Maharashtra has played a vital role in reconstituting cultural relations and anti-caste political strategies in various ways. The anti-caste movement became popular due to its cultural coherence coupled with its character and the variety of forms in which it was expressed. If one looks at post-Ambedkar Dalit politics, the Dalit Panther movement, which exhibited critical literary expression and radicalism, invoked Ambedkar's anti-caste cultural politics (Pawar, 2017). Later, the Bahujan Samaj Party (BSP) in the 1990s revitalized the Ambedkarite movement and reintroduced anti-caste consciousness in electoral politics as well. The 1990s were also a time when the debate around caste was revived by unlocking the Mandal Commission report to provide reservation to the Other Backward Classes (OBCs) in central institutions. These processes created an environment for the political and intellectual unification of oppressed communities (the Scheduled Castes [SCs], Scheduled Tribes [STs], and OBCs) to deconstruct social and cultural barriers.

However, upper-caste hegemonic consciousness retained its caste-based cultural ethos through which upper castes enjoy substantial control over the minds of the people at large. Suraj Yengde, in his essay 'Apartheid in Fancy Dress' (2020), mentions that 'India's upper caste, or so-called "twice-born" Hindus – who make up around 18 percent of the population' – have virtually dominated Indian cinema, 'passing off their own narrow, elite, turgid caste culture as a caricatured representation of pan-Indian life'. In this elite and casteist attitude of the Indian cinema industry, Dalit suppression was barely given any space, and when portrayed, it was often projected through the 'sympathetic view' of the *savarna* (upper-caste) gaze, rather than the radicalizing voice of the oppressed.

The debate around Dalit representation on the Indian cinema screen is fairly new. It has only been since a decade that anti-caste intellectuals have begun to raise concerns about the portrayal of Dalit lived realities in the Indian cinema space. An upper-caste gaze of the camera mostly attempts to depict Dalits as subjugated and pliant – in other words, they are either shunned by society or left at the mercy of dominant castes or classes (for instance, *Achhut Kannya* [1936] and *Ankur* [1974]) – and fails to capture the Dalit as an assertive force who fights for his or her dignity and self-respect. Ravi Ratan (2020) notes: 'Dr B.R. Ambedkar was treated like an "untouchable" by the casteist film-makers of Indian cinema. He was virtually erased from the backdrop of scenes for a long time'. It is only recently with the strong anti-caste resistance that a few film-makers have started to bring Ambedkar's radical approach into the cinematic sphere.

Mainstream Indian Cinema, Music, and 'Castelessness'

In mainstream literature and culture, Dalits and the oppressed sections of society are less likely to be represented in a radical manner. On similar lines, owing to its intrinsic connection to the dominant social fabric, the Indian cinema industry attempts to maintain upper-caste status quo by particularizing its dominant hegemonic culture, which Yengde (2020) refers to as 'Punjabi Khatri caste' culture. In order to counter the dominant notion of Indian cinema, scholarly engagement with an anti-caste approach becomes an important intervention in Indian cinematic studies. From the time of India's independence, Indian cinema has largely focused either on forming 'conservative' nationalism or the secular notion of the Hindu–Muslim relationship through projection of progressive liberalism and the Nehruvian socialist agenda (Margaret, 2013; Yengde, 2018). Hindi cinema's transformation into 'Bollywood' and India's mainstream culture have been globalized in multiple ways. After the opening up of the economy in the 1990s, it has captured the international market combined with subsequent changes in the political economy of 'Bollywood'. Under the cover of castelessness, Indian cinema has largely displayed dominant cultures repackaged in modern forms. Films like *Dilwale Dulhania Le Jayenge* (1995), *Sooryavansham* (1999), and *Mr. and Mrs. Iyer* (2002) showcase Indian family values, the dominant Thakur power, and conservative-versus-liberal narratives. This hegemonic depiction continues to be represented in different forms; a recent example could be Anubhav Sinha's *Article 15* (2019). Mainstream films have either depicted nationalistic values, Gandhian notions, or the Hindu–Muslim quest for (dis) unity. But the quest of the downtrodden masses and their liberation remain obscure in mainstream celluloid narratives. Question of inter-caste marriage, the Dalit world, and Dalit rights have never acquired any space in the content and imagination of 'Bollywood'.

To counter the stark reality of caste, film-makers from oppressed communities have begun to project anti-caste practices and dialogue around it in their language. This language varies from the mainstream and derives its strength from the everyday humiliation inflicted on them, with Dalit protagonists presented as assertive and articulating their struggles. Suraj Yengde eloquently captures this by noting that 'Dalit Cinema' offers a critical reading of the Hindi film industry by addressing its relationship with caste, and also underlines the transformation in the Marathi film industry. Taking up Nagraj Manjule's *Fandry* (2013) and *Sairat* (2016), two films which have discussed and debated caste and have changed the Marathi cinematic industry in the past few years,[2] Yengde states: 'Dalit cinema as a resistance movement definitely has the potential to be among the pioneers of modern artistic resistance; that potential could be harnessed by departing from traditional forms of art' (2018: 14). Although mainstream Indian cinema paints castelessness, it is the cinema of the oppressed that subtly captures everyday struggles of the marginalized. Such articulate expression and engagement by Dalits can be considered part and parcel of the Dalit resistance movement. Through cinematic streaming, an anti-caste approach is articulated, and the inner workings of caste oppression and assertion are presented. Similarly, anti-caste music also departs from the conventional and populist trend and offers dialectics of cultural assertion by combining traditional and modern art forms. This is elaborated in the section on anti-caste music.

Considering recent Marathi and Tamil cinema by anti-caste film directors such as Nagraj Manjule, Pa. Ranjith, and Mari Selvaraj, and the way they depict anti-caste aesthetics in commercial films, Manju Edachira (2020: 47–49) argues that these directors break conventional practices of film-making and disturb the viewer's sensibility in order to argue that 'the unconscious of the Indian audience is caste untouchability [and thus] what these directors make possible is an impossibility'. They break away from upper-caste hegemonic dominance in Indian cinema as it is inadequately sensible towards the representation of caste perspectives from below and unwilling to change its ways. Moreover, it is also important to note that many times showcasing religious marginalization dilutes and diverts the question of caste and reduces it to highlighting poverty (see Konda, 2020: 63). To substantiate further, Jyoti Nisha (2020) offers an insightful reading of mainstream cinema and notes: 'Bahujan characters have been either victimised or exoticised by the Indian cinema to peddle a distorted identity of secular India.' She suggests the possibility of Bahujan perspectives to present Bahujan characters. Edachira invokes the category of 'anti-caste' but limits it by exploring 'aesthetics', while Yengde and Nisha elaborate cinema through already contested as well as influential categories such as 'Dalit' and 'Bahujan' that acquire their meaning in contextual political ground. Gopal Guru (2018), in his essay 'Politics of Naming', writes:

> The accommodation of these categories into an emancipatory project is not out of convenience; it has an authenticity in it as all these categories confront various structures of domination and exploitation ... the category dalit provides both an element of negation (to state constituted categories or harijan) and permits the conjunction of categories belonging to the same logical class (Buddhist, bahujan).

It can be argued that Yengde and Nisha seem to be specifying cinema under the categories of 'Dalit' and 'Bahujan' which can be broadly situated in an anti-casteist perspective. However, the point to note from this scholarship is that mainstream Indian cinema, which previously represented 'liberalism', now seems to be hidden behind the veil of 'castelessness'. In other words, the embodied nature of Indian cinema is determined by upper-caste culture and its sentiments, which are not anti-caste but present themselves as casteless.

The Language of the Anti-Castes

From Phule to Ambedkar and beyond, the language of the anti-caste movement is not just against caste per se but also an assertion to eradicate discriminatory culturization. It is a call to establish an egalitarian society and imagine alternative possibilities of an egalitarian order. As saint Ravidas imagined, 'Begumpura' (Sorrowless City), a utopia where prosperity and equality thrive (see Omvedt, 2016: 106–07), seeks to humanize society by endorsing democratic values. 'Anti-caste' can be defined in various ways, but here in the context of music, cinema, and popular cultural realms, it can be conceived of as an assertion of everyday 'lived experiences' – patriarchy, gender discrimination, violence. The language of anti-caste narrative functions through multiple 'subcultures', but united by an Ambedkarite consciousness that celebrates the social democratic model.[3] Therefore, the predetermined condition of the anti-caste is an exertion and a restriction – a lack of freedom and liberation under caste codes. One who has not been raised in anti-caste cultural surroundings cannot formulate resistance against caste in radical and liberatory language. In an interesting short documentary called *The Discreet Charm of the Savarnas* (2020), Rajesh Rajamani wonderfully captures the perception of casteless liberal upper castes who have no 'lived experience' of caste but try to articulate it from a distance.

Anti-Caste Music: Educative and Reformatory

As quoted in the epigraph to this chapter, there was a need to disseminate Ambedkar's anti-caste thought to educate the masses about the apathy Dalits or lower castes face in caste society. Instead of accommodating anti-caste ideas to sensitize the larger masses, the mainstream public sphere reinforced the structures that perpetuate inequalities. The rise of alternative anti-caste music can be attributed to this tendency of exclusion. In a bid to unite people and bring social reform, Mahars in Maharashtra have been using singing as a tool to educate people about their revolutionary history and the agenda of anti-caste politics. The following popular saying in Marathi reveals the dialectics of caste relations:

> *Brahmanchya ghari lihina*
> *Kunbya ghari dana*
> *Mahara ghari gana*

> At the Brahmin's house you write and learn
> At the tiller's house you thresh
> At the Mahar's [Dalit's] house you sing
> —Marathi saying

As a medium of anti-caste resistance, Mahars are using the caste-based occupation of singing to spread the message of 'equality, liberty and fraternity'. The anti-caste musical tradition, from which emerging writers and singers take inspiration, can be traced back to much before independence.

In 1937, a meeting was held in Kasarwadi Dadar, Bombay (present-day Mumbai), where Bhimrao Kardak and his troupe of *shahirs*[4] performed *shahiri* to canvas Ambedkar's ideas in the presence of Ambedkar himself. Ambedkar generously said: 'Ten of the meetings and gatherings are equal to one *jalsa* by Kardak and his troupe. What else can I add? [The] *jalsa* has said all of it' (quoted in Maitreya, 2020). In the dominant musical traditions of India, lives of the oppressed rarely find space. It is through the Satyashodhak Jalsa, Ambedkari Jalsa, and later *gayan* parties that emerged during the 1990s that struggle and resistance found representation and helped in fomenting an anti-caste consciousness among the oppressed and awakened them. These *gayan* parties largely operated through public performances generally organized on the birth anniversary of Ambedkar, the conversion day on which people visit Dikshabhumi, Nagpur, and on the death anniversary of Ambedkar at Chaityabhumi, Dadar. The songs focused on the Gandhi–Ambedkar confrontations, life and struggle of Ramabai and Babsaheb, the doctrine of the Buddha and saint Kabir Das, constitutional justice, discrimination, and Dalit lives in villages as well as cities. In one song written by Dutta Paikrao and sung by Milind Shinde, they deconstruct the idea of Gandhi as a celebrated figure in mainstream culture while emphasizing Ambedkar's efforts in saving Gandhi's life and building this country. The song runs:

Kaaida Bhimacha pan photo Gandhicha,
Shobhun disto ka notavar?
Kiti shobhala asta Bhim notavar, tay un kotavar
Khara desh premi tharla Bhim ghatnakar
Vidyelahi puroon urla asa vidyadhar
Desha savarl, tya Gandhi la tarala, pena chya tya tokavar.

The law of Bhim, but photo of Gandhi
Does Gandhi's image suit on the Indian currency?
Instead, how beautiful Ambedkar would have looked in tie and coat
True lover of the country was Bhim the constitution maker
The one completely dedicated to study, the studious one
He revived the country; he saved Gandhi with the tip of his pen.[5] (Shinde, 2017)

The songs provided a critical reading of history rooted in the hierarchical order of caste and associated struggles that followed. They not only reminded people of their historical oppression but also made them aware of the hardships undergone to establish the ideals that allow them a dignified existence. They cultivated a critical consciousness among the masses and created conditions to keep the movement alive. Sharmila Rege, in her book, *Against the Madness of Manu: B. R. Ambedkar's Writings on Brahmanical Patriarchy* (2013), discusses the Ambedkarite musical tradition and calendar art and argues that:

> The representations of the personal/conjugal in the Ambedkarite booklets and musical compositions question the dominant ideal of companionate marriage that constituted Brahmanical middle class modernity. In the musical compositions on the life of Ambedkar and Ramabai, companionship transcends the realm of the private. It suggests that community, the household and the political realm are inseparable. (Rege, 2013: 36)

The songs sung as *bhajans*, disseminated through cassette culture, tell the story of the relationship between Ambedkar and Ramabai and are narrated as a lesson for the men and women of the community. They suggest that the Dalit world, whether it is private or political, cannot be separated.

Anand Patwardhan, in his documentary film titled *Jai Bhim Comrade* (2011), draws on incidents ranging from the Ramabai Nagar massacre (11 July 1997) to the Khairlanji atrocity (29 September 2006) to paint a picture of the nature of Dalit politics. Generally, we see movies or documentaries open with a disclaimer, but Patwardhan's documentary begins differently by showing a description of two traditions prevailing and operating in Indian society. Culturally dominant communities still follow the Manusmriti's code of conduct. However, in the political realm, they have to follow the constitutional codes. Patwardhan in the disclaimer shows that in the 1950s, the Manusmriti's tradition was replaced with the Indian constitution. The film moves further with the news of the suicide of a young Dalit poet and singer, Vilas Ghogre. Not only does the film make massacres and politics visible, but it also deals with questions of labour, caste, class, culture, and the way anti-caste music becomes a symbol of Ambedkarite resistance. The film brings many generations of the Dalit community together who continue to dedicate their lives to disseminate Ambedkarite philosophy through their songs. Artists like Waman Dada Kardak, Vithal Umap, Milind Shinde, Anand Shinde, Sushma Devi, and Sambhaji Bhagat by default appear on the frontlines.

Thus, singing is not merely a profession or labour for Dalits; rather, it is passed down as a powerful instrument for awakening people. Their songs take on the role of activists, carrying the message of social democracy and ideals advocated by Ambedkar. They remind the oppressed communities that whatever freedom they enjoy today is because of the leaders of the heterodox tradition of Phule, Ambedkar, and their families, and the sacrifices they made for the Dalit cause.

Kadubai Kharat, who is a street singer from Aurangabad, points this out eloquently in her songs. Although she is illiterate, through her powerful voice and intensity of Ambedkarite thought, she continues to spread the revolutionary teachings of Ambedkar to the masses. In an interview with ABP Majha (2018), a Marathi channel, she sang:

> A child in arm, broom in hand, and burden of dung on head.
> No clothes to wear, nothing to eat, an unimaginable humiliating condition it was.
> But my Bhim (Babasaheb), my Bhim has filled my pot with gold.[6]

And the second song which gained her huge popularity across the country is as follows.

> There is more of Babasaheb's grace in your life than of your father and mother.
> The bread you eat, Babasaheb has signed on it.[7]

The lyrics here highlight how Dalits had to live in servile conditions and pursue caste-imposed occupations, but owing to Ambedkar's efforts, their lives have changed dramatically, with improved living conditions and a better social position. All this became possible due to Ambedkar alone.

Music has transcended language barriers by using a fusion of languages and instruments to disseminate anti-caste thought among culturally varied masses. Sambhaji Bhagat, a *shahir*, attempts to deconstruct Brahmanical and capitalist philosophy and the caste–class structure through his Ambedkari Jalsa. In addition, he criticizes socio-techno-cultural 'cyber capitalism'. In his songs, he combines local and global vocabularies of resistance as well as local and modern musical instruments. At the outset of his performance, Bhagat gives a disclaimer: 'I am not here to entertain you, I am here to disturb you.' He and his troupe started a YouTube channel called 'The War Beat' in 2017; a notable song by the troupe is 'Blue Nation':

> Lovers of freedom come on, come on ...
> The slogan of Jai Bhim is [more] lovable to us than our life
> It is not a play on words but it is our *inquilab* [revolution] ...
> Jai Bhim is not a slogan of a particular caste, creed
> Jai Bhim is the slogan of every oppressed person. (The War Beat, 2017)

This song brings three generations and three languages (Hindi, English, and Marathi) together with traditional and modern musical instruments and a fusion of folk and pop singing styles. It is a song addressing oppression and seeking constitutional rights – an assertion of human rights. There are new forms of inequalities and thus new forms of expression to counter them. Rahi Gaikwad, a Mumbai-based journalist in her piece, 'An Equal Music' (2016), which appeared in *The Hindu* writes:

> Today, the singers have bigger dreams … [and] a far more universal appeal than their older counterparts did. Not so long ago, playback singers and musicians were known to hide their caste identity. The new lot flaunts it. Their lyrics are from their history, their videos replete with Ambedkar photos and Buddhist iconography.

Along with folk music, *shahiri*, and ballads, there is also the emergence of Dalit pop, rap, and band culture, with Ginni Mahi and Sumeet Samos being some of the popular singers. Recently, in early 2021, Swarup Dangle, a 10-year-old rapper, released a song on YouTube called 'Khambir Pidhi' (A Powerful Generation of Your Thought). In rap, Swarup sings:

> Babasaheb [Bhimraya], my father tells me the story of your struggle and makes me listen to songs of equality. He points his finger towards your photo, he points his finger toward Bhimshala. I shall get educated, I shall fight, and these are my words to you, Bhima. I will not get hurt nor will I bend; have faith in me, Bhima.[8] (Dangle, 2021)

These powerful lyrics symbolize the way Babasaheb's photo and the story of his struggle prepare successive generations to fight for an anti-caste space. Further, they show that it is the anti-caste message that fuels the resistance to fulfil the dream of 'social democracy' and 'associate living' envisioned by Ambedkar. Thus, it can be argued that anti-caste music not only offers a strong critique of dominant narratives of music and its production, but also engenders a larger process of de-casteing the production and consumption of music itself. Drawing from the past, it operates as a mirror of reflection and assertion for upper-caste and ex-untouchable audiences, respectively, making it relevant in contemporary politics.

Moving further, along with Maharashtra, Tamil Nadu has also nurtured a strong anti-caste base. The state is inspired not only by Ambedkar's idea of democracy but also by Periyar's non-Brahmin movement. In this context, the films of Pa. Ranjith are relevant and can be considered as representing the sociocultural vibrancy of the state. Two of his films, *Kabali* (2016) and *Kaala* (2018), have generated great interest in and debate on the question of caste, locally and globally. In March 2018, Ranjith also started the organization

Neelam Cultural Centre through which he tries to bring anti-caste artists together. 'Casteless Collective', a YouTube channel, is part of this initiative. Tenma and Arivu, members of 'Casteless Collective', mentioned in an interview: 'As the casteless collective they blend traditional Gana[9] music with hip hop and rock to challenge the caste system' (Webb, 2020).

A number of generations of Dalit musicians have performed during various festivals and also for the entertainment of dominant communities. But after the renaissance initiated by Phule and Babasaheb, they have been using music and instruments as a method of assertion and resistance.

Anti-Caste Cinema

In the regional Marathi cinematic sphere, if we consider the appearance of assertive Dalits, specifically after the 1990s, a good example would be *Mukta*, directed by Jabbar Patel (1994). The movie represents Dalit Panthers co-founder Namdeo Dhasal's activism, inter-caste relationship, and the class pride and power of Maratha–Kunbi landholders. The movie also weaves in the question of race when Mukta's friend, Julian, who is Black, comes from America to visit India. Although the movie fails to bring out the subtlety of caste society, it does manage to bring the caste–class and race contexts together. If one looks at the historical context of *Mukta*, it highlights race and Dalit representation and how both these movements (Black and Dalit) stand against domination and systemic suppression. The movie was released at the same time as when the Marathwada University in Aurangabad was renamed 'Dr Babasaheb Ambedkar Marathwada University'. It was a 20-year-long struggle in which a number of Dalit families sacrificed their lives.[10] On 14 January every year, Dalit leaders and activists celebrate this achievement by organizing conferences and other programmes around the university area. In addition, Patel also made a biopic, *Dr Babasaheb Ambedkar: The Untold Truth* (2000) in the same decade. The film depicts Ambedkar's life, struggle, and fight for the depressed masses. It also shows his anti-caste assertion and his efforts in drafting the Indian Constitution and making the 'Hindu Code Bill' as the first law minister of independent India. Damini Kulkarni (2018) revisits this biopic in the aftermath of the Bhima Koregaon violence (1 January 2018) and writes:

> As Ambedkar gradually transforms himself into a leader of his people, the film captures his motivations behind the protest organised at Mahad in 1927, the burning of the *Manusmriti* later that year, and the agitation at the Kalaram temple in 1930. The film is at its most articulate and poignant when it dwells on his call to Dalits to 'Educate, Organise, Agitate'.

Apart from these events, the movie also shows how Ambedkar was influenced by the Buddha and Kabir in his early life as his family was a follower of Kabir *panth*.

If we see mainstream films on caste and its functioning, an important issue is of gender and patriarchy in relation to Dalit women. For example, Shekhar Kapur's *Bandit Queen* (1994) is a biographical movie based on Phoolan Devi, who belonged to the Mallah community, classified as SC, and considers the subtlety of caste and 'Brahmanical patriarchy'. It opens in 1968 Uttar Pradesh (UP) with the practice of child marriage, conventional among lower-caste households, as little Phoolan faces domestic violence and abuse becomes an everyday reality. The movie goes on to tell the story of her exploitation at the hands of the dominant Thakur caste. However, it does not show her resistance or how she fought against systemic exploitation in a radical manner. It attempts to settle the matter at the end of the film, where anti-caste cinema would end – by opening the matter for dialogue. Therefore, the intervention of anti-caste cinema becomes important. One of the major contentions brought forth through anti-caste cinema is the stereotypical representation of Dalits instead of an 'embodied sensibility' as Edachira (2020) would call it.

To understand the quest differently, one can look at short films such as *The Discreet Charm of the Savarnas*, a 20-minute film directed by Rajamani. This film raises a pertinent question about the predilection of the '*savarna* gaze'. It revolves around three upper-caste people looking for a 'Dalit' to act in their film. The binaries of the *avarna* (lower caste) and *savarna* are highlighted in a subtle but significant manner. The three characters, depicted as 'progressive', want to project oppression and yet never realize their own prejudices and compliance in it. A scene that stands out in the movie is when, at the end, they do find a Dalit character, and one of them remarks how she is too pretty to be a Dalit. The casteless, liberal-progressive *savarna* characters here fail to escape their own biases, and the director uses this to make subtle gibes at the saviour complex of the oppressor towards the oppressed. For example, the character Swami, a film director, remarks how a Dalit actor and an actor playing a Dalit are different things; yet for his movie, he is apparently searching for a 'real Dalit'. The *savarna* narrative involves Dalit identity which satisfies their ingrained biases of how a Dalit should look like or be. He or she cannot be too pretty because the attempt is to 'look' like a Dalit. This movie succeeds in 'deflecting the Savarna gaze back at them' (see Singaravel, 2020), which, Rajamani writes, was the singular resolve of the script. Another major arc is that the Dalit character is nameless. The intellectualization of oppression while failing to actually see it is something that this short film showcases.

An anti-caste cinematic space helps in unfolding the myth of Dalit representation. *The Discreet Charm of the Savarnas*, through the use of satire, raises a striking question prevalent throughout its narrative: is it the *savarnas* who get to decide how, when, and in what manner should the 'lived experiences' of the Dalit community, which they have been complicit in oppressing, be depicted? The quick answer lies in the making of the narrative of this short film. The film was created under the banner of Ranjith as a step forward in establishing an anti-caste space through sensitive independent film-makers who are situated in the semantics of Dalit identity. Historically, Indian cinema has appropriated the Dalit narrative and labour. Dalit narratives have been mostly told by progressive-liberal upper castes, specifically by men, which failed to bring about any radical shift in the telling of suppressed narratives, thus being unjust to their cause.

Another film that can be discussed in this context is *Masaan* (2015), directed by Neeraj Ghaywan. *Masaan*, when it came out, was appreciated for having a Dalit protagonist. Since the 1990s and the post-liberalization world, Indian cinema's mainstream narratives have depicted socially homogeneous couples. Caste as an undertone sometimes holds a partial, secondary role where class- or caste-based patriarchy is often established through generally accepted traditional and obscure ritualistic practices looming large over individual choices. *Masaan* scores big on this front. With two parallel storylines, it confluences the binary and tries to amalgamate it into one. *Masaan* features caste as a narrative but never really seeks to present an alternative. It rather affirms what has already seeped into the mainstream visual media: the only time when two people from vastly different social identities can have a *sangam* (union) is in death. This focuses on an important stand: the fact that caste is not redundant and shapes identities and interactions. Deepak, who belongs to the Dom community, a low-caste community of corpse burners in Varanasi, falls in love with Shalu, who is from the Bania community. The film aesthetically depicts the romance brewing between two people who have a 'chance' encounter. The two are a contradiction to the age-old divides of a society that fuels the fires of casteism through mainstream audio and visual narratives. Their coming together is a spark that flashes through the narrative, and yet the embers fade too soon. Shalu, though apprehensive at first, falls for Deepak and promises her loyalty to him even after coming to know his 'caste'.

Where the narrative differs is in the depiction of the protagonist by Ghaywan, as a Dalit himself. The protagonist is not a meek individual needing salvation. He emotes pain yet does not seek sympathy. This was a welcome change as it sought to break the stereotypical representation of Dalit identity. The film engages with caste in a nuanced manner where Ghaywan gives space to the emotions of every character, not highlighting one over the other. Another trope that this movie establishes is the omnipresence of caste in society, always followed yet never discussed. This is where it mixes aesthetics with social questions. Death here becomes a metaphor for the oppressive nature of the caste system, mixing religion and patriarchal constructs to depict life as we live it and conveniently choose not to know. Shalu dies in an accident during 'a religious pilgrimage with her family' right when she asserts her individual opinion and choice. Through an intense narrative style, the story highlights an important anti-caste stance: can we really free ourselves from societal boundaries dictated by the oppressive structures of caste without getting rid of the entire system in the first place? Death here is used as a narrative tool to depict a larger evil. By doing so, in an aesthetically informed manner, caste no longer remains the subtext casting its looming presence. The performativity of progress is then shattered through dramatic representation. *Masaan* is an important film not because of its commercial success or its narrative technique. The film is important because it humanizes the characters' loss and allows space for it to manifest. While Indian cinema keeps caste invisible as it benefits the upper levels of the 'twice-born', anti-caste cinema makes it visible to showcase how caste is a harmful institution for the larger development of Indian democratic society as it makes human dialogue impossible. Thus, it is strongly asserted that anti-caste cinema and the music of the oppressed is a step towards culturizing anti-caste consciousness within the dominant sphere.

Conclusion

To sum up, one will have to agree that caste is rooted in the so-called Indian hegemonic dominant culture, and it is strengthened and institutionalized through various processes, with the mainstream Indian 'culture industry' being one such medium. In contrast, this chapter has attempted to show how anti-caste music and cinema have played an instrumental role in generating a consciousness that breaks and alters the perception and portrayal of caste on screen and in wider society. The chapter also offers an extended meaning of caste and anti-caste resistance and the ways in which they are performed and presented through music and cinema. The ideological apparatus has tried to assimilate individuals into caste-based traditions which neutralize caste-based oppression by manifestations of a general consensus. Therefore, it is necessary to assert identities of communities who do not share the mainstream core cultures. The chapter has elaborated the way anti-caste scholarship critically looks at mainstream depictions of Dalits and oppressed masses. It has also shown how the language of the anti-castes developed, seeking to bring social equality. Through its analysis, the chapter has demonstrated that anti-caste music has evolved into different forms, ranging from traditional forms of singing to modern modes of expression, and continues to enliven the Ambedkarite anti-caste perspective. Before the coming of anti-caste cinema, it was music which was (and continues to be) used as a tool for resistance. The coming of anti-caste cinema has shaken the Indian cinematic world as these films bring a new vocabulary into the world of cinema where caste otherwise remains invisible.

Notes

1. 'Culture industry' is a critical theory coined by Theodor Adorno and Max Horkheimer (1944) in which he presents his defence of modernist art and critiques mass culture.
2. I discuss *Fandry* and *Sairat* in detail in Ingole (2022).
3. Ambedkar, in his speech before the Constituent Assembly on 25 November 1949, explained that political democracy cannot last without the base of social democracy. It is a way of life that works through the principles of 'liberty, equality and fraternity'.
4. *Shahir* refers to one who sings *shahiri*. And *shahiri* is ballad singing, also known as *jalsa*, a tradition of Maharashtra.
5. Translated by me.
6. Roughly translated by me.
7. Roughly translated by me.
8. Roughly translated by me.
9. *Gana* is a musical form performed by downtrodden communities in Chennai and other parts of Tamil Nadu. The songs used to be sung accompanied by musical instruments during funerals. For more details, see Srivathsan (2012).
10. For more details, see the excerpt from Eknath Awad's autobiography, *Strike a Blow to Change the World* (2018), translated by Jerry Pinto.

Bibliography

ABP Majha. 2018. 'Kadubainchi Bhimgeet'. YouTube. 6 December. https://www. you tube.com/watch?v=YuUw9mnPNq8. Accessed on 20 January 2021.

Adorno, T. W. 1991. *The Culture Industry: Selected Essays on Mass Culture*, edited with an introduction by J. M. Bernstein. London and New York: Routledge.

Adorno, T. W., and M. Horkheimer. 1944. 'The Culture Industry: Enlightenment as Mass Deception'. https://www.marxists.org/reference/archive/adorno/1944/culture-industry.htm. Accessed on 20 January2021.

Awad, E. 2018. 'How a 20-Year-Long Dalit Movement to Rename Marathwada University Was Met with Violence'. *Scroll.in*, 29 November. https://scroll.in/article/903555/how-a-20-year-long-dalit-movement-to-rename-%20marathwada-university-was-met-with-violence. Accessed on 28 October 2022.

Kapur, S. 1994. *Bandit Queen* (Film). Mumbai: Kaleidoscope Entertainment, Channel4.

Dangle, S. 2021. 'Khambir Pidhi'. Swarup Dangle, YouTube. 16 January. https://www.youtube.com/watch?v=EwB_xb3i0Sg. Accessed on 20 January 2021.

Edachira, M. 2020. 'Anti-Caste Aesthetics and Dalit Interventions in Indian Cinema'. *Economic and Political Weekly* 55(38): 47–53.

Gaikwad, R. 2016. 'An Equal Music'. *The Hindu*, 20 August. https://www.thehindu.com/features/magazine/An-equal-music/article14580390.ece. Accessed on 12 February 2021.

Ghaywan, N. 2015. *Masaan* (Film). Mumbai: Drishyam Films, Phantom Films, Macassar Productions, and Sikhya.

Guru, G. 2018. 'Politics of Naming'. *Seminar* 710. http://www.india-seminar.com/2018/710/710_gopal_guru.htm. Accessed on 3 January 2021.

Hall, S. 1998. 'Notes on Deconstructing "the Popular"'. In *Cultural Theory and Popular Culture: A Reader*, edited by J. Storey, 442–53. New York: Pearson Longman.

Ingole, P. 2022. 'Inter (Caste) Love Stories: Experiential Eye (I) in Fandry and Sairat'. *Economic and Political Weekly* (Engage) 57(9). https://www.epw.in/engage/article/inter-caste-love-stories-experiential-eye-i-fandry. Accessed on 28 October 2022.

Konda, G. R. 2020. 'Dalit Narrative and Dalit Representation in Indian Cinema'. *Economic and Political Weekly* 55(49): 63–64.

Kulkarni, D. 2018. 'Classics Revisited: Jabbar Patel's Ambedkar Biopic Is a Portrait of Both the Man and the Legend'. *Scroll.in*. https://scroll.in/reel/864097/classics-revisited-jabbar-patels-ambedkar-biopic-is-a-portrait-of-both-the-man-and-the-legend. Accessed on 21 January 2021.

Maitreya, Y. 2019. 'From Shahiri to Shahitya'. *Economic and Political Weekly* 54(6): 71.

———. 2020. 'Dalit Shahirs of Maharashtra: From Bhimrao Kardak to Sambhaji Bhagat, Tracing a Legacy of Anti-Caste Music and Poetry'. *Firstpost*, 23 April. https://www.firstpost.com/living/dalit-shahirs-of-maharashtra-from-bhimrao-kardak-to-sambhaji-bhagat-tracing-a-legacy-of-anti-caste-music-and-poetry-8273941.html. Accessed on 28 October 2022.

Margaret, S. 2013. 'Cultural Gandhism: Casting Out the Dalit Woman'. *Economic and Political Weekly* 48(18): 82–90.

Nisha, J. 2020. 'Indian Cinema and the Bahujan Perspective'. *Economic and Political Weekly* 55(20). https://www.epw.in/engage/article/indian-cinema-and-bahujan-spectatorship. Accessed on 28 October 2022.

Omvedt, G. 2016. *Seeking Begumpura: The Social Vision of Anti-Caste Intellectuals.* New Delhi: Navayana.

Patel, J. 1994. *Mukta* (Film). Mumbai: National Film Development Corporation Limited.

———. 2000. *Dr Babasaheb Ambedkar: The Untold Truth.* (Film). Mumbai: National Film Development Corporation Limited.

Patwardhan, A. 2011. *Jai Bhim Comrade* (Documentary). Mumbai: Patwardhan Production.

Pawar, J. V. 2017. *Dalit Panthers: An Authoritative History.* New Delhi: The Marginalised.

Rajamani, R. 2020. *The Discreet Charm of the Savarnas* (Documentary). Chennai: Neelam Productions.

Ratan, R. 2020. 'Lights, Camera, Caste: An Ambedkar Photo Made It to Bollywood after 38 Years of Independence'. *The Print*, 9 August. https://the print.in/opinion/lights-camera-caste-an-ambedkar-photo-made-it-to-bollywood-after-38-yrs-of-independence/478068/. Accessed on 21 January 2021.

Rege, S. 2013. *Against the Madness of Manu: B. R. Ambedkar's Writings on Brahmanical Patriarchy.* New Delhi: Navayana.

Shinde, M. 2017. 'Kaayda Bheemcha' (Song). T-Series Marathi, YouTube. 9 April. https://www.youtube.com/watch?v=nUiH9JTVAk4. Accessed on 15 February 2021.

Singaravel, B. 2020. 'Rajesh Rajamani's New Film Fixes the Gaze on the Self-Congratulatory, Liberal Savarna'. *The Wire*, 12 October. https://thewire.in/film/rajesh-rajamani-the-discreet-charm-of-the-savarnas-liberal-progressive-satire. Accessed on 21 January 2021.

Srivathsan, A. 2012. 'A Struggle to Elevate the Subaltern Chennai Gana'. *The Hindu*, 25 August. https://www.thehindu.com/news/cities/chennai/a-struggle-to-elevate-the- subaltern-chennai-gana/article3817592.ece. Accessed on 11 January 2021.

The War Beat. 2017. 'Blue Nation' (Music Video). Mission Manuskey, YouTube. 26 January. https://www.youtube.com/watch?v=KDtNu6qj0rM. Accessed on 26 January 2021.

Webb, E. 2020. 'The Rebel Musicians Fighting India's Caste System'. BBC Sounds. https://www.bbc.co.uk/sounds/play/w3cszdc0. Accessed on 3 January 2021.

Yengde, S. 2018. 'Dalit Cinema'. *South Asia: Journal of South Asian Studies* 41(3): 503–18.

———. 2020. 'Apartheid in Fancy Dress'. *The Baffler* 51. https://thebaffler.com/salvos/apartheid-in-fancy-dress-yengde. Accessed on 3 January 2020.

9

Portrayal of Dalits in the Media

A Study of Select Newspapers from Uttar Pradesh

Swadesh Singh

A new middle class has emerged in India in the last 70 years. This change gained momentum particularly after liberalization began in 1991. Dalits, too, have become a part of this process – first due to the positive discrimination policies of the government and later due to the opportunities created by the liberal economy. However, members of this new Dalit middle class suffer, in one way or the other, from their 'stigmatized identity' in the caste system (Ram, 1988: 118).

The Dalit middle class has played a major role in establishing Dalit polity and asserting the identity of Dalits. Even the term 'Dalit' was popularized by intellectuals belonging to the Dalit middle class. With the emergence of this middle class, the number of educated Dalit youth seeking employment in the organized sectors has also increased. The first major flow was directed towards government jobs which offered reservation, but with the onset of liberalization, this trend changed. The Indian markets now saw the rise of a vibrant private sector that offered lucrative and dynamic jobs, and like the rest of society, Dalit youth, too, were drawn to the private sector. However, it was soon realized that the private sector suffered from the same malaise as the broader society – caste prejudices were carried into this new sphere as well (Thorat and Neuman, 2010). This chapter therefore delves deeper into the questions of representation of Dalits in the private sector. These questions are approached through a sample survey in media organizations in Uttar Pradesh (UP). Since media institutions form the basis of the study, the chapter further ventures into a content analysis of select newspapers for a time period of one year to understand the impact of such representation in terms of the quality and quantity of the coverage of Dalit issues. Lastly, it finds that online and social media platforms are emerging as an important alternative for the aspiring Dalit middle class.

Representation in the Newsrooms of UP

Taking media as a segment of the private sector, this study delves into the subject of representation and exclusion of Dalits. Media was chosen as the focus because it is regarded as the fourth pillar of democracy and bears the responsibility of being representative as a 'watchdog'. As Delhi-based media has been the subject of many studies (Chamaria, Kumar, and Yadav, 2006), this study focuses on regional media. UP was chosen as the site of this study as it is the most populous state, has the largest Dalit population, and has seen a Dalit woman as the chief minister many times.

For the purpose of this research, a field survey of news organizations in Lucknow and adjoining areas was conducted wherein attempt was made to understand their social composition and identify existing patterns. The field study commenced with a quantitative survey, involving the preparation of a questionnaire,[1] which was filled by over 250 journalists. These were middle-level and new journalists from the news desk, field reporters, camera persons, and graphic designers. Interviews were conducted with senior journalists, including editors. The first phase of the survey, comprising quantitative techniques, revealed a huge gap as respondents were found reluctant to answer the second set of questions. Hence, qualitative methods comprising focus group discussions (FGDs) and structured and unstructured interviews were used in the second phase.

Some of the major findings were as follows: the upper castes, which constitute around 20 per cent of the population of UP (see Kumar, 2021; Naqvi, 2019), were found to have a representation of 54 per cent in the news-media organizations of Lucknow. Conversely, the Other Backward Classes (OBCs), which constitute 42 per cent of the population of the state, were found to have only 25 per cent representation. Dalits were limited to 8 per cent; and religious minorities, comprising mainly Muslims, were 13 per cent. Of the total percentage of upper castes represented, Brahmins, Kayasthas, Rajputs, and Baniyas were found to constitute 65 per cent, 15 per cent, 13 per cent, and 7 per cent, respectively.[2]

Five FGDs of journalists were conducted, with four to six journalists in each, in the second phase of the study. These brought up distinct points of view on the representation gap in newsrooms. Journalists from the Dalit community said that they faced exclusion and discrimination at multiple levels, ranging from hiring to allotment of assignments and awarding of promotions. Some said that there were not many government media institutes in the state, and the fee at private institutes was out of bounds for them. Some upper-caste journalists believed that the youth from marginalized sections did not take the initiative to join journalism and preferred to prepare for government jobs. Others contended that such members lagged behind due to weak skill sets and poor contacts.

Based on the responses, certain observations can be made: newsrooms have very little diversity and representation of Dalits. While some newsrooms have made a conscious decision to bring Dalit reporters on board to report on Dalit issues, the overall representation continues to be poor. Dalit journalists admitted that there is discrimination within newsrooms. The discriminatory practices range from not being provided equal opportunities to being denied increments and promotions. They also admitted that this has a cascading negative effect on their career with lesser opportunities leading to lesser achievements and lesser recognition. Some respondents also pointed out that the lack of transparency led to discriminatory salaries and arbitrary decision-making. Entering media organizations is one of the biggest hurdles for Dalit journalists. Media organizations hire by reference, and vacancies are publicized by word of mouth. All this entails knowing people who are already employed in the field and perpetuates caste, class, or regional exclusion. It was also found that Dalit journalists join media organizations late and do not get promotions on time. The survey shows that positions like bureau chief, chief reporter, news editor, and editor were occupied by upper castes. Newsrooms have failed to create space for marginalized communities despite the fact that members of these communities, particularly Dalits, are educated and ready to join the mainstream.

Coverage of Dalit Issues in the Media

An understanding of the composition of newsrooms leads to the pertinent question of how this composition affects the creation, selection, and presentation of news. This section of the study ventures into these issues through a detailed analysis of news reports concerning Dalits vis-à-vis the overall compilation of the newspaper, during a particular timeframe. The objective of this section is to undertake a comparative analysis of the content of select newspapers to determine if the coverage of Dalit issues has changed in any way over the last two decades, and make an attempt to understand the nuances of news coverage, from display and frequency to tone and texture. Attempt has also been made to look at any change in the coverage of news in the light of changes in newsrooms in particular and society and politics at large.

Though Dalits are emerging as politically empowered, upwardly mobile claimants of government jobs and beneficiaries of the liberal economy in India, there is still a long way to go. Content analysis of three newspapers in UP, which are published from Lucknow, helps us understand how the representation of

Dalits in newsrooms impacts the content of newspapers. The analysis establishes how issues concerning Dalits have been covered in the media and whether due diligence is exercised in reports concerning Dalits.

For this content analysis, three parameters were used: social (issues of atrocities), political (issues of Dalit politics [electoral and non-electoral]), and economic (issues concerning economic empowerment and reservation for Dalits). Three Hindi newspapers with different ownership and ideological leanings were chosen: the *Hindustan*, the *Dainik Jagran*, and the *Rashtriya Sahara*.[3] A time period of 12 months (from 1 April 2016 to 31 March 2017) was taken for the analysis as it marked two decades since Kenneth Cooper's landmark report in *The Washington Post* titled 'India's Majority Lower Castes Are Minor Voice in Newspapers'. In this report published on 5 September 1996, Cooper (1996) wrote: 'India's 4,000 daily newspapers publish in nearly 100 languages, but one voice is largely absent in the press of the world's largest democracy: that of the lower castes, which account for more than 70 per cent of the country's 934 million people.' The article was followed a month later by B. N. Uniyal's (1996) write-up in *The Pioneer*. Uniyal said that in his 30 years as a journalist, he had not met a fellow journalist who was a Dalit. In 2006, 10 years after the Cooper–Uniyal reports, a survey of Hindi and English newspapers and television channels failed to find any Dalit or Adivasi among 300 senior journalists in Delhi. The year 2016 also marked 25 years of liberalization. This period saw the rise of the Bahujan Samaj Party (BSP) to power, with the party forming a full-majority government in UP. It also saw the emergence of the Narendra Modi government at the centre, which took several steps for the empowerment of Dalits not just by creating opportunities for jobs but also by creating entrepreneurial avenues (Press Trust of India, 2016).

For a point of reference and better understanding, the content of the *Dainik Jagran* and the *Rashtriya Sahara* newspapers covering the period of 1 December 1998 to 20 April 1999 has also been used.[4] At the turn of the century, the *Dainik Jagran* and the *Rashtriya Sahara* covered Dalit issues, but the extent and manner were poor. The coverage of economic issues of Dalits was minimal. Even political issues were not dealt with consistently. One of the reasons for this could be that the discourse was gravitating around secularism, leaving little room for other issues. For example, incidents of attacks on Christian missionaries in Gujarat and Odisha were covered extensively while repeated attacks on Dalits in Bihar by the Ranvir Sena were relegated to the margins. A comparative analysis of three major events concerned with Dalit issues – the Bihar massacres, the BSP's role in toppling the Vajpayee government, and reservation in the appointment of judges – would help reach a better understanding.

The Jehanabad and Narayanpura massacres were major incidents of cyclical caste killings during this period. These incidents are often cited as examples of the bloody history of caste violence in the country. However, at that time, these incidents did not receive the deserved coverage. The *Dainik Jagran* refrained from mentioning that the Jehanabad victims were Dalits and the perpetrators were allegedly members of the upper-caste Ranvir Sena.[5] The *Rashtriya Sahara* also barely mentioned the Jehanabad incident. It focused on the political fallout of the BSP supporting the centre's resolution for the president's rule in Bihar in the wake of the killings. The humanitarian aspect of the incident – the lives lost and families devastated – was completely missing. The subsequent incidents of violence were covered but without any clear reference to their casteist nature. In only a few editorials, the victims' Dalit identity was mentioned. On 4 February, columnist Ram Sujan Amar wrote an editorial piece on caste violence in Bihar titled 'Dalit Massacre in Bihar'.

The biggest news of this period related to Dalit politics was the fall of Atal Bihari Vajpayee's government at the centre. While the *Dainik Jagran* was observed to refrain from covering the BSP's activities generally, in this event, it prominently covered the party's political strategy and outcome. On 19 April, the *Dainik Jagran* wrote in its editorial that the stand of the BSP in the Lok Sabha was the height of opportunism. This was the first time in five months that the BSP found mention in the newspaper's own editorial which is considered as the stand of the paper. The *Rashtriya Sahara* also covered this incident, prominently focusing on Mayawati and the BSP. However, it also mentioned other coalition partners who withdrew support and caused the government to fall. On 19 April, the newspaper reported Mayawati as stating: 'We took revenge on the BJP [Bharatiya Janata Party]. The BJP caused our MLAs to defect. Now, I feel satisfied.'[6]

The issue that was raised by the then president of India, K. R. Narayanan, with regard to the appointment of judges was covered by both the *Dainik Jagran* and the *Rashtriya Sahara*. The *Dainik Jagran*, however, carried scathing editorials criticizing the president for implying that casteism existed in the judiciary. In one such editorial, it expressed unhappiness over the statement of the president: 'It is an insult to the judiciary to think that the appointment and promotion process of the judges is biased. It is not a good sign that caste discrimination is being dragged into the appointment of judges.'[7] In his Republic Day address to the nation, the president again raised the issue of Dalit atrocities and exploitation. This provided apt ground to discuss the issue of reservation in jobs for Dalits raised by him earlier.

It is important here to understand that the media does not work in a vacuum and biases tend to creep in. Media organizations, sometimes, succumb to the pressure of the ruling establishment due to business interests or when they think there is no audience for certain issues. Individuals within media institutions have a personal understanding of the discourse which in turn affects the overall output of a newspaper. It seems that the guiding perception in newsrooms was to remain focused on secularism; hence, several news items and editorials on the subject figured prominently. The national political leadership also spoke on the issue time and again, providing news reports more fodder and action. On the other hand, silence prevailed on issues of social justice and empowerment.

In Delhi, the media reported about the BSP when they ditched the BJP during the floor test. Mayawati became a front-page subject when the BJP government led by Vajpayee fell in April 1999. Journalists conducted interviews with her and wrote about her. It can therefore be said that with the emergence of the BSP, the media started paying attention to Dalit issues, especially politics, and then slowly moved towards social and economic issues. However, at the same time, news of atrocities against Dalits was almost absent. Instances of atrocities were recorded only when they reached the scale of 'massacres'. Smaller incidents or those involving individuals never made it to the editorial list and were missing from the pages of newspapers. On the contrary, incidents of theft, burglary, or harassment of upper castes were covered on local pages regularly. Even when cases of atrocities against Dalits were reported, the voices of victims, humanitarian angles, and follow-up stories of grief, delayed justice, and anger were entirely overlooked. An important observation, however, is that though many news items related to Dalits failed to appear on the front or inner pages, they found place in the editorial sections. During the content analysis of the *Dainik Jagran* and the *Rashtriya Sahara*, it was found that editorials, stories, and poems by organic intellectuals and others were published as they were outsourced, but news items were comparatively absent.[8]

Case Study of Select Newspapers of UP (2016–17)

By analysing two newspapers published from Delhi from 1 December 1998 to 20 April 1999, this research tried to understand how issues concerning Dalits were covered in the final year of the last century. With this as a comparative yardstick, an analysis of three newspapers published from

Lucknow almost two decades later was carried out. During this period, UP had witnessed a phase of political awakening. Changes were seen in Delhi as well as Lucknow with the rise of the BSP and its leader Mayawati. The BSP formed a full-majority government in 2007–12 which had many socio-economic repercussions in the region. Under the leadership of Mayawati, the BSP got more than 4 per cent votes in successive Lok Sabha elections. In the general elections of 2009, a section of opposition parties even proposed her as a prime ministerial candidate. In the new century, Dalit politics began to find its due space with the emergence of Dalits as a potent political force. Dalit issues no longer remained the exclusive domain of the BSP as other parties too began taking ownership of these issues. Political parties, including the BJP, the Indian National Congress (hereafter Congress), and the Samajwadi Party (SP), accepted the importance of Dalit politics and started giving more representation to Dalits in their party structure, electoral tickets, and governments. The Congress gave out-of-turn promotions to Dalit leaders like Mukul Wasnik and Ashok Tanwar at the central level and others at the state level. The BJP made Thawar Chandra Gehlot[9] a member of its parliamentary board. Hence, the emergence of the BSP and Mayawati in UP brought about a change in the political discourse of the country during this period. In this changed scenario, the content analysis of the three newspapers was carried out to examine if these changes were equitably reflected in the media coverage of Dalit issues.

The analysis of news items has been divided into three parameters: social, political, and economic, along with a separate section on editorials. After analysing issues of the three newspapers over one year, it was found that the *Dainik Jagran* carried a total of 52 items related to Dalits, the *Rashtriya Sahara* carried 58, and the *Hindustan* carried 60 (Table 9.1).

Table 9.1   News and editorials covering Dalit issues in three newspapers of Lucknow, 2016–17

Newspaper	Social issue	Economic issue	Political issue	Editorial	Total
Dainik Jagran	16	3	20	13	**52**
Rashtriya Sahara	10	2	38	8	**58**
Hindustan	14	4	38	4	**60**

Source: Author's analysis of concerned newspapers.

An Analysis of Lead News Items on Dalit Issues and Their Coverage by Select Newspapers

Una Flogging

Five Dalit youths were flogged in Una, Gujarat, allegedly by upper-caste youths in July 2016 (*The Hindu*, 2016). While the primary incident had gone largely unreported in the mainstream national media, a video of the occurrence sparked protests and outrage a few days later. The incident was picked up by Delhi-based newspapers from social media. In the regional newspapers of UP, this incident found a prominent place though it was less emphasized in them as compared to national newspapers. While the primary episode did not get covered in all three newspapers, the subsequent protests and related incidents were covered in the *Dainik Jagran* and the *Rashtriya Sahara*. As a corollary to this, other regional instances of atrocities against Dalits were highlighted by all three newspapers around this time. The Una episode acquired political undertones, becoming a rallying point for the opposition, and the newspapers also carried relevant editorials in this backdrop. Some of the news items related to this incident also find mention under the 'politics' category as political parties traded charges over the issue, each accusing the other of politicizing the same.

Ambedkar's 125th Birth Anniversary and Death Anniversary

All three newspapers widely covered events related to Ambedkar's birth anniversary celebrations across party lines. Politicians and thinkers like Ramchandra Guha and Udit Raj wrote editorials. Full-page advertisements and news items were published in different newspapers. UP governor, Ram Naik, was quoted as saying: 'Ambedkar was the craftsman of the Indian state.' He was speaking at a programme organized by the Ambedkar Mahasabha in Lucknow.[10]

Coverage by all three newspapers reflects the important change in political outlook with regard to Ambedkar, with all political parties co-opting his legacy and making it a point to be seen as following the path paved by him. All of them had dedicated exclusive space to events marking Ambedkar's anniversary. Articles related to the anniversary were also given space in the editorial section of the three newspapers. Similarly, they all covered Ambedkar's death anniversary widely. A distinct improvement is thus observed in the coverage of Ambedkar and his ideas or related news.

Loans for Dalit Entrepreneurs

All three newspapers carried news related to a government scheme for loans for Dalit youth entrepreneurs. Then then union finance minister, Arun Jaitley, launched the Stand-Up India scheme to promote entrepreneurship among Dalits. He was quoted as saying that women and Dalits would be the biggest beneficiaries of the scheme. The Stand-Up India scheme aimed at creating 2.5 lakh entrepreneurs by providing loans of INR 10 lakhs to INR 1 crore.[11] This shows the turn of the Dalit discourse towards economic issues, something that was completely absent earlier. It also signifies a change in the government's outlook towards Dalit issues and attempts to take the discourse beyond the boundaries of reservations to providing jobs and livelihoods.

Engagement of Political Parties with the Dalit Electorate

All three newspapers carried a number of articles and editorials, spread out over the period under consideration, about political parties reaching out to the Dalit electorate through various means. Such attempts were not just restricted to the BSP anymore; other national parties like the BJP and the Congress were also seen taking the lead. News of political leaders reaching out to Dalit families and eating a meal with them, or other forms of outreach by political parties, were frequently reported. These are some examples:

'Modi Government is Always Silent on Dalits: P L Punia' (page 10, single column)[12]

'Ambedkar Does Not Belong to One Caste: Mulayam Singh Yadav' (at a party programme on Ambedkar) (page 2, double column)[13]

'Modi Speaks in Parliament on Violence Against Dalits' (pages 1 and 13): 'PM Modi broke his silence in Parliament and spoke on the issue of violence against Dalits. He said, '*Shoot me but don't attack Dalits*'. He further said that fake *Gaurakshak*s want to create problems, these people should get harsh punishment. He appealed to people to come forward to ensure security and respect for Dalits.'[14]

'RSS to Brainstorm on Dalit Issues' (page 11, Delhi, Vinod Shukla)[15]

Inferences from the Content Analysis of the Three Newspapers

The analysis of the content of newspapers in 1998–99 and 2016–17 raises several useful observations and inferences. The sheer volume of coverage of Dalit issues in newspapers had increased manifold in 2016–17, when compared to the coverage in 1998–99. From giving space to individual cases of atrocity to dwelling on different aspects of the Scheduled Castes and Scheduled Tribes (Prevention of Atrocities) Act, 1989, newspapers were no longer treating Dalit issues merely as fillers. Editorials exploring Dalit issues from different angles also appeared widely across all three newspapers. This view was seconded in op-eds by many journalists, thinkers, and politicians. The quantum jump in coverage, particularly of political issues, can be understood in light of the fact that Dalit politics widened its own boundaries during this period. The BSP, for example, went from 'Bahujan' to 'Sarvajan' and opened its doors to other castes, creating room and role for them in the Dalit discourse. Dalit issues and icons, which had so far remained the sole domain of the BSP, gradually began to be claimed by other political parties, thereby effecting a proportionate increase in depiction in newspapers. It must also be kept in mind that the upper-caste-dominated newsrooms too began to feel a sense of ownership as Dalit issues broke party and individual boundaries to become national issues.

However, while there was a quantitative jump in the coverage of Dalit issues, it was not always accompanied by an equivalent jump in quality and sensitivity. A big change in terms of quality, over the coverage in 1998–99, was that Dalits subjected to atrocities were now being clearly identified by their caste. News articles were displaying courage by presenting facts and leaving no ambiguity about the essential identity of the victims. The change, however, did not always extend to the caste identification of the accused. The *Dainik Jagran*'s senior editor, Rajeev Sachan, was of the view that journalists had become more sensitive in covering issues related to Dalits. He shared his experience with a journalist covering the Saharanpur issue that took place in April 2017 when a journalist of non-Dalit background regularly covered the incidence of Dalit atrocities with full sensitivity. He said this kind of coverage and sensitivity was not expected a few years ago.[16] During the content analysis, it was also observed that reports on cases of atrocities, particularly of those against Dalit women, often lacked sensitivity. Cases of rape or humiliation were summarized on the basis of the most debasing aspect of the crime to evoke outrage – for example 'woman/man stripped, paraded naked'. This lack of sensitivity clearly stems from the fact that Dalits themselves are missing from newsrooms. It can hence be inferred that while there is a new wave of awareness in newsrooms about Dalit issues, a disconnect still exists due to the lack of Dalit journalists.

A significant directional shift was observed with regard to the manner in which news reports on Dalit issues were positioned, presented, and worded.

In the content analysis, it was found that while earlier the newspapers remained passive on Dalit issues, they now showed willingness to position themselves as crusaders and champions of the cause. There were specific instances where news stories were written to elicit action from the reluctant establishment and evoke outrage. The newspapers were hence no longer silent spectators but had become active campaigners for social justice.

After an analysis of the three newspapers and having observed the coverage of Dalit issues in them, it can also be inferred that the Dalit political discourse was primed to enter a new phase. Dalit politics did go a long way through the BSP or Mayawati, but new claimants of Dalits votes too have joined the fray. These new entrants, especially the BJP, are now talking about Dalit issues and taking them forward by infusing new dimensions into them. In the recent general elections of 2014 and 2019 and the assembly elections of 2017, the BJP and other political parties have provided leadership to non-Jatav communities as well. This could be read as an attempt to venture deeper into Dalit politics and thereby create more space for its coverage.

Moreover, news reports about economic issues related to Dalits were also indicative of an emerging aspect of Dalit discourse. Earlier the discussion was around Dalit representation, political power, reservation, and atrocities. Now, besides these issues, reservation in private sector, Dalit entrepreneurship, and schemes like Stand-Up India and the Pradhan Mantri MUDRA Yojana (PMMY) have also become part of Dalit intellectual discourse. While in 1998–99 the coverage of Dalit atrocities was nominal, by 2016–17 such cases were receiving wide attention. As a result, while one came across more and more frequent mentions of Dalits being victims of crimes, one did not come across any other aspect of Dalit life. This clearly led to the stereotyping of Dalits as victims. Similarly, in political coverage, Dalits were treated as a monolithic and homogenous identity with little attempt made to understand the divisions and disparities within the segment. To break such stereotyping, newsrooms need to step up and make an effort to relook at Dalit life and politics and at the same time make newsrooms more representative. This will enable them to infuse vigour and ideas and take the discourse forward.

Countering Exclusion: Emergence of Dalit Alternative Media

As a result of the persistently poor quantity and quality of coverage by the media, as seen thus far, Dalit individuals and organizations have tried to create their own counter–public sphere and taken the path of alternative media (*Hindustan Times*, 2018). In the last 25 years, an information society has emerged, in which Dalits and other marginalized communities have been unable to take part. News were selected and curated for people who were able to pay the cost of the newspaper and buy the products advertised in it. So, even when newspapers expanded their reach, there was a section of society that was either inadequately represented or not represented at all. The conscious members of this section of society tried to create an alternative media space, their own public sphere, where they established magazines and newspapers like the *Khabar Leharia*, the *Vanchit Vani*, the *Dalit Andolan Patrika*, the *Samyak Bharat*, and the *Dalit Dastak*. While a number of such efforts have been made, it is also a fact that many of these are unable to find commercial success. However, in this era of information and technology, Dalits have taken to online platforms. While it is very hard to reach 5,000 people through a magazine, it has become easier to reach out to millions through websites and social media platforms.

The advent of the internet and social media has really strengthened the alternative media space, allowing for the coexistence of diverse voices. In recent years, Dalit youth and organizations have used this space to raise their concerns and voice their anger when they are unable to do so in the mainstream media. After 2010, websites like Roundtable India, Dalit India, Ambedkar.org, Nacdor. org, Velivada.org, Dalitcamera.org, and so on, which cover news of Dalits in detail, were started. Dalit individuals, organic intellectuals, and organizations have also used social media to be more vocal about their views and reach out to each other.

The growth of alternative media has given birth to an era of outrage by giving the marginalized, including Dalits, a platform to express their discontent, dissent, and disenchantment. This wave of outrage is, in particular, led by 'Digital Dalits'. While figures indicate an increase in literacy among Dalits and the rise of a dynamic Dalit middle class, the same is not proportionately reflected in institutions, including the mainstream media. Alternative media, however, is aptly representative of this change as a number of educated and empowered Dalits have turned to this medium to get heard. English has emerged as the language of empowerment with the onset of digital media. While the traditional media – newspapers and television – used regional languages to reach out to locally entrenched audiences, alternative media has changed the game entirely, breaking the monopoly of mainstream media organizations in disseminating news. Instead of pursuing reporters to bring their grievances to light, members of a group now take to social media or alternative media and share their problems with their peers, who further endorse it, creating a digital wave of sorts. Any content on digital media can be accessed anywhere in the world at any time, without an expiry date. This has gone a long way in getting audiences and content together. Many members of the Dalit community have established themselves as social media influencers. They effectively guide, navigate, and lead debates on Dalit issues on digital platforms, take on the government, and come to the aid of their followers.

Conclusion

The Dalit discourse in the country has been trapped in stereotypes that have identified the community with dehumanizing work, atrocities, victimhood, illiteracy, and reservations for many years. Most of these stereotypes have been perpetuated by the media. The content analysis undertaken in this study revealed that stories of violence against Dalits continue to far outnumber news reports related to Dalits in other spheres such as economics, sports, arts, and so on. This also indicates a clear lack of positive reinforcing stories about the new Dalit assertion and breaking out of old moulds. It is important to realize that Dalit paradigms vary with class, region, language, and religion. Hence, a monolithic and stereotype-ridden approach fails to provide viable solutions. A comparison with earlier surveys reveals that the numbers from marginalized sections, especially Dalits, have increased in newsrooms, but this is still not adequate, and they are yet to reach the top echelons. The number of news items concerning the marginalized sections have also increased, but these still display lack of sensitivity. To break the cycle of caste discrimination, it is essential to draw the Dalit debate out of stereotypes and address Dalit lives in contemporary India. This would be possible only if more and more Dalits are involved in the process of creating and curating information and knowledge. Moreover, involvement of Dalit journalists in reporting or deciding coverage allocation is essential to ensure humane and holistic coverage, and not just sensationalized news.

An interesting aspect of the contemporary Dalit scene that emerges in this study is that the members of the community are now working for their own empowerment without waiting for the benefits promised by the government or agencies. In the case of the media, for example, Dalits have carved out a space for themselves through alternative media, having realized that the mainstream was not suited to raise their voices. They are also using social media to reach out to each other, pool stories and experiences, and exercise power and pressure as a bloc to prevent discrimination. This breaks the monopoly of a few in deciding which information goes out to the public, hence setting the tone and agenda for the national discourse.

Notes

1. Questions were on newsroom representation in two sets. One set was on caste, gender, education, and so on, while the other was on assignment allocation, bias, discrimination, exclusion, and promotion.

2. Additionally, the survey revealed a huge gender gap, with 90 per cent men and only 10 per cent women finding representation in newsrooms.

3. Narendra Mohan, the owner and editor of the *Dainik Jagran*, was a member of parliament (MP) from the Bharatiya Janata Party (BJP) in the Rajya Sabha. Shobhana Bhartiya, who owns the Hindustan Times group, was also a nominated MP during the Indian National Congress (hereafter Congress) regime. Amar Singh, who was on the board of directors of the Sahara group which owns the *Rashtriya Sahara*, was a senior leader of the Samajwadi Party (SP).

4. I went through microfilms of the Delhi edition of the *Dainik Jagran* and the *Rashtriya Sahara* available at the Nehru Memorial Museum and Library, New Delhi.

5. 'रणवीर सेना ने 12 लोगों को मारा', *Dainik Jagran*, 12 February 1999.

6. *Rashtriya Sahara*, 19 April 1999.

7. The original Hindi lines read: 'ये मानना भी कि नियुक्ति या पदोन्नति प्रक्रिया में दुर्भावना का परिचय दिया जाता है, न्यायालय का बड़ा अपमान है । यह शुभ लक्षण नही कि न्यायाधीशों की नियुक्ति प्रक्रिया में जातिवादी भेदभाव की बात जान बूझकर लाई जा रही है ।'.

8. On the editorial pages, organic intellectuals like Chandra Bhan Prasad, Shauraj Singh Bechain, and Kanwal Bharti found space. Other columnists like Kuldeep Nayyar, Ram Sujan Amar, and Dinanath Mishra also commented on caste issues from time to time.

9. Gehlot was a prominent BJP Dalit leader from Madhya Pradesh, who served as the union cabinet minister of social justice and empowerment and was thereafter appointed governor of the state of Karnataka.

10. 'Birth Anniversary Celebrations of Dr Ambedkar', *Hindustan*, 15 April 2016 (page 7, half page). Similar news and editorials were published in other newspapers, too.

11. 'Mudra Scheme Benefited 3.32 Crore People: Jaitley', *Dainik Jagran*, 6 April 2016.

12. *Hindustan*, 1 April 2016.

13. *Hindustan*, 12 April 2016.

14. *Rashtriya Sahara*, 8 August 2016.

15. *Rashtriya Sahara*, 20 March 2017.

16. Interview with Rajiv Sachan at the office of the *Dainik Jagran* in Noida, UP, 16 June 2017.

Bibliography

Primary Sources

Chamaria, A., J. Kumar, and Y. Yadav. 2006. 'Survey of the Social Profile of the Key Decision Makers in the National Media'. New Delhi: Media Study Group.

Dainik Hindustan, Lucknow edition, 1 April 2016–30 March 2017.

Dainik Jagran, Lucknow edition, 1 April 2016–30 March 2017.

Dainik Jagran, New Delhi edition, 1 December 1998–20 April 1999.

Rashtriya Sahara, Lucknow edition, 1 April 2016–30 March 2017.

Rashtriya Sahara, New Delhi edition, 1 December 1998–20 April 1999.

Secondary Sources

Cooper, K. 1996. 'India's Majority Lower Castes ARE Minor Voice in Newspapers'. *Washington Post*, 5 September. https://www.washingtonpost.com/archive/politics/1996/09/05/indias-majority-lower-castes-are-minor-voice-in-newspapers/4acb79e3-13d6-4084-b1d9-b09c6ed4f963/?utm_term=.6b27f767e27f. Accessed on 20 February 2020.

Fernandes, L. 2006. *India's New Middle Class: Democratic Politics in an Era of Economic Reform*. Minneapolis: University of Minnesota Press.

Fraser, N. 2008. *Social Justice in the Age of Identity Politics: Redistribution, Recognition and Participation*. New Delhi: Critical Quest.

Free Press. n.d. 'Who Owns the Media?' https://www.freepress.net/ownership/chart. Accessed on 20 March 2018.

Hindustan Times. 2018. 'Meet the Dalits Who Are Using Online Platforms to Tell Stories of Their Community'. 25 May. https://www.hindustantimes.com/india-news/meet-the-dalits-who-are-using-online-platforms-to-tell-stories-of-their-community/story-nkg4lHQ1DL44DbCBiJ7CrN.html. Accessed on 10 March 2018.

Jeffrey, R. 2001. '[Not] Being There: Dalits and India's Newspapers'. *South Asia* 24(2): 225–38.

———. 2009. *India's Newspaper Revolution: Capitalism, Politics, and the Indian Language Press*. New Delhi: Oxford University Press.

Kapur, D., D. S. Babu, and C. B. Prasad. 2014. *Defying the Odds: The Rise of Dalit Entrepreneurs*. New Delhi: Penguin Random House India.

Kumar, R. 2021. 'The UP Caste Calculus: What the State's Poll History Tells Us about Who Stands Where'. News18, 4 October. https://www.news18.com/news/opinion/the-up-caste-calculus-what-the-states-poll-history-tells-us-about-who-stands-where-4283663.html. Accessed on 31 October 2022.

Kumar, V. 2006. *India's Roaring Revolution: Dalit Assertion and New Horizons*. Delhi: Gagandeep Publications.

Loyand, M. 2008. 'Politics without Television: The Bahujan Samaj Party and the Dalit Counter-Public Sphere'. In *India: Satellites, Politics and Cultural Change*, edited by N. Mehta, 62–85. London and New York: Routledge.

Mehta, V. 2014. 'YouTube Channel Becomes Rallying Point for India's Dalits'. *BBC*, 7 January. http://www.bbc.com/news/world-asia-india-25502849. Accessed on 20 March 2018.

Mondal, S. 2017. 'Indian Media Wants Dalit News but Not Dalit Reporters'. *AlJazeera*, 2 June. https://www.aljazeera.com/amp/indepth/opinion/2017/05/ indian-media-dalit-news-dalit-reporters-170523194045529.html?__twitter_ impression=true. Accessed on 15 May 2018.

Naqvi, S. 2019. 'UP's Changing Caste Equations'. *The Tribune*, 7 April. https://www. tribuneindia.com/news/archive/column/up-s-changing-caste-equations-754461. Accessed on 31 October 2022.

Ninan, S. 2007. *Headlines from the Heartland: Reinventing the Hindi Public Sphere*. New Delhi: SAGE Publications.

Press Trust of India. 2016.'Govt to Create 2.5 Lakh Dalit Entrepreneurs Under Stand Up India'. YourStory, 26 March. https://yourstory.com/2016/03/govt-dalit-entrepreneurs-stand-up-india/. Accessed on 6 August 2018.

Ram, N. 1988. 'Chapter 7: Resume: The Rise of a New Middle Class'. In *The Mobile Scheduled Castes: Rise of a New Middle Class*, edited by N. Ram. Delhi: Hindustan Public Corporation.

The Hindu. 2016.'Protests Continue in Gujarat Over Thrashing of Dalits Near Una'. 21 July. https://www.thehindu.com/news/national/Protests-continue-in-Gujarat-over-thrashing-of-Dalits-near-Una/article14501552.ece. Accessed on 6 August 2018.

Thorat, S. 2007. 'Caste and Economic Discrimination: Causes, Consequences and Remedies'. *Economic and Political Weekly* 42(41): 4121–24.

Thorat, S., and K. S. Neuman. 2010. *Blocked by Caste: Economic Discrimination in Modern India*. New Delhi: Oxford University Press.

Uniyal, B. N. 1996. 'In Search of a Dalit Journalist'. Anveshi. http://www.anveshi.org. in/broadsheet-on-contemporary-politics/archives/broadsheet-on-contemporary-politics-vol-2-no-1011/in-search-of-a-dalit-journalist/. Accessed on 10 March 2018.

10

Hierarchy in Protest

A Comparison of Dalit and Upper-Caste Agitations

Amit Ahuja and Rajkamal Singh

> We live in a *loktantra* [democracy]. But once voting is over, we are forgotten. To be seen and heard in between elections, we have to remember a democracy is also a *bheedtantra* [system of crowds]. Where a crowd alarms the state, the state wakes up. It sees. It listens. That is why it is important to protest.[1]

> Unless a child cries, even a mother does not listen. Why will the state pay attention to the poor unless they protest?[2]

Introduction

Protests mobilize citizens and represent collective action. They give voice to citizens by articulating their demands. They highlight salient concerns in the public domain. Protests are an increasingly popular form of representing grievances and aspirations across the world (*The Economist*, 2020). According to government data, India clocks more than 300 protests per day.[3] And as the two testimonies in the epigraphs point out, citizens understand the significance of protest politics. This chapter focuses on the study of identity-based protests.

Identity is a popular focal point for protest mobilization because it can be a source of shared interests, grievances, and networks. But do all identity groups turn to identity-based protests to the same degree? Around the world, societies are defined by a variety of structural inequalities. In many instances, these are rooted in ethnic and racial identities. The social and political behaviour of marginalized groups is distinct and can differ from the politics of dominant groups. Still, we know little about how these differences manifest across a variety of forms of politics, including protest activity. For instance, how does the protest behaviour of Blacks compare with that of Whites in the United States and in South Africa, or the protests of indigenous communities compare with those of Whites across Latin America, or the protests of Dalits compare with those of upper castes in India?

In this chapter, we explore Dalit protest activity within the context of hierarchical caste group relations.[4] Specifically, we ask, is the protest activity of Dalits (the lowest ranked group in the caste hierarchy) different from that of the upper castes (the highest ranked group)?[5] Using a novel event-based dataset of protest activity at Jantar Mantar in New Delhi,[6] India's most prominent state-designated protest site, we examine the record of 333 caste-based protests that occurred between 2016 and 2019.[7] We find that the protest activity of a marginalized group is distinct and differs from that of a dominant group; Dalit protest activity diverges sharply from that of upper castes. First, Dalits organize more caste-based protests (48.6 per cent) than upper castes (13.2 per cent). Second, Dalits are more likely than upper castes to ally with other caste groups in their protest activity. Third, Dalit protest demands are more likely to be hierarchy contesting, whereas upper-caste protest activity is more likely to be hierarchy preserving.[8] Our findings suggest that 75 years after Indian independence from colonial rule, caste-based protest activity at Jantar Mantar is reflective of the effects of caste hierarchy; caste disparity still mostly shapes Dalit agitation politics.

Dalits and Upper Castes

Dalits count among India's most powerless citizens (Mendelsohn and Vicziany, 1998).[9] They continue to suffer social exclusion and discrimination. They are disproportionately poor. Several social reform movements, constitutional provisions, pieces of legislation, and political agitations have come together to undermine the belief in caste in India. However, caste distinctions and stigma, and prestige associated with caste identities, survive (Chakrabarti, 2022) and inform social (Ahuja and Ostermann, 2016) and political (Suryanarayan, 2019) behaviour.[10] This has a bearing on the social relations of Dalits and how they experience the state and democratic politics.

The relationship of Dalits with the state and higher-ranked members of society remains capricious. Dalits are more easily dismissed by state functionaries; they are weakly networked with pressure groups. Dalits struggle more than higher-caste members to access laws and institutions that potentially offer them protections. The judicial process poses a variety of hurdles, and the police are more reluctant to intervene on their behalf (Ramaiah, 2011). The news media is more likely to neglect their concerns and the social injustices they suffer (Balasubramaniam, 2011). Fewer civil society organizations advocate for them (Waghmore, 2013). They face discrimination across markets (Thorat and Attewell, 2007; Thorat and Neuman, 2012). Their stigmatized identity makes them vulnerable to acts of humiliation (Guru, 2011) and violence at the whim of dominant-group members (Viswanathan, 2005). These disadvantages fuel Dalit grievances.

At the opposite end of the hierarchical social order, upper castes benefit from the prestige associated with their identity as well as the position of structural dominance their higher status has historically allowed them to enjoy. They are over-represented among the wealthy and educated (Bharti, 2018). This over-representation also extends into the national legislature and parliamentary committees,[11] upper echelons of the bureaucracy,[12] the higher judiciary,[13] media,[14] civil society, higher education,[15] and upper tiers of the corporate sector.[16]

Why Protest Politics Matters for an Identity Group

Protests are just one among many different forms of political assertion; however, they matter to a group's politics.[17] For an identity group, protests are an accessible path to autonomous self-assertion. Protests are a more attainable vehicle for citizens to express their political voice as compared to electoral collective action. Most caste-based electoral mobilization, some scholars argue, is carried out by political parties (Chhibber, 1999). Grassroots electoral collective action by caste groups is rare, and any attempt to scale it up typically runs into five challenges. First, caste groups are dispersed, and not concentrated in majorities in electoral districts. Second, caste and the lived experience of hierarchy are rooted in a local context, which can vary from one location to another. Third, India has a single-member-district plurality, winner-takes-all electoral system, where the threshold for electoral success is much higher than in the case of a proportional representation system. Fourth, the scale of mobilization required for electoral success is substantial because of high electoral district magnitude (the average parliamentary constituency had 1.5 million voters in 2019). And fifth, the financial cost of electoral mobilization is substantial. One estimate from 2018 found that for an electoral campaign a candidate needed INR 10 crore in a large urban and INR 5 crore in a rural parliamentary constituency (Deka, 2018). Moreover, according to the Centre for Media Studies (CMS), the 2019 national elections saw a total spending of USD 8.6 billion. Together these factors constrain the successful self-mobilization of caste groups in the electoral arena. Together these factors constrain the successful self-mobilization of caste groups in the electoral arena. In comparison, protest mobilization has a lower participation threshold, is more flexible with respect to its timing, and is less expensive. Protests enable the articulation of even those caste-related demands that parties either ignore or neglect. Even at a much smaller scale, protests can immediately voice a caste group's demands instead of waiting for the next election, draw attention to group concerns through disruptions, and make the group visible.[18]

The Indian constitution guarantees citizens the right to protest.[19] On the one hand, protests have a hallowed history due to their role as the primary mode of politics during the country's freedom struggle. After independence, despite state repression, India has witnessed several consequential protest movements. These have sustained the reputation of protest activity as a legitimate form of politics. Data published by the state show that the total number of protests for the country rose from 37,627 in 2004 to 1,15,837 in 2016.[20]

On the other hand, protest politics is not universally regarded as a democratic virtue; it is also viewed sceptically. In his final speech to the Constituent Assembly on 25 November 1949, B. R. Ambedkar had warned against the use of protest politics in a constitutional democracy, calling it 'Grammar of Anarchy'. The underlying assumption behind his observations was that a constitutional democracy provides institutional avenues to articulate, aggregate, and represent collective grievances and demands.

One interpretation of rising protest activity is that it is a symptom of the failure of institutional politics. But that still leaves us with important questions: Under conditions of graded identity-based inequality, who protests in the name of identity? And how do the protests of the dominant groups compare with those of subordinate groups?

Comparative Study of Protest Politics

There is rich literature on caste-related social movements and political parties; however, a systematic study of caste-based protests and their effects remains largely neglected. Is data availability to blame for this inattention across the disciplines of political science and sociology? Two data-related challenges point in this direction. First, disadvantaged groups may not rely on protests as frequently as more privileged groups, undermining the possibility for a comparative study. Research on petitioning behaviour in colonial times (Lee, 2020) and claim-making in the post-colonial era (Kruks-Wisner, 2018) finds that petitioning and claim-making through social movements and associations among Dalits lag behind those of more advantaged groups.

Still, today, Dalit protest politics is a reality. Dalits organize and participate in large and small protests. Consider some recent instances. In 2016, Dalit student and civil society organizations protested across multiple cities, when Rohith Vemula, a PhD student at the University of Hyderabad, distressed by his treatment by the university administration, committed suicide (Shantha, 2019).

Also, in 2016, the state of Gujarat witnessed Dalit protests in response to the public flogging of Dalits by a mob made up of members of dominant castes (Mondal, 2016). In 2017, Dalit protests broke out in parts of western Uttar Pradesh (UP) when Dalit symbols and icons were desecrated by upper castes (Pai and Kumar, 2017). In 2018, Dalits protested across multiple states against the dilution of the Scheduled Castes and Scheduled Tribes (Prevention of Atrocities) Act, 1989, by the Supreme Court of India (*Indian Express*, 2018). Again, in 2018, widespread protests were triggered in Maharashtra when an annual commemoration of Dalits at Bhima Koregaon, Pune district, was attacked by members of dominant castes (Shantha, 2018). Parallel to Dalit street politics, a live Dalit digital public sphere has also appeared (Ahuja, 2018).

The second challenge relates to the measurement of protest activity. Unlike outcomes related to vote share and public goods, protest activity is difficult to capture. Consequently, studies of protest activities in India usually draw on case studies of protest movements (Ray and Katzenstein, 2005). Systematic quantitative analysis of protest events is rare.

A systematic study of protests of groups requires accurate and exhaustive information on all protests, over a period of time, in a given location. The available data repositories on protest events present serious limitations in this respect. The Armed Conflict Location & Event Data Project (ACLED), for example, tracks protest activity based on selected newspaper reports in various countries including India. But newspaper-report-based datasets capture a small percentage of protest activity (McCarthy, McPhail, and Smith, 1996), and additionally, newspapers underreport protests of the poor and marginalized, making the ACLED datasets potentially susceptible to the selection bias problem. Police records of protest events provide a more complete account of protest activity (Hocke, 1996). The Indian state perceives protests as a law-and-order threat, so its records of protests tend to be more exhaustive in comparison. Still, the Indian state only releases aggregate data on protests annually, and it does not identify protesting organizations, demands, size, and date of the protest. Capturing such data for spontaneous or unauthorized protests is very difficult for a researcher. By contrast, pre-authorized protests offer an opportunity to capture substantial information on protest activity. Therefore, we turn to a state designated protest site where protests are pre-authorized, enabling the availability of information on them. Besides producing an exhaustive list of all the protest activities, we can account for protest demands, size, and tactics.

In this chapter, we compare the caste-based protest activity of Dalits with that of upper castes because the lived experience of the hierarchy differs sharply across these two groups. These are two similarly sized groups situated at the opposite ends of the caste spectrum. Dalits form 17 per cent of the population whereas the share of the upper castes stands at 20 per cent.[21] Their status in the caste hierarchy disadvantages Dalits socially, economically, and politically. By contrast, upper castes derive the benefits of their status across all arenas. Since some intermediate castes share characteristics with Dalits while others with upper castes, we exclude them from this comparison. We do report their protest activity in the chapter, however.

We focus on caste-based protest activity because it allows us to understand how caste identity in general, and status disparity more specifically, shapes agitation politics. Ultimately, a large part of the political salience of caste identity is rooted in how different castes relate to each other. By comparing the caste-based protest activity of groups situated at opposite ends of the social hierarchy, we can better understand this form of collective action in the larger context of caste-based politics.

Hierarchy and Protest Politics

Two distinct intuitions drawn from the literature on collective action inform our inquiry on how hierarchy influences protest activity. Caste identity is a source of disadvantage for Dalits, while for upper castes it remains a source of advantage. The upper caste may feel threatened by increasing lower-caste influence. Occasionally this threat perception produces protests as was visible during the agitation against the implementation of the Mandal Commission report in 1990 (Balagopal, 1990). On the whole, though, Dalits are likely to have more caste-based grievances and fewer means to address them than upper castes. We also know that protests can be a reflection of the failure of institutional politics. Since subordinate groups like Dalits are more likely to face institutional neglect than dominant groups, we should expect them to organize more protests to highlight their demands.

An opposite comparative outcome for upper-caste and Dalit caste-based protest activities may be equally plausible. We know that, historically, marginalized groups have practised politics under a variety of constraints. Short of material resources and cultural capital, vulnerable to the threat of social as well as state coercion, and poorly endowed with leadership and organizational resources, the social and electoral mobilization of marginalized groups lags behind that of more advantaged groups (Piven and Cloward, 1977; Scott, 1986). Since a marginalized group has fewer resource endowments than the dominant group, its protest activity should be more constrained than that of the dominant group. In general, we would therefore expect Dalits to indulge in fewer and smaller protests than upper castes.

In the section that follows, we draw on police records to evaluate an exhaustive list of 333 caste-based protest events that took place over 44 months (from January 2016 to August 2019)[22] at Jantar Mantar in New Delhi. We compare Dalit protest activity to that of upper castes and describe its demands and tactics. Although not an entirely representative account of caste-based protests nationwide, our analysis nevertheless offers the first systematic descriptive account of caste-based protest politics. It provides a glimpse of how hierarchy shapes protest behaviour.

The Jantar Mantar Protest Study

To assess Dalit caste-based protest activity in comparison to that of upper castes, we decided to conduct a protest-event-analysis (PEA) study at a prominent protest site.[23] We picked Jantar Mantar for our PEA study because it is the most prominent state-designated protest site in India. It is located in the national capital city, New Delhi. Its proximity to the national parliament, federal government ministries, the Supreme Court of India, and news media offices draws protesters to it from across the country. Several major protest movements in the last decade, including India Against Corruption in 2011, the Nirbhaya protests in 2012, the 'One Rank One Pension' protests in 2015–16, the farmers' movement in 2017, and, more recently, the anti-Citizenship Amendment Act (CAA) protests in 2019–20, have unfurled at Jantar Mantar.[24] The bulk of the Jantar Mantar protests, however, are small protests.

State-designated sites of protest like Jantar Mantar are a feature of the urban landscape across state capitals in India as well as many other democracies (Mantri, 2021).[25] Such spaces serve the purpose of effectively managing public order while allowing the right to dissent. Jantar Mantar became a state-designated site of protest only in 1993 (Ghoshal, 2018). Prior to the 1990s, most protests in New Delhi district were organized in the Boat Club or in front of the parliament (Sultan, 2017). However, after a clash between farmers and the federal government during a large protest in 1988, the Indian government banned protests at most sites in central Delhi, citing security and public-order concerns (Sultan, 2017). This ban continued until 1993 when the government declared Jantar Mantar as an official site of protest (Mehrotra, 2017).

Protests at Jantar Mantar are heavily regulated. To conduct protests at this site, organizers must apply for permission to the deputy commissioner of police (DCP) office of New Delhi and provide a guarantee that they will comply with the law.[26] Additionally, under the guidelines of the Supreme Court of India and the Delhi High Court, the police have also laid down specific rules and regulations that relate to the place, size, and manner of protest.[27]

Data on Jantar Mantar Protests

We collected data on all protest applications for the Jantar Mantar site submitted to the New Delhi district's DCP office between January 2016 and August 2019.

Our findings draw on the information provided by the organizers in their protest applications. Additionally, we gathered information on whether the police granted permission to protest to the organizers. In this chapter, we use information on only those protest applications that received permission from the DCP office.[28] Still, we report findings on all protest applications in the notes at relevant places.

We manually coded the caste identity of the organizers of each protest based on a predetermined set of caste-related keywords to identify protests organized by caste groups. Our first set of keywords corresponds to the names and abbreviations used for the four caste groups that we wanted to analyse – namely, Scheduled Castes (SCs or Dalits), Scheduled Tribes (STs, Adivasis or indigenous people), Other Backward Classes (OBCs, a group of socially and economically disadvantaged castes), and upper castes (UCs). The second set includes names of specific *jatis* (sub-castes) under each caste category based on the Government of India classification. Finally, in instances where the organizers' name did not have any *jati* or broad caste-group names, we examined their protest demands. When all protest demands were caste-based, we counted them as caste protests. Further, in instances where multiple caste groups collaborated on the same application, we coded them as a combination of caste groups – for instance, SC+ST, SC+ST+OBC, and SC+OBC.[29]

Descriptive Analysis

Between January 2016 and August 2019, 4,921 applications were submitted to seek permission to protest at Jantar Mantar. Of these, only 53.8 per cent (2,648 applications) received police permission to protest.[30] The share of caste-related applications among the total was 11 per cent (542). Among permitted protests, 12.6 per cent were caste-based protests (333), suggesting that caste is a prominent, not a dominant, motif of protest politics at Jantar Mantar. The permission rate for caste-related applications was 61.4 per cent, which is higher than the overall rate of permissions.[31]

Who Protests?

Out of the total 333 caste-based protests at Jantar Mantar, the share of SC-organized protests was higher than that of any other group, totalling to 36.3 per cent (121 events). The share of SC protests remained the highest among all caste groups across the 44 months. It was 36.7 per cent in 2016, 41.8 per cent in 2017, 29.4 per cent in 2018, and 38.3 per cent in 2019. By contrast, the share of upper-caste protests was the lowest across the same time period, with 13.2 per cent (44) of the total protests. The same pattern is reflected in the protest application data (see Figure 10.1).[32]

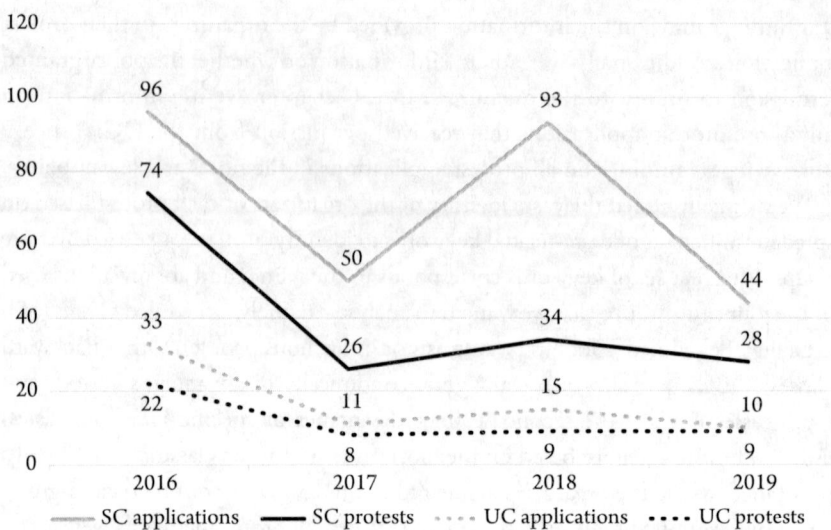

Figure 10.1   Total number of Scheduled Caste (SC) and upper-caste (UC) protests and applications at Jantar Mantar, New Delhi, between January 2016 and August 2019

Source: Data from the deputy commissioner of police's (DCP) office, New Delhi.

Note: The total number of SC protests and applications also includes those that were petitioned to be organized in coalition with ST and OBC groups.

In addition to organizing protests under their distinct identities, SCs organized protests as part of broader social coalitions with STs as well as OBCs. These coalitions were represented by single organizations such as the SC–ST Teachers Front and the National SC–ST–OBC Student and Youth Front. As Table 10.1 shows, the protest coalition between SCs and STs was the highest with 9.9 per cent (33) of the total caste-based protests. There were seven instances in which all three lower-caste groups (SCs, STs, and OBCs) came together and only one instance in which SCs collaborated with OBCs to conduct protests at Jantar Mantar. These protests increase the overall tally of SC protests from 36.3 per cent (121 events) to 48.6 per cent (162 events) of the total caste-based protests. The social coalitions between the lower-caste groups were mainly formed by employees of schools, colleges, railways, or other organizations. In contrast, we did not find a single instance of upper castes protesting in coalition with any other caste group.

Additionally, there were 17 occasions on which multiple organizations collaborated to conduct a single event at Jantar Mantar. Over 50 per cent of these events were organized by SC organizations, and these were largely within-SC collaborations.[33] For instance, the Dalit Shoshan Mukti Manch with

Table 10.1 Number and proportion of permitted protests across caste groups at Jantar Mantar, New Delhi, between January 2016 and August 2019

Caste groups	2016	2017	2018	2019	Total
SC	55 (36.7 per cent)	23 (41.8 per cent)	20 (29.4 per cent)	23 (38.3 per cent)	121 (36.3 per cent)
ST	23 (15.3 per cent)	10 (18.2 per cent)	12 (17.6 per cent)	11 (18.3 per cent)	56 (16.8 per cent)
OBC	31 (20.7 per cent)	11 (20.0 per cent)	13 (19.1 per cent)	12 (20.0 per cent)	67 (20.1 per cent)
UC	22 (14.7 per cent)	8 (14.5 per cent)	9 (13.2 per cent)	9 (15.0 per cent)	48 (14.4 per cent)
SC + ST	16 (10.7 per cent)	1 (1.8 per cent)	13 (19.1 per cent)	3 (5.0 per cent)	33 (9.9 per cent)
SC + OBC	0 (0 per cent)	0 (0 per cent)	1 (1.5 per cent)	0 (0 per cent)	1 (0.3 per cent)
SC + ST + OBC	3 (2.0 per cent)	2 (3.6 per cent)	0 (0.0 per cent)	2 (3.3 per cent)	7 (2.1 per cent)
Total	150 (100 per cent)	55 (100 per cent)	68 (100 per cent)	60 (100 per cent)	333 (100 per cent)

Source: Authors' analysis of data from the deputy commissioner of police's (DCP) office, New Delhi.

Note: SC, ST, OBC, and UC stand for Scheduled Classes, Scheduled Tribes, Other Backward Classes, and upper castes, respectively. Values in parentheses denote the share of permitted protests by each group for that particular year. Between 5 October 2017 and 16 July 2018, protests at Jantar Mantar were banned by the National Green Tribunal.

the Samta Sainik Dal and the Dalit Mahasabha with other SC organizations. By contrast, we do not observe any collaborations among upper-caste organizations or between upper-caste and other group organizations.

Size and Tactics of Dalit Protests

While anyone can apply to protest at Jantar Mantar, state regulations constrain the size and tactics of protest used. For instance, the most recent Delhi Police mandate prohibits an overall gathering of more than 1,000 people and requires protests to be organized at a designated spot, essentially restricting protest tactics like marches that involve movement from one place to another. Moreover, the area marked for protest activity is barricaded, and heavy police presence monitors and enforces the law. A newspaper report in 2017 records a DCP stating that 'at least 100 police personnel remain deployed at Jantar Mantar even on days when no large demonstrations are organized' (Goswami and Singh, 2017). Jantar Mantar was designated by the state as a protest site because it offered limited space for gatherings. As a result, most of the caste-related protests organized were relatively small, and the majority of the organizers used benign tactics in their events. The median size of SC protests was 150 and that of upper-caste protests was 200.[34]

The two most used tactics across caste categories were *dharna* (demonstration) and presentation of memorandum to authorities. We also observe other tactics to a much lesser degree, including marches, hunger strikes, effigy burning, meetings, and candlelight vigils. Among the SC protests, nearly 67 per cent used *dharna*, 51.1 per cent gave out memorandums, 8.9 per cent organized marches, 8.9 per cent held meetings, 6.7 per cent used hunger strikes, and 13.3 per cent used other tactics.[35] It is noteworthy that SC protests used a more diverse set of tactics relative to upper-caste protests. Among upper-caste protests, 70.6 per cent used *dharna* and presentation of memorandums, and 11.8 per cent used meetings as a tactic.

Protest Demands

A popular demand across all caste groups was related to reservations. Among the SC protests, 23.9 per cent (29) were organized on reservation-related issues. Of the total SC protests related to reservation, 44.8 per cent (13) sought complete implementation of reservation policies or asserted their right to reservations, and 41.3 per cent (12) pertained to the issue of sub-categorization of the existing reservation quotas.[36] In addition to the protests related to reservations, SC protests also reflected three other broad demands. First, 30.6 per cent (37) of the total SC protests were organized to seek justice in cases involving atrocities and discrimination against SC groups. Second, 11.6 per cent (14) of the protests were on issues related to SC leaders and symbols or were related to a particular *jati* within the SC group. Finally, 10.7 per cent (13) of the total protests were about seeking better working conditions, release of salaries, increase in wages, or change in existing state policies.

In comparison, among upper-caste protests, a total of 50 per cent (22) raised reservation-related demands.[37] Of the total upper-caste protests on the issue of reservations, half either demanded separate reservations for their group or asked to be inducted into quota categories for other disadvantaged groups. The other half demanded the abolition of reservation policies. Of the non-reservation related upper-caste protests, the major demands were as follows: 11.4 per cent (five) were organized against state policies and lower-caste leaders (for example, against the implementation of the recommendations of the Mandal Commission report and Mayawati), 9.0 per cent (four) were organized on issues such as murders or police encounters against upper-caste individuals (for example, the killing of the gangster Anand Pal by the police in 2017), and 6.8 per cent (three) were organized to pay tribute to security-forces personnel killed in action (for example, those killed in the Pulwama terror attack in 2019). Next, we interpret the findings of the descriptive analysis of the protest data.

What Do We Learn from the Protest Study?

The analysis of the number of applications to protest and actual protests at Jantar Mantar clearly shows that Dalits protest in substantial numbers and make a variety of demands on the state. Despite constituting 17 per cent of the population, Dalits are part of almost half the caste-based protests. Instead of lagging behind the caste-based protests of the resource-advantaged upper castes, Dalit protests far exceed them. Dalits are also more inclined to partner with other groups to make their demands. As Gopal Guru and Anuradha Chakravarty (2005: 135) remind us, for Dalits, 'organizing against caste has required organizing on the basis of caste'. The caste-based protest activity of Dalits stands in sharp contrast to that of upper castes. Besides organizing fewer caste-based protests, the upper castes also do not form protest coalitions with other groups.

This does not mean that a difference in resources does not shape caste-based protests. The median Dalit protest was smaller in size (150 participants) than the median upper-caste protest (200 participants) in this time period. In 25 one-on-one interviews conducted with protest organizers in 2021, all but one identified resources as a significant constraint for protest activity.[38] Protests demand time and resources for meeting travel, food, and (in many instances) lodging expenses. For Dalit protest organizers, fewer resources often translate into smaller protests. Since upper-caste protest organizers are more likely to be resource advantaged than their Dalit counterparts, they can organize larger protests. Our sense of the on-site protest-event observations at Jantar Mantar tells us that besides protest size, upper-caste resource advantage matters in another way. Individuals belonging to advantaged groups participate across a wide cross-section of other types of protests. Still, for them, higher resource advantage does not produce higher caste-based protest activity. They just have fewer caste-based grievances.

Can protest policing explain the gap in caste-based protest activity? Scholars argue that protests of subordinate groups are policed differently compared to other groups, with subordinate group protests receiving harsher treatment from state authorities (Davenport, Soule, and Armstrong, 2011). This argument would suggest fewer Dalit than upper-caste protests are permitted, which is not the case. Moreover, in a separate paper on protest policing we show that the caste identity of the protest group has no effect on the state's decision to permit the protest at Jantar Mantar (Singh, Hemrajani, and Ahuja 2023).

Is the difference in frequency of Dalit and upper-caste protest activities an artefact of protest type? In other words, is some aspect of permitted protest activity responsible for the difference? To answer this question, we turn to ACLED data, which capture unpermitted and permitted protest activities. It corroborates our findings and points to a similar pattern. It shows that at the national level between 2016 and 2021, caste-based protests formed a limited share, 4.2 per cent, of the total 63,488 protests. Importantly, among the caste-based protests, 1,076 (39.7 per cent) involved Dalit groups, while only 297 (11 per cent) involved upper-caste groups.[39]

This gap between Dalit and upper-caste protest activities observable across two different data sources is surprising for theories of ethnic outbidding (Rabushka and Shepsle, 1972). These would predict caste-based mobilization of Dalits to be countered by the upper castes. Observation from ranked ethnic systems, however, suggests otherwise; subordinate-group ethnic mobilization is seldom countered by mobilization of dominant groups along ethnic lines (Gisselquist, 2013). So, why are upper-caste protest organizers less likely to turn to caste-based protest than Dalit organizers? One explanation suggests that the smaller size of dominant groups as compared to subordinate groups forces the elite to turn to broader forms of electoral mobilization.[40] But upper castes and Dalits are similarly sized caste categories. Moreover, unlike electoral mobilization, protest activity has much lower thresholds of turnout and is easily supported by turning to in-group members. Alexander Lee (2020) suggests that upper-caste politicians with a potentially broad appeal are less likely to attempt to activate their narrow ascriptive identities, preferring to instead emphasize broader ascriptive identities or de-emphasize ascriptive identities entirely. By contrast, elites from poor groups, like Dalits, try to construct narrow categories in which they will not have wealthy and talented political rivals. If the fear of wealthy and talented political rivals drove more Dalit political organizers to caste-based protests, then we would expect them to be more likely to shun protest coalitions with potential rivals. As it turns out, the Jantar Mantar protest data show that Dalit protest organizers were more likely to join protest coalitions with other Dalit, ST, and OBC protest organizers. Upper-caste protest organizers did not join protest coalitions.

If hierarchy still shapes the lived experience of Dalits and upper castes, then the salience and breadth of caste-based grievances are likely to be more substantial for Dalits than upper castes, making Dalit protest organizers more likely to turn to caste than their upper-caste counterparts. Besides organizing more caste-based protests, Dalit protest demands are more wide-ranging and together most of them are directly hierarchy contesting and ask for social justice. A plurality of their protest demands is against atrocities committed against members of the group. Other significant demands relate to the implementation of state affirmative action policies and denounce the desecration of Dalit symbols. By contrast, upper-caste demands are hierarchy preserving. Half their protest demands either oppose policies promulgated for the redressal of effects of caste inequality or demand a share in these policies.[41] Upper castes also protest to oppose lower-caste leaders and their social-justice-related demands.

Protests at Jantar Mantar are limited in size, non-violent, and rely on benign tactics. In that sense, these protests are an expression of dissent, but they lack the power of disruption. This is a result of the heavy policing of protests at this site and stringent set of rules used by the state to regulate the protests. Violation of these rules can trigger a police case against the organizers and deny them permission to protest in the future. Still, Dalits use a wider repertoire of non-violent protest tactics than upper castes. Dalit protests are aimed at mainstreaming Dalit demands. A wider set of tactics reflects a stronger desire to get noticed. Upper castes, by contrast, have a significant presence in the public sphere and their sensibilities define the mainstream. Their protests are therefore more assured about being noticed and do not have to resort to a wide repertoire of protest tactics.

Conclusion

While the relationship between group status and voting behavior in multi-ethnic democracies has received substantial attention, the impact of group status on protest activity is not well understood. In this chapter, we compared caste-based protest activity of Dalits and upper castes using a novel dataset based on police records. Recent scholarship on caste has suggested that hierarchy has given way to ethnicity (Lee, 2020). Our findings on caste-based protest activity, however, indicate that hierarchy still shapes some forms of caste mobilization. The status of Dalits in the hierarchy, specifically their caste-rooted disadvantage, influences the frequency, coalition behaviour, tactics, and demands of their caste-based protests. Dalits of the new millennium have become more voiceful and turn to protest activity, but they are still protesting against the effects of hierarchy.

Notes

1. Interview with a protest organizer from Uttar Pradesh in 2019.
2. Interview with a Dalit protest leader from Tamil Nadu in 2009.
3. According to the last aggregate figure provided by the Bureau of Police Research and Development, the average protests per day in India in 2017 were 317.
4. Scholars differentiate ranked from unranked ethnic systems. As described by Horowitz, an ideal type of ranked system has an acknowledged absence of an upper class belonging to the subordinate group, a ritualized mode of hierarchy, and a leadership of the subordinates which necessarily has to enjoy the approval of the dominant groups. See Donald L. Horowitz (1985), Ashutosh Varshney (2003), and Rachel M. Gisselquist (2013).
5. We use the term 'Dalit' in our chapter in recognition of the politics it represents. The term, which means 'broken to pieces', not only weaponizes the oppression faced by the community, but also prosecutes the oppressor. The moment a people call themselves Dalit, the question arises who crushed these people? That question represents a powerful indictment.
6. We are not aware of any other study that compares the protest activity of groups at a protest site in India.
7. We would like to gratefully acknowledge the contributions of Yana Allen, Isabella Boffil, Zehra Siddiqui, Andee Brooker, Jessica Stratman, and Daniel Stone at the University of California, Santa Barbara, for their assistance with building and cleaning our dataset. We are also thankful for the insightful feedback provided by Pradeep Chhibber, the editors of the volume, and two anonymous reviewers.
8. The hierarchically arranged castes are broad categories made up of locally salient sub-castes, or *jatis*. The Hindu caste system is made up of over 3,000 *jatis*. People identify more closely with their *jatis* than castes. *Jatis* falling within a caste category share the structural conditions and their place in the purity–pollution-based ritual hierarchy.
9. In this chapter, we use 'Scheduled Castes' (SCs) and 'Dalits' interchangeably, based on the context.
10. Among others, see Tharailath Koshy Oommen (1984), Gail Omvedt (1994), S. V. Rajadurai and V. Geetha (1998), Dipankar Gupta (2000), and Myron Weiner (2001).
11. See Priyamvada Trivedi, Basim U. Nissa, and Saloni Bhogale (2019); Christophe Jaffrelot and Gilles Verniers (2019); and Dilip Mandal (2019).
12. Response to a recent right-to-information (RTI) query revealed that of the total 504 bureaucrats who hold the post of joint secretary and above in the Government of India, 451 (89.4 per cent) are from upper castes, 40 (7.9 per cent) are from SCs or Scheduled Tribes (STs), and 13 (2.57 per cent) are from Other Backward Classes (OBCs). See Sanya Dhingra (2018).

13. The caste composition of justices of the Supreme Court of India shows that more than 50 per cent of the judges come from upper castes. In fact, until 1980, not a single Supreme Court judge belonged to the SC, ST, or OBC communities. See Namit Saxena (2021).

14. In mainstream media outlets (television, newspapers, and digital news websites), upper castes dominate ownership, news broadcasting, debates, and editorial (Oxfam India, 2019).

15. For example, less than 1 percent of faculty at the 23 Indian Institutes of Technology (IITs) are either Dalit or Adivasi (Paliwal, 2023).

16. An analysis of 4,000 Indian firms listed in India and abroad showed that of the 9,052 board members, 8,387 (92.6 per cent) belonged to upper castes. See D. Ajit, Han Donker, and Ravi Saxena (2012).

17. Research suggests that agitations, demonstrations, and protests shape consequential outcomes for an identity group, including its identity (Gorringe, 2005; Waghmore, 2013), representation (Gause, 2022), electoral mobilization (Van Cott, 2005; Gillion, 2020), public opinion on the group's concerns (Cohn and Quealy, 2020), and state policies related to the group (Weldon, 2011; Gillion, 2013).

18. Research on Dalit politics, for example, has for the most part focused on institutional politics, including effects of electoral quotas on Dalit representation (Pande, 2003; McMillan, 2005; Jensenius, 2017; Chauchard, 2017), electoral performance of Dalit parties (Pai, 2002; Chandra, 2004), and Dalit voters' behaviour (Verma, 2009). Dalit protest politics, by contrast, has remained neglected.

19. In the case of *Mazdoor Kisan Shakti Sangathan v. Union of India* (Writ Petition [Civil] No. 1153 of 2017 [Judgment dated 23 July 2018]; [2018] 7 SCC 324), the Supreme Court of India interpreted Articles 19(1)(a) and 19(1)(b) of the Indian constitution to include the right to protest.

20. The government has stopped publishing protest data after 2016.

21. Since independence, the Indian census has collected data only on the SCs and the STs. The Socio-Economic and Caste Census (SECC) collected data that were to be published in 2016, but the government decided to withhold them on the grounds that there were serious classification issues to be resolved. So arriving at an accurate number for the upper castes is not possible. However, the caste composition of primary school students is available and points to an estimate. The 2019–20 data suggest that 25 per cent of India's primary school children belong to religious minorities and Hindu upper castes (Nagarajan, 2021). This suggests that the percentage of upper castes falls between 10 and 15 per cent. Another estimate uses the 2002 All-India Debt and Investment Survey to place the upper castes at 15 per cent of the population (Zacharias and Vakulabharanam, 2011).

22. Our study is confined to the time period between 2016 and 2019 because the data prior to 2016 were not made available to us by government officials.

23. For more on the PEA method, see Ruud Koopmans and Dieter Rucht (2002).

24. India Against Corruption was an anti-corruption movement led by Anna Hazare and several other civil society activists in 2011–12. Hazare's hunger strike at Jantar Mantar in April 2011 was one of the most highlighted events of the movement. The Nirbhaya protests took place in 2012 against the brutal gang-rape and murder of a 23-year-old girl in Delhi. During these protests, Jantar Mantar was one of the most important sites at which a series of public protests were organized. The 'One Rank One Pension' movement was organized by ex-servicemen to seek parity in pension for retired officers of the Indian Armed Forces. The movement continued for a total period of 320 days until the organizers were forcefully removed in October 2018 from Jantar Mantar. Then, in 2017, hundreds of farmers from the state of Tamil Nadu reached New Delhi to protest against the inaction of the central and state governments on the issues of interlinking of rivers, farmer suicides, debt, and fair remuneration. The two protests lasted for 141 days in total: 41 days in March–April 2017 and 100 days in July–October 2017. The anti-CAA protests began in December 2019 and continued till March 2020. In Delhi, Jantar Mantar was one of the sites at which anti-CAA protests were organized; the other prominent one was Shaheen Bagh.

25. National Mall in Washington, DC, and Hyde Park in London are prominent examples. In India, Azad Maidan in Mumbai, Freedom Park in Bengaluru, Statue Circle in Jaipur, and Dharan Chowk in Hyderabad are the well-known state-designated sites of protest, besides Jantar Mantar in New Delhi.

26. This is because as per the Delhi Police Act of 1978, the police have the power to regulate every public gathering in Delhi (See Section 28 of the Delhi Police Act, 1978, http://legislative.gov.in/sites/default/files/A1978-34.pdf [accessed on 30 March 2022]). While the regulatory powers conferred by the Act were granted for the more general purpose of preserving order in public places, the police have been using a permit system to regulate the organization of public processions, rallies, and protests.

27. Until July 2018, the guidelines to protest at Jantar Mantar were in accordance with the 2003 standing order numbered 309. The Delhi Police revised these guidelines and put in place a new order after the ban by the National Green Tribunal (which had banned protests at Jantar Mantar between 5 October 2017 and 16 July 2018) was lifted in July 2018. Both these orders can be found at https://criminallawstudiesnluj.wordpress.com/2020/02/06/delhi-police-circulars-standing-orders-for-regulating-protests (accessed on 30 March 2022).

28. Police officials report that permitted protests fail to take place in extremely rare instances.

29. We do not include protests organized by caste-based parties (for instance, the Republican Party of India [RPI], the Bahujan Samaj Party [BSP], and so on) in

our analysis. The only instance in which parties are counted in our analysis is if a caste-based wing of that party was the organizer (for instance, the SC–ST wing of the Indian National Congress) or if the party itself organized the protest with some other caste organization (for instance, the Dalit Shoshan Mukti Manch with the RPI). Additionally, we have coded caste-based organizations with 'Bahujan' in their name under SC protests because of their demands being specific to only the SC category. In general, there were a negligible number of party-organized protests.

30. Despite the ban on protests at Jantar Mantar by the National Green Tribunal between 5 October 2017 and 16 July 2018, organizers continued to petition to protest at the site. The permission rate during this period was only 6.1 per cent. The overall permission rate after excluding the banned period from our data was 61.3 per cent.

31. The permission rate for caste-related protests after excluding the months during which protests at Jantar Mantar were banned was 71.3 per cent.

32. The second-highest share among the caste protests across the years was of OBCs with 20.1 per cent (67) followed by that of STs with 16.8 per cent (56). We find a similar trend on analysing protest application data. The share of SC applications was the highest at 37.4 per cent followed by OBCs, STs, and upper castes with 19.6 per cent, 15.5 per cent, and 12.7 per cent, respectively.

33. Data on protest applications also show that SC organizations collaborate more than organizations of any other caste group. There were 26 applications overall in which an organization applied to protest with other organizations. Of these, 13 were by SC organizers, four by ST, three by OBC, five by SC+ST, and one by SC+OBC.

34. The median size for actual OBC and ST protests was 200 and 175, respectively.

35. Tactics-related data were available for only 121 of the 333 permitted protests and 215 of the 542 applications. Of these 121 protests, 45 were organized by SCs, 22 were by STs, 26 were by OBCs, 17 were by upper castes, and 9 were by coalition groups. Of the 215 applications, 83 were SCs, 36 were STs, 49 were OBCs, 19 were upper castes, and 28 were coalition-group applications. Most of the protests as well as applications show that organizers used multiple tactics (for example, *dharna* and presentation of memorandum). To calculate tactics for our analysis, we listed events with multiple tactics under each of the corresponding tactic categories. Hence, the sum of the reported percentages for protest tactics is greater than 100.

36. The state reserves quotas in educational institutions and state jobs for SCs.

37. Among the ST, OBC, and lower-caste coalition protests, the share of reservation-related protests was 23.2 per cent (13), 43.7 per cent (31), and 19.5 per cent (8), respectively. Furthermore, data on protest applications show a similar trend.

Of the 542 applications, 29.5 per cent (160) were on reservation-related issues. Of these, 30.6 per cent (49) were by SC organizers, 13.1 per cent (21) by STs, 33.1 per cent (53) by OBCs, 16.2 per cent (26) by upper castes, and 8.3 per cent (11) by organizers from lower-caste coalitions.

38. These interviews were conducted with protest organizers belonging to different castes in Punjab.

39. ACLED (acleddata.com) collects data on political violence and protests for more than 100 countries. The dataset contains information on location, date, actors, and type of violence. We calculated the total caste-related protests by conducting a keyword search to identify actors associated with caste groups. The keywords used were 'caste', 'Other Backward Class group', 'tribal', 'Adivasi', and when necessary, we searched for specific *jati* names (for example, 'Brahmins', 'Maratha', 'Patidars', 'Jat'). To calculate Dalit protests, we filtered the aforementioned list using keywords such as 'Dalit', 'SC/ST', and 'Valmiki'. To calculate upper-caste protests, we filtered using keywords such as 'general caste', 'Pandit', 'Brahmin', 'Thakur', and 'Rajput'. While ACLED data corroborate the trends that we find in our dataset, we believe there are some limitations to these data. Event data collected using secondary sources are generally prone to having selection and description bias. Moreover, the current data do not take into account reportage from several vernacular language newspapers (for example, the *Lokmat* in Maharashtra, the *Dainik Jagran* in the Hindi belt, the *Punjab Kesari* in Punjab, and the *Dina Thanti* in Tamil Nadu), all of which are newspapers with large circulations.

40. Rachel M. Gisselquist comes to this conclusion by drawing on cases of ranked systems in South America and Africa.

41. The upper-caste demand to be included among the beneficiaries of reservation policies should not be mistaken as a rejection of the caste hierarchy – far from it. It is only a claim to state benefits. Inclusion into the reservation bracket has not led other groups, OBCs for example, to discard their adherence to a hierarchical order or resulted in a reduction of violence and discrimination against Dalits.

Bibliography

Ahuja, A. 2018. 'Digital Dalits: Is Social Media a Game Changer for Dalit Politics?' *The Print*, 23 April. https://theprint.in/opinion/dalit-history-month/digital-dalits-is-social-media-a-game-changer-for-dalit-politics/51284/. Accessed on 3 March 2023.

———. 2019. *Mobilizing the Marginalized: Ethnic Parties without Ethnic Movements*. New York: Oxford University Press.

Ahuja, A., and S. Osterman. 2016. 'Crossing Caste Boundaries in the Modern Indian Marriage Market'. *Studies in Comparative International Development* 51(3): 365–87.

Ajit, D., H. Donker, and R. Saxena. 2012. 'Corporate Boards in India: Blocked by Caste?' *Economic and Political Weekly* 47(32): 39–42.

Balagopal, K. 1990. 'This Anti-Mandal Mania'. *Economic and Political Weekly* 25(40): 2231–34.

Balasubramaniam, J. 2011. 'Dalits and a Lack of Diversity in the Newsroom'. *Economic and Political Weekly* 46(11): 21–23.

Bharti, N. K. 2018. 'Wealth Inequality, Class and Caste in India, 1951–2012'. Master's Thesis, Paris School of Economics. http://piketty.pse.ens.fr/files/Bharti2018.pdf. Accessed on 3 March 2022.

Bureau of Police Research and Development. 2017. https://bprd.nic.in/WriteReadData/userfiles/file/databook2017.pdf. Accessed on 20 November 2020.

Centre for Media Studies (CMS). 2019. *Poll Expenditure, The 2019 Elections*. New Delhi: Centre for Media Studies.

Chakrabarti, P. 2022. 'Conceptualizing and Measuring Ethnic Inequality: Findings from India'. SSRN Scholarly Paper, Rochester, NY.

Chandra, K. 2004. *Why Ethnic Parties Succeed: Patronage and Ethnic Head Counts in India*. Cambridge: Cambridge University Press.

Chauchard, S. 2017. *Why Representation Matters: The Meaning of Ethnic Quotas in Rural India*. Cambridge, UK: Cambridge University Press.

Chhibber, P. 1999. *Democracy without Associations: Transformation of the Party System and Social Cleavages in India*. Ann Arbor, MI: University of Michigan Press.

Cohn, N., and K. Quealy. 2020. 'How Public Opinion Has Moved on Black Lives Matter'. *New York Times*, 10 June. https://www.nytimes.com/interactive/2020/06/10/upshot/black-lives-matter-attitudes.html. Accessed on 20 November 2020.

Davenport, C., S. A. Soule, and D. A. Armstrong. 2011. 'Protesting While Black?: The Differential Policing of American Activism, 1960 to 1990'. *American Sociological Review* 76(1): 152–78.

Deka, K. 2018. 'Political Funding: Who Pays for the Party?' *India Today*, 9 November.

Dhingra, S. 2018. 'Hard Fact: Despite Quotas, Dalits, Tribals Are Nowhere in the Corridors of Power'. *The Print*, 17 April. https://theprint.in/opinion/dalit-history-month/despite-quotas-dalits-tribals-are-nowhere-in-delhis-corridors-of-power/50167/. Accessed on 8 March 2022.

Gause, L. 2022. *The Advantage of Disadvantage: Costly Protest and Political Representation for Marginalized Groups*. Cambridge, UK: Cambridge University Press.

Ghoshal, A. 2018. 'End of a Protest: The Story of Jantar Mantar as a Protest Site Began in 1993'. *Indian Express*, 26 June. https://indianexpress.com/article/india/jantar-mantar-protests-ngt-end-of-a-protest-2011-lokpal-agitation-anna-hazare-4922867/. Accessed on 20 November 2020.

Gillion, D. Q. 2013. *The Political Power of Protest: Minority Activism and Shifts in Public Policy*. New York: Cambridge University Press.

————. 2020. *The Loud Minority: Why Protests Matter in American Democracy*. Princeton, NJ: Princeton University Press.

Gisselquist, R. 2013. 'Ethnic Politics in Ranked and Unranked Systems: An Exploratory Analysis'. *Nationalism and Ethnic Politics* 19(4): 381–402.

Gorringe, H. 2005. *Untouchable Citizens: Dalit Movements and Democratization in Tamil Nadu*, vol. 4. New Delhi: SAGE Publications.

Goswami, S., and K. P. Singh. 2017. 'NDMC, Delhi Police Welcome NGT Ban on Protests at Jantar Mantar'. *Hindustan Times*, 6 October. https://www.hindustantimes.com/delhi-news/ndmc-delhi-police-welcome-ngt-ban-on-protests-at-jantar-mantar/story-jbloPNSmXoqMngAjuxp7MP.html. Accessed on 20 November 2020.

Gupta, D. 2000. *Interrogating Caste: Understanding Hierarchy and Difference in Indian Society*. New Delhi: Penguin Books.

Guru, G. (ed.). 2011. *Humiliation: Claims and Context*. New Delhi: Oxford University Press.

Guru, G., and A. Chakravarty. 2005. 'Who Are the Country's Poor? Social Movement Politics and Dalit Poverty'. In *Social Movements in India: Poverty, Power, and Politics*, edited by R. Ray and M. F. Katzenstein, 134–66. Lanham, MD: Rowman & Littlefield.

Hocke, P. 1996. 'Determining the Selection Bias in Local and National Newspaper Reports on Protest Events'. Discussion Paper FS III 96–103, Social Science Center Berlin.

Horowitz, D. 1985. *Ethnic Groups in Conflict*. Berkeley: University of California Press.

Indian Express. 2018. 'Bharat Bandh Pictures: Protests Against SC/ST Act Turn Violent'. 2 April. https://indianexpress.com/photos/india-news/bharat-bandh-dalit-protest-sc-st-atrocities-act-violent-5120337/. Accessed on 31 January 2021.

Jaffrelot, C., and G. Verniers. 2019. 'In Hindi Heartland Upper Castes Dominate New Lok Sabha'. *Indian Express*, 27 May. https://indianexpress.com/article/explained/in-hindi-heartland-upper-castes-dominate-new-house-5747511/. Accessed on 8 March 2022.

Jensenius, F. R. 2017. *Social Justice through Inclusion: The Consequences of Electoral Quotas in India*. New York: Oxford University Press.

Koopmans, R., and D. Rucht. 2002. 'Protest Event Analysis'. In *Methods of Social Movement Research*, edited by B. Klandermans and S. Staggenborg, 231–59. Minneapolis: University of Minnesota Press.

Kruks-Wisner, G. 2018. 'The Pursuit of Social Welfare: Citizen Claim-making in Rural India'. *World Politics* 70(1): 122–63.

Lee, A. 2020. *From Hierarchy to Ethnicity: The Politics of Caste in Twentieth-Century India*. New Delhi: Cambridge University Press.

Mandal, D. 2019 '17th Lok Sabha Looks Set to Confirm Ambedkar's Fears: No Vocal Dalits in Parliament'. *The Print*, 8 May. https://theprint.in/opinion/17th-lok-sabha-looks-set-to-confirm-ambedkars-fears-no-vocal-dalits-in-parliament/232383/. Accessed on 8 March 2022.

Mantri, M. 2021. *Cities and Protests: Perspectives in Spatial Criticism*. Newcastle: Cambridge Scholars Publishing.

McCarthy, J. D., C. McPhail, and J. Smith. 1996. 'Images of Protest: Dimensions of Selection Bias in Media Coverage of Washington Demonstrations, 1982 and 1991'. *American Sociological Review* 61(3): 478–99.

Mcmillan, A. 2005. *Standing at the Margins: Representation and Electoral Reservation in India*. New York: Oxford University Press.

Mehrotra, N. 2017. 'How Jantar Mantar Killed the Spirit of Protest'. *Outlook*, 2 June. https://www.outlookindia.com/website/story/how-jantar-mantar-killed-the-spirit-of-protest/299180. Accessed on 20 November 2020.

Mendelsohn, O., and M. Vicziany. 1998. *The Untouchables: Subordination, Poverty and the State in Modern India*. Cambridge: Cambridge University Press.

Mondal, S. 2016. 'Dalits Protest Una Thrashing in Modi's Hometown, Blame BJP and Hindutva'. *Hindustan Times*, 23 July. https://www.hindustantimes.com/india-news/dalits-protest-una-thrashing-in-modi-s-hometown-blame-bjp-and-hindutva/story-PcDEifwFGlHn20fLwuvTOJ.html. Accessed on 31 January 2021.

Nagarajan, R. 2021. 'School Enrolment Data Indicates 45% OBCs, 19% Dalits in India'. *Times of India*, 30 July. https://timesofindia.indiatimes.com/india/school-enrolment-data-indicates-45-obcs-19-dalits-in-india/articleshow/84877162.cms. Accessed on 12 October 2022.

Omvedt, G. 1994. *Dalits and the Democratic Revolution: Dr Ambedkar and the Dalit Movement in Colonial India*. New Delhi: SAGE Publications.

Oommen, T. K. 1984. 'Sources of Deprivation and Styles of Protest: The Case of the Dalits in India'. *Contributions to Indian Sociology* 18(1): 45–61.

Oxfam India. 2019. *Who Tells Our Stories Matters: Representation of Marginalized Groups in Indian Newsrooms*. New Delhi: Newslaundry, Teamwork Arts, and Oxfam India. https://www.oxfamindia.org/sites/default/files/2019-08/Oxfam%20NewsLaundry%20Report_For%20Media%20use.pdf. Accessed on 8 March 2022.

Pai, S. 2002. *Dalit Assertion and the Unfinished Democratic Revolution: The Bahujan Samaj Party in Uttar Pradesh*. New Delhi: SAGE Publications.

Pai, S., and S. Kumar. 2017. 'Saharanpur Protests Herald a New Phase in Dalit Politics'. *The Wire*, 23 May. https://thewire.in/politics/saharanpur-protests-herald-new-phase-dalit-politics. Accessed on 31 January 2021.

Paliwal, A. 2023. 'How India's Caste System Limits Diversity in Science: In Six Charts'. *Nature*, 11 January. https://www.nature.com/immersive/d41586-023-00015-2/index.html. Accessed on 3 March 2023.

Pande, R. 2003. 'Can Mandated Political Representation Increase Policy Influence for Disadvantaged Minorities? Theory and Evidence from India'. *American Economic Review* 93(4): 1132–51.

Piven, F. F., and R. Cloward. 1977. *Poor People's Movements: Why They Succeed, How They Fail*. New York: Vintage Books.

Rabushka, A., and K. Shepsle. 1972. *Politics in Plural Societies: A Theory of Democratic Instability*. Columbus, OH: Charles E. Merrill Publishing Company.

Rajadurai, S. V., and V. Geetha. 1998. *Towards a Non-Brahmin Millennium: From Iyothee Thass to Periyar*. Kolkata: Samya.

Ramaiah, A. 2011. 'Growing Crimes against Dalits in India despite Special Laws: Relevance of Ambedkar's Demand for Separate Settlement'. *Journal of Law and Conflict Resolution* 3(9): 151–68.

Ray, R., and M. F. Katzenstein (eds.). 2005. *Social Movements in India: Poverty, Power, and Politics*. Lanham, MD: Rowman & Littlefield.

Saxena, N. 2021. 'Disproportionate Representation at the Supreme Court: A Perspective Based on Caste and Religion of Judges'. *Bar and Bench*, 23 May. https://www.barandbench.com/columns/disproportionate-representation-supreme-court-caste-and-religion-of-judges. Accessed on 8 March 2022.

Scott, J. 1986. 'Everyday Forms of Peasant Resistance'. *Journal of Peasant Studies* 13(2): 5–35.

Shantha, S. 2018. 'Dalits, Others across Mumbai Take Part in Maharashtra Bandh; Around 250 Detained in Two Days'. *The Wire*, 4 January. https://thewire.in/caste/dalits-others-across-mumbai-take-part-in-maharashtra-bandh-around-100-detained. Accessed on 31 January 2021.

———. 2019 'Rohith Vemula's Suicide Triggered a New Political Wave'. *The Wire*, 17 January. https://thewire.in/caste/rohith-vemula-suicide-triggered-a-new-political-wave. Accessed on 31 January 2021.

Singh R., R. Hemrajani, and A. Ahuja. 2023. 'Preventive Repression: Protest Policing in New Delhi'. *Journal of Urban Affairs*. https://doi.org/10.1080/07352166.2022.2147075. Accessed on 3 February 2023.

Soule, S., D. McAdam, J. McCarthy, and Y. Su. 1999. 'Protest Events: Cause or Consequence of State Action? The US Women's Movement and Federal Congressional Activities, 1956–1979'. *Mobilization: An International Quarterly* 4(2): 239–56.

Sultan, P. 2017. 'Delhi's Century-Long Tryst with Dissent, from Queen's Garden to Jantar Mantar'. *Hindustan Times*, 9 October. https://www.hindustantimes.com/delhi-news/delhi-s-century-long-tryst-with-dissent-from-queen-s-garden-to-jantar-mantar/story-KnuMmrsEvN1jkRvsSxAscM.html. Accessed on 20 November 2020.

Suryanarayan, P. 2019. 'When Do the Poor Vote for the Right Wing and Why: Status Hierarchy and Vote Choice in the Indian States'. *Comparative Political Studies* 52(2): 209–45.

The Economist. 2020. 'Political Protests Have Become More Widespread and More Frequent'. *The Economist*, 10 March. https://www.economist.com/graphic-detail/2020/03/10/political-protests-have-become-more-widespread-and-more-frequent. Accessed on 20 November 2020.

Thorat, S., and K. Neuman. 2012. *Blocked by Caste: Economic Discrimination in Modern India*. New Delhi: Oxford University Press.

Thorat, S., and P. Attewell. 2007. 'The Legacy of Social Exclusion: A Correspondence Study of Job Discrimination in India'. *Economic and Political Weekly* 42(41): 4141–45.

Trivedi, P., B. U. Nissa, and S. Bhogale. 2019. 'From Faith to Gender to Profession to Caste: A Profile of the 17th Lok Sabha'. *Hindustan Times*, 25 May. https://www.hindustantimes.com/lok-sabha-elections/from-faith-to-gender-and-profession-to-caste-a-profile-of-the-17th-lok-sabha/story-Mnp5M4pRX3aUji1UFFVy2N.html. Accessed on 8 March 2022.

Van Cott, D. L. 2005. *From Movements to Parties in Latin America: The Evolution of Ethnic Politics*. New York: Cambridge University Press.

Varshney, A. 2003. 'Nationalism, Ethnic Conflict, and Rationality'. *Perspectives on Politics* 1(1): 85–99.

Verma, R. 2009. 'Dalit Voting Patterns'. *Economic and Political Weekly* 44(39): 95–98.

Viswanathan, S. 2005. *Dalits in Dravidian Land: Frontline Reports on Anti-Dalit Violence in Tamil Nadu, 1995–2004*. New Delhi: Navayana.

Waghmore, S. 2013. *Civility against Caste: Dalit Politics and Citizenship in Western India*. New Delhi: SAGE Publications.

Weiner, M. 2001. 'The Struggle for Equality: Caste in Indian Politics'. In *The Success of India's Democracy*, edited by A. Kohli, 193–225. Cambridge: Cambridge University Press.

Weldon, L. 2011. *When Protest Makes Policy: How Social Movements Represent Disadvantaged Groups*. Ann Arbor, MI: University of Michigan Press.

Zacharias, A., and V. Vakulabharanam. 2011. 'Caste Stratification and Wealth Inequality in India'. *World Development* Volume 39(10): 1820–33.

Part III

Transformations in Ideology and Identity

11

Annihilation, Identity, Representation

Kanshi Ram and the Conundrums of Dalit Political Agency

Surinder S. Jodhka

Margins tend to be invisible. They are also generally 'inaudible' and are often spoken of by 'others' claiming to be their 'vanguards'. Marginality implies near absence of resources, not only material but also social and political. The twentieth-century revolutionary movements of peasants and the working classes were mostly led by 'outsiders', who had the luxury of not being stifled by the oppressive relational structures within which the marginals were themselves located.[1] This has, interestingly, not been the case with India's Dalits, particularly in modern times. Despite the hierarchy of caste being amongst the most vicious forms of inequality, Dalits have produced articulate leaders, a range of political elite from within their own communities. Almost every linguistic region of India has had prominent individuals who led the political struggles of their communities at the regional level[2] and often coordinated with counterparts in other regions and other marginalized caste communities. Some also acquired national and global visibility and eventually became part of India's political elite.

This process, which began during the early decades of the twentieth century, has continued to gain momentum over the years. Foremost among those who emerged from the margins of caste and became recognized as Dalit leaders at the national level is, obviously, B. R. Ambedkar, who also served as a cabinet minister of the first national government in independent India. Kanshi Ram, who founded the Bahujan Samaj Party (BSP) and served as a member of the Indian parliament, was the second to follow in this league. They both had pan-Indian presence and played significant roles in articulating the Dalit political agenda and making Dalit political agency matter in the national imagination. Though they rose to be part of the national political elite, they cultivated a social and political base from where they launched their political lives. Ambedkar, for example, worked mostly from Bombay and, more broadly, Maharashtra, his 'native' region. Kanshi Ram had a more fluid trajectory. While his family and *zaat-biradari* (kinship cluster) lived in Punjab, he emerged as a face of Dalit assertion in all of north India, with significant electoral successes in the state of Uttar Pradesh (UP). Kanshi Ram saw himself as taking forward Ambedkar's political work and was popularly seen as doing so by those who joined his politics.[3] Even those who think that 'a comparison between these seemingly incomparable personalities could be misleading' agree that he has been 'the biggest and most creative leader in the post-Ambedkar Dalit movement' (Teltumbde, 2006: 4531).

Looking back from the third decade of the twenty-first century, Ambedkar remains the most revered leader and has come to be seen as an ideologue of diverse Dalit identities and political imaginations. His influence on contemporary Dalit lives in India goes far beyond the sphere of electoral mobilization. For many across different regions and communities of ex-untouchables, he was a messiah who paved the path of liberation through a life dedicated to their cause. His legacy continues to shape and inspire a wide variety of social, religious, and political movements of Dalit communities across the subcontinent. Given his pioneering struggle and educational achievements, he has also come to be widely recognized as an important thinker of modern India, beyond the Dalit universe, and as one who provided a powerful and critical perspective about Indian society. He envisioned a radical democratic future for India but through a liberal democracy. As a thinker and activist, he wrote on almost every significant subject of his time – from the history of the Indian caste system to democratic statecraft to aspects of religious life. Having garnered academic interest across social science disciplines, his life and contributions to the Dalit cause and India's democratic politics continue to be written about.

As indicated previously, Kanshi Ram's life trajectory was different from Ambedkar's. They were not only born in different regions but also belonged to different time periods. Unlike Ambedkar, Kanshi Ram did not go abroad to do a PhD or earn a degree to practice law at the bar; nor did he write books like Ambedkar did or debate with people of the stature of M. K. Gandhi, having emerged on the national political scene nearly half a century after Ambedkar. However, he shared many similarities with Ambedkar. Kanshi Ram, by his own admission, travelled on the path that had already been laid by Ambedkar. And, quite like Ambedkar, he saw electoral politics as an instrument of social change. He too founded Dalit organizations and a political party and provided leadership to a variety of Dalit organizations and movements. While Ambedkar's party could not win electoral battles or form a government led by a Dalit, Kanshi Ram's party did. The rise of the BSP in UP, the largest and most politically important state of India, marked a phenomenal shift in the larger politics of north India. Even though the BSP could not replicate such political success in other Indian states, the impact of its electoral achievements in UP has been felt far and wide. Its rise has changed the nature of electoral arithmetic in several states of northern India and beyond. Through his strategic political thinking and its clever execution, Kanshi Ram also changed the nature of the caste–democracy relationship. In terms of the contribution of an individual leader to the shaping of an autonomous Dalit politics, and bringing it to the centre stage of national politics, Kanshi Ram remains unsurpassed, and his legacy compares very favourably with that of Ambedkar.

However, unlike Ambedkar, the persona of Kanshi Ram has attracted much less academic attention. As Vivek Kumar (2014: 73) rightly argues: 'He did not receive the kind of attention and recognition he deserved.' Even when he is remembered and written about, it is mostly in relation to the Dalit politics of UP, where the political party he founded managed to form a government with his confidant, Mayawati, as the chief minister (Pai, 2002, 2006; Narayan, 2014; Bose, 2008). He is rarely talked about as someone who contributed to the making of Indian democracy or even shaping Dalit identities. Mainstream political analysts began to forget him soon after he exited the scene. Even his death in 2006 did not evoke much public interest.

> The electronic and print media reported it but did not spend much time or space on it. While there were write-ups and obituaries in leading English daily newspapers, the accompanying photographs were of mourning relatives or VIPs placing a wreath on his body, none from the past when he played an active and determining role in politics. (Pai 2006: 1)

Despite such cold-shouldering by the mainstream media, Kanshi Ram remains an important symbol of Dalit assertion and political activism; he was a notable member of the political elite who shaped the nature of democratic and electoral politics in independent India. It is not only his persona that continues to inspire the newer generation of leaders coming from different Dalit communities, but he is also remembered for the language and idioms he injected into national politics and Dalit activism.

I revisit the legacy of Kanshi Ram in this chapter by looking at his life trajectory and the making of his politics. I further look at the manner in which his legacy continues to shape contemporary Dalit political thinking and activism. I also argue that it is his idea of caste and politics and caste in politics that remains the dominant mode of mobilization within communities of Dalits and the 'lower backwards'. I thus explore how his legacy has influenced the larger ecosystem of the democratic political process in India.

Researching India's Political Elite

As a field of enquiry, 'elite studies' has been an interdisciplinary enterprise and has seen many ups and downs over the past century. The term and its associated formulations were first proposed by a section of functionalist and 'right-wing' social scientists in the Western academy as a possible alternative to 'left-wing' and Marxist class analysis. The advocates of elite theory criticized the Marxist foretelling of a socialist revolution leading to a society where everyone would be equal. They argued that inequalities of power and resources were inevitable; all human societies have been organized around the 'iron law of oligarchy' (Michels, 1915) and are likely to remain so. The Italian sociologist Vilfredo Pareto averred that so-called revolutionary changes were mere alterations in the nature of regimes, a 'circulation of elite'. Their dispositions and sources of legitimacy changed, but elite power remained inescapable, implying that a small set of individuals always dominated political life. The same held good for other spheres of life. For him, the elite were 'a class of the people who have the highest indices in their branch of activity' (cited in Kolegar, 1967: 357). Similarly, Italian political scientist Gaetano Mosca (1939: 362) underlined the omnipresence of an elite or 'political class', who discharged 'the role of government' and thus fulfilled the 'need of management and order'.

Such a notion of inevitability of elite power lost appeal among social scientists with the rise of fascism in Europe, around the time when these theories were being propounded. However, the concept reappeared in the Western academy after a few decades. This time it was invoked as a core category in critical sociology by scholars like C. Wright Mills (1956) and Pierre Bourdieu (Wacquant, 1993). The category acquired a new lease of life with growing interest in the study of rising social and economic inequalities after the 1990s across different regions and countries of the contemporary world (see Khan, 2010, 2012; Best and Higley, 2018; Jodhka and Naudet, 2019). Over the years, it has come to be accepted as an important category of analysis across the social sciences. In their *Handbook of Political Elites*, Heinrich Best and John Higley (2018: 3) define the political elite as 'individuals and small, relatively cohesive, and stable groups with disproportionate power to affect national and supranational political outcomes on a continuing basis'. For the purpose of my discussion of Dalit political agency in this chapter, I broadly use the term to include all 'political leaders' who have been influential in shaping the nature of India's political life.

Perhaps the most important feature of India's political elite is their social diversity, which has been steadily growing over time, with diverse sections of the Indian population producing leaders and representatives from within their communities, across regions. India's political elite has also been ideologically very diverse. Their growing diversity is a reflection of the nature of change being experienced on the ground, in the economy and society. As Yogendra Singh (1973: 129–30) rightly observes, 'the changes in elite structure … might also reveal the essential nature of social changes taking place in that society'.

However, the study of the political elite has not been a very popular concern with social scientists in India. As Mukulika Banerjee (2010: xv) rightly points out, most of the social science writings on India's democratic politics revolve around '"groups", defined variously by caste, class and status'. In comparison, literature on leadership 'has been remarkably lacking'. Though there had been 'a promising beginning, when a conference was organized in 1956 in the University of California' that deliberated on the subject (Guha, 2010: 289; see Park and Tinker, 1959), it did not become a popular subject of empirical enquiry with political sociologists working on Indian democracy. However, as Banerjee argues, there have been some notable exceptions. She counts the work of Mattison Mines (1996) on 'institutional big men' and a study of three chief ministers of Karnataka by E. Raghavan and James Manor (2009) as a part of this league. In general, most writings on the subject of leadership have been in the form of biographies and autobiographies, usually written in a celebratory mode. However, they provide useful entry points for social scientific enquiry into the subject and could help us frame further questions.[4] There has also been a growing volume of literature on subjects like clientele politics and patronage democracy (see Piliavsky, 2014; Chandra, 2004), including an edited volume on political dynasties (Chandra, 2016).

Given the obvious significance of the subject, it is indeed surprising that so little has been written about the changing dynamics of India's political class and/ or its caste dynamics. Even when the question of caste is discussed in relation to India's political elite, it is invariably done in relation to the dominant caste communities and their rise on the electoral scene during the 1970s, or in the context of 'backwards' who began to become visible in regional and national politics during the 1990s. Rarely is the rise of Dalit politics and its leaders seen from the perspective of the changing dynamics of India's political elite. As indicated earlier, I hope to do exactly this by looking at the life and political legacy of Kanshi Ram in this chapter.

The Making of Kanshi Ram

Dalit biographical narratives, including those presented in autobiographical accounts, invariably begin with stories of the protagonist's childhood marked by poverty and deprivation. They also carry accounts of untouchability and humiliation, usually experienced a little later in life, in school or when they begin to move out of their home into the wider world. It is through these struggles and negotiations with the prejudices and discrimination they encounter that they tend to develop the consciousness of being Dalits, asserting their identity through the language of 'politics', seeking dignity and citizenship.[5]

Kanshi Ram did not tell any such stories about his childhood or later life. As his biographer, Badri Narayan, writes:

> Recalling his childhood and student days, Kanshiram had once said that while he saw many people around him who were affected by casteism and led pathetic lives, he himself was 'never overtly' a victim of this …'.… All my brothers were physically very strong and always ready for a fight. Our family always rejected helplessness and we were so arrogant that no one dared to touch us.' (Narayan, 2014: 17)

Kanshi Ram was born in 1934 in the north-western state of Punjab, in a family of Ramdasia Sikhs in a village of Ropar district, Punjab. Though originally belonging to the larger cluster of the Chamars, the Ramdasias are a section among them who have identified with Sikhism for long. The fourth Sikh guru, Guru Ramdas, is believed to have made them a part of the Sikh movement. Ramdasias were also one of the four groups within the Sikh community who were included in the list of Scheduled Castes (SCs) on the insistence of the Sikh representatives in the Constituent Assembly.

Though Sikh ideology decries notions of ritual hierarchy and has put in place institutional processes that weaken caste, its practice in everyday life survives and is widely accepted by scholars working on Sikhism and the region of Punjab.[6] While its presence and practice are widely acknowledged, including by the Sikh orthodoxy, it has taken on a different form and character. Perhaps the most important aspect of the regional profile of the caste system is that Brahmins have a relatively 'low' or marginal status in the social and religious life of Punjab (see Tandon, 1988 [1961]: 76). Kanshi Ram, too, acknowledged this:

> In Punjab, Brahmins were not that prominent economically or culturally. It was the Jat Sikhs who constituted the dominant community. Sikhism never encouraged Brahminism … Kanshiram once recalled in a lecture that as a small boy when he saw how some Brahman boys he knew lived, he thought that Brahmans were a *very poor, backward community*. Only much later did he come to realise that socially they were way above the dalits. (Narayan, 2014: 16–17; emphasis added)

The only memory of 'exploitation of the downtrodden' he seemed to have recalled from his personal life was the story of his father having been asked to do *begaar* (unpaid labour) by a bureaucrat, an official at the 'canal guest house' (Narayan, 2014: 17).

The nature of his childhood experience of caste perhaps had an influence on his later life. He carried himself with a sense of dignity and confidence all his life. While he was working in Pune, rarely did anyone think of him being a Dalit because he was tall and 'fair skinned'. The BSP even had to officially release 'a pamphlet' denying rumours that he was not a Dalit himself because he did not look like one.[7]

Becoming Dalit

'Dalit' is not a caste category, synonymous with ex-untouchables or SCs. It is a political construct. It represents an articulation of a specific view on the subject of caste that rejects popular anthropological theorizations which approach it as a uniquely Indian cultural reality, a consensual framework of living a Hindu life. The idea of Dalit rejects the ideology of caste and *karma* and foregrounds the experience of violence that it implied for those classified as 'untouchables'. Thus, it invokes the notion of modern citizenship, or its absence, for those who are excluded by its practice. The promise of modern citizenship required an 'annihilation of caste' as Ambedkar famously argued in 1936.

The category, however, began to acquire prominence only during the 1970s, when the Dalit Panthers movement emerged in the state of Maharashtra (Murugkar, 1991; Jaoul, 2007). The organization was formed in Bombay in 1972. The Panthers expressed their disappointment with the existing leaders of the SCs, those in the Republican Party of India (RPI), and those working with national political parties, particularly the Indian National Congress, who were all able to get elected because of quotas, or the reservation system, but did not have an independent voice. The Panthers also floated a pan-Indian organization in 1980, but their influence did not last for long.

Kanshi Ram shaped and sustained the next wave of the Dalit movement during the post-Ambedkar period. Though his movement found its realization in northern India, he, too, was 'educated' about the dynamics of caste in Maharashtra. After completing his education in science from Punjab, he joined as a junior scientist in a public-sector unit, the Explosives Research and Development Laboratory (*ERDL*), located in Pune. It was here that he closely encountered 'caste' as it was being experienced in modern organizations during those times. As the story goes, Ambedkar's birthday used to be a holiday in his organization.

However, the management suddenly decided to withdraw the holiday. Some of
the Dalit employees protested against the move, but the administration did not
concede. A class 4 employee, Dinabhana, who had led the protest, was charged
with insubordination and fired. Even though Kanshi Ram was in a senior cadre,
he openly came out in support of Dinabhana and helped him during his legal
struggle. As his biographer writes, when his upper-caste colleagues asked him to
stay away from the trade union activities of the class 4 staff, as he had nothing in
common with them,

> Kanshiram retorted that the similarity indeed existed as Dinabhana was a
> Bhangi and he himself was a Chamar; they both had the same problems and
> this struggle was not for the Class IV workers alone. (Narayan, 2014: 20–21)

This turned out to be an important turning point in Kanshi Ram's life. He saw
how caste was experienced in urban settings. Thus, his most critical encounter with
caste was far away from home, in *the office* of a modern public-sector organization,
as a member of the officially designated SCs. He decided to build a platform for
the protection of upwardly mobile Dalits like himself and set up the All India
Backward and Minority Communities Employees Federation (BAMCEF) in
1978. He actively worked with the organization for 27 years. He was so involved
in work at the BAMCEF that he decided to resign from his job. This was the time
when he developed his perspective on caste and politics. He was fascinated by
Ambedkar's writings and vision, but he grew dissatisfied with the Dalit activists
of Maharashtra. He found the RPI 'divided into many factions', which made it
incapable of any serious political action. The Panthers too 'were wasting their time
on endlessly debating the relevance of Marxism and Buddhism to the Dalit cause'.
The real need was for 'organizing a social movement' (Pai, 2006: 2). As a result,
not only did he shift his politics to north India, but he also began to conceptually
move to different modes of dealing with and overcoming caste.

Although his larger social universe of political action was composed of the
Dalit masses, he saw Dalit employees as his primary constituency. 'They were
also educated and monetarily secure.' Their training in the bureaucratic set-up
enabled them to work 'in a disciplined manner' (Kumar, 2013: 73). However,
the task of acquiring political power required popular mobilization across the
length and breadth of the country. It was with this objective in mind that he set
up a new organization called the Dalit Shoshit Samaj Sangharsh Samiti (DS4)
in 1981, followed by the BSP in 1984. Along with a group of his comrades, he
initiated a march on bicycles, which took him across the country, cycling around
3,000 kilometres over a period of 40 days.

It was during this march that he coined the famous slogans that reflected his notion of the Bahujan, the majority. Majority, for him, was a residual category, which included everyone except for the three upper-caste Hindu groups: the Thakurs, the Brahmins, and the Baniyas ('Thakur, Brahmin, Baniya chhod; Baki sab hain DS4'). In his calculation, the three, identified as the 'other' of the Bahujan, made for only around 15 per cent of the total population. Even though India became a democracy in 1947, they, the minority, had been ruling over the majority (Kumar, 2013: 81–86). They were able to do so because the majority was willing to be fooled and manipulated. This is what needed to be questioned and stopped:

Vote hamara, raj tumhara; nahin chale gaa, nahin chale gaa

Our votes, and your rule; no longer, no longer!

Moving Beyond Dalit-ness[8]

Kanshi Ram stayed firmly committed to Ambedkar's ideals of building a society grounded in the culture of equality and human dignity, free from the oppressions of caste hierarchy. He also stayed committed to the idea of electoral democracy as the only mode of bringing about change and believed that change had to come from above, through acquisition of political power, thus developing a different mode of thinking about Dalit politics. Though he may appear to be disagreeing with Ambedkar on foregrounding the agenda of *Annihilation of Caste*, nowhere did he criticize Ambedkar. His views on Dalit representation were only a restatement of Ambedkar's position on the subject, a preference for 'separate electorates' over the reservation policy. Quite like Ambedkar's, Kanshi Ram's approach to politics remained pragmatic. Recognizing that caste may be hard to annihilate, as Ambedkar had hoped, he advocated an active use of caste, as a resource to be mobilized and consolidated, the purpose of which was only to move towards making the playing field more accessible and equal for 'his people'.

Speaking at the First World Dalit Convention at Kuala Lumpur in Malaysia in 1998, he said:

When I read *Annihilation of Caste* in 1962–63, I too felt that it was possible to annihilate caste. However, when I closely looked at the caste system and how deeply it is ingrained in the lives of common people, I changed my opinion. It is hard to forget caste. Even when poor Indians migrate from their villages to urban slums, the one thing that they all carry with them is caste. If it matters so much to common people, how could we destroy it?

As I have come to understand, caste is a double-edged sword. We need to learn to *handle* it. The *suvarna*s [upper castes] have so far used it against us, even though they are only 15 per cent of the population and we are 85 per cent … If we have such large numbers, why can't we use it for ourselves? However, the challenge is to learn to use caste, politically … What appears to us as a source of all our problems could also be a source of opportunity for us. We need to use it for our own good. If we use it intelligently, we can be in power … And power is the key to all solutions. We need to be the rulers of this country. (Nath and Kureel, 1999: 1–8)[9]

He underlined the need for a new imagination and a political organization that would bring together thousands of caste communities and organize them as a united political force, the Bahujans. This, too, was born out of pragmatic considerations. Dalits were to provide leadership to this process. He called for building an autonomous politics of the Dalits and abandoning the opportunistic alliance politics of the kind being undertaken by the RPI in Maharashtra. He also criticized the widespread sense of being marginal, *dalitpan*. While caste was a useful tool and a resource for moving towards acquiring power, the obsession with Dalit-ness (*dalitpan*) was 'a reflection of a negative and defeated mindset'. The need was 'to come out of it. *Dalitpan* had become the biggest weakness of Dalits. It made them dependent like beggars. Beggars can never become rulers' (Nath and Kureel, 1999: 16).

These arguments were an extension of the ideas he had developed early in his political life, some of which were put together in the only book he wrote, *The Chamcha Age*. Published in 1982, on the fiftieth anniversary of the Poona Pact, the book was dedicated to Jyotirao Phule, B. R. Ambedkar, Periyar E.V. Ramaswamy' and 'many other rebellious spirits', who had worked hard to prepare the ground for Dalit struggles. As he explains in the book, the Poona Pact was signed between Gandhi and Ambedkar after the former sat on a fast unto death against the British decision to grant separate electorates to the 'untouchable' communities of India, represented by Ambedkar. Under the 'pact', Ambedkar was to withdraw his demand for separate electorates, and in return, the 'untouchables' (later to be classified among SCs) were to be given a quota of seats reserved for them from among the seats allocated to the Hindus. While other minorities could keep their separate, community-specific electorates, Dalits were to be elected by the common electorate. Ambedkar had worked hard to earn separate electorates from the colonial rulers, which he believed would give an autonomous or sovereign voice to Dalits. But he had to surrender them in the face of Gandhi's fast and the fear of the possible consequences his death could have had for the nascent Dalit movement.

According to Kanshi Ram, the separate electorates would have given the SCs a sense of autonomy and authority, thereby undermining the power of the upper castes, who constituted only a small proportion of India's total population. Ambedkar's success in winning separate electorates for Dalits was an indication of things to come for the upper castes, and they understood their imminent marginalization in a democratic India. This was the reason for Gandhi's hunger strike. Gandhi managed to manipulate Ambedkar into signing the Poona Pact, and this implied a defeat for Dalits. Their hope and vision of a 'Bright Age' was thus lost. *The Chamcha Age* was a direct consequence of the Poona Pact. It made Dalit leaders stooges of the upper castes. Even when a fair number of seats were reserved for them, Dalit electorates had very little say in getting their representatives elected. Given their demographic distribution across the country, no SC candidate could win without the support of upper-caste voters. This is how national parties (read: upper-caste parties) gained control over Dalit leaders and representatives. Dalits who managed to get elected as members of national parties did not represent their fellow Dalits but acted as agents and stooges of the upper castes, their *chamchas*, Kanshi Ram argued.

It was not only the elected representatives from the reserved seats who he was critical of, he also included bureaucrats in the same category. Given that Dalits do not have any say in the political system, Dalit employees also suffer. Even when they are selected, SCs are rarely given substantive positions of authority in the system. They too are therefore turned into *chamcha*s. Such opportunist mobilization of a section of Dalits in the *chamcha* age thus produces, what Kanshi Ram calls, an 'alienation of the elite'. The Dalit elite could overcome this alienation by 'payback to the oppressed and exploited society'. The mobile Dalits, who had been able to move out of their depressed positions and had benefited from the state policy of reservations which had been put in place because of the struggles of the Dalit masses, had an obligation to reciprocate. However, in the longer run, the way out of the *chamcha* age lay in claiming a share in state power, *hissedari*, which was substantive and real and would take everyone towards a new culture of equality.

The Legacy

How do we revisit the legacy of Kanshi Ram? What made him one of the most powerful politicians of his time? How was he able to transcend his immediate identity of being a Ramdasia Dalit Sikh from Punjab and emerge as the most powerful and influential of the Dalit leaders of UP? What explains the decline of Dalit politics after his departure? How do we assess his legacy in Dalit politics and Dalit leadership today?

Kanshi Ram developed much of his political imagination away from home, in Maharashtra, while interacting with local Dalit organizations and reading Ambedkar's writings. Unlike the local Dalits of Maharashtra, who saw each other in terms of their *jati* identity, Kanshi Ram could easily identify himself with the aggregated official category of 'SCs'. It is perhaps also for this reason that his understanding of caste, and the political rhetoric around which he framed his politics in later years in north India, was through governmental language and the caste hierarchy produced by it. He saw caste as a national system, which could be classified into three groupings: the Brahmins and other upper-castes (the General category), the backwards (the OBCs), and the Dalits (the SCs). His notion of the *bahujan samaj* too was additive, made of the officially classified OBCs and SCs, plus religious minorities. This, for him, was a matter of alliance building. His own goal was to mobilize and empower Dalits, giving them a sense of confidence, which would enable them to become capable leaders of their communities and of the larger alliance of Bahujans, eventually emerging as rulers.

His initial activities remained focused on making common Dalits aware of their shared situation of marginality and how they could convert their votes into a source of change. The next move was to work out an additive strategy of visualizing Indian society and arguing for an identity-based representational space for communities in the Indian political system. An important implication of such an imagination of the Indian political process was to turn the logic of caste from its existing vertical frame to a horizontal one: 'jiski jitnee sankhya bhari, uski utnee hissedari' (political representation of each community in proportion to their numbers). For this to happen, he needed the Dalit political elite to come out of the patronage of the upper-caste elite. To him, SC politicians working with mainstream political parties were all *chamcha*s. Such an imagination of Dalit liberation would have required a shift in focus, away from 'caste annihilation' towards consolidation of caste communities. It was only through numbers, and the consciousness of communities seeking their legitimate share in the power structure, that Dalits could move forward, taking them closer to the representational politics of the rural 'dominant caste'. His language of politics also gave a new lease of life to Dalit activism, a new confidence and hope of becoming rulers and sharing power. His success was quite evident.

However, his vision of democratization in the political domain through community-based *hissedari*, representational power sharing, soon confronted a major block. While it was easy to visualize the additive idea of *bahujan*, its realization on the ground required a very different kind of vision and political language. A Bahujan imagination needed to be produced through a politics that could transcend *jati*-specific boundaries and invoke a completely different kind of language. This was neither visualized in this framework nor attempted. The ground realities of social and economic life in a region like UP made it very difficult to bring Dalits and 'backwards' together for common political action. This was even more difficult in the absence of a vocabulary that visualized caste as being different from *jatis*. If *jati* and caste were to be the primary mode of mobilization, why would 'backwards' cede leadership space to Dalits?

The growing self-awareness of social deprivation and political marginalization among Dalits through the language of identity does not necessarily bring them together as a political community. Identity politics based purely on the principle of *hissedari* could go either way, towards consolidation or fragmentation. If demographics matter, it would also matter across Dalit *jatis* and in their proportions of representation. Though it might appear contradictory, the rise or success of the BSP and its constant reminder of caste identity would have likely produced an aspirational elite within the individual *jatis*, aware of their numbers and accounting for their possible *hissa* (share). The post-Mandal moment of politics that expanded space for caste-based political mobilization would have only enabled such a process of sharpening *jati*-specific community identities. The idea of a Bahujan alliance in the absence of a language that did not go beyond the additive process of *jati* and caste coming together could at best be short-lived.

The process of caste-based mobilization and *jati*-based fragmentation has also had implications for the relationship of caste with electoral politics at a broader level. It made everyone available for political manoeuvring for viable electoral alliances. Its translation is quite evident in electoral politics after 2014, when leaders of the Bharatiya Janata Party (BJP), with superior resources at their command, were able to successfully carry out such a manoeuvring. At the local level, every *jati* has its own leaders, and they negotiate for their share in the power that can be acquired through electoral politics. Growing mobilization for sub-classification of SCs and OBCs across India further sharpened the internal divisions within the officially classified categories.

This is not to say that there has been a decline of Dalit politics or a disappearance of the caste question from electoral politics or that caste differences and hierarchies no longer matter in everyday social life. On the contrary, increasing mobilization and active organizational processes have produced a newer form of Dalit politics and leadership, which is more awakened and assertive. In other words, the BJP's ability to secure Dalit votes does not necessarily imply the triumph of Hindutva over caste. If the realities of caste persist – exclusionary, inequitable, and humiliating – it would be very hard for any political formation to take their support for granted.

However, to move forward, the new generation of Dalit leadership would need to invent a different kind of politics, beyond the tokenism of *hissedari*. It would need to embed itself in an imagination that promises citizenship and substantive equality through democratic politics. It would also have to engage with the broader debates on questions of individual rights versus communitarian cultures and their representation. While democratic politics with a focus on social change finds it hard to engage with ascription-based identities, it can hardly ignore them in societies divided around caste, race, and ethnicity where the presence of diverse communities is not merely a matter of cultural difference but also a source of denial and discrimination.

Notes

1. See the literature on the famous 'middle peasantry thesis' in Hamza Alavi (1965).
2. Very few people may know the name of Mangoo Ram outside Punjab. However, the Ad Dharm movement during the 1920s and 1930s had a significant empowering impact on the community in the Doaba region of Punjab (see Juergensmeyer, 1988; Ram, 2017; Jodhka, 2009).
3. A popular slogan among the BSP activists of UP is 'Baba tera mission aadhura; Kanshi Ram karega poora …' (O, Baba, Kanshi Ram is here to fulfil your mission) (quoted in Kumar, 2014: 77).
4. Scholarship on the subject is gaining ground though the pace remains slow. See Paul Brass (2011); Philip Oldenburg (2018); Pamela Price and Arild. E. Ruud (2010).
5. See, for example, Omprakash Valmiki (2008).
6. See, for example, W. H. McLeod (1996); I. P. Singh (1977); Surinder S. Jodhka (2002, 2004, 2017); Harish K. Puri (2003); Paramjit S. Judge and Gurpreet Bal (2009); Ronki Ram (2009).
7. As Kumar (2013: 71) writes: 'Some people call him a Brahmin, others call him a civil servant … To do away [with] these mysteries [the] BSP's central office released a pamphlet …'
8. Some arguments presented in this section draw from Jodhka (2021).
9. Translated and paraphrased by me.

Bibliography

Alavi, H. 1965. 'Peasants and Revolution'. *Socialist Register* 2: 241–77.

Ambedkar B. R. 1979. 'Annihilation of Caste'. In *Dr. B.R. Ambedkar: Writings and Speeches*, edited by V. Moon, 23–96. Mumbai: Government of Maharashtra.

Banerjee, M. 2010. 'Foreword'. In *Power and Influence in India: Bosses, Lords and Captains*, edited by P. Price and A. E. Ruud, xv–xvii. New Delhi: Routledge.

Best, H., and J. Higley (eds.). 2018. *The Palgrave Handbook of Political Elites*. London: Palgrave Macmillan.

Bose, A. 2008. *Behenji: A Political Biography of Mayawati*. New Delhi: Penguin.

Brass, P. R. 2011. *An Indian Political Life: Charan Singh and Congress Politics, 1937 to 1961*. New Delhi: SAGE Publications.

Chandra, K. 2004. *Why Ethnic Parties Succeed: Patronage and Ethnic Head Counts in India*. New York: Cambridge University Press.

———. 2016. *Democratic Dynasties: State, Party and Family in Contemporary Indian Politics*. New Delhi: Cambridge University Press.

Guha, R. 2010. 'Chapter 19: Political Leadership'. In *The Oxford Companion to Politics in India*, edited by N. G. Jayal and P. B. Mehta. New Delhi: Oxford University Press.

Jaoul, N. 2007. '"Political and Non-Political" Means in the Dalit Movement'. In *Uttar Pradesh: Identity, Economic Reforms and Governance*, edited by S. Pai, 191–200. New Delhi: Pearson.

Jodhka, S. S. 2002. 'Caste and Untouchability in Rural Punjab'. *Economic and Political Weekly* 37(19): 1813–23.

———. 2004. 'Sikhism and the Caste Question: Dalits and Their Politics in Contemporary Punjab'. *Contributions to Indian Sociology* 23 (1–2): 165–92.

———. 2009 'The Ravi Dasis of Punjab: Global Contours of Caste and Religious Strife'. *Economic and Political Weekly* 44(24): 79–85.

———. 2017 'Caste From a Contemporary Perspective'. In *Brill's Encyclopedia of Sikhism* vol. 1, edited by K. A. Jacobsen, G. S. Mann, K. Myrvold, and E. Nesbitt, 236–42. Leiden: Brill.

———. 2021. 'Kanshi Ram and the Making of Dalit Political Agency: Leadership Legacies and the Politics of Hissedari'. *Economic and Political Weekly* 56(3): 35–41.

Jodhka S. S., and J. Naudet (eds.). 2019. *Mapping the Elite: Power, Privilege and Inequality*. New Delhi: Oxford University Press.

Judge, P. S., and G. Bal. 2009. *Mapping Dalits: Contemporary Reality and Future Prospects in Punjab*. Jaipur: Rawat Publications.

Juergensmeyer, M. 1988. *Religious Rebels in the Punjab: The Social Vision of the Untouchables*. Delhi: Ajanta Publications.

Khan, S. R. 2010. *Privilege: The Making of an Adolescent Elite at St. Paul's School*. Princeton: Princeton University Press.

———. 2012. 'The Sociology of Elites'. *Annual Review of Sociology* 38: 361–77.

Kolegar, F. 1967. 'The Elite and the Ruling Class: Pareto and Mosca Re-examined'. *Review of Politics* 29(3): 354–69.

Kumar, V. 2013. *Dalit Assertion & Bahujan Samaj Party: A Perspective From Below*. New Delhi: Samyak Prakashan.

———. 2014. *Prajatantra Mein Jati, Aarakshan Avam Dalit* (Hindi). New Delhi: Samyak Prakashan.

McLeod, W. H. 1996. *The Evolution of the Sikh Community: Five Essays*. New Delhi: Oxford University Press.

Michels, R. 1915. *Political Parties: A Sociological Study of the Oligarchical Tendencies of Modern Democracy*. London: Jarrold & Sons.

Mills, C. W. 1956. *The Power Elite*. New York: Oxford University Press.

Mines, M. 1996. *Public Faces, Private Voices: Community and Individuality in South India*. Berkeley: University of California Press.

Mosca, G. 1939. *The Ruling Class* (Elementi de Scienza Politica). New York: McGraw Hill.

Murugkar, L. 1991. *Dalit Panther Movement in Maharashtra: A Sociological Appraisal*. Bombay: Popular Prakashan.

Narayan, B. 2014. *Kanshi Ram: Leader of the Dalits*. Delhi: Penguin Viking.

Nath, M. G., and K. Kureel. 1999. *Jativiheen Samaj ki Sathapana Ke Liye Aapko Desh ka Hanuman Banana Hoga* (Hindi). New Delhi: Baba Sahib Dr Ambedkar Press.

Oldenburg, P. 2018. 'Political Elites in South Asia'. In *The Palgrave Handbook of Political Elites*, edited by H. Best and J. Higley, 2003–24. London: Palgrave Macmillan.

Pai, S. 2002. *Dalit Assertion and the Unfinished Democratic Revolution: The Bahujan Samaj Party in Uttar Pradesh*. New Delhi: SAGE Publications.

———. 2006. 'Kanshi Ram: "The Man and His Legacy": An Essay'. EconPapers. https://econpapers.repec.org/paper/esswpaper/id_3a639.htm. Accessed on 26 October 2019.

Park, R. L., and I. Tinker (eds.). 1959. *Leadership and Political Institutions in India*. Princeton: Princeton University Press.

Piliavsky, A. (ed.). 2014. *Patronage as Politics in South Asia*. New Delhi: Cambridge University Press.

Price, P., and A. E. Ruud (eds.). 2010. *Power and Influence in India: Bosses, Lords and Captains*. New Delhi: Routledge.

Puri, H. K. 2003. 'Scheduled Castes in Sikh Community: A Historical Perspective'. *Economic and Political Weekly* 38(26): 2693–701.

Raghavan, E., and J. Manor. 2009. *Broadening and Deepening Democracy: Political Innovation in Karnataka*. New Delhi: Routledge.

Ram, K. 1982: *The Chamcha Age: An Era of Stooges*. Delhi: DS-4 Office.

Ram, R. 2009. 'Regional Specificities and Caste Hierarchies in Punjab'. *Indian Journal of Politics* 43(2): 15–29.

———. 2017. 'The Genealogy of a Dalit Faith: The Ravidassia Dharm and Caste Conflicts in Contemporary Punjab'. *Contributions to Indian Sociology* 51(1): 52–78.

Singh, I. P. 1977. 'Caste in a Sikh Village'. In *Caste Among Non-Hindus in India*, edited by H. Singh, 66–83. New Delhi: National Publishing House.

Singh, Y. 1973. *Modernization of Indian Traditions*. Delhi: Thomson Press.

Tandon, P. 1988 [1961]. *Punjabi Century (1857–1987)*. New Delhi: Viking Press.

Teltumbde, A. 2006. 'An Enigma Called Kanshi Ram'. *Economic and Political Weekly* 41(43–44): 4531–32.

Valmiki, O. 2008. *Joothan: A Dalit's Life*. New York: Columbia University Press.

Wacquant, L. J. D. 1993. 'From Ruling Class to Field of Power: An Interview with Pierre Bourdieu on *La noblesse d'état*'. *Theory, Culture and Society* 10(3): 19–44.

12

Reading Caste and Class Together

A Dalit–Bahujan–Left Alliance?

Dwaipayan Bhattacharyya*

'In the swirl of contradictions that envelope India, no other pair of terms has had as baleful a consequence for the politics and future of this country as caste and class,' wrote Anand Teltumbde. 'These two words have divided the working-class movement into two camps – movements oriented towards class struggle and those against caste, each driven by the ideological obsessions of their protagonists through divergent paths that led to the eventual marginalisation of both.' While they have different conceptual horizons, 'the similarity between the two is enough to build a unified emancipatory struggle – a potential that both these movements have failed miserably to realise' (Teltumbde, 2018: 91). One can have no quarrel with Teltumbde on the fact that both class-blind caste movements and caste-blind class struggle have reached an impasse in contemporary Indian politics. The parties that fought upper-caste domination are now split and fragile, and the class-based left parties, sequestered as they are, have turned largely ineffective. A serious rethinking of class and caste politics, therefore, is needed to imagine a popular politics as alternative to the hegemonic surge of authoritarian populism in today's India.[1]

The surge is represented by the Bharatiya Janata Party (BJP) with its Hindu majoritarian ideology. This has a telling effect on India's secular constitution, her public institutions, as well as the political space for articulating protest and dissent. For the survival of India's democracy, it is necessary to have an array of counter-hegemonic popular mobilizations which cannot be constituted in the absence of a confluence between two distinct solidarity positions: of the

* I thank the editors of this volume, the participants of the workshop in which the draft of this chapter was presented, and the anonymous reviewer for comments and suggestions. I also appreciate the constant support I receive through my association with the M. S. Merian–R. Tagore International Centre of Advanced Studies 'Metamorphoses of the Political' (ICAS:MP).

oppressed Dalit and Bahujan castes and of the grossly exploited informal working classes. While Dalit and Bahujan mobilizations had scaled new heights in India's democracy and altered its polity's representational character, they barely breeched the limit of symbolic recognition for marginal social groups. On the other hand, the parliamentary left and the social democratic parties are now faced with a crisis emerging from their inability to move beyond the economic demands of the organized working class and failure to adequately politicize the rural proletariat. The challenge, therefore, is to overcome the extant approaches of both caste and class politics and imagine a concrete possibility for a reciprocal, non-reductive exchange between the two.

Caste and Class: Politics, Possibilities, Limits

In the 1990s, politics in India revolved around a triangular contest between the three Ms – *mandir*, Mandal, and the market.[2] In India's northern Gangetic plain, caste and class assertions delivered electoral gains. While the Janata Dal was the initial platform for the Other Backward Class (OBC) and Dalit alignments, the Bahujan Samaj Party (BSP) and the Samajwadi Party (SP) in Uttar Pradesh (UP) and the Rashtriya Janata Dal (RJD) in Bihar were eventually their greatest beneficiaries (Pai, 2002; Jaffrelot, 2003). Trade and Kisan Union opposition to privatization and deregulation helped the communists strengthen their base among the organized working class, and in rural West Bengal, the ruling Left Front headed by the Communist Party of India (Marxist) (CPI-M) – thanks to the support of sharecroppers and landless farm workers – appeared invincible.[3] In the decades that followed, however, everything changed. In UP and Bihar, the BJP replaced the BSP, the SP, and the RJD; in West Bengal, the left got virtually decimated, with its vote share shrinking to an all time low in the face of the BJP's meteoric rise. Why, then, did caste and class assertions fail to galvanize the poor and the marginal communities while Hindutva forces gained an unprecedented traction?

A short answer to the question is this: while the parties aligned to caste identities promised the oppressed social groups social and political rights for their symbolic recognition and representation, they offered no policy for redistribution of economic assets. On the other hand, the communists treated the poor as collectives constituted principally around economic demands for distribution of agricultural land or subsistence wages in abstraction from the conditions of social injustice or cultural marginality that the poor routinely found themselves in.[4]

The limits of symbolism in caste politics were evident in Narendra Modi's landslide victory in the 2014 national elections, followed by another emphatic win in 2019. Modi, an OBC, tactically changed the narrative of positive discrimination into one of acquiring individual skills for development in conjunction with an invitation to a larger identity: the Hindutva fold of religious nationalism. This attracted the marginal *jatis* from both the OBCs and Dalits – the non-Yadav OBCs (such as Gadariyas, Kushwahas, Telis, and Lodhis) and the non-Jatav Scheduled Castes (SCs) (such as Dhobis, Koris, and Dharikars) – who reckoned that their rising aspirations were suppressed by the forward sections of their own communities for the past quarter century. The micro-foundation of the BJP's social penetration was laid at the expense of the educated and professional leaders in established OBC and Dalit political parties.[5]

These changes are irreversible; a return to the older form of caste mobilization is difficult, if not impossible. The wooing back of the marginal *jatis* under the leadership of dominant caste groups is unlikely for two reasons. First, the promises of expanding the scope of affirmative action through reservation in government jobs or educational placements have reached a dead end with the judiciary restricting the total amount of reservation to 49 per cent. Second, since the early 1990s, the proportion of permanent government employees among non-farm permanent employees has shrunk rather consistently and, of late, stridently (from 23 per cent in 2004–05 to 18 per cent in 2010–12) (Thorat, 2019: 225–26). These limits put a bar on the appeals of parties like the SP or the RJD for job reservations on caste lines. Rather, a large section of these marginal groups now perceives the BJP's promise of induction into the Hindu fold, however cosmetic, as an alternative route to prestige and prosperity. With the help of a large section of pliant media, and its unmatched financial prowess, the rise of the BJP as a popular force among the under castes has been sharp and rapid.

While the foundational ideas of Hindutva remained essentially an upper-caste ideology (Drèze, 2020), the BJP has managed to profit by projecting an aspirational unity of the Hindus which is nothing short of a Bahujan coalition of an alternative kind that makes the locationally dominant sub-castes its 'other' (Yadavs in UP and Bihar, Jats in Haryana, and Marathas in Maharashtra, for example). What potentially began as an identarian antidote to the Hindu majoritarian onslaught in the early 1990s now appears to have run its course. It is thus imperative to imagine a new logic of mobilizing the under castes to build an alternative democratic constituency.[6]

The defeat of the old caste politics is matched by attacks on working-class organizations. Since 2014, in the name of 'labour law reforms', the National Democratic Alliance (NDA) has recommended a slew of changes in employment contracts. Measures like easy hiring and firing, reducing minimum wages, restricting social benefits, removing administrative oversight, and so on were recommended avowedly to attract investments or for 'ease of doing business'.

Rajasthan under the BJP took the lead and changed its labour laws in 2014 to empower employers to shut down factories without government approval. The Government of India's *Economic Survey*, 2018–19, commended such steps as an example for other states to emulate in order to 'foster job creation and capital accumulation' (Ministry of Finance, 2019: 21–22). Several states followed suit. In 2015, the central government proposed to club all 44 labour laws within four codes – on wages, industrial relations, social security and occupational safety, and health and working conditions – ostensibly to simplify labour relations and reduce litigation. The proposal was perceived widely as anti-worker and pro-industry, forcing the government – to the lament of big businesses – to backtrack in the face of opposition from even the Bharatiya Mazdoor Sangh, the BJP's trade-union wing. When the economy had to be shut down in March 2020 due to the pandemic, three BJP-ruled states (Gujarat, Himachal Pradesh, and Madhya Pradesh) spent no time in diluting the Factories Act, 1948, to lengthen daily working hours from 8 to 12, and weekly hours from 48 to 72. UP went far ahead. With the COVID-19 lockdown as a pretext, the state government introduced an ordinance to suspend 'the operation of all labour laws for a period of three years'. Gujarat, of course, was quick to take the cue and introduced a similar Bill applicable to new industrial and manufacturing establishments.[7]

It is evident that those who stood for the solidarity of oppressed castes and those for the unity of working classes failed to protect their respective constituencies. Empirically, there is little surprise that the marginal castes and the economically poor classes significantly overlap on the socio-economic matrix. As the data from the National Election Studies' (NES) 2004 survey conducted by Lokniti, Centre for the Study of Developing Societies (CSDS), New Delhi, covering a large cross-section of respondents at the national level, suggest, castes and classes manifestly converge at the top and the bottom of the hierarchy: the upper-castes were over-represented in white collar jobs, and the lower castes, Dalits, in the manual and menial jobs at the bottom (Vaid, 2012: 395–422). While the upper castes were not entirely cushioned against a downward slide on the class line, Dalits were almost always barred from upward mobility, making India's caste–class convergence – however nuanced it might be – somewhat a picture of continuity rather than profound change (Kumar, Heath, and Heath, 2002: 4091–96). The celebrated 'upsurge' of the marginal castes, defining a turning moment in India's post-Mandal politics (Yadav, 2000: 146–75), it seems, did not alter much the economic base of the caste–class confluence. It probably helped the forward or better-off classes from the lower castes to make an instrumental use of affirmative action for upward mobility, enlarging the material gap between them and the poorer classes within the same caste groups, a gap that Hindutva majoritarian politics decades later exploited to its advantage. Therefore, channels for representation of the marginal castes against oppression, in absence of redistributive policies to lessen class exploitation, run the risk of making the poor and the marginal social groups vulnerable to counter-democratic machinations.

Oppression and Exploitation

To distinguish exploitation and oppression *analytically*, Michael Burawoy and Erik Olin Wright (2002: 471) offer a useful sociological approach. Are Dalits *exploited* by the upper castes or *oppressed* by means of social exclusion? Exploitation, from a Marxian position, is a process by which a society is stratified by (*a*) an unequal protection of legal rights (such as property rights) and powers (juridical, political, or social) over productive resources and (*b*) an ability of those with such rights and powers to appropriate surplus generated by those without. When only the first condition prevails, social divisions are primarily oppressive and when both occur, social inequalities are markedly exploitative. This suggests, for class exploitation, the exploiter and the exploited are not only subjected to an asymmetric relation of power, they are also mutually dependent in organizing production and reproduction. By contrast, when a group with privileged access to resources deprives another group of benefits – as the white settlers did to the native Americans – racial oppression occurs, not class exploitation. However, in the settler colonies of Africa, where the indigenous population was both barred from accessing the resources and made to labour to produce surplus for plantations and farms, class exploitation occurred on racial grounds. This explains why while oppression can cause a genocidal wiping out of the oppressed, exploitation requires that the exploited be protected from extinction. How, within this field of distinction, does one locate caste in India?

Dalits and marginal castes face both caste oppression and economic exploitation, and they mutually reinforce each other. Caste oppression runs through the ritual injunctions that block Dalits and 'backwards' from escaping their designated places for producing social values other than the ones that serve the advanced castes. Even a symbolic breach is treated as defiance of the rigid hierarchy, as encroachment on upper-caste privileges, and put down violently.[8] The three top castes are linked to pedagogic values of intellect, disciplinary values of politics, and material values of the economy, while those below are meant to produce surplus, which can be appropriated by the upper castes. Of course, in practice, these rules are regionally diverse and reasonably diluted – except perhaps endogamy – but such fissures are roundly resented and frequently acted upon by upper castes. Caste stigma and humiliation are umbilically conjoined with extraction of surplus value.[9]

Caste oppression puts up a screen on class exploitation and renders the latter either invisible or legitimate by destiny. It means, if the Marxists were to engage with the working class (and turn the 'class-in-itself' into a 'class-for-itself'), they cannot possibly get any lead unless they *simultaneously* establish their struggle against the social and cultural oppression of castes. In the same vein, the problem of caste oppression can only be resolved by unravelling the tissues of material exploitation that reinforce caste oppression. It requires the adoption of a distributive agenda for material equality along with representational mobilization for recognition and social justice. A transformative agenda to counter both oppression and exploitation requires unravelling what one may call the class effects in culture and the caste effects in economy. We shall return to this after an excursion into the immense intellectual influence of B. R. Ambedkar and Karl Marx in positioning the politics of caste and class in India.

Caste and Class: Conceptual Horizons

Caste, as Ambedkar pointed out, stands for 'graded inequality', internal to the logic of *chaturvarna*, a religiously sanctioned hierarchy that makes Brahmins the greatest beneficiaries of a system but offers relative benefits to other *varna*s along 'an ascending scale of reverence and a descending scale of contempt'. As a result, the monopoly of contempt at the top never faces a united opposition from *varna*s below: each *varna* has a stock of systemic reverence to protect from those below in rank, which perpetuates the oppressive hierarchy (Ambedkar, 2020). This differs radically from the Marxian definition of class hierarchy in which the proletariat as an exploited class is expected to discover its historical role of defying and destroying the exploitative order it is subjected to. That capitalism proved more durable than such theoretical anticipations has been explained by Marxists as the prevalence of 'false consciousness', which allegedly allured sections of the working class to assume that possibilities for upward mobility and graded benefits can be availed within the system. This split the working classes on racial, national, and ethnic lines and, at times, in sectors of industry.[10] Indeed, religion also played a key role in its making, but not centrally as it did for caste. 'Graded inequality', after all, *is* Hinduism.

Ambedkar placed caste in the global contexts in which race and class were taken as commensurate categories of caste. He took pains to 'translate' caste in class and racial terms, focusing on the analogous character of deprivation appended to each. This was important also to base his anti-caste struggle on liberal values such as enlightenment, equality, freedom, and fraternity. In short, caste never stood as 'anthropological exceptionalism' for the anti-caste warriors; rather, they treated the particular experience of caste in consonance with the universal struggle for class and racial justice. However productive such efforts at commensuration – of caste and race and of caste and class – might have been, 'they were unstable and ultimately insufficient due to caste's relationship with Hinduism' (Rao, 2018: 135). Ambedkar himself never stopped drawing attention to the distinctive character of caste, especially in relation to class. In response to the Gandhian view that the caste system had roots in the division of labour, Ambedkar famously remarked that it instead stood for a 'division of *labourers* and not just *labour*' and the caste order spins on a penal system to stall any possible transgression, which the Gandhian attempt to de-stigmatize labour could scarcely undo (Rao, 2018: 141). Nonetheless, Anupama Rao (2018: 126–46) has recently iterated that unlike many nationalists of his time, Ambedkar (and before him Jyotirao Phule) drew inspiration from global revolutionary currents and placed caste within a universalistic project of human emancipation from multiforms of inequality and injustice.

Ambedkar's theory of caste and the Marxist understanding of class both shared a strong egalitarian ethos, a belief in the instrumental capacity of the state to either perish or protect equality. However, they differed in one crucial respect: while the 'Marxist tradition had to note the factual existence of caste as social practice but subsumed it as a relatively minor part of a general class analysis', Ambedkar – by contrast – 'subsumed class into an analysis which asserted the analytical primacy of caste structures' (Kaviraj, 2009: 197). Ambedkar's understanding of the relation between caste and class changed over the years; yet he remained critical of the 'economic reductionism' associated with Marxism, which treated the caste–class dichotomy through the binary of economic base and religious superstructure. For Ambedkar (1979a: 43), religious or moral principles had a primacy in governing collective social lives, and radical politico-economic changes followed – rather than preceded – socio-religious reforms. He treated caste as a cohort of class, especially in his critique of atomistic individualism: 'To say individuals make up society is trivial,' he argued. 'Society is always composed of classes.' Suggesting that caste and class were 'next door neighbours', his invitation was for determining 'what was the class that made itself into a caste' in early Hindu society. 'A Caste is an Enclosed Class,' he concluded (Ambedkar, 1979b: 15). Despite his deep intellection on class in a caste-society, drawn to John Dewey's rejection of violent class struggle and the Fabian faith in gradual transition to socialism, Ambedkar all along maintained his philosophical autonomy vis-à-vis Marxism.

If caste was an enclosed class for Ambedkar, for Marx – writing half a century earlier around roughly the period of Phule – caste appeared as a marker of divisions producing an immobile society that 'has no history at all', and thereby creating grounds for foreign invasion. Marx knew, for sure, that the British were introducing machinery and means of communication to this 'fabulous country' to fulfil their own extractive mission; yet he also had little doubt that modern industry 'will dissolve the hereditary divisions of labour, upon which rests the Indian castes, those decisive impediments to Indian progress and Indian power' (Marx, 2007: 223). So, in holding caste as originally linked to relations of labour, as an impediment to social progress, and as deserving liquidation, Marx was not entirely antithetical to Ambedkar. Where Marx differed, however, was in his early enthusiasm for the imminent dissolution of caste in the wake of economic expansion under colonialism. Even when he revised his initial optimism, it was in recognition of capitalism's *failure* to transform India's village economy.[11] Ambedkar (1979a: 70–71), by contrast, firmly held that the Brahmin intelligentsia, which was among the top beneficiaries of colonial rule, was never to take up the cause of social reforms for annihilation of castes. The more they changed under colonial modernity, he argued, the more they remained the same.

Marx's 'labour theory of caste' and his optimism that economic modernity would sweep aside ritual hierarchy influenced the works of even the most sensitive Marxist scholars who made close and prolonged studies of India's social and cultural history. For instance, Damodar Dharmananda Kosambi (1950: 262), while arguing that the caste system and religion sanctified 'the function of naked violence', also maintained that this was meant to serve not religious function but that of class domination.[12] Religion, for him, effectively 'minimized the need for internal violence, thereby leading all social manifestations of class struggle in India into religio-philosophical channels of expression' (Kosambi, 1950: 263). The equivalence of caste and class appeared complete. 'Caste is class at a primitive level of production,' wrote Kosambi, 'a religious method of forming social consciousness in such a manner that the primary producer is deprived of his surplus with the minimum coercion' (quoted in Roy, 2008: 79). In the end, however, Kosambi's optimism, much like that of Marx noted earlier, was based on a faith in the modernist erasure of caste with the building of railways, factories, and cities: 'Its [the caste system's] supposed unshakeability and inherent strength vanish as soon as new forms of production come in …' (quoted in Roy, 2008: 79).

In sum, subsumption of caste within the texture of industrial modernity continues in the writings of many Marxist scholars even to this day. Similarly, many scholars on Dalits and marginal castes tend to reduce the issue of social justice to an imagined cultural essence, abstracted from the context of class exploitation. To break such parallel circuits of circular reasoning that either subsume 'culture' to 'economy' or vice versa *analytically*, and to make the two engage meaningfully with each other, we need (as mentioned before) to explore caste effects in economy and class effects in culture. We will take a brief detour to understand Ambedkar's complex relationship with Marxism and communism in his time.

Ambedkar and the Communists

There are three different perspectives available in the literature on Ambedkar's relationship with Marxism and Marxist politics. Gail Omvedt suggests that Ambedkar was close to the Marxist tradition in the 1930s, but by the 1940s he increasingly distanced himself to adopt a more eclectic social democratic position. In 1936, Ambedkar described his recently founded Independent Labour Party (ILP) as a worker–peasant party and chose to hoist a red flag. 'The ILP grew and became the only party in India which led struggles against capitalists and landlords along with agitations against caste oppression, calling for a radical opposition to the "brahmin–bourgeois Congress" and seeking to pull in non-brahmans as well as Dalits' (Omvedt, 2011: 49–50). It participated in joint campaigns with the communists in 1938, most notably in anti-landlord stirs (the landlords were mainly Brahmins, with some being upper-caste Marathas) to protect Kunbi and Mahar tenants in the Konkan region. It also joined the communists in a united working-class strike in the textile mills against the 'black bill' of the Indian National Congress (hereafter Congress) government that outlawed industrial action. In his appreciation of Marxism, Ambedkar wrote:

> I have definitely read studiously more books on the Communist philosophy than all the Communist leaders here. However beautiful the Communist philosophy in these books … the test of it has to be given in practice. And if work is done from that perspective, I feel that the labour and the length of time needed to win success in Russia will not be so much needed in India … in regard to the toilers' class struggle, I feel the Communist philosophy is closer to us. (quoted in Omvedt, 2011: 50–51)

However, such an affable approach to the communists depleted eventually as a radical alternative to the Congress under Gandhi failed to take off in the 1930s. The communists moved closer to the nationalist cause against imperialism and softened their class line to characterize the Congress as essentially a united anti-imperialist movement. Once the Soviet Union got involved in the Second World War, the communists adopted a more congenial approach to the British war efforts. Ambedkar, on his part, retreated from his class–caste radicalism and, in 1942, founded the All India Scheduled Castes Federation with a larger spread but a narrower focus on caste. He now joined the government with the aim of gaining maximum concessions from the colonial state, the days of which were numbered.

A second perspective suggests that Ambedkar was generally disinterested in Marxism, though his encounter with communist politics was disjointed yet continuous. 'As a matter of fact,' wrote Teltumbde (2017), 'Ambedkar was never close to a Marxist position and had never accepted Marxist economics. However, in the same breath, it can be certainly said that he was always interested in communism and that the interest never waned.' For this view, the anti-communist rhetoric that Ambedkar employed in the 1940s had to do not so much with his abhorrence of communism as a philosophy as with his anxiety to protect his own constituency on the ground from a possible communist influence. So, Ambedkar's anti-communist rhetoric cannot be read in abstraction from its 'political context' – of attacks on him by the communists for 'fragmenting their constituency' and, by equal measure, Ambedkar's concern about 'the potential attraction of communism to Dalits'. 'After all', as the argument goes, 'their constituencies hopelessly overlapped each other' (Teltumbde, 2017).

In a later piece, Teltumbde offers a more nuanced analysis than citing competitive politics as a major determinant in conditioning Ambedkar's mind. In *Republic of Caste*, he tracks the long lineage of Marx's somewhat generic and broad-brush understanding of caste which 'did not constitute the core concern' for his social and economic analyses (Teltumbde, 2018). Drawing references to 'caste' in Marx right from *German Ideology* (1846) through *Poverty of Philosophy* (1847), *A Contribution to the Critique of Political Economy* (1859), the *New York Tribune* essays (1853), and finally *Capital* (1867), Teltumbde establishes that Marx's 'insightful description of the caste system is impressive and anticipates Ambedkar's disdain for it; it also indicates that caste was not extraneous to the frame of historical materialism' (Teltumbde, 2018: 106). Rather, for Marx, caste was a special case of class division of labour ingrained in an idyllic and utterly regressive 'self-sufficient' village community as a mode of surplus extraction. On this Ambedkar did not have any quarrel; rather, he extensively used the idiom of 'class' to depict caste in his writings in line with 'his desire to bring all the untouchable castes together as Depressed Classes of Dalits' (Teltumbde, 2018: 101). Where Ambedkar differed with Marx, and radically so, was in his refusal to treat class as a universal agent for social revolution: 'to Ambedkar it [class] was a culture-specific interest group that could accomplish its goal by forcing through a series of changes in its situation' (Teltumbde, 2018: 101). Influenced by the Fabians and the pragmatist philosopher Dewey, Ambedkar's social change was both enlightened and gradual with the intelligentsia as its leading force working its way through a liberal institutional order. 'Ambedkar did not find anything in Marx that could be of help to him in dealing with the problem of caste' (Teltumbde, 2018: 103).

Apart from being 'interested in' or 'indifferent to' Marxism, Ambedkar at times was also quite scornful of the Brahminic pedigree of the Indian communists and their mechanical rendition of the philosophy. While the *telos* of communism with its egalitarian promises was indeed attractive, he was disapproving of the invocation of violence, 'the dictatorship of the proletariat', and the 'mythification' of the 'base–superstructure' metaphor. He was condescending to the communist leadership whose upper-caste orientation, he reckoned, failed to make them realize the 'caste question' in class struggles. In his interviews to the American journalist Selig Harrison in 1953, Ambedkar stated:

> The Communist Party was originally in the hands of some brahmin boys – Dange and others. They have been trying to win over the [M]aratha community and the Scheduled Castes. But they have made no headway in Maharashtra. Why? Because they are mostly a bunch of brahmin boys. The Russians made a great mistake to entrust the Communist movement in India to them. Either the Russians didn't want communism in India – they wanted only drummer boys – or they didn't understand. (quoted in Teltumbde, 2018: 113–14)

Economy of Caste

A major constraint in reading caste and class together, as we noted earlier, is the essentialist evocation of caste as a sociocultural or political category, and of class as primarily economic in character. What if one attempts to trace the caste effects in economy and the class effects in the social and cultural realms of experience? To reframe caste–class relations, to understand how caste is shaped in the economic and class in the cultural, a radical rethinking of the existing caste and class politics is necessary.

A recent essay has brought together a growing literature that approaches caste identity in 'relation to modern economy – a domain in which caste identity and hierarchy are often understood to be absent or eroded by market processes' (Moss, 2020: 1226). It is rather surprising, we are told, that while the transformative potential of caste in modern India is often viewed both culturally, as ritual practices, or politically, as a category for representation, 'less attention has been paid to the caste effects in the economy' (Moss, 2020: 1225). Indeed, such decoupling of caste from the economy is not accidental. '[T]he modern market economy is a field in which the pervasive effects of caste are rendered invisible in ways that may serve selected interests by concealing processes of advantage and discrimination' (Moss, 2020: 1227).

One traces several key moments in the decoupling of caste from economic processes in modern India, some of which David Moss himself refers to. At the beginning of India's economic planning, caste was treated as a premodern relic, of little value in building the nation or explaining poverty and inequality. Launching the first Five-Year Plan, the then home minister fondly hoped that the new measures would lead to 'the establishment of our society on the socialist pattern' in which 'social and other distinctions will disappear' (Jaffrelot, 2006: 178–79). In 1953, the Kaka Kalelkar Commission was asked to prepare a list of the 'Backward Classes' – that is, *classes* other than the SCs and the Scheduled Tribes (STs) which were educationally and socially backward. It was only after a gap of eight decades that in 2011 a Socio Economic and *Caste* Census was conducted in the face of bureaucratic pushback at the highest level (its data are yet to be made fully public). As this is being written, a demand to conduct a caste census is gathering momentum in civil society, primarily to expose the essentially caste character of economic deprivation in the country.[13]

Moss thinks that even Marxist historians have failed to escape the culturalist rendition of caste. Despite his rejection of Dumont's premise (that the reality of caste could only be known at the ideological or intellectual level and was not to be grasped at the level of politics or economics) and bringing much evidence that solidly placed the history of caste on an economic base, Irfan Habib concluded 'that the modern economy ... has so shaken the traditional hereditary division of labour that caste survives only in its religious and personal aspects that Dumont is criticised for privileging' (Moss, 2020: 1230). This reflects rather blatantly the self-definition of the 'Indian modern', the post-colonial elite, which 'inscribed itself silently' as upper-caste and thus rendered the lower castes not only as the 'other' but also as non-modern. The history of Indian nationalism, from the elite modern standpoint, largely remained a uniform history of contesting the colonial state and the colonial capital. The 'internal colonialism' of caste oppression was alien to such schema. Dalit scholars, on the other hand, inspired by Ambedkar, narrated a history that resisted 'the submersion of caste into the analysis of class as much as into colonialism' (Moss, 2020: 1233). Paradoxically, while the upper-caste elite invisibilized ascriptive identities in their story of economic extraction, Dalit scholars, on their part, tended to make the economic disappear in their story of social discrimination by disavowing class. In both versions, caste remained a de-economized category.

Even the policy of affirmative action, as we noted earlier, failed to address the issues of economic redistribution. In absence of any serious challenge to the prevailing systemic inequality, or the legal structure that protects India's highly polarized economy, the policy of 'quota', as it is known, remained a mere managerial technique that the state deployed for 'caste abatement' (Jayal, 2015: 124). The onset of neoliberal reforms seemingly changed it all. It put the market at the centre, promising a new horizon for Dalit emancipation, sans the state. If Dalits and marginal castes were to emerge as entrepreneurs in the globalized market, they were expected to undermine the caste order and get treatment at par with the upper castes. Chandra Bhan Prasad, an ideologue of 'Dalit capitalism', invoked capital to fight caste. '[C]aste and capitalism cannot coexist,' he asserted. 'Dalit capitalism will soon turn the caste order into a relic of sorts' because the 'market is a great leveller'. 'Dalits can't buy social markers', but they can buy 'material markers', and one day 'Dalits will be served by non-Dalits, purely for material gain'.[14] While appearing to offer an economic theory of caste, what 'Dalit capitalism' did was to treat the market as an abstraction, a great level playing field. A host of scholars refuted this view. They cited the market's ideological 'embeddedness' (Prakash, 2018: 55), its 'low intensity spectacles' of selective Dalit induction (Guru, 2012: 41–49), its patently 'intercaste restrictions' (Thorat, 2004: 2560), or its 'quasi-legal or illegal networks' (Harriss-White and Prakash, 2010). By disembedding the market from the social, Dalit capitalism ended up invoking the economic not as a potent site for progressive transformation but as an inert abstraction.

Culture of Class

To understand how belonging to a marginal caste – or being Dalit–Bahujan – can play a vital part in the *making* of the Indian working class, one may draw upon an essay by Dipesh Chakrabarty (2013: 207–12)[15] written as a tribute to the great historian E. P. Thompson's magnum opus, *The Making of the English Working Class*. Here, Chakrabarty revisits the idea of how the working class, which shares a class experience determined by relations of production, can simultaneously be *English* in Thompson's 'schema … for historical and cultural differences' (Chakrabarty, 2013: 211). In other words, Chakrabarty explores the way Thompson negotiates myriad ambiguities strewn in the path of the *making* of the working class as it experiences capitalism as a universal mode of production, but does so from a location in culture which differs in one country, in one context, from another. Although the British historian's reliance on a 'stadial history' (the idea that the history of English industrialization foreshadows in some way industrial histories in the non-Western world) and his fond hopes in the early 1960s in the Third World's potentials for establishing socialism turned eventually into 'lost causes', Thompson's critical and creative treatment of *culture* in the making of working-class consciousness remained, a far cry from economic determinism or structural sociology in the Marxian tradition.[16]

Thompson wrote in an intense passage:

> The making of the working class is a fact of political and cultural, as much as of economic, history. It was not the spontaneous generation of the factory system. Nor should we think of an external force – the 'industrial revolution' – working upon some nondescript undifferentiated raw material of humanity and turning it out at the other end as 'fresh race of beings'. The ... Industrial Revolution [was] imposed, not upon a raw material, but upon the free-born Englishman – and the free-born Englishman as Paine had left him or as the Methodist had moulded him. The factory hand or stockinger was also the inheritor of Bunyan, of remembered village rights, of notions of equality before the law, of craft traditions ... The working class made itself as much it was made. (Quoted in Chakrabarty, 2013: 207)

One pauses and wonders, what if a class is made not as the 'free-born Englishman' inspired by citizen Paine's radical republicanism in the closing years of the eighteenth century, but as one bonded and bounded by structures of ignominy sanctioned by religious laws? How does *that* working class make itself or get made, culturally?

To put it in a formulaic fashion, three propositions implicit in the passage are (*a*) the *process* of making a class, (*b*) *economy* as the foundation of class experience, and (*c*) *cultural tradition* as the enabler of class consciousness. 'I am convinced,' wrote Thompson, 'that we cannot understand class unless we see it as a social and cultural formation, arising from processes which can only be studied as they work themselves out over a considerable historical period.' While class experience is defined largely in economic terms, class consciousness is different. It is a matter of handling the universal raw materials of class experience 'in cultural terms: embodied in traditions, value-systems, and institutional forms' that vary from one part of the world to another (Chakrabarty, 2013: 209–10). Thompson continues:

> If the experience appears as determined, class-consciousness does not. We can see a logic in the responses of similar occupational groups undergoing similar experiences, but we cannot predicate any law. Consciousness of class arises in the same way in different times and places, but never in just the same way. (Chakrabarty, 2013: 209)

'It was precisely in the assumed gap between class-experience and class-consciousness,' Chakrabarty (2013: 211) tells us, 'that Thompson made room for "culture" (such as the tradition of the "free-born Englishman") that processed class-experience in different ways in different historical spaces. Hence his mention of a similar logic, but no law, of the "same way" but "not just the same way", and so on.' Based on this, Chakrabarty asked in his own work as part of the Subaltern Studies Collective: 'What would happen in the histories of men and women who filled the ranks of the industrial working classes in a country like India but whose cultural heritage was significantly different from that of their counterparts in England?' (Chakrabarty, 2013: 207).

One may extend Chakrabarty's question on national differences and ask how variations in the cultural location of caste matter in the making of the Indian working class. Do caste divisions in our society defeat the universality of class experience *a la* Thompson and deny it a relative uniformity? How can an upper-caste, working-class experience be equivalent to the Dalit working-class experience? Even if 'equality before law' or 'the free-born Englishman' does not define the cultural trait of the Dalit, lower-caste narratives – as sociologist Dipankar Gupta shows – carry an implicit idea of caste inversion. 'All these stories of various hues, pedigree and provenance point to the central fact: that no caste thinks that it is inferior to any other; in fact, they presume a certain superiority in most cases' (Gupta, 2005: 146). In any case, class consciousness – even if one follows Thompson's schema – cannot be dissociated from cultural traditions which, for the Dalit and the Bahujan, are made of the democratic desire to expand in the economy and polity for representation and equality. Therefore, caste in class matters *both* at the levels of experience and consciousness, in the making of working-class solidarity against an oppressive social system *as well as* an exploitative economy. Any emancipatory project for the working class in India can ignore the caste–ethnic dimensions at its own peril. This makes the tracing of caste in class, and simultaneous (not sequential) engagement with the issues of class in caste, so important for the parties on the left if they aspire to build a counter-hegemonic collective.

Conclusion

To engender a deeply transformative politics, Marxist or Dalit activists need to discover appropriate languages and strategies to simultaneously engage with equality–recognition, distribution–representation, deprivation–humiliation, and exploitation–oppression. Small steps in the direction are rare but not absent. Kancha Ilaiah Shepherd has recently recorded such initiatives in Telangana. Reporting on the Telangana Mass and Social Organisations (T-MASS), formed in July 2017 as a 'Bahujan Left Front', Shepherd (2018b) writes: '[U]nder its broad umbrella many

Ambedkarist, Phuleite, communist, humanist, women organizations are working with a broad philosophical framework of Mahatma Phule, Ambedkar and Karl Marx. Its banners always carry the portraits of these thinkers and perhaps it should add Savitribai Phule's portrait too.' Another such experiment is the Satyashodhak Communist Party, founded by Sharad Patil, whose lifelong endeavour has been to explore caste society through Marx and Phule.[17]

Acknowledging that the early Indian communists suffered from 'streaks of [the] economic reductionist approach to Marxism' which prevented them from recognizing Ambedkar's 'radicalism', the Communist Party of India (Marxist–Leninist) (CPI-ML) states that the party works 'for the accentuation of class differentiation among various castes'. It further highlights the important task of annihilating caste because that 'facilitates class formation, accentuates class polarization and makes class struggle more open, broad and direct, and brings out the class in a purer form' (CPI-ML, 2001). India's largest parliamentary communist party, the CPI-M, has recently adopted a resolution on the plight of the Dalits in its 22nd Congress (April 2018) (CPI-M, 2018: 33–34). As Shepherd (2018a), an attendee, points out: 'For the first time in the communist movement (including the CPI and other small parties and groups), a communist party leader – the CPM general secretary … said the new experiment of building an alliance involving the communists and the Ambedkarites called the Bahujan Left Front (BLF) is the politics of the future.'

David Harvey (2020), in a recent lecture, remarked: 'Somebody said to me … if you start a movement with race and class together, you are asking for trouble. Malcolm X and others started to talk about class and race … As soon as class and race get together, it's a dynamite!' A 'unified emancipatory struggle', as Teltumbde had put it, bringing class and caste together may have immense potentials to strike at the root of authoritarian populism and explode its foundation.

Notes

1. For a recent narrative, see Priya Chacko (2018). In this chapter, I am keeping myself confined to northern Indian politics alone. Caste and class politics is of a significantly different character in the south of the Vindhyas in setting the sequence for social reforms and political empowerment, civic engagement, and electoral mobilization. For a recent work on caste politics in southern India, see Hugo Gorringe (2017). For a comparison between left politics in Kerala and West Bengal, see Manali Desai (2001).

2. Three representative studies of this period are Thomas Blom Hansen (1999), Christophe Jaffrelot (2003), and Rob Jenkins (2000).

3. Communists in West Bengal failed to effectively include the informal working class in its organized politics and had to pay a heavy price for this. See Rina Agarwala (2013).

4. For a review of symbolic politics in UP, see Chapter 4 in this volume. For the left's neglect of caste issues in West Bengal, see the works of Uday Chandra, Geir Heierstad, and Kenneth Bo Nielsen (2016) and Dwaipayan Bhattacharyya (2016).

5. For the post-Mandal scenario, see Christophe Jaffrelot (2020).

6. This argument needs to be qualified on the following grounds. While caste equations indeed have altered, that alone does not explain the tectonic shifts in the northern Indian states of UP and Bihar. The BJP's communication with the electorate and the effects of its policies demand closer scrutiny for explaining the dramatic expansion of the party's social base. See, for instance, Gilles Verniers (2019a, 2019b).

7. These developments were reported extensively, especially on digital platforms. See Arvind Narrain, Maitreyi Krishnan, and Clifton D. Rosario (2020), Arundhati Roy (2020), and Ramapriya Gopalakrishnan (2020).

8. The National Crime Records Bureau (NCRB) reported that India registered a 6 per cent annual increase in atrocities against Dalits in 2019. Of these, 84 per cent crimes were committed in just nine states, home to 54 per cent of the Dalit population. UP topped the chart of atrocities in absolute numbers. More alarmingly, the conviction rate in offences under the Scheduled Castes and Scheduled Tribes (Prevention of Atrocities) Act, 1989, was just 32 per cent nationally, and the pendency rate of cases was a whopping 94 per cent (*Times of India*, 2020).

9. To illustrate this, the informal working class in India, by and large, is treated as Dalit. In most upper-caste middle-class families (including liberal, enlightened, so-called 'woke' families), domestic workers are not allowed to use the household artefacts or utensils. This is also true of visitors to the household for performing specific duties (such as driver, carpenter, plumber, delivery man, or any gig worker). Being a *shramik*, or belonging to the working class, carries no pride. Even amongst communist parties, one rarely finds actual working-class members in leadership or policy-making bodies. Being a *chaiwallah* (tea seller) can become a matter of revelation only after one occupies the high table of power and prestige by overcoming the status of a worker. Service, in conditions of intense informality and hyper social hierarchy, turns into servitude; it is more of an institution than an occupation and can scarcely be understood as wage work in the classical forms of capitalist reproduction (Ray and Qayum, 2009: 2). Also see Baby Halder (2006) and Samita Sen and Nilanjana Sengupta (2016).

10. As is well known, 'false consciousness' as a category to explain the reproduction of capitalism and weakness of working-class solidarity was not particularly helpful

in the non-European context. In its bare minimum it resembled the ideological structure of 'graded inequality' as was elaborated from Friedrich Engels' use of the term by György Lukács (1971: 64) and Karl Mannheim (1979 [1936]: 84–87). It was in Antonio Gramsci's work (1992 [1971]: 187) that a more useful idea of 'common sense' opened up a field for the contest between ruling-class hegemony and the counter-hegemonic subaltern forces.

11. Marx (1991: 922) revised his optimism in his *Capital*, vol. 3, where he indicated the continuity of a 'genuine natural economy' in Indian village communities where modern industry was yet to decouple agriculture from manufacturing.

12. Kosambi (1950: 262), as is well known, contested Marx's reading of 'Asiatic' societies as immobile and rejected the Stalinist straitjacketing of Indian history within the modular stages of slavery–feudalism–capitalism. India, he pointed out, escaped slavery with the bondage of its caste system, which he suggested can be interpreted by creatively adopting Marx's methods rather than by remaining mechanically aligned to his classifications.

13. 'The sentimental excesses of poverty as a political metaphor served to mask the corrosive caste dimension of our inequalities. A caste census threatens to push this dimension into the open, making it impossible for the political class to continue to hide behind euphemism and circumvention' (Deshpande, 2021). Also see Prasenjit Bose (2021).

14. Quoted in Aseem Prakash (2018: 51–56, 53), taken from S. Anand (2016).

15. All quotations from Thompson are from this essay by Chakrabarty. The page marks from the article are shown in parentheses in the main text.

16. Thompson famously contrasted his Marxism with that of the French 'structuralist' Louis Althusser, whose epistemology, he argued, 'has no category (or way of handling) "experience" (or social being's impingement upon social consciousness)'. See Thompson (1995: 5–6).

17. One of Patil's early essays seeks to theorize caste as class in pre-colonial India (Patil, 1979: 287–96).

Bibliography

Agarwala, R. 2013. *Informal Labour, Formal Politics, and Dignified Discontent in India*. Cambridge: Cambridge University Press.

Ambedkar, B. R. 1979a. 'Annihilation of Caste'. In *Dr Babasaheb Ambedkar: Writings and Speeches*, vol. 1, 23–96. Mumbai: Education Department, Government of Maharashtra.

———. 1979b. 'Castes in India'. In *Dr Babasaheb Ambedkar: Writings and Speeches*, vol. 1, 5–22. Mumbai: Education Department, Government of Maharashtra.

———. 2020. 'Who Were the Shudras?'. In *Dr Babasaheb Ambedkar: Writings and Speeches*, vol. 7. New Delhi: Dr Ambedkar Foundation.

Anand, S. 2016. 'Capitalism Will Turn Caste Order into a Relic' (Interview with Chandra Bhan Prasad). *Outlook*, 6 April.

Bhattacharyya, D. 2016. *Government as Practice: Democratic Left in a Transforming India*. New Delhi: Cambridge University Press.

Bose, P. 2021. 'No Excuses Please, India Awaits a Full Caste Headcount'. *The Hindu*, 20 October.

Burawoy, M., and E. O. Wright. 2002. 'Sociological Marxism'. In *Handbook of Sociological Theory*, edited by J. H. Turner, 459–86. New York: Kluwer Academic and Plenum Publishers.

Chacko, P. 2018. 'The Right Turn in India: Authoritarianism, Populism and Neoliberalisation'. *Journal of Contemporary Asia* 48(4): 541–65.

Chakrabarty, D. 2013. 'The Lost Causes of E. P. Thompson'. *Labour: Journal of Canadian Labour Studies* 72 (Fall): 207–12.

Chandra, U., G. Heierstad, and K. B. Nielsen. 2016. *The Politics of Caste in West Bengal*. London: Routledge.

Communist Party of India (Marxist) (CPI-M). 2018. 'Dalits: Worsening Plight'. Political Resolution Adopted by the 22nd Congress of the CPI-M, Hyderabad, 18–22 April.

Communist Party of India (Marxist–Leninist) (CPI-ML). 2001. 'Caste, Class and Dalit Question'. Paper presented at Central Party School of CPI(ML), 28–30 November, Bhuvaneshwar. http://www.archive.cpiml.org/liberation/year_2002/april/article%20caste%20and%20class.htm. Accessed on 17 March 2021.

Desai, M. 2001. 'Party Formation, Political Power, and the Capacity for Reform: Comparing Left Parties in Kerala and West Bengal, India'. *Social Forces* 80(1): 37–60.

Deshpande, S. 2021. 'Who's Afraid of a Caste Census?'. *Indian Express*, 13 August.

Drèze, J. 2020. 'The Revolt of the Upper Castes'. *India Forum*, 20 February. https://www.theindiaforum.in/article/revolt-upper-castes. Accessed on 17 March 2021.

Economic Survey 2018–19, Volume 1, 'Shifting Gears: Private Investment as the Key Driver of Growth, Jobs, Exports, and Demand'. https://www.indiabudget.gov.in/budget2019-20/economicsurvey/doc/vol1chapter/echap01_vol1.pdf. Accessed on 17 March 2021.

Gopalakrishnan, R. 2020. 'Changes in Labour Laws Will Turn the Clock Back by over a Century'. *The Wire*, 20 May. https://thewire.in/labour/labour-laws-changes-turning-clock-back. Accessed on 17 March 2021.

Gorringe, H. 2017. *Panthers in Parliament: Dalits, Caste, and Political Power in South India*. New Delhi: Oxford University Press.

Gramsci, A. 1992 (1971). *Selections from Prison Notebooks*, translated by Q. Hoare and G. N. Smith. New York: International Publishers.

Gupta, D. 2005. 'Caste Today: The Relevance of a Phenomenological Approach'. *India International Centre Quarterly* 32(1): 138–53.

Guru, G. 2012. 'Rise of the "Dalit Millionaire": A Low Intensity Spectacle'. *Economic and Political Weekly* 47(50): 41–49.

Halder, B. 2006. *A Life Less Ordinary: A Memoir*. New Delhi: Zubaan Books.

Hansen, T. B. 1999. *The Saffron Wave: Democracy and Hindu Nationalism in Modern India*. Princeton: Princeton University Press.

Harriss-White, B., and A. Prakash. 2010. 'Social Discrimination in India: A Case for Economic Citizenship'. OIWPS VIII, Oxfam India Working Paper Series, September Oxfam India, New Delhi.

Harvey, D. 2020. 'Anti-Capitalist Chronicle: Race and Class'. YouTube video, 25 June. https://www.youtube.com/watch?v=Na7LQDSVNIs. Accessed on 17 March 2021.

Jaffrelot, C. 2003. *India's Silent Revolution: The Rise of the Lower Castes in Northern India*. New York: Columbia University Press.

———. 2006. 'The Impact of Affirmative Action in India: More Political Than Socioeconomic'. *India Review* 5(2): 173–89.

———. 2020. 'Mandal Moment: 30 Years On'. *Indian Express*, 22 August.

Jayal, N. G. 2015. 'Affirmative Action in India: Before and After the Neoliberal Turn'. *Cultural Dynamics* 27(1): 117–33.

Jenkins, R. 2000. *Democratic Politics and Economic Reforms in India*. Cambridge: Cambridge University Press.

Kaviraj, S. 2009. 'Marxism in Translation: Critical Reflections on Indian Radical Thought'. In *Political Judgement: Essays for John Dunn*, edited by R. Bourke and R. Guess, 172–200. Cambridge: Cambridge University Press.

Kosambi, D. D. 1950. 'On a Marxist Approach to Indian Chronology'. *Annals of the Bhandarkar Oriental Research Institute* 31(1–4): 258–66.

Kumar, S., A. Heath, and O. Heath. 2002. 'Changing Patterns of Social Mobility: Some Trends Over Time'. *Economic and Political Weekly* 37(40): 4091–96.

Kumar, V. 2016. 'Caste, Contemporaneity, and Assertion'. *Economic and Political Weekly* 51(50): 84–86.

Lukács, G. 1971. *History and Class Consciousness: Studies in Marxist Dialectics*, translated by R. Livingstone. Cambridge, MA: MIT Press.

Mannheim, K. 1979 (1936). *Ideology and Utopia: An Introduction to the Sociology of Knowledge*. London: Routledge and Kegan Paul.

Marx, K. 1991. *Capital: Critique of Political Economy*, vol. 3, translated by D. Fernbach. London: Penguin Books and New Left Review.

———. 2007. 'The Future Results of British Rule in India: August 8, 1853'. In *Dispatches for the New York Tribune: Selected Journalism of Karl Marx*, with foreword by F. Wheen and introduction by J. Ledbetter, 219–24. London: Penguin Books.

Ministry of Finance. 2019. *Economic Survey 2018–19*, vol. 1. New Delhi: Ministry of Finance, Government of India.

Moss, D. 2020. 'The Modernity of Caste and the Market Economy'. *Modern Asian Studies* 54(4): 1225–71.

Narrain, A., M. Krishnan, and C. D. Rozario. 2020. 'Covid-19 Lockdown: Uttar Pradesh and Madhya Pradesh Watering Down Labour Laws Is a Body Blow to the Working Class'. *Firstpost*, 11 May.

Omvedt, G. 2011. *Understanding Caste: From Buddha to Ambedkar and Beyond*. New Delhi: Orient Blackswan.

Pai, S. 2002. *Dalit Assertion and the Unfinished Democratic Revolution: The Bahujan Samaj Party in Uttar Pradesh*. New Delhi: SAGE Publications.

Patil, S. 1979. 'Dialectic of Caste and Class Conflicts'. *Economic and Political Weekly* 14(7–8): 287–96.

Prakash, A. 2018. 'Dalit Capital and Markets: A Case of Unfavourable Inclusion'. *Journal of Social Inclusion Studies* 4(1): 51–61.

Rao, A. 2018. 'Deprovincializing Anticaste Thought: A Genealogy of Ambedkar's Dalit'. In *The Postcolonial Contemporary: Political Imaginaries for the Global Present*, edited by J. K. Watson and G. Wilder, 126–46. New York: Fordham University Press.

Ray, R., and S. Qayum. 2009. *Cultures of Servitude: Modernity, Domesticity and Class in India*. Redwood City, CA: Stanford University Press.

Roy, A. 2020. 'Enough of Cheap Theatrics. We Need Brains. We Need Heart. We Need Accountability' (Book Excerpt). *Scroll.in*, 18 November. https://scroll.in/article/961480/arundhati-roy-enough-of-the-cheap-theatrics-we-need-brains-we-need-heart-we-need-accountability. Accessed on 17 March 2021.

Roy, K. K. 2008. 'Kosambi and Questions of Caste'. *Economic and Political Weekly* 43(30): 78–84.

Sen, S., and N. Sengupta. 2016. *Domestic Days: Women, Work and Politics in Contemporary Kolkata*. New Delhi: Oxford University Press.

Shepherd, K. I. 2018a. 'Notes from the CPM Congress'. 25 April. http://www.kanchailaiah.com/2018/04/25/notes-from-the-cpm-congress/. Accessed on 17 March 2021.

———. 2018b. 'T-MASS: A New Experiment in Ambedkarite–Marxist Alliance'. 1 February. http://www.kanchailaiah.com/2018/02/01/t-mass-a-new-experiment-in-ambedkarite-marxist-alliance/. Accessed on 17 March 2021.

———. 2019. *Buffalo Nationalism: A Critique of Spiritual Fascism*. New Delhi: SAGE Publications.

Teltumbde, A. 2017. 'Introduction'. In *B. R. Ambedkar, India and Communism*. New Delhi: Leftword. E-book.

———. 2018. *Republic of Caste: Thinking Equality in the Time of Neoliberal Hindutva*. New Delhi: Navayana.

Thompson, E. P. 1995. *Poverty of Philosophy*. London: Merlin Press.

Thorat, S. 2004. 'On Reservation Policy for Private Sector'. *Economic and Political Weekly* 39(25): 2560–63.

———. 2019. 'Dalits in Post-2014 India: Between Promise and Action'. In *Majoritarian State: How Hindu Nationalism is Changing India*, edited by A. P. Chatterji, T. B. Hansen, and C. Jaffrelot, 217–36. New York: Oxford University Press.

Times of India. 2020. 'Nine States Have 54% of Dalits, See 84% of Crime against SCs'. 2 October. https://timesofindia.indiatimes.com/india/nine-states-have-54-of-dalits-see-84-of-crime-against-scs/articleshow/78439021.cms. Accessed on 17 March 2021.

Vaid, D. 2012. 'Caste–Class Association in India: An Empirical Analysis'. *Asian Survey* 52(2) (March–April): 395–422.

Verniers, G. 2019a. 'Breaking Down the Uttar Pradesh Verdict: In Biggest Bout, Knockout'. *Indian Express*, 28 May.

———. 2019b. 'How UP Was Conquered'. *Indian Express*, 25 May.

Yadav, Y. 2000. 'Understanding the Second Democratic Upsurge: Trends of Bahujan Participation'. In *Transforming India: Social and Political Dynamics of Democracy*, edited by F. Frankel, 146–75. New York: Oxford University Press.

13

Towards Radical Democracy

The Dalit–Bahujan Claim for Political Power

Harish S. Wankhede

> We do not want a little place in the brahmin alley. We want to rule the whole country. We are not looking at persons but at a system. Change of heart, liberal education, etc. will not end our state of exploitation. When we gather a revolutionary mass, rouse the people, out of the struggle of this giant mass will come the tidal wave of revolutions.
>
> —*Dalit Panthers' Manifesto* (1973)

Liberal Democracy and Dalits

Democracy's relationship with marginalized communities is often seen as a benevolent gesture of modernity, by which the disadvantaged communities that were hovering outside the purview of power can now be accommodated and represented in the new regime (Phillips, 1990). The modern nation builders of India acknowledged that the historically marginalized communities must have proportionate representation in the new institutions of power, and, reasonably, the erstwhile untouchables and Adivasis are identified as the new shareholders, bargainers, or participants in the nation-making process. It was recognized that accommodation and representation of the lower strata in mainstream civil and political life is crucial for India's nascent democracy. Heralding the objectives of social justice, the state became the prime force for empowerment and emancipation of marginalized communities, especially the ex-untouchable castes. Through various laws and policy mechanisms (like the reservation policy for the Scheduled Castes [SCs] and Scheduled Tribes [STs]), it was assumed that the empowerment of Dalits would soon be achieved.

In post-independence India, these communities welcomed the new constitutional state with the hope that due to their significant numbers, they may have a substantive share in power and would thus influence or determine the nature of state functioning. In this chapter, I have argued that though the politics of social justice has remained one of the major tools to imagine an empowered position for Dalits in the modern state, it is their quest to become the political ruling class that has radically emancipated them from their depressed social location. In the normal social science discourse, the Dalit movement is highlighted as a dynamic force that aspired to democratize modern institutions by ensuring sizeable participation of socially marginalized groups. However, its 'political' counterpart has not necessarily endorsed such a passive statist position; instead it visualizes that Dalit advancement in electoral battles will radically transform the 'social elite centric' function of power, thus laying the groundwork for a substantive form of democracy.

Any discussion on representation often addresses marginalized communities as a mere filler, patch, or token in the discourse of power, allowing the conventional authority (mainly social elites) to retain and hegemonize power in various institutions of the state. It prevents marginalized communities from claiming centrality in the discourse of power. In contrast, Dalit democratic aspirations are not merely about communitarian representation, institutional accommodation, or becoming symbolic subjects of policy documents alone. Instead, they aspire that Dalits shall represent the general idea of the nation and lead the state towards democratic socialism. The Dalit–Bahujan political agency aims to radicalize the current norms of liberal democracy.

For Dalits, democracy is the possibility of revolutionary transformation through republican–constitutional means. In one of his presentations at the University of Delhi, Gopal Guru had suggested that the Ashok Chakra on India's national flag metaphorically represents that phenomenon.[1] The spokes of the wheel are the representation of various communities that revolve cordially, allowing each community to take the top position once during its motion–thus periodically distributing power amongst all the stakeholders fairly. Further, socialism is an additional virtue that heralds the state as an ethical mechanism promising welfare of the worst-off social groups. It means an organic collaboration between poor and marginalized people for economic empowerment and social emancipation.

Democracy signifies the possibility that 'anybody' can rise to the pinnacle of power. It offers the chance to even the worst-off communities to become powerholders or the legitimate authority in the state. Dalits wish to avail this democratic possibility by representing the 'others' without prejudices and discomfort. The Dalit parties are not formed to remain passive subjects of social justice policies, but to elevate their stature as equal upholders and bearers of political power and, consequentially, to establish democratic socialism. Democracy therefore is not only an arrangement between the dominant political elites (the social elites), power brokers (the middle classes and the dominant castes), and token shareholders (Dalits, Adivasis, and Muslims) to run the state machinery.

Instead, democratic processes must ensure that high echelons of powers or the elite authority or conventional throne-grabbers can periodically be replaced by new people, especially from the worst-off social groups.

Dalit politics is an aspirational value that challenges the parental gaze of the nationalist parties over the lower castes and proposes that Dalit–Bahujan parties can provide substantive leadership to them. To secure social and political justice, strong electoral advancement of the Dalit–Bahujan masses becomes imperative. Rather than allowing the social elites to represent and rule the general masses perpetually, the Dalit–Bahujan political agenda proposes that the traditional elites shall have limited access to power. In order to secure the general welfare of the masses, the social order, the state institutions, and the market should perform under Dalit–Bahujan ideological guidance.

To fulfil such an agenda, the politics of socially marginalized people has introduced nuanced collective nomenclatures, showcasing their political ambitions. In this context, the chapter examines the making and trajectories of three political identities – namely, Dalit, Bahujan, and now Vanchit. Though these identities emerged in three different historical periods, they are bonded with a desire of elevating the socially marginalized communities as the leading claimants of state power.

Ambedkar and the Quest for Political Power

Babasaheb Ambedkar noted that the hierarchical cleavage between the social elites and marginalized groups does not allow them to form a fraternal association. He approached the colonial state and the new generation of nationalist elites to make them aware of precarious class conditions and social oppression that untouchables faced in their everyday lives. He hoped that the upcoming industrial development, democratic institutions, and republican values would form the basic structure for the liberation of untouchables from the terrible Brahminical feudal order. He hoped that with radical social reforms, social designations based on graded hierarchies would cease over time, making the modern public sphere more accommodative of marginalized communities.

From 1919 onwards, Ambedkar started demanding that untouchables should be treated as an integral part of political deliberations and the colonial state should grant them special rights in the political, economic, and educational fields. Ambedkar wanted to liberate the socially depressed classes from their assigned location of subjugation and oppression. He argued that the deprivation of untouchables might be reduced if the state promises them better schooling facilities, enacts laws to end social discrimination, and allows them to take positions of power in modern institutions. He advocated that the state must assure the depressed classes special representation in legislative bodies through separate communal representation. This democratic assertion is often belittled as a narrow political act and is used to look down upon Ambedkar as a merely sectarian leader.

Ambedkar accused the nationalist parties (especially the Indian National Congress [hereafter Congress]) of representing the interests of the Hindu social elites while relegating those of the Bahujan masses (including Muslims and the Other Backward Classes [OBCs]) to the periphery, thus reproducing the hierarchical social cleavage in the political milieu. During the Third Round Table Conference in London that debated the proposed Constitution of India in 1932, Ambedkar made a fierce demand for treating untouchables as equal citizens and also claimed that the community shall be constituted separately (by granting them separate electorates), equivalent to the status given to other religious minorities (Vundru, 2018: 28). However, his campaign to launch untouchables as independent participants in political democracy troubled Mahatma Gandhi the most.

Gandhi looked at Ambedkar's demand as an attempt to break Hindu unity and claimed that the Congress under his leadership was more concerned with and committed to the welfare of untouchables. Gandhi decided to oppose the Communal Award granted by the British government and launched an indefinite hunger strike at Yerwada Jail to defeat the proposal. Under extremely coercive conditions and a deep emotional predicament, Ambedkar decided to sign a compromise with the Congress leadership in 1932. That deal is often remembered as the 'Poona Pact'. Though Ambedkar failed in his first inning and made necessary compromises, it introduced him as a dedicated and sincere leader of the depressed classes at the national level.

Ambedkar's fearless challenge to Gandhi's paternal and moralist appeal was based on the assessment that the social elites lack ethical convictions when it comes to the emancipation of untouchables. Ambedkar continued his political journey as a sharp critic of nationalist social elites and wanted to posit the depressed classes as the new political opponents of the Congress. At different points in time, he formed three political parties to represent the interests of the most marginalized communities. These functioned as a distinct political bloc that wanted to introduce the socially marginalized communities as a new political class in order to restrict the hegemonic domination of the social elites over all spectrums of power. Like all political parties, the parties formed by Ambedkar also had the grand ambition of elevating their leaders and members as ruling elites in the democratic process.

Ambedkar visualized that a political camaraderie with other marginalized groups and religious minorities would form a significant majority to defeat the social elite-led Congress in the elections. However, the first party that Ambedkar formed in 1936, the Independent Labour Party (ILP), had socialist motives and highlighted the issues of the working classes in its manifesto. The ILP was mostly functional in the Bombay Presidency and often had to engage with communist–socialist organizations on various workers' issues. Though Ambedkar started his political party for general working-class people, he was aware that untouchable labourers in modern industries, especially in textile mills, needed support. During the general strikes of labourers in Mumbai, Ambedkar raised the problems faced by untouchable workers and demonstrated how these workers were discriminated against and exploited not only by factory owners, but also by their own colleagues and fellow workers, including communist-led workers' unions. They often faced discrimination because of their low-caste identity.

In 1942, Ambedkar established his second political party, the All India Scheduled Castes Federation (SCF). The party was meant to organize and promote the interests of the diversified untouchable castes on one national platform. Soon, it enlarged into a nation-wide structure, developing branches in all major states with new regional leaders and patrons. Ambedkar introduced the SCF as an arch-rival of the Congress and as a harsh critic of Gandhi's leadership. The Congress was depicted as an association of social elites and as a party that mainly served the interests of rural and urban elites.

Ambedkar introduced the SCF when hectic deliberations were taking place between Congress nationalists, representatives of smaller political parties, and community leaders over the framing of the Constitution of India. It was an acceptable political norm that in the new constitution, different religious communities and groups would be granted political safeguards according to their numerical strength and historical experiences. Ambedkar wanted to establish untouchables as one of the prime actors in the nation-building process and suggested that, like other minorities, his community should be granted a separate electorate and related safeguards.

Both the political parties formed by Ambedkar had a comprehensive political programme, attractive new leadership, and zeal to challenge the hegemony of the social elites; however, in electoral battles, they often failed to perform commendably. In general and assembly elections, the SCF only received meagre support from non-Dalit general voters. It was marked as a Mahar-centric party, and other caste groups, including many castes within Dalits, remained distanced from both parties. In a tragic tale of electoral politics, in the two elections for Lok Sabha seats that Ambedkar contested, Mumbai North (1952) and Bhandara (1954), he lost to his nearest Congress opponents.

To overcome the stereotype that his party only represented the SCs, Ambedkar deliberated and decided to launch the Republican Party of India (RPI) in 1956. He envisaged the RPI as a secular–socialist political front that drew its ideological essentials from Buddhist principles and sought to represent the poor and socially marginalized masses. Before his death, he only managed to draft a rough blueprint of the party programme and suggested its basic organizational formations. The RPI improvised the SCF's community-centric stereotype and wanted to present itself as a party of the socially marginalized communities, farmers, and working classes. It aimed at galvanizing deprived communities and providing a substantive ideological programme and vision for political transformation, under the leadership of Dalits.

Episodes of Ambedkar's political life showcase the arrival of untouchables into the modern public sphere as a substantive class. His political achievements are not his personal victories, because in each attempt the ex-untouchables had improvised their locations as dignified political actors. Ambedkar's engagement with the British regime and the nationalist elites as a spokesperson of the depressed classes over time established the untouchables as a permanent component of political deliberations at the national level, secured necessary safeguards to protect their rights in the social sphere, and also introduced them as an integral part of state institutions. Ambedkar's political activism thus raised untouchables out of the deep social filth that had clutched them for a very long time.

Post-Ambedkar Dalit Imagination of a Democratic Revolution

In the post-Ambedkar period, the Dalit (constituted by the radical Dalit Panthers Movement), the Bahujan (crafted by Kanshi Ram), and recently the Vanchit (proposed by Prakash Ambedkar) identities have introduced nuanced ideological versions to understand the relationship of marginalized communities with democracy and power. All three identities have an agnostic relationship with grand elite constructions like 'Hindu', 'Citizen', and 'Proletariat' for their abstract nature. As an alternative, the Dalit–Bahujan and the Vanchit are projected as indigenous and organic collectives that represent the actual social and political interests of the worst-off communities.

The Roar of the Panthers

The initial political activism of the RPI in Maharashtra was impressive. It appeared that the party could combine class and caste issues and would represent the downtrodden and marginalized communities sincerely.

The RPI portrayed the possibility that the ex-untouchables may enter democracy as the new vanguards and lead the political battle on behalf of the oppressed sections, including the agrarian labour class, backward castes, Muslims, and Adivasis. However, the social and ideological differences within the party soon become insurmountable, and finally, the party ruptured because of the petty personal deviations of its own leadership.

From the early 1970s, the RPI was fragmented into multiple factions having only a peripheral impact on the politics of the state. The RPI was divided into as many as 11 different factions, and Mahar-caste leadership dominated most of them. The RPI not only failed to mobilize the worst-off social groups against the ruling Congress, but also failed to convince the non-Mahar Dalits to join it. Furthermore, in its desperate move to remain visible in the power structure, it forged opportunistic alliances with the Congress. This made it a 'stooge' of the ruling elites, and soon it became a negligible force in Maharashtra's politics. It heralded the importance of conversion to Buddhism in most of its public meetings, but hardly tried to develop a sound synthesis and mass mobilization over the economic and political problems faced by the deprived sections of the state.

It is in the social, cultural, and intellectual domains that Dalit voices have sharpened their intervention and created an alternative ideological force to challenge the hegemony of the social elites. In Mumbai, the rise of the Dalit Panthers in 1972 was an important event, as it produced a new language, political rhetoric, and militancy within the Dalit youth, and transformed the moribund lethargy that had crippled the Dalit political movement earlier. It borrowed its ideological values from many revolutionary sources like the Black Panthers, the radical left, the Civil Rights movement in the United States, and so on, but it adapted these values to make them suitable to resolve the crisis and struggles under which the untouchables were surviving at that time.

'Dalit' was a radical political category that not only challenged the liberal promise of citizenship, but also targeted the Marxist identity of the 'proletariat class'. 'Dalit' is introduced as a mélange category that suffers from social and economic exploitation simultaneously. The activism of the Dalit Panthers highlighted the sufferings of caste and class oppression and wanted to imagine 'Dalit' as a common category to represent caste–class deprivation, thus demonstrating the possibility of representing a large majority of the poor under one rubric. The Panthers highlighted the embeddedness of Dalits in historical experiences of humiliation and exploitation, and from that vantage point, they made assertive claims for liberation. Under the revolutionary philosophy of Ambedkar and Karl Marx, it was assumed that Dalits could emerge as a powerful vanguard of the oppressed communities.

Interestingly, the Panthers also showed little faith in the Ambedkarite hope in constitutional democracy, the discourse of rights, and electoral politics, and wanted untouchables and other oppressed communities to unite and wage a radical non-compromising battle against social and political elites. Such militancy pushed many Dalits away from the Panthers' programme, and it became a club of creative and intellectual pamphleteers without much consideration of everyday political and social issues of the deprived communities. On the political front, it failed to promote any suitable alternative, and later, under the burden of its internal ideological conflicts,[2] it failed to make durable inroads into mainstream politics. By the mid-1980s, the heroic assertion of Dalit youths weakened and started collapsing towards a slow death. It is only in Marathi Dalit literature that we can notice its glowing remnants.

The Bahujan Collective

In the mid-1980s, with the inception of the Bahujan Samaj Party (BSP) in Uttar Pradesh (UP) under the leadership of Kanshi Ram, Dalit politics witnessed a new turn. Kanshi Ram learnt a lot from his initial experiences as an RPI activist in Maharashtra and wanted to provide a new identity, organizational setup, and political language to Dalit politics. 'Bahujan' thus broadened the horizon of Dalit politics positively and liberated the category from the militant prison that the Panthers had constituted. Kanshi Ram proposed that the class-sensitive Dalit identity is inadequate for representing the heterogenous social and cultural habitat. His creation of the 'Bahujan' acknowledges that there are plural and often conflicting social identities that SC-centric Dalit or Buddhist identities cannot represent. The Bahujan identity allows varied lower castes to retain their social values while formulating a grand political alliance at the national level.

The notion of 'Bahujan' that Kanshi Ram coined was one of the most imaginative political categories, and it sought to overturn the dominant generalization that the deprived classes are always submissive bearers of political power. The Bahujan identity also rejected mainstream formulations based on class, religion, and secularism because they favour and legitimize the control of upper castes over the rest. The political philosophies of the social elites disregard the aspirations of Dalits and lack any radical programme to bring about social transformation. Challenging the limitations of these national parties, the BSP argued that an inclusive and representative social engineering of lower castes and minorities is the most appropriate formula for power sharing (Wankhede, 2008).

This alternative conceptualization of a political party based on a 'majority–minority' dichotomy mirrors the classical Marxist categories, but with new cultural attires suitable to the Indian context. Social identity not only replaces the class category in this mode, but also democratizes the whole structure by sanctioning autonomy to every cultural, social, and religious group, before forming the alliance. The Bahujan identity neither believes in the total submission of all deprived communitarian identities to become one nor does it philosophize a complete suppression of the minority ruling elites to achieve its political ideals. The Bahujan identity is a democratic political alliance between the politically deprived caste groups under the leadership of the most exploited castes of Indian history, Dalits. This coalition of all deprived minority communities (SCs, STs, OBCs, and minorities), in a practical sense, represents the majority of the population in India (Hasan, 2004: 382). The BSP mobilizes its voters under this newly carved metanarrative by making one grand promise that political power is the *guru killi* (master key) that enables its wielders to open every lock, whether social, political, economic, or cultural (Dubey, 2001: 228–310).

Being the formulators and leaders of the Dalit–Bahujan category, the ex-untouchables are also the most stringent advocates of the BSP's political strategies. They have discovered a pan-national legacy of 'Bahujan' leaders as their ideologues and constructed a distinct political discourse based on Ambedkar's thoughts. Being Dalits, they have the foremost zeal and ambition to overthrow the perpetuating domination of the Hindu social elites. They imagine themselves as part of a grand 'Bahujan' collective and want to lead the other oppressed communities towards substantive democracy.

The Idea of 'Vanchit' and the New Bahujan Politics in Maharashtra

In the 2019 general elections in Maharashtra, the Bharatiya Janata Party (BJP) and the Shiv Sena alliance drowned both the Maratha-led parties, mainly the Congress and the Nationalist Congress Party (NCP). The National Democratic Alliance (NDA)'s voting percentage rose to a whooping 47 per cent as voters reposed their faith in the leadership of Narendra Modi, cutting across communities and castes. The NDA won a majority of seats with huge margins, allowing the opposition to win only 7 seats out of 48. However, alongside the news of the decimation of the United Progressive Alliance (UPA), it was the emergence of the Vanchit Bahujan Aghadi (VBA) as an impressive Third Front that received great attention.

The VBA, under the leadership of Prakash Ambedkar, is technically a nascent party, but it can also be seen as an improvised version of his earlier party, the Bharatiya Bahujan Mahasangh. The VBA garnered an impressive 7.08 per cent vote share in the 2019 Lok Sabha elections but was able to win only one

Lok Sabha seat, Aurangabad (in alliance with the All India Majlis-e-Ittehadul Muslimeen). In the same year, in the state assembly elections, it retained its vote share at close to 5 per cent, and its candidates stood at second position in 10 seats. Though the VBA did not win any seat in the assembly, it announced the re-arrival of Dalit politics in the state. Interestingly, the party created a new bloc of 'Vanchit castes', which mostly comprised other marginalized and backward communities as the new players in India's democracy. These communities were conventionally voting for national parties; however, they hardly found any visibility in mainstream political spaces. By forming the 'Vanchit' identity, Ambedkar provided a new platform for their issues and grievances.

The VBA confidently promotes the politics of the 'Vanchit' (excluded) castes and suggests that these communities form the 'Bahujan' (majority) in Maharashtra. Numerically, it appears that the VBA is eyeing a large consolidation of many neglected communities that have remained away from mainstream power. It has estimated that Dalits (12 per cent), Adivasis (9 per cent), Muslims (11 per cent), the vast lower sections of the OBCs, and other neglected tribal and caste groups like the Dhangars, Agri-Kolis, Telis, Bagdis, Koshtis, Malis, and so on, constitute a large proportion of the population in Maharashtra. These sections form the largest chunk of the Dalit–Bahujan population, at 25 to 40 per cent in every constituency. The VBA highlights that national parties (including the NCP) led by Brahmin–Maratha elites have neglected and deprived these communities persistently. The VBA's politics is to engage these communities in democratic discourses not only as passive participants but as new assertive leaders. It promises vital recognition to the issues and concerns of these left-out groups and to provide them respectable space at each political stage. It pledges the formation of a grand social alliance to challenge the conventional powerful domination of the social elites (Brahmins), affluent Marathas, and rich Kunbi sections.

Prakash Ambedkar realizes that building such mega unity is a huge political task and just crunching empirical data on social identities will not be sufficient. There is also a need to have a populist socio-economic agenda to attract the poor masses to the VBA platform. In light of this, the party has announced its economic agenda by pushing the issues of poor farming communities, tenants, and landless labourers. In Maharashtra, especially in semi-urban and rural areas, agrarian distress has surmounted manifold, and there are no substantive political voices that have been able address this issue.

Importantly, the VBA is targeting those communities and castes that had been voting for the BJP–Shiv Sena alliance till the recent past. During the 2019 assembly elections, VBA candidates highlighted that the social and economic conditions of most of the 'Dalit–Bahujan' voters have remained precarious and they have a negligible share in institutions of power. The rhetoric of social justice was reintroduced in political circles, assuring swift remedies for the concerns of the worst-off communities. There are very few takers within these sections for the BJP's rhetoric of development, but socially backward communities have remained its constant supporters due to cultural attachment to right-wing politics. The NCP and the Congress had failed to treat the farmers' problems substantively, and it is the VBA that has taken the issues of poor farmers more seriously than its counterparts.

The VBA has promoted impressive ideological assertion based on the values of social justice and socialism in order to dismantle the BJP's brand of elite-led social engineering. It has aggressively highlighted the socio-economic problems of these sections and promoted organic leadership at local levels. Prakash Ambedkar has emerged as a visionary leader who wishes to bridge the gap between Dalits and Bahujan groups and has readily accepted leaders from other communities as equal partners in the formation of the VBA.

Importantly, the VBA has challenged the negative stereotypes attached to Dalit–Bahujan politics. The allegation that Dalit politics often perpetuates Mahar domination and is interested mainly in protecting their social and political rights is refuted by offering a new political nomenclature that essentially speaks about peripheral, vulnerable, and deprived castes. The VBA wished to expand its social base beyond the Mahar or the Neo-Buddhist section and connected other marginalized groups as leading partners. Lower-caste communities that are often seen as crucial associates of right-wing politics, mainly the lower OBC groups like the Dhangars and the Agri-Kolis, have been proposed as the new flag bearers and leaders in the VBA's politics. It has created an umbrella party comprising more than 200 big and small social, political, and cultural organizations. It has expanded its social base to ensure greater participation of poor classes and most vulnerable castes in the party's functioning and power structure, making the VBA a broad federal platform of marginalized and neglected groups.

As was done by the BSP during its inception in UP politics, the VBA is redefining the politics of social justice in Maharashtra on similar grounds. The VBA promises to represent the most marginalized castes and communities and thus contests the BJP in its own game of social engineering. Evoking collective grief about marginalization and exclusion within the vast lower-caste and backward communities, the VBA claims that it will be the new platform that would represent the voices of excluded communities. Despite a promising start, the expectation that marginalized castes and communities would rally behind a Dalit party for political and social emancipation has not been achieved yet. Will the trust-deficit syndrome that is intrinsically attached with Dalit–Bahujan parties ever be reduced?

Trust-Deficit Syndrome in Dalit Politics

Dalit, Bahujan, and the recently formed 'Vanchit' are the three distinct political categories that claim to represent the masses (not only the ex-untouchable castes but also the others). The Dalit–Bahujan ideological force constructed the idea of the nation as a compartmentalized hierarchical building, in which the powerful top floors are appropriated by social elites while relegating the Dalit–Bahujan mass into its nadir for perpetual suffering. Dalits wished to overturn the floor arrangement so that every community could get equal access to the apparatus of power and change its social and economic location with freedom and dignity.

Ambedkarite politics is visualized as a difficult process that wishes to humanize social relationships and transform power structures. Establishing democratic socialism through parliamentary processes is one of the grand objectives that Ambedkar and post-Ambedkar Dalit politics have persistently sought. Engagement with Dalit–Bahujan categories empowers marginalized communities as conscious political players. It allows them to escape the hegemonic paradigm crafted by the social elites to discover their own potential in political battles. However, the political or social construct that Dalits have offered for bringing democratic change has been subjected to criticism, hatred, prejudice, anxiety, and even casteist remarks. The labelling of Ambedkar as a Dalit leader or the making of the BSP as a Dalit party are visible examples of such distrust and prejudice.

There are few takers for the Dalit–Bahujan political imagination. Only in states like UP, Maharashtra, Tamil Nadu, and, in some respects, Bihar, we see a credible making of a 'Dalit–Bahujan' identity that challenges the cultural and political hegemony of the social elites. Even within the Dalit populace, only the visible sections (like the Mahars or the Neo-Buddhists in Maharashtra and the Jatavs in UP) have adopted such a political construct as their prime ideological alternative. The rest of the Dalit communities often pursue their political options strategically and are comfortable in staying distanced from Dalit–Bahujan political activism. A vast majority of the socially marginalized communities are delinked from the revolutionary consciousness that Dalit–Bahujan politics offers. Therefore, there are more stories about the failure or decline of the Dalit movement and hence more obituaries of the same. Interestingly, it is the BJP that has learnt a lot from the ideological and organizational arrangements of the BSP and restructured its electoral politics around the cultural questions of the lower castes.

In the current scenario, the BJP has been appreciated as a more organized force in mobilizing the Dalit and Bahujan sections. The BJP's plan is now an open strategy (known as Hindutva's social engineering) that says that the inherent social contradictions and historic divides between the politically assertive lower castes (the Mahars in Maharashtra and the Jatavs in UP) and the worst-off lower-caste sections need to be exploited. The politically deprived social groups are engaged through creative cultural strategies and such association is utilized during the electoral process.

Here, the BJP has successfully crafted the section of 'political activists' within Dalit and OBC groups as the new 'social enemy' while erasing the historical memory that the same castes have consistently struggled against injustice, provided leadership, and formed political organizations in defence of social justice. A new social alliance is now offered in which the worst-off Dalit groups are expecting that the BJP, under the leadership of social elites, would bring them the profits of social justice and would also empower them and uplift them from their economic condition (Bansal, 2019). It appears that the BJP has successfully established the Ambedkarite Dalits as a new social enemy, alongside the Muslims as its political enemy. For example, in the UP assembly elections of 2017, it was projected that the Jatav–Yadav–Muslim votes are not required by the BJP as everyone else is voting for the Hindutva party. Parties like the Rashtriya Janata Dal (RJD) in Bihar and the BSP and the Samajwadi Party (SP) in UP largely remained passive and yet had to reinvent their own political models to challenge the BJP's cunning social engineering in their respective states (Narayan, 2019).

The political representation of the Dalit–Bahujan has been operative under crude Brahminical hegemony. They are often represented as degraded social bodies burdened with undignified social roles and therefore unable to operate as free beings. Dalit–Bahujans are perpetually compartmentalized as the poor other, whereas the social elites operate as the dignified claimants of the nation's historic heritage and therefore as the legitimate authorities over the assets of the nation. The social elites suggest that they can operate beyond their social and cultural embeddedness and can act ethically on behalf of the general masses. The masses can be represented through nationalist ideas ('citizenship'), ethnic political convictions ('Hindutva'), or class affinities ('proletariat') under the able leadership of the social elites. By evoking such abstract collectivist notions, all the major institutions of power are controlled and managed under the authoritative clutch of the social elites, whereas the Dalit–Bahujan mass is seen as a passive recipient of the benefits showered by them.

The social elites can represent the idea of the nation, and invariably the different components of the nation are also represented by them. They can perform on behalf of general interests and shared national values; however, such virtue is not allowed to the socially marginalized groups, especially Dalits. Dalits are seen as exclusive inanimate bodies that operate without moral or ethical capacities and cannot think or act beyond their bodily integrity. They are regarded as people who only reinforce their caste affinities and thus disturb the prospect of grand political ideas that seek to connect the citizens for a utilitarian purpose. Such assertion is considered antagonistic to the classical values of nationalism, Hindu religious affiliation, and even to ideas of secular citizenship. Dalit identity has been reprimanded by right-wing ideologues for undermining the collective Hindu consciousness and challenging the possibility of social harmony and national unity.

Conclusion: Will the Trust-Deficit towards Dalit Parties Ever Be Reduced?

The possibility that Dalits can represent the 'others' or the nation is still a utopian idea. The democratic political process has no radical channel to transform these psychological boundaries between Dalits, Bahujans, civil society, and the social elites. Instead, the differences are often reproduced and structured on caste lines and often benefit the ideological agenda of the social elites.

Any fraternal collaboration can be achieved only under political norms promoted by the social elites. The social elites often create an organic unity between different social segments on the basis of citizenship (Indian), religion (Hindu), or class (workers and labourers), and undermine or repress the call for social justice as sectarian, deviant, or unity-breaking. The nationalist parties functioning under the aegis of social elites (the Congress, the BJP, the left, and regional parties) are presented as successful in accommodating and representing Dalit–Bahujans under their ideological umbrella; however, when Dalits form similar ideological constructs or political metanarratives to represent the others, their failure becomes inevitable.

Though Dalit–Bahujan–Vanchit political ideas are radical with ethical persuasions, they are not seen as a possible articulation of a national vision. Dalit politics is contaminated by the 'trust-deficit syndrome', whereas the politics organized by the social elites is seen as collectivist or nationalist and therefore accommodative or sensitive. Dalit politics has failed to build necessary equivalence between various sections of marginalized people so as to create a durable communication network or formidable 'Bahujan' alliance. Ironically, the political ideology that promises power, prestige, and intellectual vibrancy has been rejected by sections within the depressed classes, who thus become an alibi or partner for the projects designed by the social elites. Most of the sections within the Dalit–Bahujan populace mistrust and have developed critical aggression towards each other, thus failing to organize and unify the communities for a substantive political battle. Though the new politics of 'Vanchit' addresses the issues of trust deficit between the Dalit–Bahujan groups and aspires to provide political consciousness to the worst-off vulnerable groups, it is too early to suggest that such an innovative political project will be successful.

Notes

1. Gopal Guru delivered the keynote address in the national seminar on 'Indian Republic at Sixties: Appraisal from the Margins' at Ram Lal Anand College (Evening), University of Delhi, on 21 March 2012.
2. A debate started between the founding members of the Dalit Panthers, Raja Dhale and Namdeo Dhasal, over the ideological tools that need to be given primacy in building the future of the organization. Dhale proposed 'Buddhism' whereas Dhasal emphasized the collective consciousness of large oppressed communities under the rubric of 'class'. Dhasal was accused of deviation and called a communist stooge.

Bibliography

Bansal, S. 2019. 'How India Voted in 2019 Election? Here Is What India Today–Axis My India Post-Poll Study Tells Us'. *India Today*, 31 May. https://www.indiatoday.in/diu/story/how-india-voted-2019-lok-sabha-election-india-today-axis-my-india-poll-1539617-2019-05-31. Accessed on 17 September 2019.

Dalit Panthers. 1973. *The Dalit Panthers' Manifesto*. https://raiot.in/dalit-panthers-manifesto/. Accessed on 17 September 2019.

Dubey, A. K. 2001. 'Anatomy of a Dalit Power Player: A Study of Kanshi Ram'. In *Dalit Identity and Politics*, edited by G. Shah, 289–310. New Delhi: SAGE Publications.

Hasan, Z. 2004. 'Representation and Redistribution: The New Lower Caste Politics in North India'. In *Parties and Party Politics in India*, edited by Z. Hasan, 370–96. New Delhi: Oxford University Press.

Narayan, B. 2019. 'Gathbandhan vs Gathbandhan: Social Coalition Crafted by BJP Trumped BSP–SP–RLD Caste Alliance'. *Indian Express*, 24 May. https://indianexpress.com/article/opinion/columns/narendra-modi-grand-alliance-bsp-sp-alliance-mayawati-akhilesh-yadav-uttar-pradesh-5745367/. Accessed on 15 August 2019.

Phillips, A. 1990. *The Politics of Presence*. Oxford: Oxford University Press.

Vundru, R. S. 2018. *Ambedkar, Gandhi and Patel: The Making of India's Electoral System*. New Delhi: Bloomsbury.

Wankhede, H. S. 2008. 'The Political and the Social in the Dalit Movement Today'. *Economic and Political Weekly* 43(6): 50–57.

14

Liberation Panthers and the Dalit Challenge to Hindutva in Tamil Nadu

Meena Kandasamy and Hugo Gorringe

On 27 September 2020, a small group called the European Periyar Ambedkar Comrades' Federation organized a webinar on 'Periyar and Indian Politics'. The address was delivered by Thol. Thirumavalavan, the leader of the Viduthalai Chiruthaigal Katchi (VCK, or Liberation Panther Party), the largest Dalit-led party in Tamil Nadu, and he focused on Periyar's feminism. In the lecture, Thirumavalavan outlined why Periyar had attacked Hindu scriptures: 'As per Hindu Dharma, all women are created by God as prostitutes. They are prostitutes as per Hindu Dharma ... Manu Dharma. The status of all women is less than that of a man.'[1] In so doing, Thirumavalavan was following in the footsteps of Periyar, Ambedkar, and others in highlighting the ideological underpinnings of 'Brahminical patriarchy' (Chakravarti, 1993). A video clip of these comments, however, was seized upon and widely circulated by Hindu-right groups in Tamil Nadu, especially the Bharatiya Janata Party (BJP), which accused Thirumavalavan of calling *all* women prostitutes. They filed a case against him, called for his arrest, and sought to organize protests to condemn his remarks. Faced by this onslaught, Thirumavalavan doubled down on his comments and demanded a ban on the Manusmriti instead.

What is this party which has aroused the ire of the BJP? The VCK emerged as a radical Dalit movement fighting caste inequality, but it has consistently rallied under the slogan of uprooting Hindutva. Their opposition to the Rashtriya Swayamsevak Sangh (RSS) dates back to L. K. Advani's infamous *rath yatra* in the early 1990s, the inflammatory dangers of which the Dalit Panthers compared to Hanuman setting fire to Lanka and against which they organized cycle rallies and poster campaigns.[2] The party has never had more than four members of the legislative assembly (MLAs) or two members of the parliament (MPs) at one time, does not have a recognized symbol yet, and has always contested elections in alliance with larger and more established allies. Despite this, it is regularly singled out for attacks by the BJP–RSS in Tamil Nadu and remains a thorn in the side of Hindutva.

Indeed, the VCK and its founder-president, Thirumavalavan, have been argued to be the greatest ideological threat to the BJP and Hindutva groups in Tamil Nadu at present, representing a key bulwark against the breach of the Dravidian fortress and spearheading the ideological battle against Sanatana Dharma (Damodaran and Gorringe, 2019). Our chapter will subject this claim to scrutiny by documenting and analysing the strategies and ideology of the party and the BJP's attacks upon it. The VCK has reframed current Indian politics as a struggle between the RSS–BJP–Sangh forces on the one hand and Ambedkarites on the other. In so doing, it offers a forceful counter-narrative to Hindutva. Although the VCK is compelled to work with larger Dravidian parties and operate within the sociopolitical parameters of Tamil politics, we conclude by echoing Gail Omvedt's (2003) call to 'look South'. To begin with, we offer a brief introduction to the Viduthalai Chiruthaigal.

The Panthers and the BJP in Tamil Nadu

The VCK is a small, Dalit-led party which emerged from the Tamil branch of the Dalit Panthers of India in the late 1990s. Like the Dalit Panthers, the VCK named named 'power, wealth, price; landlords, capitalists, money-lenders, and their lackeys; those parties who indulge in religious or casteist politics, and the Government which depends on them' as the enemies of Dalits (Contursi, 1993: 326–27). Its key aims and objectives are captured in the flag of the party: a white five-pointed star superimposed upon blue and red stripes. The blue is a reference to the ideals of Ambedkar, and the red indicates a commitment to Marxism and workers' struggles. Each point of the star is then linked to a core demand: caste annihilation, women's liberation, proletarian liberation, Tamil-linguistic nationalism, and anti-imperialist struggle. Whilst not explicit here, due to the party's emergence in opposition to Dravidian parties, Periyar's more radical anti-caste thinking is also central, as we shall see.

Were we to measure the success of the VCK in electoral terms alone, looking at seats won and vote share (seven MLAs and three MPs to date in 21 years, with never more than four MLAs at any one time), we would regard them as a marginal organization with minimal influence (Gorringe, 2017; Wyatt, 2010). Such analysis, however, neglects that political recognition and impact extend beyond electoral results. Analysis of the VCK thus needs to probe their interaction with, and possible effect on, other parties and social relations more generally. Writing for *The Caravan*, Sujatha Sivagnanam (2020) described the VCK as a 'political heavy-weight in the state' due to their committed cadre-base, which saw them rally 80,000 people at a protest event in Tiruchy at short notice. In the context of Tamil Nadu, where the BJP has failed to gain electoral purchase, the VCK has greater grassroots presence.

Despite its national dominance, the BJP has had marginal vote gains in Tamil Nadu. Its inability to break into the state has been attributed to the domination of strong regional parties (Subramanian, 1999; Schakel, Sharma, and Swenden, 2019). Its increase from 3.3 to 5.47 per cent of vote share in 2014 (Ramajayam, 2014: 272) was viewed as 'a substantial achievement since support for the BJP and its ideology in these regions was almost entirely absent before' (Schakel, Sharma, and Swenden, 2019: 334). At the national level, they rightly anticipated that the BJP's win in 2019 would return India to a one-party dominant system where it would 'forcefully assert its ideology, not just dominance' (Schakel, Sharma, and Swenden, 2019: 350). Eswaran Sridharan (2020: 176), however, argues that the dominance of this ideological hegemony 'can be challenged electorally at the state level and ideologically at a broader level'. Indeed, in 2019, the BJP's vote share in Tamil Nadu slipped back to 3.66 per cent as it lost all five seats it contested (Vasudevan, 2019).

It should, perhaps, be no surprise that the BJP's hegemony should be challenged in Tamil Nadu. Since 1967, the state has been dominated by two parties that emerged from the radical, anti-Brahminical Dravidar Kazhagam (DK; Dravidian Federation). In their analysis of the 2019 election, C. Manikandan and Andrew Wyatt (2020: 314) observe that the death of two political giants, Jayaram Jayalalithaa (leader of the All India Anna Dravida Munnetra Kazhagam [AIADMK]) and Muthuvel Karunanidhi (leader of the Dravida Munnetra Kazhagam [DMK]), left a political vacuum in the state, but 'scepticism of centralized power in New Delhi along with enthusiasm for Tamil culture and state autonomy' remain central to Tamil politics. This was reflected in the fact that #GoBackModi trended on Twitter each time prime minister Modi campaigned here (Manikandan and Wyatt, 2020: 320). To offset its weakness in the state, the BJP was allied to the AIADMK (which had contested alone in 2014). Standing against them, the DMK's campaign stressed that it would save Tamil honour ('Tamizh maanam kaappom') (*Business Standard*, 2019a). The regional focus of the two main Tamil parties comes to the fore here: one allying with the national BJP to shore up ties with the centre, and the other foregrounding the cultural nationalism that has become the hallmark of Dravidian politics (Barnett, 1976).

As against this *regional* focus, the Liberation Panthers brought opposition parties together under the banner of 'Desam Kaappom' (Save the Nation) rallies in January 2019 and February 2020, which linked local and national issues.

Local, Tamil concerns over education policy and language rights were raised, but the main thrust of the conferences was on national politics. The first rally was an explicitly anti-BJP event and was attended by national figures like the Communist Party of India (Marxist) (CPI-M) general secretary, Sitaram Yechury, and the Communist Party of India (CPI) secretary, Sudhakar Reddy (*The Hindu*, 2019a). It was no coincidence that DMK president, M. K. Stalin, made the fervent call to isolate the BJP in Lok Sabha polls from this platform (*The Hindu*, 2019a). The second Desam Kaappom rally was held in the aftermath of the Citizenship Amendment Act, the National Register of Citizens, and the National Population Register (CAA–NRC–NPR) being passed by the Modi government. Broadening the criticism around the CAA–NRC–NPR exercise as anti-Muslim, Thirumavalavan reiterated that it was anti-women, anti-Dalit, anti-poor, and anti-people (he noted that his own mother had no papers, illustrating the wider implications of the Act) and that it was in everyone's interests to challenge it (*The Hindu*, 2020). Thirumavalavan raised questions around federalism as well as social justice, the reservation policy, citizenship, and democracy. It is the Liberation Panthers' ideological challenge and resistance to this forceful assertion of BJP–RSS ideology, thereby preventing the Sangh Parivar[3] from making inroads in Tamil Nadu, that we seek to unpack in this chapter. As Hanna Herzog (1987: 317) argues, 'minor' parties are often considered to be unimportant, but 'they play an active and significant role in the negotiations on the socio-political boundaries and rules of the game of a given political system'. This is undoubtedly true of the VCK and is evident in its relations with the Hindu right.

The Parivar and the Panthers

In the opening to this chapter, we saw how the BJP has singled the VCK out for attention. In an interview to NewsClick (2019), Thirumavalavan – leader of the VCK – attributed the narrowness of his victory in the Chidambaram constituency in 2019[4] to the efforts of the Hindu Munnani (Hindu Front) and the Sangh Parivar in campaigning against him. Vignesh Karthik and Jeyannathann Karunanithi (2020) give a flavour of these tactics, noting how the BJP-linked Hindu Makkal Katchi (Hindu People's Party) sought to discredit Dalit leaders using religion. Thirumavalavan, for example, is seen as unfit to represent the concerns of the Scheduled Castes (SCs) because 'he is a Buddhist'. Not only is this claim false, it also neglects the fact that Buddhists are also included in the SC category. It reflects the BJP's attempts to appeal to Dalits in the state by presenting themselves as the representatives of all 'Hindus'. Given that Dalits were only included as 'Hindu' during the independence struggle (Viswanath,

2014) and are still subject to discrimination and exclusion by their 'co-religionists' (Ramachandran, 2014), the BJP has used identity politics, installing L. Murugan, an Arundhathiyar and the former vice chairman of the National Commission for Scheduled Castes (NCSC), as its state president in Tamil Nadu.[5] The aim here is to mobilize this non-dominant SC group behind the party (Karthik and Karunanithi, 2020).

These attempts to woo Dalit voters go alongside efforts to discredit the VCK. The BJP's national secretary, H. Raja, demonstrated that the party was firmly in their sights, when he tweeted that Thirumavalavan must be arrested for a speech on Hindu temples, and called him 'the embodiment of all evil forces' (Hemavandhana, 2019). The *Business Standard* (2019b) reported on then BJP state president Tamilisai Soundarajan's attempts to isolate the VCK from other parties following a speech in which Thirumavalavan had criticized Gandhi's views on Hinduism, whilst defending Kamal Haasan's depiction of Godse as a Hindu terrorist. 'Thirumavalavan has gone to the worst extent to term Gandhi a Hindu extremist,' she is reported to have said. 'Now what will other parties say to this?' As VCK cadres have sought to oppose BJP campaigns at every step, tensions have grown between members of both parties leading to violence in several places (DTNext, 2017). Apart from the Manusmriti row, which the chapter began with, the VCK cadre have also reported threats from the special branch to arrest them for distributing material against the Manusmriti.[6]

Some of these attacks also play on Thirumavalavan's caste status. H. Raja, for instance, appealed to his Brahmin and dominant-caste Hindu base, saying: 'The party which is touched by Thirumavalavan will not be touched by the people' (NDTV Tamil, 2018). In 2016, they alleged that Thirumavalavan was working with 'extreme' Muslim outfits to promote conversion to Islam (Hindu Existence, 2016). Alongside portraying the VCK as anti-national and inadequately Hindu, the BJP has joined caste-based outfits in Tamil Nadu to accuse the VCK of encouraging *nadaka kaathal* (staged love or love jihad). Dalit men are allegedly being advised by the VCK to 'entrap' Hindu and Shudra women in marriages or love affairs (Mohan, 2016). Whilst this narrative of transgressive love undermines the emphasis on 'Hinduness', it has been seized upon by the BJP to make inroads amongst dominant-caste voters. BJP leader H. Raja used old footage of a speech by Thirumavalavan on intercaste marriages – where he is heard saying that a woman might fall in love with a Dalit man because he has *sarakku* (stuff, or in context, he has what it takes) and *midukku* (vitality or majesty) to conjure the spectre of predatory Dalit masculinity.[7] Thirumavalavan's speech was critiquing claims of 'love jihad' and noting that there might be many reasons why a woman would fall in love with a Dalit man. In twisting this into an accusation that Dalit men are deliberately seeking to ensnare upper-caste women, the BJP presented the VCK as a casteist gang *and* exposed young Dalit men to violence.

In 2016, H. Raja similarly falsely claimed that Thirumavalavan had said that 'none of the men in Tamil society have any masculinity except us' (purportedly referring to Dalit men) and that he was responsible for creating caste wars (NewsGlitz, 2016). Efforts to sustain such propaganda place the BJP alongside casteist parties like the Pattali Makkal Katchi (PMK; Toiling People's Party), which has been regularly articulating such claims (Mohan, 2016). Recently, these claims have filtered into the cultural realm in films such as *Draupadi*, which justifies violence against cross-caste marriages (Shekhar, 2020a).[8] This position further reinforces the gendered politics of caste; Dalit women marrying dominant-caste men is a non-issue, but when it is a question of non-Dalit women (or 'our women' to caste-Hindu parties), it becomes a site of confrontation (Irudayam, Mangubhai, and Lee, 2011). Speaking after the death of Illavarasan, a Dalit youth who married a Vanniyar woman, before being forcibly separated and dying in mysterious circumstances, Thirumavalavan noted that caste and politics had combined to create 'social torture' and called for legislation against so-called 'honour killings' (Lakshmipathi, 2013).

These differences over cross-caste marriages reveal the battle between a caste-annihilating ideology continuing the legacy of the Self-Respect Movement and the caste-sustaining ideology of right-wing caste outfits. Under Periyar, 'self-respect marriages' were popularly referred to as *jaati maruppu thirumanam* (literally, marriages denying or opposing caste) (Geetha and Rajadurai, 2011). Periyar himself was seen as a revolutionary and a feminist who conducted these marriages, signalling a break from tradition and a shattering of the caste system. Less than 50 years after his death, cross-caste marriages between Dalit men and caste-Hindu women, which happen on their own accord, are occasions for violence and murder (so-called honour killings). Thirumavalavan is blamed for encouraging such marriages or relationships and is accused of fomenting love jihad (Mohan, 2016). Whilst this partly reflects how *Dalit* leadership is demonized by the same people who appreciated the revolutionary potential of Periyar, it also speaks to arguments about a dilution of 'Dravidian ideology'.

VCK as the Ideological Heir of Periyar?

V. Geetha (2020) has recently discussed the regression of Dravidian ideology and the Hindu-right wing moving into the gaps. She argues: 'Dravidian governance has thus belied the ideological and normative basis of a politics that Periyar identified with social justice, women's liberation and Dalit emancipation.'

Although newspapers frequently speak of 'the land of Periyar', especially when explaining the failure of national parties in making inroads, we are tempted to ask whether either Dravidian party is really Periyarist anymore. In an interview to *Mint* in 2017, Thirumavalavan was asked why caste atrocities continued in Tamil Nadu despite Periyar's influence. His response is instructive:

> One cannot agree that the DMK as a political party – a splinter group of Periyar's *Dravida Kazhagam* (DK) – has fully imbibed the ideals of Periyar. AIADMK stands eons away from the principles of Periyar. These political parties do not wish to invite the wrath of caste Hindus, as they function under their control. Whenever there is an instance of Dalit atrocity, they fail to take any initiative against the dominant caste groups and in the last 50 years, crimes against Dalits have been on the rise. (Thangavelu, 2017)

We echo Thirumavalavan's analysis here. Of the many Ambedkarite organizations that came up in Tamil Nadu in the late 1980s, the VCK stood out in its embrace of Periyar, including in marking Periyar's birth and death anniversaries, a feature that had been restricted to the DK and the Dravidian parties. In an interview conducted for this chapter, Thirumavalavan recounted how 'I took Periyar into the villages and spoke about him in meetings saying Ambedkar and he are one and the same. Both fought for caste annihilation and against Brahmin domination, both wanted to uproot Hindutva culture and both criticized Sanatana Dharma'.[9] External recognition of this is seen in how the VCK has worked closely with the DK on issues of reservation and Tamil rights over the past two decades. DK president, Krishnasamy Veeramani, has often remarked that just as the DK–DMK used to be called a double-barrelled gun when working together, the VCK–DK–DMK is a triple-barrelled gun to destroy Sanatana (Brahminism).[10]

Several commentators would question our portrayal of the VCK as a Periyarist party. S. Anand (2004) quotes Thirumavalavan as saying that 'Periyar had no separate agenda for Dalits'. Similarly, party propaganda secretary, Gowthama Sannah, argued that 'the notion that the Periyarist movement achieved anything significant for the downtrodden is simply an illusion'.[11] Importantly, both these points are critical of the inadequate implementation of Periyar's radical ideas rather than opposing the ideas themselves. Critics within the party accept the Panthers' Periyarist claims, but question their actions in this regard:

> We had three leaders: Ambedkar, Periyar and Prabhakaran. He said it is these three leaders who will guide our path, but he has betrayed each of these leaders. He has not done what Periyar said – he has not fulfilled the

objective of eliminating God. He has not fully taken on board Ambedkar's call for blood union to end caste. He has not stood firm for Prabakharan's Eelam liberation either.[12]

The assertion here is that the VCK does lay claim to Periyar but fails to live up to his ideals in much the same way as others. There is, however, more to Periyar than 'godlessness' as Thirumavalavan avers saying that Periyar's atheism should be read as a 'strategy towards gaining social justice', in alliance with Ambedkarism and democracy.[13]

Lest these be seen as just words, note that VCK weddings *do* continue many of the traditions espoused by Periyar. They have not systematically campaigned for cross-caste marriages (even amongst Dalit castes), but even without such a campaign, we have seen the political vitriol cast at them because cross-caste marriages occur. Crucially, the VCK has always upheld a couple's right to choose their partners and conduct simple 'self-respect-style marriages' in which bride and groom are urged to 'follow the path of Revolutionary leader Ambedkar and Periyar. Join the party to spread their ideologies and to eradicate caste and casteism'.[14]

At a meeting for potential post-holders, Thirumavalavan spelled out the party's position:

> All can love the party, all can join and take responsibility in the party – those who are in agreement with caste eradication, who accept Ambedkar's principles, who follow Periyar's principles, who have faith in democracy, who want to fight for the freedom of marginalized and weaker sections, who believe that there are oppressed people out there, who believe that people are denied power, who believe in egalitarianism – all can join the party.[15]

In espousing an anti-caste, Tamil nationalism and relentlessly supporting struggles for social justice – whether that is reservations for the Other Backward Classes (OBCs) and women, expressing solidarity with minorities, or demanding equal respect for Tamil language education – the VCK is clearly Periyarist.

Soft Hindutva and the Dalit Challenge

As the struggle for social justice, reservations, women's empowerment, and Bahujan articulation gains momentum throughout India, Periyar is once again being reclaimed,[16] but the Dravidian parties remain in their soft-Hindutva corners, and there has been a steady erosion of his rationalist critique of religion. Indeed, C. J. Fuller (2001: 1608) argues that Hindutva ideas have seeped into the everyday 'common sense' of people in Tamil Nadu. He further notes that despite its electoral weakness in the state, the BJP here is well-organized and frequently allied to one or another of the Dravidian parties. Although the national president of the BJP launched a scathing attack on the DMK in late August 2020, accusing them of 'inciting anti-national feelings' (Shanmughasundaram, 2020), the party allied with the DMK for the 1999 Lok Sabha and the 2001 legislative assembly elections. The ideological atrophy in the Dravidian party can be seen in its fierce condemnation of the repeal of Article 370 in Kashmir (Karthik and Karunanithi, 2019), whilst maintaining a studied silence on the Ayodhya verdict. Following an incident in July 2020, in which the Periyarist Karuppar Kootam (Black Collective) posted material on social media that was said to insult the popular god Murugan, the DMK was split, with some harking back to Periyar and others emphasizing their Hinduness (Shekhar, 2020b).[17]

With the BJP aggressively playing the 'Hindu card', even the VCK has been forced to assert that most of its members are Hindu and that it is not an 'anti-Hindu party' (Yazhiniyan, 2019). The BJP has therefore also attacked Periyar directly. While only fringe saffron outfits were involved in desecrating his statue and mounting a symbolic onslaught online (Bose, 2020), BJP leaders must shoulder some of the responsibility.[18] In August 2020, BJP leader Kalyanaraman (whose account has since been suspended for violating Twitter rules) tweeted that the golden era of Tamil Nadu will rise on the day when Tamils equate pictures of Periyar with viewing shit.[19] Where the BJP sees Periyar as its supreme ideological enemy, the VCK sees Periyar as a leader on par with Ambedkar, inevitably setting them at loggerheads with each other.

The VCK's close alignment with the DMK has led to accusations that it has become institutionalized and lost its radicalism. Some even portray it as little more than the 'SC/ST Wing of the DMK' (Gorringe, 2017). Such a portrayal does injustice to the VCK's outspoken protests against caste atrocities and national policies like the CAA or the National Education Policy (NEP), which demonstrate the ideological clarity of the party. Further, unlike the other Dalit parties in Tamil Nadu, the VCK has sought to retain a *certain pan-Indian sense of Dalitness* in its interventions in the public sphere, condemning atrocities in other states and allying with Dalits elsewhere in highlighting local cases.[20] On 14 April 2020, the day Dalit Marxist intellectual Anand Teltumbde surrendered before the National Investigation Agency (NIA) in Pune under the Bhima Koregaon case, Thirumavalavan arranged a joint, cross-party letter[21] by Dalit Parliamentarians and leaders.[22] The VCK's vociferous presence in this campaign aligns with its fervent critique of oppressive state machinery. Demanding the repeal of the draconian Unlawful Activities (Prevention) Act, 1967 (UAPA) – which permits the state to designate an individual as a terrorist without trial – Thirumavalavan also pointed out that Teltumbde's politics as both a Marxist and an Ambedkarite made him particularly dangerous for Hindutva forces.

It is worth noting that although the DMK is numerically stronger in the parliament, the party has not had a cogent criticism of state power or draconian legislation like the National Security Act (NSA) or the UAPA in recent years – in part, perhaps, because it has used (at least in the 1990s) punitive legal measures to crush dissent, including against the Panthers (Gorringe, 2005). It is, perhaps, to be expected that a small party that grew out of a radical Dalit movement should protest against caste discrimination and government repression. The VCK, however, has also been vocal on OBC reservations and was the first to make a representation on two key issues: OBC reservation in medical college admissions (Thirumavalavan, 2020) and challenging the exclusion of 'creamy layer' OBCs from reservations (Harad, 2020).[23] While the BJP makes inroads into the OBCs (Tamil Nadu's dominant castes) by using caste pride and feelings of superiority consistent with a Periyarist outlook, the VCK's approach towards the OBCs is to not paint them as oppressors or enemies, but to identify them as democratic forces who also require social justice. Crucially, the party critiques the BJP–RSS stance on reservation as upholding brahmin supremacy and seeking a return to Varnashrama Dharma. As Thirumavalavan argued in his analysis of the NEP in 2020:

> Today's National Education Policy is also grounded on the same agenda: RSS, the Sangh Parivar, and their political wing BJP are all united in their objective that OBC and socially backward classes should not get education, they should not aspire for power. If they get educated, get degrees and occupy government jobs, who will sweep the streets? Who will wash the toilets? Who will do the agricultural work? Who will weave clothes? Who will do carpentry? Who will make the pots? Who will make the jewellery? Who can do all this work in their place? (Maktoob, 2020)

The VCK stands out as an Ambedkarite party in such speeches but also in its embrace of Periyarism and adjacency to Marxism. In an address to the party cadre on 7 July 2020, Thirumavalavan explained that Marxism and Ambedkarism are not opposed to each other, but are ideological weapons in the fight for equality and against Hindu fascism:

> We are duty-bound to ask: who are today's ruling class? If we have to identify them in terms of their ideology, they are fascists. We can also call them capitalist forces. We can call them Brahminical forces. We can call them chauvinists and racists. We can call them communal fanatics and caste fanatics. We can also call them patriarchs and misogynists.[24]

The ideological challenge to Hindutva, as articulated by the VCK, moves beyond a critique of Brahminism and graded social inequality to highlight the BJP's intimate ties with capitalists. Even in critiquing the scrapping of Article 370, thus removing the special status of Jammu and Kashmir, the VCK's criticism highlighted that corporates would now buy land in Kashmir. Indian nationalist hegemony was countered along with the corporate agenda (Sreerag, 2019). Where Dalit parties like the Bahujan Samaj Party (BSP) welcomed the reading down of Kashmir's special status (*India Today*, 2019), the VCK was vociferous in its condemnation. In line with Thirumavalavan's assertion that the VCK is not 'just' a Dalit party, this reveals sharp insight into the workings of India's federal system and the crony capitalism of the supposedly nationalist BJP. In a recent television interview, Thirumavalavan labelled the BJP an anti-people party, an *anti-Hindu party*, and enumerated the reasons why keeping the BJP out of Tamil Nadu was a priority:

> They are breaking everyone [political parties] here; they are taking steps to weaken Dravidian parties; they separate and divide the Dalit community itself on the basis of caste backgrounds to prevent them from raising forward as a unified force; they have likewise pulverized the OBC communities on a national level; they have taken up an autocratic approach of 'One Nation, One Culture'; they are a threat at the national level also, so we cannot ruin the unified opposition to the BJP.[25]

It is in this frame that the VCK's embrace of Tamil Nationalism must be understood. Thirumavalavan spelled out the party's position on the rise of the BJP:

> One religion that is Hindu, one language that is Hindi and one nation that is Hindu Rashtra. So, Hindu Hindi Hindustan, BJP is working only for this agenda ... Real federalism is nationalism. Federalism means pluralism. But the Modi government and RSS are thinking that one nation, one culture is nationalism. (Sreerag, 2019)

The Panthers and Political Pluralism

Critics frequently assert that the VCK's entry into party politics, following a decade-long boycott of elections, was attended by a dilution of their radicalism. As one observer put it:

> 'The liberation pussy-cats!' They used to be Panthers, but now like pussy-cats they have gone flocking round Jayalalithaa. They are selling their people. There can be exploitation by movements against exploitation too.[26]

We are not suggesting that the VCK is beyond reproach or that it has not compromised for any of the contortions of electoral competition (see Chapter 5). There is also some truth in the claim that it lacks a clear blueprint for social change. Veteran journalist Punitha Pandian notes how the party has not embraced Ambedkar's social agenda which includes conversion out of Hinduism.[27] Similarly, whilst the VCK now has union branches that raise workers' issues in large companies, it can be said to lack a clear programme of action to address class inequalities. Some, like the critic quoted earlier, take this to illustrate that the VCK's engagement with Ambedkar, Periyar, and Marx is mostly rhetorical or symbolic. Party propaganda secretary Sannah's response here is important:

> Now, we, in the VCK, need to tackle court cases, protest, lead struggles, stand against caste-Hindus, stand against exploiters, stand against the police, address the concerns and doubts of party comrades, address the concerns of non-Dalits in the party – it is within this multitude of concerns that we have to address any problem ... In some areas we get an immediate resolution. In others – like in Munjanur[28] – it took 20 years to get a solution. In those 20 years what will the people have said? They will have said: 'This lot come and go, and come and go.' That is what they will have said. Today we were successful on the back of continued protests – this was not a one-off demonstration or a problem that arose the other day ... It takes years of sustained protests. If the VCK back off from such protests, then you can condemn us. If they accuse us of selling out even when protests are ongoing, then it is our job to help them understand the ground realities.[29]

The VCK, as noted at the outset, is a small party. Moreover, as the largest Dalit-led party in Tamil Nadu, it not only leads protests against caste atrocities in the state but is vilified and subject to caste discrimination itself. It is for this reason that Gorringe (2005: 55) argues that:

> The Liberation Panthers are perhaps best described as *issue based*, in that they articulate a coherent set of principles and demands, but *incident sensitive*, in that they react to the aggression of others more often than campaigning on issues. This is not necessarily a criticism, since the highlighting of abuses is a crucial part of the search for justice.

Given this, what can we learn from the example of the Panthers? We maintain that institutionalization has not fully tamed the Panthers. Indeed, in a scenario where the land of Periyar seems ever more vulnerable to Hindutva, especially of the soft-cultural variant (see Fuller, 2001), the VCK stands as a bulwark against this. They do so, we contend, because they continue to articulate the most coherent critique of the Hindu right in the state and mobilize both their own cadre and other parties on this basis. The 2019 and 2021 election campaigns in Tamil Nadu demonstrated that ideological clarity matters in communicating to voters and in withstanding the soft-Hindutva tide that has swept much of the country.

If the BSP's recent travails suggest that there *is* something of an impasse in Dalit politics, the ideologically driven campaigns of the VCK illustrate that electoral politics need not entail deradicalization. This is why the BJP is wary of them. In calling out the BJP for its communal agenda, pointing to its corporate interests, raising the issue of federalism, and foregrounding the question of linguistic pluralism, the VCK has offered a consistent and ideologically clear programme that has proved attractive to voters and offers lessons to politicians elsewhere, echoing Omvedt's (2003) argument to 'look South'. In calling out the hypocrisy of the BJP, which spent fortunes to erect a statue of Sardar Patel, and then claimed to have no money for education or the National Rural Employment Guarantee Act (NREGA), the VCK revealed the vacuity of the BJP's development agenda.[30] We can only hope that BJP leader J. P. Nadda's accusation that the DMK was a 'sheltering ground for those people not working in the best interest of the nation' (Press Trust of India, 2020) is not the harbinger of a new wave of repression. Unlike Narendra Subramanian (1999), we view political pluralism in Tamil Nadu as the result of continued mobilization by radical actors rather than a lasting legacy of Dravidianism and argue that the Panthers are central to the process. As Thirumavalavan argued in 2003, all of Ambedkar's work can be condensed into the one line: 'We shall uproot Hindutva. Hindutva is opposed to equality … Hindutva is against democracy. So, Viduthalai Chiruthaigal is against Hindutva' (Thirumavalavan, 2004: 172).

Notes

1. Translated by Meena Kandasamy. See an account in Kandasamy (2020).
2. Thirumavalavan recalled this history in a recent speech on the occasion of Muhammad Ismail's (popularly known as Quaid-e-Millat [Father of the Nation]) birth anniversary on 5 June 2020. See the speech at Thol. Thirumavalavan (@thirumaofficial), 'கண்ணிய தமிழர் காயிதே மில்லத் பிறந்த நாள் விழா; திருமாவளவன் சிறப்புரை', Twitter, 5 June 2020, 11:57 a.m. https://twitter.com/thirumaofficial/status/1268791438076076032. Accessed on 10 October 2022.
3. The Sangh Parivar refers to the association of Hindu nationalist organizations clustered around the RSS, including the BJP, the Bajrang Dal, and the Vishva Hindu Parishad.

4. This was an incredibly close-fought election with the lead changing hands several times. Thirumavalavan eventually won by 3,219 votes (*The Hindu*, 2019b).

5. Murugan served as Tamil state president of the BJP from March 2020 to July 2021, when he was made a union minister in the BJP government.

6. Tamizharasan, personal communication with the authors, December 2020.

7. See H. Raja's Facebook post, 24 April 2019, 9:31 a.m., https://www.facebook.com/HRajaBJP/posts/2092431330874206?comment_id=2092452054205467&reply_comment_id=2093805800736759. Accessed on 10 October 2022.

8. See the trailer of *Draupadi* at IMDb, https://www.imdb.com/title/tt11581264/?ref_=vp_vi_tt (accessed on 10 October 2022). Thugs in the film are identified as Dalit through the use of well-known VCK political slogans and are portrayed as seeking to ensnare Vanniyar women who are forced to fight back to defend their honour.

9. Thirumavalavan, interview with Kandasamy, September 2020.

10. Veeramani has made this claim in a number of speeches. See, for example, this speech from 2 December 2018: 'திராவிட சிந்தனையின் மூன்று குழல் துப்பாக்கிகள் தி.க, திமுக, விசிக என்று - தி க தலைவர் கி.வீரமணி', YouTube video, 2 December 2018, https://youtu.be/Sho9Dk_ZHS0 (accessed on 25 October 2022).

11. Gowthama Sannah, interview with Gorringe, April 2012.

12. Interview with Gorringe, February 2012.

13. Thirumavalavan's speech, translated by Kandasamy, PeriyarTV, YouTube video, 29 November 2018, https://www.youtube.com/watch?v=ylSi3AFn8-M&t=849s (accessed on 10 October 2022).

14. Party wedding, Gorringe's fieldnotes, February 2012.

15. Thirumavalavan, Gorringe's fieldnotes, May 2012.

16. See the monuments to Periyar erected by the Bahujan Samaj Party (BSP) and the numerous Ambedkar–Periyar Study Circles, for example.

17. Notably, the DMK's touted ideological younger generation leader, Udhayanidhi, posted pictures of a Vinayakar idol in his home shortly afterwards (Bharathi, 2020).

18. When Lenin's statue was toppled in Tripura, for example, BJP leader H. Raja tweeted that the same should happen to Periyar (*Deccan Chronicle*, 2018). Following a furore, he backtracked and said it was done by his internet admin.

19. Kalyanaraman (@bjpkalyaan), Twitter, 21 August 2020, https://twitter.com/BjpKalyaan/status/1296633232293756928 (accessed on 10 October 2022).

20. Note the inclusion of Ram Vilas Paswan in protests around the Paramakudi firing in 2011 (*Times of India*, 2011).

21. Read the full letter at *The Caravan* (2020).

22. See the VCK press note and tweet at Thol. Thirumavalavan (@thirumaofficial), 'It is unacceptable that Dr. Anand Teltumbde, who has not committed any

crime, against whom there is no evidence of having committed a crime, is being imprisoned …', Twitter, 13 April 2020, 3:31 p.m., https://twitter.com/thirumaofficial/status/1249638937858998274 (accessed on 10 October 2022).

23. The party even launched a hashtag called 'VCK for OBCs'. See Thol. Thirumavalavan (@thirumaofficial), 'Modi Government's proposed decision to make amendments to "creamy layer" is an effort to ensure that majority OBCs will not be able to avail reservation', Twitter, 9 July 2020, 4:09 p.m., https://twitter.com/thirumaofficial/status/1281176018049327104 (accessed on 10 October 2022).

24. Thirumavalavan's speech at a book-discussion meeting, translated by Kandasamy, 7 July 2020. See the advertisement for the event at Thol. Thirumavalavan (@thirumaofficial), 'தும் செயலியில் இணைந்திடுவோம்…', Twitter, 7 July 2020, 5:56 p.m., https://twitter.com/thirumaofficial/status/1280478227157315584 (accessed on 10 October 2022).

25. See the full interview at 'Kelvikkenna Bathil: Exclusive Interview with Thirumavalavan (VCK)', Thanthi TV, YouTube video, 22 September 2020, https://www.youtube.com/watch?v=WJD9LdCS0CU (accessed on 10 October 2022).

26. Gnanasekharan, interview with Gorringe, July 1999.

27. Punitha Pandian, interview with Gorringe, April 2012.

28. This is referring to struggles to secure Dalit access to burial and cremation grounds. For details, see *The Hindu* (2012).

29. Sannah, interview with Gorringe, April 2012.

30. See Thirumavalavan's speech delivered at the 2020 Save the Nation conference at Red Pix 24x7, YouTube video, 24 February 2020, https://www.youtube.com/watch?v=BTZb_RlhjaU (accessed on 10 October 2022).

Bibliography

Anand, S. 2004. 'Iconoclast, Or Lost Idol?'. *Outlook*, 24 September (updated 5 February 2022). https://www.outlookindia.com/magazine/story/iconoclast-or-lost-idol/225173. Accessed on 10 October 2022.

Barnett, M. R. 1976. *The Politics of Cultural Nationalism in South India*. Princeton, NJ: Princeton University Press.

Bharathi, S. 2020. 'Udhay Stalin's Vinayagar Idol Photo on Twitter Draws Flak from Supporters and Opposition'. *News Minute*, 24 August. https://www.thenewsminute.com/article/udhay-stalin-s-vinayagar-idol-photo-twitter-draws-flak-supporters-and-opposition-131462. Accessed on 10 October 2022.

Bose, R. 2020. 'Why Has Periyar's Statue Been Vandalised with Saffron Paint? It Starts with a YouTube Video'. News18, 17 July. https://www.news18.com/news/buzz/why-has-periyars-statue-been-vandalised-with-saffron-paint-it-starts-with-a-youtube-video-2720541.html. Accessed on 10 October 2022.

Business Standard. 2019a. 'Campaign Ends in TN; AIADMK, DMK Make Final Bid to Woo Voters'. 16 April. https://www.business-standard.com/article/pti-stories/campaign-ends-in-tn-aiadmk-dmk-make-final-bid-to-woo-voters-119041601025_1.html. Accessed on 10 October 2022.

———. 2019b. 'TN BJP Flays VCK Leader for Terming Gandhi a Hindu Extremist'. 19 May. https://www.business-standard.com/article/news-ians/tn-bjp-flays-vck-leader-for-terming-gandhi-a-hindu-extremist-119051900905_1.html. Accessed on 10 October 2022.

Chakravarti, U. 1993. 'Conceptualising Brahmanical Patriarchy in Early India: Gender, Caste, Class and State'. *Economic and Political Weekly* (Special Article: April): 579–85.

Contursi, J. 1993. 'Political Theology: Text and Practice in a Dalit Panther Community'. *Journal of Asian Studies* 52(2): 320–39.

Damodaran, K., and H. Gorringe. 2019. 'Panthers in Parliament: Why Thiruma's Win Matters the Most'. *The Wire*, 25 May. https://thewire.in/politics/panthers-in-parliament-why-thirumas-win-matters-the-most. Accessed on 10 October 2022.

Deccan Chronicle. 2018. 'BJP Leader H Raja Deletes Post Warning Periyar Statue Will Be Pulled Down Too'. 6 March. https://www.deccanchronicle.com/nation/current-affairs/060318/bjp-h-raja-deletes-tweet-warning-periyar-statue-pulled-down-too.html. Accessed on 10 October 2022.

DTNext. 2017. 'VCK, BJP Cadre Clash at Karur'. 25 October. https://www.dtnext.in/News/TopNews/2017/10/25015932/1050014/VCK-BJP-cadre-clash-at-Karur. Accessed on 10 October 2022.

Fuller, C. J. 2001. 'The "Vinayaka Chaturthi" Festival and Hindutva in Tamil Nadu'. *Economic and Political Weekly* 36(19): 1607–16.

Geetha, V. 2020. 'The Periyar Sun Has Set … Or Has It? Finding the Afterlife Of Dravidianism'. *Outlook*, 24 August. https://www.outlookindia.com/magazine/story/india-news-opinion-is-india-racist-dravidian-governance-has-debunked-ideological-basis-of-politics-that-periyar-identified-with-da/303554. Accessed on 10 October 2022.

Geetha, V., and S. Rajadurai. 2011. *Towards a Non-Brahmin Millennium*, 2nd revised edition. Kolkata: Samya.

Gorringe, H. 2005. *Untouchable Citizens*. New Delhi: SAGE Publications.

———. 2017. *Panthers in Parliament: Dalits, Caste, and Political Power in South India*. New Delhi: Oxford University Press.

Harad, T. 2020. 'VCK Going to Hold Online Demonstration against "Creamy Layer" Rule for OBCs'. *The Satyashodhak*, 10 July. https://thesatyashodhak.com/vck-going-to-hold-online-demonstration-against-creamy-layer-rule-for-obcs. Accessed on 10 October 2022.

Hemavandhana. 2019. 'Thirumavalavan Should Be Arrested'. Tamil OneIndia, 19 November. https://tamil.oneindia.com/news/chennai/h-raja-tweeted-arrest-vck-thirumavalavan-368992.html. Accessed on 10 October 2022.

Herzog, H. 1987. 'Minor Parties: The Relevancy Perspective'. *Comparative Politics* 19(3): 317–29.

Hindu Existence. 2016. 'Islamist's Conversion Plot Foiled in Tamil Nadu'. 12 August. https://hinduexistence.org/2016/08/12/islamists-conversion-plot-foiled-in-tamil-nadu/. Accessed on 10 October 2022.

India Today. 2019. 'BSP Supports Govt on Scrapping of Article 370 for J&K'. 5 August. https://www.indiatoday.in/india/story/bsp-article-370-jammu-kashmir-1577348-2019-08-05. Accessed on 10 October 2022.

Irudayam, A., J. Maghubhai, and J. Lee. 2011. *Dalit Women Speak Out.* New Delhi: Zubaan Books.

Kandasamy, M. 2020. 'Why Feminists Must Join the Movement against the Manusmriti'. *The Wire*, 24 October. https://thewire.in/caste/why-feminists-must-join-the-movement-against-the-manusmriti. Accessed on 10 October 2022.

Karthik, V., and J. Karunanithi. 2019. 'Federalism Is at the Heart of DMK's Tryst with Jammu and Kashmir'. *The Wire*, 11 September. https://thewire.in/politics/dmk-jammu-and-kashmir-article-370-federalism. Accessed on 10 October 2022.

———. 2020. 'Will BJP's UP Model of Mobilising Scheduled Castes Work in Tamil Nadu?'. *The Wire*, 18 March. https://thewire.in/politics/bjp-tamil-nadu-mobilise-scheduled-castes-l-murugan. Accessed on 10 October 2022.

Lakshmipathi, B. 2013. 'Caste Combined with Politics Is the Culprit: Thirumavalavan'. Round Table India, 17 July. https://www.roundtableindia.co.in/caste-combined-with-politics-is-the-culprit-thirumavalavan. Accessed on 10 October 2022.

Maktoob. 2020. 'BJP Govt's New Education Policy Targets OBC Communities: Thol. Thirumavalavan MP'. 12 August. https://maktoobmedia.com/2020/08/12/bjp-govts-new-education-policy-targets-obc-communities-thol-thirumavalavan-mp/. Accessed on 10 October 2022.

Manikandan, C., and A. Wyatt. 2020. 'Tamil Nadu: Political Pluralism and Party System Changes'. In *India's 2019 Elections: Modi-Led BJP Wave*, edited by P. Wallace, 313–28. New Delhi: SAGE Publications.

Mohan, R. 2016. 'Jeans, "Love Drama" and the Electoral Spoils of Tamil Nadu's Hidden Caste Wars'. *The Wire*, 6 May. https://thewire.in/politics/tamil-nadus-hidden-caste-wars. Accessed on 10 October 2022.

NDTV Tamil. 2018. 'Seeman Rages about H. Raja's Abuse of Thiruma'. 12 December. https://www.ndtv.com/tamil/seeman-slams-h-raja-over-thiruma-issue-1961574. Accessed on 10 October 2022.

NewsClick. 2019. 'Sangh Parivar Works Against Dalits, Attempted to Defeat Me: Dr. Thol. Thirumavalavan'. 9 June. https://www.newsclick.in/sangh-parivar-works-against-dalits-attempted-defeat-me-dr-thol-thirumavalavan. Accessed on 10 October 2022.

NewsGlitz. 2016. 'Thirumavalavan is Creating Caste Wars: H. Raja Speech'. YouTube video, 6 August. https://www.youtube.com/watch?v=2GKPmd5JuHI. Accessed on 10 October 2022.

Omvedt, G. 2003. 'Introduction: Thunder Out of the *Cheri*'. In R. Thirumavalavan, *Talisman: Extreme Emotions of Dalit Liberation*, translated by Meena Kandasamy, xiv–xxiv. Kolkata: Samya.

Press Trust of India. 2020. 'DMK Shelters Those Not Working for National Interest, Says BJP Chief JP Nadda'. *The Print*, 24 August. https://theprint.in/politics/dmk-shelters-those-not-working-for-national-interest-says-bjp-chief-jp-nadda/488259/. Accessed on 10 October 2022.

Ramachandran, V. 2014. 'Introduction'. In *Dalit Households in Village Economies*, edited by V. Ramachandran and M. Swaminathan, 1–23. New Delhi: Tulika Books.

Ramajayam, P. 2014. 'Tamil Nadu: Countering the National Wave'. *Research Journal Social Science* 22(2): 271–81.

Ravikumar. 2006. 'Re-Reading Periyar'. *Seminar* 558. http://www.india-seminar.com/2006/558/558%20ravikumar.htm. Accessed on 10 October 2022.

Schakel, A., C. K. Sharma, and W. Swenden. 2019. 'India after the 2014 General Elections: BJP Dominance and the Crisis of the Third Party System'. *Regional and Federal Studies* 29(3): 329–54.

Shanmughasundaram, J. 2020. 'Tamil Nadu Is Shelter for Anti-nationals, Says JP Nadda'. *Times of India*, 25 August. https://timesofindia.indiatimes.com/city/chennai/tamil-nadu-is-shelter-for-anti-nationals-says-j-p-nadda/articleshow/77732346.cms. Accessed on 10 October 2022.

Shekhar, G. 2020a. 'Darkness Talks Back', *Outlook*, 16 March. https://www.outlookindia.com/magazine/story/entertainment-news-darkness-talks-back/302920. Accessed on 10 October 2022.

———. 2020b. 'Tamil Nadu Assembly Elections: The Lord Murugan Factor and How BJP Can Ride'. *Outlook*, 10 August. https://www.outlookindia.com/magazine/story/india-news-tamil-nadu-assembly-elections-the-lord-murugan-factor-and-how-bjp-can-ride/303500. Accessed on 10 October 2022.

Sivagnanam, S. 2020. 'Massive Rallies Unite Periyarists and Ambedkarites against the BJP in Tamil Nadu'. *The Caravan*, 13 March. https://caravanmagazine.in/politics/massive-rallies-unite-periyarists-and-ambedkarites-against-the-bjp-in-tamil-nadu. Accessed on 10 October 2022.

Sreerag, P. 2019. 'All Corporates Will Purchase Jammu and Kashmir: VCK President Thol Thirumavalavan'. *The Caravan*, 2 September. https://caravanmagazine.in/politics/thol-thirumavalavan-mp-tamil-nadu. Accessed on 10 October 2022.

Sridharan, E. 2020. 'India in 2019: A New One-Party Hegemony?' *Asian Survey* 60(1): 165–76.

Subramanian, N. 1999. *Ethnicity & Populist Mobilization*. New Delhi: Oxford University Press.

Suganthi. 2017. 'H. Raja Questions Whether Seeman and Thirumavalavan Are Mentally Well: Video'. Tamil OneIndia, 20 June. https://tamil.oneindia.com/news/tamilnadu/thirumavalavan-seeman-do-not-have-mental-balance-said-h-raja-286786.html. Accessed on 10 October 2022.

Thangavelu, D. 2017. 'A Party Founded by a Dalit Remains a Dalit Party: VCK's Thirumavalavan'. *Mint*, 14 April. https://www.livemint.com/Politics/l32niffcDHYAaE7X8ATbRI/A-party-founded-by-a-Dalit-remains-a-Dalit-party-VCKs-Thir.html. Accessed on 10 October 2022.

The Caravan. 2020. 'Dalit Leaders Condemn Anand Teltumbde's Arrest on 14 April—Ambedkar Jayanti'. 12 April. https://caravanmagazine.in/noticeboard/dalit-leaders-condemn-anand-teltumbde-arrest-on-ambedkar-jayanti. Accessed on 10 October 2022.

The Hindu. 2012. 'Dispute over Pathway to Burial Ground'. *The Hindu*, 10 June. https://www.thehindu.com/todays-paper/tp-national/tp-tamilnadu/dispute-over-pathway-to-burial-ground/article3511043.ece?test=2&textsize=small. Accessed on 10 October 2022.

———. 2019a. 'Time to Isolate BJP in Lok Sabha Polls: Stalin'. 24 January. https://www.thehindu.com/news/national/tamil-nadu/time-to-isolate-bjp-in-lok-sabha-polls-stalin/article26074179.ece. Accessed on 10 October 2022.

———. 2019b. 'Thirumavalavan Wins by a Slender Margin in Chidambaram'. *The Hindu*, 25 May. https://www.thehindu.com/news/national/tamil-nadu/thirumavalavan-wins-by-a-slender-margin-in-chidambaram/article27241533.ece. Accessed on 10 October 2022.

———. 2020. 'BJP Trying to Redraft Constitution, Says VCK'. 23 February. https://www.thehindu.com/news/national/tamil-nadu/bjp-trying-to-redraft-constitution-says-vck/article30892105.ece. Accessed on 10 October 2022.

Thirumavalavan, Thol. 2004. *Uproot Hindutva: The Fiery Voice of the Liberation Panthers*, translated by M. Kandasamy. Kolkata: Samya.

———. 2020. 'OBC Reservation in Medical Education: VCK Gives Call for Protest'. *The Satyashodhak*, 6 June. https://thesatyashodhak.com/obc-reservation-in-medical-education-vck-gives-call-for-protest/. Accessed on 10 October 2022.

Times of India. 2011. 'Paswan Raps Jaya for Comments'. 21 September. https://timesofindia.indiatimes.com/city/madurai/Paswan-raps-Jaya-for-comments/articleshow/10058931.cms. Accessed on 10 October 2022.

Vasudevan, L. 2019. 'How Dravidian Heartland Closed Its Door on Modi'. *India Today*, 6 June. https://www.indiatoday.in/india/story/tamil-nadu-lok-sabha-elections-1543891-2019-06-06. Accessed on 10 October 2022.

Viduthalai (Liberation). 2017. 'DK–DMK–VCK Are a Three-Barrelled Gun to Bring Down Sanathanam'. 14 February. http://viduthalai.in/page-6/137566. html. Accessed on 10 October 2022.

Viswanath, R. 2014. *The Pariah Problem: Caste, Religion and the Social in Modern India*. New York: Columbia University Press.

Wyatt, A. 2010. *Party System Change in South India*. London: Routledge.

Yazhiniyan. 2019. '"90 Per Cent of My Supporters Are Hindus": Thol Thirumavalavan'. DTNext, 11 April. https://www.dtnext.in/tamilnadu/2019/04/11/90-per-cent-of-my-supporters-are-hindus-thol-thirumavalavan. Accessed on 10 October 2022.

15

Dalit-Bahujan Politics

Crisis and Future

Badri Narayan

This chapter aims to focus on the process and causes of the gradual decay of the Bahujan Samaj Party (BSP)-led Dalit–Bahujan movement in India. It will critically evaluate Dalit politics and the Dalit movement in north India – its forms and content, its language and epistemology, its issues and agendas, and the mobilizational politics followed by it. In the chapter, I would like to discuss how and why the Dalit movement in north India is facing a crisis, why internal weaknesses are being produced within it, and how these weaknesses are contributing to the gradual weakening of the mainstream Dalit movement. We will also explore the challenges to the Dalit movement which are emerging from rival political forces. Thus, this chapter will try to present a critical review of Dalit politics in north India and assess its future in the country. This chapter has evolved through an amalgam of historical methodology for mapping the crisis of the Dalit–Bahujan movement. Drawing on my own fieldwork over many years in varied villages of Uttar Pradesh (UP), I have tried to understand the longue durée, or long-run processes, historical structures, and relations of the Dalit–Bahujans. I have also used various newspaper reports to substantiate and support my arguments here.

Called the 'Bahujan movement' following the name given to the Dalit movement by Kanshi Ram, since Dalits and lower castes constitute the *bahujan*, or the majority population, the movement in the state of UP in north India took the form of a political movement under a political party – the BSP – launched in 1984 (Pai, 2002). The party saw a sharp rise in support under its next leader, Mayawati, but unfortunately, the Bahujan movement did not focus on social issues concerning Dalits like their exploitation, killing, and rape (Pai, 2020).

It is true that the BSP has not launched any big social movement for the last few decades (Narayan, 2012). It mainly focuses on fighting for electoral success, but since 2007, when it swept the assembly elections in UP, it has not seen any major achievements in electoral politics either in UP or in any other part of India.

These electoral defeats are in a way symptomatic of a deeper crisis prevailing in the Dalit–Bahujan movement in India, especially in the Hindi-speaking region.

Mapping the Crisis

This crisis in the Dalit movement occurs at both ideological and political levels. Nothing like a pan-Indian Dalit movement probably exists today, though scattered Dalit movements are found in some form or the other at various state and regional levels. The common factor in all these movements is that they are based on Babasaheb Ambedkar's ideas and have evolved from them. Some of these forms developed as local versions of the Ambedkarite movement (Narayan, 2014).

The emergence of Kanshi Ram on the political scene is undoubtedly the second biggest wave in the history of the Dalit movement since Ambedkar started the movement in the country. It is true that the Dalit–Bahujan movement in UP was inspired by Ambedkar and was born from the womb of Ambedkarism. However, it contains an inherent tension between Ambedkar's values and ideals-based ideology on the one hand and Kanshi Ram's practical and pragmatic politics on the other. Kanshi Ram organized the Dalits of UP into a wider category called the *bahujan samaj*. Mayawati later tried to bring all the lower castes under the bigger umbrella of *sarvajan* (all inclusive) and sought to fight elections after 2007 with a coalition of all castes forming the *sarvajan*. Unfortunately, the experiment failed in the 2017 and 2022 UP assembly elections, and the Bharatiya Janata Party (BJP) won with a resounding majority.

Ambedkar provided an ethical context to the politics of Dalit liberation since morality was very important for him. On the other hand, Kanshi Ram chose to be pragmatic in his attempt to politically empower Dalits. He was unconcerned about the means of acquiring political power, emphasizing the end – that is, the attainment of political power. If he was criticized for his 'opportunism', he would immediately reply that if Brahmins could become influential by being opportunistic, then Dalits too could use opportunism to empower themselves. Kanshi Ram believed that until a casteless society was formed, it was necessary for Dalits to strategically use their caste as a tool for emancipating themselves and dethroning Brahminism. While Ambedkar saw the abolition of the caste system as vital for Dalit emancipation, Kanshi Ram and Mayawati favoured the awakening of Dalit and backward identities in order to link these with the Bahujan movement. Kanshi Ram and Mayawati transformed Ambedkar's slogan, 'Abolish the caste system' – propagated in his undelivered speech *Annihilation of Caste* (1936) – into 'Promote the caste system' to mobilize Dalits towards the restoration of their caste identity and self-esteem (Narayan, 2014).

Kanshi Ram viewed caste as a double-edged sword, to be used to benefit the Bahujans, while simultaneously destroying Brahminical hegemony. Despite all these differences, Kanshi Ram believed in Ambedkar's idea of power being the master key for Dalit emancipation, which he used to call *guru killi*.

So, the two foundational notions which the Dalit–Bahujan movement revolves around are (*a*) evoking caste identities of Dalit communities with pride and (*b*) capturing democratic state power for Dalit emancipation. Both notion-based strategies initially worked well, but the 2012 UP assembly elections in which Mayawati was defeated and lost power indicated a growing crisis for the BSP movement in the state. We have observed that caste-identity-based politics has almost faded in UP in the past few years. One possible reason is that the belief among the marginalized and subalterns that their problems will be resolved when representatives from their own *jati–biradari* (own caste) come into power seems to have shattered now. Also, their belief that leaders from their own caste will disseminate democratic and state-led benefits among them has become weaker. In spite of great trust in Ambedkarite ideology, common Dalits have also understood the problem of the 'master key' idea suggested by Ambedkar – namely, capturing state power through votes will not resolve all their problems and sufferings. They experienced a long period of governance under BSP chief Mayawati in UP, which succeeded to some extent in providing them dignity and a share in governance and state-led projects and opportunities, but could not fulfil the expectations of a large section of the Dalit community.

Political and Electoral Crisis

In the 2009 Lok Sabha elections, the BSP won 27.42 per cent of the votes and 20 seats in UP (Narayan, 2014). In 2014, it garnered 19.6 per cent votes – nearly 8 percentage points less – and did not win a single seat.

Not only in UP, but all over India Dalit politics is losing its influence and electoral significance. In the recent 2019 assembly elections in Maharashtra and Haryana, Dalit political parties performed poorly. The BSP won just one seat in Haryana and none in Maharashtra, while no Republican Party of India (RPI) faction could win a seat in Maharashtra. In the 2019 Lok Sabha elections, the BSP, despite fielding candidates from a larger number of constituencies, won only 10 seats in UP. The RPI factions also could not win even a single seat in Maharashtra.

Dalit politics has never been able to consolidate its energies in one party; neither is there any one form of Dalit politics in the country. It is struggling to maintain its identity in different states in different forms and under different names. The agenda of empowering Dalits, liberating them from exploitation and oppression, and ensuring a good life for them seems to exist, but if we look beyond the BSP in UP, most other Dalit parties have been subsumed by mainstream political parties or become their adjuncts, negotiating for a small share of the pie of political power. This situation is mostly visible in Maharashtra, the home state of Ambedkar, the messiah of Dalits. When Ambedkar started developing Dalit politics in India, it was his belief that a day would come when Dalit political parties would emerge powerful in electoral politics and marginalize Brahminical forces. He formed the RPI in 1957 to ensure a better future for Dalits. By 1970, however, it had become so marginalized in Maharashtra that it had to bargain with the Indian National Congress (hereafter Congress) for even two seats (Verniers, 2019).

Kanshi Ram wrote a book called *The Chamcha Age: An Era of the Stooges* (1982) based on what he witnessed in Maharashtra, where he lived for some time. In his thesis, he advised Dalit parties to shun the tendency to merge with major political parties for a few seats and instead asked them to strengthen themselves politically. He said that Dalits and Bahujans should grow out of their 'begging' tendency and become givers rather than takers. He showed the way by developing a powerful Dalit–Bahujan movement in UP and other parts of northern India and then forming the BSP in 1984 (Narayan, 2014).

He developed his politics around the fact that Bahujans, comprising nearly 85 per cent of the population and including the Scheduled Castes (SCs), Scheduled Tribes (STs), and Other Backward Classes (OBCs), formed the largest social group in the country and could become electorally influential and shape the politics of power (Narayan, 2014). For some years, it seemed like his dream was coming true, and Mayawati, his protégé and the leader of the BSP, became the chief minister of UP four times. In 2007, her party swept the UP assembly polls through her strategy of social engineering, or *sarvajan* politics, taking everyone by surprise. However, the BSP has been pushed to the fringes again as her *sarvajan* politics failed to resist the rise of Hindutva.

Elsewhere in India, the Dalit vote is divided among the larger political parties. In Punjab, the two big Dalit social groups, namely the Ravidas Jatavs and the Valmikis, are now part of the social bases of the Congress and the Akali Dal, respectively. Since Kanshi Ram failed to bridge the division between the Ravidas Jatav and the Valmiki communities, a strong Dalit party could not emerge in the state. Similarly, electorally effective Dalit politics could not develop in the southern states of Karnataka, Tamil Nadu, Kerala, and Andhra Pradesh. In these states, Dalit political parties either did not emerge or were appropriated by the Congress and regional parties when they did.

The future of Dalit politics in India is thus bleak. The opportunism of a section of the political leadership, the inner division and conflict among influential

Dalit castes, the appropriation of Dalit communities by major political parties, the conduct of Dalit groups in begging the bigger parties for seats, the tendency to be takers rather than givers, and the emphasis on *sarvajan* politics over *bahujan* politics are some reasons for this state of affairs.

Hindutva Appropriation and the New Challenge

The assertive mobilizational campaign by the Rashtriya Swayamsevak Sangh (RSS) among Dalits, especially *ati*-Dalit (very Dalit) and *atipichda* (very backward) communities in India, has become another challenge for Dalit politics in the country. At its 2017 Vrindavan convention, the RSS decided to give importance to Dalits in its sociocultural campaigns (Ramchandran, 2019). Meant for intensifying its *samajiksamrasta* (social harmony) campaign and forging links with Dalits, *vanchit*s (deprived), and other oppressed social groups, this strategy comes in the wake of reports that BSP supremo Mayawati is losing her hold over the Dalit masses (Vij, 2020).

The door through which the RSS has tried to access Dalit communities is its counter mission of mobilizing non-Jatav Dalits under the Hindutva fold. This space appears to be an open field for the RSS campaign, because the Bahujan movement has failed to include these communities in the political sphere, especially in UP.

In its first phase, under Kanshi Ram, the BSP had tried to bring together the marginalized, backward, and Muslim communities under one party. But after his death, Kanshi Ram's efforts to link these communities with the Bahujan movement were not continued properly. Dalit communities are not homogeneous; there are various levels and layers in terms of political consciousness and development (Narayan, 2016). On analysing the grassroots reality, we find that among the large number of Dalit castes, it is only the Jatavs who are the core voters of the BSP. In addition, castes like Pasi, Dhobhi, Kori, Khatik, and so on, are considered the 'Bahujan voters' of the party. Among the 65 Dalit castes, more than 55 are numerically small and scattered, with almost negligible presence, some examples of which being Basor, Sapera, Kuchbadhiya, Musahar, Begaar, Tantwa, Rangrej, and Sarvan. At the local level, these communities often vote under the influence of prominent Dalit, backward, and *savarna* castes. Political parties are either unaware of their presence or do not give them much importance as they constitute a weak vote bank (Narayan, 2016).

These numerically small castes mostly reside in hamlets comprising 10–20 huts. Even in large, multi-caste hamlets, only two or three of their huts can be seen. Though their votes are given due importance in *panchayat* (local village council) elections, the same is not true of Lok Sabha and assembly elections. Even the BSP, which is actively involved in Dalit–Bahujan politics, takes them for granted. Candidates from these castes do not get tickets during elections and are also not allowed to participate politically. Thus, we see such castes living in penury and existing as an invisible social group in Indian democratic politics. Tragically, access to political power and representation and recognition as subaltern citizens are being denied to them even after seven decades of independence.

Though they come under the categories of 'Dalit' and 'Bahujan', their presence is almost negligible in Dalit and Bahujan politics. They get a minor share of the resources distributed to the poor and the marginalized, do not have leaders from their own communities, and political parties hesitate in giving them leadership roles. Economically weak, they lack access to education, and only when an economically strong group emerges from their communities, can they develop their own politics.

The RSS is actively propagating its *samrasta* (harmony) programmes among these groups in villages in the border region between UP and Nepal, which extends from Gorakhpur to Bahraich, Awadh, and some areas of eastern UP. It organizes programmes for the cleanliness of hamlets and *samrastabhoj* (community meals) with residents and runs primary schools there. It also runs its *shakha*s (sessions) in gardens and parks near the hamlets of marginalized Dalits, endeavouring to produce activists from among them (Narayan, 2008).

The Sangh Parivar's[1] efforts may produce activists who can take on leadership roles, but it is difficult to estimate how long these marginalized communities would need to carve out a place in the BJP's politics. During my field visits in 2017, I observed that in the executive training camps organized in the areas adjoining Allahabad, the RSS was making efforts to establish a connection with activists from 'small' Dalit castes.

There is a competitive tension between dominant Dalits and marginalized Dalit castes, whom the RSS has been trying to bring into the BJP fold through its 'social harmony campaign'. By giving tickets to Pasis, Sonkars, and Rawats, the BJP has tried to woo the most marginalized Dalit castes away from the BSP. The BJP has tried to convince voters that Mayawati had not worked in their favour, invoked Ambedkar and other Dalit heroes, promised a Bharat Ratna for Kanshi Ram, and arranged political meetings in Dalit hamlets with the help of RSS-affiliated social organizations. It has also participated in the caste associations of the Most Backward Castes (MBCs) and stoked Hindu polarization in the wake of the Muzaffarnagar riots to make further inroads into the BSP's vote bank. Relatedly, the BJP has portrayed Mayawati, who was seen as a beneficiary of Muslim consolidation, as unsympathetic to Hindus (Narayan, 2014). The MBCs were also promised that the social justice committee report prepared by the Rajnath Singh-led BJP government in UP would be implemented and that reservations in education and jobs would be granted (Mishra, 2018).

Through its campaigns and strategies of cultural politics, the RSS is raising the aspirations of Dalit communities, especially the most marginal Dalits, for them to be considered a part of the high order and socially important communities. It is also working to channelize the hidden desire of Dalit communities of being included with upper castes through cultural participation, religious inclusion, and creating inter-community dining opportunities for them. Through *sevakarya* (social service) for them, such as opening schools, organizing medical camps, and conducting cleanliness projects, the RSS is trying to facilitate the idea that social dignity and well-being may be acquired through the Sangh's agenda of *samajiksamrasta* (Bhattacharjee, 2019). Prime minister Narendra Modi, through the use of state policies, and the Sangh, through its social service activities and cultural politics, are transforming Dalit communities into aspirational communities. This is the counter-process of the politics of evoking Dalit-caste and sub-caste identities which has remained the basis of Dalit politics for a long time in UP.

Another phenomenon that may be observed while working in the grassroots is that the Sangh Parivar has succeeded in creating a Hindutva common sense among Dalits, making them think and express themselves like Hindus. They have not only generated this desire, but have also organized it in such a way that it can be politically mobilized at any time by using polarizing language.

New Desires and Non-Response

The Bahujan politics formulated by Kanshi Ram sought to build a grand alliance of various caste-based identities. This politics accorded respect to Dalit and backward-caste identities and created space for their participation in power politics. Both Dalits and backward castes benefitted from state-led development. Exposure to democratic politics, the market, and globalization, in turn, triggered new aspirations among sections of Dalits and backward castes, especially those who were early beneficiaries of social mobility.

BSP politics under Mayawati, however, has failed to respond to these aspirations as it continues to speak solely in terms of building caste and community alliances. Mayawati seems unable to develop a political language that can address the new aspirations of the fast-changing Dalit community, weakening her hold over the old BSP base. Although, in recent years, a creamy layer and a middle class have emerged among Dalits, a large section continues to be marginalized and remains on the periphery of society. Both these sections subscribe to the Dalit identity, but their concerns and aspirations are not the same, which Mayawati has failed to understand and evoke in her politics.

The BSP will also be forced to redefine its relationship with other Bahujan castes in the wake of the BJP's outreach to them. A big part of Kurmi society was associated with the BSP when it was a movement. Kurmi leaders like Sone Lal Patel were linked to the party and close to Kanshi Ram. Also, literate and educated OBC groups like Kori, Kushwaha, Kanchi, and Chaurasia identified with the BSP's politics of emancipation. But gradually these groups have become alienated from the party. A dominant middle class that was tech-savvy and used social media had already emerged in the backward castes. The BSP was unable to communicate with this group, while the BJP and Narendra Modi were adept at such outreach.

Crisis of Political Language

The crisis of Mayawati is also related to the political language of the BSP. She uses old, middle-class, non-governmental organization (NGO) language, which is not resonating with a large section of the Dalit community. The community is constantly evolving. Many Dalits are now wealthy and aspiring to integrate with the broader identity of being Hindu, which is why a large section is moving towards Dalit–Hindu aspirations.

Even in this time of crisis, there is no denying that Mayawati is a champion of Dalit identity, and it is too early to discount her. Having said that, if she does not change her language and align it with new Dalit aspirations, she will lose the game to the RSS. I say 'RSS' because she is in clear confrontation with the Sangh for Dalit support, and not with the BJP.

Economic growth has led to changes in the Dalit community, as argued, due to which Mayawati's political language fails to align with changed Dalit aspirations. If we look at the Jatav caste, which is her core vote base, the wealthy Jatavs are moving towards a Dalit–Hindu identity. Wealth has earned them respect in society, but they want full respect and total equality. This is where religion comes into the picture. The RSS is working to bring Jatavs closer to the Hindu identity through various upper-caste Hindu rituals, which Jatavs find respect in. The invisible Dalit castes, most of whom are illiterate, struggle for development and, most importantly, social respect, which comes with socio-religious integration. This is being addressed by the RSS. On the other hand, Mayawati is stuck in 'Dalit middle-class language'. In order to develop a new, accommodative language, Mayawati needs to interact with the community at the grassroots, which Kanshi Ram practised but she has not. She needs to appeal to both Ambedkarite and Hindu aspirations, which characterize the evolved, heterogenous Dalit community.

The Dalit movement in India is also suffering from an epistemological crisis. A section of Dalits finds itself in a dilemma about using the term 'Dalit' for their empowerment and are raising questions about their identity as Dalits. Some castes that fall within the SC category have objected to being called Dalit. They have asserted that they should be referred to by their caste names instead. But many falling under the SC category prefer to be called Dalit as it helps homogenize their social identity. The term 'SC' appears neutral when used for administrative purposes. It denotes only those castes that have been classified under the SC group. However, the term 'Dalit' includes OBCs, lower-caste Muslims, and other marginalized and subaltern groups. This word signifies a group which faces subordination and exploitation.

The word 'Dalit' emerged from the Sanskrit word *dalan*, which means 'oppressed' (Narayan, 2006), and so assigns an identity to the whole group of people oppressed under the caste system in Indian society. This word is also politically significant because of its popular use by Dalit and Bahujan leaders like Jyotirao Phule and Ambedkar. So, the use of the term 'SC' may end up diluting its cultural and political significance. Mayawati's mentor, Kanshi Ram, himself frequently used the word 'Dalit' in his political discourse. He evolved a larger identity for the oppressed in Indian society as 'Bahujan', which included SCs, OBCs, STs, and Muslims.

We observe that, on the one hand, the term 'Dalit' represents political desire for socially and politically contesting communities who acquire dignity and political power. However, on the other hand, the way Dalit consciousness is being formed at the social level enables them to obtain dignity and power through various social strategies – namely, contestation, adoption, and accommodation. The influence of popular sects on Dalit consciousness facilitates acquiring dignity through interaction and develops space for accommodation.

With the help of a research team from G. B. Pant Social Science Institute, Allahabad, I had conducted a study on popular Dalit religious and cultural sects in four states in 2017–18: UP, Bihar, Madhya Pradesh, and Odisha. These sects included the Kabir Panth, Satnaami Panth, and Mahima Dharma. It was interesting to note that the daily lives of Dalits – their behaviour, intelligence, and folk knowledge – developed mostly under the influence of these sects. a.

While interviewing Dalit groups residing in various villages across the four states, it was observed that Kabir Das, Ravidas, Guru Ghasidas, and Mahima Swami featured prominently in many of their songs and stories (Narayan, 2018a). The influence of Swami Achhutanand of the Aadi Hindu Panth on the consciousness of these Dalits was also observed (Narayan, 2018a). Their spiritual thoughts and rituals, beginning from birth to death, are all inspired by the ideologies of these saints and traditional sects. Though it is said that saints do not belong to any particular caste, it is also seen that numerous saints of the Dalit and backward castes – like Ravidas, Dhana, and Peepa – were born during the Bhakti period. The Bhakti saints spread feelings of self-respect and humanity, which deeply influenced Dalit culture (Burchett, 2009).

At the same time, Ambedkar played a great role in arousing a democratic culture based on constitutional values among Dalits. He taught them how to become responsible citizens and helped them develop amicable relations with the state.

It thus becomes clear that the development of social and cultural consciousness among Dalits was inspired by reformist sects and Ambedkar. We can say that they were the decisive elements of their consciousness and that the Dalit consciousness is formed by the interplay of these two elements. This might be a drawback for political parties which try and understand Dalit consciousness only through the eyes of Ambedkar.

In the absence of either of these elements, it is not possible to understand Dalits' consciousness and their inner self in a holistic manner. Many organizations like the RPI, which wish to consider Dalits only through the Ambedkarvadi lens or want to engage in polarization around Ambedkar, may find little success. Kanshi Ram understood this fact, evident in his speech at the Ram Navami fair in Chhattisgarh, where Dalits thronged in huge numbers (Akela, 2006). He also worked with the Satnamis and developed the Bahujan leadership. Simultaneously, he associated himself with Ambedkar's symbolism and actively visited Ambedkar fairs. He gave importance to Ambedkar's ideology, albeit in a selective manner. However, as his opinions on various issues contrasted with those of Ambedkar, he developed his own brand of pragmatic politics.

There was a point in Kanshi Ram's life when due to the immense pressure of Ambedkarite intellectuals and groups, he had thought of embracing Buddhism, but ultimately, he did not convert (Narayan, 2014). Kanshi Ram knew very well that in states like UP and Punjab, and also in other parts of India, large numbers of Dalits were Kabir *panthi* or Ravidasi. He understood that if he embraced Buddhism, it might have a bad effect on the party's politics as it would lose the symbolic power of getting associated with these sects.

Mayawati, who grew politically under Kanshi Ram's guidance, has always revered the saints and gurus of Dalit society, and this has been one of the biggest reasons behind the accomplishments of her party. But of late there has been a decrease in the use of names of Dalit saints and gurus in the party's discussions. Why did this happen?

Production of Leaders and the BSP Movement

Understanding the issue of leadership is crucial to explain the weakening of Bahujan politics in north India. From the 1980s to 2016, the movement asserted itself largely through the BSP under the hegemonic influence of the Kanshi Ram–Mayawati combine (Salim, 2020). Around 2016, it saw the emergence of aggressive youth leaders like Jignesh Mevani in Gujarat and Chandrashekhar Azad in UP.

> These youth leaders used the assertive Dalit vocabulary against the 'dominant others', which the BSP employed during its early phase. Over time, the BSP went beyond aggressive language against other sections of society and adopted a partly inclusive discourse, which suited its move to bahujan and sarvajan politics. Chandrashekhar, who formed the Bhim Army, was imprisoned for his alleged involvement in the Saharanpur and Shabbirpur caste violence cases. (Narayan, 2018b)

His release from jail on 14 September 2018 is being perceived in two ways. Some analysts and political leaders believe that his release is part of the BJP's plan to gain his support and appease the SC public. This could create sympathy among Dalits and prepare a political climate in which the votes of the Mayawati-led BSP could be divided. Another set of political observers believes that his release will strengthen the Mahagathbandhan (Grand Alliance)[2] politics in UP. Chandrashekhar had declared his support for the Mahagathbandhan in opposition to the BJP in the 2019 election. He had also declared his deep respect for Mayawati, calling her his *bua* (aunt). Mayawati spurned his claim to a *bua–bhatija* (aunt–nephew) relationship and described his release as a BJP strategy.

While Mayawati is trying to sideline Chandrashekhar, the Bhim Army is expanding its activities. For example, after Yogi Adityanath's 2018 statement claiming Hanuman was a Dalit, Chandrashekhar organized a massive rally in Muzaffarnagar and appealed to Dalits to appropriate Hanuman temples. He also demanded that Dalit priests be appointed at such temples (Bhardwaj, 2018).

Mayawati needs to handle the emergence of Dalit–Bahujan youth leaders cautiously. She should either absorb them in the BSP's rubric of the Bahujan movement or try to neutralize their political impact through her own campaigns in the future. These leaders can pave the way for erosion and fragmentation of the political base of the BSP, of which a section of Dalits is looking for political space in other parties like the BJP. These situations are producing a churning in Dalit politics in UP which is generating new leaders such as Chandrashekhar.

Double Dilemma

The Dalit–Bahujan movement in north India is suffering from a double dilemma: handling caste and religion together and balancing Hindu and Muslim groups to expand the vote base of the BSP. We have already discussed the first dilemma while dealing with the political language issue. We shall now discuss the second dilemma associated with handling Hindu and Muslim communities. During the 2017 assembly elections, the BSP under Mayawati tried to extend the reach of the Bahujan movement by proposing a new social alliance that was called the Dalit–Muslim alliance. The strengthening of the Dalit–Muslim alliance is an important part of the BSP's plan. To do so, the party worked to form a core team of local and regional Dalit and Muslim leaders to spread fraternal feelings at the grassroots.

BSP leaders have started visiting Dalit and Muslim *basti*s (slums). Local leaders of the party visited Muslim slums targeting the 'BJP–SP [Samajwadi Party] undeclared and invisible alliance' and claimed that 'there won't be any riots after Mayawati's return to power'.[3] Besides targeting the BJP amidst the Dalit–Muslim electorate, the BSP also made Muslims suspicious of the SP, the party they had supported for nearly 25 years. In order to strengthen the alliance, Mayawati planned to bring the Muslim community closer by providing them electoral representation. In the 2017 UP assembly elections, the BSP provided tickets to more than 100 Muslim candidates.

Though the BSP perceives Muslims as a singular entity, its focus is on OBC and Dalit Muslims, or the Azlaf and Arzal Muslims. The party is increasingly active in the hamlets and slums of Muslim social groups like Ansari, Gaddi, Tatwa, Fakir, Halalkhor, and so on. This time, the party is not attempting to exploit class and caste differences among Muslims, though it often highlights the issues of poor Muslims. The phrase 'poor Muslim' invokes the category of class, without breaking away from Kanshi Ram's idea of poor Muslims being a part of Bahujan unity, which includes Dalits, MBCs, and OBCs.

In the process of forging a Dalit–Muslim alliance, Mayawati is facing a double dilemma. On the one hand, she has to try sociopolitical alliances like a Dalit–Muslim alliance during elections; on the other, she has to retain the section of Dalits who have evolved an upper-caste Hindu mindset in the BSP fold. She tried to work out her politics in the broader Hindu framework, but she soon realized that religion was the turf of the BJP–RSS and she would lose her ground there. As a last resort, to save the section influenced by her, the BSP leader has talked about converting middle-class Dalits to Buddhism. However, she is caught between the Ravidas and Kabir sects of Dalit communities, who are influenced by Hinduism, and middle-class Dalits, who are Buddhists, both of whom she wants to please.

The Pandemic and Dalit Politics

The COVID-19 pandemic has brought about two important shifts in the political discourse about subalterns and the marginalized in north India. First, the lockdown caused suffering to vulnerable labourers, migrants, and the poor, and brought them to the centre of deliberations. Second, the space of subalterns in the public health system and the safety of their bodies emerged as a major concern in public discussion. However, the issues and concerns of Dalits specifically remained disguised in these debates under the broader subaltern categories of poor, vulnerable, labourer, and marginalized. Before the pandemic, 'Dalit' was one of the key concerns of deliberation about the subalterns. The pandemic resulted in a shift in the politics of language about the marginalized in north India. In contemporary debates, there is a reappearance of class-based terms, vocabularies, and categories, which are overshadowing all important discussions. The identity issues around caste and other related concerns have become either invisible or visible as a fragment of this larger domain. It seems that Dalit leaders like Mayawati and Chandrasekhar have not been able to effectively engage with these new shifts. They could not carve out a specific location in these new debates for their politics. They have to reorient their caste-identity-based political language and reshape their political discourse to engage with class-oriented political debates, which have emerged in these virus-centred times.

Dalit leaders are in a dilemma of how to address their constituencies in class terminology, failing to support the labour, migrants, and poor, who suffered the most during the pandemic, despite the fact that the majority are Dalits and OBCs. This dilemma is causing a crisis of language of politics for Dalit leaders in north India, making them almost passive in the political discourse. The coronavirus converted us to a bare biological body from a social body, which appears as a condition of bare life as observed by the eminent theoretician Giorgio Agamben (2020). The pandemic has also blunted the edge of the Dalit-versus-non-Dalit dichotomy temporarily, creating a further dilemma for Dalit politics in terms of using this conventional strategy, earlier the most important source of Dalit mobilization in India. It is possible that these shifts in political debates may also continue in the post-pandemic phase at least for a few years.

Most economists are predicting economic slowdown, as the virus has produced a situation which may result in increased vulnerability and marginalities at a horizontal level across castes and religions. The Dalit movement in north India is habituated to dealing with caste-based binaries in its mobilizational language but has failed to develop flexibilities to respond to the changing political diction with the changing times.

Conclusion

In fact, Dalit politics, especially in north India, has not changed its political diction for 30 years, retaining the language which had evolved with the Kanshi Ram-led Bahujan movement. It has failed to develop new social programmes in its politics of democracy and Dalit empowerment, which may prepare a solid ground for Dalit emancipation. What we are observing is that this movement is facing a crisis of agendas and social programmes. The constant repetition of unfulfilled claims and commitments, and similar programmatic slogans and promises, has created disillusionment in a section of their support base.

Another issue is that the Dalit movement in north India is grappling with a leadership crisis. This crisis has appeared due to a break in the *nabhi-nal* (umbilical cord) relationship between 'movement' and 'party'. In states like UP, Bihar, Madhya Pradesh, Punjab, and Rajasthan, Dalit assertions are mostly centred around the electoral politics of Dalit–Bahujan political groups and parties. Some alternative social movements like those led by Jignesh Mevani and Chandrashekhar Azad also could not restrain their electoral aspirations. During the Bahujan movement in the 1990s, the idea was that the movement and the party may facilitate each other. But the BSP, which emerged from the Bahujan social movement, gradually developed as a pyramidically structured party, discontinuing its reciprocity with the Dalit movement under Mayawati. Further, within the BSP, the development of political leaders from various Dalit–Bahujan castes froze. This caused erosion in its broader social base and ultimately weakened the Dalit movement in north India. A contradictory situation emerged in the Dalit movement which disturbed the growth of the party horizontally. On the one hand, the Bahujan movement gave a strong boost to political aspirations within various numerically important Dalit–Bahujan castes and communities; on the other, this unnatural freezing of the flow of emergence of political leadership at various levels smashed political ambitions and initiatives of the cadres and hampered the natural growth of the party and the movement.

The Dalit movement in north India is constantly facing new situations and challenges, but those who are leading it are not able to change their strategies, diction, forms, and grammar of politics to respond to them. Under the influence of Ambedkarite ideologies and Dalit–Bahujan movements, an assertive and politically aware Dalit consciousness was being formed among a section of Dalit groups. Hindutva intervention among Dalits posed a new challenge to this process by producing a Hindutva common sense among a section of Dalits. The Dalit movement has not yet reached its aspired heights, and a proper consciousness has not been disseminated among grassroots Dalits. The intervention by Hindutva groups filled the blanks and mobilized a section of the most marginalized Dalits under the Hindutva flag. Now, the pandemic has also posed a new challenge for the Dalit movement in north India. This challenge has arisen because the pandemic has relegated caste-based identities and concerns, which were earlier an ideological resource base for the Dalit movement in the region, as a secondary discourse. This virus-centred situation has produced anxiety for personal safety and health, which is beyond caste and religion. This new challenge may be temporary, but it may bring a paradigmatic shift for Dalit politics in north India.

The Dalit movement and politics in north India need to come out of their epistemological crises, and they may need a great deal of effort to invent something new in form and content to respond to new challenges. They also need to evolve new social strategies for expansion, based on current social mapping. Dalit leaders must realize that the Dalit community and society have changed drastically and are not in the same situation in which they were in the decades of the 1940s and 1990s – that is, during the lifetimes of Ambedkar and Kanshi Ram.

Notes

1. The Sangh Parivar refers to the association of Hindu nationalist organizations clustered around the RSS, including the BJP, the Bajrang Dal, and the Vishva Hindu Parishad.
2. The Mahagathbandhan is an alliance of opposition parties formed against the BJP.
3. Interview with a BSP party worker.

Bibliography

Agamben, G. 2020. 'The Enemy Is Not Outside, It Is within Us'. Book Haven (Blog), Stanford University, CA. https://bookhaven.stanford.edu/2020/03/giorgio-agamben-on-coronavirus-the-enemy-is-not-outside-it-is-within-us/. Accessed on 26 October 2022.

Akela, A. R. 2006. *Manyavar Kanshi Ram Saahab Ke Sakshatkaar*. Aligarh: Anand Sahitya Sadan.

Bhardwaj, V. 2018. 'Dalit Group in Muzaffarnagar Tries to Take Possession of Hanuman Temple, Muzaffarnagar'. *Hindustan Times*, 5 December. https://www.hindustantimes.com/lucknow/dalit-group-in-muzaffarnagar-tries-to-take-possession-of-hanuman-temple/story-UAwWTXINORlLofy8tN9EcM.html. Accessed on 14 October 2022.

Bhattacharjee, M. 2019. *Disaster Relief and the RSS: Resurrecting Religion through Humanitarianism*. New Delhi: SAGE Publications.

Burchett, P. 2009. '*Bhakti*'. *International Journal of Hindu Studies* 13(2): 115–41. https://jstor.org/stable/40608021. Accessed on 6 November 2022.

Dhoomil. 2018. *Sansad se Sadak Tak*. New Delhi: Rajkamal Prakashan.

Mishra, S. 2018. 'BJP Follows Rajnath's OBC Quota Template'. *Times of India*, 3 May. https://timesofindia.indiatimes.com/city/lucknow/bjp-follows-rajnaths-obc-quota-template/articleshow/64009540.cms. Accessed on 2 December 2022.

Narayan, B. 2006. *Women Heroes and Dalit Assertion in North India*. New Delhi: SAGE Publications.

———. 2008. 'Demarginalisation and History: Dalit Re-Invention of the Past'. *South Asia Research* 28(2): 169–84.

———. 2012. 'Ambedkar and Kanshi Ram: So Alike, yet So Different'. *The Hindu*, 11 July.

———. 2014. *Kanshiram: Leader of the Dalits*. New Delhi: Penguin Books.

———. 2016. *Fractured Tales: Invisibles in Indian Democracy*. New Delhi: Oxford University Press.

———. 2018a. 'Field Diary 2017–18'. G. B. Pant Social Science Institute, Prayajraj.

———. 2018b. 'The Battle for the Bahujan'. *Indian Express*, 4 December.

Pai, S. 2002. *Dalit Assertion and the Unfinished Democratic Revolution: The Bahujan Samaj Party in Uttar Pradesh*. New Delhi: SAGE Publications.

———. 2020. 'Future of Dalit Politics Swings between Decline and Regeneration'. *The Wire*, 25 March. https://thewire.in/politics/dalit-politics-chandra-shekhar-aazad. Accessed on 26 October 2022.

Ram, K. 2015. *The Chamcha Age: An Era of the Stooges*. New Delhi: Siddharth Books.

Ramchandran, S. K. 2019. 'Focus on Dalits, Minorities, RSS Tells BJP'. *Hindustan Times*, 12 July. https://www.hindustantimes.com/india-news/focus-on-dalits-minorities-rss-tells-bjp/story-st9nMix8518SMjudEH6VpK.html. Accessed on 13 November 2022.

Salim, S. 2020. 'Kanshi Ram, Mayawati & BSP: Rise of Bahujan Politics in India'. *Heritage Times*, 16 February. https://heritagetimes.in/kanshi-ram-mayawati-bsp-rise-of-bahujan-politics-in-india/. Accessed on 23 November 2022.

Verniers, G. 2019. 'Maharashtra Wasn't the Cakewalk the BJP Thought It Would Be: 34 Charts and Maps Explain the Verdict'. *Scroll.in*, 30 October. https://scroll.in/article/941968/why-wasnt-maharashtra-the-cakewalk-the-bjp-thought-it-would-be-34-charts-explain-the-verdict. Accessed on 26 October 2022.

Vij, S. 2020. 'The Mayawati Era Is Over. Bye Bye Behenji'. *The Print*, 27 January. https://theprint.in/opinion/the-mayawati-era-is-over-bye-bye-behenji/354887/. Accessed on 6 November 2022.

Part IV
Aspirations and Anxieties

16

Technology in the Lives of Young Dalits

Snigdha Poonam and Samarth Bansal

Ved Prakash, a young Dalit man from Bihar, had a postgraduate degree and a teaching job at a government-run school when he decided to study journalism. 'I had been teaching for five years when I quit my job. I thought if I don't do this job, someone else [from my community] can do it. But we have no one in the media.'

So, he searched the internet for journalism colleges and came across the Indian Institute of Mass Communication, New Delhi. 'I applied right away and cleared both the written test and interview,' he said. He chose to study television journalism. In 2014, he got his first major job as a business reporter for the *Dainik Bhaskar* in Patna. 'It was a good job. Mainly, I would receive business-related press releases and turn them into news reports.'

Some of those press releases came from Dalit organizations. 'I was receiving a lot of news about Dalits.' But he noticed that his articles were often missing from the next day's newspaper. The desk was killing them, he said. 'If I asked them why they weren't publishing my articles day after day, they would say I shouldn't complain as long as I was being paid a salary.'

He was told to keep quiet and carry on. 'Kranti nahin karni hai. Naukri karo' (Don't start a revolution; do your job). So he quit. 'My whole purpose was to highlight the voices of my people in the media.'[1]

Upper castes have a stranglehold across print, television, and digital media. According to a 2019 Newslaundry–Oxfam study, as many as 106 of the 121 managerial positions in the surveyed newsrooms were held by upper-caste individuals; three out of every four anchors (among a total of 40 anchors on Hindi channels and 47 on English channels) of news debates were upper-caste; only 5 per cent of all articles in English newspapers were written by Dalits or Adivasis (Hindi newspapers scored slightly higher at around 10 per cent); and 72 per cent of by-lined articles on news websites were written by upper-caste journalists.

Years earlier, in 2006, the Centre for the Study of Developing Societies (CSDS), New Delhi, had surveyed 37 Delhi-based platforms and found that 90 per cent of the decision-makers in English-language print publications and 79 per cent in English-language television channels were upper-caste (*Indian Express*, 2019).

Across regional media, too, it is rare to find salaried Dalit journalists. In a survey of news organizations in Lucknow published in this volume, Sandesh Singh found that only 8 per cent of the staff were Dalits (see Chapter 9). His analysis of the content published in three Hindi newspapers in Uttar Pradesh (UP) shows the impact of this disparity on the coverage of Dalit issues. While Dalit issues found relatively more space in newspapers – across news and editorial pages – in 2016–17 as compared to 1998–99 – the quality of the articles did not see an equivalent improvement. Cases of atrocities, especially against Dalit women, were handled insensitively, perpetuating casteist stereotypes. Stories of violence against Dalits outnumbered reports concerning other aspects of Dalits' public life: economics, sports, and arts, among other things. So, while the awareness of Dalit issues has increased, Singh argues the disconnect persists due to the lack of Dalit journalists in newsrooms.

Over the past few years, many Dalits have launched their own media platforms using the internet as an ally. In 2016, Prakash created his news channel on YouTube and became his own boss. 'I lost trust in mainstream media. On YouTube, there is no gatekeeper, only an audience – as big as any newspaper can claim.'[2]

As of September 2022, his one-man channel, Activist Ved, has 1.25 million subscribers who await every report of his from Bihar – ranging from corruption scandals to election campaigns. Shooting through the day and editing at night, Prakash, who is the only prominent Dalit political journalist in Patna, covers Bihar's messy politics through a clear-cut lens: caste.

'Dalits across the world were angry. Online, they could be angry together and turn that fury into something potent,' writes Yashica Dutt in her memoir, *Coming Out as A Dalit* (2019: 165). She describes how Hyderabad University student Rohith Vemula's suicide in 2016, following persistent caste-based discrimination on the campus, brought into focus many existing digital outlets run by Dalits and inspired several others.

'Large numbers of people now started following RTI [Round Table India], Ambedkar's Caravan, Savari, Velivada and Dalit Camera for updates they couldn't find elsewhere,' Dutt (2019: 166) wrote. Some of them use text, some video, and some both. Their coverage is wide-ranging: breaking news to data-based journalism, op-eds to listicles. YouTube already hosts more than a dozen channels

(Dalit Dastak, Awaaz India, Bahujan TV, and so on) that cover Dalit–Bahujan issues ignored by the mainstream media as well as mainstream issues from the Dalit–Bahujan perspective.

Prakash argues, however, that many more Dalits would have to enter the media to make a real difference. A journalism career remains inaccessible to most. 'They don't go in for media education. Many don't even know that these courses and degrees exist. Because of that, they are cut off from opportunities.'[3]

Another reason is the lack of approval for the high-risk and low-reward journalism jobs within Dalit communities. 'There is still a craze for government jobs no matter how small,' Prakash said. However small they may be, government jobs guarantee income security and social influence.

> My own mother thinks I still have a government job in Patna. If she finds out that I no longer do, she will worry that finding a bride for me will be an issue. It doesn't matter that I earn more than I did as a schoolteacher or that I have five post-graduate degrees or that lakhs of people watch my videos. She hasn't seen any of them.[4]

Meanwhile, Prakash's channel gains hundreds of thousands of followers every day. 'We are reaching 10 lakh [1 million] people every day,' he recently posted on Facebook, where the views for his videos even surpass those accrued on YouTube. His ad-based earnings are divided across the two platforms. 'I am making decent money – more than I would have at a government job.' He says most of his viewers are from backward castes, but his content is keenly watched by upper-caste internet users as well. 'They are curious to know if they are being criticized.' Some of them go on to threaten him in the comments. 'One of them recently said "Zinda ya murda pakdo inhein" [Catch him dead or alive]'. He will not be backing off anytime soon, however. 'Dar toh hamare andar hai nahin' (I have no fear in me).

His attitude may be unique, but his experiences would resonate with many Dalits of his generation. The majority of India's 200 million Dalits (Census of India, 2011) have limited access to mainstream technologies, but these are increasingly central to the lives of those who do.

The internet claims the top spot. Young Dalits are using the internet in greater numbers every day: asserting identities, expressing views, finding communities, organizing protests, learning skills, reporting news, creating entertainment, passing time, and finding love. These are usual online activities for internet users belonging to any background, but for young Dalits, many of them are often fraught with the same tensions, risks, and threats that mark their physical worlds.

The freedoms offered by the internet can be conditional. Asserting caste pride online can result in real-life vengeance; trying to find love can be frustrating; the support mobilized for a cause can be fleeting; and many voices remain unheard. The inequalities are not limited to the internet alone. Dalits continue to face discrimination in tech education and jobs in India as well as abroad. But many of them are pushing back in wide-ranging ways for more agency, solidarity, and opportunities. The outcomes are often unexpected.

Getting around Gatekeepers

In September 2019, when Bollywood director Neeraj Ghaywan posted a job call on Twitter seeking out assistant writers and directors from Dalit, Bahujan, and Adivasi (DBA) communities (Shanta, 2019), he was bombarded with threats for being 'casteist' and even subjected to a police complaint.

Ghaywan's intention was to use Twitter as a platform to open up access to Bollywood opportunities for DBA aspirants.

> We haven't had an acknowledged Dalit or Adivasi artist in all of [Hindi film] history, whether in front of or behind the camera. I am the first Dalit director in Hindi cinema's 100-plus-year history. If you look at population figures, Dalits and Adivasis make up 26 per cent together even if we are citing a dated census. We have ghosted that entire population in the industry and in the cinema.[5]

The results of that exclusion are clear on the screen. In 2015, *The Hindu* analysed all Hindi movies released over the previous two years and found an upper-caste monopoly on characters and plots (Rukmini and Naig, 2015). In 2013 and 2014, only two movies each featured lead characters from explicitly backward castes. The leading men and women were shown to be upper-caste Hindus in most other films. The article further noted that the overwhelming majority of nearly 750 actors and actresses who were in more than five movies over the last decade happen to be upper-caste Hindus, followed by Muslims.

If Dalit characters appear on screen at all, they are shown as either victims or villains – a selective and stereotypical portrayal. As Prashant Ingole argues in this volume, film-makers ignore Dalits as an assertive force that also fights for dignity and self-respect (see Chapter 8). Ingole writes that while mainstream movies evoke nationalistic and Gandhian values or the quest for Hindi–Muslim unity, the stories of downtrodden masses and their liberation remain missing. Bollywood has largely ignored, he says, questions of inter-caste marriage and Dalit rights – in fact, the word 'Dalit' itself is hard to come by.

Ghaywan believes an obvious answer is to include more Dalits on and off camera. And that makes a difference: over the past few years, multiple regional films made by Dalit artists – writers, directors, actors – have told brilliant stories (*Fandry*, *Chauthi Koot*), and some have also broken box-office records (*Kabali*, *Sairat*).

'I have tried to speak to like-minded [Bollywood] film-makers. They say we want to do it, but don't know how to do it because it is rude to ask someone what their caste is,' Ghaywan says. It just shows how Hindi film-makers avoid confronting caste.

That is where, he said, technology can help. 'Tech puts you on a platform with somebody who is not your equal. It gives you access. You can actually go and ask a director on Twitter. Access is the most difficult aspect [for an aspirant]. Earlier, the biggest challenge used to be "How do you get the phone number of a director?"'

But technology can only do so much, Ghaywan pointed out. A year after his Twitter job call, his inboxes remained flooded with CVs from DBA aspirants, but in the absence of an industry-wide interface, he said he would not have the time, money, and other resources to train more than a few. 'That's what I am grappling with. I don't know if I can help all of them, and I feel guilty, and the guilt pushes you into a vicious cycle where you don't look at any of their messages.'[6]

Some believe the emergence of streaming platforms such as Netflix and Amazon Prime could improve inclusion. 'At least there is an acknowledgement that there is a lot more scope for that,' says Anushka Shah who runs Civic Studios, a Mumbai-based film lab set up to create civic-themed entertainment. 'The web series is a longer medium. There is more space for nuance and complexity. Among recent productions, *Mirzapur* [Amazon Prime, 2018], *Pataal Lok* [Amazon Prime, 2020], and *Inside Edge* [Amazon Prime, 2017] featured Dalit characters ... If you need to create an impact, representation is key,' she said.[7]

Ghaywan, who has directed parts of a web series for Netflix (*Sacred Games*) remains sceptical. 'Some of the directors are doing it, but the studios aren't consciously going after hiring diverse talent.'[8]

To many DBA film aspirants, YouTube offers a way to get around gatekeepers. 'If the content they put up is good, it goes viral. I recently heard about an Odisha singer who did something with beatbox on YouTube. It became viral and led to Bollywood offers,' said Ghaywan. The aforementioned singer is a 27-year-old Dalit migrant worker, Duleswar Tandi, of Kalahandi district in Odisha, who raps about the woes of the rural poor through songs such as 'Hashtag Farmer' and 'Sarkar Jabab De'. In July 2020, Bollywood composer Vishal Dadlani tweeted to him a public offer (DH Webdesk, 2020) to record and release his music. This, Ghaywan says, is among the limited uses of technology. 'The idea of virality is that it helps transcend the barriers.'

An Unequal Industry

While many Dalits are using technology to enter previously inaccessible professions, it is the tech jobs themselves that prove the hardest to land.

Most tech jobs continue to be dominated by upper-caste engineers and managers. In its 2018 report on Facebook and hate speech, Equality Labs, a Dalit civil rights organization that works for caste, gender, and racial equity, argued that part of the problem stems from the lack of diversity in the company (Soundararajan et al., 2019).

'Facebook staff lacks the cultural competency needed to recognize, respect, and serve caste, religious, gender, and queer minorities,' the authors said, arguing that 'hiring of Indian staff alone does not ensure cultural competence across India's multitude of marginalized communities. Minorities require meaningful representation across Facebook's staff and contractor relationships' (Soundararajan et al., 2019: 7).

Many technology professionals, especially in top executive positions, are graduates of the Indian Institutes of Technology (IITs) or other elite engineering colleges. At the IITs, 15 per cent of seats are reserved for the Scheduled Castes (SCs), 7.5 per cent for the Scheduled Tribes (STs), and 27 per cent for the Other Backward Classes (OBCs). But Dalit students in the IITs have reported facing caste-based discrimination for a long time.

In a 2015–16 survey conducted at IIT Varanasi by World Bank researchers, students from the SC and ST categories reported facing negative attitudes from fellow students. 'Almost everyone in both the general and reserved caste categories believes that general caste students have higher or the same ability as others,' the study noted, and 'a majority of students in both caste categories believe that reserved category students are less able. Almost no one in any of the caste categories believes that the reserved category students have more ability than others' (Pandey and Pandey, 2018). These beliefs and perceptions, the authors concluded, create a psychological barrier to the academic performance of students from lower-caste groups and serve as regular reminders of their caste identity in their everyday life on campus.

'Engineers really invest in this mythology of their own castelessness,' said Ajantha Subramanian, a professor of anthropology at Harvard University, at an online panel discussion on 'Caste in Tech' organized by Equality Labs.[9]

Subramanian, who has researched caste discrimination at IITs, said most engineers 'believe their academic and professional successes are due entirely to their own merit or intellect or innate abilities and have nothing to do with being long-standing beneficiaries of caste privilege'.

This idea of Dalit students being less deserving, which typically shows up in a university setting, extends to the workplace as well. In June 2020, the California government filed a civil rights lawsuit against Cisco for caste-based discrimination against an Indian–American Dalit engineer. The case involved Sunder Iyer, a Brahmin engineer at Cisco, who revealed to his colleagues that the complainant, a Dalit engineer, made it to IIT through reservation quota – a fact he knew because both of them went to IIT Bombay at the same time. When the Dalit engineer reported this to the company's human resources (HR) department, the case was sidelined because going by the books, caste discrimination was not unlawful (Mukherji, 2020). Following the complaint, Iyer took away the role of the Dalit engineer as the lead on two technologies, and over the next two years, his professional growth was stalled, bonuses denied, and promotions put on halt.

'Caste-based discrimination doesn't just affect the employees; it also affects the companies,' said Maya Kamble, a software engineer and founding member of the Ambedkar Association of North America, at the 'Caste in Tech' panel discussion. 'If you lose Dalit employees, you are not just losing one employee; you are losing a big market space as well. It's in the interest of the tech industry to have caste as a protected category for themselves.' The next billion users of the internet, she reminded her audience, will come largely from marginalized communities. She stressed that Dalits are the best representatives of their own problems as well as the solutions that technology can provide.

Political Mobilization on Social Media

In April 2018, tens of thousands of Dalits across India took to the streets to protest against a Supreme Court judgment that diluted the provisions of the Scheduled Castes and Scheduled Tribes (Prevention of Atrocities) Act, 1989.

The 'Bharat *bandh*' was unprecedented in many ways, starting with the fact that there was no central leadership or established political party behind the nationwide protests. Instead, Dalits were mobilized, in less than two weeks, through repeated messages shared through a network of WhatsApp and Facebook groups. Real-time photos and videos were circulated on the day of the protest to get more people out.

The protests illustrate the transformative power of social media for Dalit politics. In a 2020 paper, Arvind Kumar Thakur, an independent researcher, argued that without the viral diffusion of videos and trending social media hashtags, many violent attacks on Dalit youth and the offline mobilizations that followed would have gone ignored. This network-driven mobilization has reduced the dependence of Dalit activists on 'non-Dalit leaders and intelligentsia to express their political views' (Thakur, 2020).

Digital platforms have also enabled local movements to take on a national character, breaking down traditional geographical and cultural boundaries (Harad, 2018). 'The imagination of the Dalit community has begun to expand beyond the confines of the neighbourhood, city, and the state,' Amit Ahuja (2018), an associate professor of Political Science at the University of California, Santa Barbara, wrote in *The Print*. 'Exposed to online Dalit discourse from different parts of the country, youths have begun to imagine themselves as part of a larger community across language and cultural divides.'

These interactions extend internationally, too. 'When Dalit youth, connected through social media, see the power of Black Lives Matter, when they see how the protest movement in summer 2020 in the United States led to a moment of reckoning for many white folks, it spreads globally,' notes Dutt.[10]

> The pop culture of the United States, like TV shows, in many ways defines pop culture across the world and has a huge cultural impact. When civil rights and protest movements occur, they resonate with Dalits in India. There is an instant sense of kinship … India has already seen a series of protests in the last five years. The public, especially Dalits, already understand how important protests are. So, when the Black Lives Matter movement happened in the summer, it was like the perfect storm.[11]

This thread of Dalit movements being inspired by Black movements is not new and has happened over the decades. 'We are natural allies,' Dutt observes. The transnational social media connections speed up the visibility of a trend.

Conversations on social media are also changing the construction of political identities. 'Identity and representation are very important when people are getting used to social media,' says Tejas Harad, an anti-caste social commentator. 'There are more users now and the assertion of identity has grown. When people watch others [from their community] feeling confident they also start to feel confident, and slowly they become comfortable talking about their positions.'

But there is no one fixed approach in asserting identity. Harad says the youth Dalit leader Jignesh Mevani, an independent member of the legislative assembly (MLA) in Gujarat, completely sidesteps caste identity and turns attention to economic issues – a class-based approach to look at the caste system. At the same time, with more users talking about caste-based issues from different geographical locations, diverse Dalit voices are emerging. 'People are getting radicalised at a younger age, even those who aren't from activist families. People in Maharashtra are usually immersed in the movement from their childhood, but today people in other parts of India also start getting politicised at younger ages,' he says.[12]

When a protest movement gathers attention, it appears that Dalits speak as a monolith. But Dutt says that view is reductive as it ignores the multiple layers of Dalit resistance rooted in individual experiences. 'Sub-castes in India are a reality of the caste system,' she notes, pointing to the inequities within the Dalit community. 'When we are talking about [the] Dalit movement, we are talking about 25 million people. That's a huge number. We can't go and say this one person represents the entire movement.'[13]

But some scholars argue that the promise of these movements may be short-lived, with their impact weakened by their ephemerality. In his paper, Thakur (2020) shows that Dalit hashtag activism over an issue loses momentum after a few months, and the multiplicity of online Dalit narratives, alongside the dominance of upper-caste Hindu narratives, are hurdles for effective networked resistance.

In an interview with the International Dalit Solidarity Network, Anju Singh (2017), a Dalit woman activist working with the All India Dalit Women's Rights Forum, highlighted the broader challenges in digital mobilization. First is the lack of access. 'Online spaces are highly dominated by dominant-caste and English-speaking people,' Singh said. Seventy-five per cent of India's tribals and 71 per cent Dalits have no social media exposure, according to a survey by Lokniti, CSDS (2019), compared to 54 per cent upper-caste people. 'Social media space has always been upper-caste dominated and continues to be so,' the survey report noted (Lokniti, 2019: 23). The inequity also exists within Dalit communities. 'Majority of our Dalit communities struggle with issues of basic access to food, land, water, sanitation, education, employment,' Singh said. 'So the use of social media among our communities is restricted to the few people who have managed to gain some amount of upward mobility, which means access to a smartphone and basic internet connection.'

The second issue concerns language. 'Language is another hurdle that divides us and keeps us from sharing ideas across regions,' Singh said. 'In a country like India, which has more than 2000 languages, you can only imagine the complexity of navigating the digital space.'

The third issue pertains to constant backlash and trolling. 'When I started tweeting from my handle @dalitawaz, I had a lot of trolls attacking me, making threats on my life and sexually harassing me online,' Singh said.

Whenever Dalits speak about caste or caste crime on social media, she said, 'non-Dalit people, especially young people, start arguing about reservation – which is our constitutional right' (Singh, 2017).

Despite this, Singh stays determined. 'It is important for us to put out our counter histories because official histories are always written from the perspective of the dominant caste,' she said. As part of the social media training Singh conducts for Dalit youth, she teaches basic digital security tips like password protection, privacy settings, careful use of pictures and videos, and how to stop someone bothering or threatening them.

Right to Virality

Rashi Shinde started using TikTok at the age of nine. Her parents believe the 11-year-old can copy any Bollywood actress. Rashi proves them right one 30-second video after another. She became famous lip-synching to Bollywood hits from the 1990s while acing the expressions of the top heroines from that era: Sridevi's spontaneity, Madhuri Dixit's intensity, and Juhi Chawla's playfulness. In the viral world of short-video platforms, Rashi has made her name as an 'expressions queen'. In June 2020, when TikTok was banned in India, Rashi lost 1,56,500 followers, but she quickly built a fanbase on a new platform called 'Snack' where millions of people followed her in quick succession. She went on to earn a salary of INR 10,000 from the platform. Rashi releases at least one video every day, and on some days, she dances not to Bollywood numbers but Ambedkar songs, each reflecting a different mood: devotion, anger, hope, solidarity.

Of Ambedkar's place in her life, Rashi says: 'If he didn't exist, we wouldn't either.'[14] The comments on her videos comprise cascades of 'Jai Bhim', often followed by blue-heart emojis. Many of these are posted by young Dalits who post similar content across the short-video universe, comprising Instagram reels and Roposo, using TikTok's song-and-dance style to assert caste. They find each other by tagging commonly followed handles like @jaibhimarmy and searching common hashtags such as #jaibhim, #dalit, #jaibhimgirls, and #jaibhimboys, and often go on to post duets, meet offline, or simply chat in the comments.

Hundreds of Dalit girls and boys count as social media influencers today with hundreds of thousands of followers each. Rashi's father, Amol Shinde, says her stardom has gone beyond caste. 'Her followers are from every caste – upper, middle, lower. They are from everywhere – Bengal, Bihar, Delhi.'[15] Love and hate both flow freely in the comments. However, the threats and insults can easily be traced to users with upper-caste names.

'Indian casteist hate speech is part of an ecosystem of violence designed to shame, intimidate, and keep caste oppressed communities from asserting their rights and participating as equals in society,' a 2019 report by Equality Labs noted on the basis of 1,000 samples of hate speech in Facebook posts in six different Indian languages (Soundararajan et al., 2019: 40). Forty per cent of all casteist posts attacked reservations, and the remaining included caste slurs, derision of caste-based menial labour (like manual scavenging), anti-Ambedkar messages, and anti-inter-caste personal relationships content.

Amol, who works as a computer operator in Maharashtra's Kopargaon village, says, Dalit internet users, who still form a majority of Rashi's followers, 'take pride in one of their own girls reaching such heights. It's not easy for us. The upper castes don't let us rise.'[16]

In 2015, Rashi's 23-year-old maternal uncle was kidnapped and then killed in the same village by a group of Maratha and OBC men after his phone rang in public and an Ambedkar song played out. 'They had warned him against it, saying they don't like it,' Rashi's mother, Ashwini Shinde, said.[17] The case drags on in a local court as of the writing of this chapter, while the suspects have been out on bail. The family is constantly aware of the risks in cultivating a public profile for Rashi, but they believe social media allows them to escape the iron grip of caste in the village. Ashwini was the first in the family to post short videos, and she and her husband make up Rashi's production team today. After Snack also shut down, Rashi moved on to Instagram, YouTube, and another TikTok-like short-video app called Moj. Her work hours are longer today, and her status as an influencer is unshakable, but the caste slurs keep coming.

Many expect that internet-driven democratization and social media access will act as a catalyst to transform society. However, after a 15-month-long ethnographic study of social media usage in Tamil Nadu, anthropologist Shriram Venkatraman (2017) concluded that the exact opposite is happening: social media itself has been transformed by deeply rooted cultural realities. 'We can only come to appreciate what social media is in South India when we recognise that within a few years, social media has become a powerful expression of a much older and wider story of Tamil society itself' (Venkatraman, 2017: 24).

Venkatraman documented how people bring their offline traditions onto social media, especially by friending people mostly from similar backgrounds – specifically with regard to caste and class. 'This kind of in-group behaviour also gives rise to the sense of online "otherness" as represented by everyone else,' Venkatraman (2017: 4) wrote.

Even if people achieve equality of access – which itself has a long way to go – it does not translate into social equality. As Vekatraman (2017: 4) points out: 'Merely because one is capable of "friending" people from different backgrounds does not mean that anyone will, especially if one of the people is from a lower socio-economic background.'

Caste in Online Matchmaking

Cultural realities block the prospects of love and marriage even further. Ninety per cent of marriages in India are still arranged, caste being central to the equation. In 2017, the CSDS released the results of a sample survey of 6,122 respondents aged between 15 and 34 years across 19 states (*Indian Express*, 2017). One of its key findings was that 92 per cent of those married had intra-caste weddings.

The fear of inter-caste love and marriage leads men belonging to certain caste groups to consider Facebook a dangerous influence for women in their families, Venkatraman noted in his ethnography. 'Such a perception of Facebook comes from their use of the platform as a tool to flirt, the fear of inter-caste romances, their communities' perception of cross-gender friendship and the fear of losing family honour within their community if others become aware that a girl has been exposed to such friendships' (Venkatraman, 2017: 37). This, he wrote, limits women's access to mobile phones and social media to varying degrees, from restricted use to outright bans and constant surveillance.

Some online matchmaking platforms for Indians are built on caste segregation whereas others operate in denial. Matrimony websites put caste front and centre; it is among the first questions users must answer while creating a profile. Some platforms even use technologies to make sure upper-caste users do not come across Dalit profiles. In 2020, Shaadi.com, which claims to be the 'world's oldest and most successful matchmaking service', was exposed by the UK's *Sunday Times* for designing their algorithm to keep SC profiles out of the upper-caste radar (Rudra, Urwin, and Calver, 2020). Their spokesperson denied the allegation.

Most online dating platforms project themselves as 'caste-agnostic'. A Tinder spokesperson told us their users typically do not care for caste.[18] The chief executive officer (CEO) of Truly Madly, a dating app with six million active profiles, Snehil Khanor, said their 'whole proposition is to cater for a generation that doesn't believe in the arranged marriage set-up of caste, gotra, religion and cooking skills'. Their users, he stressed, have rejected caste-based matrimony. Multiple marriages sparked off by Truly Madly involve people from different cultures, he pointed out.[19] He is technically right. Thanks to the dating app, a woman from Kerala could find a man from Lucknow; and a 9-to-5 banker could woo a freelance graphic designer. However, most of the intercultural marriages showcased by the platform, whether it is a Vyas marrying a Tiwari or a Menon marrying a Sood, appear to preserve rather than reject caste hierarchies.

The answer perhaps lies in more anti-caste and not merely inter-caste love. 'For a Dalit woman or a Dalit queer person or an upper-caste person dating them, the oppositions are always there in their mind. Pyar hai, sab kuch hai, par parents se kaise milwaoge? [There is love, there is everything, but how will you introduce your partner to your parents?]' says Jyotsna Siddharth, who in 2018 launched the Instagram page 'Project Anti-Caste Love' to understand how caste plays out in romantic relationships. 'There is this thing about control of women's sexuality and property, and inheritance, but then there is something deeper which is making people uncomfortable,' Jyotsna says. The page, which has thousands of followers, showcases stories, interviews, movie recommendations, and love letters written by couples in inter-caste and inter-religious relationships. The project is an extension of her MPhil research which was sparked off by her own online and offline dating experiences as a Dalit woman. 'Dating apps seem anonymous. You don't have to talk about your caste or religion. But I feel that it is only a matter of time. Initially, yes, people are going by looks and personality but at some point, when you really want to know more, you begin to ask questions.'[20]

For Dalits, however, revealing their caste is never optional in a romantic scenario.

> I know that sooner or later it will come up. But your response is to delay it. You need to allow the circumstances and comfort for people to reveal things and not just expect that people will start talking about it. That's not something upper-caste people have to do. In spite of running the project, many times I don't know how to respond. I can't immediately have a sassy response and shut somebody up. I am not there yet.[21]

And that's when, she said, 'I get reminded that that's the reason I started this project.'

One of the people featured on 'Project Anti-Caste Love' is Dhiren Bhorisa, an urban sexual geographer whose doctoral research is centred on caste, class, and queerness. In a phone interview, Bhorisa, who teaches law at Jindal University, said that outside of big cities like Delhi, young people enter the realm of desire not through a dating app but Facebook.

> Social media is for many people one way in which they negotiate their sexuality. They can create fake accounts. In those fake accounts, what they are constructing is more real. When I made my first social media account,

on Orkut, it was a fake account, and I gave myself a Sankritized name: Sanidhya. Nobody poor and downtrodden would have that name. But I didn't stop there. When I had to give myself a second name, I called myself Sanidhya Sharma. Because I knew that people would talk to me.[22]

On queer dating apps, Bhorisa says, 'Caste does not just remain caste. It takes on a racialized form.' It is common for dominant-caste users to flaunt their identity on an app like Grindr.

> In the Delhi–Haryana region, most profiles you'd see would be of Jats and Gurjars. They are not Brahmins, but they are dominant castes. By identifying themselves as Jats and Gurjars, they are racializing their bodies to suggest what a Jat or Gurjar person looks like. Their bodies are constructed through the caste location. Some even go on to say 'Jat 10 inches' or 'Gurjar 9 inches'. They are not merely flaunting their caste identity but also talking about power, dominance, and a particular body aesthetic. In southern India, you will find Reddys and Gaudas [doing the same] because caste also operates in a regional framework. You strangely are able to gain more leverage in the sexual encounter. Even if you don't put up a picture on your profile, you will still get a lot of people saying 'hi'.[23]

In their research on queer dating apps, Bhorisa has also come across profiles that only show interest in members of their own caste. 'There are profiles that say "Brahmins only". I have a lot of screenshots of this kind. There is one that said, "Brahmin ka chora with jat ke shouk" [Brahmin boy with Jat tastes].' Recently, however, they have begun to see Dalit users mention their caste in their Grindr profiles. 'I found one that said, "I am a Valmiki boy." Valmiki is a Dalit community. You are locating yourself in a very unequal terrain of sexual desire. People always reject you after asking questions; they always figure out where you live, so why don't I say it upfront.'[24]

Bhorisa believes technology can both exacerbate and undermine the grip of caste on love:

> It helps reveal a lot of these tensions but also allows possibilities of assertion. You are hopeful that certain boundaries which have come to us as very rigid can be slightly renegotiated. My Instagram bio says 'awkward Dalit queer'. Because my Instagram is linked to my Grindr profile, I often get messages saying, 'Why do you have to say you are Dalit?' But why does a Jat boy have to say he is Jat in his profile? They are like, 'It's a bad thing and I shouldn't do it, and if I do, I am casteist.' I tell them caste is already there. Sometimes I get threat messages saying, 'Mujhe pata hai tum kahan rehte ho. Bahar milna toh dikhate hain tumhein caste kya hota hai' [I know where you live. Meet me outside and I will show you what caste is]. I say to them, 'You are proving my point.'[25]

Bhorisa's hopes are grounded not in the wonders of technology but in the power of love. 'People are coming together, falling in love with each other. I see hope in love. Maybe the algorithms may not make us match, but there are other ways we will devise for love to survive.'

Notes

1. Ved Prakash, phone interview with the authors, 2020.
2. Ved Prakash, phone interview with the authors, 2020.
3. Ved Prakash, phone interview with the authors, 2020.
4. Ved Prakash, phone interview with the authors, 2020.
5. Neeraj Ghaywan, phone interview with the authors, 2020.
6. Neeraj Ghaywan, phone interview with the authors, 2020.
7. Anushka Shah, phone interview with the authors, 2020.
8. Neeraj Ghaywan, phone interview with the authors, 2020.
9. Equity Labs, 'Caste in Tech', YouTube video, 01:54 hrs, 24 August 2020, https://www.youtube.com/watch?v=_Yv1IgDqjps (accessed on 25 October 2022).
10. Yashica Dutt, phone interview with the authors, January 2021.
11. Yashica Dutt, phone interview with the authors, January 2021.
12. Tejas Harad, phone interview with the authors, 2020.
13. Yashica Dutt, phone interview with the authors, January 2021.
14. Rashi Shinde, phone interview with the authors, 2020.
15. Amol Shinde, phone interview with the authors, 2020.
16. Amol Shinde, phone interview with the authors, 2020.
17. Ashwini Shinde, phone interview with the authors, 2020.
18. Anonymous Tinder spokesperson, phone interview with the authors, 2020.
19. Snehil Khanor, phone interview with the authors, 2020.
20. Jyotsna Siddharth, phone interview with the authors, 2020.
21. Jyotsna Siddharth, phone interview with the authors, 2020.
22. Dhiren Bhorisa, phone interview with the authors, 2020.
23. Dhiren Bhorisa, phone interview with the authors, 2020.
24. Dhiren Bhorisa, phone interview with the authors, 2020.
25. Dhiren Bhorisa, phone interview with the authors, 2020.

Bibliography

Ahuja, A. 2018. 'Digital Dalits: Is Social Media a Game Changer for Dalit Politics?'. *The Print*, 23 April. https://theprint.in/opinion/dalit-history-month/digital-dalits-is-social-media-a-game-changer-for-dalit-politics/51284. Accessed in February 2022.

Census of India. 2011. 'Primary Census Abstract: Data Highlights'. New Delhi: Office of the Registrar General and Census Commissioner of India.

Deccan Herald. 2020. 'Meet Odisha Migrant Worker Duleswar Tandi Who Raps to Express His Anguish'. 10 July. https://www.deccanherald.com/national/north-and-central/meet-odisha-migrant-worker-duleswar-tandi-who-raps-to-express-his-anguish-859392.html. Accessed in January 2022.

Dutt, Y. 2019. *Coming Out as A Dalit.* New Delhi: Aleph Book Company.

Harad, T. 2018. 'Towards an Internet of Equals'. *Mint*, 31 August. https://lifestyle.livemint.com/news/talking-point/towards-an-internet-of-equals-111645092715631.html. Accessed in April 2022.

Indian Express. 2017. 'Lokniti–CSDS–KAS Survey: Mind of the Youth'. 3 April. https://indianexpress.com/article/explained/lokniti-csds-kas-survey-mind-of-the-youth-4597199. Accessed in February 2022.

———. 2019. 'From the Margins, a New Era for Dalit Media'. 3 November. https://indianexpress.com/article/opinion/columns/indian-media-dalit-issues-reporting-upper-caste-diversity-6100055/. Accessed on 25 October 2022.

Lokniti. 2019. *Social Media & Political Behaviour.* New Delhi: Centre for the Study of Developing Societies (CSDS).

Mukherji, A. 2020. 'The Cisco Case Could Expose Rampant Discrimination against Dalits in Silicon Valley'. *The Wire*, 8 July. https://thewire.in/caste/cisco-caste-discrimination-silicon-valley-dalit-prejudice. Accessed in February 2022.

Oxfam India. 2019. *Who Tells Our Stories Matters: Representation of Marginalized Groups in Indian Newsrooms.* New Delhi: Newslaundry, Teamwork Arts, and Oxfam India. https://www.oxfamindia.org/sites/default/files/2019-08/Oxfam%20NewsLaundry%20Report_For%20Media%20use.pdf. Accessed in February 2022.

Pandey, P., and S. Pandey. 2018. 'Survey at an IIT Campus Shows How Caste Affects Students' Perceptions'. *Economic and Political Weekly* 53(9): ISSN 2349-8846. https://www.epw.in/engage/article/Survey-at-an-IIT-Campus-Shows-How-Caste-Affects-Students-Perceptions. Accessed on 25 October 2022.

Prakash, V. 'The Activist'. YouTube Channel. https://www.youtube.com/c/theActivist. Accessed in February 2022.

Rudra, P., R. Urwin, and T. Calver. 2020. 'Indian Dating Site Deems Untouchables Undatable'. *Sunday Times*, 2 February. https://www.thetimes.co.uk/article/indian-dating-site-deems-untouchables-undateable-08xhkpd6b. Accessed in February 2022.

Rukmini, S., and U. Naig. 2015. 'In Bollywood, Storylines Remain Backward on Caste'. *The Hindu*, 28 June. https://www.thehindu.com/news/national/in-bollywood-storylines-remain-backward-on-caste/article7362298.ece. Accessed in March 2022.

Shanta, S. 2019. 'Interview: Director Neeraj Ghyawan on Why His Job Call Seeks Bahujan Talent'. *The Wire*, 13 September. https://thewire.in/caste/neeraj-ghaywan-interview-job-call-diversity-bollywood. Accessed in March 2022.

Singh, A. 2017. 'Anju Statement – UN Minority Forum'. International Dalit Solidarity Network. https://idsn.org/wp-content/uploads/2017/12/Anju-statement-UN-Minority-Forum.pdf. Accessed in March 2022.

Soundararajan, T., A. Kumar, P. Nair, and T. Greely. 2019. *Facebook India: Towards the Tipping Point of Violence: Caste and Hate Speech*. Los Angeles: Equality Labs. https://static1.squarespace.com/static/58347d04bebafbb1e66df84c/t/5d0074f6 7458550001c56af1/1560311033798/Facebook_India_Report_Equality_Labs. pdf. Accessed in April 2022.

Thakur, A. K. 2020. 'New Media and the Dalit Counter-Public Sphere'. *Television and New Media* 21(4): 360–75.

Venkatraman, S. 2017. *Social Media in South India*. London: UCL Press.

17

Dalit Middle Class

Aspirations, Networks, and Social Capital

Gurram Srinivas

The Dalit middle class constitutes a significant segment of the Indian middle class (or middle classes) today, as a distinctive sociopolitical and cultural community. Though small in numbers within an ever-growing Indian middle class as well as Dalit population, middle-class Dalits have created political agency of their own within India's middle classes (seemingly apolitical) as well as the Dalit community (with a political identity self-attributed by Scheduled Castes [SCs]). The emergence of a minuscule Dalit middle class is an indication of limited socio-economic mobility among Dalits in the last seven decades. Despite several safeguards existing in the Indian Constitution to ameliorate the structural disadvantages faced by Dalits in society, their socio-economic mobility has been limited mainly due to limited socio-economic transformation in Indian society (Deshpande, 2003). The existence and growth of the Dalit middle class is often considered not only an indicator of achieved upward socio-economic mobility among them, but also, more significantly, a source of inspiration for the rest of the Dalit population. However, the emergence of a middle class among Dalits has not improved their socio-economic or political status in the caste hierarchy (Guru, 2002). Like poor Dalits, middle-class Dalits are also subjected to inequality, discrimination, and exclusion in their lifeworld (G. Srinivas, 2016; Saavala, 2001).

Therefore, in the last four decades, a large number of studies have focused on middle-class Dalits to understand social and economic mobility among them (see Kulke, 1976; Ram, 1988; Omvedt, 2001). Both empirical and conceptual analyses of the Dalit middle class largely focus on tracing the trajectory of the Dalit middle class and its characteristics, contributions to the Dalit cause, potential to fight social and economic inequality, and contributions towards socio-economic development and political empowerment of Dalits. From its inception, the Dalit middle class has garnered scholarly interest in its growth pattern as well as in its interaction with other sections of society. One of the earliest conceptualizations about the formation of the Dalit middle class has aptly emphasized it as the process of upward mobility of the very best, and often most talented, among Dalits (Dushkin, 1979).

Scepticism to Wonder

The Dalit middle class has attracted varied responses from both critics as well as champions. A number of scholars and researchers focus on multitudes of themes such as caste, class, education, occupation, social mobility, and social change; and contemporary analyses of the Dalit middle class do not vary vastly from initial conceptualizations about its composition, characteristics, and politics.[1] As a new middle class that emerged merely four decades ago, the Dalit middle class is growing numerically and geographically and is also becoming internally diverse, going much beyond the initially enumerated modern occupations and professions, like public-sector employment, that were largely confined to bigger cities. In the last two decades, more and more new instances of formation of a small yet sizeable Dalit middle class are being recorded beyond the urban sprawls of bigger cities – increasingly so in smaller towns and urban hinterlands in all corners of the country.[2] Much like the general middle class in India, the Dalit middle class is also becoming internally more diverse as its members are increasingly drawn from some of the numerically smaller SCs that were earlier marginalized in accessing education and employment opportunities in comparison to the numerically larger communities of the SCs. At the same time, internal competition among the SCs is also at an all-time high, given the limited educational and employment resources in the public sector, and it is time for them to look towards creating and accessing new opportunities in the private sector and in entrepreneurship.[3]

The major focus of enquiry into the Dalit middle class when its emergence was being analysed for the first time was its integration and incongruity with the general middle class in India (Kulke, 1976).[4] Later, the focus shifted to the distinctiveness of the Dalit middle class as a new middle class, different from the general middle class in the country (Ram, 1988);[5] at both these stages, the concern was about the extent to which middle-class Dalits were a class in themselves and how integrated they were with the general middle class in India. However, today, the Dalit middle class is considered a formidable section of the Dalit community, one that is championing the cause of the entire community by taking on the pivotal roles of inspiration, mobilization, and political action (G. Srinivas, 2016).

Historically, Dalits have gone through various phases of mobilization and collective struggles aspiring for equality, socio-economic mobility, and political rights – especially so in the post-independence period – which are intrinsically intertwined with the emergence of the Dalit middle class.[6] The members of the Dalit middle class are championing the civil, economic, cultural, and political rights of all Dalits as their upward social and economic mobility warrants and affords them (Omvedt, 2001). It is in this context that the aspirations, networks, and social capital of the Dalit middle class need to be analysed to understand the similarities and distinctions with other castes and communities.

It is evident from both empirical accounts and conceptual generalizations of the Dalit middle class that the life circumstances of this class are manifestly different from others, especially the general Indian middle class. Considering the abundant accounts that have profiled the middle class in India,[7] the Dalit middle class satisfies all the important features of middle classes in India, besides some other features that are unique to this section alone. The most important aspect of Dalit middle-class uniqueness is generally attributed to its atypical location, which necessitates that it deal with varied forms of caste-based discrimination while achieving and retaining economic mobility at the same time.[8] In order to reach a middle-class position, Dalits have to pursue social as well as economic mobility simultaneously. This is a double burden as far as Dalits are concerned, who have been far too long condemned to be socially and economically excluded communities in India. In comparison with Dalits, the 'caste-Hindu middle class' enjoys a privileged social status independent of its economic attributes, and the middle classes in other societies are also not subjected to such kinds of socially hierarchical and unequal circumstances.[9]

Even after middle classes belonging to different marginalized castes, tribes, ethnicities, regions, and religions have been empirically enumerated and conceptually analysed as distinctive from the general middle class in India, there persists an effort to equate the caste-Hindu middle class with the Indian middle class. Such generalizations invariably attempt to illustrate the general middle class by providing basic descriptions of their socio-economic profiles, interests, and perceptions on various issues concerning their own lives and intermittently on some societal issues and identification with various sociopolitical issues.[10] Similarly, studies on the Dalit middle class also engage with such issues in addition to emphasizing caste and identity.[11]

Middle-class Dalits are faced with the question of identity at both the individual and the collective levels. Their reference points regarding mobility (individual as well as family aspirations) proportionally depend on the social and economic networks and social capital they acquire as part of their education and economic mobility, to effectively develop a common resource pool to aid each other. This process makes them devise and adapt new strategies to ensure that their social and economic mobility is substantive and enduring. The Dalit middle class is still not free of the life situations of Dalits in general, and is still influenced by the social reality of resistance to their social and economic mobility and the restrictions imposed on them by the caste system over generations (Gokhale, 1986; Kulke, 1976).

From 'Dalits in the Middle Class' to 'Dalit Middle Class'

When new occupations and professions such as teachers, doctors, engineers, and bureaucrats at various levels of the administration, requiring modern education and technical skills, emerged during the colonial period, they were devoid of purity and impurity principles as well as ritual, occupational, and traditional caste rankings as criteria of entry. Thus began the process of delinking social rank and status from caste and instead attaching the same to occupation, for the first time in the history of the caste system. However, the general middle class that emerged in this process, known as the new middle class, was largely constituted by the 'upper castes' – the ruling classes or traditionally propertied classes in India. As evinced in numerous analyses of changing occupational structures and formation of classes in India, even during this period, entry into middle-class occupations was largely based on ascription for the upper castes, which could easily translate their access to resources to form a *jati*-specific middle class or enter the existing general middle class. In contrast, given their discriminated social status and lack of resources and opportunities, Dalits and other 'lower castes' could not achieve middle-class status until an enabling social environment was created by the policies of the government in the post-independence period, and even after achieving socio-economic mobility they could not enter the general middle class.[12]

The provision of access to education and occupations in the modern sphere enabled Dalits to aspire for middle-class occupations and professions.[13] The emergence of the middle class in India is generally attributed to the British who created a section of educated people from among the natives to be employed in the middle-level bureaucracy to run the administration. In that process, the literate 'upper castes' were recruited into these 'new' occupations during the initial stages itself and have continued to maintain their dominance ever since.

However, the aspirations of the lower castes to obtain such positions led them to improve their educational level, and in the process, a few of them have succeeded in entering the middle class. In order to enable more marginal social groups gain access to modern education and employment, in the post-independence period, the Indian state provided reservations. Thus, for the first time, Dalits and other marginalized communities who availed the benefits of reservations entered modern occupations at all levels. As the social background and orientations of these new entrants are different compared to those of the 'upper castes' who dominated the middle class, the former are generally considered the 'new middle class' in India.

Historically, the upper castes dominated the social, economic, and political spheres of society due to the 'higher' status accorded to them by their 'ritual purity' in the traditional social structure. In modern India too they secured higher positions in society by monopolizing modern education, thereby extending their hold over the upper and middle classes (Deshpande, 2003). In both cases, a vast majority of Indian society remained dispossessed as 'lower castes' in the caste structure and as wage-labouring 'lower classes' in the class structure.

In the post-independence period, Dalits have gradually made an entry into modern occupations and professions, with the help of sociopolitical changes enabling social and economic mobility in general and with state-provided reservations in education and employment in particular. Reservations have supported Dalits, like other disadvantaged sections of society, in enhancing their social and economic status and reaching middle-class positions, which were hitherto monopolized by upper castes. The long periods of 'social reform' (pre-independence) and 'social justice' (post-independence) enabled at least a few Dalits to seek education and enter a class structure that is amenable to their social and economic aspirations. Dalits have been able to enter middle-class occupations and professions only in the post-independence period, with increased access to education and growth of the public sector.[14] Now they are represented in all modern occupations, but such presence over a very long period is not proportionate to their population, and they are unequally distributed across various occupations and among the positions within them There are no reliable data about the number of middle-class Dalits across India or the proportion of Dalits that are middle class. However, 5–10 per cent of Dalits are estimated to have so far become part of the middle and upper classes.

Amidst many contradictory claims and analyses surrounding its representation in modern occupations, its social and economic mobility, its attempts to enter the middle class by 'forfeiting' its roots, and so on, the Dalit middle class is required to be carefully examined to assess its presence in these fields vis-à-vis its priorities and politics (Guru, 2002). The very nature and extent of its shifting of grounds, and whether its entry itself is an achievement or trouncing of social and economic mobility, need to be examined. Many Dalits who are represented in these modern occupations are the first generation in their respective families to do so, and their level of achievement is significant in terms of 'grandeur' and 'noteworthiness'. In such a context, the Dalit middle class is largely comprised of persons who have achieved social and economic mobility. The Dalit middle class is also caught between non-recognition of its achievement by society on the one hand, and 'jealousy' and 'expectations' from other Dalits on the other. Middle-class Dalits are thus, in a sense, 'untouchable' to society and 'outcastes' for other Dalits.

The existence of the Dalit middle class is mainly attributed to the 'reservation policy' which aimed at uplifting individual Dalits from the disadvantaged positions of their earlier generations to be part of an egalitarian society. In post-independence India, a few Dalit individuals, who witnessed mobility as compared to the social and economic class of their parents formed 'a new Dalit middle class'.[15] Therefore, it is considered distinct from the general middle class.[16] In the absence of a full-fledged assimilation and integration process, middle-class Dalits largely remain a close-knit community with a distinct political temperament. They arrange their lives around each other, heavily confining their social relations, especially at the family level, to fellow Dalits.

A Community with Aspirations

In the last 200 years, Dalits have availed every opportunity within their reach to rise from the subjugation, marginalization, and various other exclusions imposed by the caste system. This modern awakening began with the utilization of the nominal representation provisions under British rule and continued with the various constitutional safeguards made available to them in the post-independence period. The important factors that contributed towards this include the religious movements during the Bhakti period, the social reform movements in the nineteenth and twentieth centuries, the anti-caste movements led by Jyotirao Phule and Periyar, the Dalit movement initiated by B. R. Ambedkar, and, in the post-independence period, a number of Dalit movements in various states asserting Dalit ideology and identity.

The social consciousness engendered by various forces and factors like Dalit movements, government welfare programmes, modern education, wider social interaction with other communities, and so on, has resulted in rising aspirations among Dalits. Having become aware of their rights, Dalits now participate in all important spheres of national life. The last few generations of Dalits have been consciously nurturing a fascination for modern lifestyle, democratic values, and secular outlook, which have accorded them a distinct identity – the Dalit identity (Omvedt, 1990). Since then, Dalits have been enthusiastically taking to modern education, for it is a major source of increased economic and social status (Sharma, 2001).

Today, Dalits are not mere 'passive participants'; they have a systematic programme, and their aspirations for social, economic, and political equality lead them to strategies and means for their realization (Roy and Singh, 1987; Raj, 1998). They have not restricted themselves to government jobs alone; they have entered various other occupations and professions and achieved a considerable level of improvement in their socio-economic status. They are also nurturing aspirations equal to those of caste Hindus in educational, occupational, political, and cultural fields, though their entry has had a brief and sometimes unsuccessful history compared to that of caste Hindus. Ever since they have experienced social and economic mobility, Dalits are resisting the increasing opposition to their social mobility and the growing number of atrocities being committed upon them by the 'upper castes', and they have come together as a collective identity.

Most middle-class Dalits are the first generation in their families to achieve the required education levels for employment in white-collar jobs. After entering such jobs and professions, they have had to contribute portions of their earnings towards the educational and entrepreneurial needs of the members of their paternal and maternal families and, in some cases, even the extended family. Such sharing of limited economic resources is an additional burden on their salaries; it negatively affects their limited economic mobility and impacts their overall consumption levels and lifestyle.

A Networked Class

The mobility of individuals and castes in Indian society is not a new phenomenon. The mobility of the intermediary castes per se, from one occupation to another and taking on the name of another caste, was permitted in the past. M. N. Srinivas (1956) named this process 'Sanskritization'. Upward mobility of the lowest castes or 'outcastes' was tabooed in the traditional caste order, with several restrictions imposed to curtail changes in their occupations and lifestyles. There were no changes in the positions of the two polarities: the topmost and the bottom in the caste hierarchy. Dalits located at the bottom of the hierarchy could not raise their social status until the caste system was attacked from outside by the British and modern social reformers. Under British rule, Dalits were employed in secular jobs and, for the first time, brought into continuous contact with caste Hindus. Social reformers mainly tried to educate Dalits and instil 'awareness' among them, in addition to attacking the caste hierarchy.

The process and fruits of modernization were initially not accessible to all castes. Even among caste Hindus, the degree of mobility, to a great extent, depended on their location in the caste hierarchy. Those who enjoyed a better social and economic status traditionally, by virtue of their caste, moved 'up' more easily than those who were placed 'below' them. In all, the process of modernization largely reflected the traditional status system rather than any other criteria. In a way, the modern social order is superimposed on the traditional social order. Caste plays a significant role in one's access to education, particularly with regard to one's attitudes, consciousness, and participation in social relations.

Now, Dalits have entered new occupations to which they did not have access earlier, such as entrepreneurship, sales, business, medicine, law, engineering, government jobs, and so on. However, such mobility has not been without its problems. They have had to face obstacles in the form of social conflict, resistance from upper castes, non-implementation of reservations in employment and promotions, continued caste discrimination at the workplace and in residential areas, and so on. In the face of these socio-economic disabilities, their numerical strength, better economic opportunities, urban contact, improved communication, enhanced exposure to mass media, assistance from external leadership, and stronger participation in the political process have helped them in the process of development by providing greater resources to engage in political action.

The members of the Dalit middle class were instrumental in framing many development policies and programmes for the upliftment of the SCs and the Scheduled Tribes (STs) – ranging from the 1979 Special Component Plan (SCP) to the 1989 Scheduled Castes and Scheduled Tribes (Prevention of Atrocities) Act. They have generated awareness among the Dalit masses about constitutional safeguards and human rights and were successful in placing Ambedkar's ideology in the popular imagination of the nation. They have organized themselves in the workplace and in professional associations, as well as in literary, cultural, educational, development, and rights-based organizations that successfully led many protests, agitations, and movements against discrimination, exclusion, and atrocities at the local, regional, and national levels.[17]

Dalit Identity as Social Capital

The social awareness and assertion of Dalit identity today is an outcome of social change that was contributed to by various historical developments and sustained efforts of the 'marginalized' and deprived sections to build a 'Dalit' identity that is more assertive in nature. The trajectory of Dalit consciousness, as has been developed by middle-class Dalits, is a common resource at the disposal of the Dalit community as a whole. Middle-class Dalits tend to use their Dalit identity at the individual and group levels for mobilizing and organizing themselves and in the Dalit community at large; their Dalit identity is an instrument that provides them the required social capital within the middle class, which they generate by pooling their individual resources together to augment a common group resource. The social capital of Dalits is very limited in comparison to that of other communities, especially the dominant castes and 'twice-born' caste Hindus, who have managed to amass disproportionate social and economic capital in the post-independence period (Deshpande, 2003). Occupational mobility, increased urbanization, and transnational migration are some successful strategies adopted by Dalits in recent decades, which have enabled them to acquire both upward social mobility and social capital.

Such a process of generation of social capital among middle-class Dalits has positive outcomes for the Dalit community at large. Even if only a limited number of Dalits were able to access the new 'secular' occupations and benefit from the protective discrimination policies of the state, it produced long-lasting effects for the Dalit community as a whole. P. G. Jogdand (2017) analyses the 'paying-back' tendency among middle-class Dalits, in the context of unfavourable depictions of and unreasonable 'expectations' from the Dalit middle class, with the help of empirical evidence from Maharashtra. He observes:

> Available literature tends to show that there is 'individual mobility' at the cost of group stagnation. A few individuals are the beneficiaries of the welfare policies and the programmes. Although it is small in size, it has played an important role in the process of resource mobilisation. It is a significant sector in initiating and perpetuating [D]alit resistance in all spheres of life. Our empirical experiences show the positive narrative of [the] [D]alit middle class (DMC) that emerged in Maharashtra. (Jogdand, 2017: 303)

However, it is important to note that such social mobility lacks uniformity and has substantial limitations. It has not been able to effect changes in all spheres of upward mobility – namely, social, economic, political, and cultural – for all Dalits equally.[18]

The process of formation of social capital among Dalits is analysed in many empirical accounts, variously focusing on their educational and occupational mobility or on the emergence of an elite section or middle class among them (see Sachidananda, 1974; S. Singh, 1987; Roy and Singh, 1987). The generation and augmentation of social capital among the Dalit middle class takes place in the context of similar socio-economic backgrounds of other Dalits and disparity with non-Dalits in the workplace or professional environment. Middle-class Dalits are often faced with situations of limited reciprocal social relations with non-Dalits beyond the workplace; they feel compelled to justify their suitability for the positions they are occupying and prove their ability to perform professional roles more efficiently than non-Dalits (G. Srinivas, 2016). However, instances of cooperation and congenial work relations with non-Dalits are on the rise in recent times, compared to the hostility experienced by middle-class Dalits in various professions in the past. This is an indication of increased integration of middle-class Dalits in the workplace, but their acceptance at the societal level has still not been established by empirical evidence. Beyond professional ranks and designations in the workplace, many middle-class Dalits still struggle to establish social relations and engage in social interaction based on respect and dignity with non-Dalit middle classes, in residential or neighbourhood settings (Saavala, 2001).

Conclusion

The very emergence of a Dalit middle class suggests that it is distinct from the general middle class in its identity and politics. Often, when it is opposed to the ideals and values of the general middle class, the same is manifested in its own priorities and politics. As its social composition, formation process, and shared values and beliefs indicate, the Dalit middle class is ordained to be distinct from the general middle class. The fostering of a separate identity from the general middle class is itself the product of a protest ideology that has been shaping up over the centuries. The protest ideology that was articulated by Ambedkar is now being revived by middle-class Dalits.

The commonality of shared traits, similar background, and a collective future drive individual recruits of the Dalit middle class to band together. Similarly, the external environment, particularly their interaction with caste Hindus, has a bearing on their level of integration into the general middle class. The very emergence of the Dalit middle class is attributed to the reservation policy. It runs contrary to the expectations of the independent Indian state that prioritized the goal of achieving integration in society over quicker development of disadvantaged groups, thereby choosing the reservation system over community based 'special development packages'. Thus, the reservation policy was originally aimed at individual-based upward mobility among Dalits, with the intention to integrate them into the 'mainstream'.

When contrasted with their socio-economic background and their middle-class location, middle-class Dalits' life situation indicates a uniqueness that is specific to the Dalit middle class, in terms of education and employment.

Similarly, the identity patterns of the Dalit middle class are distinctive when compared to those of others. The ideals, values, and goals nurtured and developed by them suggest that the Dalit middle class is developing the grand vision of achieving socio-economic and political equality for Dalits on par with others. Thus, the Dalit middle class is interpreting, reshaping, and developing a more comprehensive Dalit ideology. It is being shaped by the common experiences and collective beliefs of Dalits belonging to the middle class.

The Dalit middle class, as it has emerged in contemporary India, is the outcome of various historical developments – mainly the state policy of protective discrimination which provided it with educational and employment opportunities. Similarly, other factors like social reform and social change inspired by modernization further facilitated this process. It is in this context that we can understand how social and economic mobility helped Dalits invoke a community identity and in what ways their community and Dalit identity influenced their social and economic mobility in turn.

Notes

1. Christophe Jaffrelot (2008: 48) tries to explore the nature of the 'political culture of Dalit middle class'.
2. It is important to note that most analyses of Dalits today reference the Dalit middle class more often than in the past, and not only in the context of educational and occupational mobility.
3. Sudha Pai (2008: 228) advocates for this in the context of economic liberalization and emergence of a competitive market in India.
4. It primarily focused on whether economic mobility also leads to social mobility among Dalits.
5. The Dalit middle class is a new middle class for Nandu Ram as, unlike the general middle class, members of the new middle class comprise those who reach middle-class status through upward mobility.
6. Jayashree B. Gokhale (1986: 281) notes that the emergence of the Dalit middle class in Maharashtra was facilitated by the educational mobility provided by schools and colleges run by the People's Education Society (PES, established by B. R. Ambedkar in 1945).
7. See B. B. Misra (1961) for a historical account of the emergence and typology of middle classes in India and Bhagwan Prasad (1968) and Gurchain Singh (1985) for the characteristics of middle classes in India.
8. Lelah Dushkin (1979: 661) poignantly analyses the opposition to educational and employment mobility among Dalits and the formation of a middle class among them.

9. Some exceptions are Blacks in the United States and ethnic minority groups in societies like Japan, Malaysia, and so on.

10. See Pavan K. Varma (1998, 2004); Leela Fernandes (2006). A contrary view can be found in S. S. Jodhka and Aseem Prakash (2016).

11. See Eckeharde Kulke (1976); Nandu Ram (1988); Gurram Srinivas (2016); Minna Saavala (2001).

12. In the case of Dalits, they could achieve social and economic mobility but not thorough access to the general middle class; see Kulke (1976) and Ram (1988) for a similar analysis.

13. Many empirical studies that focused on educational, occupational, and economic upward mobility among Dalits indicated either the formation of an elite section or middle class among Dalits (see Ram, 1988; Kulke, 1976).

14. Gopal Guru (2002: 142–43) holds that the formation of the Dalit middle class is a post-independence phenomenon, which was confined in its initial phase to the national and state capitals, and more so in southern and western India.

15. In this context, Ram (1988: 7–11) identifies areas where the SCs have progressed due to constitutional measures – namely, access to religious and other public places and lessening of ritual and social distance; growing integration of different caste groups including the SCs in schools, colleges, and universities; growing share in political power; and occupational mobility.

16. Regarding upwardly mobile Dalits, Kulke (1976: 253) argues that the social environment of middle-class Dalits is different from that of their community of origin, and they have not as yet been fully integrated into the 'mainstream' middle-class culture that is largely dominated by upper castes. Also, the specific problems faced by middle-class Dalits are due to their newly acquired economic status.

17. One such organization, the All India Backward and Minority Communities Employees Federation (BAMCEF), ended up giving birth to the Bahujan Samaj Party (BSP) and other political parties.

18. Anand Teltumbde considers the Dalit middle class as one of the main hurdles for the development of the Dalit masses: 'The tiny [D]alit middle class has hegemonic hold over the [D]alit masses as it was to be the custodian of their interests' (Teltumbde, 2017: 550).

Bibliography

Deshpande, S. 2003. *Contemporary India: A Sociological View*. New Delhi: Penguin Books.

Dushkin, L. 1979. 'Backward Class Benefits and Social Class in India 1920–1970'. *Economic and Political Weekly* 14(14): 661–67.

Fernandes, L. 2006. *India's New Middle Class: Democratic Politics in an Era of Economic Reform*. London: University of Minnesota Press.

Gokhale, J. B. 1986. 'The Sociopolitical Effects of Ideological Change: The Buddhist Conversion of Maharashtrian Untouchables'. *Journal of Asian Studies* 45(2): 269–92.

Guru, G. 2002. 'Dalit Middle Class Hangs in the Air'. In *Middle Class Values in India & Western Europe*, edited by A. Imtiaz and H. Reifeld, 141–51. New Delhi: Social Science Press.

Jaffrelot, C. 2008. '"Why Should We Vote?": The Indian Middle Class and the World's Largest Democracy'. In *Patterns of Middle Class Consumption in India and China*, edited by C. Jaffrelot and P. van der Veer, 35–54. New Delhi: SAGE Publications.

Jodhka, S. S., and A. Prakash. 2016. *The Indian Middle Class*. New Delhi: Oxford University Press.

Jogdand, P. G. 2017. 'Social Benefits of Reservation: Mapping Social Mobility and the "Paying-Back" Tendency among the Middle Class'. *Sociological Bulletin* 66(3): 302–15.

Kulke, E. 1976. 'Integration, Alienation and Rejection: The Status of Untouchables'. In *Aspects of Changing India*, edited by S. D. Pillai, 244–54. Bombay: Popular Prakashan.

———. 1983. 'The Problems of the Educated Middle Class Harijans'. In *Social Inequality and Political Structures*, edited by J. P. Neelson, 133–47. New Delhi: Manohar.

Misra, B. B. 1961. *The Indian Middle Classes: Their Growth in Modern Times*. London: Oxford University Press.

Omvedt, G. 1990. '"Twice-Born" Riot against Democracy'. *Economic and Political Weekly* 25(39): 2195–97, 2199–201.

———. 2001. 'The Dalits: Dynamic Upsurge'. *The Week*, 30 December.

———. 2004. 'Untouchables in the World of IT'. Panos Features, February. http://www.indiasocial.org/cgi/news.asp?id=3048&sel=1. Accessed on 24 August 2014.

Oommen, T. K. 1977. 'Sociological Issues in the Analysis of Social Movements in Independent India'. *Sociological Bulletin* 26(1): 14–37.

———. 1994. 'Panchamas to Dalits: The Context and Content of Identity'. *Times of India*, 11 May.

Pai, S. 2008. 'Changing Dialectics of Dalit Aspirations: Demand for Affirmative Action'. *Indian Journal of Industrial Relations* 44(2): 227–33.

Prasad, B. 1968. *Socio-Economic Study of Urban Middle Classes*. Delhi: Sterling Publishers.

Raj, M. C. 1998. 'Paths of Dalit Liberation'. *Integral Liberation* 2(3): 148–54.

Ram, N. 1988. *The Mobile Scheduled Castes: Rise of a New Middle Class*. New Delhi: Hindustan Publishing Corporation.

————. 1995. *Beyond Ambedkar: Essays on Dalits in India*. New Delhi: Har-Anand Publications.

Roy, R., and V. B. Singh. 1987. *Between Two Worlds: A Study of Harijan Elites*. Delhi: Discovery Publishing House.

Saavala, M. 2001. 'Low Caste but Middle-Class: Some Religious Strategies for Middle-Class Identification in Hyderabad'. *Contributions to Indian Sociology* 35(3): 293–318.

Sachidananda. 1974. *The Harijan Elite*. New Delhi: Thompson Press.

Shah, G. 2001. 'Dalit Movements and the Search for Identity'. In *Dalit Identity and Politics*, edited by G. Shah, 195–213. Delhi: SAGE Publications.

————. (ed.). 2001. *Dalit Identity and Politics*. New Delhi: SAGE Publications.

————. (ed.). 2002. *Dalits and the State*. New Delhi: Concept Publishing Company.

Sharma, K. L. 2001. 'Caste and Class in the Emergence of Dalit Identity and Movement'. In *Reconceptualising Caste, Class and Tribe*, 75–100. Jaipur: Rawat Publications.

Sheth, D. L. 1999. 'Secularisation of Caste and Making of New Middle Class'. *Economic and Political Weekly* 34(34–35): 2502–10.

Singh, G. 1985. *The New Middle Class in India: A Sociological Analysis*. Jaipur: Rawat Publications.

Singh, S. 1987. *Scheduled Castes of India: Dimensions of Social Change*. Delhi: Gian Publishing House.

Srinivas, G. 2016. *Dalit Middle Class: Mobility, Identity and Politics of Caste*. New Delhi: Rawat Publications.

Srinivas, M. N. 1956. 'A Note on Sanskritization and Westernization'. *Far Eastern Quarterly* 15(4): 481–96.

———— (ed.). 1996. *Caste: Its Twentieth Century Avatar*. New Delhi: Penguin Books.

Teltumbde, A. 2017. 'Envisioning Dalit Futures'. In *Alternative Futures: India Unshackled*, edited by A. Kothari and K. J. Joy, 536–54. New Delhi: AuthorsUpfront Publishing Services.

Varma, P. K. 1998. *The Great Indian Middle Class*. New Delhi: Viking.

————. 2004. *The New Middle Class in India*. Noida: HarperCollins Publishers.

Zelliot, E. 1992. *From Untouchable to Dalit: Essays on the Ambedkar Movement*. New Delhi: Manohar.

18

The Persisting Developmental Gap
A Case for Restitution and Reparations

Amit Thorat

How long should it take Dalits, the 'ex-untouchables' of India, to overcome their historical (and continuing) disadvantage and be able to flourish at the same standards of living as those of the so-called *general castes*, or, if not match, come close to them in terms of the many indicators of development and well-being? This is an often debated and contested question, which seems to have emerged yet again in contemporary political, legal, and popular debates, with arguments put forth on both sides of the spectrum.

On the one hand, it is contested that 73 years of constitutional provisions, such as the law against the Hindu (but not restricted to Hinduism) practice of untouchability and for protection from caste atrocities, as well as reservations in educational institutions, public-sector jobs, and the legislature, are policy tools which have been instituted for long enough to help Dalits rise from their deplorable condition to a status of respect, socio-economic well-being, and upward mobility. These arguments claim that these laws are no longer required and that the practices of untouchability, discrimination, and exclusion are vestiges of ancient and medieval history, because India is now progressing on the path of creating a casteless social order.

On the other hand, contrary to the aforementioned arguments, evidence shows that while the Dalits of India have indeed come a long way from their untouchable and enslaved status as a community, the developmental gap between them and the so-called general category (excluding the tribal and the Other Backward Class [OBC] population) is glaring and persistent. Whichever indicator of human development we examine – economic, social, cultural, health, and so on – it is easy to see that Dalits lag far behind the rest. In this chapter, we will examine how this gap has evolved over time. The continuation of caste atrocities is another grave matter that would require an independent study and, while important, will not be a focus of this chapter.

The chapter will closely look at the *persisting gap* in as many different aspects of life as available data would let us, and we will try to understand how much of it emerges from *down-the-stream outcomes* of the historical practice of enslavement and the denial of human and civil rights. The chapter will also show how many of these effects might be compounded by continuing practices of exclusionary and discriminatory behaviour in the economic, social, public, and market spaces.

The chapter comprises the following sections: The first section looks at existing studies and evidence that try to ascertain the condition of ex-untouchables as *enslaved* in the ancient, medieval, and colonial periods. This section is based on the author's ongoing study that is part of a Lancet Commission study on reparation and distributive justice,[1] soon to be published. The second section will examine available data to measure the quantum and nature of the gap that persists between Dalits and others in various spheres of human well-being. The next section will re-look at research that collects evidence of continuing exclusion and discrimination, along with evidence which attempts to ascertain people's mindsets and stated behaviours reflecting continuing belief in the inherent inequality of humans and prejudice against those deemed lowly. The fourth section will examine ways in which we should start thinking of correcting for historical denials and deprivations and also look at new ways of addressing continuing discrimination and exclusion.

A Brief History of Enslavement

Continually emerging research and turn-of-the-century studies clearly indicate the existence of caste-based enslavement in India. It is an often overlooked fact, one that is either not acknowledged willingly, or not accepted by all, or not reflected upon seriously, and so it has not formed a substantive part of seriously formulated arguments that support continuation and expansion of constitutional and institutional provisions for Dalits.

Caste untouchability is generally believed to date back to *c.* 200 BCE, and, according to some scholars (Jha, 2018), further back to *c.* 600 BCE. The accuracy of the dates notwithstanding, it still remains the oldest continuing practice of prejudice, possibly anywhere in the world, spanning a period of 2,200 to 3,000 years. As untouchables, particular groups and sub-groups amongst the broad category of the Shudras were deprived of their human and civil rights, denied the right to education, trade, enterprise, or vocation, could not undertake farming or accumulate assets or wealth, were forced to live in segregated communities and subjected to social isolation, and were considered ritually and spiritually defiling because of being *deemed* to have been born impure. While these facts are not unknown and are often restated, it needs to be understood that these have prevailed for the entire length of the historical period mentioned earlier. It is difficult, if not impossible, to find a parallel to this experience elsewhere.

Over and above this social status, many untouchable *jati*s, or sub-groups, came to be designated as *enslaved sub-castes* as far back as *c.* 600 BCE (Chanana, 1962), a category that continued to exist for another 2,500 years till the British formally decreed *enslavement* illegal in 1843 (Banaji, 1937). While untouchability was as close as one could get to being enslaved, designating certain untouchable castes, *socially or legally*, as enslaved completed their enslavement to the so-called *savarna*s (upper castes).

In the *Dharmashastras* compiled and presented as law by Manu, he says, 'a Shudra, whether bought or un-bought, should be reduced to slavery because he is created by God for the service of a Brahman' (Buhler, 2006 [1886]: 24). Manu further says:

> Even if a Shudra is made free from the services of a master one should not consider this as his absolute freedom from slavery, because servitude remains in him as [an] integral part of his nature or it is one of his basic tendencies to serve others from which no one can actually disassociate him. (Sahoo, 2013: 453, *Manusmṛti* 8.417)

What rendered enslavement in India most bewildering to Europeans, however, was its relations, or, precisely, the way it was superimposed on India's caste system (Temperley, 2000: 178).

Studies (Saradamoni, 1980; Mohan, 2015) show the nature of untouchable slavery of the Pulayas and Parayas in southern India in the nineteenth century. The studies detail the specific rights of the enslaved, trade in enslaved people, types of work they were made to do, the wages they received, and their living conditions. As an enslaved caste, the Pulayas did not have the right to property. They could be sold, leased, or mortgaged, and could be offered as presents to friends or as gifts to temples. The enslaver could transfer them, separate children from parents and wives from husbands, and offer them as dowry for a daughter's wedding or as debt payments. The Pulayas therefore had no agency over their own lives and were akin to owned property.[2]

K. Saradamoni (1980) and P. Sanal Mohan (2015) show that considered untouchable and impure, these castes were not allowed inside villages and towns, let alone households for domestic work. Consequently, they were employed as enslaved labour on agricultural fields on the periphery of towns and villages. They were not allowed to miss a single day of work, had to tend to the fields from early morning till late evening, and would be punished for missing work. They were considered a part of the livestock on the farm and even ploughed fields along with bullocks and buffaloes. Their remuneration was only two-thirds of that paid for any form of labour to Shudras at large and was so meagre that they barely survived, consuming boiled leaves of the *thakara* plant (*Senna tora*) for half a year, and for the rest they ate wild yams foraged from the forest. Many a time, driven by hunger and temptation, they would steal jackfruit and coconuts from plantations. In addition, they were restricted from consuming certain food items as part of the rules that governed their lives.

The studies by Saradamoni (1980) and Mohan (2015) go on to describe the clothing and housing conditions of the enslaved. An ex-enslaved recounts that they were not allowed to wear clothes and had to tie leaves and branches around their naked bodies. Their living quarters were small, makeshift rudimentary huts that they built near the fields they worked on. The author describes them as nothing more than 'large baskets' (Mohan, 2015). They even spent their nights on trees to watch over the fields they worked on.

The hard labour, poor nourishment (barely enough to survive), and miserable living conditions had adverse impacts on their health, driving them closer to death. Hard labour included digging, carrying, planting, lifting heavy loads, and often working for hours in water. This led to rheumatism, fever, cholera, and other severe health conditions that proved fatal and led to death way before they reached old age.

Punishment for the enslaved was harsh. The enslaver, or master, had the legal right to pronounce offences and administer punishment. While cutting of body parts such as the nose, and so on, was not uncommon in earlier times, in the later period that seems to have been largely replaced by flogging. The transfer deeds of the enslaved mentioned and gave the enslaver the right to chain, flog, and even deprive them of their life.

While the rules governing the rights, trade, and treatment of the enslaved might have varied in time over history, it is clear that enslavement of particular sub-castes of the Shudras continued right through the medieval period and the Mughal period (*c.* 900–1772 CE) and the 71 years of established British Raj in India (1772–1843 CE) till it was formally banned in 1843.

The British in India instituted the Anglo-Indian law in 1772, which was finally constituted in 1798. However, from 1772 till 1843, they appointed a Brahmin law officer, whose job was to advise the British on the relevant Hindu laws that applied based on the *Dharmashastras*, sign reports, and assist in passing judgments. The 1772 law states: 'In suits regarding succession, inheritance, marriage and caste, and all religious usages and institutions, the Hindu laws with regard to Hindus are to be considered the general rules by which the judges are to form their decision.' An example from 1824 is where the appointed Hindu law officer to the British court was asked to clarify Hindu enslavement; he simply recounted the seven descriptions of the enslaved as mentioned in the *Manusmriti* (Adam, 1840: 54–55). Thus, the Hindu laws of enslavement were in effect applicable uninterrupted from 200 BCE to 1772 CE and further till 1843 CE, when the British finally abolished them. It cannot be overemphasized that the British accepted the caste laws as they existed at that time in India and did not 'invent' the caste system, as some scholars would have us believe!

In their attempts to understand the caste system and identify the people and communities they were to govern, the British conducted cadastral surveys and clubbed the thousands of *jatis* they encountered into broad classifications for their convenience – this in no sense implies they were the creators of caste in India. They might have been the first to use different terminologies and names to understand and simplify the graded system of innumerable *jatis* for administrative governance, but anyone who would go as far as to credit or blame the British for 'recreating' or 'inventing' the caste system is surely attempting to mislead themselves or others.

Amongst other reports and documents, the Law Commission of India's report of 1840 made observations on the practice of slavery as it existed at the time. It stated that on the basis of extensive surveys undertaken, it was found that around the eastern and western coast of the southern peninsula, and very likely elsewhere in the country, whole castes were regarded as impure and subjected to agricultural slavery for a long time in history (Adam, 1840). These findings of the commission finally led to a law banning caste slavery in India.

The Gap

Given this 2,000-odd-year-long history, from about 200 BCE till 1843 CE, we are bound to see the *down-the-stream* effects and manifestations of enslavement and untouchability. It is possibly the longest any group or community has suffered in a continuous manner in the history of humanity. Then to wish away the grave consequences of this past and to focus solely on the post-independence period of merely 75 years to consider the harms and expect a people to overcome their disadvantage is in itself a continuation of the same mindset and injustice. To think that laws and policy interventions over this period of less than a hundred years should suffice – and that the incalculable harm in terms of loss of human rights, loss of economic wealth in terms of incomes and assets, personal and group humiliation, trauma, and the resulting psychological, social, and cultural harm would be undone – is another form of oppression.

One needs only to look at the gap that still persists, despite the many laws and policy interventions to safeguard against the continuing prejudice, discrimination, exclusion, violence, and atrocities. In the following section, we shall examine this gap, as it exists between Dalits (Scheduled Castes [SCs], or ex-untouchables) and upper castes.

Land

The desire to call a piece of land one's own possibly emerged in humans as soon as they learnt how to cultivate plants for food and began to live in permanent settlements. Even if, historically, the early ancestors of enslaved and untouchable communities owned land, individually or collectively, they subsequently lost all rights to own land and work it, possibly even homestead land. They were forced to work lands owned by others either as enslaved agricultural labour or as untouchables serving other caste groups. Historical evidence is scant, and more research is needed to understand if this ancient practice continued unabated through medieval and modern times till slavery was formally outlawed or certain concessions were made for them to be able to own land. It is likely that some did manage to acquire land and till it; however, one can safely assume that the share of such households would be miniscule at the time of independence.

While the policy of land reforms, after independence, was aimed at redressing the huge inequalities in land ownership between landlords and cultivators, this largely failed to transfer land to the actual tiller, except in some small pockets, and most of the transfers were appropriated by middle tenants, rent collectors, and so on, the go-betweens for landlords and cultivators.

The gap that existed in land ownership between 2003 and 2013 shows that while the non-reserved or general-category (non-SC or non-ST or non-OBC) household on an average owned 2.03 acres of land, the SC household owned 0.67 acres on average (Table 18.1). This might not seem like much, but this can be the difference between owning homestead land plus a small kitchen garden versus an acre or two of agricultural land that can be cultivated to provide food and/or income, as well as work (for instance, in the absence of migrant work during the COVID-19 lockdown), collateral for borrowing money, economic and social security, and much more.

If we look at household distribution (Table 18.2), we find that in 2013, of the total SC households in India, 90.5 per cent fall in the marginal and small-land ownership category as compared to 79.3 per cent of general-category households. The latter would also have access to higher levels of education and assets as we shall see further.

Table 18.1   Distribution of households, land area, and average land size in India, 2003 and 2013

Social groups	Households (per cent)		Area (per cent)		Average land size (hectare)		Average land size (acre)	
	2003	2013	2003	2013	2003	2013	2003	2013
Scheduled Tribes	10.5	11.9	11.1	13.1	0.77	0.65	1.90	1.61
Scheduled Castes	21.6	20.1	9	9.2	0.3	0.27	0.74	0.67
Other Backward Classes	41.6	44.8	43.5	45.7	0.76	0.6	1.88	1.48
Others	26.3	23.2	36.3	32	1	0.82	2.47	2.03
All	100	100	100	100	0.73	0.59	1.80	1.46

Source: Author's calculations with data from the Land and Livestock Survey of India, 2013.

Assets

The major assets data at the household level, collected by the Debt and Investment Survey organized by the National Sample Survey Office (NSSO) of India in 2013, included land, buildings, livestock, farm and non-farm equipment, transport vehicles, financial assets (for example, shares, debentures, deposits, and so on), and gold ornaments. We find that in terms of the combined value of all these assets, SCs owned 7.6 per cent of the total value of assets in India in 2013, while Hindu upper castes (excluding other religious denominations) owned 41 per cent. In terms of the average value of assets owned per household, this translates to 6,20,000 rupees for SCs, as against a staggering 27,70,000 rupees for Hindu upper castes (Tagade, Naik, and Thorat, 2018).

Clearly, 75 years of post-independence access to education and federal jobs through reservations is too short a time period for SCs to accumulate enough assets and land to be at par with upper-caste Hindus and match the intergenerational accumulation of assets and wealth over thousands of years. This was also at the cost of the former by appropriating the remunerations for their hard labour and denying them savings and asset ownership, continuing exclusion and discrimination notwithstanding. In his recent book, Arun Kumar (2017), writing about the *black economy* of India and using three different methods to

Table 18.2 Distribution of households across land-size classifications by socio-religious groups in India, 2013

Class	Scheduled Tribes (per cent)	Scheduled Castes (per cent)	Other Backward Classes – Hindu (per cent)	Upper castes – Hindu (per cent)	Muslim (per cent)	Others (per cent)	Total (per cent)
Landless (0.002 hectare)	9.4	7.2	6.8	7.3	8.0	7.5	7.4
Marginal (0.002–1.000 hectare)	68.8	85.7	73.8	66.3	84.3	69.4	75.4
Small (1.000–2.000 hectares)	14.6	4.8	11.4	13.0	5.1	10.6	10.0
Semi-medium (2.000–4.000 hectares)	5.7	1.8	5.6	8.6	2.0	7.4	5.0
Medium (4.000–10.000 hectares)	1.4	0.5	2.2	4.2	0.5	3.9	1.9
Large (> 10.000 hectares)	0.0	0.0	0.2	0.6	0.0	1.4	0.2
Total	100	100	100	100	100	100	100

Source: Author's calculations with data from the Land and Livestock Survey of India, 2013.

triangulate, comes up with an estimate predicting that 62 per cent of India's economy is black! One can then imagine how much more wealth particular groups own than is visible through state-sponsored national-level surveys; what we report here is just the tip of the iceberg.

Education

We know that the right to acquire education was historically denied to untouchables and the enslaved under Hindu religious and social code. Due to the notion of purity and pollution, untouchables had no access to any social institutions, including schools. Access to schooling began systematically only after the British arrived in India. In 1892, under the guidance and demand of B. R. Ambedkar, the British set up special schools for untouchables as well as allocated budgets for scholarships (Jaffrelot, 2006). The principalities of Mysore and Baroda, whose rulers came from farming Shudra communities, also encouraged the education of untouchables and gave reserved seats in their civil administration. This late an access to education for them is apparent as Dalit students and even academics that one encounters at present are either first- or second-generation learners. Rarely does one find third-generation learners from the community.

While access to education and schooling have improved slowly over time, it is quite well known that Dalit students were and are not treated similarly inside classrooms. They had to, and are still made to, sit separately or at the back of the class in many rural schools, if not urban ones. They are not encouraged and mentored in the same methods and manner of knowledge acquisition as others and are therefore often neglected and near abandoned. There are numerous cases of Dalit children, as reported in the media, facing discrimination and untouchability while being served food as part of the government's mid-day-meal scheme in schools (*Times of India*, 2019; *Hindustan Times*, 2021). They are many a time denied food or served less, are assigned separate plates that are colour-coded differently from the rest, made to sit separately while eating, and so on. Instances of them being forced to clean school toilets have also been reported.[3]

Even when Dalit students manage to reach elite educational institutions in the country, they face constant discrimination, humiliation, and exclusion from students, faculty, and staff. Suicide rates are amongst the highest for graduate and postgraduate students and do not seem to fall.

As a result, there exists a substantial gap between the educational achievements of Dalits and others. The policy of reservation for Dalits in institutions of higher education has significantly encouraged them to try and access education, as has the fact that Ambedkar ensured these policy measures were constitutionally mandated and urged the ex-untouchables and enslaved to educate themselves. This has resulted in Dalits managing to enter institutions and access education over the past 50 years or so. One wonders what their fate would have been had reservations not been state policy.

The gross enrolment ratio of upper-caste Hindus (28.2) was nearly thrice that of Dalits (10.1) in 2007–08 (Table 18.3). Even after 10 years, by 2017–18, we find that the gap had reduced only by a third and still persists. The dropout rate of Dalits in 2017–18 was 14 per cent as compared to 9.6 for upper-caste Hindus (Table 18.4).

Table 18.3 Gross enrolment ratio in higher education in India, 1956–2018

Social groups	2017–18	2014	2007–08	1995–96
Scheduled Tribes	14.9	15.1	6.4	3.9
Scheduled Castes	19.2	20.2	10.1	3.9
Other Backward Classes – Hindu	26.0	28.6	13.3	
Upper-caste Hindus	38.1	43.4	28.2	
Muslim	15.3	15.3	8.4	
Total	24.3	26.9	14.8	7.3

Source: National Sample Survey (NSS) data on social consumption, 2017–18 and 2014; NSS, 1995–96 and 2007–08.

Table 18.4 Dropout rate in education in India, 2017–18

Social groups	Dropout
Scheduled Tribes	18.8
Scheduled Castes	14.0
Other Backward Classes – Hindu	11.1
Upper-caste Hindus	9.6
Muslim	15.6
Total	12.6

Source: Author's calculations with data on education from the 75th round of the National Sample Survey (NSS), 2017–18.

Health

Similarly, it is no surprise that the health gap between the two groups is still significant and persisting. Table 18.5 gives the rates of neo, infant, and under-five mortality in 2015–16, based on the National Family Health Survey (NFHS) data. We see that the rates for SCs are nine percentage points higher than the others for neo and infant mortality, and around 17 percentage points for under-five mortality. Table 18.6, based on NFHS data, indicates that the rate of stunting and underweight among children under five years is much higher for SCs in comparison to children from OBCs or the general category. The Scheduled Tribe (ST) children, however, are worse off on these indicators.

Table 18.5 Childhood morality rate by social groups in India, 2015–16 (per 1000)

All-India	Scheduled Castes (per cent)	Scheduled Tribes (per cent)	Other Backward Classes (per cent)	Others (per cent)
Neo-natal morality rate	33	31	30	24
Infant mortality rate	45	44	42	33
Under-five mortality rate	56	57	51	39

Source: Author's calculations with data from the National Family Health Survey (NFHS), 2015–16.

Table 18.6 Stunting and underweight rates for children under five years by social groups in India, 2015

Social groups	Stunted	Underweight
Scheduled Castes	43	39
Scheduled Tribes	44	45
Other Backward Classes	39	36
Others	31	29
Total	39	36

Source: Author's calculations with data from the National Family Health Survey (NFHS), 2015–16.

Poverty

Seventy-five years of independence have seen the country work hard to try and reduce the number of people who live in poverty. And poverty has fallen substantially over the years, seeing significant reductions after 2010 and falling to the lowest level of 22 per cent in 2011–12. While these reductions are welcome, one finds that the relative differences across social groups in rates of poverty remain more or less similar. If the incidence of poverty of SCs was 20 percentage points higher than that of the others in 2004–05, by 2011 the gap had reduced to 17 percentage points, a reduction of only three percentage points (Table 18.7).

Moreover, a disproportionately large segment of the landless agricultural and non-agricultural wage workers in rural areas and urban areas, small and marginal farmers, and other casual workers in the informal sector are comprised of the SC (and ST) population. These groups of people also own low levels of assets, hardly any land (except small and marginal farmers and homestead land), and suffer from wealth deprivation.

One can only imagine their plight – losing their job, not being able to find work, denied pay or receiving pay for just a day or week or at most a month after the first nation-wide lockdown was announced during the pandemic. One would not be surprised to find that the incidence of poverty has risen substantially as a direct consequence of the loss of work and income due to the COVID-19 lockdown, which was implemented suddenly, without any prior warning for people to plan and make provisions.[4] This severely affected most of the population

Table 18.7 Headcount poverty rates by social groups in India, 2004–05 and 2011–12

Social groups	2004–05 (per cent)	2011–12 (per cent)
Scheduled Castes	47.6	43.0
Schedule Tribes	36.8	29.4
Other Backward Classes	26.7	20.7
Others	16.0	12.5
Muslim	29.2	25.4
Total	28.3	22.0

Source: Author's calculations with data on consumption expenditure from the National Sample Survey (NSS).

but was especially grave for the SC and ST populations, who have lower levels of savings and assets to liquidate for emergency use. It would be safe to assume that the lockdown would have pushed a large section of the vulnerable population below the poverty line, especially Dalits and tribals.

Continuing Mindsets and Discrimination

Compounding this historical legacy of enslavement and denial of basic human rights, and its outcomes in terms of persisting vulnerabilities, is the continuation of the mindset, belief, and behaviour of the so-called *savarna*, or non-Dalit social groups. Despite the constitutional ban on the practice of untouchability, a pan-India survey in 2011–12, the India Human Development Survey (IDHS; Thorat and Joshi, 2020), found that 30 per cent and 27 per cent of households in rural and urban India, respectively, accepted practising untouchability. A social-group-wise break up of these households shows that 52 per cent of Brahmin, 24 per cent of forward-caste, 33 per cent of OBC, and 22 per cent of ST households reported practising untouchability.

Since this was a face-to-face survey, many respondents either refused to answer the question on untouchability or gave politically correct responses. When the same two questions were asked, verbatim in a telephonic survey, called the Social Attitudes Survey, India (SARI) in rural and urban Uttar Pradesh (UP), Rajasthan, Delhi, and Mumbai, the response rates rose significantly. In rural and urban Rajasthan, 66 and 50 per cent of respondents, respectively, reported that either they themselves or a family member practised untouchability. These rates were 64 and 48 per cent in rural and urban UP, and 39 and 21 per cent in Delhi and Mumbai, respectively (Coffey et al., 2018). Since the incidence of inter-caste marriages is very low in India, around 5 per cent, according to the IHDS (2011–12), the SARI survey asked respondents if they would support a law against inter-caste marriages. The same study reports that the percentage of those supporting such a ban ranged from 60 per cent in rural Rajasthan to 40 per cent in Delhi!

These responses indicated a worsening of personal and familial belief systems and mindsets towards Dalits. This is then reflected in how Dalit children, youth, and others are treated in schools, colleges, and institutes of higher education, where they seek an escape from the social context they grow up in and their family members face on a daily basis, especially in rural areas of the country. Even when Dalit youth manage to complete their education by surmounting prejudice and bigotry in educational institutions, they face the same discrimination in the job market.

In a study of private-job-market hiring, it was found (Thorat and Attewell, 2007) that in a sample of Dalits, Muslims, and upper-caste job applicants, the first two had significantly lower chances of even being called for an interview, when the basic qualifications of applicants from all three groups were identical. Dalits had only 0.67 and Muslims 0.33 of the odds that an upper-caste applicant had of being called for an interview.

As a result of historical denial of access to wealth, assets, and education, as well as continuing discrimination, it is not surprising to see that the Dalit work force is disproportionately engaged in casual labour and self-employed work rather than regular salaried work as opposed to upper castes who are found to be over-represented in regular salaried employment (Table 18.8).

While the share of Dalits (Thorat, Madeshwaran, and Vani, 2020) in the total national workforce in 2004–05 and 2017–18 was around 18 per cent, their share

Table 18.8 Percentage distribution of workers (UPSS) by social groups and work status in India, 2004–05 and 2017–18

Socio-religious groups	2004–05				2017–18			
	Workforce	SE	RW	CL	Workforce	SE	RW	CL
Scheduled Tribes	8.8	8.0	3.8	12.9	9.3	9.8	4.6	12.2
Scheduled Castes	18.5	13.3	15.5	30.4	18.2	13.8	15.6	29.9
Other Backward Classes	36.6	39.5	30.7	33.7	35.6	38.4	33.3	31.8
Upper-caste Hindus	20.2	22.5	33.6	9.1	20.5	22.0	29.4	9.2
Muslims	10.2	11.1	9.0	9.0	10.6	10.7	9.7	11.2
Others	5.7	5.6	7.4	4.9	5.8	5.2	7.4	5.6
Total	100	100	100	100	100	100	100	100

Source: Thorat, Madeshwaran, and Vani (2021), based on unit-level data from the National Sample Survey (NSS), 2011–12, and the Periodic Labour Force Survey (PLFS), 2017–18.
Note: UPSS: Usual Principal and Subsidiary Status; SE: self-employed; RW: regular worker; CL: casual labour.

amongst casual wageworkers was around 30 per cent (disproportionately higher) in the first period and remained the same in the second. Upper castes, who made up about 20 and 22 per cent of the labour force in the first and second round, had a share of 33 and 29 per cent amongst the regular salaried category.

Using Oaxaca decomposition and Neilson's non-linear employment decomposition analysis, Thorat, Madheswaran, and Vani's study (2021) further finds that 47 per cent of the difference in wages between Dalits and forward castes is squarely due to discrimination. Additionally, the decomposition of the difference in the gross employment rate between the two groups indicates that 83 per cent of the gap is again due to discrimination.

Together, both employment and wage discrimination have severe implications for Dalits in terms of incomes earned, savings, asset accumulation, and overall well-being, as well as levels of poverty. These measures imply that 1.9 million Dalit regular workers in 2004–05 and 1.2 million in 2017–18, would have been out of poverty in the absence of discrimination!

Conclusion and Recommendations

When observed over the short span of the post-independence period (about 75 years till date), the sociocultural and economic situation of Dalits seems to suggest that Dalits have indeed come a long way from their position of being actual or near enslaved or being bonded or attached labour and have managed to rise in status, socially and economically. While incidents of violence and atrocities still occur on a regular basis, civil society organizations, Dalit human right commissions, and so on are seen to work hard to fight for justice for the community. However, impatience of the larger population with the policy of reservations and specific laws such as those protecting Dalits against atrocities, and so on, is a product of this myopic gaze.

Oppression, exclusion, and discrimination against Dalits, when seen from a historic perspective of about 2,200 to 2,500 years, however, makes us realize a different truth; which is that the *down the stream* consequences of historic injustices are not only grave and deep but also long-lasting and persistent. Many of these are now so structurally institutionalized that they are indistinguishable from social, economic, and cultural normative behaviour. To expect a community to forget this past and pretend that the historic wrongs are a figment of their imagination, without any bearing or disadvantages on them, and compete as equals with the rest of the population, that has grown, progressed, and prospered by exploiting and appropriating the surplus that rightfully belonged to the labouring classes of Dalits (and others), is in itself a form of continued prejudice, insensitivity, and arrogance of an unparalleled inhuman nature.

Before Dalits are expected to suddenly become *meritorious* in a generation or two, culturally and socially at par with the rest, and compete as equals with those who denied them their human, civil, economic, and social rights, amongst many others, as well their share of land, assets, wealth, income, wages, and so on, non-Dalits must first accept their part in this historic injustice, offer an apology, and finally offer *Reparations and Restitution*. This is the debt that society and the state owe them.

Philosophical Arguments for Reparations

Before an argument for reparations can be made, it would be helpful to understand the meaning of the terms compensation, restitution, and reparation; how they seem to overlap in meaning and could be seen as similar; and how they essentially differ from each other.

Restitution, simply put, is 'the act of giving back something that was lost or stolen to its owner', according to the *Oxford Advanced Learner's Dictionary*. It is conditional on separation of something from its rightful owner. It does not, however, take for granted always that a wrongdoing has occurred in the act of separation. For instance, if A steals B's bike (or finds it) and then simply returns it, without any explanation or expression of remorse or apology, one can say restitution has taken place (but not reparation).

Reparation can take place only after any loss or damage has occurred from a wrongdoing. Reparation is a right or cluster or rights, while restitution is not always a right. Going by the aforementioned example, if A returns B's bike and also apologizes for the wrongdoing, then one can say there is reparation as not only has the bike been returned (restitution), but the apology also helped make amends for the emotional distress caused to B. In this example, if the stolen bike is lost or destroyed and A apologizes for it, and B feels satisfied with the apology, then reparation has taken place without restitution. Restitution is therefore not a necessary condition for reparations.

Compensation, however, while sounding similar to both reparation and restitution in meaning in some sense, is in essence different from both. It implies merely covering up any loss, harm, or damage that was caused by either a wrongdoing or otherwise. 'Something fully compensates a person for a loss if and only if it makes him or her no worse off than he or she would otherwise have been; it compensates person X for person Y's action A, if X is no worse off receiving it, if Y had not done A' (Nozick, 1974: 57).

As mentioned, compensation does not therefore presuppose that a wrongdoing has occurred. Damage or loss could be suffered by someone without being wronged by another. In that case compensation is due but not reparation.

Quite often when reparation is due, as a result of a wrongdoing, it would include restitution – that is, the return of what was taken away – and in case restitution is not possible, then compensation might be given, in an attempt to make the person no worse off than what she was before the wrongdoing occurred. However, restitution for that which can be returned and compensation for that which cannot be, by themselves, do not amount to reparation (though some might feel it is enough) unless accompanied by an admission of the wrongdoing by the harming party and an expression of remorse and or apology.

John Locke on Reparations

John Locke can be credited with being one of the first to propose a cogent argument for reparations. His propositions have formed the basis for many subsequent arguments put forth for Black reparations. He believed that people have natural rights that they derive directly from natural law. These rights were equal for all, and people were naturally disposed to live in peace and harmony (Locke, 1998). This was in contravention to the 'state of nature' argument of Thomas Hobbes, who asserted that people were naturally disposed to be in a state of competition, conflict, and chaos (see Malcolm, 1996).

To discourage the defiance of these natural rights of people, Locke proposed punishment. 'Punishment must be administered 'with so much Severity as will suffice to make it an ill bargain to the Offender, give him cause to repent, and terrifie others from doing the like' (Locke, 2013 [1689]: sec. 8). To restore the harm that crime 'commonly' causes 'some person or other', Locke proposed reparations. He states, reparation must give the 'satisfaction due to any private Man, for the damage he has received' (Locke, 2013 [1689]: sec. 11). For him, the right to reparations emerges from the right to self-preservation. These rights could be demanded only against the 'goods and services of the offender' (Locke 1689: sec. 11). This implies that the victim of a wrongdoing has rights to reparation only from the wrongdoer. This, however, does not imply that the recipient has to be the immediate victim of the wrongdoer. He was of the opinion that a crime usually harms 'some person or other'. For example, if a girl's parents are murdered, she has a claim to reparation for the harm and ensuing hardships of life that this act causes her. Even when a harm does not lead to material loss for the victim, it causes damage to the victim's 'self-respect and moral standing' and she deserves an admission of the harm done and an apology from the wrongdoer, and if all of these require the wrongdoer to be punished, then repentance and reparations for the victim may also include punishment.

Locke, however, makes a distinction between the right to reparations and the right to punish; the latter he gives to the state. Even when the wrongdoer does not gain monetarily from the act or harm, reparations are due to the victim for the latter's mental, personal, and psychological satisfaction. In the event the wrongdoer does get enriched, then reparation may include restitution and/or compensation.

The Harm Argument

The harm argument relies on the idea that the transgressions of slavery [*caste untouchability, caste enslavement*] initiated an unbroken chain of harms linked as cause and effect that began with the slaves [*ex-untouchables and ex-caste-enslaved*] and continues among U.S. blacks [*Dalits*] to the present day. Therefore, since the transgressions of slavery [*caste untouchability, caste enslavement*] harm present day U.S. blacks [*Dalits*], they have rights to reparations against those who committed those transgressions. (Boxill, 2003)

While this argument is made to justify reparation to the present-day Black descendants of slavery, it applies to the descendants of the *caste-enslaved* and near-enslaved *ex-untouchables* or to any other present-day group in equal measure, who in the past or whose ancestors faced similar harm.

The Inheritance Argument

The inheritance argument for black [*Dalit*] reparations states that the freed people [*ex-enslaved*] had rights to reparations for their injuries; that they held these rights against the slave holders [*owners*] and also against the state and federal governments for failing in their duties to protect them from the slave holders; that these rights were never honored; and finally, that they passed on the right of inheritance to present day U.S. blacks [*Dalits*] who are their descendants and heirs [*ex-untouchables and ex-caste-enslaved*]. (Boxill and Corlett, 2010)

While this argument is specifically in the context of Black slavery, it applies to the case of Dalits in equal measure.

In the year 1843, the British in India legally abolished *caste enslavement* under Anglo-Indian law. Till then caste-based enslavement was a historic practice, largely as agrestic slavery, but not confined to it, and had continued unabated. Once the law was passed to abolish caste-based enslavement, the freed caste enslaved had a right to reparation for the denial of human (including civil, social, economic) and other rights. The British government and the subsequent governments that came to power post-independence made no formal announcements for any form of compensation, restitution, or reparations for them.

The British Crown owes reparations to the Dalits of India for delaying the enactment of the anti-caste-enslavement law for 10 years after it abolished slavery in England. Even after the enactment of the anti-caste-enslavement law in India, they failed to announce any form of reparative measures for the *caste-enslaved*, for instance, of the kind that were declared for freed Black slaves in the United States, such as providing forty acres and a mules. A reparative measure of this sort would have helped them get detached from their agrestic masters and start anew.

In the absence of any such reparative proclamations which could have made the *enslavers* liable to make reparative transfers or payments, the *caste-enslaved*, despite being legally now termed as free on paper, had no means whatsoever of an alternative source of livelihood. As a consequence, they had no option but to continue to work for their masters, but now as attached, bonded, or indentured labour which was no different from the earlier situation in all practical senses.

The Spiritual Renewal Argument

The spiritual renewal argument states that while compensation and restitution are essential and the starting points in the process of healing and reconciliation, true reparations would demand in addition that there also be an acceptance of historic crimes and injustices and that these have led to a causal chain of events that carried forward and affected (and continue to) the lives of the descendants of the victims of *untouchability and caste enslavement*.

> What I'm talking about is more than recompense for past injustices – more than a handout, a payoff, hush money, or a reluctant bribe. What I'm talking about is a national reckoning that would lead to spiritual renewal … Reparations would mean a revolution of the American consciousness, a reconciling of our self-image as the great democratizer with the facts of our history. (Coates, 2014)

While Ta-Nehisi Coates makes this argument in the context of Black slavery, it very well applies to the context of caste enslavement and untouchability. Without a recognition of historical facts, crimes, violence, denials, and that these and their harmful consequences are passed on inter-generationally to their present-day descendants (and further on), and without a sense of atonement and apology, people, groups, and the country cannot truly move forward on a path of reconciliation, healing, and growth of a new national consciousness.

For each of the arguments put forth above, there are problems or counter criticisms posed by many who feel the need to argue against the idea of reparations. In return, these counter arguments have been responded to and addressed quite adequately in the literature. However given the scope of this particular piece, it is not possible to go into the arguments in this long-standing debate at length.

The Way Forward

Once we agree that reparations are morally and ethically just and necessary, then the task ahead will be to decide the form reparations would take. Experience from around the world has taught us that each case is different, and the nature and form that reparations take vary from one country to another.

Such an initiative will begin with, first, an acknowledgment by the state as well as by the descendants of the enslavers and those who benefitted from the labour of untouchables and the enslaved, of *enslavement* and near enslavement of a large section of society in the form of *untouchability*, it various forms, its implementation and day-to-day practice historically and in the present, and its grave harm to its victims.

Second, it would require accepting responsibility for these transgressions and offering an unconditional apology for this grave historic wrong. Third, it would involve setting up a *reparation commission* that would look into all aspects of this long and slow process. The commission should constitute separate committees with subject experts from the Dalit community, practitioners, and policymakers to examine and suggest compensation, restitution, and reparation measures in different spheres of the lives of Dalits. These spheres could be but are not limited to the following:

1. economic reparations: land redistribution; wealth redistribution through a tax or cess, especially targeting the top 10 percentile of the population; share in the financial markets, in terms of a proportion of top executive decision-making seats in firms reserved, seats on the board reserved, proportion of shares, equity, and other financial instruments earmarked, buying of financial instruments or of goods, inputs, services, and so on from enterprises owned by minority community members; amongst others; access to cheaper credit over longer durations and many other such provisions in every aspect of people's economic life;
2. access to better and cheaper healthcare, education, housing, transportation, public spaces, and so on;
3. encouraging inter-caste marriages, dining, cohabitation, and other social, political, and cultural interactions.

Not only will this initiative and process be necessary for the Dalit community to feel that the injustices they endured are acknowledged and to some extent an attempt is set in motion for a healing process to begin, but it is essential for changing the national social psyche (of the non-Dalit population) and transformation of the nation's social structure.

Notes

1. See Harvard University, 'Lancet Commission on Reparations and Redistributive Justice: Advanced Seminar at the Radcliffe Institute', 12–13 November 2019, https://projects.iq.harvard.edu/lancet-reparations/home (accessed on 24 October 2022).
2. While the status of caste slaves might seem very similar to that of black slaves, there are vital differences. First, the transatlantic slave trade involved forcefully abducting African people and shipping them to the plantations and farms and as manual labour to South America, North America and Europe. The caste slaves, on the other hand, were born into designated slave castes and slave labour, agrestic or otherwise, which was their ascribed hereditary occupation. Second, the transatlantic slave trade was the consequence of colonial expansion and the need for free or forced labour. The emergence of caste slavery happened over a long period of hierarchical categorization of population by status and ascribing specific occupations as well as selective ascription of categories for new entrant groups in the Hindu fold, all religiously and divinely ordained.
3. See *The Hindu* (2022); Deepak Lavania (2017); Pramod Madhav (2021).
4. This caused the unemployment rate to rise from 11 per cent to 22 per cent for the SCs and the STs in the rural regions of India as opposed to a rise from 10 per cent to 20 per cent for the general-category population.

Bibliography

Adam, W. 1840. *The Law and Custom of Slavery in British India, In a Series of Letters to Thomas Fowell Buxton, Esq*. Boston, MA: Weeks, Jordan & Company.

Ambedkar, B. R. 1979. *Dr. Babasaheb Ambedkar: Writings and Speeches*, vol. 1, compiled by V. Moon. Bombay: Government of Maharashtra.

———. 1990. *Dr. Babasaheb Ambedkar: Writings and Speeches*, vol. 3, compiled by V. Moon. Bombay: Government of Maharashtra.

———. 1990. *Dr. Babasaheb Ambedkar: Writings and Speeches*, vol. 7, compiled by V. Moon. Bombay: Government of Maharashtra.

America, R. F. 1993. *Paying the Social Debt: What White America Owes Black America*. Santa Barbara, CA: ABC-CLIO.

Banaji, D. R. 1937. *Slavery in British India*. Bombay: Taraporewala Sons and Co. Kitab Mahal.

Boxill, B. R. 2003. 'A Lockean Argument for Black Reparations'. *Journal of Ethics* 7(1): 63–91.

Boxill, B. R., and J. A. Corlett. 2010. 'Black Reparations'. In *The Stanford Encyclopedia of Philosophy* (Spring 2022 edition), edited by E. N. Zalta. https://plato.stanford.edu/archives/spr2022/entries/black-reparations/. Accessed on 26 October 2022.

Buchanan, F. H. 1807. *A Journey from Madras through the Countries of Mysore, Canara, and Malabar, Performed under the Orders of the Most Noble the Marquis Wellesley, Governor General of India*, vol. 1. London: Cadell.

Buhler, G. 2006 (1886). *The Law of Manu*. Delhi: Motilal Banarsidass Publications.

Chanana, D. R. 1962. *Slavery in Ancient India: As Depicted in Pali and Sanskrit Texts*. India: People's Publishing House.

Coates, T-N. 2014. 'The Case for Reparations'. *The Atlantic*, June.

Coffey, D., P. Hathi, N. Khurana, and A. Thorat. 2018. 'Explicit Prejudice: Evidence from a New Survey'. *Economic and Political Weekly* 53(1): 47.

Feagin, J. R. 2004. 'Documenting the Costs of Slavery, Segregation, and Contemporary Racism: Why Reparations Are in Order for African Americans'. *Harvard BlackLetter Law Journal* 20: 49–81.

Hindustan Times. 2021. 'Dalit Students Made to Sit Separately for Meals in Amethi Village, Probe On'. 1 October. https://www.hindustantimes.com/india-news/dalit-students-made-to-sit-separately-for-meals-in-amethi-village-probe-on-101633064747438.html. Accessed on 26 October 2022.

Jaffrelot, C. 2006. 'The Impact of Affirmative Action in India: More Political than Socioeconomic'. *India Review* 5(2): 173–89.

Jayashree, C. H. 1989. 'Agrestic Slavery in Mirasi-Tenures of Tamil Nadu during 19th Century'. *Proceedings of the Indian History Congress* 50: 580–87.

Jha, V. 2018. *Candala: Untouchability and Caste in Early India*. Delhi: Primus Books.

Indian Law Commissioner, East Indies (India Office). 1841. 'Appendix to the Report from Indian Law Commissioners Relating to Slavery in the East Indies'. https://dspace.gipe.ac.in/xmlui/handle/10973/19931. Accessed on 20 February 2023.

Kotani, H. (ed.). 1997. *Caste System, Untouchability and the Depressed*. Delhi: Manohar.

Kumar, A. 2017. *Understanding the Black Economy and Black Money in India: An Enquiry into Causes, Consequences and Remedies*. New Delhi: Aleph Book Company.

Lavania, Deepak. 2017. 'Dalit Student Made to Clean Toilets, Thrashed by Social Welfare Officer in Uttar Pradesh'. *Indiatimes*, 15 September. https://www.indiatimes.com/news/india/dalit-student-made-to-clean-toilets-thrashed-by-social-welfare-officer-in-uttar-pradesh-329776.html. Accessed on 26 October 2022.

Locke, J. 1998 (1960). *Second Treatise on Civil Government* (*Il Secondo Trattato Sul Governo*). https://english.hku.hk/staff/kjohnson/PDF/LockeJohnSECONDTREATISE1690.pdf. Accessed on 26 October 2022.

———. 2013 (1689). 'Two Treatises of Government, 1689'. In *The Anthropology of Citizenship: A Reader*, edited by S. Lazar, 43–46. Hoboken, NJ: Wiley.

Lorenzo, A. M. 1945. 'Agrestic Serfdom in Northern India'. *Indian Journal of Social Work* 5: 133–41.

Madhav, Pramod. 2021. 'School Teacher Suspended for Making Dalit Students Clean Toilets in Tamil Nadu's Tirupur'. *India Today*, 19 December. https://www.indiatoday.in/cities/story/tirupur-school-teacher-suspended-for-making-dalit-students-clean-toilets-1889556-2021-12-19. Accessed on 26 October 2022.

Malcolm, N. (ed.) 1996. *Thomas Hobbes: Leviathan*. Oxford: Oxford University Press.

Mohan, P. S. 2015. *Modernity of Slavery: Struggles against Caste Inequality in Colonial Kerala*. New Delhi: Oxford University Press.

Nozick, R. 1974. *Anarchy, State, and Utopia*. New York: Basic Books.

Sahoo, P. C. 2012. 'Slavery, Manu and Human Rights'. *Bulletin of the Deccan College Research Institute* 72: 451–56.

Saradamoni, K. 1980. *Emergence of a Slave Caste: Pulayas of Kerala*. New Delhi: People's Publishing House.

Sharma, R. S. 1958. *Sudras in Ancient India: A Survey of the Position of the Lower Orders Down to circa AD 500*. Delhi: Motilal Banarsidass Publishers.

Tagade, N., A. K. Naik, and S. Thorat. 2018. 'Wealth Ownership and Inequality in India: A Socio-Religious Analysis'. *Journal of Social Inclusion Studies* 4(2): 196–213.

Temperley, H. 2000. 'The Delegalization of Slavery in British India'. *Slavery and Abolition* 21(2): 169–87.

Thomas, K. T. 1999. 'Slaves: An Integral Part of the Production System in Malabar (19th Century)'. *Proceedings of the Indian History Congress* 60: 600–10.

Thorat, A., and O. Joshi. 2020. 'The Continuing Practice of Untouchability in India'. *Economic and Political Weekly* 55(2): 37–45.

Thorat, S., N. Tagade, and A. K. Naik. 2016. 'Prejudice against Reservation Policies: How and Why'. *Economic and Political Weekly* 51(8): 61–69.

Thorat, S., and P. Attewell. 2007. 'The Legacy of Social Exclusion: A Correspondence Study of Job Discrimination in India'. *Economic and Political Weekly* 42(41): 4141–45.

Thorat, S., S. Madheswaran, and B. P. Vani. 2021. 'Caste and Labour Market in India: Employment Discrimination and Its Impact on Poverty'. Economic and Political Weekly 56(21). https://www.epw.in/journal/2021/21/special-articles/caste-and-labour-market.html. Accessed on 26 October 2022.

Times of India. 2019. 'Dalit students made to sit separately during mid-day meal in Mandi School'. 11 December. https://timesofindia.indiatimes.com/city/shimla/dalit-students-made-to-sit-separately-during-mid-day-meal-in-mandi-school/articleshow/72465065.cms. Accessed on 26 October 2022.

The Hindu. 2022. 'Dalit Boy Forced to Clean Toilet in School near Coimbatore'. 5 April. https://www.thehindu.com/news/cities/Coimbatore/dalit-boy-forced-to-clean-toilet-in-school-near-coimbatore/article65292946.ece. Accessed on 26 October 2022.

Viswanath, R. 2010. 'Spiritual Slavery, Material Malaise: "Untouchables" and Religious Neutrality in Colonial South India'. *Historical Research* 83(219): 124–45.

Wilson Anti-Slavery Collection. 1834. *Slavery in India: Papers Relative to Slavery in India*. Manchester: John Rylands University Library, University of Manchester.

Yamazaki, G. I. 1997. 'Introduction: Social Discrimination in Ancient India and Its Transition to the Medieval Period'. In *Caste System, Untouchability and the Depressed*, edited by H. Kotani, 3–20. New Delhi: Manohar.

19

Dalit Capitalism

Adversity, Opportunity, and Agency

D. Shyam Babu

The empowerment of Dalits has been linear. There was a time when an 'educated Dalit' was more of a mythical beast than reality; the same was the case with a Dalit doctor, a Dalit officer, a Dalit minister, or a Dalit governor. It has been a progression of sorts in the sense that without education Dalits could not have entered the civil services, and without their electoral participation – through a quota system for Dalit candidates under universal adult franchise[1] – even a few of them would not have ended up as ministers, governors, and so on.

The story of their upward mobility, a journey that has yet to reach its destination, began in the mid-nineteenth century which witnessed two radical developments in the history of India. First, schools were thrown open to Dalit children from 1853 onwards. Though this proved to be a symbolic act on paper, unacceptable to broader society, its transformative potential came to be realized in subsequent decades. The second development was even more radical, and its impact proved to be long-lasting. In 1862, the Indian Penal Code (IPC) came into force, decreeing at the stroke of a pen that all Indians were equal before the law, irrespective of their caste, creed, or gender. That a crime attracts the same punishment for all was an alien idea, but it forever changed the fate of lower castes for the better.[2] The introduction of the Code of Criminal Procedure (CrPC) two decades later laid a firm foundation for a rule-based society.

The two aforementioned developments triggered numerous popular movements and policy initiatives, a list of which is too long to enumerate here. The process culminated in the Constitution of India which embodies the universal values of liberty, equality, and fraternity, and contains an entire section (Part XVI) on the upliftment of Dalits and other weaker sections through welfare measures such as job quotas. Job quotas by nature tend to benefit only a tiny section of any group, and only a fraction of Dalits entered public employment, thus forming the nucleus of a Dalit bourgeoisie.

A caveat may be in order at the outset. Dalit capitalism rankles both the left revolutionary and the right reactionary. Even equanimous scholars remain sceptical as they feel it promises more than it can ever deliver. Shorn of ideological arguments, Dalit capitalism is a simple idea to encourage Dalits to invest in occupational diversity, mobility, and agency. As a slogan it aims to change the negative image of Dalits about themselves that they are destined to operate within a set of occupations, while entrepreneurship is for the Banias (traditional merchant castes). Similarly, the hope behind the concept is to demonstrate to society and the government that Dalits can succeed as entrepreneurs under non-discriminatory conditions.

This chapter makes an attempt to analyse the latest stage of the quest of Dalits for upward mobility which is captured by the slogan 'Dalit capitalism.' The first section contextualizes adversity and opportunity by tracing, till the end of the twentieth century, the forces that paved the way towards a more inclusive society. In a case of remarkable continuation, independent India has not only followed (so far) the templates created by the colonial government, but also scaled them up and framed myriad new interventions. The second section discusses the pathways of Dalit capitalism, specifically what objective conditions are necessary for this new class to thrive. A major highlight of the section is the story of how Dalits, having realized the new opportunities that the 1991 economic reforms had created, assumed agency to effect occupational diversity and forayed into entrepreneurship. The third section flags how electoral mobilization has proved to be a double-edged sword, giving the community a voice while simultaneously triggering resentment among non-Dalits. The past three decades have witnessed lower-caste political mobilization with slogans of 'social justice' and *bahujan* which were based on the assumption that the discriminated groups being in the majority could and must come together to capture political power. It has become painfully clear now that any caste-based mobilization would end up strengthening the caste system, which is not a favourable outcome for Dalits. The final section assesses where the community stands at the moment with regard to its civil, political, and social status. It raises the question whether the lack of social citizenship among Dalits would result in the erosion of their civil and political rights.

Adversity and Opportunity

It is the contention of this chapter, using the framework of Thomas H. Marshall's influential essay on citizenship (1950) that civil, political, and social dimensions form the triumvirate of citizenship for Dalits, and they have been unfolding since the mid-nineteenth century. There are two distinct aspects of the essay that are relevant to Dalits and, more generally, India. First, citizenship, or full membership in society, comes in historical progression. In the context of England, Marshall (1950: 14) assigned civil, political, and social dimensions of citizenship 'without doing too much violence to historical accuracy' to the eighteenth, nineteenth, and twentieth centuries, respectively. In the case of India, the lag of a century is evident as the progression traversed the nineteenth, twentieth, and twenty-first centuries, even as social citizenship still remains in a nascent stage.

As mentioned earlier, the IPC from 1862 onwards accorded to all Indians a modicum of civil rights, such as equality before the law, due process, and so on. After independence, Indians began enjoying the fruits of political citizenship in exercising universal adult franchise and complete freedom to seek elected office. Dalits have even been guaranteed a fixed number of seats in the lower houses of legislature, proportionate to their population.[3]

The third dimension – social citizenship – has been a tricky one, at least in the context of Dalits. The reasons are obvious. Whereas civil and political rights can be had through the fiat of the state, it cannot enforce social rights. It would be one thing for the state to forbid non-Dalits from discriminating against Dalits, but it would be quite another to decree that Dalits be treated by non-Dalits as their fellow human beings. Coincidentally in 1949, the same year in which Marshall delivered his lecture (which was published the following year), Ambedkar, in his final address to the Constituent Assembly, raised the same point: 'What does fraternity mean? Fraternity means a sense of common brotherhood of all Indians – of Indians being one people. It is the principle which gives unity and solidarity to social life' (Ambedkar, 1949: para 326).

The second distinct aspect to Marshall's essay is his analysis of the views of well-known economist Alfred Marshall who was ready to accept or condone quantitative or economic inequalities as natural or irremediable while condemning qualitative or social inequalities (Marshall, 1950: 7). Citizenship on the social plain assumes a certain sense of oneness among members of a society without which there is no basis for a group to live together. The Ambedkarite conception of social citizenship is fraternity, as expounded by Ambedkar himself in 1936:

An ideal society should be mobile, should be full of channels for conveying a change taking place in one part to other parts. In an ideal society there should be many interests consciously communicated and shared. There should be varied and free points of contact with other modes of association. In other words, there must be social endosmosis. This is fraternity, which is only another name for democracy. (Ambedkar, 2020: 57)

The progress or mobility of Dalits has indeed been linear, but with a twist. True, the dawn of the IPC meant they could theoretically be equal with others before the law. However, even today the country needs special laws, such as the 1989 Scheduled Castes and Scheduled Tribes (Prevention of Atrocities) Act, to safeguard their civil liberties. Similarly, Dalits exercise their franchise and enjoy full representation in the lower houses of legislature. But there is much to be desired in the substantive exercise of their civil and political citizenship. Several chapters in this volume, such as Chapter 18, testify to this dichotomy – formal or de jure rights in stark contrast to de facto subordination.

Therefore, for Dalits, adversity and opportunity are not two successive phases, moving from the former to the latter; in fact, the community moves back and forth. Adversity and opportunity are the twine that cannot be separated. Few would question the forward march of Dalits to regain their humanity. The progress, however, is slow enough for many scholars to miss it altogether.

Take the case of the second half of the twentieth century. We tend to flag how the Constitution abolished untouchability and granted reservations for the Scheduled Castes (SCs) and Scheduled Tribes (STs), as well as the landmark laws to punish those who resort to violence against the community. However, the functioning of liberal democracy itself, imperfect though it has been, has helped Dalits in numerous ways. The nationalization of banks in the late 1960s ensured Dalits could receive wages in the form of cash, instead of kind, though it took a generation to reach them. The Green Revolution ended starvation which had hitherto disproportionately affected Dalits. Similarly, the abolition of the practice of bonded labour in the mid-1970s must be regarded for its long-term transformative impact (Kapur et al., 2010: 47).[4] Even a secular matter like increased road-connectivity meant the state's ability to reach remote areas where previously its writ did not run at all.

The experience thus far teaches us that three preconditions need to converge for Dalits to make progress in all three spheres of citizenship. The foremost is the existence of a civil society wherein equality before the law and universal adult franchise are a reality. By the end of the twentieth century, India fulfilled this condition. There was (and indeed is) a gap between the extent of civil and political citizenship available to Dalits and others,[5] but we must compare Dalits' own past with their current status. For example, even the increase in violence must be regarded as a backlash of society against the progress made by Dalits (Chakraborty, Babu, and Chakravorty, 2006: 2480). The second precondition – that the Indian economy must grow fast and high for Dalits to reap its benefits – may sound trite and self-evident. Not so. Non-Dalits, especially upper castes, enjoyed economic prosperity and a vibrant civil society, while Dalits were denied even minimum standards of living. Ambedkar (2020: 40) recounted an incident in Rajasthan (something that even now happens sporadically) wherein Dalits were punished for the 'crime' of consuming ghee (clarified butter).

The third precondition builds on the previous two. Exercising occupational diversity and spatial mobility translates into agency for the community. In a survey of lifestyle changes among Dalits in two blocks of Uttar Pradesh (UP) in 1990 and 2007 (Table 19.1), it was found that

> ... over this relatively short period, half or more of households had added someone working as a migrant, in a profession, or in business, so that by 2007, about four-fifths of Dalit households in these two blocks had at least one family member, and sometimes more in one of these three activities. (Kapur et al., 2010: 47)

Migration, coupled with occupational diversity, triggered profound changes in the areas surveyed. To begin with, labour shortage helped Dalits increase their bargaining power. There is anecdotal evidence of similar dynamics in operation in other parts of the country. Before the economic reforms of 1991, Dalits had neither the freedom to migrate nor access to opportunities in cities.

Thus, the state employed all the means at its disposal to accord civil and political citizenship to Dalits, and what was left out – social citizenship – was in any case outside the purview of the state. That progress has been tardy with regard to the civil and political fields is due to society's resistance. Ambedkar put this succinctly, noting that formal legal rights would not mean much if society refused those rights to Dalits. A different force was needed to effect social change that would ultimately accommodate them as equal citizens.

Table 19.1 Occupational diversity and mobility of Dalits in Uttar Pradesh, 1990 and 2007

	1990	2007
Farm workers	61	33.05
Households doing sharecropping	10.8	21.4
Masons, tailors, or drivers	11.65	39.5
Grocers, tea or *paan* vendors, and so on	5.1	23.85
Households dependent on government jobs	6.15	7.1
Factory workers in cities	10.3	39.5

Source: Kapur et al. (2010: 47).

Capitalism as an Agent for Social Change

At the turn of the twenty-first century, India was at a crossroads. It was evident that while the 1991 reforms were working, the process needed to be accelerated. There was a consensus that, coupled with a free society, freer markets would put the country on a high-growth trajectory (Babu, 2003: 21). Dalits too needed a reset because, as Surinder S. Jodhka (2010: 41) put it, the 'growing privatisation of India's economy and declining avenues of employment in the state sector also meant shrinking of jobs available under the quota system for reserved categories'. Therefore, for the community, the time was ripe to expand and diversify. The Bhopal Conference of Dalit intellectuals and activists, which took place in January 2002 (sponsored by the government of Madhya Pradesh), proved to be the catalyst (Pai, 2010; Prakash, 2010).

The conference was unique in several respects. It was the first of its kind in that never before had such a huge all-India Dalit conference (with more than 250 participants from all over the country) taken place to take stock of the situation. It was more policy-oriented than academic. Moreover, though the conference was organized by the Madhya Pradesh government, which provided infrastructural and financial support, it was Dalit activists who determined the agenda, sessions, speakers, and so on. Aditya Nigam, a sympathetic but sceptical observer who attended the conference, wrote:

> It was clear to those attending the conference that though [the chief minister] Digvijay Singh and his government were hosting the event, it was almost entirely conducted by a committed group of Dalit intellectuals and activists. Probably, there was a mutual dependence of both sides on each other but clearly, the agenda and the discussions reflected an almost complete autonomy of the intellectual content of the conference. (Nigam, 2002: 1193)

At the outset, the conference accomplished a policy breakthrough as the chief minister announced from the venue itself that the state government would help Dalit entrepreneurs by implementing 'supplier diversity'.[6] This 'accomplishment', though it proved to be short-lived in the state, established supplier diversity in favour of Dalits as a policy option,[7] which has been emulated by several states.[8] The *Times of India* commended the effort, remarking that 'promotion of supplier diversity may well be the alternative to jobs that are simply not there' (*Times of India*, 2003). Far more substantial has been the influence of 'Dalit capitalism' which came out of the conference as a slogan.

The organizers were motivated by two concerns. First, job quotas are an inherently narrow policy instrument. Only a fraction of Dalits would benefit even if their full quota of government jobs was given to them. Job quotas in any case bypass the less educated and illiterate Dalits. Therefore, reservations per se would never be able to bring Dalits on par with others. Probably nothing would.

Second, the organizers were also convinced that entrepreneurship offered several possibilities. An illiterate Dalit can open a grocery store in their village, as many do, while an educated one can access capital from banks to start a business *at their level*. It was also evident by the turn of the new millennium that a nascent bourgeoisie had emerged among the community, which is urban, educated, and unemployed. What was needed was a slogan, a 'spectacle' (Guru, 2012), to catch the imagination of Dalits to think away from reservations. Therefore, Dalit capitalism is more of a strategy about seeking to change perceptions and very little about capitalism as an economic system. In her assessment of the Bhopal Conference, Sudha Pai (2010: 471) is equanimous:

> It acknowledged that older policies such as protective discrimination were no longer as useful as in the past and a free and frank discussion was required to chalk out the path ahead. The participants urged that a new societal consensus was needed on the Dalit Question before any new policies could be put forward and this could only emerge out of dialogue between the dominant and disadvantaged groups.

In about two decades of its existence as an idea and a possibility, Dalit capitalism has been fairly successful. Dalit entrepreneurs are no doubt statistically insignificant, but their very presence as a category has added a new positive dimension to Dalit identity. In this respect, Dalit capitalism treads the same trajectory as that of its inspiration, Black capitalism. Hardly a generation ago, scholars pronounced Black enterprises a failure, but today these enterprises are a force to reckon with. For example, as per the data for 2012 there were '2.58 million Black-owned businesses in the United States, generating $150 billion in annual revenue and supporting 3.56 million U.S. jobs' (Association for Enterprise Opportunity [AEO], n.d.: 4). One may dismiss these accomplishments as being trivial by comparing them with the size of the US economy. A better way of comparison, for both Blacks and Dalits, however, is to measure their current condition with that of their past.

Several studies since the early 2000s indicate upward mobility of most social groups in India as a result of economic reforms. Kapur et al. (2010: 49) have even emphasized that during 1990 and 2007, 'as per their own self-assessment, the social well-being of large numbers of Dalits advanced even faster than their material well-being'. The aforementioned work was followed up with a book,

Defying the Odds (2014), which celebrated the dawn of Dalit capitalism. Implicit in the two studies is the belief that marrying India's liberal democracy with freer markets would not only put the country on a high-growth trajectory, but would help even Dalits to improve their socio-economic conditions. The belief was not so much in the virtues of capitalism as an economic system as in its historical role as a social disrupter.

Has Dalit capitalism lived up to its promise à la Black capitalism? Are two decades good enough time to make a definitive assessment? Dalit entrepreneurs as a class effectively debunk the negative stereotype that Dalits would remain backward without the prop of reservations. Their role as agents of social change is buttressed by two facts.

First, none of the 21 Dalit entrepreneurs that *Defying the Odds* profiled had accessed any government scheme to start their businesses. In fact, this was the observed trend even in the survey that was the basis for the book. Indurkar (2018: 206), in his thesis on Dalit entrepreneurs, found that 'about 77.3 per cent Dalit entrepreneurs have started their ventures with their own sources and savings as an initial capital and they did not avail any loans from the financial institutions'. Aseem Prakash's book, *Dalit Capital* (2015), too, found the same phenomenon among the 90 Dalit entrepreneurs he interviewed and inferred that 'this often meant a very high interest rate' (Prakash, 2015: 76).

Seeking to strike a balance between the optimism in the aftermath of the Bhopal Conference and the reality of very few Dalits in businesses, Iyer, Khanna, and Varshney (2013: 53) pose two important questions: 'Dalit millionaires may have burst on the scene, but how far do they represent the general state of Dalit entrepreneurship in the country? More widely, what is the relationship between caste and entrepreneurship?' Terming the underrepresentation 'widespread', they cite that in 2005, Dalits owned only 9.8 per cent of all enterprises, 'well below their 16.4% share in the total population' (Iyer, Khanna, and Varshney, 2013). The underrepresentation of Dalits in businesses, where they enjoy no quota system, may be contrasted with their numbers in the bureaucracy where, in 1950 the community was granted reservations proportionate to their share in the population. In 2001 Dalits accounted for 11 per cent of Group A and B (managerial and supervisory) posts in the government, and by 2019 the number had increased to 15 per cent (Babu, Kapur, and Prasad, 2022).

The fact that the mobility of Dalits is in any case slow is no answer to the questions raised by Iyer and colleagues. Prima facie, Dalits owning about 10 per cent of enterprises may appear impressive, but we do not know their size, nature, turnout, or the jobs they have created. Much more important are the sustainability and growth of these enterprises. As for the other question on how far caste remains an impediment to entrepreneurship among Dalits, while Iyer and colleagues report widespread underrepresentation, Prakash (2010) is emphatic that Dalit entrepreneurs face caste discrimination. But *Defying the Odds* differs in a significant way. It records the trials and tribulations of its heroes but reports not many insurmountable hurdles *due to caste discrimination*. We need more studies from anthropology and sociology to determine issues related to caste.

Second, many Dalit entrepreneurs are first generation, semi-literates, or illiterates, who were not rich enough to pursue higher education but determined enough to succeed in entrepreneurship. Their growth belies the assumptions of the Bhopal Conference that second- or third-generation educated Dalits ('Dalit bourgeoisie'), whose parents and grandparents accessed reservations, would, with the dwindling job opportunities in the government, embrace entrepreneurship. Their success proves the simple point that what Dalits need is equal opportunities coupled with a robust regime of the rule of law. This also explains why so few success stories received so much publicity.

Hence, we have the 'spectacle' of Dalit capitalism, a slogan to influence national discourse, a new pathway for the community's upward mobility, and a public-policy choice for any willing government. Therefore, it will remain tantalizing, being a source of hope for the believer no matter how much the sceptic scorns it.

Electoral Mobilization as a Force against Social Change

Pertinent to our discussion is *The Narrow Corridor* (2019) by Daron Acemoglu and James A. Robinson, who in their historical–comparative analysis of how the creative tension and contestation between society and state produced or failed to produce liberty around the world squarely implicate caste in India's poverty and backwardness, especially of Dalits. They state their thesis thus:

> A strong state is needed to control violence, enforce laws, and provide public services that are critical for a life in which people are empowered to make and pursue their choices. A strong, mobilized society is needed to control and shackle the strong state. (Acemoglu and Robinson, 2019: 13)

A strong state and a strong society while counteracting each other would produce 'a narrow corridor' for liberty to survive and thrive. The bane of India – insofar as Dalits are concerned – is the brittleness of the state. The state grants civil liberties to Dalits, society violates them. The state grants preferential policies in favour of Dalits, society keeps throwing hurdles in their way. The ideals of the state, as enumerated in the preamble to the Constitution, are anathema to the spirit of society.

Ironically, the country's electoral politics has produced this stalemate. In most heterogeneous countries, such as India, it is difficult to separate the political from the social. Social identities determine the ideologies of groups and even their religious denominations. For example, in the United States, conservatism with limited government as its credo finds more traction among Whites than among Blacks and other minority groups, because Whites tend to prefer status quo, while other groups seek change through proactive governments that would favour them.

With a few exceptions, therefore, ruling arrangements at the centre and in the states are comprised of social coalitions that have been stitched together and are sometimes known by appealing acronyms. The phenomenon is not limited to lower-caste parties which, in any case, openly cater to specific caste(s); even national parties like the Indian National Congress (hereafter, Congress) and the Bharatiya Janata Party (BJP) seek to build on social coalitions. For example, in the 1970s, the Congress in Gujarat was successful in bringing together Kshatriyas, Harijans, Adivasis, and Muslims (KHAM) under its fold. The party now appears to be in terminal decline because it has been losing the support of one social group after the other. At present the BJP enjoys the support of upper castes and the Most Backward Classes (MBCs).

Since caste remains an important social marker for many Indians, it is but natural that it seeps into the realm of politics. However, since no one caste enjoys geographic concentration in sufficient numbers to muster a legislative majority, it is always a coalition of castes that forms the majority. It has been the experience that upper castes by and large retain their primacy by co-opting a few lower castes and minorities. While under the Congress, upper castes stitched together KHAM kind of arrangements everywhere in the country, under the BJP they brought together a new coalition of most backwards plus most Hindu groups, excluding Harijans (Dalits), Adivasis, and Muslims, as well as other minorities.

There would be nothing wrong in a caste-driven society if its politics were entrenched in caste. However, two aspects are salient to our discussion. First, successful social coalitions brought together by upper castes, such as the Congress governments in the past and that of the BJP now, are more often rooted in big-tent politics peppered with some sentiments that pass off as ideologies, if not ideologies per se. For example, whereas the Congress had non-alignment in foreign policy and claims of a mixed economy, secularism, and so on, in domestic policy, the BJP has Hindutva in that it not only represents Hindus but its ideology and vision are also derived from the Hindu ethos.

Second, though lower-caste mobilizations have sworn by social justice and their being in numerical majority (such as the Bahujans in the Bahujan Samaj

Party [BSP]), they have never managed to accord a modicum of dignity to their avowed ideals. Hence, their coalitions have proved to be short-lived, especially in the Hindi belt. There is never anything larger than the sum of a coalition's parts. Each of these formations – such as the BSP, the Samajwadi Party (SP), the Rashtriya Janata Dal (RJD), and so on – has reduced itself to a single-caste party, finally descending into a family outfit, fulfilling the prophetic words of late Ram Vilas Paswan that many of these parties 'will have to shut shop by 2020' (Press Trust of India, 2019). Though all these parties are very much around, their decline and disappearance are not in doubt.

The failure of lower-caste electoral mobilization in the north, especially in UP, has resulted in further marginalization of Dalits in two respects. First, Dalits have effectively ceased to be a part of the electoral process in the state. No party cares to campaign in Dalit hamlets. The BSP being a party representing Dalits has no compulsion to campaign amongst them as it is certain of their support, while non-BSP parties too skip Dalits because they are also certain that Dalits would not support them (Babu, 2019). The state's political system has evolved in such a way that upper castes, who more often provide the critical mass for a social coalition, do not count Dalit votes in devising their electoral arithmetic. Second, the very natural process of electoral polarization and consolidation on caste lines has ended up isolating Dalits from other castes, especially upper castes.

Therefore, the electoral process that held a promise for lower castes and Dalits to claim their just share in political power has proved to be counterproductive. In other words, the attempts of Dalits to maximize their citizenship rights in the realm of politics resulted in a backlash against them in the social realm.

Conclusion

At the beginning of the third decade of the twenty-first century, can we assert that Dalits are closer to achieving social citizenship? Is the fraternity, which Ambedkar insisted on, a reality? Just like in the case of their civil and political citizenship, a categorical assertion in one way or the other about their social citizenship misses the point. Empowerment of persecuted minorities like Blacks and Dalits has never been an event, like a country's independence, but a process that often moves so slow that many do not see any movement. Moreover, as mentioned earlier, unlike civil and political rights which could be granted by the state, social rights are to be accepted by society. It has been our experience over the past seven decades that there is no finality on the civil rights of Dalits which could be violated with impunity; as for their political rights, there has been steady progress.

There hangs a huge question mark on the full citizenship rights of Dalits. One feature of Hindutva that must trouble Dalits is the apparent triumph of society over state. Only time will tell whether the civil and political citizenship that Dalits gained in the nineteenth and twentieth centuries, respectively, will remain strong enough in the twenty-first century to accord them social citizenship, or, conversely, whether their lack of social citizenship would result in the erosion of their civil and political rights.

Notes

1. The Constitution of India provides (in addition to job quotas) reserved constituencies in the lower houses of legislature at the centre and in states wherein only Dalit candidates can contest.
2. This was the fulfilment of the sentiment that T. B. Macaulay articulated against the prevalent separate penal codes for Hindus and Muslims. He said in the House of Commons on 10 July 1833 that 'though I fully believe that a mild penal code is better than a severe penal code, the worst of all systems was surely that of having a mild code for the Brahmins … while there was a severe code for the Sudras' (Macaulay, 1833: para. 528).
3. Articles 330 and 332 of the Constitution provide quotas in legislature for Dalits and tribals, respectively.
4. The Bonded Labour System (Abolition) Act, 1976, proved to be a landmark legislation that helped the country end all forms of forced labour to realize the fundamental rights of equality and individual freedom.
5. See also the section 'Electoral Mobilization as a Force against Social Change'.
6. Supplier diversity, being implemented in the United States, refers to the principle and practice of a company or agency procuring its requirements from diverse suppliers to benefit minority groups, such as African Americans.
7. Though in the 1970s the central government began allocating petrol stations to SCs and STs, it never became a template.
8. For example, many southern states, especially Telangana, have introduced several measures to promote entrepreneurship among Dalits. Moreover, a Google search of the phrase 'supplier diversity in India' would lead to many instances of multinational companies in India following supplier diversity in the country.

Bibliography

Acemoglu, D., and J. A. Robinson. 2019. *The Narrow Corridor: States, Societies, and the Fate of Liberty*. New York: Penguin Books.

Ambedkar, B. R. 1949. *Constituent Assembly Debates*, vol. 11, 25 November. https://www.constitutionofindia.net/constitution_assembly_debates/volume/11/1949-11-25. Accessed on 29 April 2022.

———. 2020. 'Annihilation of Caste'. In *Dr. Babasaheb Ambedkar: Writings and Speeches*, vol. 1. New Delhi: Dr Ambedkar Foundation, Ministry of Social Justice and Empowerment, Government of India.

Association for Enterprise Opportunity (AEO). n.d. *The Tapestry of Black Business Ownership in America: Untapped Opportunities for Success*. Washington, DC: Association for Enterprise Opportunity. https://www.aeoworks.org/images/uploads/fact_sheets/AEO_Black_Owned_Business_Report_02_16_17_FOR_WEB.pdf. Accessed on 21 October 2022.

Babu, D. S. 2003. 'Dalits and New Economic Order: Some Prognostications and Prescriptions from the Bhopal Conference'. RGICS Working Paper 44, Rajiv Gandhi Institute for Contemporary Studies, New Delhi.

———. 2019. 'From Empowerment to Disenfranchisement: Lower Caste Mobilisation Appears to Have Run Its Course'. *Times of India*, 28 August. https://timesofindia.indiatimes.com/blogs/toi-edit-page/from-empowerment-to-disenfranchisement-lower-caste-mobilisation-appears-to-have-run-its-course/. Accessed on 28 April 2022.

Babu, D. S., D. Kapur, and C. B. Prasad. 2022. 'Reimagining Merit in India: Cognition and Affirmative Action'. In *Making Meritocracy: Lessons from China and India, from Antiquity to the Present*, edited by T. Khanna and M. Szonyi, 287–306. New York: Oxford University Press.

Chakraborty, D., D. S. Babu, and M. Chakravorty. 2006. 'Atrocities on Dalits'. *Economic and Political Weekly* 41(24): 2478–81.

Guru, G. 2012. 'Rise of the "Dalit Millionaire": A Low Intensity Spectacle'. *Economic and Political Weekly* 47(50): 41–49.

Indurkar, C. B. 2018. 'Dalit Entrepreneurs: Their Challenges and Strategies'. PhD Thesis, Tata Institute of Social Sciences, Mumbai.

Iyer, L., T. Khanna, and A. Varshney. 2013. 'Caste and Entrepreneurship in India'. *Economic and Political Weekly* 48(6): 52–60.

Jodhka, S. S. 2010. 'Dalits in Business: Self-Employed Scheduled Castes in North-West India'. *Economic and Political Weekly* 45(11): 41–48.

Kapur, D., C. B. Prasad, L. Pritchett, and D. S. Babu. 2010. 'Rethinking Inequality: Dalits in Uttar Pradesh in the Market Reform Era'. *Economic and Political Weekly* 45(35): 39–49.

Kapur, D., D. S. Babu, and C. B. Prasad. 2014. *Defying the Odds: The Rise of Dalit Entrepreneurs*. Gurgaon: Random House India.

Macaulay, T. B. 1833. 'East-India Company's Charter'. https://hansard.parliament.uk//Commons/1833-07-10/debates/bf333819-5f71-4ad5-96cd-a41a08c999dd/East-IndiaCompanySCharter. Accessed on 21 October 2022.

Marshall, T. H. 1950. *Citizenship and Social Class*. Cambridge: Cambridge University Press.

Nigam, A. 2002. 'In Search of a Bourgeoisie: Dalit Politics Enters a New Phase'. *Economic and Political Weekly* 37(13): 1190–93.

Pai, S. 2010. *Developmental State and the Dalit Question in Madhya Pradesh: Congress Response*. New Delhi: Routledge.

Prakash, A. 2010. 'Dalit Entrepreneurs in Middle India'. In *The Comparative Political Economy of Development: Africa and South Asia*, edited by B. Harriss-White and J. Heyer, 291–317. London and New York: Routledge.

———. 2015. *Dalit Capital: State, Markets and Civil Society in Urban India*. New Delhi: Routledge.

Press Trust of India. 2019. 'Parties like SP, BSP, RJD Will Shut Shop by 2020: Ram Vilas Paswan'. *Times of India*, 4 June. https://timesofindia.indiatimes. com/india/parties-like-sp-bsp-rjd-will-shut-shop-by-2020-ram-vilas-paswan/ articleshow/69654014.cms. Accessed on 24 March 2022.

Times of India. 2003. 'Reserved Signs: Politicians Can Only Offer Job Quotas but No Actual Jobs'. 2 June.

Part V
Discrimination and Representation

20

Do Scheduled Caste Reservations for Political Office Improve the Lives of Dalits?

Simon Chauchard and Francesca R. Jensenius

Over the past 20 years, much empirical work has examined the impact – on a variety of outcomes – of political reservations for members of the Scheduled Castes (SCs) in India. In this chapter, we provide an overview of what we know about the effects of reservations in the Indian parliament, state legislatures, and local-level elected bodies, to date.

Before we set out, we want to clarify what this chapter is *not* about. Reservation policies can be normatively justified or opposed. However, positioning ourselves in this debate is not our aim here. Nor are we able to say much about what the effects *would have been* if the system had been designed differently, if it were to be removed, or if it had been implemented elsewhere. Our goal is rather to lay out what empirical research and data tell us about the current system as implemented in India. We focus here on the individuals we know best: politicians elected in seats reserved for the SCs across India.[1] These are often unknown political actors. Yet they constitute a sizable share of all elected officials in the country: as of September 2022, 84 of 543 members of parliament (MPs), 625 of 4,099 members of legislative assemblies (MLAs), and 15 to 17 per cent of all those elected to over 2,83,000 local elected bodies in villages, blocks, and districts were representatives from seats reserved for the SCs.

While India's political reservation system is unique in its massive scope and duration, many types of electoral quota systems are in place across the world. The extensive normative literature on *descriptive representation* highlights the importance of including individuals from disadvantaged or marginalized groups in office.[2] Yet the effects of such inclusion are not clear. One common argument is that political representatives are better at representing people *like them* because of shared experiences or shared interests (Mansbridge, 1999; Duflo, 2005). Empirical research focusing on the United States finds evidence for such patterns: the inclusion of minority groups in politics has been found to boost political participation, increase trust in political institutions, and enhance pride and self-respect (Marschall and Ruhil, 2007; Gay, 2002; Broockman, 2013).

The empirical evidence for such effects in other parts of the world is sparser and more mixed. In a study of quota policies for women across Latin America, for instance, Mala Htun (2016) demonstrates that these quotas have had few effects beyond boosting the number of women in politics. Increasingly, scholars argue that the effects of different forms of policies of inclusion will depend on context – on institutional design, the type of group that is included, the political culture, and so on. However, group-based quotas comparable in design and scope to Indian caste-based reservations have not been implemented elsewhere. As a result, it is hard to meaningfully compare the Indian experience with differently designed quota systems elsewhere.

What have the effects of political reservations for SCs been in India? We approach this question by looking at four types of outcomes that have been studied empirically in the Indian context in recent years: the impact on political and electoral outcomes, on material or developmental outcomes broadly defined (public goods provision, educational achievements, health, and so on), on state–citizen relations (such as access to the bureaucracy and police), and, finally, on caste relations, conflict, and untouchability-related behaviours. In what follows, we detail each of these effects before reflecting on their potential drivers.

A few caveats are in order regarding the scope and methodology of this review. First, the evaluation of different forms of reservation policies (in politics, education, and public jobs) has generated renewed and considerable interest over the past 20 years (since Pande, 2003; Chattopadhyay and Duflo, 2004), especially so in American academia. The reasons behind this interest have admittedly been largely methodological, as the social sciences have become increasingly focused on studying micro-level phenomena where one can cleanly identify causal effects. The way the Indian system of political reservations has been designed helps researchers study their *causal impact*. Our focus here is on this recent wave of scholarship that has sought to empirically measure the impact of political reservations.

Second, it is important to highlight a number of likely biases in the literature we review. Two biases seem especially worth mentioning. To start with, for data reasons, the majority of empirical studies of SC reservations in India are of SC MLAs and SC village council presidents (*pradhan*s or *sarpanch*es); by contrast, very few works focus on the impact of SC MPs, SC members of municipal corporations or village councils, or SC representatives at the block and district levels. This suggests that much work remains to be done. Our intuition, however, is that the findings we report on are likely to also apply in these understudied contexts. Beyond this institutional bias, we cannot exclude the possibility that a form of publication bias might exist – in this case, favouring scholarship emphasizing that reservations *do* have an impact, as opposed to those arguing that reservations have no impact at all. This should qualify our own conclusions: where we find these reservations to have mixed, often minor, impacts on relevant outcomes, the reality may actually be that they have even weaker effects since studies finding no impact are often not published.

A third and final caveat is that the extensive scholarship on the impact of reservations does not only concern *political* reservations or *political reservations for SCs*, our mandate in this chapter. In fact, relatively few of the works on the impact of political reservations focus solely on political reservations for the SCs. They are often also about reservations for the Scheduled Tribes (STs), women, and the Other Backward Classes (OBCs). It does not make much sense to exclude the evidence presented in studies of political quotas for other groups insofar as their impact does comparatively inform the Dalit experience. Besides, many of the papers and books on which we rely *jointly* study the impact of several types of reservation categories. Accordingly, in most sections of this chapter, we report on two kinds of arguments and evidence: general evidence about the impact of political reservation, as well as findings specific to SC reservations, when such work exists.

How Did Political Reservations Come to Be?

The particular design of the quota system in the Lok Sabha and the lower houses of India's state assemblies – reserved territorial constituencies with joint electorates – was the result of several decades of political negotiations. The discussion first revolved around reserving positions for Muslims, and then gradually changed to being mainly about the 'depressed classes' (Dalits) and women. Whether or not to reserve positions for Dalits was controversial for many years until the signing of the Poona Pact in 1932, where Mahatma Gandhi and B. R. Ambedkar agreed that Dalits should be granted reserved seats with *joint electorates*, meaning that voters from all caste groups could vote in them (Jensenius, 2017).

Following the Poona Pact, the Indian Constitution granted the SCs (as well as the STs) reserved seats with joint electorates both in the Lok Sabha and in India's state assemblies. These reservations have been effectively implemented since India's first post-independence elections (1951–52). The reservations were originally put in place for 10 years, but they have since been extended.[3] The reserved seats were first moved after every census, but it was then decided to freeze the constituencies (and with it the location of reserved seats) as delimited after the 1971 census. Since then Indian constituencies have only been delimited once following the 2001 census – the delimitation that came into effect in 2008.[4]

The intentions of the drafters of the Indian Constitution were quite clear: to break down social boundaries and allow the SCs a seat at the table. This arguably undermined merit as the main organizing principle of political representation in India (Varshney, 2022). Still, there was confusion about what outcomes to expect from reservations among later generations of politicians, as well as among other actors. The debates in the Lok Sabha relating to the extension of the quotas every 10 years vacillated between arguments about how quotas were implemented to help the SCs get elected in a plurality voting system and assertions that they will result in the development ('upliftment') of the SC community in general (see Jensenius, 2017: ch. 2). This disjuncture between *intended* effects and *expected* effects – which is typical of many discussions of quotas around the world – has led some to declare these quotas a failure, although they have been very successful at preventing the systematic exclusion of members of the Dalit community from politics.

When it comes to local-level institutions, the Indian parliament enacted two constitutional amendments in 1992 that mandated the establishment of elected institutions of local government (*panchayat*s) from the village to the district level in rural areas and their equivalents (municipalities) in urban areas. As amended, the Constitution now provided, in addition to reservations for women, reservation for members of the SCs and STs in proportion to their percentage in the population (most states later added OBC quotas).

The Effects of Political Reservations for the SCs

Political reservations for the SCs have been strictly implemented: in reserved constituencies and wards, only those able to document belonging to a SC are able to run for elections. Since SC candidates are also allowed to run for elections in general seats, and a few of them are successful in winning these positions, the share of the SCs in elected office in India is actually somewhat *higher* than their share of the population (Jensenius, 2016: 456).

So, who are these members of the SCs that are elected? Marc Galanter (1979: 442) reported that SC MPs and MLAs were younger than other politicians; they were more likely to be from rural areas, had less formal education, and were less likely to be professionals. This gap in age and educational attainment seems, however, to have gotten smaller over time (Jensenius, 2017: 149–50).

The party composition in reserved and general constituencies is also remarkably similar. Looking at the party affiliation of MLAs elected to reserved and general seats between 1974 and 2007 across India, there is virtually no difference in what parties they were elected from, although the Bharatiya Janata Party (BJP) was somewhat more successful in reserved seats (Jensenius, 2017: 78). A key difference between those brought to power through reserved seats and general seats, however, is that the ones in reserved seats tend to be less experienced in politics – particularly when these positions have recently been moved. This is partly because reserving seats usually prevents non-SC incumbents from rerunning, opening the space for new entrants into politics. It is also because a smaller share of the SCs run for re-election (Jensenius, 2017: 109).

Another important characteristic of those elected to reserved seats in state assemblies and in the Lok Sabha is that they tend to be less wealthy and less likely to be criminals compared to politicians in general seats (Vaishnav, 2017). SC politicians are also less likely to belong to political dynasties or to have a relative in politics – reflecting the lower bargaining power that Dalits enjoy within the main political parties (Chauchard, 2016). At both the state and national levels, those elected to reserved seats are also more likely to be women compared to those elected in general seats, arguably because political parties have responded to the demands to increase the share of women in politics by increasing the share of women in seats reserved for SCs or STs (see Jensenius, 2016). This is, however, not the case in reserved positions in *panchayati raj* elections, where positions are also explicitly reserved for women.

It is important to note that most studies of SC politicians report that they are perceived to be less powerful than other politicians, including by themselves (Galanter, 1984). Jensenius (2017) notes that SC politicians are often talked of as less 'effective', 'impressive', or 'glamorous' than other politicians. Additionally, while we so far lack good data on this phenomenon, SC politicians – particularly at the village level – are more often described as proxies for more powerful political actors (Chauchard, 2017).

With these descriptive statistics in mind, it remains that elected SC politicians exist in large numbers. This matters in and of itself, as it means that Dalits are elected to political office in contemporary India and that these political reservations now hardly raise eyebrows. Insofar as this massive presence in office generates some hope for changes in society beyond a mere presence in politics, it is not entirely evident what effects we might expect or how long it should take for changes to take place.

The Impact on Political and Electoral Patterns

The first type of effects we look at are related to political and electoral patterns. Reservations alter electoral rules and thereby constitute a direct intervention in the political process. How does this guaranteed inclusion of SC politicians in the political system affect electoral competition? To answer this question, we distinguish between direct effects on political competition and indirect 'spillover' effects.

Effects on Political Competition

Reservations for SCs have strong effects on how competitive elections are, the number of candidates running for election, how close elections are, and electoral turnout. Adam Auerbach and Adam Ziegfeld (2020) explore the effect of political reservations on political competition. They hypothesize that by constraining the number of potential candidates, seat reservations diminish not only the number of major candidates, but also the presence of smaller parties and independents, to the benefit of larger parties. Drawing on rich electoral data at multiple levels, they find that the effective number of candidates is indeed lower in electoral districts with reservations, meaning that there are fewer viable candidates competing for power. Similarly, vote shares for independent candidates are lower and major parties are higher. These effects are the largest in local elections and the smallest in national elections.

Electoral races are also less tight in reserved constituencies, both in terms of the winning vote share and the margin of victory (Jensenius, 2017: ch. 5), although these differences – as most differences between reserved and general constituencies – grow smaller the longer the reservations are in place. The same holds for electoral turnout. There has been a substantial and persistent turnout gap between SC-reserved and general constituencies, though the gap has grown smaller over time. Jensenius (2017) provides some evidence that the gap owes less to caste bias, or to a feeling of being disempowered, than to comparatively weaker networks and mobilizational capacity of SC politicians. Sacha Kapoor and Arvind Magesan (2018) demonstrate that the lower turnout in reserved constituencies may also result from the smaller number of candidates in such constituencies.

Spillover Effects

Another set of political outcomes that has interested scholars is that of 'spillover effects' – namely, who is elected when the reserved seats are withdrawn (in case of rotation or redistricting), and whether political reservations help increase access to higher-level political or partisan positions.

Let us first consider what happens when reservations are withdrawn. A long-term goal of these quotas is that they should no longer be needed – society should change in a way that individuals from all segments have an equal chance of winning elections. Yet, as noted previously, the reserved positions for the SCs have been repeatedly extended exactly because it is unlikely that many SCs would be elected if the quotas are withdrawn.

Since the quotas remain in place, we cannot know what would happen if they were discontinued altogether. It is, however, interesting to see what happens when the reserved seats rotate from one place to another. In some sense, we should not expect the SCs to run in general seats once the reserved seat is moved elsewhere, as parties seem to consider general seats as 'reserved' for general-category candidates. Further, the SCs may be less likely to get a ticket from large parties since they are perceived to have lower chances of winning – due to social bias, their lower level of wealth, and weaker political networks. On the other hand, we should expect to see at least some SCs rerun for office due to their incumbency advantage – as has been shown for the case of local-level reservations for women (Bhavnani, 2009) – or that the exposure of voters to SC leadership makes them less biased against them, similar to what studies of women in politics in India show (Beaman et al., 2009).

Our expectations may be ambiguous, but the empirical evidence is quite clear: the SCs are unlikely to run for re-election and even less likely to be re-elected once reservations are withdrawn, and the chances of other SCs gaining political office are not higher in formerly reserved areas than elsewhere (Bhavnani, 2017). At the village level, only limited evidence exists (Chauchard, 2017, explored the case of Rajasthan), but a similar conclusion appears to apply: once reserved seats are moved, we are *not* likely to see more SC candidates or greater vote shares for SC candidates.

Another type of spillover effect that is generating increasing interest is whether reserved positions at lower levels of government result in the recruitment and training of political talent, which boosts representation at higher levels of politics. This question is particularly relevant for women in politics in India, since women have reserved positions in the *panchayati raj* system, but not in state assemblies or the parliament. Recent works (O'Connell, 2018; Goyal, 2020; Maitra and Rosenblum, 2021) do suggest that such an effect occurs for women. We are unfortunately not aware of published studies finding a similar effect for the SCs.

And, finally, a third form of spillover might take place at the level of the executive, where there are no reserved positions for the SCs. Both Galanter (1979) and Jensenius (2017) report such effects, looking at recruitment into cabinet positions. As noted by Galanter (1979: 444), the large contingents of SC (and ST) parliamentarians provide 'a quantitative basis for Scheduled Caste and Tribe participation in leadership at the cabinet level'. Relying on data from 1977–2007, Jensenius (2017: ch. 5) shows that SC MLAs have increasingly been given cabinet positions across India, although they are still less likely than other politicians to be given the highest-ranked positions.

Impact on Developmental Outcomes

Do political reservations for members of the SCs in turn lead to increased redistribution towards Dalits, greater access to public and private goods, or other material benefits?

Before we detail the empirical evidence on this point, it is important to reiterate that the expectations of these policies were and are unclear and even contradictory. As noted in our discussion of the historical trajectory of SC reservations, one of the expectations of this policy was that it would help improve the material or socio-economic standing of the SC community at large. This expectation or hope for material benefits is also reflected in some of the academic studies we subsequently report.

The reservation policy for the SCs was arguably designed to avoid the activism in office of members of the SCs who would specifically work for SC interests (Galanter, 1979). At least two contributions, published 40 years or so apart, provide important intuitions about the incentives and behaviours of Dalit MPs and MLAs in this regard: Galanter (1979) and Jensenius (2017). The two reach remarkably similar conclusions, highlighting the fact that little has changed over the past decades. Debating the pros and cons of political reservations, Galanter (1979) observes that the electoral incentives of SC politicians likely make them refrain from advocating for their group insofar as their constituencies are populated overwhelmingly by others. Jensenius (2017: ch. 3) supports this intuition 40 years later. She draws on qualitative data to note that Dalit MLAs 'respond to the incentives of the electoral system' (Jensenius, 2017: 12) and that we should not expect SC politicians elected to SC-reserved seats to be particularly responsive to the SC community.

Thad Dunning and Janhavi Nilekani (2013) as well as Chauchard (2014, 2017) reach similar conclusions about politicians elected to village-level institutions (*gram panchayats*). Chauchard (2017) notes that politicians competing for the position of village president (*sarpanch*) typically belong to a coalition in which several caste groups are included. Qualitative interviews (see Chauchard, 2017: ch. 4) suggest that coalitions that transcend caste boundaries are needed for two reasons. The first is that many villages are extremely fractionalized, and the votes of several caste groups are usually required in order to become the *sarpanch*. The second relates to the fact that reservations are implemented on a rotating basis, and rotation creates incentives for inter-caste coalition-building.

Rotation accordingly provides an incentive for various groups to join forces to ensure that the benefits received by members of different groups remain more or less constant over several electoral periods. Both sets of authors conclude that the incentives of SC village-council heads are not geared towards favouring members of the SCs at the expense of other villagers. This is especially true where and when the *sarpanch* also has a partisan or non-ethnic affiliation, since that official's incentives would then be to target *all* members of his or her coalition, whether or not they are co-ethnics. This effect is possibly compounded by the perverse incentives that rotation creates for upper-caste incumbents (and also those elected in reserved seats), who may have a short-term interest in discriminating in favour of their own group members (Parthasarathy, 2017). In line with this second, more pessimistic view, remarkably little evidence seems to suggest that SC elected officials are inclined to favour their own caste members.

These insights have not, however, prevented a swathe of scholars from looking for policy effects, overall development effects, or effects on handouts. Early studies of reservations (especially gender-based reservations, though the logic of the authors was not necessarily specific to gender) suggested that the provision of public goods may better reflect the needs of members of these groups when 'one of their own' is in public office (Chattopadhyay and Duflo, 2004). Several prominent studies found significant positive effects of women or women-friendly leaders on policies that women wanted (Chattopadhyay and Duflo, 2004; Clots-Figueras, 2011). Other studies found worse development outcomes where women were in power (Bardhan, Mookherjee, and Torrado, 2010; Afridi, Iversen, and Sharan, 2017). Increased representation of disadvantaged castes in political office has sometimes been found to bring benefits for these castes, though the impact of SC reservations has generally been found to be weaker than the impact of ST reservations (for example, Pande, 2003; Gulzar, Haas, and Pasquale, 2020).

More recent studies, however, cast doubt on these conclusions. Studies of village-level reservations report no effects (Dunning and Nilekani, 2013), or suggest that effects may only concern a subset of the groups they target (Bardhan, Mookherjee, and Torrado, 2010; Chauchard, 2017) or that they are not consistent across outcomes (Chauchard, 2017). Aimee Chin and Nishith Prakash (2011), looking for an effect of the share of the SCs in state assemblies on poverty, find no significant effect of SC reservation on any of their poverty measures and, in fact, cannot rule out a weak negative effect of SC representation on the urban poverty rate. In a study of the long-term trajectories of various development indicators for SC-reserved state assembly constituencies compared to very similar non-reserved constituencies, Jensenius (2015, 2017: ch. 4) also finds no effect on overall development or on the development of the SC community in particular.

Several papers extend this scholarship by looking at the impact of reservations on less obvious development-related outcomes at the state level. Elizabeth Kaletski and Nishith Prakash (2016) examine the impact of state-level reservation on child labour in India and, in turn, focus on the impact of reservations on health-worker visits (Kaletski and Prakash, 2017). Finally, Chon-Kit Ao and Somdeep Chatterjee (2018) explore the impact of political reservations on credit access and borrowing composition. All three papers reach a similar conclusion: reservations have a beneficial effect among the STs, but not among the SCs.

Overall, then, SC reservations do not seem to benefit Dalits in material ways. Still, these studies look at the effects of increasing the share of SCs in state legislatures or compare similar areas with and without SC politicians. As such, based on this evidence, we cannot rule out that the overall development trajectory of the SCs in India might have looked different had the reservation system not been in place or had another type of reservation system been in place. It may have been the same, or better, or worse, but we simply do not have any empirical evidence that allows us to draw conclusions about these counterfactual scenarios.

Impact on State–Citizen Relations

Next, we turn to the impact SC reservations have had on state–citizen relations. While reservations may not lead to substantial developmental changes, they may be beneficial insofar as they help Dalits get better access to the state, the police, or the bureaucracy.

This should be especially true of representation at the most local level of politics: the village council. Iyer et al. (2012) make such a claim about gender-based village reservations. Their evidence suggests that there is an increase in reporting crimes against women with an increase in female representation in local governments, which should be considered good news, as it is driven by greater reporting rather than greater incidence of such crimes. In contrast, they find no increase in crimes against men or in gender-neutral crimes.

Chauchard (2017: chs. 3 and 4) develops a similar argument in his study of the impact of SC reservations in village councils. He finds that reservation for a SC *sarpanch* appears to create a new channel of communication between the village's SC community and local institutions. Because of low upward social mobility and economic dependence on wealthier villagers, SC communities often remain deprived of access to local institutions, such as local political institutions at higher levels of the government and various administrative offices, including police services. This lack of contact with the outside world often contributes to their plight. In the absence of such contacts outside the village, SC villagers who are blatantly discriminated against, cheated, or verbally abused will find it difficult to lodge a complaint, let alone get potential offenders punished under the stringent anti-untouchability acts[5] on the books. Reservation for an SC *sarpanch* appears to improve this state of affairs by creating an obvious channel of communication between the village's SC community and these institutions. Because *sarpanch*es attend numerous meetings at higher levels of the government and are typically engaged in a multitude of dealings with various actors of local politics and business, reservations offer the SC community access to a network of relatively powerful individuals that was previously out of reach. Whereas Chauchard's observations suggest that this linkage was less likely to extend to police forces – whom all his SC interlocutors, including *sarpanch*es, systematically accused of bias – these links may still imply fairer treatment by police forces insofar as the *sarpanch*es' new contacts at the block level could intercede in favour of the SC community.

Impact on Caste-Related Attitudes and Behaviour

Finally, we turn to effects on caste-related attitudes and behaviour. Works on gender quotas in India suggest that descriptive representation may lessen discrimination against future cohorts of women in politics (Beaman et al., 2009; Bhavnani, 2009) and increase aspirations and educational attainment of girls (Beaman et al., 2012). Building on this literature, Chauchard (2014, 2017) looks at the effects of political reservations for the SCs in village councils on the *psychology* of intergroup relations. Relying on a detailed exploration of the case of SCs in rural Rajasthan, he argues that backlash effects are relatively unlikely to occur and that citizens from dominant groups will tend to to go on with their lives over time, unfazed by the access of a new group to political representation.

This peaceful acceptance of minority inclusion opens the door to subtle but positive changes in patterns of intergroup relations. Descriptive representation may have an impact on intergroup relations because the *taste* for members of newly represented groups changes or because individuals *strategically* update their behaviours upon perceiving that norms of interaction are changing. While both mechanisms can lead to meaningful, beneficial changes in interpersonal behaviours, they have very different implications in terms of the kind of change we should expect to observe, as well as different implications for the permanence of those changes. Empirically, Chauchard finds that stereotypes are sticky, deeply anchored, and inherently resistant to disconfirming information. Contrary to what optimistic findings in empirical studies of descriptive representation have so far suggested (for examples, Hajnal, 2005; Beaman et al., 2012), this indicates that descriptive representation is likely to improve interpersonal relations neither because it changes what individuals perceive to be the characteristics of members of stigmatized groups nor because it progressively leads them to a new appreciation of these groups. Instead, it matters by signalling to individuals that their fellow citizens or political institutions are becoming more tolerant and that they should adapt to this new worldview.

In her study of SC reservations at the state level, Jensenius (2017: chs. 7 and 8) also explores attitudinal effects. She presents qualitative evidence suggesting that quota politicians are often referred to as 'weak', 'inefficient', and 'useless' by other elites (Jensenius, 2017: 202). Using data from an original survey in Uttar Pradesh (UP), however, she shows that voters for the most part feel similarly about SC politicians and other politicians, and that those who have lived in a reserved constituency for a long time are somewhat more likely to evaluate SC politicians positively. Last but not the least, looking at the impact on the treatment of SCs in society more generally, she considers how quotas have affected caste-based discrimination. She presents evidence from two surveys indicating that there has been a reduction in caste-based discrimination in SC-reserved areas.

Recent papers complement and extend these results. Victoire Girard (2018) looks at the impact of village-level reservations on discrimination, proxied with caste-based exclusion from the streets. She finds that SC quotas reduce the likelihood of such discrimination by about one-fifth. The results, however, imply that the effect is not persistent: it disappears with the end of the SC quota. Further, in a different paper, she reports that inter-caste tensions as measured by household surveys increase when SC quotas are introduced, indicating that whereas there may have been improvements with regards to discrimination in the public sphere, there is evidence of backlash in the private sphere (Girard, 2021). Abhay Aneja and S. K. Ritadhi (2020), in turn, consider whether representation in the government can reduce violence suffered by Dalits. To answer this question, they examine the impact of political parties formed with the primary purpose of representing SCs. They address the endogenous selection of minority-favouring parties using state-level variation in aggregations of close election outcomes. They find that a 10 percentage-point increase in representation reduces the minority murder rate by three percentage points. An analysis of possible causal mechanisms indicates that politicians respond to minority constituents by increasing police effort in responding to the victimization of the SCs, which may have the effect of deterring future offenders. Moreover, improvements in self-reported attitudes toward government institutions (including the police) suggest that these results are not the product of negative reporting bias in government crime statistics.

They emphasize, however, that the results are driven by an increase in the representation of SC parties, not by SC reservations.

Conclusion

Overall, the results reported here do not provide evidence that SC reservations have had a deep and rapid transformational impact on society at large. The effects on political competition are generally negative or at least null. There are some spillover effects into higher-level political positions, but this is happening slowly; material effects are weak, if there at all; and while there are effects on state–citizen relations, inter-caste relations, and attitudes, they are not dramatically large and they are smaller in the private sphere than in the public sphere. Some readers might assess this account as disappointing insofar as political reservations are often (undeservedly, in our opinion) expected to lead to more impressive changes. However, patterns of social inequality are hard to change, and the reservation policy is just one out of many possible tools to do so.

Why do we not see more of a change? As discussed previously, we believe *institutional incentives* best explain these weak and inconsistent effects. In the absence of separate electorates, SC politicians elected at all levels of the government rarely see it as valuable from an electoral standpoint to be seen as strong Dalit advocates. The reason is simple: the way Indian reservations are designed, the SCs are almost always in a minority in reserved constituencies, and since all the candidates are SCs, the SC vote is split between them. SC politicians therefore need to appeal to non-SCs for votes. If SC politicians are assumed to be motivated by career incentives and re-election, as is usually assumed of politicians in traditional voting models, we should not expect to see much difference in the behaviour of politicians in reserved and general constituencies; whereas they may have a shared experience of hardship and exclusion, SC politicians elected through reserved seats simply do not have the incentives to work for their own groups because they are elected mostly by non-SCs. Our respective studies suggest this to be the case both for MLAs (Jensenius, 2017) and for SC *sarpanch*es (Chauchard, 2017). Partisan politics is at least partly to blame for how these incentives play out. Parties in India have generally been controlled by non-SC leaders, and SC politicians may never be given the opportunity to run for office if they are not palatable to the party leadership (Jensenius, 2015).

Would separate electorates for Dalits have been better at improving the situation of Dalits in India? It is impossible to tell. In addition to this institutional change being highly unlikely, evidence from other contexts does not suggest that it makes minorities better off (see, for example, work by Lublin [2014] on Maoris in New Zealand, Htun [2016] on Colombia, and Allen [2018] on Croatia). Separate electorates may help groups to politically mobilize around a group identity, and form group-specific parties, but the result tends to be that the representatives of these group-specific parties end up being marginalized in legislative debates. They end up outside the dominant political discourse rather than as part of it. For a group that mainly shares a history of exclusion and discrimination, rather than a separate identity that they wish to safeguard, this does not necessarily emerge as a particularly desirable alternative.

With all this in mind, we should also not lose sight of the positive changes that seem to have resulted from the reservation system. Political reservations do, at the very least, allow for the entry of the SCs as politicians – something that would not have been likely to have happened otherwise. Over time this new political elite is likely to gain more political influence because they are better integrated within the main parties; and this may, in turn, reduce inter-caste tension to the extent that the SCs may be elected without reservations.

Notes

1. We have each written a book about the effects of SC reservations: Chauchard (2017) about SC heads of village councils and Jensenius (2017) focusing on members of legislative assemblies (MLAs).
2. Descriptive representation refers to the idea that a politician represents those that share an ascriptive trait – someone who 'looks like' them. It is also used to talk about how well legislative assemblies 'mirror' the entire population (see Pitkin, 1972).
3. The policy was last extended up to 25 January 2030 in 2019.
4. See the Delimitation of Parliamentary and Assembly Constituencies Order, 2008.
5. For instance, the Scheduled Castes and Scheduled Tribes (Prevention of Atrocities) Act, 1989.

Bibliography

Afridi, F., V. Iversen, and M. R. Sharan. 2017. 'Women Political Leaders, Corruption, and Learning: Evidence from a Large Public Program in India'. *Economic Development and Cultural Change* 66(1): 1–30.

Allen, G. 2018. 'Presence and Impotence: The Perils of Guaranteed Descriptive Representation'. Dissertation, September, University of California, Santa Barbara.

Aneja, A., and S. K. Ritadhi. 2021. 'How Representation Reduces Minority-targeted Crime: Evidence from Scheduled Castes in India'. *Journal of Law, Economics, and Organization*. DOI: 10.1093/jleo/ewab028.

Ao, C-K., and S. Chatterjee. 2018. 'The Effects of Political Reservations on Credit Access and Borrowing Composition: New Evidence from India'. GLO Discussion Paper No. 227, Global Labor Organization, Maastricht, Netherlands.

Auerbach, A. M., and A. Ziegfeld. 2020. 'How Do Electoral Quotas Influence Political Competition? Evidence From Municipal, State, and National Elections in India'. *Journal of Politics* 82(1): 397–401.

Bardhan, P., D. Mookherjee, and M. P. Torrado. 2010. 'Impact of Political Reservations in West Bengal Local Governments on Anti-poverty Targeting'. *Journal of Globalization and Development* 1(1). DOI: 10.2202/1948-1837.1025.

Beaman, L., E. Duflo, R. Pande, and P. Topalova. 2012. 'Female Leadership Raises Aspirations and Educational Attainment for Girls: A Policy Experiment in India'. *Science* 335(6068): 582–86.

Beaman, L., R. Chattopadhyay, E. Duflo, R. Pande, and P. Topalova. 2009. 'Powerful Women: Does Exposure Reduce Bias?' *Quarterly Journal of Economics* 124(4): 1497–1540.

Bhavnani, R. R. 2009. 'Do Electoral Quotas Work after They Are Withdrawn? Evidence from a Natural Experiment in India'. *American Political Science Review* 103(1): 23–35.

———. 2017. 'Do the Effects of Temporary Ethnic Group Quotas Persist? Evidence from India'. *American Economic Journal: Applied Economics* 9(3): 105–23.

Broockman, D. E. 2013. 'Black Politicians Are More Intrinsically Motivated to Advance Blacks' Interests: A Field Experiment Manipulating Political Incentives'. *American Journal of Political Science* 57(3): 521–36.

Chattopadhyay, R., and E. Duflo. 2004. 'Women as Policy Makers: Evidence from a Randomized Policy Experiment in India'. *Econometrica* 72(5): 1409–43.

Chauchard, S. 2014. 'Can Descriptive Representation Change Beliefs about a Stigmatized Group? Evidence from Rural India'. *American Political Science Review* 108(2): 403–22.

———. 2016. 'Disadvantaged Groups, Reservation, and Dynastic Politics'. In *Democratic Dynasties: State, Party and Family in Contemporary Indian Politics*, edited by K. Chandra, 173–206. Cambridge, UK: Cambridge University Press.

———. 2017. *Why Representation Matters: The Meaning of Ethnic Quotas in Rural India*. Cambridge, UK: Cambridge University Press.

Chin, A. and N. Prakash. 2011. 'The Redistributive Effects of Political Reservation for Minorities: Evidence from India'. *Journal of Development Economics* 96(2): 265–77.

Clots-Figueras, I. 2011. 'Women in Politics: Evidence from the Indian States'. *Journal of Public Economics* 95(7–8): 664–90.

Duflo, E. 2005. 'Why Political Reservations?' *Journal of the European Economic Association* 3(2–3): 668–78.

Dunning, T., and J. Nilekani. 2013. 'Ethnic Quotas and Political Mobilization: Caste, Parties, and Distribution in Indian Village Councils'. *American Political Science Review* 107(1): 35–56.

Galanter, M. 1979. 'Compensatory Discrimination in Political Representation: A Preliminary Assessment of India's Thirty-Year Experience with Reserved Seats in Legislatures'. *Economic and Political Weekly* 14(7–8): 437–54.

———. 1984. *Competing Equalities: Law and the Backward Classes in India*. Berkeley: University of California Press.

Gay, C. 2002. 'Spirals of Trust: The Effect of Descriptive Representation on the Relationship between Citizens and Their Government'. *American Journal of Political Science* 46(4): 717–33.

Girard, V. 2018. 'Don't Touch My Road: Evidence from India on Affirmative Action and Everyday Discrimination'. *World Development* 103 (March): 1–13. DOI: 10.1016/j.worlddev.2017.10.008.

———. 2021. 'Stabbed in the Back? Mandated Political Representation and Murders'. *Social Choice and Welfare* 56: 595–634.

Goyal, T. 2020. 'Local Female Representation as a Pathway to Power: A Natural Experiment in India'. https://papers.ssrn.com/sol3/papers.cfm?abstract_id=3590118. Accessed in January 2021.

Gulzar, S., N. Haas, and B. Pasquale. 2020. 'Does Political Affirmative Action Work, and for Whom? Theory and Evidence on India's Scheduled Areas'. *American Political Science Review* 114(4): 1230–46.

Hajnal, Z. 2005. *Changing White Attitudes toward Black Political Leadership*. New York: Cambridge University Press.

Htun, M. 2016. *Inclusion without Representation in Latin America: Gender Quotas and Ethnic Reservations*. New York: Cambridge University Press.

Iyer, L., A. Mani, P. Mishra, and P. Topalova. 2012. 'The Power of Political Voice: Women's Political Representation and Crime in India'. *American Economic Journal: Applied Economics* 4(4): 165–93.

Jensenius, F. R. 2015. 'Development from Representation? A Study of Quotas for the Scheduled Castes in India'. *American Economic Journal: Applied Economics* 7(3): 196–220.

———. 2016. 'Competing Inequalities? On the Intersection of Gender and Ethnicity in Candidate Nominations in Indian Elections'. *Government and Opposition* 51(3): 440–63.

———. 2017. *Social Justice through Inclusion: The Consequences of Electoral Quotas in India*. New York: Oxford University Press.

Kaletski, E., and N. Prakash. 2016. 'Does Political Reservation for Minorities Affect Child Labor? Evidence from India'. *World Development* 87 (November): 50–69.

———. 2017. 'Can Elected Minority Representatives Affect Health Worker Visits? Evidence from India'. *Review of Development Economics* 21(1): 67–102.

Kapoor, S., and A. Magesan. 2018. 'Independent Candidates and Political Representation in India'. *American Political Science Review* 112(3): 678–97.

Lublin, D. 2014. *Minority Rules: Electoral Systems, Decentralization, and Ethnoregional Party Success*. New York: Oxford University Press.

Maitra, P., and D. Rosenblum. 2021. 'Upstream Effects of Female Political Reservations'. *European Journal of Political Economy* 71(C): e102061.

Mansbridge, J. 1999. 'Should Blacks Represent Blacks and Women Represent Women? A Contingent "Yes"'. *Journal of Politics* 61(3): 628–57.

Marschall, M., and A. Ruhil. 2007. 'Substantive Symbols: The Attitudinal Dimension of Black Political Incorporation in Local Government'. *American Journal of Political Science* 51(1): 17–33.

O'Connell, S. D. 2018. 'Can Quotas Increase the Supply of Candidates for Higher-Level Positions? Evidence from Local Government in India'. *Review of Economics and Statistics* 102(1): 65–78.

Pande, R. 2003. 'Can Mandated Political Representation Increase Policy Influence for Disadvantaged Minorities? Theory and Evidence from India'. *American Economic Review* 93(4): 1132–51.

Parthasarathy, R. 2017. 'Ethnic Quotas as Term-Limits: Caste and Distributive Politics in South India'. *Comparative Political Studies* 50(13): 1735–67.

Pitkin, H. 1972. *The Concept of Representation*. Berkeley: University of California Press.

Vaishnav, M. 2017. *When Crime Pays: Money and Muscle in Indian Politics*. New Haven: Yale University Press.

Varshney, A. 2022. 'Merit in the Mirror of Democracy: Caste and Affirmative Action in India'. In *Making Meritocracy: Lessons from China and India, from Antiquity to the Present*, edited by Tarun Khanna and Michael Szonyi, 20–41. New York: Oxford University Press.

21

Are Dalit Legislators Performing Their Oversight Role?

Evidence from the Question Hour in the Lok Sabha and Select State Legislatures

Kaushiki Sanyal

After independence, India opted for quota-based reservation[1] for Dalits and Adivasis (Scheduled Castes [SCs] and Scheduled Tribes [STs]) in the national and state legislatures.[2] The need for such representation arose from the idea that universally defined rights of political citizenship are insufficient to guarantee representation of ascriptively defined social groups. Scholars such as Will Kymlicka (1995), Anne Phillips (1995), Melissa Williams (2000), and Niraja Gopal Jayal (2006: 6) support group representation within the institutions of representative democracy, which promise formal equality but, in reality, systematically under-represent the historically marginalized.

The original goal of reservation was to bring the SCs, or Dalits, into the mainstream (Jensenius, 2015). However, much of the research that studied the performance of Dalit legislators has focused on their role as representatives of their community and whether they were effective in developing their community. The majority of such studies found political reservation to have almost no effect on the condition of Dalits (Galanter, 1979; Dushkin, 1972; McMillan, 2005; Yadav, 2008; Jensenius, 2012, 2015). Aimee Chin and Nishith Prakash's (2011) study found no significant impact of reserved seats in reducing poverty among the SCs but reported a better positive correlation between reserved seats and reduction of poverty among the STs. Only Rohini Pande's (2003) study showed that political reservation had increased redistribution of resources in favour of groups which benefitted from such reservation. However, she also argued that existing political institutions could not enforce full policy commitment. Simon Chauchard and Francesca Jensenius in this volume (see Chapter 20) provide a review of the empirical research on the impact of political reservation on the SC community in India. The present chapter begins with a brief history of political reservation in India.

A Brief History of Political Reservation in India

As the British started opening up legislative bodies to Indians during the colonial period, the oppression of 'untouchables' became a prominent social and political matter. By 1919, religious minorities in India (Muslims, Sikhs, Indian Christians, and Europeans) were politically represented through separate electorates.[3] B. R. Ambedkar, an erudite, foreign-educated economist, took up cudgels on behalf of his community and started arguing for universal adult franchise and political representation for untouchables on the basis of their proportion in the population. He first appeared before the Southborough Commission in 1919, but none of his demands were accepted by the British.

Interestingly, Ambedkar (2013: 350–55) severely criticized separate electorates for Muslims as a means of representation on the following grounds:

1. Separate communal electorates intensified communal feelings, with both sides not feeling any responsibility towards each other.
2. The Muslim community was not so distinct from others that they had different interests. Any special concerns of the community could be represented through reserved seats and the general electorate.
3. Separate communal electorates tended to make a community a permanent minority towards whom the majority felt no responsibility. A combination of a joint electorate and universal adult suffrage would serve minorities better.
4. A separate electorate was a violation of the 'doctrine of consent'. Although legislators elected through separate electorates got to decide on all policies, they only represented the community that elected them.
5. Muslims could counter the threat of their vote getting diluted due to the larger presence of Hindus by opting for universal adult franchise to increase their voting strength.

The next opportunity came in 1927 when the Simon Commission was formed to review electoral reforms. Ambedkar reiterated his demand with a caveat that if such reservation and suffrage were not given, he wanted separate electorates for Dalits. The Simon Commission recognized Dalits as a distinct political group and allotted reserved seats to them from those of the Hindus. However, any Dalit who wanted to contest elections had to be declared fit for the purpose by the governor of the state. Ambedkar attacked the British government for their stance (Vundru, 2018).

His next opportunity came at the three Round Table Conferences (1930–32) organized by the British to work on the future Constitution of British India.[4] In both the first and second conferences, Ambedkar forcefully made his case for

Dalit representation through reservation and universal adult franchise, with the same caveat. The British did not grant universal adult suffrage but acceded to his demand for separate electorates in August 1932.

Almost immediately, M. K. Gandhi went on a fast unto death opposing separate electorates for Dalits as well as seat reservation. His opposition seemed to stem from the fear that it would create division within the Hindu community and could even lead to bloodshed (Jyoti, 2019).

Ambedkar refused to budge, but as Gandhi's health deteriorated, pressure mounted on him to compromise. It was finally agreed that 18 per cent of the seats allotted to the general electorate for British India in the central legislature would be reserved for the depressed classes. But while Ambedkar wanted a referendum among Dalits after 15 years to decide on whether to continue with reserved seats, Gandhi wanted to hold it after five years. The stalemate continued till Ambedkar had to give in due to Gandhi's health, and the Poona Pact was signed on 24 September 1932. It was decided to do away with the referendum clause. Instead, the Poona Pact provided for reservation in provincial and central legislatures to continue 'until determined by mutual agreement between both the communities concerned in the settlement' (Vundru, 2018). The elections of 1937 and 1946 were held under the panel system of the Poona Pact.

Contours of the Study

Keeping in mind both the original goal of reservation (mainstreaming) and the core function of oversight, this chapter studies the performance of SC members of parliament (MPs) and members of the legislative assembly (MLAs) during the Question Hour in the Lok Sabha and the Uttar Pradesh (UP) legislative assembly. These choices were made based on the fact that only the lower house has reserved seats, and UP has about 21 per cent SC population (Census of India, 2011).The chapter (*a*) examines whether Dalit legislators are performing their oversight role effectively; (*b*) assesses whether there are structural and procedural issues that constrain Dalit legislators in the execution of their functions; and (*c*) recommends tweaks to the rules of procedure that may improve the ability of Dalit legislators to discharge their duties more effectively.

The Question Hour,[5] chosen as proxy for measuring the performance of a legislator's oversight role, has been quantitatively and qualitatively analysed. For the quantitative analysis of the Lok Sabha, data were taken for the entire 16th Lok Sabha and the 17th Lok Sabha (till the Monsoon session 2020). For the UP legislative assembly, data for the 17th legislative assembly (till August 2020) were taken. The data for national and state legislatures have been collated by the PRS Legislative Research as part of their 'MP and MLA Track' database.[6]

For the qualitative analysis, the questions for four sessions in the Lok Sabha and three sessions in the UP legislative assembly were used. The four sessions for the Lok Sabha were chosen to include sessions from both the 16th and the 17th Lok Sabha. Snapshots of the data that were analysed are provided in Table 21.1.[7] For the Lok Sabha, the accepted number of questions per session was used instead of what got answered on the floor of the house since the idea is to study the intent of the legislator rather than the outcome (disruptions are not in their control).

However, for the UP legislative assembly, only the questions that were asked on the floor of the assembly were taken since listed questions were not available. Also, the data for only three sessions were available (see Table 21.2).

Table 21.1   Snapshot of Lok Sabha data (84 out of 545 seats reserved for Scheduled Castes [SCs]), 2018–19

Sessions	Dates	Total questions asked by SC MPs		
		Starred	Unstarred	Total
Winter 2018	11 December–8 January	78	914	992
Budget 2019 (pre-election)	31 January–13 February	26	356	382
Budget 2019 (post-election)	17 June–26 July	92	934	1026
Winter 2019	18 November–13 December	85	885	970

Source: Collated from the official website of Lok Sabha, https://loksabha.nic.in (accessed in October 2022).

Table 21.2   Snapshot of Uttar Pradesh legislative assembly data (84 out of 404 seats reserved for Scheduled Castes [SCs]), 2019–20

Sessions	Dates	Total questions asked by SC MLAs		
		Starred	Unstarred	Total
1	5–18 February 2019	6	14	20
2	18–26 July 2019	15	59	74
3	2–24 October 2019	No questions asked		
4	26 November 2019–2 January 2020	4	23	27

Source: Collated from the official website of Lok Sabha, https://loksabha.nic.in (accessed in October 2022).

The Question Hour, as an oversight tool, is unique because it gives equal opportunity to all legislators to ask questions irrespective of party affiliation or position; they are not subject to the party whip, debate, vote, or motion, and the questions are chosen through a lottery. Only starred and unstarred questions were analysed because these alone are chosen by ballot (Lok Sabha, n.d.a). Short-notice questions are allowed only if the minister agrees to answer them, and even if he does, the speaker can disallow this, if not of an urgent nature (Lok Sabha, n.d.b).

The chapter aims to determine whether Dalit legislators are performing their oversight role effectively by showing the trends in the following:

1. frequency of participation in the Question Hour by Dalit MPs and MLAs versus other MPs and MLAs;
2. frequency of participation in the Question Hour by gender, age, education level, and experience;
3. types of questions asked (information, action, policy); and
4. nature of questions asked (SC-community oriented or of general interest).

Effectiveness of Dalit Legislators

While representing constituents is a key function of legislators, there are other equally important core functions: making laws, approving budgets, and oversight – that is, holding the executive accountable. Since India does not strictly follow the principle of separation of powers, the executive (government), not the legislature, is the main initiator of legislation and the budget. The legislature debates and passes these. Consequently, the primary function of the parliament and its members is to hold the government accountable. Also, individual legislators have limited power to initiate[8] or amend laws and policies.[9]

It is incorrect to expect that Dalit legislators should only be representing their communities. While reserved constituencies will have a majority of Dalits, there are also other communities in the same constituency. In fact, political theorists such as Edmund Burke (1790 [1968]) and James Madison (Madison, Hamilton, and Jay, 1987 [1787–88]) were clear that the elected representative's first obligation is to the nation. Therefore, while citizens have the right to elect a candidate who they feel will best represent their interests, once elected, representatives have the 'undemocratic' prerogative to act contrary to the views of their constituents if they feel it is in the national interest (Mezey, 2008: 34). Also, individual legislators have a limited role in initiating or implementing development projects in their constituencies. This is backed by evidence from a variety of literature surveyed by Chauchard and Jensenius (see Chapter 20).

MP and MLA local area development (LAD) schemes only allow individual legislators to recommend works in their constituencies based on a set of guidelines (with specified allocations for SC-majority areas in all constituencies in the case of the MPLAD).[10] MLALAD scheme guidelines differ across states. For example, in Delhi each MLA can recommend works for up to INR 10 crores every year, while in UP the amount is INR 3 crores (*Times of India*, 2021).

The Question Hour as an Oversight Mechanism

Given that the primary function of a legislator is to hold the government accountable, the Question Hour is a powerful tool. It offers various advantages: (*a*) legislators participate in it extensively (*Economic Times*, 2019); (*b*) legislators can ask questions about any aspect of administrative activity, and the government is obliged to answer orally or in writing; and (*c*) questions are chosen by ballot so presiding officers of the house have no discretion about which questions get asked.

In contrast, other mechanisms of oversight such as adjournment motions, calling attention, half-an-hour discussion, and special mention[11] can only be initiated by a legislator if the party leader or the presiding officer of the house permits it.

Although parliamentary committee membership is another way of influencing policy, who becomes a member is decided by the party leadership. Recent research by IndiaSpend (Sharma, 2021) on membership in parliamentary committees in the 17th Lok Sabha shows that only 8 of the 27 committees (24 department-related standing committees and three financial committees) have adequate SC representation. These eight committees in the 17th Lok Sabha pertain to external affairs, social justice, chemicals, coal and steel, labour, water resources, law and justice, and tourism.

Country-specific studies that examine the behaviour of legislators through parliamentary questions are many. These include works on Canada (Franks, 1985), Denmark (Damgaard, 1994), Norway (Rasch, 1994), Sweden (Mattson, 1994), Turkey (Hazama, Gençkaya, and Gençkaya, 2007), and the United Kingdom (Chester and Bowring, 1962; Franklin and Norton, 1993; Cole, 1999). The first study of the Question Hour in the Indian parliament was conducted by Mohapatra (1969), and it laid down a methodological approach to use content analysis to understand response styles, questioning frequencies, and question types. Subsequent studies were carried out by Datta (2008) and Srikrishna Ayyangar and Suraj Jacob (2014).

A few studies have focused exclusively on marginalized communities (Kumar, 2008; Imtiyaz and Zaman, 2019; Ambagudia, 2019; Bhogale, 2018). In his paper, Kumar studied legislators' interventions in the Lok Sabha between 1985 and 1995 to formulate policies for the inclusion of marginalized SC or

ST communities. It concluded that although the parliament does deliberate on these issues, the quality is poor, and the responses of the government are confined to extension or modification of existing policies rather than any paradigm change. Aisha Imtiyaz and Fakhruz Zaman compared the questions raised by SC and ST members to non-SC or ST members to study the 'representativeness' of the former between 1996 and 2016 in the Lok Sabha. They found that SC MPs were closely connected to the interests of their community, confirming that reserved-seat MPs are able to provide substantive representation to their community.

However, none of the literature focuses on the oversight role of Dalit legislators at the national or state level. This chapter aims to address the gap.

How Active Are Dalit MPs and MLAs Compared to Their Non-SC Counterparts?

The number of seats reserved in the Lok Sabha and legislative assemblies is proportionate to the SC population in each state. As such, a key indicator of whether SC MPs and MLAs are carrying out their oversight role is how frequently they ask questions as opposed to general-category MPs. Figures 21.1 and 21.2 show how many questions, on average, each MP or MLA asked in the entire duration of the session. Figure 21.1 looks at data for SC legislators, non-SC legislators, and all MPs and MLAs.

There is a significant difference between the number of questions asked by non-SC legislators and SC legislators in both the Lok Sabha and the UP legislative assembly. Non-SC legislators, on a per-head basis, ask more questions than SC legislators. Analysing the data by gender, a similar pattern emerges (Figure 21.2). Non-SC male and female legislators ask more questions than their SC counterparts. Also, the difference in questions asked between male and female MPs and MLAs in the case of Dalits is higher than for non-SCs.

Who are more active during the Question Hour? According to Figure 21.3, younger MPs asked more questions per head in both the 16th and the 17th Lok Sabha. But this is the reverse in the case of SC MPs. The data shows a similar trajectory in UP, too. Younger, non-SC MLAs ask more questions, but the reverse happens in the case of SC MLAs. Younger SC MLAs ask about half the number of questions per head compared to older legislators.

Figure 21.4 shows that, on average, non-SC MPs who have only passed school ask more questions than their higher-educated counterparts. But this trend is reversed when it comes to SC MPs and MLAs. Across the board, higher-educated SC legislators ask more questions than their less-educated counterparts.

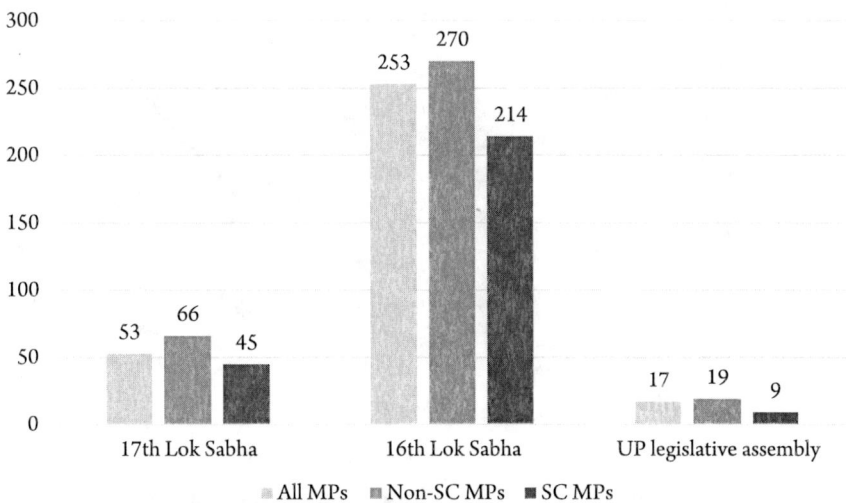

Figure 21.1 Frequency of participation in the Question Hour by Scheduled Caste (SC) legislators and non-SC legislators

Source: Author's calculations based on data collated by the PRS Legislative Research.

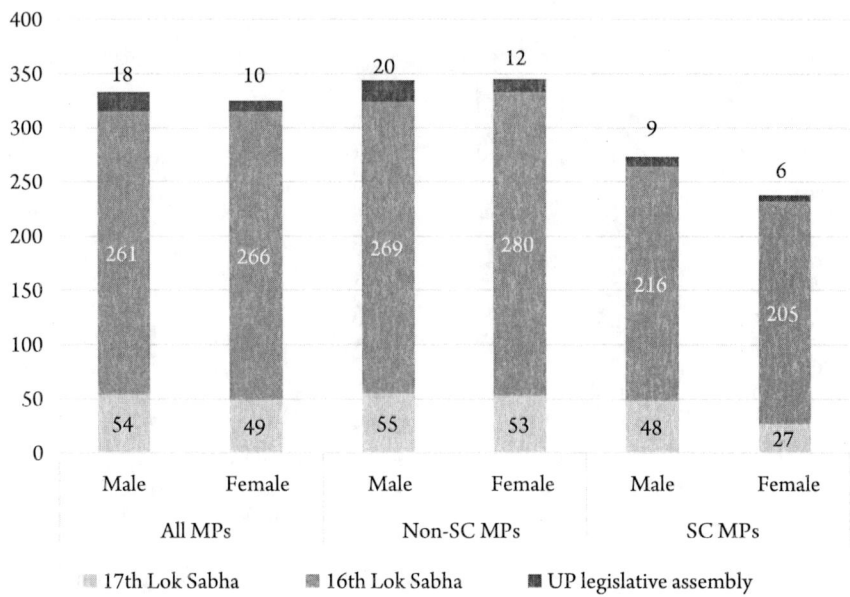

Figure 21.2 Frequency of participation in the Question Hour by gender of Scheduled Caste (SC) legislators and non-SC legislators

Source: Author's calculations based on data collated by the PRS Legislative Research.

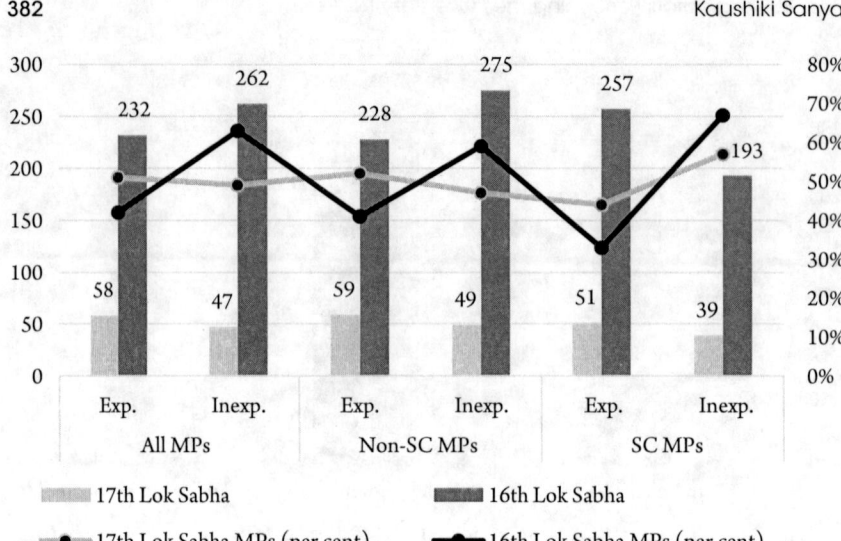

Figure 21.3 Frequency of participation in the Question Hour by age of Scheduled Caste (SC) legislators and non-SC legislators

Source: Author's calculations based on data collated by the PRS Legislative Research.

Note: Young: 25–50 years; old: above 50.

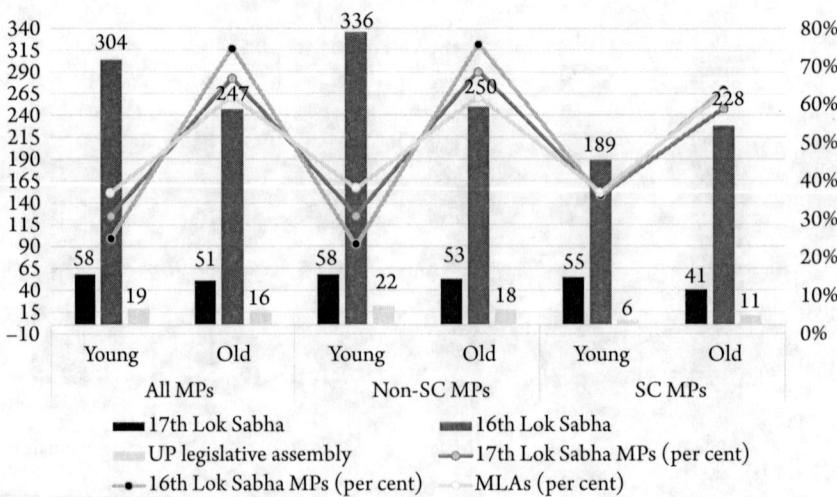

Figure 21.4 Frequency of participation in the Question Hour by education level of Scheduled Caste (SC) legislators and non-SC legislators

Source: Author's calculations based on data collated by the PRS Legislative Research.

Note: Only first-term MPs are classified as inexperienced; rest are classified as experienced. Data for Uttar Padesh on experience of MLAs were not available and therefore could not be computed.

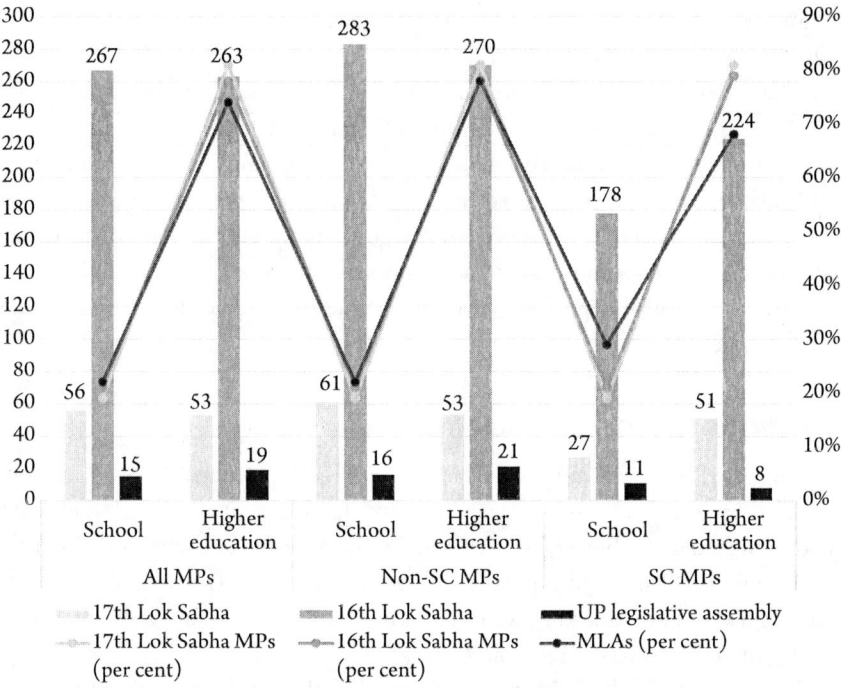

Figure 21.5   Frequency of participation in the Question Hour by experience among Scheduled Caste (SC) legislators and non-SC legislators

Source: Author's calculations based on data collated by the PRS Legislative Research.

Do more experienced MPs ask more questions? Figure 21.5 shows this is decided by the proportion of MPs who are first-timers or experienced. In the 16th Lok Sabha, where the proportion of first-time non-SC MPs was high, they asked more questions. It was the reverse in the 17th Lok Sabha. But this is not the case for SC MPs. Even though there were more first-time MPs among SCs in both terms, they asked less questions than their more experienced counterparts.

Nature of Questions Asked by Dalit MPs and MLAs

This section attempts to analyse the questions qualitatively in order to understand the substance of the issues raised by SC legislators. Are they asking questions to elicit information or making a demand for policy change? Are they raising mostly SC-related questions? Is the focus on the country or the state or their constituency?

In order to analyse the nature of the questions, they were classified into (*a*) type, (*b*) category, and (*c*) level.

The types of questions were further classified as follows: information (to obtain data), policy (to demand information related to specific policies), and action (to ask the government about any action it intends to take on an issue). This classification has been used in Akirav's (2011) paper on the effectiveness of the Israeli parliament. In terms of category, the questions were divided into SC-related questions and those that were general in nature. In terms of level, the questions were sub-categorized based on whether they were at the national, state, or constituency level.

Findings for the Lok Sabha

In the Lok Sabha, the top 10 ministries to which questions by SC MPs were directed included railways, human resource development, finance, agriculture, and home affairs (Table 21.3). Surprisingly, given the lower human development indicators for Dalits, the ministries of social justice, rural development, health and family welfare, drinking water and sanitation, and labour were not among those which were targeted the most.

The majority of the questions asked by SC MPs sought to elicit information about various government schemes and initiatives (~80 per cent); thereafter were questions related to policy (~15 per cent) and, finally, action-oriented questions (~5 per cent). Information-related questions covered a diverse range of issues such as drug de-addiction cases, minimum support price (MSP) for organic

Table 21.3 Top five ministries to whom questions are targeted in the Question Hour

Ministries	Type of questions	
	Starred	Unstarred
Human Resource Development	8	75
Finance	9	74
Agriculture	2	72
Railway	20	69
Home	2	69

Source: Collated from the official website of Lok Sabha, https://loksabha.nic.in (accessed in October 2022).

produce, and coastal security. Policy-related questions pertained to the telecom policy, non-motorized-transport policy, and policy to eradicate leprosy. Action-oriented questions included steps taken by the government to deal with natural calamities, simplification of legal formalities to set up micro, small, and medium enterprises (MSMEs), and action against malpractices by private hospitals.

Most of the questions were general in nature. But about 40 per cent of them focused on SCs. These primarily related to reservations in jobs or promotions in government departments, procurement policies for MSMEs, manual scavenging, and atrocities against the SCs and STs. For instance, starred questions raised the issues of reservation in the Indian Institutes of Technology (IITs), status of constitution of district courts to try cases under the Scheduled Castes and Scheduled Tribes (Prevention of Atrocities) Act, 1989, and reservation of posts in central universities. Surprisingly there were a number of questions about tribal welfare asked by SC MPs, but fewer questions about minorities. The larger proportion of the questions related to the national level (70 per cent), followed by questions specific to states (20 per cent). A much lower number of questions were about constituency-level issues (10 per cent).

Party interest in a topic seemed to dictate the nature of the questions asked. A large number of Bharatiya Janata Party (BJP) members from the SC community asked about yoga or Ayurveda and the efforts made to promote them. However, there were no questions related to cow vigilantism, lynchings, demonetization, or Kashmir by any of the ruling-party members.[12]

Findings for the UP Legislative Assembly

Contrary to the Lok Sabha, questions in the UP assembly were mostly action-oriented (~90 per cent), followed by questions seeking information (~5 per cent), and those concerning policy (~5 per cent). They were also largely at the constituency level. But similar to the pattern in the Lok Sabha, most questions were not SC-related.

Most of the questions related to departments such as health and family welfare, education, *panchayati raj*, rural development, water resources, public works, and home affairs. These demanded action from the government at various levels. A large number of questions were focused on Lucknow and Prayagraj.

The few SC-related questions pertained to reservation in various government bodies, and only one question asked for data about cases of atrocities committed against the SCs.

There were many more constituency-related questions here than in the Lok Sabha, with MLAs raising queries on specific villages. For example, Ujjwal Raman

Singh, the MLA from Karchana constituency, asked an unstarred question on 23 July 2019: 'Will the Minister of Panchayati Raj be pleased to state that about 500 metres from the canal to the house of Janki Prasad in the Gram Sabha Lakhanpur Karan in the assembly constituency Soraon of Prayagraj district is dilapidated? If yes, will the government undertake interlocking in the above? If yes, for how long? If no, why?'

A few questions related to AYUSH (Ayurveda, Yoga and Naturopathy, Unani, Siddha, and Homeopathy) and construction of cow sheds, both issues of interest to the ruling party. But most of the questions were concerned with agricultural infrastructure, education, and healthcare.

Observations and Recommendations

Are Dalit legislators performing their oversight role effectively? The quantitative data show that across various parameters (caste, gender, age, educational qualifications, and experience), Dalit legislators ask fewer questions per head than their non-Dalit counterparts. Further analysis reveals younger, female, and less-experienced SC legislators ask fewer questions than their older, male, and more experienced counterparts. Interestingly, this is contrary to the trend shown in the case of non-Dalit legislators.

Although it is difficult to pinpoint the exact reasons for this without more in-depth research, it is possible that SC legislators have less access to resources, mentorship, and training than their non-SC counterparts. Individual legislators in India do not have trained research staff to assist them in their work, unlike in other countries such as the United States, the United Kingdom, Australia, and Canada. Legislators may employ staff on their own initiative or through non-government agencies.[13] Major parties field Dalit candidates from reserved constituencies but rarely from unreserved constituencies, with the implication that they do not consider them winnable otherwise. This may adversely affect how much mentorship and training, young, female, and first-time legislators get from their own parties.

Second, the Rules of Procedure of the Lok Sabha may inhibit SC legislators from asking community-specific questions since they do not allow MPs to ask a starred question which is related to a limited section of society or which relates to representation in the services of communities protected under the Constitution, such as the SCs, STs, and Other Backward Classes (OBCs), in which no question of policy is involved. These have to be admitted as unstarred questions (Lok Sabha Secretariat, 2019).

Third, disruptions of the Question Hour have become a common feature of Indian legislatures. At most, out of the 20 starred questions allowed in a day, five are answered on the floor of the house by the concerned minister. So, unless the legislators are able to ensure their question is among the first five on the list, it gets the status of unstarred (written) question.

However, a qualitative analysis of the questions shows that SC legislators do ask hard-hitting questions and that their questions span a wide range of subjects rather than having a narrow focus on their communities. This may not show them in a positive light if viewed solely as representatives of their communities. Nonetheless, a legislator is elected by their entire constituency, which includes people from various castes and communities, and is supposed to represent the national interest. Viewed from such a perspective, SC legislators do fulfil their role as effectively as non-SC legislators. Such a broadening of interest also indicates that SC legislators have become part of the mainstream.

In order to ensure that Dalit legislators, especially young, female, and first-timers, have a level playing field, it is important for the parliament, state legislatures, and political parties to invest in providing them training, mentorship, and resources. This would ensure higher quality of participation and performance in the legislature and even increase the winnability of the candidate in the next election. In addition, the Lok Sabha could increase the duration of the Question Hour to accommodate more questions. It could also allow questions about the welfare of reserved communities as starred questions.

If the primary purpose of reservation is to drive the agenda of development of the SC community, then it is clear from previous research as well as the present study that reservation may not be the right mechanism. Options such as separate electorates or dual-member constituencies may be explored. However, if the purpose is to broaden the representative character of the legislature without forcing legislators to be identity-focused, then the current system of reservation can continue. The advantage of such a system is that we not only broaden the representative character of the legislature, but also gain from their knowledge and experience in diverse fields.

Conclusion

The study of political representation is at the core of political science. Most substantive studies on this issue in India have focused on the overall outcome in terms of improvement in the socio-economic condition of marginalized groups. However, there are limits to what an MP or an MLA can achieve in a parliamentary democracy. Their role is confined to developing laws and policies, overseeing budgetary allocations, keeping the executive in check, and representing their constituents. The execution of laws, government orders, and schemes falls to the bureaucracy, over which elected representatives have limited control.

Therefore, it is unfair to expect legislators to bring about sweeping changes in the socio-economic conditions of their constituents. We should judge them by what they are actually supposed to do.

As the data in the chapter show, SC legislators have performed reasonably well on this count. They ask questions, with some being related to the conditions of the SCs while others are related to policy or the performance of the government. Some of the constraints they face are lack of institutional support for research, the nature of party politics in India, and so on, which limit their participation and need political reforms.

This information about revealed preferences of MPs and MLAs, through the qualitative data from the Question Hour, gives us some insight into the agenda-setting dynamics within the political system. Importantly, the Question Hour in the Lok Sabha cannot be characterized as an ineffective instrument for all its legislators – clearly, some legislators find greater value in making use of the Question Hour than others.

This chapter provided a glimpse into the rich material to be mined from parliamentary and legislative assembly proceedings. As most states start putting data in the public domain, it opens up a key avenue of research to understand the dynamics of state politics and centre–state relations. In this volume, Badri Narayan and Gurram Srinivas, on the distinct nature of aspirations of the Dalit middle class, provide further scope for research on how connected Dalit legislators are with their voters (see Chapters 15 and 17). In this era of competitive and cooperative federalism, this would be an important area for scholars of legislative studies to explore.

Notes

1. Presently, 84 seats are reserved for SCs in the Lok Sabha and 1–85 seats in state legislative assemblies. Allocation of seats at the national and state levels is made on the basis of the proportion of their population to the total population in the respective states. The present delimitation of constituencies was carried out on the basis of the 2001 census figures, and this shall continue till the first census after 2026 as per the Delimitation of Parliamentary and Assembly Constituencies Order, 2008.

2. Reservation is only applicable to the Lok Sabha and legislative assemblies (not upper houses) as legislators are elected by direct election.

3. Known as the Lucknow Pact, in 1916, the Indian National Congress and the Muslim League signed an agreement on seat-sharing in elections for the provincial legislature, where a separate electorate for Muslims was accepted. The pact was incorporated in the Government of India Act, 1919.

4. A series of three such conferences was held during 1930–32.

5. Questions are used to obtain information from governments and to monitor their actions. In India, the first hour of a parliamentary or legislature session is reserved for questioning the government.

6. MP and MLA Track, PRS Legislative Research, https://www.prsindia.org/mptrack (accessed on 6 October 2020).

7. The total number of questions asked by MPs in the starred and unstarred categories are put in a random ballot. From the ballot in the Lok Sabha, 20 starred questions are picked for answering during the Question Hour, and 230 are picked for written answers (unstarred). Ministries receive the questions 15 days in advance so that they can prepare their ministers for the Question Hour. They also have to prepare for follow-up questions (supplementary) they can expect to be asked in the house. Government officers are close at hand in a gallery so that they can pass notes or relevant documents to support the ministers in answering a question.

8. Individual MPs, irrespective of party affiliation, can introduce proposed legislation known as a private member's bill. However, in India not a single private member's bill has been passed since 1970.

9. The decision to enact a law or policy is taken by the respective ministers and approved by the cabinet. It is also possible to pass laws without amendments with a simple majority. Individual legislators can influence Standing Committee reports through their interventions if they are members (standing committees are formed with members of both houses to examine Bills and other policy-related matters). But these reports are recommendatory.

10. See Ministry of Statistics and Programme Implementation (2016) for the guidelines.

11. These are various tools to raise matters of public importance and initiate discussions. Some of them require voting while others do not.

12. Cow vigilantism and lynching are issues of special interest for Dalits since the primary targets of such forms of violence are minorities and Dalits who sell and consume beef. Demonetization and removal of the special status of Kashmir were steps taken by the BJP.

13. For examples, the Legislative Assistants to Members of Parliament (LAMP) Fellowship and the Swaniti Initiative.

Bibliography

Akirav, O. 2011. 'The Use of Parliamentary Questions in the Israeli Parliament, 1992–96'. *Israel Affairs* 17(2): 259–77.

Ambagudia, J. 2019. 'Scheduled Tribes, Reserved Constituencies and Political Reservation in India'. *Journal of Social Inclusion Studies* 5(1): 44–58.

Ambedkar, B. R. 2013. *Dr Babasaheb Ambedkar: Speeches and Writings*, vol. 2. Bombay: Government of Maharashtra. https://www.mea.gov.in/Images/attach/amb/Volume_02.pdf. Accessed on 22 February 2022.

Ayyangar, S., and S. Jacob. 2014. 'Studying the Indian Legislature: What Does Question Hour Reveal?' *Studies in Indian Politics* 2(1): 1–19.

Bailer, S. 2011. 'People's Voice or Information Pool? The Role of, and Reasons for, Parliamentary Questions in the Swiss Parliament'. *Journal of Legislative Studies* 17(3): 302–14.

Bhogale, S. 2018. 'Querying the Indian Parliament: What Can the Question Hour Tell about Muslim Representation in India?'. Working Paper 2018-1, Trivedi Centre for Political Data (TCPD), Ashoka University, Sonepat.

Birch, A. H. 1971. *Representation*. London: St Martin's Press

Bird, K. 2005. 'Gendering Parliamentary Questions'. *British Journal of Politics and International Relations* 7(3): 353–70.

Burke, E. 1790 (1968). *Reflections on the Revolution in France*. London: Penguin Books.

Chester, N., and N. Bowring. 1962. *Questions in Parliament*. Oxford: Oxford University Press.

Chin, A., and P. Nishith. 2011. 'The Redistributive Effects of Political Reservation for Minorities: Evidence from India'. *Journal of Development Economics* 96(2): 265–77.

Cole, M. 1999. 'Accountability and Quasi-Government: The Role of Parliamentary Questions'. *Journal of Legislative Studies* 5(1): 77–101.

Damgaard, E. 1994. 'Parliamentary Questions and Control in Denmark'. In *Parliamentary control in the Nordic countries*, edited by M. Wiberg, 44–76. Tampere: Finnish Political Science Association.

Datta, S. 2008. 'Television Coverage and Political Voice: Evidence from Parliamentary Question Hour in India'. Working Paper No. 1281627, Social Science Research Network (SSRN).

Disch, L. 2015. 'The Constructivist Turn in Democratic Representation: A Normative Dead-End?' *Constellations* 22(4): 487–99.

Dovi, S. 2002. 'Preferable Descriptive Representatives: Or Will Just Any Woman, Black, or Latino Do?' *American Political Science Review* 96(4): 745–54.

Dryzek, J., and S. Niemeyer. 2008. 'Discursive Representation'. *American Political Science Review* 102(4): 481–93.

Dushkin, L. 1972. 'Scheduled Caste Politics'. In *The Untouchables in Contemporary India*, edited by J. M. Mahar, 165–226. Tucson, AZ: Arizona University Press.

Economic Times. 2019. 'Wayanad MP Ready with a Barrage of Questions'. 19 November. https://economictimes.indiatimes.com/news/politics-and-nation/wayanad-mp-ready-with-a-barrage-of-questions/articleshow/72118956.cms?from=mdr. Accessed on 17 February 2022.

Franks, C. E. S. 1985. 'Debates and Question Period in the Canadian House of Commons: What Purpose Do They Serve?' *American Review of Canadian Studies* 15(1): 1–15.

Franklin, M. N., and P. Norton. 1993. *Parliamentary Questions*. Oxford: Clarendon Press.

Galanter, M. 1979. 'Compensatory Discrimination in Political Representation: A Preliminary Assessment of India's Thirty-Year Experience with Reserved Seats in Legislatures'. *Economic and Political Weekly* 14(7–8): 437–54.

Grant, R., and R. O. Keohane. 2005. 'Accountability and Abuses of Power in World Politics'. *American Political Science Review* 99(1): 29–44.

Hazama, H., Ö. F. Gençkaya, and S. Gençkaya. 2007. 'Parliamentary Questions in Turkey'. *Journal of Legislative Studies* 13(4): 539–57.

Imtiyaz, A., and F. Zaman. 2019. 'Evaluating Reserved Seats as a Measure of Substantive Representation for Scheduled Castes and Scheduled Tribes through the Analysis of Parliamentary Questions in the Lok Sabha (1999–2016)'. *Contemporary Voice of Dalit* 11(2): 119–29.

Jaffrelot, C. 2003. *India's Silent Revolution: The Rise of the Lower Castes in North India*. London: C. Hurst & Co. Publishers.

Jayal, N. G. 2006. *Representing India: Ethnic Diversity and the Governance of Public Institutions*. New York: Palgrave Macmillan.

Jayal, N. G., and P. B. Mehta. 2010. *The Oxford Companion to Politics in India*. New Delhi: Oxford University Press.

Jensenius, F. 2012. 'Political Quotas in India: Perceptions of Political Representation'. *Asian Survey* 52(2): 373–94.

———. 2015. 'Development from Representation? A Study of Quotas for the Scheduled Castes in India'. *American Economic Journal: Applied Economics* 7(3): 196–220.

Jyoti, D. 2019. 'Gandhi, Ambedkar and the 1932 Poona Pact'. *Hindustan Times*, 1 October. https://www.hindustantimes.com/india-news/gandhi-ambedkar-and-the-1932-poona-pact/story-5WuyrphB8OwtRp5lC9XQGP.html. Accessed on 15 March 2022.

Khilnani, S. 1997. *The Idea of India*. London: Hamish Hamilton.

Kumar, N. 2008. 'Formulation of Inclusive Policies in Parliament'. *Economic and Political Weekly* 43(29): 80–87.

Kymlicka, W. 1995. *Multicultural Citizenship: A Liberal Theory of Minority Rights*. Oxford: Clarendon Press.

Locke, J. 1689 (1988). *Two Treatises of Government*, edited by P. Laslett. Cambridge: Cambridge University Press.

Lok Sabha. n.d.a. 'Seventeenth Lok Sabha: Procedure Relating to Questions'. Lok Sabha. http://loksabhaph.nic.in/Questions/ProcedureRelating.aspx. Accessed on 29 October 2020.

———. n.d.b. 'Seventeenth Lok Sabha: Procedure for Short Notice Questions'. Lok Sabha. http://164.100.47.194/Loksabha/Questions/ProcedureForShortNotice. aspx. Accessed on 29 October 2020.

Lok Sabha Secretariat. 2019. *Procedure and Practice: Question Branch*, vol. 1. New Delhi: Lok Sabha Secretariat.

Madison, J., A. Hamilton, and J. Jay. 1987 (1787–88). *The Federalist Papers*, edited by I. Kramnick. Harmondsworth: Penguin Books.

Mansbridge, J. 1999. 'Should Blacks Represent Blacks and Women Represent Women? A Contingent "Yes"'. *Journal of Politics* 61(3): 628–57.

———. 2003. 'Rethinking Representation'. *American Political Science Review* 97(4): 515–28.

Martin, S. 2011. 'Parliamentary Questions, the Behaviour of Legislators, and the Function of Legislatures: An Introduction'. *Journal of Legislative Studies* 17(3): 259–70.

Mattson, I. 1994. 'Parliamentary Questions in the Swedish Riksdag'. In *Parliamentary Control in the Nordic Countries*, edited by M. Wiberg, 276–356. Helsinki: Finnish Political Science Association.

McMillan, A. 2005. *Standing at the Margins: Representation and Electoral Reservation in India*. New Delhi: Oxford University Press.

Mezey, M. L. 2008. *Representative Democracy: Legislators and Their Constituents*. Lanham, MD: Rowman & Littlefield.

Ministry of Statistics and Programme Implementation. 2016. 'Guidelines on Members of Parliament Local Area Development Scheme (MPLADS)'. https://www.mplads. gov.in/MPLADS/UploadedFiles/MPLADSGuidelines2016English_638.pdf (accessed on 24 March 2022).

Mohapatra, M. K. 1969. 'Questioning Behavior in Lok Sabha in 1952: A Methodological Exploration in Behavioral Research on Indian Legislatures'. *Indian Journal of Political Science* 30(4): 362–72.

Pande, R. 2003. 'Can Mandated Political Representation Increase Policy Influence for Disadvantaged Minorities? Theory and Evidence from India'. *American Economic Review* 93(4): 1132–51.

Pennock, J. R., and J. Chapman (eds.). 1968. *Representation*. New York: Atherton Press.

Phillips, A. 1995. *Politics of Presence*. New York: Clarendon Press.

Pitkin, H. 1967. *The Concept of Representation*. Los Angeles: University of California Press.

Plotke, D. 1997. 'Representation Is Democracy'. *Constellations* 4(1): 19–34.

Rasch, B. E. 2011. 'Behavioural Consequences of Restrictions on Plenary Access: Parliamentary Questions in the Norwegian Storting'. *Journal of Legislative Studies* 17(3): 382–93.

Rehfeld, A. 2005. *The Concept of Constituency: Political Representation, Democratic Legitimacy and Institutional Design.* Cambridge: Cambridge University Press.

Saward, M. (ed.). 2000. *Democratic Innovation: Deliberation, Representation and Association.* London: Routledge.

Sharma, S. 2021. 'Reservations Can Take the Disadvantaged to Parliament, But Not in Key Positions'. IndiaSpend, 15 June. https://www.indiaspend.com/governance/reservation-scheduled-castes-tribes-representation-social-justice-755256. Accessed on 15 March 2022.

Times of India. 2021. 'After One Year Pause, Govt to Release MLALAD Funds'. 14 April. https://timesofindia.indiatimes.com/city/lucknow/after-one-year-pause-govt-to-release-mlalad-funds/articleshow/82056919.cms. Accessed on 24 March 2022.

Vundru, R. S. 2018. *Ambedkar, Gandhi and Patel: The making of India's Electoral System.* New Delhi: Bloomsbury Publishing.

Williams, M. 2000. 'The Uneasy Alliance of Group Representation and Deliberative Democracy'. In *Citizenship in Diverse Societies*, edited by W. Kymlicka and W. Norman, 124–53. Oxford: Oxford University Press.

Yadav, Y. 2008. 'The Paradox of Political Representation'. *Seminar* 586. https://www.india-seminar.com/2008/586/586_yogendra_yadav.htm. Accessed in October 2022.

22

Why Are Some Backward Castes Demanding Scheduled Caste Reservation?

Arvind Kumar

The Constitution of India, under article 16(4), makes provision for reservation in 'favour of any backward class of citizens'[1] in the distribution of public offices, employment, and educational opportunities. The insertion of the provision on 'backward class of citizens' in the Constitution had initiated intense debate in India's Constituent Assembly.[2] The members deliberated upon the meaning of 'backward classes' and arrived at one conclusion that ex-untouchable castes and tribal communities, which had been enumerated as Scheduled Castes (SCs) and Scheduled Tribes (STs) under the Government of India Act, 1935, were a section of the backward classes. Therefore, they were placed under articles 341 and 342 of the Constitution. However, there were castes and communities which were not included in the list of SCs and STs but were backward. To identify them, article 340 was inserted in the Constitution, empowering the president of post-colonial India to appoint a commission for investigating the condition of socially and educationally backward classes and suggesting possible measures for removing their disabilities.

Under article 340, three backward-classes commissions have been appointed till date. The Jawaharlal Nehru government had appointed the first commission in 1953, under the chairmanship of Kaka Kalelkar, which submitted its report in 1955. The Janata Party government of Morarji Desai appointed the second commission in 1978, under the chairmanship of B. P. Mandal, which submitted its report in 1980. On the recommendations of these commissions, particularly the second commission, popularly known as the Mandal Commission, a third category of backward classes emerged – namely, the Other Backward Classes (OBCs). Although the term 'classes'[3] has been used in official documents, it is a euphemism for a grouping of castes in the middle of the caste hierarchy, distinct from upper castes, intermediate castes, SCs, and STs. On the recommendation of the Mandal Commission, the OBCs have been given reservation in public offices, employment, and educational institutions.

The Narendra Modi government appointed the third backward-classes commission in 2017, under the chairpersonship of G. Rohini, which is yet to submit its report despite multiple extensions of its tenure (Pandey, 2022).

In a nutshell, 'backward classes of citizens' have been divided into three categories – OBCs, SCs, and STs – under the provisions of articles 340, 341, and 342, and have been provided 27 per cent, 15 per cent, and 7.5 per cent reservation, respectively, in the public offices, employment, and educational institutions of union government. Likewise, state governments also provide reservation to the OBCs, SCs, and STs. However, over the past few years, some castes of the OBC category, popularly known as Most Backward Castes[4] (MBCs) in the northern Indian states, particularly Uttar Pradesh (UP), have been demanding inclusion in the SC category. In response to this demand, successive governments in UP led by Mulayam Singh Yadav,[5] Mayawati,[6] and Akhilesh Yadav[7] made recommendations to the union government for inclusion of such castes in the SC category, but all of them were rejected. In 2019, the Bharatiya Janata Party (BJP) government in the state, led by Yogi Adityanath, made another attempt to include these castes in the SC category by ordering district officials to issue caste certificates, but the High Court of Allahabad stayed this order (Srivastava, 2019).

While such rejection has mostly been premised on the dubious legality of whimsically including castes and communities in the list of SCs and STs, increasing demands for inclusion force one to move beyond the legalese and reflect on what social and economic forces are producing such demands. This question is intriguing because castes included in the SC category continue to face social oppression including boycott even today. While economic and social backwardness are in no way limited just to the SCs, caste-based oppression, especially through the practice of untouchability, is more common against their members. Ajay Gudavarthy (2012) argues that backwardness produces a citizen capable of speaking and asserting the language of rights, legal and constitutional entitlements, and of pointing towards the limitations of planning and public policy in the past, and hence backward castes in comparison to SCs have been seen to be sociologically distinct in terms of being internally heterogeneous and culturally, socially and economically differentiated; their sociopolitical mobilisation has always been conscious of such differentiations. Contrary to this, untouchability, unlike backwardness, produces a victim-subject whose subjective perception is constructed either with self-contempt or a stigmatised victimhood (Gudavarthy, 2012). The sociopolitical mobilisation of Dalits began as a cohesive movement of various sub-castes that were culturally different and hierarchized but were economically similar.

This dissimilarity and practice of untouchability is a source of stigmatization of castes included in the SC category. The demand for SC status is thus implicitly accompanied by the possibility of such stigmatization and humiliation; that MBCs have made this demand in spite of such social costs is a phenomenon that calls for consideration.

In this chapter, I examine the causes for the rising demand for SC status among MBCs. I find that MBCs are worried about deterioration of their socio-economic conditions due to changing economic policies and social structures. Their worry has also an element of fear of being placed at the bottom of Indian society. Hence, their primary concern is that of improving their social status through material advancement. To augment their demand for inclusion in the SC category, they also claim to have been victims of untouchability, albeit to a lesser degree. And finally, rather than drawing the social stigma of untouchability, MBCs see their inclusion in the SC category as political ammunition against possible caste-based oppression.

This chapter is divided into following sections. The second section theoretically examines the sources of stigma of untouchability, its ill effects, and its possible solutions to overcome such stigma. The third section takes an inductive leap and provide a broad overview of sub-castes, or *jatis*, which are considered to be MBCs. This section also traces the genealogy of MBC category. The fourth section provides brief details of the castes and *jatis* of UP which have been demanding to be included in the SC category, with their social status and traditional occupations. The fifth section elaborates the data and methodology adopted for this study. The sixth section explains the socio-economic conditions of MBCs and their claim for SC status through empirical analysis of elite interviews. The seventh section analyses the factors which are fuelling the demand for SC status among MBCs. The eighth section explains how the ingrained sense of hierarchy in Indian society has also been contributing to the demand for the extension of SC status. The final section wraps up by providing a summary and conclusion of this chapter.

Stigma of Untouchability and Its Consequences

Untouchability has multiple negative consequences for the life prospects of castes and communities which are victims of this practice (Shaha, et al. 2006). Such castes and communities are categorized as SCs and also referred to as Dalits.[8] Conventionally, untouchability was seen as an archaic social practice responsible for the backwardness of Dalits because it reduces their choices and opportunities in sociopolitical and economic spaces. However, there is increasing scholarship which tries to look at the ill-effects of untouchability from the perspective of moral philosophy or psychology (Guru, 2009; Gudavarthy, 2012). This perspective broadly understands the issue of untouchability through the theory of 'the tribal stigma of race, nation, and religion, these being stigma that can be transmitted through lineages and equally contaminate all members of a family' (Goffman, 1990: 14). In addition to this tribal stigma, there are stigmas of abominations of the body arising from physical disabilities, and blemishes of the individual character, such as weak will, domineering or unnatural passions, treacherous and rigid beliefs, and dishonesty (Goffman, 1990).

Stigma is further understood to be a product of the emotion of disgust which can be traced to the deep history of the human species, including magical ideas of contamination, impossible aspirations to purity, immortality, and non-animality (Nussbaum, 2004). It is a social and political construct which replaces the 'sense of self' with a stigmatized self and public shame (Gudavarthy, 2012). The sense of shame in public domain reduces public efficiency of individuals. Furthermore, stigmatization is 'adding insult to injury' of misrecognition and deprivation (Fraser and Olson, 1999). In Indian context, 'the oppressive Brahmanical knowledge tradition imagined the body of members of untouchable castes and communities through their contact with death and waste matter' (Chakrabarty, 2018: 5). Such imagination of the 'Dalit body' resulted in deprivation of something profoundly important to human beings – that is the touch of other humans (Guru and Sarukkai, 2012). This created untouchability resulting into the marginalization of its victims. Moreover, it produces humiliation in the everyday life of victim castes (Guru, 2009).

Stigma in the Indian context goes beyond castes and communities to include the policies which have been designed for empowering marginalized castes. For example, the reservation policy is mocked in India through the logic of merit, so whenever this policy is opposed, protesters start polishing shoes or cleaning streets to mark their grievance. Even when the report of Mandal Commission was implemented, a section of upper-caste women students had protested with banners claiming they would not find suitable husbands (Chakravarthi, 2003). Moreover, employees belonging to the SCs or the STs are often referred to as *sarkari damad*[9] (Guru, 2009). These examples illustrate how the stigma of caste persists in public life, and merely bringing policies is not sufficient to remove it.

Three possible ways are discussed to overcome the stigma of untouchability: first, treating every human being as a 'mind' without reference to the socially marked identity of their body; second, looking beyond the social identity of people and thinking about the material which forms the human body[10] and also connects all bodies to the matter making up our universe – ancient atomic and sub-atomic particles (Chakrabarty, 2018); and, third, forcing tormentors to eradicate their prejudice of making judgments about the bodies of others. It is argued that the bodies of untouchable castes become untouchable because the imagination of Brahmins proclaims their own body as pure (Chakrabarty, 2018). So, unless the idea of pure body is devalued radically, the idea of impure body cannot be eradicated and, hence, the stigma of untouchability cannot be overcome. This is the reason why Ambedkar (2014 [1936]) suggested questioning the very sanctity of the religious scriptures of the Brahminical tradition which are the sources of purity and pollution.

Genealogy of the MBC Category

With the beginning of the twenty-first century, a section of OBCs has started identifying itself as MBCs, and there is growing political consciousness about this new identity. In one of her unpublished papers, Sudha Pai argues that the OBCs in the states of Hindi heartland fall into three categories based on their caste and class criteria: social status, income, and educational abilities. These are, first, the numerically small, economically well off, and comparatively better-placed, and socially and politically important 'forward' or upper-backward classes; second, a middle category – largely landowning, constituting the dominant castes in rural areas, upwardly mobile, and gradually improving its socio-economic and educational status; and third, the MBCs, or EBCs, who are the most backward in terms of social status, income, and educational abilities. The last category has not been much known, but it has acquired prominence due to its electoral support to the BJP.

While the MBCs are part of the OBCs, the genesis of this category goes back to the recommendations of the first backward-classes commission formed under the chairmanship of Kaka Kalelkar in 1953. The commission had prepared a list of 2,399 backward castes or communities for the entire country, out of which 837 castes were classified as 'most backward' (Government of India, 1955). The report of the commission was tabled in the parliament but was rejected. However, the government of India had asked state governments to conduct a survey for identifying backward castes and take necessary measures for removing backwardness (Galanter, 1984).

In the decade of 1970s, the governments of Bihar and UP appointed backward-classes commissions in their respective states. Bhola Paswan Shastri, the chief minister of Bihar, appointed the Mungeri Lal Commission in 1971, which submitted its report in 1976. This commission recommended reservations for OBCs, MBCs, women, and economically weaker sections, besides SCs and STs. The chief minister Karpoori Thakur implemented the report of the commission in 1978. In UP, a similar commission was constituted by the chief minister Hemwati Nandan Bahuguna in 1975 under the chairmanship of Chhedi Lal Sathi. The Sathi Commission submitted its report on 17 May 1977. The commission categorized backward classes into three groups: most backward castes, upper backward castes, and Muslim backward castes. It had recommended 17, 12, and 2.5 per cent reservation in government jobs to respective category, but its recommendations were never implemented.

The Mandal Commission in its report did not make any separate provision for the MBCs, although one member of the commission, L. R. Naik, had given a dissent note in support of recognizing the MBCs as a separate category (Government of India, 1980). With the implementation of the report of the Mandal Commission in 1989, the category of MBCs lost significance for a decade.

Although the Mandal Commission had bulldozed the concept of MBCs, this category became alive once again with the formation of the social justice committee in UP in 2001 under the chairmanship of Hukum Singh. The committee identified 79 sub-castes within the OBCs and divided them into three categories: backward classes, more backward classes, and most backward classes (Table 22.1) (Verma, 2001).

Rising Demand of MBCs for SC Status

The social justice committee under the chairpersonship of Hukum Singh identified 70 castes as MBCs and recommended sub-categorization of the OBCs, but the High Court of Allahabad stayed its implementation. The attempt to sub-categorize reservation was opposed by Mulayam Singh Yadav[11] and Mayawati[12] (Verma, 2001). To counter the BJP's strategy of dividing backward castes, just before the general election in 2004, Mulayam Singh Yadav recommended inclusion of 17 MBCs – namely, Kahar, Kashyap, Kewat, Nishad, Bind, Bhar, Prajapati, Rajbhar, Batham, Gaur, Tura, Majhi, Mallah, Kumhar, Dheemar, Godia, and Machua in the SC category. The succeeding governments of Mayawati and Akhilesh Yadav also made similar recommendations. In 2018, Yogi Adityanath's government in UP appointed another social justice committee under the chairmanship of Raghvendra Kumar.[13] This committee is also reported to have recommended sub-categorization of OBC reservation. Instead of implementing the report of this committee, the Yogi Adityanath

Table 22.1 Sub-categorization of the Other Backward Classes (OBCs) by the Hukum Singh Committee

Schedule	Nomenclature of the category	Number of castes	Name of the castes
A	Backward Classes	1	Yadav: Ahir, Gwala, Yaduvashiya
B	More Backward Classes	8	Sonar, Sunar, Swarnkar, Jat, Kurmi, Chanau, Patel, Patanwar, Kurmi-Mall, Kurmi-Sainthwar, Giri, Gujjar, Gosain, Lodh, Lodha, Lodhi, Lot, Lodh-Rajput, Kamboj
C	Most Backward Classes	70	Arakh, Arakvanshiya, Kachchi, Kachchi Kushwaha, Shakya, Kahar, Kashyap, Kewat, Mallah, Nishad, Kisan, Koeri, Kumhar, Prajapati, Kasgar, Kunjra, Raeen, Gareria, Pal Vaghel, Gaddi, Ghoshi, Chikwa, Qassab Qureshi, Chak, Chhippi, Chipa, Jogi, Jhoja, Dhafali, Tamoli, Barai, Chaurasia, Teli, Samani, Rogangar, Sahu, Rauniar, Gandhi, Arrak, Darji, Idrisi, Kakutstha, Dhiver, Naqqal, Nat (those not included in SCs), Naik, Lohar, Lahar-Saifi, Lonia, Nonia, Gole-Thakur, Lonia-Chauhan, Rangrez, Rangwa, Marchcha, Halwai, Modanwal, Hajjarn, Nai, Salmain, Savita, Sriwas, Rai Sikh, Sakka-Bhisti, Bhisti-Abbasi, Dhobi (those not included in SCs or STs), Kasera, Thathera, Tamrakar, Nanbai, Mirshikar, Shekh, Sarwari (Pirai), Peerahi, Mev, Mewati, Koshta, Koshti, Ror, Khumra, Sangatarash, Hansiri, Mochi, Khagi, Tanwar, Singharia, Faqir, Banjara, Ranki, Mukeri, Mukerani, Barhai, Saifi, Vishwakarma, Pachaal, Ramgadhiya, Jangir, Dhiman, Bari, Beragi, Bind, Biyar, Bhar, Rajbhar, Bhurji, Bharbhunia, Bhooj, Kandu, Kashaudhan, Bhathiara, Mali, Saini, Sweeper (those not included in SCs), Halalkhor, Katuwa, Maheegeer, Dangi, Dhakar, Gada, Tantawa, Joria, Patwa, Patahara, Patehara, Deovanshi, Kalal, Kalwar, Kalar, Manihar, Kacher, Lakhara, Murao, Murai, Maurya, Momin (Ansar), Muslim Kayastha, Mirasi, Naddaf (Dhuniya), Mansoori, Kandere, Kadere, Karan (Karn)

Source: Verma (2001).

government in 2019 made another unsuccessful attempt to include the MBCs in the SC category, indicating that the BJP has changed its previous stance of dividing OBC reservation (Kumar, 2019a).

The castes mentioned in Table 22.2, which have been demanding SC status in UP, can be further broadly clubbed into four castes or communities based on their traditional occupations: (*a*) fisherfolk (fishermen): Kashyap, Kewat, Nishad, Bind, Batham, Gaur, Tura, Majhi, Mallah, Dheemar, Godia, and

Table 22.2 Traditional occupations and social status of the Most Backward Castes (MBCs)

Name of caste	Traditional occupation	Social status
Kahar	Cooking and litter-bearer	Service caste
Kashyap	Fishing	Service caste
Kewat	Fishing	Service caste
Nishad	Fishing	Service caste
Bind	Fishing	Service caste
Bhar	Making rice puffs and litter-bearer	*Harwaha* (agriculture labour) caste
Prajapati	Pot-making	Artisan caste
Rajbhar	Mason, Litter-bearer	*Harwaha* (agriculture labour) caste
Batham	Fishing	Service caste
Gaur	Fishing	Service caste
Tura	Fishing	Service caste
Majhi	Fishing	Service caste
Mallah	Fishing	Service caste
Kumhar	Pot-making	Artisan caste
Dheemar	Fishing	Service caste
Godia	Fishing	Service caste
Machua	Fishing	Service caste

Source: Prepared by the author based on interviews of MBC leaders of various political parties and caste associations.

Machua; (*b*) Kahar; (*c*) Bhar or Rajbhar; and (*d*) Prajapati or Kumhar. The status of some of these *jati*s changes in some states. For instance, castes such as Bind, Keot (Kevat), and Mallah are SCs in West Bengal whereas Bhars or Rajbhars are STs in Chhattisgarh, Madhya Pradesh, and Maharashtra, since they have been declared a sub-caste of Gond tribe (see the list of STs of the Ministry of Tribal Affairs). These discrepancies have also fuelled the demand for inclusion of castes in the same category across the country.

The MBCs are not the only castes which have been demanding the change of category. Some OBCs have also made similar demands in Hindi-speaking areas such as Jharkhand and Rajasthan. The Kurmis of Jharkhand (*The Telegraph*, 2003) and West Bengal (Chakraborty, 2021) and Gujjars of Rajasthan (Press Trust of India, 2005) have been consistently seeking ST status. The demands of Gujjars to be included in the ST category have also resulted in violent conflict with the Meenas (*Financial Express*, 2007). Similarly, dominant intermediary castes like the Jats of Haryana, Patidars of Gujarat, and Marathas of Maharashtra have also been pressing for reservation, but they seek either inclusion in the OBC category or separate reservation. This demand of backwardness by these dominant communities is seen as reverse aspiration (Devara, 2021).

Exploring the Demand of MBCs: Data and Methodology

The demand for SC status by the MBCs in UP has accelerated since 2013, when Gayatri Prasad Prajapati, a minister from the MBC community in the Akhilesh Yadav government, had launched a Rath Yatra[14] in this regard. During that period, in the months of January and February 2014, I decided to conduct interviews with 10 MBC leaders belonging to five political parties: BJP, Bahujan Samaj Party (BSP), Indian National Congress (INC), Samajwadi Party (SP), and Gareeb Samaj Party. Along with their membership of parties, these respondents have also been members and office bearers of caste associations such as All India Gond Mahasabha, All India Nai Mahasabha, Rashtriya Nishad Ekta Parishad, All Bharatiya Rajbhar Sangathan, All India Backward and Minority Communities Employees Federation, and so on. They became key respondents, and two of them had been part of the Rath Yatra.

These persons were selected because of their influential position of being political mobilizers and opinion-makers among their castes. It is well argued that an important objective of political science research is to understand policymaking, for which interviewing political elites becomes indispensable because they might hold exclusive information by virtue of being significant position-holders (Halperin and Heath, 2017). Interviewing social and political elites in India has another advantage: social elites are often office bearers of caste associations and federations, so their status plays a significant role in political mobilization and shaping of public opinion towards policies; they thus have insights into people's opinions on regional issues (Jaffrelot, 2003). The participants in the interview were predominantly from Awadh and eastern UP, but their position as office bearers in caste associations allows us to assume that the issues which they would be raising would have universal presence in their castes across the state.

The interviews, which were conducted in January–February 2014, primarily followed a semi-structured questionnaire covering broad themes of the stigma of untouchability, socio-economic status, and willingness to struggle against the stigma of untouchability (see Table 22.3).

Table 22.3 Overview of the interview questionnaire

Theme	Questions
Stigma of untouchability	1. Did their caste members agree with the decision of the Uttar Pradesh government to include them in the SC category?
	2. The castes included in the SC category have historically faced untouchability. Their inclusion in this category would bring them the identity of ex-untouchables; would their caste be ready to face this?
Socio-economic status	3. What do they feel about the existing OBC category?
	4. Does their community feel closer to members of the backward castes or members of the SCs?
	5. Is non-implementation of reservation the only reason for backwardness or are other policies of the government also responsible?
Willingness to struggle against the stigma of untouchability	6. Did they accept Dalit icons such as Ambedkar as their own?
	7. Would their caste start accepting Buddhism like Dalits?

Describing the Claims for SC Status

The most striking finding of this research is that the demand among the MBCs for SC status has persevered over the last four decades, with Gayatri Prasad Prajapati's Rath Yatra fuelling it further in 2013. The respondent from the Rajbhar caste illustrated this point cogently: 'The first time such a demand emerged was in 1980, when Doodhnath Rajbhar, an INC MLA from the Mubarakpur assembly constituency of Azamgarh district, submitted a memorandum in the UP legislative assembly demanding inclusion of the Rajbhar or Bhar caste in the ST category, but the state government sent a proposal for inclusion of this caste in the SC category which got rejected by the union government.'[15] The respondent from the Gaur caste also pointed out a comparable story about the representatives of his caste making similar demands to prime ministers Indira Gandhi, Charan Singh, and V. P. Singh.[16] He said that nowadays each caste has its own caste association or federation[17] which has been fuelling these demands. Based on the intensity of these demands, state governments have sent proposals to the union government for including these castes in the SC category, but these have never been accepted.[18] Overall, there has been widespread support among the MBCs for being included in the SC category.

Even if such demands had been persistently made in the past, this does not resolve the puzzle present here: relatively 'superior' castes wanting SC status to upend commonly held hierarchized notion of the system. Interviews with these caste leaders were important in understanding the reasons behind such demands. When asked about the stigma of untouchability, the respondent from the Nai (barber) caste said that his caste had already been engaged in doing unclean work inside the houses of upper castes, whereas SCs had done the same work outside the house.[19] The respondents from the Gaur and Nishad castes informed me that their castes still face untouchability, and similar observations were made by the respondent from the Rajbhar caste. One respondent from the Nishad caste, who happened to be a local leader of the INC, suggested that traditional forms of untouchability were declining rapidly.[20] Similarly, the respondents from the Prajapati or Kumhar caste informed me that their caste does not face untouchability and neither does the young people in their caste.[21]

The respondents from the Nishad, Gaur, and Rajbhar communities told me that their castes are similar to the castes in the SCs and therefore they should be included in the SC category. However, the respondent from the Prajapati caste said that their caste is similar to the Yadav, Kurmi, and Kushwaha castes, but argued for their own inclusion in the SC category. One respondent from the Nishad caste associated with the Gareeb Samaj Party, while explaining similarities between Nishads and Chamars, mentioned that upper castes identify women of Nishad and Chamar castes with red and yellow colours of their sarees (cloths).[22] When asked about choosing a solution between inclusion in the SC category, and the division of OBC reservation in the three sub-categories as suggested by the Hukum Singh Committee, the respondents from the Gaur, Nishad, and Rajbhar castes asserted that they should be included in the SC category because their social and economic status has been like that of the SCs. To further substantiate their point, these respondents cited the practice of bonded labour (*begar*). The respondents from the Gaur and Nishad castes informed that like untouchable castes, occasionally their castes had to work in agricultural fields, although their main occupations were as fisherfolk and boatsmen. These fisherfolk had to supply fish to upper-caste landlords whenever asked to do so. For all services and fish provided, no payment was made. The respondents from the Kumhar or Prajapati caste also had similar observations regarding payment for pottery. The respondent from the Bhar caste said that the Bhar, Rajbhar, and Kahar castes were not paid for the work done for upper-caste landlords.

Despite having a similar socio-economic status to that of the SCs, when respondents were asked, 'Why were the MBCs not included in the SC category previously?', they stated that their caste was misguided in the 1930s, when the list of SCs was being prepared. One respondent from the Nishad caste said that during that time, their caste was misled by the propaganda of nationalist leaders that claimed by including them in the SC category, the British government was making them Chamars; so their forefathers rejected the proposal to be included in the SC category.[23] This claim is verified in the note of E. A. H. Blunt (1932), a member of the executive council in the United Provinces government, about the Bhar or Rajbhar caste, where he writes: 'In the Uttar Pradesh, they call themselves *Rajbhar*. They are good agriculturists and masons. They have strong Panchayats and they agitated for the removal of their caste from the list of Scheduled Castes.' The assertion of the MBC leaders and this document show that these lower castes in north India made collective claims to higher ritual ranks in the caste hierarchy through 'Sanskritization' to obtain concessions from the colonial authorities (Rudolph and Rudolph, 1967). In states such as West Bengal where the impact of 'Sanskritization' was less, fisherman castes are included in the SC category. Even in undivided UP,[24] the carpenter caste, named Badhai or Vishwakarma, is in the SC category in hill districts but in the OBC category in the plains. In post-colonial India, caste associations and federations increased political mobilization, and hence they also started demanding correction in such anomalies.

Factors Fuelling the Demand for SC Status

The demand of 17 MBCs for SC status in UP has intensified since the publication of the Hukum Singh Committee's report in 2001. There are two factors – changing social structure and status inequality – which have been fuelling this demand.

India has undergone tremendous social changes since independence. Introduction of land reforms, the community development programme, universal adult franchise, the rule of law, and so on, have changed the power dynamics of Indian society (Jodhka, 2010) and resulted in the decline of the old social order (Rao and Frankel, 1989). The changing of the social order has resulted in the decline, but not elimination, of the practice of untouchability. Alongside, the stigma of untouchability is also declining. Meanwhile, the country introduced a new economic policy in 1991. This policy broke down the *jajmani* system (the practice of lower castes rendering various services to the upper castes in exchange for grain or other goods), resulting in these castes being deprived of their traditional occupations, and also filled the domestic market with machine-made goods rendering the products of artisan castes useless. A section of MBCs, such as Kumhars (pot makers), Bhars, Rajbhars, Badhai (carpenter), and so on, have been directly impacted.

The new economic policy also unleased rapid urbanization which is resulting in the contamination of rivers, making them unfit for the survival of fishes. Sand mining in rivers has also adversely impacted aquatic life. The cumulative outcome of all these is that the fisherman castes, which had been dependent on the river, are gradually losing their occupation. The construction of bridges has further resulted in the loss of their traditional occupation as boatsmen.

The loss of traditional occupations due to the emergence of a market-based economy is forcing the MBCs to enter the job market as labourers. In rural India, these castes, particularly fishermen and Bhars or Rajbhars, are becoming agricultural labourers. The increasing engagement in agriculture as labour exacerbates the potential of them facing verbal abuse and physical violence. Their demand for inclusion in the SC category is thus also guided by the fact of getting penal protection under the Scheduled Castes and Scheduled Tribes (Prevention of Atrocities) Act, 1989.

Rapid social and economic change has infused a sense of status inequality among the MBCs. This was evident in the replies of respondents from the Nishad and Gaur castes who claimed that one cannot find Indian Administrative Service (IAS) and Indian Police Service (IPS) officers (in local terms DM [district magistrate] and SP [superintendent of police]) from their castes,[25] and there are very few people from their castes in Class I, Class II, and Class III government jobs[26] as well. Affluent backward castes such as Yadavs, Kurmis, and Kushwahas get the lion's share of OBC reservation.[27] So whenever the government launches any scheme for improving the socio-economic status of MBCs, they fail to avail the benefit of such schemes because of the lack of a network in public offices.

Race against the Bottom

One constant complaint among the respondents was that their exclusion from government jobs has made their situation worse than that of Dalits or Chamars. The abysmal presence of members of the MBCs in public institutions seems to be creating a sense of powerlessness and anxiety among them. The relative improvement of the social and economic status of Dalits has been further increasing anxiety among the MBCs because it has generated a threat of falling to the lowest social order of Hindu society.

The frequent invocation of Dalits for explaining the MBCs' own socio-economic status points to the ingrained hierarchical nature of Indian society, wherein Dalits have been imagined at the bottom of the social order. The MBC castes and communities seem to be not only worried about their declining socio-economic status but also vigilant that their situation should not get worse than that of Dalits, which would place them at the bottom of the social order. Therefore, most of the decisions of the MBCs including the demand for SC status seem to be guided by such strategic considerations (Kumar, 2019b), which can be called the race against the bottom section of Indian society.

Conclusion

The MBCs in north Indian states, particularly UP, have been demanding their inclusion in the SC category. This demand has received momentum since the publication of the report of the Hukum Singh Committee, but it is not very new. Empirical evidence suggests that the history of this demand goes back to the third decade of post-colonial India. However, political parties and caste associations and federations have recently accelerated this demand.

The MBCs have been demanding SC status despite the threat of the stigmatized label of untouchability. This is because these castes have already faced some degree of untouchability at the local level. Also, the practice of untouchability is declining with time. Therefore, instead of bringing the stigma of untouchability, they see their inclusion in the SC category as an instrument for increasing their social status and material empowerment, since it would provide reservation in legislatures, government jobs, educational opportunities; material resources; and the ammunition of the Scheduled Castes and Scheduled Tribes (Prevention of Atrocities) Act against caste-based oppression.

The rapid socio-economic change and political development since the liberalization of Indian economy in 1991 have played a major role in the rising demand for SC status. The neoliberal economic policy has led to the deterioration of the socio-economic conditions of the MBCs, resulting in the decline of social status, which in turn has become a source of anxiety for them. The abysmal presence of these castes in public institutions has prevented them from availing the benefits of state-sponsored schemes. Besides, the improving social and economic status of Dalits is further increasing anxiety among them because it has generated a fear of falling to the lowest level of the Hindu social order; to avoid this, their demand also seems to be guided by strategic considerations of the race against the bottom section of Indian society.

Notes

1. Article 15(1) and (4), article 16(1), (2), and (4), and article 46 in the Constitution deal with backward classes.
2. The Constituent Assembly debate on backwardness and reservation took place mainly on 23 August and 14 October 1949. See 'Constituent Assembly Debates', vols. 9 and 10, https://www.constitutionofindia.net/constitution_assembly_debates (accessed on 20 December 2020).
3. In *R. Chitralekha and Anr v. State of Mysore and Ors*, AIR 1964 SC 1823, the Supreme Court of India had held that 'classes [of citizens] is not synonymous with castes. It may be that for ascertaining whether a particular citizen or a group of citizens belong to a backward class or not, his or their caste may have some relevance, but it cannot be either the sole or the dominant criterion for ascertaining the classes to which he or they belong'. See 1964 AIR 1823, 1964 SCR (6) 368, https://indiankanoon.org/doc/203735/ (accessed on 31 January 2021).
4. Instead of MBCs, the term 'Extremely Backward Classes' (EBCs) is used in Bihar. In Rajasthan, the term Mool or Asli backward classes is used by the MBCs in the ongoing process to differentiate themselves from the OBCs.
5. In 2004, the Mulayam Singh Yadav government made the first attempt for the inclusion of MBCs in the SC list by bringing a resolution in the state assembly. Then, his government amended the UP Public Services Act, 1994, including 17 OBCs in the SC category, but the Allahabad High Court quashed the decision, declaring this move unconstitutional and void since the power to declare any caste as SC rests with the centre (*The Hindu*, 2019).
6. In 2008, the Mayawati government sent another proposal to the union government for the inclusion of 16 MBCs in the SC category. However, this proposal also demanded increasing percentage of SC reservation. The union government did not accept this proposal (Zee News, 2008).

7. In November 2013, the Akhilesh Yadav government send a third proposal for the inclusion of 17 MBCs in the SC category, but the union government once again rejected this proposal in 2015 (*The Pioneer*, 2015).

8. The term 'Dalit' became popular in south-west India with the formation of the Dalit Panthers in 1972. Later, it also got popularized in north India with the formation of the Dalit Shoshit Samaj Sangarsh Samiti (DS4) in 1981. However, its use dates back to the colonial period. Prior to the Government of India Act, 1935, castes and communities that were victims of untouchability were referred to as 'depressed classes'. The Act designated depressed classes as SCs, but the term's Marathi translation, 'Dalit', remained in political use. Even B. R. Ambedkar's party, the All India Scheduled Castes Federation (AISCF), used this term in the Marathi edition of its election manifesto in 1946 (Chandan, 2015).

9. *Sarkari damad* translates to son-in-law of the government.

10. In the Sankhya school of Indian philosophy, every organic body is argued to be made of equal quantities of five constituents called *panchamahabhute*: earth (*kshiti*), water (*jal*), fire (*pavak*), air (*samira*), and space (*gagan*). See Gopal Guru (2012).

11. To derail the process of implementation of the report of the social justice committee, Mulayam Singh Yadav asked members of the legislative assembly (MLAs) from his party to resign collectively so that early elections could be called (Verma, 2001).

12. Mayawati had initially welcomed the move of revision of reservation, but latter opposed it (Verma, 2001).

13. Other members of the committee included J. P. Vishwakarma, Bhupendra Vikram Singh, Ashok Rajbhar, and Mahesh Kumar Gupta (secretary). The committee was tasked with evaluating backwardness among OBCs, as well as Jats, and analysing government schemes implemented for backward castes and plans and policies for their empowerment (Sharma, 2018).

14. For mobilizing the popular support of MBCs, the SP organized 'Samajik Nyay Adhikar Yatras' several times in the last two decades. The first Yatra was held in 2007 before the assembly elections, then in 2009 ahead of the Lok Sabha elections, and again in 2011 before the state assembly elections in March 2012. The last such Yatra was organized from November 2013 to March 2014 ahead of the 2014 Lok Sabha elections (*The Pioneer*, 2015).

15. Pancham Rajbhar, the former general secretary of the All Bhartiya Rajbhar Sangathan, in a telephonic interview with the author on 28 January 2021. According to Pancham Rajbhar, Doodnath Rajbhar was the first MLA from the Rajbhar or Bhar caste in the UP legislative assembly. Documents provided by Pancham Rajbhar confirm that the UP legislative assembly had discussed sending a proposal for including Bhars or Rajbhars in the ST category, but

somehow the official proposal was sent to include this caste in the SC category. The registrar general and census commissioner rejected this proposal on 28 June 1983 on the ground that this caste does not face untouchability.

16. Respondent from the Gaur caste, in an interview with the author on 31 January 2014, in Bandipur, Ambedkar Nagar, UP.

17. Lloyd Rudolph and Susanne Hoeber Rudolph (1967) discuss the role of caste associations and federations.

18. The state governments sent a proposal to the union government because under articles 341 and 342, only the parliament is empowered to add and remove castes in the list of SCs and STs.

19. Respondent from the Nai (barber) caste, in an interview with the author, on 5 February 2014, in Paikoli Bazar, Ambedkar Nagar, UP. He further added that his caste was not included in the proposal sent by the SP government, but the BSP government had included his caste in its proposal.

20. Respondent from the Nai (barber) caste, in an interview the author.

21. Respondents from the Prajapati or Kumhar caste, interview with the author on 2 February 2014, in Bandipur, Ambedkar Nagar, UP.

22. Respondent from the Nishad caste, in an interview with the author on 2 February 2014, in Bandipur, Ambedkar Nagar, UP.

23. Respondent from the Nishad caste, in an interview with the author on 2 February 2014, in Bandipur, Ambedkar Nagar, UP.

24. Taking out the hilly districts of UP, a new state, Uttaranchal, was formed in 2000, which was renamed as Uttarakhand in 2007.

25. Respondents from the Nishad and Gaur castes, in an interview with the author on 2 February 2014, in Bandipur, Ambedkar Nagar, UP.

26. Government jobs in India are categorized as Class I, Class II, Class III, and Class IV. Employees of Class I jobs are ranked the highest in terms of appointment and authority. They are appointed at various managerial positions across government departments. Class II employees do supervisory work. Class III employees do supportive but non-supervisory work at the grassroots level. Class IV employees are bottom-ranked in government work.

27. Cases have been filed on this issue in the Supreme Court, which is exploring various solutions. For a brief summary of possible solutions, see Kumar (2020).

Bibliography

Ambedkar, B. R. 2014 (1936). *Annihilation of Caste*. In *Dr. Babasaheb Ambedkar: Writings and Speeches*, vol. 1, edited by V. Moon. New Delhi: Dr Ambedkar Foundation.

Blunt, E. 1932. *Explaining the Origin & Nature of Depressed & Backward Classes.* Lucknow: Government Branch Press.

Chakrabarty, D. 2018. 'The Dalit Body: A Reading for the Anthropocene'. In *The Empire of Disgust: Prejudice, Discrimination, and Policy in India and the US*, edited by Z. Hasan, A. Z. Huq, M. C. Nussbaum, and V. Verma, 1–20. New Delhi: Oxford University Press.

Chakraborty, S. 2021. 'Kurmis Seek ST Status'. *The Telegraph*, 8 January. https://www.telegraphindia.com/west-bengal/kurmis-seek-scheduled-tribe-status/cid/1803016. Accessed on 30 January 2021.

Chakravarthi, U. 2003. *Gendering Caste: Through a Feminist Lens*. New Delhi: SAGE Publications.

Chandan, S. 2015, 'Ambedkar ki Kuch Durlab Tasverein' (Hindi). BBC Hindi, 14 April. https://www.bbc.com/hindi/india/2015/04/150413_ambedkar_photo_feature_vr?SThisFB%3FSThisFB. Accessed on 30 January 2021.

Devara, R. 2021. 'Demanding "Backwardness": A Reverse Aspiration by Dominant Communities in India'. https://blogs.lse.ac.uk/southasia/2021/01/25/demanding-backwardness-a-reverse-aspiration-by-dominant-communities-in-india/. Accessed on 30 January 2021.

Financial Express. 2007. 'Gujjar, Meena Clash Leaves 5 Dead, 20 Hurt'. 1 June. https://www.financialexpress.com/archive/gujjar-meena-clash-leaves-5-dead-20-hurt/200757/. Accessed on 31 January 2021.

Fraser, N., and K. Olson. 1999. *Adding Insult to Injury*. New York: Verso.

Galanter, M. 1984. *Competing Equalities: Law and the Backward Classes in India.* New Delhi: Oxford University Press.

Goffman, E. 1990. *Stigma: Notes on the Management of Spoiled Identity*. London: Penguin Books.

Government of India. 1955. *Report of the Backward Classes Commission*, vols. 1–3 (K. Kalelkar). Shimla: Government of India Press.

———. 1980. *Report of the Backward Classes Commission*, parts 1 and 2, vols. 1–7 (B. P. Mandal). New Delhi: Government of India Press.

Gudavarthy, A. 2012. 'Can We De-Stigmatise Reservations in India?' *Economic and Political Weekly* 47(6): 55–62.

Guru, G. 2009. *Humiliation: Claims and Context*. New Delhi: Oxford University Press.

Guru, G., and S. Sarukkai. 2012. *The Cracked Mirror: Indian Debate on Experience and Theory*. New Delhi: Oxford University Press.

Halperin, S., and O. Heath. 2017. *Political Research: Methods and Practical Skills.* London: Oxford University Press.

Jaffrelot, C. 2003. *India's Silent Revolution: The Rise of the Lower Castes in North India.* New Delhi: Permanant Black.

Jodhka, S. S. 2010. 'Caste and Politics'. In *The Oxford Companion to Politics in India*, edited by N. G. Jayal and P. B. Mehta, 154–63. New Delhi: Oxford University Press.

Kumar, A. 2019a. 'Forget about Subcategorisation of OBC Reservation, BJP Has Changed Its Stance'. *The Print*, 2 July. https://hindi.theprint.in/opinion/forget-obcs-split-bjp-changes-stance/71754/. Accessed on 31 January 2021.

———. 2019b. 'Taking Hierarchy Seriously: Uncovering the Race against the Bottom'. https://theblahcksheep.com/taking-hierarchy-seriously-uncovering-the-race-against-the-bottom/. Accessed on 30 January 2021.

———. 2020. 'Both Upper Caste and Quota Creamy Layer Cite Merit. But Their Goals Are Different'. *The Print*, 29 July. https://theprint.in/opinion/both-upper-caste-and-quota-creamy-layer-cite-merit-but-their-goals-are-different/470092/. Accessed on 31 January 2021.

Ministry of Tribal Affairs. n.d. 'State/Union Territory-Wise list of Scheduled Tribes in India'. New Delhi: Ministry of Tribal Affairs, Government of India. https://tribal.nic.in/downloads/statistics/LatestListofScheduledtribes.pdf. Accessed on 31 January 2021.

Nussbaum, M. C. 2004. *Hiding From Humanity*. Princeton, NJ: Princeton University Press.

Pai, S. n.d.. 'Understanding "Backwardness" for Affirmative Action: The Most Backward Castes/Classes in Uttar Pradesh'. Unpublished paper.

Pandey, N. 2022. 'Polls Round the Corner, Modi Govt Set to Grant 12th Extension to Justice Rohini Panel on OBCs'. *The Print*, 4 January. https://theprint.in/india/polls-round-the-corner-modi-govt-set-to-grant-12th-extension-to-justice-rohini-panel-on-obcs/794273/. https://tribal.nic.in/downloads/statistics/Latest ListofScheduledtribes.pdf. Accessed on 4 February 2021.

Press Trust of India. 2005. 'Gurjars Demand Reservation in ST Category'. *Times of India*, 22 August. http://timesofindia.indiatimes.com/articleshow/1206778.cms?utm_source=contentofinterest&utm_medium=text&utm_campaign=cppst. Accessed on 4 February 2021.

Rao, M., and F. Frankel. 1989. *Dominance and State Power in Modern India: Decline of a Social Order*. New Delhi: Oxford University Press.

Rudolph, L. I., and S. H. Rudolph. 1967. *The Modernity of Tradition: Political Development in India*. Chicago: Chicago University Press.

Shaha, G., H. Mander, S. Thorat, S. Deshpande, and A. Baviskar. 2006. *Untouchability in Rural India*. New Delhi: SAGE Publications.

Sharma, P. 2018. 'Committee to Evaluate Backwardness among OBCs, Jats, Formed'. *Times of India*, 25 July. https://timesofindia.indiatimes.com/city/bareilly/committee-to-evaluate-backwardness-among-obcs-including-jats-formed/articleshow/64724421.cms. Accessed on 4 February 2021.

Srivastava, P. 2019. 'Allahabad HC Stays Yogi Order to Expand SC List'. *The Telegraph*, 16 September. https://www.telegraphindia.com/india/allahabad-high-court-stays-yogi-order-to-expand-supreme-court-list/cid/1705473. Accessed on 4 February 2021.

The Hindu. 2019. 'UP Adds 17 OBC Groups to Scheduled Castes List'. 30 June. https://www.thehindu.com/news/national/other-states/up-adds-17-obc-groups-to-sc-list/article28231615.ece. Accessed on 4 February 2021.

The Pioneer. 2015. 'Centre Rejects SP Government's MBC Proposal'. 26 August. https://www.dailypioneer.com/2015/state-editions/center-rejects-sp-govts-mbc-proposal.html. Accessed on 4 February 2021.

The Telegraph. 2003. 'Kurmis Clamour for Tribal Status: Demand for ST Listing'. 6 July. https://www.telegraphindia.com/jharkhand/kurmis-clamour-for-tribal-status-demand-for-st-listing/cid/1580243. Accessed on 4 February 2021.

Verma, A. K. 2001. 'BJP's Caste Card'. *Economic and Political Weekly* 36(48): 4452–55.

Zee News. 2008. 'UP Recommends Inclusion of 16 OBC Communities in SC List'. 4 March. https://zeenews.india.com/news/nation/up-recommends-inclusion-of-16-obc-communities-in-sc-list_428277.html. Accessed on 4 February 2021.

23

Measuring Caste-Based Discrimination

Victoire Girard, Cléo Chassonnery-Zaïgouche, and Peter Mayer

Over 70 years after being outlawed, caste-based discrimination and the practice of untouchability against Dalits still regularly make the newspaper headlines. For a recent example, in 2018, in Mumbai, Sudharak Olwe held a photo exhibition on the stories of families who have lost a member as a result of caste hatred. Reported triggers of hate crime range from a phone having a ring tone paying tribute to the famous anti-caste figure B. R. Ambedkar to a lower-caste man speaking with an upper-caste woman. It is usually accepted that caste-based discrimination is a persistent phenomenon within Indian society. An open question, however, is whether the rising consciousness of its extent reflects an increase in the practice of caste-based discrimination or whether it reflects a shift in public attention and sensibility. Answering such a question requires a measure of discrimination to assess how the phenomenon has varied over time and, ideally, across place.

Discrimination is difficult to measure, be it via numbers or by using qualitative approaches. The concept is usually defined as the unequal treatment of equals based on the use of prohibited criteria linked to group identity. Discrimination occurs in a variety of contexts – in the labour market and other markets, during selection processes, or in many social interactions. While the existence of unequal treatment may already be hard to prove, partialling out the causes of that treatment is even harder. The main measurement challenge faced by researchers and policymakers has been the way an outcome is defined and isolated as the result of discriminatory behaviour when other causal factors coexist.

Overcoming the challenge of measuring discrimination is, however, key to be able to assess the extent of the phenomenon, its evolution, and where to target efforts to fight it. Researchers and policymakers in India and beyond have typically resorted to three main approaches. These are decomposition methods, direct data collection, and experimental methods (mainly correspondence and audit studies).

Decomposition methods, coming from Economics and Demography, allow one to analyse differential rates of one outcome (death, income) in relation to the affiliation to a particular demographic group (Kitagawa, 1955; Oaxaca, 1973; Blinder, 1973). In so far as they rely on aggregate data sets and not on the direct observation of behaviours, decomposition methods have been framed as indirect measures of discrimination. As a result, the main limitation of these methods is to isolate the effect of group identity as coming from discrimination alone, rather than an omitted variable bias.

Direct data collection through interviews, ethnographic methods, or qualitative surveys has also been used to determine the extent of discrimination (Dubet, 2013). These methods usually rely on the actors' narratives of their experiences. The main limitation is the subjective aspect of the procedure, as it incorporates a large amount of interpretation and perception. Sociological approaches to institutional discrimination also rely on various types of qualitative and quantitative analyses (Small and Pager, 2020).

Experimental methods, by contrast, have been framed as direct methods to measure discrimination. The main examples of these are correspondence testing (using written applications) and audit studies (which use matched pairs of applicants), whose only difference is their group membership (Anderson, Fryer, and Holt, 2006). Differential treatment of otherwise identical individuals is then attributed to discrimination (Pager, 2007). These methods produce results in a controlled environment, but the external validity of the results in other contexts is difficult to establish.

In this chapter, we focus on and compare the uses of two different sets of data to measure new aspects of the spectrum of caste-based discrimination in India. One data set may be seen as indirect, coming from administrative records of caste-based crimes; the other is direct, based on survey data.

To date, the use of crimes as a proxy to measure discrimination has received limited attention in the literature on discrimination in Economics, which has mostly focused on labour market outcomes. We highlight in the next section the results of various scholars who have used indirect, direct, and experimental methods to measure discrimination against Dalits and its evolution.

The spectrum of discrimination ranges from differential treatment to murder. In particular, Smriti Sharma (2015) refers to crimes targeting members of the Dalit community as hate crimes and notes: 'Hate crimes are characterized by a deliberate intention to victimize an individual because of his membership in a certain social group. The most crucial element that differentiates hate crimes from similar non-hate crimes is the underlying motivation.' Although crime data has received limited attention in the literature so far, this data has interesting features: it is available at low cost, is country-wide, and has occurred over time.

The set of crime data comes from first information reports (FIRs) on caste-based crimes filed at police stations. The Indian police separately record crimes that target Dalits when the perpetrator of the crime belongs to a higher caste. On accounting for the size of the Dalit population, to partial out scale effects, these crimes may be considered as an original measure of one (extreme form) of inter-caste tension (as used in Aneja and Ritadhi, 2020; Bros and Couttenier, 2015; Girard, 2020; Sharma, 2015).

We are particularly interested in two types of crimes: caste-based murders targeting Dalits (henceforth murders) as well as a range of offences including those of a symbolic nature related to caste-based discrimination (henceforth atrocities). Atrocities encompass offences recorded under the headings of the Protection of Civil Rights Act, 1955, and the Scheduled Castes and Scheduled Tribes (Prevention of Atrocities) Act, 1989. The administration refers to Dalits as members of the Scheduled Castes (SC), and we use both terms in this chapter.[1]

If one wishes to consider crimes as a measure of discrimination, we argue that an important distinction must be made between the measure of murders and the measure of atrocities. While both data series are informative about some parts of the spectrum of discrimination practices, the rate of murders across space and time is prone to less reporting and recording bias than the measure of atrocity cases. To show this, we compare the data from administrative records to household survey data. The survey data come from the nationally representative India Human Development Survey (IHDS). The IHDS 2012 (Desai and Vanneman, 2015) indeed contains two direct survey measures of one form of caste-based discrimination, as the survey straightforwardly asks individual respondents whether they practise untouchability or suffer from untouchability practices.

We show how these fundamentally different approaches to the measure of discrimination relate to each other. We argue that caste-based murders are a more relevant measure of caste-based tensions than atrocity cases, given the spatial patterns present in the crime data and their relation to the survey data on untouchability practices in contemporary India. We also put together nearly 40 years of data on murder to explore the historical experience of India's Dalits at moments of mobilization for asserting their rights. We close by discussing that atrocity cases might encompass both a component of crime perpetration and of crime records, and thus part of the increase in atrocity cases may be interpreted as a form of political voice and assertion.

The Measure of Caste-Based Discrimination: Complementary Approaches

Existing knowledge about the phenomenon of caste-based discrimination in India is based on the use of indirect, direct, and experimental approaches. Each of these approaches suffers from the limitations outlined earlier in the chapter. However, each approach allows as to gain partial insight. The combination of results based on the different approaches provides the first important picture of the prevalence and evolution of the different dimensions of discrimination before turning to the discussion of crimes data.

Analyses of caste-based labour discrimination in India may paint a more optimistic evolution than the recent rise of recorded caste-based crimes. In a comprehensive study, Viktoria Hnatkovskay, Amartya Lahiri, and Sourabh Paul (2012) used decomposition methods to analyse caste differences in education, occupations, wages, and consumption patterns for the period 1983–2005 (using data from the National Sample Survey [NSS]). They found a significant convergence in these outcomes. Despite this, convergence levels of discrimination may stay high. Sukhadeo Thorat, S. Madheswaran , and B. P. Vani used the Kitagawa–Oaxaca–Blinder decomposition method to estimate the degree of discrimination experienced by Dalits in India's formal urban employment markets in 2017–18. They found a persistent adverse daily wage gap in both private and public employment of nearly INR 70 for Dalits. The decomposition indicated that 44 per cent of the difference in salaries was due to discrimination. The probability of access to regular employment for Dalits was 0.477 as compared to 0.547 for higher castes; discrimination explained 73 per cent of the difference between castes (Thorat, Madheswaran, and Vani, 2021).

Direct measures of discrimination also paint a contrasting picture. Relying on a direct measure of discrimination, Girard (2018) documents a reduction in the reported practice of one form of caste-based discrimination: caste-based street exclusions. In the Hindi belt, the percentage of Dalit households that declare that they have been prevented from entering some street in their village due to their caste decreased from 65 per cent in 1996 to (still very high) 45 per cent in 2006. Moreover, during the period in which there was a Dalit *pradhan* (head of the village assembly), exclusion of Dalits from village roads fell by about one-fifth. However, the effect disappeared after the term in office of the Dalit *pradhan* ended (Girard, 2018). In the urban setting of the New Delhi region, interviews of 26 individuals who were seeking accommodation reveal that discrimination against Dalits and Muslims produced 'an unending story full of painful experiences, many compromises and undesirable outcomes for the communities concerned' (Thorat and Attewell, 2007: 52).

In parallel, the most recently published correspondence studies show a persistence of discrimination, albeit not widespread. Using names as a signal of caste and religion, Abhijit Banerjee, Marianne Bertrand, Saugato Datta, and Sendhil Mullainathan (2009) found no discrimination against lower castes in recruitment for software jobs, but found a significant level of statistical discrimination in call-centre recruitment, based on the use of caste as a signal of English language ability. Zahra Siddique (2011) finds *some* evidence of discrimination against lower-caste female applicants in front-office administrative jobs. These long-term patterns are usually not discussed in relation to the recent rise in recorded caste-based violence, which we aim to shed light on in this chapter.[2]

Caste-Based Murders

Administrative data – in particular, data on caste-based murders – allow us to further deepen our understanding of the extent and evolution of caste-based discrimination.

The National Crime Records Bureau (NCRB) of the government of India maintains annual records of murders of Dalits, whom the administration refers to as members of the SCs. SC murders are recorded as such, if and only if (*a*) the victim belongs to an SC and (*b*) the perpetrator is from a higher caste (hence neither an SC nor a Scheduled Tribe [ST]). Otherwise, the murder is recorded in the general crime category. SC murders are often interpreted as a signal of targeted caste-based violence.

We use Dalit murders as a benchmark to compare the performance of the two other data sources we are interested in (presented in the sections that follow). We use it as a benchmark in the sense that it is a measurement of the level of violence targeting members of the SCs which exhibits the lowest reporting bias, if only because a body is hard to hide. As a result, it makes it hard to manipulate the data on murder records, much harder than responding with some conscious or unconscious bias to a survey question on the practice or experience of untouchability, and also much harder than assessing a police officer who refuses to file a complaint about an atrocity that has been committed. This approach has been used in recent research in India (Iyer et al., 2012; Bros and Couttenier, 2015; Mayer, 2017; Girard, 2020; Aneja and Ritadhi, 2020). The main limitation of the data from a statistical point of view is that murders of Dalits remain relatively rare events, with 600 murders on average observed in all of India each year.

Thus, in order to observe meaningful variations in this benchmark, we need to resort to units that are large enough. Here we will turn to the 21 major states of India.

Atrocity Cases

With the aim of fighting caste-based discrimination, the Indian state passed the Scheduled Castes and Scheduled Tribes (Prevention of Atrocities) Act, 1989,[3] reinforcing the Protection of Civil Rights Act, 1955. Both laws focus on offences related to the persistence of caste-based practices (that are outlawed today) and the intentional humiliation of members of the lower castes. The Scheduled Castes and Scheduled Tribes (Prevention of Atrocities) Act and the Protection of Civil Rights Act provide stronger punishment than the penal code does, for a range of issues that are crucial from the perspective of human rights and which are also symbolically sensitive – for example, if a member of a higher caste denies access to a water source to a member of an SC or ST (for the complete list, see Sharma, 2015). The atrocity cases that we consider here correspond to caste-based offences listed in the Scheduled Castes and Scheduled Tribes (Prevention of Atrocities) Act or the Protection of Civil Rights Act.

As a result, an increase in atrocity statistics is often interpreted as a signal of caste-based discrimination and increase in tensions. For example, such an interpretation is commonly reported in the press:

> Union minister of state for social justice and empowerment … cautioned Telangana government on the high number of cases booked under the Scheduled Castes and Tribes (Prevention of Atrocities) Act, 1989 after the state formation … At a press conference, he said that the state has a much bigger number of cases compared to many bigger states. (Vadlapatla, 2019)

However, is a higher number of atrocities an unbiased measure of caste violence? Atrocity statistics depend on interactions between at least three actors. The recording of any atrocity indeed requires not only the perpetration of an atrocity, but also the willingness of the victims to report and of the police to record the atrocity – as stressed by Lakshmi Iyer, Anandi Mani, Prachi Mishra, and Petia Topalova (2012) for crimes targeting women. Hence, heightened tensions may not always translate into a higher number of atrocity cases. One crucial element is that caste-based discrimination may prevent the recording of an atrocity case. Discriminatory behaviours by police officers may take the form of attempts to actively prevent the recording of offences or an expectation that discrimination may deter victims from trying to report the offences (Narula, 1999; Deswal, 2013; Kumar, 2015; Minj, 2018).

Survey Declarations on Untouchability

Survey declarations come from the IHDS 2011–12 (Desai and Vanneman, 2015). We create a dummy variable called 'untouchability practice'. It is equal to 1 if a household answers 'yes' to question TR4A ('Do you practise untouchability?'). Based on this data, we compute the average, by state, of the answers on untouchability practice by rural households belonging to a higher caste (excluding the SCs or STs). The variable 'untouchability victim' tells the state-average answer of rural Dalit households to question TR4C ('Have some household members experienced untouchability?'); the dummy is equal to one if the respondent answers 'yes'.

This measure, like every survey measure relying on the interpretation of the respondent, is subject to declaration bias. The measure is also subject to a desirability bias, where one may expect that perpetrators under-report the true extent to which they practise discrimination, as discrimination is both a symbolically loaded phenomenon and an anti-constitutional action. Nonetheless, and despite untouchability and caste-based discrimination having been declared illegal in India for over half a century, it is striking to note that the answers of higher-caste households do reveal a high prevalence of discrimination (see Figure 23.2). In addition, the IHDS results are quite similar to those reported in random phone surveys conducted in Rajasthan, Uttar Pradesh (UP), Delhi, and Mumbai (Coffey et al., 2018) and are broadly comparable to discrimination practised in Gujarat villages (Armstrong et al., 2010). These data shed light on the characteristics of untouchability perpetrators (Borooah, 2017; Thorat and Joshi, 2020).

Comparing the Data Patterns

To compare the different data sources to one another, we consider the data patterns at the state level. Our sample covers 21 large states of India as currently defined.[4] To put the scales into perspective, the states in our sample account for more than 90 per cent of the crimes committed in each of the crime categories.

Data on crimes against members of the SCs are rescaled by the Dalit population in each state, to account for mechanical scale effects. We consider crime rates per 1,00,000 Dalits. Moreover, to be able to compare these data with the survey answers, we focus our analysis on the year 2012.

If crimes against the SCs by higher castes are a mere random subset of other crimes, it should be possible to explain the dynamics of these crimes by accounting for the changing number of general crimes and the share of SCs in the population of a state. However, this is not the case. In 1992, the NCRB recorded two atrocity cases per 1,00,000 Dalit population in our sample of states. Twenty-one years later, in the last year of our sample, the number of atrocities per Dalit population had more than tripled. The absolute increase observed in atrocities could be good news if it were due to an increase in reporting, thus signalling stronger self-confidence or confidence in the system among victims and better access to the police. But this increase might also indicate a backlash effect.

Dalit Murders Correlate with Other Measures of Inter-Caste Tensions; Atrocity Cases Do Not

The visual representation of Dalit murder and atrocity cases casts serious doubt on the suitability of the use of atrocity cases as a measure of caste-based discrimination. Figure 23.1 shows that atrocity cases display no clear pattern, not even in states of the Hindi belt. In contrast, murder records are the highest in the states of the Hindi belt. Rajasthan, for example, records relatively few atrocity cases per 1,00,000 Dalits, while it is one of the states witnessing the highest rate of Dalit murders.

On comparing police cases to household-survey answers, we see that household-survey answers on untouchability, when averaged by state, document a pattern that is strikingly consistent with that of caste-based murders. Figure 23.2 documents that untouchability practices, unlike atrocity cases, are particularly widespread in the Hindi belt and are lower elsewhere. The distribution of answers is quite similar if we look at either the share of higher-caste households declaring that they practise untouchability (focusing on rural households which belong neither to an SC nor to an ST) or the share of rural Dalit households declaring that they suffer from untouchability.

Aside from concerns with respect to social desirability bias in household answers, the daily practice of untouchability may seem far from committing a murder. Yet the murders and household-survey measures appear to display a strong cross-sectional correlation.

For a statistical test of the visual correlations in Figures 23.1 and 23.2, Table 23.1 displays the Pearson correlation matrix. The Spearman correlation rank – discussed in Girard (2020) to account for the limited number of observations – gives similar conclusions. Murder statistics are positively correlated with the declaration by households of either perpetrating untouchability or suffering from untouchability practices. By contrast, atrocity statistics are not significantly correlated with either murder statistics or the households' declarations.

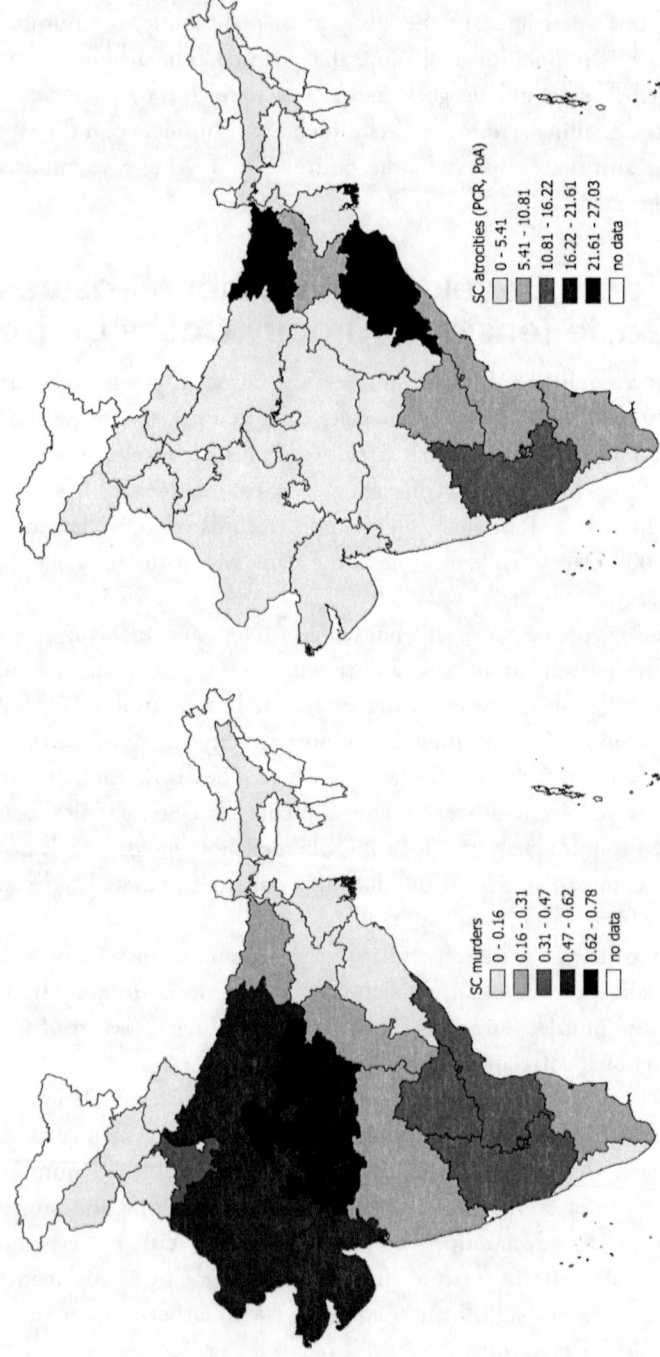

Figure 23.1 Murders of members of the Scheduled Castes (SCs) and atrocity cases, 2012

Source: Authors' calculations based on police FIR and census population data.

Note: Maps not to scale and do not represent authentic international boundaries.

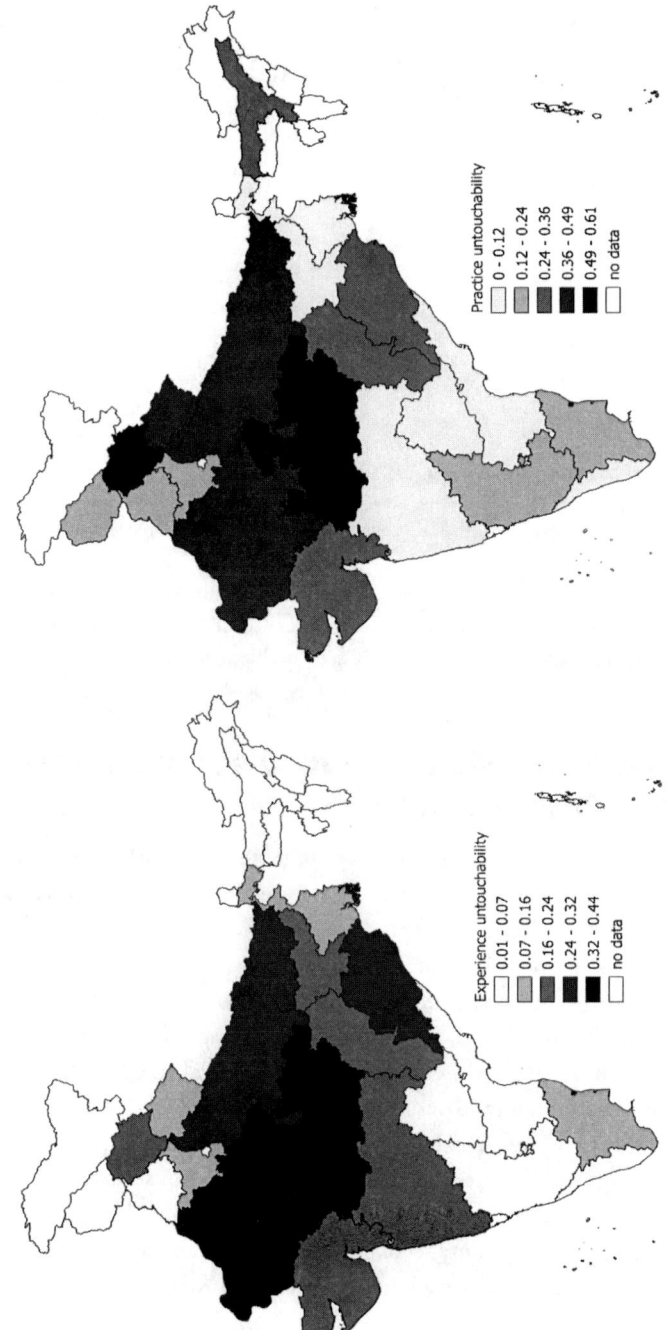

Figure 23.2 Untouchability practice and victims, 2012

Source: Authors' calculations based on India Human Development Survey (IHDS) data.

Note: Maps not to scale and do not represent authentic international boundaries.

Table 23.1   Correlation between police statistics and household survey answers (Pearson pairwise correlation matrix)

	Dalit murders	Atrocities	Practise untouchability	Face untouchability
Dalit murders	1			
Atrocities	−0.065	1		
	(0.779)			
Practise untouchability	0.396	0.232	1	
	(0.076)	(0.311)		
Face untouchability	0.465	0.203	0.650	1
	(0.034)	(0.378)	(0.001)	

Source: Authors' calculations based on FIR, census, and India Human Development Survey (IHDS) data.

Note: p-value in parenthesis. At the state level, the number of murders per 1,00,000 Dalits in 2012 displays a 0.465 correlation with the share of rural Dalits who declare having faced untouchability practices, and this correlation is statistically significant – at the standard 95 per cent threshold.

Trends in Dalit Resistance to Discrimination and Upper-Caste Violence

Another way to approach the information contained in the Dalit murder data is historical. This is the approach we pursue in this section, comparing qualitative accounts on Dalit mobilization and upper-caste reaction to this mobilization with a long-term time series on Dalit murders.

Dalit mobilization and resistance to discrimination by upper castes have met with varied reactions in different places and times. In some, there has been restrained acceptance as in eastern UP (Kapur et al., 2010). In western UP, there was 'considerable discontent, lack of trust and even conflict between caste groups' (Pai, 2001). In western Odisha, Dalit assertion was met by violent upper-caste groups who torched Dalit houses, rendering 45 families homeless (Sarangi et al., 2012). We have seen that there is a strong correlation between the percentage of households which said, in 2011–12, that they discriminated against Dalits and the murder rate of Dalits at that time.

If we examine the time series for murders between 1977 and 2019, we see that the differences between states in murder rates (per 1,00,000) of Dalits are generally consistent in that period; states such as West Bengal and Himachal Pradesh have few, if any, Dalit murders in the period; those with high rates such as UP or Madhya Pradesh tend to be consistently high.[5] But there are also significant changes over time within states which allow us to identify periods of assertion and repression.

Bihar offers a particularly striking case study. In the violent 1980s and 1990s, landowning castes and landlord armies notoriously sought to repress lower-caste assertion by acts of arson, rape, and murder; it is possible to mention only a few here.[6] Notorious massacres of Dalits occurred in Parasbigha and Pipra in 1980 and in Bhagwanpur in 1981 (Prasad, 1982; People's Union for Democratic Rights, 1983). A senior inspector of police said that 50 Dalits were killed (some in police firing) in Patna district alone in 1982–83 (People's Union for Democratic Rights, 1983). Jehanabad district was a centre of organized resistance by Dalits and other rural poor in 1986. Firing by the police in Arwal village killed 20 (Commissioner for Scheduled Castes and Scheduled Tribes, 1988).

In the 1990s, attacks on Dalits increased again. In 1991, landlord armies beheaded 16 Dalit labourers in two villages. In the mid-1990s, a new well-equipped landlord army, the Ranvir Sena, emerged in Bihar. Although it was banned by the Bihar government in 1995, '[t]he organization is believed to have killed more than 400 Dalits in rural Bihar between 1995 and 1999' (*Sabrang India*, 2020). The Sena murdered 21 Dalits in the Batani Tola massacre in 1996 (People's Union for Democratic Rights, 1997); they killed another 59 in Laxmanpur-Bathe the following year (Khan, 2019).[7] In 1999, vicious attacks, again led by the Sena, took place in Shankarbigha and Narayanpur villages (Chaudhuri, 1999).

The explanation of the causes of these acts of assertion and repression offered by B. D. Sharma, the commissioner for Scheduled Castes and Scheduled Tribes, in his 1988 report, applies to most of these murders:

> [D]isputes over wages and occupation of land have been at the root of recurrent killings in Bihar, particularly [in] Jehanabad District … While Jehanabad presents the aftermath of organized initiative by members of the Scheduled Castes to assert their rights … more typical situations in the field pertain to purely local disputes between the stronger groups and the Scheduled Castes. (Commissioner for Scheduled Castes and Scheduled Tribes, 1988: 233)

The violence for the repression of Dalit assertion can be seen with clarity in Figure 23.3. There we see sharp increases in the 1980s and again in the early 1990s.

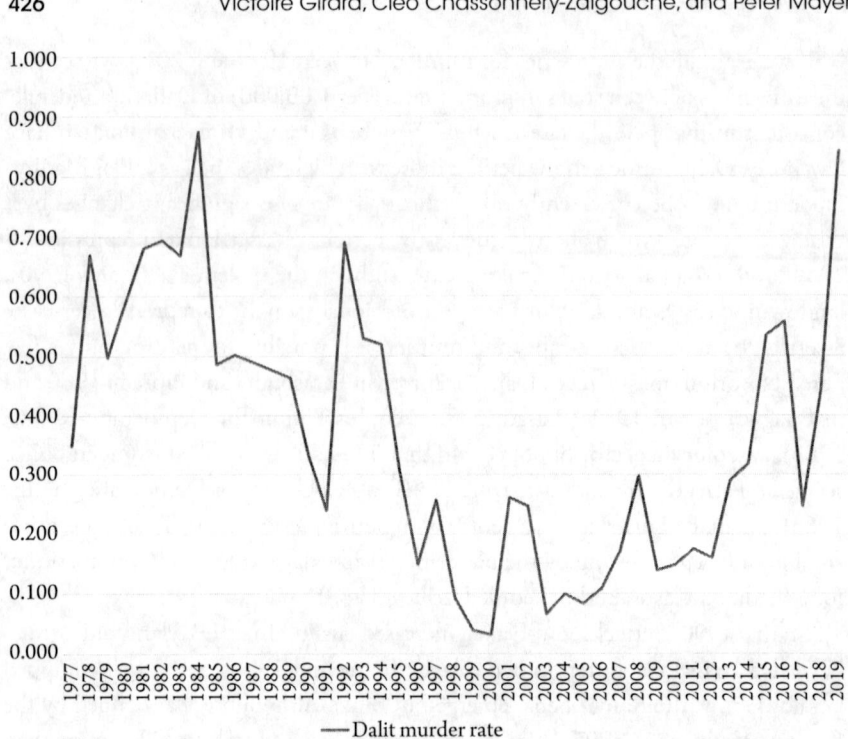

Figure 23.3 Dalit murder rate in Bihar, 1977–2019

Source: Compiled by the authors from National Crime Records Bureau (NCRB) data.

Thereafter, murder rates fell to quite low levels in the early years of the new millennium. What is a cause for concern is that the murder rates of Dalits in Bihar have increased since then, rising to an extremely worrying level in 2019. This upward trend in the murder rates of Dalits in the second decade of the twenty-first century is also noticeable in other states. This trend stands in marked contrast to the murder rates of non-Dalits which in general have been falling since the mid-1990s.

Discussion

The case of caste-based discrimination and violence in India calls for the use of a plurality of data sources and operationalization of specific measurements in relation to the institutions and political context of the country. The set of comparisons provided so far brings out three important observations.

First, murders and survey declarations consistently reveal heterogeneities in inter-caste tensions across states, while atrocity statistics do not. This observation leads us to insist on murder statistics as a useful measure of the evolution of caste-based tensions across space and time. We illustrate the relevance of this data through the case of Bihar. Dalit murders in Bihar, recorded yearly since 1977, provide an accurate mirror to the notorious events of repression against movements for Dalit advancement which took place in the 1980s and early 1990s. This murder measure, however, has limitations, as caste-based murders are overall relatively rare events, calling for supplementation with other measures of caste-based discrimination, leading us to our second point.

Second, state-level averages over two survey measures of untouchability practices reveal spatial patterns that are surprisingly consistent to the patterns of the murder data. This observation suggests that a comparison across time of even a straightforward question on the practice of untouchability by households belonging to higher castes (excluding the SCs and STs) or untouchability faced by Dalit households may bring useful policy insights.

Lastly, statistics from offences recorded under the Scheduled Castes and Scheduled Tribes (Prevention of Atrocities) Act or the Protection of Civil Rights Act – aimed at protecting members of the SCs and STs – should be interpreted with much caution. To take an extreme illustration, these statistics could be at similar levels in (*a*) a place where there is almost no reporting to the police of highly prevalent discriminatory practices and (*b*) a place where there is systematic reporting of the few instances of discriminatory practices.

The understanding of the potential voice component in the reporting and recording of atrocity cases calls for further research. As a preliminary investigation, we can correlate the trust that households have in the police with the number of atrocity cases: the more rural Dalit households trust the police,[8] the higher may be the number of recorded atrocities (a pairwise correlation at 28 per cent, with a p-value at 0.22). In contrast, the correlation between trust in the police and murder reports is, if anything, negative (a negative correlation at 31 per cent, with a p-value at 0.17). These suggestive statistics open an avenue to allow for the recording of atrocity cases to reflect the full extent of the atrocities that they aim at covering and ultimately preventing.

In the contemporary literature on caste in India, it is increasingly argued that in its modern essence, caste is primarily to be understood in terms of hierarchical power and domination. Surinder S. Jodhka (2015: 5) has criticized older approaches which conceptualize caste in terms of tradition and the cultural specificity of India instead of recognizing it as 'a material reality, shaping the economics of inequality and exploitation in the countryside'. Hugo Gorringe, Jodhka, and Opinderjit K. Takhar (2017: 232) also stress that 'the inequalities of caste are as much about power as are those of race, ethnicity or gender'.

Such a claim directly questions the relation between untouchability practices and the political participation of Dalits.

As an illustration, the use of violence to suppress Dalit claims to equal status is evident in Tamil Nadu in

> caste competition ... [especially] at the panchayat level, where local patrons directly encounter the elevation of lower-caste individuals and feel threatened by Dalit assertion and the SC/ST Prevention of Atrocities Act. As a consequence, panchayats reserved for SC candidates have witnessed violence, threats and cancelled elections. Furthermore, many elected Dalits have found it impossible to carry out their work due to upper-caste interference. (Gorringe, 2012)

These observations suggest the need for continuous investment in institutional support against caste-based discrimination. Such institutional support is crucial to allow Dalits to voice the discrimination they face, to make sure that perpetrators cannot engage in illegal actions without sanctions, and to hopefully slowly reduce, if not erradicate, the extent and severity of discriminatory practices.

Notes

1. The term 'Scheduled Castes' is used in the Constitution of India.
2. For further reviews of the literature, see Ashwani Deshpande (2011), Sukhadeo Thorat and Katherine Newman (2010), and Kaivan Munshi (2019).
3. Since 1850, this is the 22nd law that banned caste-based discrimination in India.
4. India comprises 28 states and 8 union territories. The states included in our sample are Andhra Pradesh, Assam, Bihar, Chhattisgarh, Gujarat, Haryana, Himachal Pradesh, Jammu and Kashmir, Jharkhand, Karnataka, Kerala, Madhya Pradesh, Maharashtra, Odisha, Punjab, Rajasthan, Tamil Nadu, Telangana, Uttar Pradesh (UP), Uttarakhand, and West Bengal. As Telangana became a separate entity from Andhra Pradesh only in 2014, which is subsequent to the data we are using, we attribute to Telangana the values of Andhra Pradesh.
5. In every state, the murder rate for non-Dalits is much higher than that for Dalits. At the height of oppression by landlord armies in Bihar in 1983, for example, the non-Dalit murder rate was more than five times that for Dalits (3.641 per 1,00,000 versus 0.693).
6. People's Union for Democratic Rights (1983) and Smita Narula (1999) summarize the events in Bihar, including the role of the Ranvir Sena.
7. The accused in both massacres were acquitted on appeal.
8. The information on trust in the police comes from the IHDS 2005 and 2012 surveys. It is a dummy variable equal to 1 if the respondent answered 'a great

deal' to the question 'I am going to name some institutions in the country. As far as the people running these institutions are concerned, would you say you have', where the institution at stake is 'the police – to enforce the law', and possible answers are 'a great deal of confidence = 1', 'only some confidence = 2', and 'hardly any confidence at all = 3'.

Bibliography

Anderson, L. R., R. G. Fryer, and C. A. Holt. 2006. 'Discrimination: Experimental Evidence from Psychology and Economics'. In *Handbook on the Economics of Discrimination*, edited by W. M. Rodgers III, 97–115. Cheltenham, Gloucestershire: Edward Elgar Publishing.

Aneja, A., and S. K. Ritadhi. 2020. 'How Representation Reduces Minority-targeted Crime: Evidence from Scheduled Castes in India'. *Journal of Law, Economics, and Organization*. DOI: 10.1093/jleo/ewab028.

Armstrong, D., C. Davenport, A. M. Klasing, M. Macwan, M. Pradeep, S. Vania, A. Stam, and M. K. Varma. 2010. *Understanding Untouchability: A Comprehensive Study of Practices and Conditions in 1589 Villages*. Washington, DC: Navsarjan Trust and Robert F. Kennedy Center for Justice and Human Rights.

Banerjee, A., M. Bertrand, S. Datta, and S. Mullainathan. 2009. 'Labor Market Discrimination in Delhi: Evidence from a Field Experiment'. *Journal of Comparative Economics* 37(1): 14–27.

Blinder, A. S. 1973. 'Wage Discrimination: Reduced Form and Structural Estimates'. *Journal of Human Resources* 8(4): 436–55.

Borooah, V. K. 2017. 'Caste and Regional Influences on the Practice of "Untouchability" in India'. *Development and Change* 48(4): 746–74.

Bros, C., and M. Couttenier. 2015. 'Untouchability, Homicides and Water Access'. *Journal of Comparative Economics* 43(3): 549–58. DOI: 10.1016/j.jce.2014.12.001.

Chaudhuri, K. 1999. 'Carnage in Narayanpur'. *Frontline*, 27 February–12 March.

Coffey, D., P. Hathi, N. Khurana, and A. Thorat. 2018. 'Explicit Prejudice: Evidence from a New Survey'. *Economic and Political Weekly* 53(1): 46–54.

Commissioner for Scheduled Castes and Scheduled Tribes. 1988. *Report of the Commissioner for Scheduled Castes and Scheduled Tribes: 28th Report, 1986–87*. New Delhi: Commission for Scheduled Castes and Tribes, Government of India.

Desai, S., and R. Vanneman. 2015. *India Human Development Survey-II (IHDS-II), 2011–12*. Ann Arbor, MI: Inter-University Consortium for Political and Social Research.

Desai, S., R. Vanneman, and National Council of Applied Economic Research. 2005. *India Human Development Survey (IHDS)*. ICPSR22626-v8. Ann Arbor, MI: Inter-university Consortium for Political and Social Research.

Deshpande, A. 2011. *The Grammar of Caste: Economic Discrimination in Contemporary India*. New Delhi: Oxford University Press.

Deswal, V. 2013. 'Burking of Crimes by Refusal to Register FIR in Cognizable Offences'. *Journal of the Indian Law Institute* 55(3): 361–75.

Dubet, F. 2013. *Pourquoi Moi? L'expérience des Discriminations*. Paris: Seuil.

Girard, V. 2018. 'Don't Touch My Road. Evidence from India on Affirmative Action and Everyday Discrimination'. *World Development* 103(C): 1–13. DOI: 10.1016/j.worlddev.2017.10.008.

———. 2020. 'Stabbed in the Back? Mandated Political Representation and Murders'. *Social Choice and Welfare* 56(4): 595–634. DOI: https://doi.org/10.1007/s00355-020-01294-8.

Gorringe, H. 2012. 'Caste and Politics in Tamil Nadu'. *Seminar* 633. https://www.india-seminar.com/2012/633/633_hugo_gorringe.htm. Accessed on 13 October 2022.

Gorringe, H., S. S. Jodhka, and O. K. Takhar. 2017. 'Caste: Experiences in South Asia and Beyond'. *Contemporary South Asia* 25(3): 230–37. DOI: 10.1080/09584935.2017.1360246.

Hnatkovska, V., A. Lahiri, and S. Paul. 2012. 'Castes and Labor Mobility'. *American Economic Journal: Applied Economics* 4(2): 274–307.

Iyer, L., A. Mani, P. Mishra, and P. Topalova. 2012. 'The Power of Political Voice: Women's Political Representation and Crime in India'. *American Economic Journal: Applied Economics* 4(4): 165–93. DOI: 10.1257/app.4.4.165.

Jodhka, S. 2015. 'Ascriptive Hierarchies: Caste and Its Reproduction in Contemporary India'. *Current Sociology* 64(2): 228–43. DOI: 10.1177/0011392115614784.

Kapur, D., C. B. Prasad, L. Pritchett, and D. S. Babu. 2010. 'Rethinking Inequality: Dalits in Uttar Pradesh in the Market Reform Era'. *Economic and Political Weekly* 45(35): 39–49.

Khan, M. I. 2019. 'Elections 2019: Two Decades after Worst Dalit Massacre in Jehanabad, Kin Still Await Justice'. NewsClick. https://www.newsclick.in/Jehanabad-Dalit-Massacre-Bihar-Elections-2019. Accessed on 23 January 2021.

Kitagawa, E. M. 1955. 'Components of a Difference Between Two Rates'. *Journal of the American Statistical Association* 50(272): 1168–94.

Kumar, T. K. V. 2015. 'Impact of Demographic Characteristics of Crime Victim on Interaction with Police in India: Gender, Caste, Class and Police Response'. *South Asian Survey* 22(1): 54–77. DOI: https://doi.org/10.1177/0971523117714091.

Mayer, P. 2017. 'The Better Angels of Their Natures? The Declining Rate of Homicides against India's Dalits'. *Studies in Indian Politics* 5(2): 1–22. DOI: 10.1177/2321023017727956.

Minj, J. 2018. 'Offences against Schedule Castes and Schedule Tribes'. *Journal of Human Rights Law and Practice* 1(1): 12–17.

Munshi, K. 2019. 'Caste and the Indian Economy'. *Journal of Economic Literature* 57(4): 781–834.

Narula, S. 1999. *Broken People, Caste Violence Against India's 'Untouchables'*. New York: Human Rights Watch.

Oaxaca, R. L. 1973. 'Male–Female Wage Differentials in Urban Labor Markets'. *International Economic Review* 14(3): 693–709.

Pager, D. 2007. 'The Use of Field Experiments for Studies of Employment Discrimination: Contributions, Critiques, and Directions for the Future'. *Annals of the American Academy of Political and Social Science* 609(1): 104–33. DOI: 10.1177/0002716206294796.

Pai, S. 2001. 'Social Capital, Panchayats and Grass Roots Democracy: Politics of Dalit Assertion in Uttar Pradesh'. *Economic and Political Weekly* 36(8): 645–54.

People's Union for Democratic Rights. 1983. *And Quiet Flows the Ganga: A Documentary Report on the Political Killings in Rural Bihar*. New Delhi: Peoples Union for Democratic Rights.

———. 1997. *Agrarian Conflict in Bihar and the Ranbir Sena*. Delhi: People's Union for Democratic Rights.

Prasad, N. 1982. *Rural Violence: A Case Study of Parasbigha and Pipra Violence in Bihar*. Varanasi: Gandhian Institute of Studies.

Sabrang India. 2020. 'Outlawed Caste-based Militia Ranvir Sena Issues Death Threats Over Social Media in Bihar!'. 30 June. https://sabrangindia.in/article/outlawed-caste-based-militia-ranvir-sena-issues-death-threats-over-social-media-bihar. Accessed on 24 January 2021.

Saranagi, D., K. Sunami, Nigam, and R. Padhi. 2012. 'The Price of Dalit Assertion: On the Burning Down of Dalit Houses in Lathore, Odisha'. *Economic and Political Weekly* 47(35): 19–22.

Sharma, S. 2015. 'Caste-Based Crimes and Economic Status: Evidence from India'. *Journal of Comparative Economics* 43(1): 204–26. DOI: 10.1016/j.jce.2014.10.005.

Siddique, Z. 2011. 'Evidence on Caste Based Discrimination'. *Labour Economics* 18: S146–S159.

Small, M. L., and D. Pager. 2020. 'Sociological Perspectives on Racial Discrimination'. *Journal of Economic Perspectives* 34(2): 49–67.

Thorat, A., and O. Joshi. 2020. 'The Continuing Practice of Untouchability in India: Patterns and Mitigating Influences'. *Economic and Political Weekly* 55(2): 36–45.

Thorat, S., and K. S. Newman. 2010. 'Introduction: Economic Discrimination, Concept, Consequences, and Remedies'. In *Blocked by Caste: Economic Discrimination in Modern India*, edited by S. Thorat and K. S. Newman, 208–29. New Delhi: Oxford University Press.

Thorat, S., and P. Attewell. 2007. 'The Legacy of Social Exclusion: A Correspondence Study of Job Discrimination in India'. *Economic and Political Weekly* 42(41): 4141–45.

Thorat, S., S. Madheswaran, and B. P. Vani. 2021. 'Employment Discrimination and Its Impact on Poverty: Caste and Labour Market'. *Economic and Political Weekly* 56(21). https://www.epw.in/journal/2021/21/special-articles/caste-and-labour-market.html. Accessed on 22 October 2022.

Vadlapatla, S. 2019. 'Check High Number of SC/ST Act Cases in Telangana: Ramdas Athawale to Chief Minister'. *Times of India*, 21 September.

24

Dalit Suicides in India

Vikas Arya, Andrew Page, Gregory Armstrong, and Peter Mayer

As the previous chapters have highlighted, Dalits in India have historically endured marginalization and been among the most disadvantaged populations in the country. Since suffering has been known as one of the major reasons for voluntarily ending one's life (Minois, 2001), suicide rates among Dalit populations are expected to be high, especially compared to 'general' populations.

Suicide is a serious, yet preventable public health issue. Initially recognized as an entirely psychological phenomenon, suicide is now ubiquitously accepted as a multifaceted issue with various social, cultural, psychological, and biological aspects usually underlying the causal pathway. One of the indicators of suicide being a multidimensional issue is the consistent variation observed within and between countries and regions by different socio-demographic variables, instead of simply fluctuating between areas with higher or lower prevalence of mental health issues. In 2016, there were an estimated 7,93,000 suicides worldwide, a rate of one suicide every 40 seconds (World Health Organization [WHO], 2016). The global suicide rate in 2016 was 10.6 per 1,00,000 population, with higher male suicide rates (13.5 per 1,00,000 population) than female (7.7 per 1,00,000 population) (WHO, 2016). Overall, approximately 79 per cent of all suicides occurred in low-and-middle-income countries (LMICs).

India has some of the highest suicide rates in the world. According to the Global Burden of Disease (GBD) study estimates, in 2016, there were more than 2,00,000 suicides in India accounting for 25 per cent of male and 37 per cent of female suicides globally (Dandona et al., 2018). Rates in India are higher among males (21 per 100,000) than females (15 per 100,000), and while rates have declined among females, male rates have remained stable for the last 30 years (Dandona et al., 2018). Nevertheless, in 2016, India had the third highest female suicide rate in the world (WHO, 2016). Suicide rates in India are known to differ by socio-demographic factors such as geography, age, sex, marital status, method, and markers of educational achievement (Mayer, 2010; Arya et al., 2018; Arya et al., 2019a). While studies in the past have hypothesized that suicide rates in India likely differ by religion and caste status, very few studies have reported suicide rates by religion, while almost none have reported them by caste status. Importantly, barring a solitary study (Arya et al., 2019b), none of the recent studies have reported national or state-wise suicide rates in India by religion or caste status.

Paucity of Data on Dalit Suicides

Why have studies largely ignored reporting suicide rates by religion and caste status at the national or state level? A key explanation relates to the lack of recording of suicide cases in India by religion and caste status. The National Crime Records Bureau (NCRB) is a government organization that records and reports crime data based on police reports collected from each state and union territory in India. The NCRB has been reporting on suicide cases in India since 1967 and is the only national-level, publicly available data source on suicide in the country. Suicide data in India are first recorded at the local level, then aggregated at the district level, then at the state level, and finally at the national level, which are then presented in NCRB reports (NCRB, 2018). While the NCRB provides suicide cases stratified by factors such as sex, age, and method, among others, they do not report suicides by religion or caste status. The reasons for this are not clear, but it might be because of the perceived sensitivities around religion and caste status and fears relating to the politicization of suicide in India (Mayer, 2010).

There is another data source for suicides in India which is based on the Sample Registration System (SRS). Despite the Registration of Births and Deaths Act of 1969, which makes it compulsory to report births and deaths, birth and death registrations are under-enumerated in most Indian states (SRS, 2020). To counter this problem, the SRS, which uses the verbal autopsy method to record all the births and deaths in a nationally representative sample of 1.1 million households, came to be used (SRS, 2020). The SRS recorded suicide deaths between the years 2004 and 2013. While SRS data better enumerates suicide deaths than NCRB data (Arya et al., 2020), verbal autopsy data are not publicly available. Furthermore, similar to NCRB reports, the SRS and GBD data do not report suicide cases by religion or caste status.

Dalit Suicides in 2014 and 2015

In 2014 and 2015, the NCRB recorded information on the caste and religion of suicides for the first time; however, they are yet to publish this information.

Arya, one of the authors of this chapter, managed to obtain this information under the Right to Information (RTI) Act (Roberts, 2010).[1] The NCRB provided suicide cases by religion and caste status for 2014 and 2015, stratified by all states and union territories but not by any other demographic factors normally presented in the publicly available NCRB reports (for example, sex and age).

The NCRB data showed that there were a total of 38,106 Dalit suicides in India in 2014 and 2015 with a national rate of 9.4 per 1,00,000 population. In contrast to the hypothesis that Dalits might have the highest suicide rates, higher suicide rates were noted among members of the Scheduled Tribes (STs) (10.7 per 1,00,000) and 'general' populations (15.0 per 100,000) (Arya et al., 2019b). However, there was substantial geographic heterogeneity in Dalit suicide rates observed across different regions in India (Figure 24.1), with

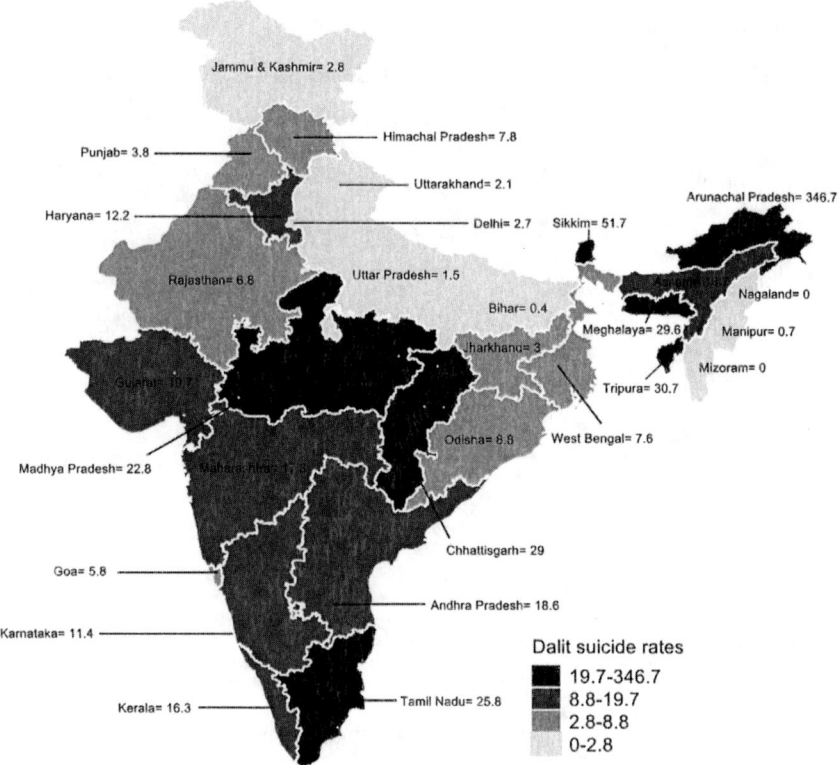

Figure 24.1   Dalit suicide rates in India, 2014–15

Source: Map compiled by the authors.

Note: Map not to scale and does not represent authentic international boundaries.

some of the highest Dalit suicide rates observed in the states of Chhattisgarh, Madhya Pradesh, and Tamil Nadu. Some of the north-eastern states also noted high Dalit suicide rates, but that is due to the small Dalit population numbers in this region; also the number of Dalit suicides in this region were generally low (Table 24.1).

Table 24.1   State-wise Dalit suicide rates and Dalit population percentage, 2014–15

	Dalit suicide rate/1,00,000 (95 per cent CI)	Dalit population by state (per cent)
North India		
Jammu and Kashmir	2.8 (2.1–3.7)	7.4
Himachal Pradesh	7.8 (6.9–8.8)	25.2
Punjab	3.8 (3.5–4.1)	31.9
Chandigarh	13.3 (10.5–16.7)	18.9
Uttarakhand	2.1 (1.6–2.6)	18.8
Haryana	12.2 (11.5–12.9)	20.2
Delhi	2.7 (2.3–3.1)	16.8
Rajasthan	6.8 (6.5–7.1)	17.8
Uttar Pradesh	1.5 (1.4–1.5)	20.7
North–east India		
Sikkim	51.7 (35.1–73.3)	4.6
Arunachal Pradesh	346.7 (258.9–454.6)	0.6
Nagaland	–	–
Manipur	0.7 (0.0–4.0)	3.4
Mizoram	–	0.1
Tripura	30.7 (27.7–33.8)	17.8
Meghalaya	29.6 (12.8–58.4)	0.6
Assam	18.7 (17.5–20.0)	6.9

(*Contd*)

Table 24.1   *(Contd)*

	Dalit suicide rate/1,00,000 (95 per cent CI)	Dalit population by state (per cent)
East India		
Bihar	0.4 (0.4–0.5)	15.7
West Bengal	7.6 (7.3–7.8)	23.5
Jharkhand	3.0 (2.6–3.4)	12.1
Odisha	8.8 (8.3–9.3)	17.1
Central India		
Chhattisgarh	29.0 (27.6–30.5)	12.8
Madhya Pradesh	22.8 (22.0–23.7)	15.6
West India		
Gujarat	19.7 (18.7–20.6)	6.7
Daman and Diu	5.4 (0.1–30.0)	2.5
Dadara and Nagar Haveli	26.3 (7.2–67.4)	1.8
Maharashtra	17.3 (16.8–17.8)	11.8
Goa	5.8 (1.6–15.0)	1.8
South India		
Andhra Pradesh	18.6 (18.1–19.1)	16.2
Karnataka	11.4 (10.9–11.9)	17.1
Lakshadweep	–	–
Kerala	16.3 (15.4–17.3)	9.1
Tamil Nadu	25.8 (25.1–26.4)	20
Pondicherry	54.0 (47.7–60.8)	15.7
Andaman and Nicobar Islands	–	–
Total	**9.4 (9.3–9.5)**	**16.6**

Source: Arya et al. (2019b).

Table 24.2   Dalit suicides and social discrimination

Correlations	
Social discrimination variables (per cent)	**Scheduled Caste (SC) suicide rate, 2014–15**
Households practising untouchability	Pearson correlation = –0.029
	Significance (2-tailed) = 0.908
Dalits who have experienced untouchability	Pearson correlation = –0.049
	Significance (2-tailed) = 0.846
Dalit women with body mass index (BMI) < 18.5, 2005–06	Pearson correlation = –0.034
	Significance (2-tailed) = 0.893
Dalit infant mortality rate, 2005–06	Pearson correlation = –0.237
	Significance (2-tailed) = 0.345
Dalit with no latrine, 2008–09	Pearson correlation = –0.038
	Significance (2-tailed) = 0.881
Rural poverty ratio, 2004–05	Pearson correlation = –0.180
	Significance (2-tailed) = 0.474
Dalit population, 2011	Pearson correlation = –0.421
	Significance (2-tailed) = 0.082

Source: Desai (2015); Mehrotra et al. (2011); EPW Research Foundation (2011); Census of India (2011).

Note: This and the following table do not include Goa, Jammu and Kashmir, Assam, Sikkim, the union territories, and the states of north-east India.

Given the disadvantaged position of Dalit populations in Indian society, it is surprising to find lower suicide rates among Dalit populations compared to 'general' populations. Furthermore, there was no correlation between Dalit suicide rates and the practice or experience of untouchability or with measures of economic deprivation (Table 24.2).

Minority Status and Dalit Suicides

Emile Durkheim's (1897) work on suicide, which is perhaps the most influential exploration of suicide in the field of science in general, and sociology in particular, argued that in certain circumstances minority status might have a protective effect on suicide (for example, the hostility faced by minority populations might 'toughen' them). By contrast, the minority stress theory posits that the discrimination and hostile social environment toward minority populations are associated with increased mental health problems and suicidal behaviour (Meyer, 2003). In the Indian context, it is conceivable that Dalits residing in regions with higher Dalit populations endure a less hostile and stressful environment compared to regions with a lower percentage of overall Dalit populations. Social deviancy theories also support this argument where social deviancy is not related to individual deviant behaviour but is based on interpersonal relationships constructed through the availability of peer groups (Wechsler and Pugh, 1967).

Despite these hypothesized relationships, we find that there was only a weak negative correlation between the state-wise Dalit population percentage and Dalit suicide rates (Table 24.2). This supports a general pattern of higher Dalit suicide rates among states with a lower percentage of Dalit populations compared to states with higher Dalit populations (this was the case for the ST and the Other Backward Classes (OBC) categories as well) (Arya et al., 2019b).

Dalit Suicide and Education

Dalit suicide rates were found to be positively corelated with some of the indicators of human development (for example, Dalit enrolment percentage in higher-secondary education) (Table 24.3). This is a curious finding given that increasing education is generally perceived as empowering. Furthermore, generally, suicide rates are higher among less educated groups compared to more educated groups, especially in high-income countries (Phillips and Hempstead, 2017). However, higher levels of education have been associated with higher suicide rates in India (Mayer, 2010; Patel et al., 2012; Arya et al., 2018). One reason for this disparity might be that literacy rates are an indicator of modernization and social change in India. Modernization and social change might result in an increasing gap between expectations and reality, especially among Indian youth, leading to higher suicide rates (Arya et al., 2018). For example, while female literacy rates have improved dramatically over the past decades, India continues to remain a largely patriarchal society, which might be resulting in increasing stress and suicidal behaviour among younger females in the country (Petroni, Patel, and Patton, 2015). It is conceivable that Dalit populations with higher levels of education are facing similar issues as the 'general' populations with higher education levels, resulting in increased risk of suicide.

It is also possible that as Dalit students attain higher levels of education, they constitute smaller percentages of the population at those levels, so their

Table 24.3 Dalit suicides and human development

Correlations	
Education variables (per cent)	**Scheduled Caste (SC) suicide rate, 2014–15**
Dalit primary enrolment ratio, 2007–08	Pearson correlation = 0.570* Significance (2-tailed) = 0.013
Dalit upper-primary enrolment ratio, 2007–08	Pearson correlation = 0.591** Significance (2-tailed) = 0.010
Dalit secondary or higher secondary enrolment ratio, 2007–08	Pearson correlation = 0.662** Significance (2-tailed) = 0.003
Dalits in higher education, 2018–19	Pearson correlation = 0.329 Significance (2-tailed) = 0.182

Source: Mehrotra et al. (2011); Census of India (2011); Planning, Monitoring, and Statistics Bureau (2019).
Note: *Correlation is significant at the 0.05 level (2-tailed). **Correlation is significant at the 0.01 level (2-tailed).

supportive communities become smaller and their risk of suicide rises. Rakesh K. Maurya (2018: 24–25) reports:

> Participants [in a university in Uttar Pradesh] shared that they rarely face or feel caste prejudice and discrimination during elementary, middle, or high school from fellow UC [upper-caste] students. Caste-based social identities of students take shape gradually as they move towards higher education when UC students start harboring a feeling of caste-based superiority over Dalit students.

Indeed, discrimination against students belonging to Dalit or ST categories at universities has been documented previously. It has been argued that some suicide cases (for example, Rohith Vemula and Payal Tadvi) were a direct result of discrimination and abuse faced by the departed (Acharya, 2019). The coverage of such suicides by the media in India is of special concern. Indian media often reports suicides in lurid detail and ignores international best practice by presenting explicit details of suicide methods (Mayer, 2010). Research suggests that such sensationalized and simplistic media coverage of suicide may lead to 'copycat suicides' (Westerlund, Schaller, and Schmidtke, 2009). While some researchers argue that copycat suicides based on media reporting are mostly limited to celebrity suicides, most researchers agree that thoughtless media coverage of any suicide can potentially lead to 'copycat suicides' (Westerlund, Schaller, and Schmidtke, 2009). In the context of Dalit suicides, other Dalits in similar positions, as some of the departed mentioned previously (for example, facing harassment at university), might feel 'encouraged' to follow a similar route as a 'way out' of abusive or disadvantaged situations while also perceiving their act as a sacrifice for the greater cause. What are almost always lacking in the Indian media are links to suicide prevention organizations or helpline numbers for anyone who feels distress after reading an article.

Oppressed Minorities and Suicide

It is an obvious error to refer to 'Dalits' as though all are identical. The historical and regional experiences of India's many Dalit communities are diverse, and this observation is equally true of suicides. Dalit suicide rates are virtually identical to those of the general populations amongst whom they live ($r = 0.814$; sig @ 0.000).

Although there is overwhelming evidence that Dalits in all parts of India experience discrimination, there is an apparent paradox concerning suicide: where overt discrimination is highest, mainly in north India, Dalit suicide rates are very low (it must be noted here that suicide rates in general are low in north India compared to those in other parts of India). These are the same states where murder rates of Dalits are the highest (see Chapter 23). These relationships suggest some plausibility of Andrew F. Henry and James F. Short's 'frustration–aggression' hypothesis that where external constraints are greatest, aggression is directed outward, against others. Conversely, where external constraints are lower, these forces are directed inward (Henry and Short, 1954).

We know almost nothing about either the risk factors for suicides among Dalits or the protective factors. We find it instructive, therefore, to consider what is known of these factors, especially for adolescents and young adults, in the African-American community in the United States (Molock et al., 1994).

Historically, African Americans had low rates of suicide. According to Kevin E. Early and Ronald L. Akers (1993), suicide was actually thought to be a 'White thing' which did not happen in the African-American community. Since the 1960s, adolescent African-American suicide rates have been rising and are now virtually the same as those of European Americans (Droege, Robinson, and Jason, 2017; Oh et al., 2020). Rheeda Walker (2020) suggests that young African Americans may be 'hidden' suicide ideators, who find it difficult to share their thoughts with others or to seek counselling or other assistance.

Some of the risk factors for suicide among African Americans include the experience of racism, poverty, exposure to community violence – especially police violence – discrimination in access to education, and the strains of having to negotiate 'dual cultural contexts' (Oh et al., 2020; Walker et al., 2008). Conversely, factors of preservation include dense social networks and family support, high self-esteem, higher economic status, and religiosity (Droege, Robinson, and Jason, 2017).

If these factors of risk and preservation seem strongly parallel with those faced by Dalits in India, of equal relevance are some of the policy responses found in the United States. These include appropriate training for health and mental health professionals, access to such professionals – especially from one's own background – and appropriate online resources (Oh et al., 2020; Walker, 2020).

In India, suicide prevention remains largely at the zero-kilometre marker. Despite the urging of some of the nation's most distinguished psychiatrists, there is still no national suicide prevention strategy such as those developed elsewhere (Vijaykumar, 2007; Mayer, 2016). Given the paucity of mental health facilities or trained psychiatrists for most of India's population, especially its rural population, that there is no specific national strategy for the prevention of Dalit suicides requires no further comment.

This chapter highlights that there is an acute lack of data on Dalit suicides in India. The available government data from 2014–15 shows that in most states Dalit suicide rates are lower than suicide rates among 'general' populations. However, Dalit suicide rates are generally higher among regions with smaller Dalit populations (compared to regions with larger Dalit populations), perhaps reflecting greater hostility in these regions.

One of the most enduring observations in the study of suicide is that suicide rates are lowest in the most traditional societies and tend to rise with modernization and more individualistic outlooks (Durkheim, 1897). We can observe this in the geographic distribution of Dalit suicides in India which shows that suicide rates are lowest in the states of north India and higher in the south (Figure 24.1). The persistence of the multi-generational or 'joint' family serves as a proxy for the degree to which traditional social ideas remain dominant. Household size appears to be a 'lagging indicator': traditional attitudes seem to persist, even as household sizes shrink over time. Household sizes are largest in northern states such as Uttar Pradesh, Bihar, Haryana, and Rajasthan; they are smallest in Tamil Nadu, Andhra Pradesh, Kerala, and West Bengal. The correlation between the Dalit suicide rate in 2014–15 and the average household size in this period is moderately strong and in the predicted direction, but it is not statistically significant ($r = -0.368$; not sig @ 0.133). The correlation is stronger with family sizes in earlier years (2005: $r = -0.702$; sig @ 0.002; 1994: $r = -0.720$; sig@ 0.002). Madhya Pradesh and especially Chhattisgarh (which was separated from Madhya Pradesh in 2000), both of which have larger average family sizes and relatively high Dalit suicide rates, appear as significant exceptions to the general pattern of geographic distribution. Larger household size in 2015 is also positively correlated with the practice of untouchability (r = 0.539; sig @ 0.021) and the experience of untouchability (r = 0.573; sig @ 0.013).

Access to education is often associated with all aspects of human development. Generally, higher suicide rates in India are found to be associated with increases in education level. Dalit suicide rates, too, were found to be associated with measures of higher levels of education. It is possible that the reasons behind the association between higher suicide and higher education rates are impacting all population groups, including Dalits. However, it is also possible that this is because as Dalit students attain higher levels of education, their entry meets with hostility and their support systems become smaller (as they constitute smaller percentages of the population at higher education levels), increasing their suicide risk.

To that end, policymakers should turn their focus back to the recommendations from the Thorat report, which, despite its compelling findings, seems to have been relegated to the annals of the past. In 2007, the then prime minister of India, Manmohan Singh, commissioned the Thorat committee to investigate allegations of differential treatment based on the caste status of students in the All India Institute of Medical Sciences (AIIMS), Delhi (Thorat, Shyamprasad, and Srivastava, 2007). The committee found a myriad of problems related to caste-based discrimination and consequently made recommendations to tackle those issues, including remedial coaching in English; equal opportunity cells; sensitivity training for academics, administrative staff, and students; and objectivity in examinations for Dalit students. However, these recommendations are yet to be implemented in any of the Indian universities, including AIIMS. It is imperative that these recommendations are implemented in universities, not least because they might help curb suicides among Dalit or ST students. These recommendations can also be adopted in workplaces (for example, sensitivity training and objectivity for job appraisals), which might help Dalit and ST employees feel valued and secured in government or corporate environments.

Conclusion

The results of this chapter are based on preliminary data (two years of national-level data, not stratified by sex or age), and hence further research needs to be undertaken to better understand the epidemiology of Dalit suicides in India. First, the NCRB reports must include the caste status of suicides. For this to happen, all the suicides recorded at the local level (that is, police stations), which eventually inform the NCRB reports, must record and disseminate the caste status of suicides. The NCRB reports must, at a minimum, dissect this data by gender, age, method, and occupation at the state level. Second, suicide researchers in India should start focusing on the association between caste status and suicides. This includes such things as the incidence of depression and suicidal ideation among young Dalits, their relative confidence in seeking appropriate counselling, and the importance of potentially protective forces such as spirituality. Also, at the all-India level, we need to understand the reasons why in regions with relatively lower or smaller Dalit populations, their suicide rates are generally higher. Third, the phenomenon of 'copycat suicides' in India should be investigated to establish whether one suicide impacts or predicts rise in future suicide incidence, especially in the short term and among similar population groups (for example, among Dalit students after a Dalit student suicide). Finally, it can be predicted, with reasonable certainty, that as Dalits attain greater parity in education, especially at secondary and tertiary levels, their suicide rates will increase; this already appears to be the case in states like Madhya Pradesh and Andhra Pradesh where just over 50 per cent of Dalits are enrolled in secondary education and suicide rates are relatively high. In the absence of national suicide prevention strategies, non-governmental organizations (NGOs) working with Dalits should also work to develop community-specific strategies which can help prevent this predictable tragedy.

Note

1. The Right to Information Act, adopted by the Indian parliament in 2005, gives citizens of India a right to acquire information held by public authorities.

Bibliography

Acharya, S. 2019. 'Student Suicides: Why Do Numbers Disproportionately Tilt towards Dalits?' *BloombergQuint*, 23 June. https://www.bloombergquint.com/opinion/student-suicides-why-do-numbers-disproportionately-tilt-towards-dalits. Accessed on 28 September 2019.

Arya V, A. Page, J. River, G. Armstrong, and P. Mayer. 2018. 'Trends and Socio-Economic Determinants of Suicide in India: 2001–2013'. *Social Psychiatry and Psychiatric Epidemiology* 53(3): 269–78.

Arya V, A. Page, D. Gunnell, R. Dandona, H. Mannan, M. Eddleston, and G. Armstrong. 2019a. 'Suicide by Hanging Is a Priority for Suicide Prevention: Method Specific Suicide in India (2001–2014)'. *Journal of Affective Disorders* 257: 1–9.

Arya V, A. Page, R. Dandona, L. Vijayakumar, P. Mayer, and G. Armstrong. 2019b. 'The Geographic Heterogeneity of Suicide Rates in India by Religion, Caste, Tribe, and Other Backward Classes'. *Crisis: The Journal of Crisis Intervention and Suicide Prevention* 40(5): 370–74.

Arya V., A. Page, G. Armstrong, G. A. Kumar, and R. Dandona. 2020. 'Estimating Patterns in the Under-Reporting of Suicide Deaths in India: Comparison of Administrative Data and Global Burden of Disease Study Estimates, 2005–2015'. *Journal of Epidemiology and Community Health* 75(6): 550–55.

Census of India. 2011. 'Census of India 2011 Data'. New Delhi: Office of the Registrar General of India, Ministry of Home Affairs, Government of India. https://censusindia.gov.in/2011-common/censusdata2011.html. Accessed on 2 October 2019.

Dandona, R., G. A. Kumar, R. S. Dhaliwal, M. Naghavi, T. Vos, D. K. Shukla, L. Vijayakumar, G. Gururaj, J. S. Thakur, A. Ambekar, and R. Sagar. 2018. 'Gender Differentials and State Variations in Suicide Deaths in India: The Global Burden of Disease Study 1990–2016'. *Lancet Public Health* 3(10): e478–89.

Desai, S., and R. Vanneman. 2015. *India Human Development Survey-II (IHDS-II) 2011–12*. https://www.icpsr.umich.edu/web/pages/DSDR/ihds-II-data-guide.html. Accessed on 5 October 2019.

Droege, J. R., W. I. Robinson, and L. A. Jason. 2017. 'Suicidality Protective Factors for African American Adolescents: A Systematic Review of the Research Literature'. *SOJ Nursing and Health Care* 3(2): 1–5.

Durkheim, E. 1897. *On Suicide*, translated by R. Buss. London: Penguin Books.

Early, K. E., and R. L. Akers. 1993. '"It's a White Thing": An Exploration of Beliefs about Suicide in the African-American Community'. *Deviant Behavior* 14(4): 277–96.

EPW Research Foundation. 2011. *India: A Pocket Book of Data Series, 2010–11*. New Delhi: Academic Foundation.

Henry, A. F., and J. F. Short. 1954. *Suicide and Homicide*. Glencoe: Free Press.

International Institute for Population Sciences (IIPS) and ICF. 2017. *National Family Health Survey (NFHS-4), 2015–16*. Mumbai: International Institute for Population Sciences. http://rchiips.org/pdf/INDIA_REPORT_DLHS-3.pdf. Accessed on 2 October 2019.

Lester, D. 2015. *Minor Sociological Theories of Suicide. Theories of Suicide: Past, Present and Future*. Springfield, IL: Charles C Thomas.

Maurya, R. K. 2018. 'In Their Own Voices: Experiences of Dalit Students in Higher Education Institutions'. *International Journal of Multicultural Education* 20(3): 17–38.

Mayer, P. 2010. *Suicide and Society in India*. London and New York: Routledge.

———. 2016. 'Thinking Clearly about Suicide in India – III: Youth and Young Adult Suicide in Australia and India'. *Economic and Political Weekly* 51(52): 85–94.

Mehrotra, S., A. Gandhi, C. Kumar, P. Saha, B. K. Sahoo, and A. Sharma. 2011. *India Human Development Report 2011: Towards Social Inclusion*. New Delhi: Oxford University Press.

Meyer, I. H. 2003. 'Prejudice, Social Stress, and Mental Health in Lesbian, Gay, and Bisexual Populations: Conceptual Issues and Research Evidence'. *Psychological Bulletin* 129(5): 674–97.

Minois, G. 2001. *History of Suicide: Voluntary Death in Western Culture*. Washington, DC: American Psychological Association.

Molock S. D., R. Kimbrough, M. B. Lacy, K. P. McClure, and S. Williams. 1994. 'Suicidal Behavior among African American College Students: A Preliminary Study'. *Journal of Black Psychology* 20(2): 234–51.

National Crime Records Bureau (NCRB). 2019. *Accidental Deaths and Suicides in India*. New Delhi: Government of India. https://ncrb.gov.in/adsi-reports-of-previous-years. Accessed on 2 November 2020.

Oh, H., K. Waldman, A. Koyanagi, R. Anderson, and J. DeVylder. 2020. 'Major Discriminatory Events and Suicidal Thoughts and Behaviors amongst Black Americans: Findings from the National Survey of American Life'. *Journal of Affective Disorders* 263 (February): 47–53.

Patel, V., C. Ramasundarahettige, L. Vijayakumar, J. S. Thakur, V. Gajalakshmi, G. Gururaj, W. Suraweera, and P. Jha. 2012. 'Suicide Mortality in India: A Nationally Representative Survey'. *The Lancet* 379(9834): 2343–51.

Petroni, S., V. Patel, and G. Patton. 2015. 'Why Is Suicide the Leading Killer of Older Adolescent Girls?' *The Lancet* 386(10008): 2031–32.

Phillips, J. A., and K. Hempstead. 2017. 'Differences in US Suicide Rates by Educational Attainment, 2000–2014'. *American Journal of Preventive Medicine* 53(4): e123–30.

Planning, Monitoring, and Statistics Bureau. 2019. *All India Survey on Higher Education 2018–19*. New Delhi: Department of Higher Education, Ministry of Human Resource Development, Government of India.

Roberts A. 2010. 'A Great and Revolutionary Law? The First Four Years of India's Right to Information Act'. *Public Administration Review* 70(6): 925–33.

Sample Registration System (SRS). 2020. *Statistical Report 2020*. New Delhi: Office of the Registrar General of India, Ministry of Home Affairs, Government of India. https://censusindia.gov.in/Vital_Statistics/SRS/Sample_Registration_System.html#2. Accessed on 3 October 2020.

Thorat, S., K. M. Shyamprasad, and R. K. Srivastava. 2007. *Report of the Committee to Enquire into the Differential Treatment of SC/ST Students in All India Institute of Medical Science, Delhi*. https://atrocitynews.files.wordpress.com/2008/05/reports-aiims.pdf. Accessed on 28 January 2021.

Vijaykumar, L. 2007. 'Suicide and Its Prevention: The Urgent Need in India'. *Indian Journal of Psychiatry* 49(2): 81–84.

Walker, R. 2020. 'Black Kids and Suicide: Why Are Rates So High, and So Ignored?' *The Conversation*, 17 January. https://theconversation.com/black-kids-and-suicide-why-are-rates-so-high-and-so-ignored-127066. Accessed on 27 January 2021.

Walker, R. L., L. R. Wingate, E. M. Obasi, and T. E. Joiner Jr. 2008. 'An Empirical Investigation of Acculturative Stress and Ethnic Identity as Moderators for Depression and Suicidal Ideation in College Students'. *Cultural Diversity and Ethnic Minority Psychology* 14(1): 75–82.

Wechsler, H., and T. F. Pugh. 1967. 'Fit of Individual and Community Characteristics and Rates of Psychiatric Hospitalization'. *American Journal of Sociology* 73(3): 331–38.

Westerlund, M., S. Schaller, and A. Schmidtke. 2009. 'The Role of Mass-Media in Suicide Prevention'. In *Oxford Textbook of Suicidology and Suicide Prevention: A Global Perspective*, edited by D. Wasserman and C. Wasserman, 515–23. Oxford: Oxford University Press.

World Health Organization (WHO). 2016. 'Suicide Rates Estimates, Age-Standardized Estimates by WHO Region'. https://apps.who.int/gho/data/view.main.MHSUICIDEASDRREGv?lang=en. Accessed on 29 February 2021.

About the Contributors

Amit Ahuja is Associate Professor in the Department of Political Science at the University of California, Santa Barbara. His research focuses on the processes of inclusion and exclusion in multi-ethnic societies, which he has studied within the context of ethnic parties and movements, military organization, inter-caste marriage, and skin-colour preferences in South Asia. His book *Mobilizing the Marginalized: Ethnic Parties without Ethnic Movements* (2019) was the winner of the 2020 New India Foundation Kamaladevi Chattopadhyay Book Prize. He is currently working on a second book-length project entitled 'Building National Armies in Multiethnic States'. He is also the co-editor of *Internal Security in India: Violence, Order, and the State* (2023).

Gregory Armstrong is a mental health researcher with a PhD in International Health from the University of Melbourne, and Senior Research Fellow at the Melbourne School of Population and Global Health, University of Melbourne. He undertakes research in Australia and in low- and middle-income countries (LMICs), with specialization in population mental health, suicide prevention, and substance misuse. He has published over 80 peer-reviewed journal articles, is the deputy editor of the *International Journal of Mental Health Systems*, and is a member of the Research Advisory Committee for Beyond Blue, Melbourne, and the National Research Committee for the Australian Association of Social Workers, Melbourne.

Vikas Arya is a research fellow in mental health at the University of Melbourne. He has a PhD in Epidemiology from Western Sydney University. His doctoral research investigated socio-economic and cultural determinants of suicide in India which entailed complex statistical modelling, data visualization, and the management and curation of large-scale datasets. He has previously worked as Research Officer for the International Association for Suicide Prevention (IASP), Washington, DC, and is currently part of the International COVID-19 Suicide Prevention Research Collaboration (ICSPRC) of the IASP, which involves the investigation of impacts of the COVID-19 pandemic on international trends in suicide.

D. Shyam Babu is Senior Fellow at the Centre for Policy Research, New Delhi. A former journalist, he now focuses on how economic changes in India have been shaping social change and transformation for the benefit of marginalized sections, especially Dalits. He is the co-author (with Devesh Kapur and Chandra Bhan Prasad) of *Defying the Odds: The Rise of Dalit Entrepreneurs* (2014), which brought to light the phenomenon of Dalit businesspersons hitherto ignored by both intellectuals and policymakers.

Samarth Bansal is an independent journalist based in India who has reported on the intersection of technology, politics, and policy. His writing has appeared in *The Hindu*, the *Hindustan Times*, *Mint*, *India Today*, and *The Atlantic*. He has a bachelor's degree in mathematics and scientific computing from the Indian Institute of Technology, Kanpur.

Dwaipayan Bhattacharyya is Professor at the Centre for Political Studies, Jawaharlal Nehru University, New Delhi. He has worked and published on the issues of decentralization, local democracy, agrarian politics, social policies, and left-wing governance in a manner that generated explanatory frameworks for political processes based on extensive field studies. His book *Government and Practice: Democratic Left in a Transforming India* (2016) offers an analysis of the long Left Front rule in West Bengal through the prism of 'party society'. Previously, he was Fellow at the Centre for Studies in Social Sciences, Kolkata, and held visiting positions at several universities in India and abroad.

Cléo Chassonnery-Zaïgouche is a historian of economics, specialized in the history of wages, discriminations, and labour. She is an assistant professor of history of economics at the University of Bologna and a research associate at the Joint Center for History and Economics, University of Cambridge.

Simon Chauchard is Associate Professor and Distinguished Researcher (Investigador Distinguido) at the University Carlos III de Madrid (University Charles III of Madrid) and a member of the Instituto Carlos III–Juan March (IC3JM) (Carlos III–Juan March Institute), Madrid. His works have appeared in the *Political Opinion Quarterly*, the *American Political Science Review*, the *Comparative Political Studies*, the *Journal of Politics*, and the *Asian Survey*, among other research outlets. His book, *Why Representation Matters: The Meaning of Ethnic Quotas in Rural India* (2017), combines qualitative work and a series of innovative surveys to explore the impact of caste-based reservation policies on everyday intergroup relations in India's villages.

Michael A. Collins is Postdoctoral Fellow at the Centre for Modern Indian Studies (CeMIS), University of Göttingen, where he teaches courses on democracy, political representation, and nationalism in South Asia. He has published on modern Dalit politics, elections, and political finance.

Victoire Girard is a researcher and professor at the Nova School of Business and Economics, Carcavelos, Portugal; a resident member of NOVAFRICA; a research affiliate of the Orléans Economic Laboratory, University of Orléans; and a fellow of the Global Labor Organization, an international network and virtual platform on labour. Her research in development economics, political economy, and environmental and natural resources economics have been published in leading journals in the fields of economics and social sciences. She uses applied micro-econometric approaches to deal with topics related to violence, inequality, social identity, and natural resources.

Hugo Gorringe is Senior Lecturer in Sociology and former Co-Director of the Centre for South Asian Studies at the University of Edinburgh. His research focuses on the interplay between caste, politics, and Dalit movements in Tamil Nadu. He is the author of *Untouchable Citizens: Dalit Movements and Democratization in Tamil Nadu* (2005) and *Panthers in Parliament: Dalits, Caste and Political Power in South India* (2017), as well as numerous articles and essays on identity, violence, space, caste, and politics.

Pranav Gupta is a PhD candidate in the Department of Political Science at the University of California, Berkeley. His research interests include political ideology, voting behaviour, and party politics.

Prashant Ingole is Postdoctoral Fellow in Humanities and Social Sciences at the Indian Institute of Technology, Gandhinagar, Gujarat. His current project focuses on environmental casteism and social justice. He is engaged in interdisciplinarity research with focus on Dalit and cultural studies.

Francesca R. Jensenius is Professor of Political Science at the University of Oslo, Norway, and Research Professor at the Norwegian Institute of International Affairs, Oslo. She specializes in comparative politics, comparative political economy, and research methods, with a regional focus on South Asia. Much of her research is related to state approaches to empowering minorities and women, in India and elsewhere. In her book *Social Justice through Inclusion: The Consequences of Electoral Quotas in India* (2017), she explores the long-term effects of electoral quotas for the Scheduled Castes. She has also published extensively on party politics and voting patterns in India and on how this relates to local-level development patterns.

Surinder S. Jodhka is Professor of Sociology at Jawaharlal Nehru University, New Delhi. He researches on social inequalities and the processes of their reproduction. Empirical focus of his work has been on caste, agrarian and rural change, and community identities. His recent publications include *Agrarian Change in India*

(2022), *India's Villages in the 21st Century: Revisits and Revisions* (2019), *Mapping the Elite: Power, Privilege and Inequality* (2019), *A Handbook of Rural India* (2018), *Caste in Contemporary India* (2015), and *Caste* (Oxford India Short Introduction Series) (2012).

K. Kalyani is Assistant Professor in the School of Arts and Sciences at Azim Premji University, Bengaluru. She was awarded her doctorate degree in Sociology from the Centre for the Study of Social Systems, Jawaharlal Nehru University, New Delhi. Her ethnographic research has explored different forms and practices of resistance, particularly by engaging with the question of caste, gender and culture through a subaltern perspective. She also engages with public discourse through her writings in *The Print* and NewsClick, among others, and she has been a speaker at several International forums.

Meena Kandasamy is a poet, novelist, and translator based in India. Her writing focuses on resistance movements for caste annihilation, feminism, and self-determination. These themes have been explored in her books of poems – *Touch* (2006) and *Ms Militancy* (2010) – as well as her three novels, *The Gypsy Goddess* (2014), *When I Hit You* (2017), and *Exquisite Cadavers* (2019). She was Fellow at the University of Iowa's International Writing Program (2009) and the Charles Wallace India Trust (2011). She has been writing on the Viduthalai Chiruthaigal Katchi (Liberation Panthers; VCK) for the last two decades. She has translated two volumes of VCK leader Thol. Thirumavalavan's writings and speeches: *Talisman* (2003) and *Uproot Hindutva* (2004).

Arvind Kumar is a PhD scholar at the Department of Politics and International Relations and Philosophy at the Royal Holloway, University of London. He is also Associate Fellow of Higher Education Academy (AFHEA), United Kingdom. His areas of research are caste, inequality, and voting behaviour in India. His broader research interests include caste and ethnic inequality, electoral behaviour, party politics, political economy, political theory, judicial politics, and South Asian politics. He was Guest Lecturer of Political Science at Satyawati College, University of Delhi, and Sessional Tutor of South Asian Politics at Royal Holloway, University of London. He is also a contributing columnist for *ThePrint*, *India Today*, and *Firstpost*.

Peter Mayer is Associate Professor of Politics and Visiting Research Fellow at the University of Adelaide, Australia. He has written on many aspects of Indian politics, international relations, economics, history, anthropology, and sociology. His recent publications have examined issues including a zone of weak governance in the Indus–Ganges plains, India's engagement with economic reforms, long-term trends in the real wages of agricultural labourers in the Kaveri delta, why elections in India appear to defy Duverger's law of party competition, the declining rate of massacres of India's Dalits, and the multiple causes of murder for dowry in India's states.

Badri Narayan is Director at the Govind Ballabh Social Science Institute, Prayagraj, Uttar Pradesh. His research interests include ethnography of marginalized politics, popular culture and identity formation, Dalit and subaltern issues, and language and the question of power. Besides having written a number of articles both in English and Hindi, he has authored *Republic of Hindutva* (2021), *Kanshiram* (2014), *The Making of the Dalit Public in North India* (2011), *Fascinating Hindutva* (2009), and *Women Heroes and Dalit Assertion in North India* (2006). He has also published more than 50 research papers in reputed international and national level research journals.

Andrew Page is Professor of Epidemiology in the Translational Health Research Institute, Western Sydney University. He has extensive research experience in epidemiology, psychology, and public health, with particular interests in the study of suicide and mental health, the social determinants of health, injury prevention, breast cancer screening, and maternal and child health. He also has interests in the application of systems science and simulation approaches to epidemiological evidence in order to inform policy and health service decision-support tools.

Sudha Pai is former Professor, Centre for Political Studies, Jawaharlal Nehru University, New Delhi, and former Rector of the same university. She was National Fellow at the Indian Council of Social Science Research, New Delhi (2016–17) and Senior Fellow at the Nehru Memorial Museum and Library, New Delhi (2006–09). Some of her well-known works include *Dalit Assertion and the Unfinished Democratic Revolution: The BSP in Uttar Pradesh* (2002), *Political Process in Uttar Pradesh: Identity, Economic Reforms and Governance* (2007), *Everyday Communalism: Riots in Contemporary Uttar Pradesh* (2018), and more recently *Constitutional and Democratic Institutions in India: A Critical Analysis* (2020).

Snigdha Poonam is a journalist and a writer. Her first book, *Dreamers: How Young Indians Are Changing the World*, won 2018's Crossword Award for non-fiction. She has reported on national affairs for the *Hindustan Times* in Delhi. Her work has also appeared in *Scroll.in*, the *Times of India*, the *New York Times*, *The Guardian*, *Foreign Policy*, and the *Financial Times*.

Kaushiki Sanyal is Fellow at JustJobs Network, a global research firm. She co-founded and headed Sunay Policy Advisory Pvt Ltd, a policy research consultancy in Gurgaon. Her professional experience includes stints with New Delhi Television Ltd (NDTV), the PRS Legislative Research, the Bharti Institute of Public Policy (Indian School of Business), the Vidhi Centre for Legal Policy, the World Bank, and the Rajiv Gandhi Foundation.

She has co-authored three books – *Public Policy in India* (2017), *Shaping Policy in India: Alliance, Advocacy, Activism* (2018) and *Artificial Intelligence and India* (2020) – and writes regularly in the popular media. She has a PhD in International Relations and a Master of Arts degree in Political Science from Jawaharlal Nehru University, New Delhi.

Dwaipayan Sen is an independent historian of modern South Asia. He has authored the book *The Decline of the Caste Question: Jogendranath Mandal and the Defeat of Dalit Politics in Bengal* (2018), as well as articles and essays in assorted volumes and journals. His current research interests concern caste and the census in modern India.

Abhinav Prakash Singh is Assistant Professor of Economics at Ramjas College, University of Delhi. He is the national vice president of the Bharatiya Janta Yuva Morcha, the youth wing of the Bharatiya Janata Party (BJP), and a member of the central team of Samajik Samvad, a focused Dalit outreach program of the BJP. He is also a regular bilingual columnist in Hindi and English in various publications.

Rajkamal Singh is a PhD candidate in the Department of Political Science at the University of California, Santa Barbara. His research interests include the study of protest politics and social movements in India.

Satnam Singh is pursuing PhD at the Centre for Historical Studies, Jawaharlal Nehru University, New Delhi. He is a Dalit activist and a popular Dalit writer. He has published several books with Samyak Prakashan, Delhi.

Swadesh Singh is Assistant Professor of Political Science at Satyawati College, University of Delhi University. He holds a PhD from Jawaharlal Nehru University, New Delhi. He has co-authored the book *Electoral Reforms: Ushering a Just Political Regime* (2015) and edited the books *New Dalit Agenda for 21st Century* (2016) and *Cultural Nationalism: The Indian Perspective* (2014). He also holds a postgraduate diploma in Mass Communication from the Indian Institute of Mass Communication, New Delhi, and has worked as a journalist with news organizations like the British Broadcasting Corporation (BBC) and New Delhi Television Ltd (NDTV). His core areas of interest are party politics, social justice, caste, Hindutva, and media.

Gurram Srinivas is Associate Professor at the Centre for the Study of Social Systems, School of Social Sciences, Jawaharlal Nehru University, New Delhi. His research interests include digital media and youth, social movements, sociology of Dalits, sociology of environment, Indian society, and urban sociology. His published works include *Dalit Middle Class: Mobility, Identity and Politics of Caste* (2016),

Intersecting Identities: Dalit Middle Class in South India (2014), and *Dalits: Studies in Continuity and Change* (co-edited with Vivek Kumar, 2014).

Amit Thorat is Assistant Professor of Economics Jawaharlal Nehru University, New Delhi. Prior to this, he was Associate Fellow at the National Council for Applied Economics Research, New Delhi, where he was part of the India Human Development Survey team. His research has focused on issues of income, educational, and health inequalities in general and across social, ethnic, and religious groups in particular, in the context of India. His work focuses on understanding people's beliefs around personal and social identity in India and its implications for social behaviour, individual distress, economic outcomes, and intergenerational transfer of wealth and trauma for social groups.

Rahul Verma is Fellow at the Centre for Policy Research, New Delhi, and Visiting Assistant Professor in the Department of Political Science, Ashoka University, Sonepat. He has a PhD in Political Science from the University of California, Berkeley. He is a regular columnist for various news platforms and has published papers in many academic journals. His co-authored book with Pradeep Chhibber, *Ideology and Identity: The Changing Party Systems of India* (2018) develops a new approach to defining the contours of what constitutes an ideology in multi-ethnic countries such as India.

Harish S. Wankhede is Assistant Professor at the Centre for Political Studies, Jawaharlal Nehru University (JNU), New Delhi. He was awarded the Raman Fellowship in 2013 and was associated with the Centre for South Asia, Stanford University, as a visiting scholar. His PhD thesis was on 'Secularism and Social Justice: Religious Minorities and Quest for Equality' under the supervision of Professor Valerian Rodrigues at JNU. He has contributed research articles and essays for major Indian journals, newspapers, and popular online portals. He is currently working on a book project on Dalit representation in Hindi cinema.

Index

Aadhaar database, 5, 102
Aadi Hindu Panth, 275
Aam Aadmi Party (AAP), 4, 26–27, 49
abominations of the body, stigmas of, 397
Acemoglu, Daron, 348
Achhutanand, Swami, 275
A Contribution to the Critique of Political Economy (1859), 219
Ad Dharm movement, 46–47, 206*n*2
Adityanath, Yogi, 70, 277, 395, 399
Adivasis, 238
Advani, L. K.
 rath yatra, 247
affirmative action, 179, 212–13, 221
Against the Madness of Manu: B. R. Ambedkar's Writings on Brahmanical Patriarchy (2013), 140
Agamben, Giorgio, 279
agrarian-feudal social order, 98
agrarian labour class, 238
Akali Dal (Shiromani Akali Dal [SAD]), 4, 47, 270
Akhil Bharatiya Vidhyarthi Parishad (ABVP), 103
All Bharatiya Rajbhar Sangathan, 402, 409*n*15
alliance building, 204

All India Anna Dravida Munnetra Kazhagam (AIADMK), 82–83, 249, 253
All India Backward and Minority Communities Employees Federation (BAMCEF), 11, 90*n*2, 116, 200, 402
all-India Dalit conference, 345
All-India Debt and Investment Survey (2002), 181*n*21
All India Gond Mahasabha, 402
All India Institute of Medical Sciences (AIIMS), Delhi, 443
All India Majlis-e-Ittehadul Muslimeen (AIMIM), 241
All India Nai Mahasabha, 402
All India Scheduled Castes Federation (AISCF), 46, 50, 219, 236, 409*n*8
All India Trinamool Congress (TMC), 27, 51
Amar, Ram Sujan, 154
Amazon Prime, 289
Ambedkar, B. R., 3, 7, 39, 49, 86, 134, 169, 193, 202, 215, 225, 268, 324–25, 375, 414
 125th birth anniversary, 157
 advocacy for separate electorates, 87

All India Scheduled Castes
    Federation, 46
anti-caste cultural politics, 134
challenge to Gandhi's paternal and
    moralist appeal, 235
and the Communists, 218–20
confrontation with Gandhi, 139
Dalit movement initiated by, 307
death anniversary of, 116
founding of All India Scheduled
    Castes Federation, 219
ideals of building a society, 201
ideology of, 9
launching of the Republican Party of
    India (RPI), 237
political activism, 237
quest for political power, 234–37
relationship with Marxism and
    Marxist politics, 218
social agenda, 258
success in winning separate electorates
    for Dalits, 203
understanding of the relation between
    caste and class, 216
VCK's engagement with, 258
Ambedkarism, 3, 9–10, 254, 256, 268
Ambedkarite Dalits, 244
Ambedkarization, process of, 7–8
Ambedkar Mahasabha, 157
Ambedkar.org, 161
Ambedkar, Prakash, 3, 240–42
Ambedkar Village Programme, for
    upliftment of the entire village
    community, 63
Anand, S., 253
Anganwadi programme for children, 63
Anglo-Indian law (1772), 319
Annihilation of Caste (1936), 201, 268
anthropological exceptionalism, for the
    anti-caste warriors, 216

anti-CAA protests (2019), 182*n*24
anti-caste aesthetics, in commercial
    films, 136
anti-caste Bhakti movement, of
    medieval India, 101
anti-caste cinema, 143–46
anti-caste consciousness, 115, 119,
    133, 134
  of the 1980s, 130*n*1
anti-caste cultural politics, 134
anti-caste movement
  defined, 138
  language of, 137–38
anti-caste music, 136
  educative and reformatory, 138–43
  rise of alternative, 138
anti-caste political strategies, 134
anti-caste practices, 136
anti-caste resistance, 138
anti-caste songs, 126
anti-caste struggle, on liberal values,
    215
anti-Citizenship Amendment Act
    (CAA), 172
anti-communist rhetoric, 219
anti-Dalit ethos, 51
anti-Hinduism, politics of, 97
antyodaya (welfare of people at the
    bottom of the socio-economic
    pyramid), 101
anxiety, 2, 12, 219, 281, 408
Apna Dal, 103
Armed Conflict Location & Event Data
    Project (ACLED), 170
Article 15 (2019), 136
Article 370, repeal of, 255, 257
Arzal Muslim, 278
ascription-based identities, 206
Association for Democratic Reforms
    (ADR), 81

Association for Enterprise Opportunity (AEO), 346
Athawale, Ramdas, 29
ati-Dalit (backward Dalit) community, 271
atipichda (very backward) community, 271
atomistic individualism, 216
atrocities against Dalits, news of, 155
atrocities on Dalits, protests against, 61
atrocity cases, 419
Attali, Jacques, 125
Auerbach, Adam, 362
authoritarian populism, 210, 225
avarna (lower caste), 144
Ayushman Bharat, 5
Azad, Chandrashekhar, 3, 10–11, 36, 126, 279
    support for the Mahagathbandhan in opposition to the BJP, 277
Azad Samaj Party, 10, 124, 126
Azlaf Muslim, 278

backward-caste identities, 273
backward castes, 238
Backward Classes, 221
    of citizens, 394
    commissions, 394–95
backwardness of Dalits, 396
Bagdis, 52
Bahuguna, Hemwati Nandan, 399
Bahujan *andolan* (agitation), 119
Bahujan collective, 239–40
bahujan, idea of, 119, 130n1, 204
Bahujan identity and consciousness, 10, 239–40
'Bahujan' leaders, pan-national legacy of, 240
Bahujan Left Front (BLF), 224–25
Bahujan mission, 115, 123

Bahujan movement, 9, 124
bahujan politics, 271
    formulated by Kanshi Ram, 273
bahujan samaj, 202, 268
Bahujan Samaj Party (BSP), 11, 47, 81, 103, 134, 193, 211, 349
    alliance with SP and RLD, 70
    budget expenditure in selected sectors by, 64–65
    construction of memorials commemorating Dalit leaders, 68
    Dalit–Bahujan movement in India, 267
    Dalit support base, 90n2
    Dalit voter base, 25, 30
    decline of, 4–5, 154
        impact on Dalit politics, 6
        in North India, 30–34
        in Punjab, 47
    defeat in elections, 59–60, 67–68
    ditching of the BJP during the floor test, 155
    dominance among Dalits, 26
    emergence of, 4
    eroding base in the UP assembly elections, 33
    formation of, 116
    inception under the leadership of Kanshi Ram, 239
    Jatav voters, 4
    as pan-India party, 30
    performance in the Lok Sabha elections since 1989, 31
    political language of, 274
    programme of retributive social justice, 62
    return to the Dalit agenda, 66–67
    rise of, 153
    rubric of the Bahujan movement, 277
    shortcomings of, 49

stand on Kashmir's special status, 257
strategy for securing political power,
    48
strengthening of the Dalit–Muslim
    alliance, 278
success under the leadership of
    Mayawati, 59
vote share
    among the Jatavs, 61
    in UP, 30, 32
Bahujan Sanghatak, 120
Bahujan songs, 7, 116, 117, 118
Bahujan voters, 271
Balakot incident (2019), 71, 74*n*9
Bala, Poonam, 119, 121–22
Balmikis, 47–48, 60, 67
Bandit Queen (1994), 144
Bandyopadhyay, Sekhar, 50
Banerjee, Abhijit, 13
Banerjee, Mukulika, 197
Bangar, Mohan, 120
bastis (slums), 278
becoming Dalit, 199–201
'Begumpura' (Sorrowless City), 137
Behalpuri, Harnam Singh, 122–24
below the poverty line (BPL), 62, 91*n*7
Bhagat, Sambhaji, 141
Bhakti saints, 276
Bharat *bandh*, 291
Bharatiya Bahujan Mahasangh, 240
Bharatiya Janata Party (BJP), 154, 247,
    268, 349, 360, 385, 395
    ability to secure Dalit votes, 205
    alliance with Shiv Sena, 240–41
    ascendance to power at the national
        level, 1
    attraction as a political alternative for
        the Dalit castes, 95
    brand of elite-led social engineering,
        242

campaign to reach out poor
    beneficiaries, 5
class-based differences in support for,
    34
'conversion' process, 5
crorepatis candidates filed by, 81
Dalits' electoral preferences in favour
    of, 6
Dalit support base, 4, 68
Dalit votes, 25–26
    ditched by the BSP during the floor
        test, 155
electoral campaigns by, 5
electoral decline in UP, 30
electoral politics, 205
electoral success among the Dalit
    communities, 36
ethno-political majoritarianism, 5
Hindu card, 255
Hindu majoritarian ideology, 210
Hindutva politics of, 98
inroads into West Bengal, Assam, and
    Tripura, 29
under leadership of Modi and Amit
    Shah, 100
lobbying for party posts, 101
long-term changes, 95–98
massive mandate won in 2014 and
    2019, 95
Muslims as political enemy of BJP, 244
per cent of Jatav and non-Jatav
    votes, 70
performance in UP 2014 elections, 69
politics of Dalit inclusion, 68–69
popularity among Dalit voters, 34–36
preference among Dalit voters, 5
profile of support for, 35, 36
reasons for Dalit shift towards,
    36–40, 59
    ideological or electoral shift, 71–72

rise of, 6
  under Narendra Modi, 1, 4
  in West Bengal, 4, 53
'Samajik Samvad' campaign, 102
share of seats reserved for Dalits, 26
shift of Dalit voters towards, 95, 107
social engineering strategy, 38, 102
in Tamil Nadu, 248–50
ties with capitalists, 257
trade-union wing, 213
views across caste groups on issues
  raised by, 40
Bharatiya Mazdoor Sangh, 213
Bhattacharya, Dwaipayan, 51
bheedtantra (system of crowds), 166
BHIM (Bharat Interface for Money), 39
Bhima Koregaon violence (1 January
  2018), 143, 255
Bhim Army, 3, 70, 277
  formation of, 36
  Jatavs in, 71
  rise of, 73
Bhimrao Ambedkar Rural Integrated
  Development Programme, 63
Bhopal Conference of Dalit (2002), 13,
  345, 347
Bhorisa, Dhiren, 297
Biju Janta Dal (BJD), 27, 28
bipolar political system, 82
Black capitalism, 347
black economy, of India, 322
Black Lives Matter, 292
Black Panthers, 79, 238
black slaves, 336n2
Blunt, E. A. H., 405
Boat Club, 172
Bollywood, 288
  Hindi cinema's transformation into, 135
  and Hindi film industry, 136
  political economy of, 136

Bombay Presidency, 236
bonded labour (*begar*), practice of, 343,
  405
Bonded Labour System (Abolition) Act
  (1976), 351n4
Bourdieu, Pierre, 196
Brahmanical knowledge tradition, 397
Brahmanical patriarchy, 144
Brahmanism, ideology of, 97
Brahmin–Baniya tag, 100
brahmin–bourgeois Congress, 218
Brahmin domination, 253
Brahminical patriarchy, 247
brahmin supremacy, 256
Bright Age, 203
British Crown, 334
British Raj, 319
bua–bhatija (aunt–nephew)
  relationship, 277
Buddhism, 200, 278
  conversion to Buddhism, 238
building memorials, politics of, 66
Burawoy, Michael, 214
Bureau of Police Research and
  Development, 180n3
Burke, Edmund, 378
Business Standard (2019), 251
Byapari, Manoranjan, 54

campaign finance regulations, 83
campaign-incurred debt, 84
Capital (1867), 219
capitalist economy, of India, 98
caste and class, concept of, 215–18
caste atrocities, protection from, 316
caste-based crimes
  atrocity cases, 419
  first information reports (FIRs) on,
    416
  inter-caste tensions, 421–24

murders targeting Dalits, 416,
    418–19
rise of, 417
survey declarations on untouchability,
    420
caste-based cultural ethos, 135
caste-based discrimination, 96, 291
    comparing the data patterns on,
        420–21
    Dalit resistance to, 424–26
    against Dalits, 414
    Kitagawa–Oaxaca–Blinder
        decomposition method for
        evaluating, 417
    measure of, 417–18
    phenomenon of, 417
    practice of, 414
    untouchability and, 420
caste-based electoral mobilization, 168
caste-based grievances, 177, 179
caste-based identities, 281
caste-based labour discrimination, 417
caste-based matrimony, 296
caste-based menial labour, 295
caste-based mobilization, of Dalits, 178,
    341
caste-based murders, targeting Dalits,
    416, 418–19
    in Bihar, 426–27
caste-based protest activity, 172
caste-based protests, 9, 167, 169, 177
caste-based violence, 418
caste–class confluence, in India, 213
caste–class relations, 220
caste-driven society, 349
caste effects in economy, 215, 218, 220
caste enslavement, 333
caste fanatics, 85
caste hierarchy, 309
caste-Hindu middle class, 304

caste identity, 171, 268
    politics based on, 269
    in relation to modern economy, 220
caste inversion, idea of, 224
Casteless Collective (YouTube channel),
    143
castelessness, 9, 135–37, 290
caste oppression, 215
caste slavery in India, law banning, 320
caste stigma and humiliation, 215
caste untouchability, 137, 317
caste violence and discrimination, 36,
    154, 162
Chaturthha Duniya, 54
Centre for Media Studies (CMS), 80,
    168
Centre for the Study of Developing
    Societies (CSDS), New Delhi,
    26, 213, 286
ceri (Dalit colonies), 92n17
Chaitya Bhoomi, in Mumbai, 39
Chakrabarty, Dipesh, 222, 224
Chakravarty, Anuradha, 177
Chatterjee, Partha, 51–52
chaturvarna, logic of, 215
Chhibber, Pradeep, 71
childhood morality rate, by social
    groups in India, 326
child marriage, practice of, 144
Chin, Aimee, 365
Christian missionaries, attacks on, 153
cinema, 8, 133, 135, 136
    anti-caste, 143–46
    Dalit Cinema, 136–37
    Marathi, 136, 143
    Tamil, 136
    Telugu, 8
cinema industry, in India, 135
    Dalit representation on, 135
circulation of elite, 196

Citizenship Amendment Act (CAA) (2019), 29, 54, 250
citizenship rights, of Dalits, 351
civil and political citizenship, to Dalits, 344
civil society organizations, 167, 330
class and racial justice, 216
class consciousness, 223
class division, of labour, 219
class domination, 217
class exploitation, 214–15, 218
class hierarchy, Marxian definition of, 215
class struggle, 210, 216–17, 220, 225
clientele politics, 197
Code of Criminal Procedure (CrPC), 340
colonial modernity, 217
Coming Out as A Dalit (2019), 286
communal polarization, 4
Communist movement, in India, 220
Communist Party of India (CPI), 92*n*20, 250
Communist Party of India-Marxist (CPI-M), 92*n*20, 211, 225, 250
Communist philosophy, 218
communist politics, 219
communist–socialist organizations, 236
community development programme, 406
community identity, 312
'conservative' nationalism, 135
Constituent Assembly of India, 50, 342, 394
Constitution of India, 235, 236, 302, 340
  article 16(4) of, 394
  article 341 of, 394
  article 342 of, 394
  article 370 of, 255, 257

Cooper, Kenneth, 153
Copeland , Nicholas, 92*n*18
copycat suicides, 441
corporate patronage, 81
coverage of Dalit issues, 150, 152–55, 157, 158, 159, 160
COVID-19 pandemic
  crisis of migration during, 71
  and Dalit politics, 279
  lockdown, 213, 321
  loss of work and income due to, 327
cross-caste marriages
  between Dalit men and caste-Hindu women, 252
  differences over, 252
  violence against, 252
cross-gender friendship, 296
cultural changes, 2, 72, 134
cultural inclusion, process of, 71
cultural industry, in India, 133–34
cultural mobilization, 69
cultural nationalism, Hindutva ideology of, 39
cultural resistance, 8, 18
culture of class, 222–24
cyber capitalism, 141

daily *bhatta* (informal wages), 82–83
Dainik Bhaskar (Hindi newspaper), 285
Dainik Jagran (Hindi newspaper), 153–54, 156, 157, 163*n*3
Dalit activism, 204
Dalit advocacy, dilution of, 86
Dalit Agenda, 13
Dalit alternative media, emergence of, 160–62
Dalit Andolan Patrika, 161
Dalit aspirations, heterogeneity of, 99

Dalit–Bahujan
  identity, 243
  ideology, 11
  music, 116
  musical practices, 116
  political activism, 243
  political agency, 233
  political representation of, 244
  politics, 125
  sociopolitical history, 115
  voters, 242
Dalit, Bahujan, and Adivasi (DBA)
  communities, 288
Dalit–Bahujan movement
  agenda of empowering Dalits, 269
  crisis of, 267
  crisis of political language, 274–76
  double dilemma, 278
  foundational notions of, 269
  Hindutva appropriation and, 271–73
  by Kanshi Ram, 267
  mapping the crisis, 268–69
  new desires and non-response,
    273–74
  in north India, 280
  political and electoral crisis, 269–71
  political consciousness and
    development, 271
  production of leaders and the BSP
    Movement, 277
  relations of, 267
  in UP, 268
Dalit–Bahujan politics, 272
Dalit body, imagination of, 397
Dalit bourgeoisie, 340
Dalitcamera.org, 161
Dalit Capital (2015), 347
Dalit capitalism, 13, 14, 222, 341
  adversity and opportunity, 341–44
  as an agent for social change, 345–48

discourse of, 99
  influence of, 345
Dalit castes
  exclusion and marginalization of, 101
  socio-economic mobility of, 107
Dalit Chamber of Commerce, 13
Dalit Cinema, 136
Dalit civil rights organization, 290
Dalit communities, 69
  aspirations and anxieties among, 12–15
  BJP's electoral success among, 36
  caste identities of, 269
  as claimants of government jobs, 152
  consciousness of, 9
  conversion to Buddhism, 278
  cultural identity, 8
  educated class and government
    employees, 104
  emergence of class differentiation
    within, 100
  empowerment of, 153
  as 'ex-untouchables' of India, 316
  journalism jobs within, 287
  'lived experiences' of, 145
  of Maharashtra, 204
  migrants from Bangladesh, 29
  migration from villages to cities, 98
  religious and cultural sects, 275
  representation in the private sector, 150
  Sanskritization and Hinduization of,
    97
  self-identity and ideology, 10
  social and political life of, 7
  as social media influencers, 162
  struggle for dignity and self-respect, 8
  as target of hate crimes, 415
  unrest over dilution of the Scheduled
    Castes and Scheduled Tribes
    (Prevention of Atrocities) Act
    (1989), 106

and upper castes, 167–68
views on Hindu nationalism, 39
voting pattern among (*See* voting
    patterns, among Dalits)
Dalit consciousness, 276, 309
Dalit Dastak, 161
Dalit electoral politics, 4
Dalit electoral preference, 4
Dalit electorate, 34
    engagement of political parties with,
    158
Dalit emancipation, 222
    democratic state power for, 269
Dalit entrepreneurs, 13, 345–48
    loans for, 158
    Stand-Up India scheme for, 158
Dalit hashtag activism, 293
Dalit-Hindu aspirations, 274
Dalit–Hindu identity, 274
Dalit identity, 245, 346
    ideological formulations of, 10
    pan-India creation of, 3
    politics of, 48
    semantics of, 145
    as social capital, 309–11
    stereotypical representation of, 145
Dalit ideology, 10, 307, 312
Dalit India, 161
Dalit intellectuals and activists, 345
Dalit *jati*s, 38
Dalit journalists, 286
Dalit leadership, 6, 206
    and BSP Movement, 277
    legacy of Kanshi Ram in, 203–6
    production of leaders, 277
Dalit legislators, 376
    comparison with non-SC
        counterparts, 380–83
    effectiveness of, 378–79
    interventions in the Lok Sabha, 379

nature of questions asked by, 383–86
    role at national or state level, 380
Dalit literature, emergence of, 8
Dalit masculinity, 251
Dalit Massacre in Bihar, 154
Dalit middle class (DMC)
    as community with aspirations,
        307–8
    creation of, 99
    distinctiveness of, 303
    emergence of, 150, 302, 304
    identity patterns of, 312
    in Maharashtra, 310
    as networked class, 308–9
    occupations and professions, 305
    reservation policy, 307
    rise of, 6, 14
    role in establishing Dalit polity, 150
    socio-economic and political equality
        for, 312
    socio-economic mobility of, 305
    socio-economic profiles of, 304
    special development packages, 311
Dalit middle-class language, 274
Dalit mobilization, effect of partition
    on, 50
Dalit movements, 1, 2, 11, 59, 61, 202
Dalit–Muslim alliance, 278
Dalit Muslims, 278
Dalit organizations, 2
dalitpan, sense of, 202
Dalit Panthers Movement, 134, 199,
    237–39
    and BJP in Tamil Nadu, 248–50
Dalit Panthers of India, 9, 79
    aims and objectives of, 248
    and political pluralism, 257–59
    Sangh Parivar and, 250–52
    Tamil branch of, 248
Dalit Parliamentarians, 255

Dalit political agency, 193, 196
Dalit political autonomy, demands for,
    50
Dalit political elite, 204
Dalit political parties, 212, 270
    decline of, 2
    fiscal constraints faced by, 82–85
    formation of, 88, 92n20
    impact of coalition politics on, 85
    in India, 79
    intractable balance, 85–88
    mass disenchantment, 99
    possibility of reduction in trust-deficit
        towards, 245–46
    social and economic capital, 81
Dalit politics, 9, 140, 159, 239, 269
    Ambedkarite politics, 243
    aspirational value, 234
    axes of
        anxieties, 3
        aspirations, 3
    claims of political disunity, 48
    comparisons and contrasts between
        Punjab and West Bengal, 55–56
    COVID-19 pandemic and, 279
    crisis facing, 3
    decline of, 205
    decline of the BSP and its impact
        on, 6
    and desire for social justice, 72
    evolution of, 12
    and fall of Atal Bihari Vajpayee's
        government, 154
    functioning of, 2
    future of, 41–42
    heterogeneity of, 99
    legacy of Kanshi Ram in, 203
    in Lok Sabha elections (2014), 26
    Mahar domination, 242
    in Punjab, 46–50

    rise in, 197
    and soft Hindutva, 254–57
    transformative power of social media
        for, 291
    trust-deficit syndrome in, 243–45
    in UP and Bihar, 3
    upheaval within, 98–100
    weakening of, 100
    in West Bengal, 50–55
Dalit popular culture, 7
Dalit pradhan (head of the village
    assembly), 417
Dalit public sphere, rise of, 8
Dalit reality, 3
Dalit representation, through
    reservation and universal adult
    franchise, 376
Dalit representatives, ethnography of,
    86–87
Dalit resistance movement, 136
Dalit Sahitya Sanstha, 54
Dalit Shoshan Mukti Manch, 174,
    183n29
Dalit Shoshit Samaj Sangharsh Samiti
    (DS4), 7, 90n2, 115, 200,
    409n8. See also DS4 singers,
    ethnographic accounts of
    beginning of, 116
    emergence of, 118
    history and emergence of, 116–18
    musical traditions, 118–20
Dalit social and cultural movements,
    104
Dalit social citizenship, 14
Dalit social groups, 270
Dalit society, characteristics of, 98
Dalit suicides, incidence of, 17–18
    in 2014 and 2015, 434–38
    and education, 439–41
    geographic distribution of, 442

and human development, 440
in India, 435
minority status and, 438–39
oppressed minorities and, 441–43
paucity of data on, 434
Payal Tadvi's case, 440
Rohith Vemula's case, 16, 36, 70, 106, 169, 440
and social discrimination, 438
state-wise, 436–37
Dalit suppression, 135
Dalit symbols, desecration of, 179
Dalit-versus-non-Dalit dichotomy, 279
Dalit vote, division of, 270
Dalit voters
ideological leanings of, 40
preference for the BJP among, 5
Dalit voting patterns, 25
Dalit writings, 7
Dalit youth, flogging of, 25
Das, Shahad, 122
decision-making, 107
decomposition methods, 414–15, 417
'Deeksha Bhoomi' in Nagpur, 39
Defying the Odds (2014), 347–48
Delhi Police, 175
Delhi Police Act (1978), 182*n*26
Delimitation of Parliamentary and Assembly Constituencies Order (2008), 388*n*1
demand for SC status
exploring the, 402–3
factors fuelling, 406–7
Hukum Singh Committee's report on, 406
by most backward castes (MBCs), 396, 399–402
race against the bottom, 407
democracy, 8, 11, 78, 88, 98–99, 140, 142, 153, 197

democratic politics, 10, 78, 81, 85, 206
democratic revolution, 78–79
post-Ambedkar Dalit imagination of Bahujan collective, 239–40
Dalit Panthers, activism of, 237–39
democratic socialism, 233
DeNora, Tia, 117
Depressed Classes of Dalits, 219
deputy commissioner of police (DCP), 172
Dera movement, 8
*dera*s, 48
Desai, Morarji, 394
'Desam Kaappom' (Save the Nation) rallies, 249–50
Desiya Murpukku Dravida Kazhagam (DMDK), 91*n*10
developmental gap, among Dalits, 320–28
assets, 322–24
education, 324–25
health, 326
land, 321
poverty, 327–28
Devi, Phoolan, 144
Devi, Usha, 120
Dewey, John, 216
Dhale , Raja, 246*n*2
Dharmashastras, 318–19
dharna (demonstration), 176
Dhasal, Namdeo, 143, 246*n*2
Digital Dalits, 161
digital platforms, 292
Dilwale Dulhania Le Jayenge (1995), 136
division of labour, 216
Dom community, 145
'double marginalization' of Dalit women, 131*n*6
downtrodden masses, stories of, 288

Draupadi (film), 252
Dravida Munnetra Kazhagam (DMK),
    27, 29, 82–83, 249, 253
  'rising sun' election symbol, 90*n*4
Dravidar Kazhagam (DK), 249, 253
Dravidian Federation. *See* Dravidar
    Kazhagam (DK)
Dravidian governance, 252
Dravidian ideology, dilution of, 252
Dravidian parties, 89
  pre-poll coalitions, 91*n*10
Dr Babasaheb Ambedkar Marathwada
    University, 143
*Dr Babasaheb Ambedkar: The Untold
    Truth* (2000), 143
DS4 singers, ethnographic accounts of
  Bala, Poonam, 121–22
  Behalpuri, Harnam Singh, 122–24
  Gautam, Kasturi, 124–25
Dufflo, Esther, 13
Dunning, Thad, 364
Durkheim, Emile, 438
Dutt, Yashica, 286

ease of doing business, 212
economically weaker sections (EWS),
    15
economic downturn, 107
economic empowerment
  need for, 13
  via support to Dalit entrepreneurship,
    102
economic extraction, 221
economic inequality, 302
economic mobility, 1
economic reductionism, notion of, 216
economic reforms, 98–99, 341, 344,
    346
economic wealth, loss of, 320
economy of caste, 220–22

Edachira, Manju, 136
educated Dalits, 340
educational and job quotas, 15
education in India, dropout rate in, 325
election campaigns, financing of, 82
Election Commission of India (ECI),
    80
electoral bonds, 80–81
electoral democracy, idea of, 201
electoral mobilization, 178
  as a force against social change,
    348–50
  lower-caste, 341, 350
electoral politics, 4–7
electoral quota systems, 357
Eleventh Plan (2007–12), 62, 66
empowerment of Dalits, 153, 340
enslavement
  Anglo-Indian law on, 333
  brief history of, 317–20
  caste-based, 317
  enslaved sub-castes, 318
  harm argument, 333
  Hindu laws of, 320
  in India, 318
  inheritance argument, 333–34
  practice of, 317
  punishment for, 319
enslavers, liability of, 334
entrepreneurship, 14–15, 99, 102, 158,
    160, 303, 309, 341, 346–48
equality before law, notion of, 224
Equality Labs, 290, 295
ethnic outbidding, theories of, 178
ethno-political majoritarian index, 39
ethno-political majoritarianism, 39, 89
European Periyar Ambedkar Comrades'
    Federation, 247
exclusions, 56, 96, 101, 105, 151,
    160–62, 307

Explosives Research and Development Laboratory (ERDL), Pune, 199
Extremely Backward Classes (EBCs), 103, 408n4
ex-untouchable castes, 394
ex-untouchables, communities of, 194
'ex-untouchables' of India, 316

Fabian faith, 216
Facebook, 290–91, 297
Factories Act (1948), 213
false consciousness, prevalence of, 215
fanaticism, rise of, 104
Fandry (2013), 136
farmers' movement of 2017, 172
film-making, practices of, 136
Finnegan, Ruth, 117
first information reports (FIRs), on caste-based crimes, 416
First World Dalit Convention (1998), 201
Firth, Simon, 115
Five-Year Plan, 221
forced labour, 336n2
free-born Englishman, notion of, 224
Fuller, C. J., 254

Galanter, Marc, 360
Gandhi, Indira, 404
Gandhi, M. K., 87, 194
 Ambedkar's challenge to paternal and moralist appeal of, 235
 confrontation with Ambedkar, 139
 fast unto death opposing separate electorates for Dalits, 376
 hunger strike, 203
 opposition to the Communal Award granted by the British government, 235
 on welfare of untouchables, 235

Ganga and Yamuna expressways, 63–64
Gareeb Samaj Party, 402
 Nishad caste associated with, 404
Gaurakshaks, 158
Gautam, Devi Dayal, 105
Gautam, Kasturi, 124–25
Geetha, V., 252
Gehlot, Thawar Chand, 156
gender-based reservations, 365
gendered politics of caste, 252
general castes, 316
German Ideology (1846), 219
Ghaywan, Neeraj, 145, 288
Girard, Victoire, 368
Global Burden of Disease (GBD) study, 433
globalization, 2, 9, 12–13, 60, 273
#GoBackModi campaign, 249
Gorringe, Hugo, 87, 225n1
gotra, 97
Gotra and Puranic identity, 97
Government of India, 173
Government of India Act (1919), 388n3
Government of India Act (1935), 3, 394
government policies and programmes, 101
*gram panchayat*s (village councils), 63, 364
Green Revolution, 343
gross domestic product (GDP), 66
group identity, 415
Guha, Ramchandra, 157
Gujjars of Rajasthan
 conflict with the Meenas, 402
 demand for ST category, 402
Gupta, Dipankar, 224
Guru, Gopal, 137, 177, 233, 246n1
guru killi (master key), 240, 269

Haasan, Kamal, 251
  depiction of Godse as a Hindu
    terrorist, 251
Habib, Irfan, 221
Hall, Stuart, 115
Harad, Tejas, 292
Harvey, David, 225
hate crimes, Dalits as target of, 415
Hazare's hunger strike (2011), 182*n*24
Herzog, Hanna, 250
higher education, 82, 168
  gross enrolment ratio in, 325
high-income countries, 439
Hindi film industry, 136
Hindu–Muslim unity, 288
Hindu castes, social coalition of, 106
Hindu Code Bill, 143
Hindu consciousness, 245
Hindu Dharma, 247
Hindu enslavement, 320
Hindu Hindi Hindustan, 257
Hindu identity, 10, 61, 69, 96
Hindu Makkal Katchi (Hindu People's
    Party), 250
Hindu Munnani (Hindu Front), 250
Hindu–Muslim relationship, 135
Hindu nationalism
  construction of, 1
  Dalit community's views on, 39
  ethno-political majoritarian index, 39
Hindu political identity, 98
Hindu Rashtra, 257
Hindu religious affiliation, 245
Hindu religious and social code, 324
Hindu revivalist movements, 97
Hindu social laws, codification of, 96
Hindustan (Hindi newspaper), 153, 156
Hindutva, 5, 351
  Dalit–Bahujan movement and,
    271–73

ideology of cultural nationalism, 39
  localization of, 103
  mobilizing non-Jatav Dalits under,
    271
  myths to link Dalits to, 69
  non-Brahminical, 69
  social engineering, 243
  soft Hindutva, 254–57
  subaltern Hindutva, 61, 98
  sustainability of, 106
  VCK ideological challenge to, 257
Hindutva majoritarian politics, 214
Hindutva politics, rise of, 11
hissa (share), 205
hissedari, principle of, 205–6
Hnatkovskay, Viktoria, 417
Hobbes, Thomas, 332
honour killings, legislation against, 252
housing security schemes, 63
Htun, Mala, 358
Hukum Singh Committee (2001),
    405–7
Human Development Index, 66
human development, indicators of, 439
hyper-nationalism, use of, 71

identity and ideology, transformations
    in, 9–12
identity-based protests, 166
identity politics, 60
  based on the principle of *hissedari*, 205
Illavarasan, death of, 252
impure body, idea of, 398
inclusion, 2, 15–17, 61, 71, 96
  BJP's politics of, 68–69
  cultural, 73
  of minority groups in politics, 357
  in OBC category, 402
  religious, 273
  in SC category, 404

Independent Labour Party (ILP), 218, 236

India
Hindu character, reassertion of, 96
Majority Lower Castes Are Minor Voice in Newspapers (1996), 153
political elite, researching on, 196–97

India Against Corruption movement (2011), 172, 182*n*24

India Human Development Survey (IHDS), 328, 416, 420

Indian Administrative Service (IAS), 62, 406

Indian caste system, 194

Indian cultural reality, 199

Indian Institutes of Technology (IITs)
caste discrimination at, 291
reservation for SCs, STs, OBCs, 290, 385

Indian middle class, rise of, 12

Indian National Congress (INC), 4, 47, 81, 96, 156, 199, 270, 349
Dalit disenchantment with, 36
monopoly over Dalit votes, 25
social bases of, 270
working-class strike in the textile mills against the 'black bill' of, 218

Indian nationalism, 221

Indian nationalist hegemony, 257

Indian Penal Code (IPC), 340

Indian Police Service (IPS), 406

Indian social structure, analysis of, 134

Indian working class, making of, 222

IndiaSpend, 379

indigenous communities, protests of, 166

Indira Awas Yojana (IAY), 63

inequality, 14, 51, 169, 179, 215, 247, 257, 302

information society, 161

Ingole, Prashant, 288

Inside Edge (Amazon Prime, 2017), 289

Instagram, 297

institutional politics, failure of, 171

inter-caste coalition-building, 364

inter-caste differences, in vote choice, 34

inter-caste marriage, 136, 288, 328

inter-caste relationship, 143

intercaste restrictions, 222

inter-caste tensions, 421–24

inter-group tensions, across Indian states, 17

'internal colonialism' of caste oppression, 221

internal ideological conflicts, 239

internet, 12–14, 161, 286–88, 291, 293, 295

iron law of oligarchy, 196

jaati maruppu thirumanam, 252

Jaffrelot, Christophe, 78, 117, 131*n*2

Jai Bhim Comrade (2011), 140

Jaitley, Arun, 158

jajmani system, 108*n*1, 406
breakdown of, 99

jalsa, 139

Jammu and Kashmir, removal of special status of, 257

Janata Dal, 211

Jan Dhan Yojana, 5

Jantar Mantar (New Delhi), protest activity at, 167, 171, 172–77
caste-based protests, 173–75
data on, 172–73
descriptive analysis of, 173–77
Hazare's hunger strike (2011), 182*n*24
lessons learned from, 177–79
limits of, 179

Nirbhaya protests (2012), 182*n*24
on-site protest-event, 177
policing of, 179
protest demands, 176–77
size and tactics of Dalit protests, 175–76
Jatavs, 61, 68, 71
Jatav–Yadav–Muslim votes, 244
jati-biradari (own caste), 269
jati identity, 204
*jati*s, 180*n*8, 205, 318, 320, 396
Jat Sikhs, 198
Jawahar Rozgar Yojana (JRY), 63
Jayalalithaa, Jayaram, 249
Jayal, Niraja Gopal, 2
Jehanabad and Narayanpura massacres, 154
Jensenius, Francesca, 15
Jinnah, M. A., 87
job losses, among Dalits, 107
job market, discrimination in, 328
job opportunities, for DBA communities, 288
under British rule, 308
getting around gatekeepers, 288–90
unequal industry and, 290–91
job quotas, 345. *See also* reservation for Dalits
of government jobs, 346
group-based, 358
Jodhka, Surinder S., 345, 427
Jogdand, P. G., 310
journalism jobs, within Dalit communities, 287
Juergensmeyer, Mark, 46

Kaala (2018), 142
Kabali (2016), 142
Kabir *panth*, 144, 275
Kabir *panthi*, 276

Kaka Kalelkar Commission (1953), 221
Kalelkar, Kaka, 394, 398
Kamble, Maya, 291
Kanshi Ram Sahari Gareeb Awaas Yojana (KSGAY), 63
Kanwar *yatra* (journey), 105
Kapoor, Sacha, 362
Kapur, Shekhar, 144
Kardak, Bhimrao, 139
karma, 199
Karpoori Thakur formula, 103
Karthik, Vignesh, 250
Karunanidhi, Muthuvel, 249
Karunanithi, Jeyannathann, 250
Khabar Leharia (newspaper), 161
Khairlanji atrocity (29 September 2006), 140
Khambir Pidhi, 142
Kharat, Kadubai, 141
Kosambi, Damodar Dharmananda, 217
Kovind, Ram Nath, 10, 39
Kshatriyas, Harijans, Adivasis, and Muslims (KHAM), 349
Kulkarni, Damini, 143
Kumar, Arun, 322
Kumar, Ashok, 118
Kumari, Saroj, 118
Kumar, Raghvendra, 399
Kumar, Vivek, 195
Kurmis of Jharkhand and West Bengal, 402
Kushwaha, Babu Singh, 67

labourers, division of, 216
labour law reforms, 212
labour theory of caste, 217
Lahiri, Amartya, 417
Lancet Commission, 317
land ownership, inequalities in, 321
land reforms, policy of, 321

Law Commission of India, 320
leadership. *See* Dalit leadership
lead news items on Dalit issues,
     analysis of
  Ambedkar's 125th birth anniversary
     and death anniversary, 157
  engagement of political parties with
     the Dalit electorate, 158
  loans for Dalit entrepreneurs, 158
  Una flogging, 157
Lee, Alexander, 178
Left Front, 27, 51, 211
legal rights, protection of, 214
Legislative Assembly, 376, 404
liberal democracy, 11
  and Dalits, 232–34
Liberation Panthers Party. *See* Viduthalai
     Chiruthaigal Katchi (VCK)
lived experiences, 138
local area development (LAD) schemes,
     379
Lok Janshakti Party (LJP), 29
Lokniti-CSDS, 26, 33, 36, 213
Lok Sabha, 154, 361
  Dalit legislators' interventions in, 379
  elections, 25, 26, 67, 80, 156, 236,
     269
  findings for, 384–85
  Question Hour, 376, 378, 379–80,
     386
  Rules of Procedure of, 386
loktantra (democracy), 166
love jihad, claims of, 251
low-and-middle-income countries
     (LMICs), 433
low-caste identity, consciousness of, 7
lower-caste communities, 174, 242
  upward mobility of, 308
lower-caste political mobilization, 341,
     350

Macaulay, T. B., 351n2
Madison, James, 378
Magesan, Arvind, 362
Mahagathbandhan (Grand Alliance)
     politics, 71, 277, 281n2
Mahamaya Awas Yojana (MAY), 63
Mahamaya Garib Balika Ashirvad
     Yojana, 63
Mahamaya Sarva Awas Yojana (MSAY),
     63
Mahaparinirvan Sthal, Delhi, 39
Mahar-caste leadership, 238
Mahars of Maharashtra, 97, 105, 138,
     243–44
Mahatma Gandhi National Rural
     Employment Guarantee Scheme
     (MNREGS), 63
majoritarianism, 5, 39, 42, 71, 89
Mallah community, 144, 399–402
Mandal, B. P., 394
Mandal Commission report (1990),
     134, 171, 394, 397, 399
  recommendations of, 177
Mandal, Jogendranath, 50
Manikandan, C., 249
Manjule, Nagraj, 136
manual and menial jobs, 213
Manusmriti, 251, 320
  code of conduct, 140, 143
manuvadi, 60
Manyawar Shri Kanshiram Ji Green Eco
     Garden, 66
Maratha–Kunbi landholders, 143
Marathi cinematic industry, 136
Marathi film industry, 136
marginalized communities, 235, 237,
     290, 306
  democracy's relationship with, 232
  empowering of, 397
market-based economy, emergence of, 406

Marshall, Alfred, 342
Marshall, Thomas H., 341
Marumalarchi Dravida Munnetra
      Kazhagam (MDMK), 91n10
Marxism, 200
Marxist economics, 219
Marx, Karl, 215, 217, 225
   labour theory of caste, 217
   revolutionary philosophy of, 238
Masaan (2015), 145–46
Mata Shabari temple, 69
matrimony, 296
Matua Mahasangha, 54
Maurya, Keshav Prasad, 70
Maurya, Rakesh K., 440
Mayawati, 7, 30, 59, 121, 154–55, 195,
      268, 272, 274, 279, 395, 399
   bua–bhatija (aunt–nephew)
      relationship, 277
   handling of Dalit–Bahujan youth
      leaders, 277
   inauguration of Noida Metro, 66
   leadership of, 156
   loss of popularity of, 5
   popularity among Dalits, 33
   Sarvajan strategy, 62–66
   style of political campaigning, 34
member of the legislative council
      (MLC), 108n10
members of legislative assemblies
      (MLAs), 53, 357, 376
members of parliament (MPs), 357, 376
memorandum, presentation of, 176
Mendelsohn, Oliver, 86
Mevani, Jignesh, 3, 11, 292
micro, small, and medium enterprises
      (MSMEs), 385
middle class Dalits. *See* Dalit middle
      class (DMC)
migration, 46, 52, 71, 98, 107, 310

Mills, C. Wright, 196
Mines, Mattison, 197
minority representation, 79, 85, 87, 89
minority stress, 439
Mirzapur (Amazon Prime, 2018), 289
Mishra, S. C., 67
Mission Geet, 117, 124–25
MLALAD scheme, 379
modern citizenship, notion of, 199
Modi, Narendra, 1, 4, 25, 29, 59, 100,
      103–4, 240, 274
   appointment of the third backward-
      classes commission, 395
   caste-wise distribution of preference
      for, 38
   emergence of, 153
   as follower of B. R. Ambedkar, 39
   Gujarat model, 68
   leadership and the delivery of welfare
      benefits, 37
   mechanism of public service delivery
      and welfare schemes, 102
   mobilizational strategies, 68
   New Welfarism of the Right, 71
   personal popularity of, 5
   rise of, 96
   'Stand-up India' scheme, 39
   transforming of Dalit communities
      into aspirational communities,
      273
   victory in the 2014 national elections,
      211
   visit in 2018 to 'Boro Ma', 54
Mohan, P. Sanal, 318–19
'money power' in elections, implications
      of, 82, 84
Mood of the Nation (MotN) survey
      (2018), 36, 71
moolnivasi, 99
moral corruption, 86

Mosca, Gaetano, 196
Moss, David, 221
most backward castes (MBCs), 17, 30,
    272–73, 349, 395
  concept of, 399
  demand for SC status, 396, 399–402
    exploring the, 402–3
    factors fuelling, 406–7
  genealogy of, 396, 398–99
  hierarchy in Indian society, 396
  in north Indian states, 407
  in public institutions, 407
  sense of
    powerlessness and anxiety, 407
    status inequality, 406
  socio-economic conditions of, 396,
    407
  traditional occupation and social
    status of, 401
'MP and MLA Track' database, 376
Mr. and Mrs. Iyer (2002), 136
mukhiya (village headman), 124
Mukta (1994), 143
Mungeri Lal Commission (1971), 398
murders. *See* caste-based murders,
    targeting Dalits
Murugan, L., 251
Musahars, 69
muscular nationalism, 5
Muslim League, 388*n*3
Muslims, 238
  as political enemy of BJP, 244
  poor Muslims, idea of, 278
Muzaffarnagar riots, 272

nabhi-nal (umbilical cord) relationship,
    280
Nacdor.org, 161
nadaka kaathal (staged love or love
    jihad), 251

Nadda, J. P., 259
Naik, L. R., 399
Naik, Ram, 157
Namasudras, 6, 50, 52, 56
Namasudra votes, 29
Narayanan, K. R., 154
Narayan, Badri, 198
National Commission for Scheduled
    Castes (NCSC), 251
National Crime Records Bureau (NCRB),
    16, 226*n*8, 418, 420, 434
National Democratic Alliance (NDA),
    29, 74*n*9, 212
  voting percentage, 240
National Education Policy (NEP), 255
National Election Studies (NES), 25–26
  2004 survey, 213
National Family Health Survey
    (NFHS), 326
National Green Tribunal, 182*n*27
National Investigation Agency (NIA),
    255
Nationalist Congress Party (NCP), 240
national political leadership, 155
National Population Register (CAA–
    NRC–NPR), 250
National Register of Citizens, 250
National Rural Employment Guarantee
    Act (NREGA), 259
National Sample Survey (NSS), 417
National Sample Survey Office
    (NSSO), 322
National SC–ST–OBC Student and
    Youth Front, 174
National Security Act (NSA), 256
National Thermal Power Corporation
    (NTPC), 66
nation-building process, 232, 236
Nehruvian patronage system,
    beneficiaries of, 98

Nehruvian secularism, decline of, 6, 96
neo-Buddhist puritanism, 104
neoliberal reforms, 222
neo-middle class, 98
Netflix, 289
net state domestic product (NSDP), 66
new class of Hindu castes, 98
new millennium, 1–4, 13, 15, 59, 346
Newslaundry–Oxfam study (2019), 285
newspapers, 9, 80, 133, 150, 152–61
newsrooms, 159, 160, 286
  representation in, 151–52
New Welfarism of the Right, 71
New York Tribune essays (1853), 219
Nigam, Aditya, 345
Nilekani, Janhavi, 364
Nirbhaya protests (2012), 172, 182n24
nirgun bhakti, 101
Nishads, 69
Nisha, Jyoti, 137
Noida Metro, 66
non-Brahminical Hindutva, ideology
  of, 69
non-Dalit parties, 59
non-governmental organizations
  (NGOs), 54, 274
non-hate crimes, 416
non-linear employment decomposition
  analysis, 330
non-Mahar Dalits, 238
non-peripheral castes, 105–6

occupational diversity and mobility of
  Dalits, 344
occupational mobility, of Dalits, 310
occupations and professions, 303,
  305–6, 308
old social order, decline of, 406
Omvedt, Gail, 218, 248
'One Nation, One Culture', 257

'One Rank One Pension' (OROP)
  protests (2015–16), 172, 182n24
online matchmaking platforms, 296
  caste in, 296–99
oppressed castes, solidarity of, 213
oppressed communities, 238
oppression and exploitation, of Dalits,
  214–15
organizational leadership, 100
Other Backward Classes (OBCs),
  11, 30, 53, 67, 90n1, 96, 103,
  130n1, 134, 211, 235, 270, 316,
  386, 394, 439
  exclusion of 'creamy layer' from
    reservations, 256
  sub-categorization under Hukum
    Singh Committee, 400
  VCK's approach towards, 256
oversight, 16, 376, 378, 379

Pal, Anand, 177
panchayat (local village council)
  elections, 272
panchayati raj system, 363, 385
  elections, 67, 361
panchteerth (five holy places), 39
Pandian, Punitha, 258
pan-Indian Dalit discourse, 3
*panna pramukh*s, 101, 108n6
Pareto, Vilfredo, 196
Pasis, 60, 67, 69, 105, 272
Paswan, Ram Vilas, 29, 350
Paswan, Sanjay, 102
Pataal Lok (Amazon Prime, 2020), 289
Patel, Sone Lal, 274
Pattali Makkal Katchi (PMK), 91n10,
  252
Patwardhan, Anand, 140
Paul, Sourabh, 417
Pearson correlation matrix, 421

peripheral castes, 105–6
'Periyar and Indian Politics' webinar, 247
Periyarist Karuppar Kootam (Black Collective), 255
persecuted minorities, empowerment of, 350
personal and familial belief systems, 328
Phule, Jyotirao, 202, 225, 275
Planning Commission, 62
political awakening, 156
political citizenship, rights of, 374
political competition, effect of political reservations on, 362
political consciousness and development, 271
political economy, emergence of, 1
political elite class, 15, 72, 78, 193, 195, 196–97, 204
political favours for campaign finance, exchange of, 81
political institutions, 358, 366, 368, 374
political language, crisis of, 274–76
political leadership, 270
political marginalization, among Dalits, 205
political power, acquisition of, 201
political reservation in India, brief history of, 375–76
political reservations for SCs, effects of, 358, 360–69
  for an SC *sarpanch*, 367
  impact on
    caste-related attitudes and behaviour, 367–69
    developmental outcomes, 364–66
    political and electoral patterns, 361–62
    political competition, 362
    state–citizen relations, 366–67

incentives for inter-caste coalition-building, 364
observations and recommendations, 386–87
pros and cons of, 364
spill-over effects, 362–64
political transformation, 49, 237
politics of power, 270
politics of unfreedom, 102
Poona Pact, 202–3, 235, 376
poor Muslims, idea of, 278
popular culture, 3, 7–9, 115–16, 133, 292
portrayal of Dalits, in the media
  analysis of lead news items on Ambedkar's 125th birth anniversary and death anniversary, 157
  engagement of political parties with the Dalit electorate, 158
  loans for Dalit entrepreneurs, 158
  Una flogging, 157
coverage of Dalit issues, 152–55
economic issues, 153, 160
editorials exploring Dalit issues, 159
emergence of Dalit alternative media, 160–62
issue of reservation in jobs for Dalits, 154
news of atrocities against Dalits, 155
representation in the newsrooms, 151–52
select newspapers
  case study of, 155–56
  inferences from the content analysis of, 158–60
post-Ambedkar Dalit movement, 194
post-Mandal politics, 213
Poverty of Philosophy (1847), 219
power brokers, 233

Pradhan Mantri Awas Yojana, 5, 72
Pradhan Mantri Mudra Yojana
        (PMMY), 102, 160
Pradhan Mantri Ujjwala Yojana, 72
Prajapati, Gayatri Prasad, 402, 404
Prakash, Aseem, 347
Prakash, Nishith, 365
Prakash, Ved, 285
  news channel on YouTube, 286
Prasad, Chandra Bhan, 222
prime minister, preference among
        different caste groups, 37
private-job-market hiring, 329
private sector, rise of, 18
Project Anti-Caste Love, 297
proletariat class, Marxist identity of, 238
Protection of Civil Rights Act (1955),
        15, 416, 419
protest data, 177–78, 181n20
protest demands, 167, 170, 173,
        176–77, 179
protest-event-analysis (PEA), 172
protest policing, 178
protest politics
  for an identity group, 168–69
  caste-based protest activity of Dalits,
        170
  comparative study of, 169–71
  Dalit and upper-caste protest
        activities, 178
  gap between Dalit and upper-caste
        protest activities, 178
  hierarchy and, 171–72
  lessons learned from, 177–79
  policing of, 178
protest site, 9, 167, 170, 172, 180n6
protest tactics, 176, 179
public employment, in India, 107
public-private partnership (PPP), 66,
        74n4

public-sector employment, 15
public-sector organization, 200
Pulayas, 318
Pulwama terror attack (2019), 71,
        74n9, 177
Punjab
  Balmikis of, 48
  Dalit political history in, 46–50
  decline of Bahujan Samaj Party (BSP)
        in, 47–48
  Mazhabhis of, 48
  SC population of, 49
'Punjabi Khatri caste' culture, 135

Question Hour, 376, 378, 379–80, 386
quota, policy of, 222. See also job quotas
  and caste-based reservations, 358
  group-based, 358

racial oppression, 214
radical Dalit political assertion, 45
radical social reforms, 234
Raja, H., 251–52
Rajamani, Rajesh, 138
Rajbanshis, 6, 52, 56
Rajbhar, Doodhnath, 404
Rajbhar, Pancham, 409n15
Rajbhar, Sukhdev Singh, 62
Raj, Udit, 157
Ramabai Nagar massacre (11 July
        1997), 140
Ramaswamy, Periyar E.V., 202
Ram, Babu Jagjivan, 39, 103, 105
Ramdasia Sikhs, 198, 203
Ram Janmabhoomi (Birthplace of Ram)
        movement, 96, 100–01
Ram, Kanshi, 7, 10, 11, 12, 30, 32, 47,
        103, 115, 116, 119, 121, 124,
        130n1, 193, 275
  approach to politics, 201

Bahujan politics formulated by, 273
bahujan samaj, 268
birth of, 198
on caste-democracy relationship, 195
The Chamcha Age: An Era of the Stooges (1982), 270
Dalit political agenda, 193
as face of Dalit assertion in all of north India, 194
as leader in post-Ambedkar Dalit movement, 194
legacy of, 203–6
life trajectory compared to Ambedkar's, 194
making of, 197–99
moving beyond Dalit-ness, 201–3
poor Muslims, idea of, 278
speech at the Ram Navami fair, 276
ranked ethnic systems, 178
Ranvir Sena, 153–54, 425, 428
attacks on Dalits in Bihar, 153
upper-caste, 154
Rao, Anupama, 216
Rashtriya Janata Dal (RJD), 211, 244, 350
Rashtriya Lok Dal (RLD), 70
Rashtriya Nishad Ekta Parishad, 402
Rashtriya Sahara (Hindi newspaper), 153–54, 157, 163n3
Rashtriya Swayamsevak Sangh (RSS), 7, 37, 53, 102, 271
L. K. Advani's *rath yatra*, 247
Sangh Parivar, 250, 259n3, 272, 281n1
samrastabhoj (community meals), 272
samrasta (harmony) programmes, 272
samskaras (ceremonies or rites), 97
shakhas (sessions), 272
Ratan, Ravi, 135
Ravidas Jatavs, 270
Ravidassia music, 116, 117, 131n3

R. Chitralekha and Anr v. State of Mysore and Ors, 408n3
Reddy, Sudhakar, 250
Rege, Sharmila, 131n6, 140
Registration of Births and Deaths Act (1969), 434
religious conservatism, 39
religious denominations, 322
religious minorities, 204, 235
religious pilgrimage, 146
reparations
economic, 335
philosophical arguments for, 331–32
reparation commission, 335
spiritual renewal argument for, 334–35
views of John Locke on, 332–33
Republican Party of India (Athawale) (RPI[A]), 29
Republican Party of India (RPI), 9, 46, 182n29, 199–200, 237, 269
political activism in Maharashtra, 237
Republic of Caste, 219
reservation for Dalits, 15, 307, 357
brief history of, 375–76
goal of, 374
in Indian Institutes of Technology (IITs), 290
in institutions of higher education, 324
in jobs, 154, 273
origin of, 359–60
reservation policies
abolition of, 177
implementation of, 176
reservation-related demands, 176
reserved constituencies, in India, 30
reserved seats, 15, 29, 86–87, 103, 105, 359, 361–62, 374–76
resistance, 3, 9, 11, 37, 118

resource mobilisation, process of, 310
reverse migration, issue of, 107
Right to Information (RTI) Act (2005),
    180n12, 435
right-wing caste outfits, caste-sustaining
    ideology of, 252
right-wing politics, 242
ritual hierarchy, notion of, 198
Robinson, James A., 348
Rohini, G., 395
Round Table Conferences (1930–32),
    375
Roundtable India, 161
rule-based society, 340
rule of law, 406
rural infrastructural programmes, 63
rural-to-urban migration, 98

Sachan, Rajeev, 159
sadhe satiya, 105
sagun bhakti, 101
Sairat (2016), 136
samajiksamrasta (social harmony)
    campaign, 271
'Samajik Samvad' campaign, 102,
    108n11
Samajwadi Party (SP), 30, 60, 70, 103,
    156, 211, 244, 350
    Samajik Nyay Adhikar Yatras, 409n14
Sambara, Kewal, 120
Sample Registration System (SRS), 434
Samyak Bharat, 161
Sanatana Dharma, 248, 253
    agenda of *samajik samrasta*, 273
    and the Panthers, 250–52
Sankhya school of Indian philosophy,
    409n10
Sanskritization, impact of, 405
Sanskritized Dalits, 96
Saradamoni, K., 318–19

sarvajan, 268
    challenge of inclusive development,
        62–66
    Sarvajan alliance, 59
    sarvajan politics, 270–71
Sathi, Chhedi Lal, 399
Sathi Commission (1977), 399
Satnaami Panth, 275
Satyashodhak Communist Party, 225
Saubhagya Yojana, 5
*savarna*s (upper castes), 105, 318, 328
    gaze, 144
    mindsets and discrimination against
        Dalits, 328–30
*Savitri Bai Phule Balika Shiksha Madad
    Yojana*, 63
Scheduled Caste (SC), 15, 47, 130n1,
    134, 198, 250, 270, 343, 394
    data on crimes against members of, 420
    literacy rates of, 48
    murders of members of, 422
    as political ammunition against caste-
        based oppression, 396
    political reservations for, 357
    poverty of, 327–28
    programmes for the upliftment of,
        309
    in Punjab, 49
    reservation policy for, 232
        effects of, 360–69
    social identity of, 275
    welfare of, 63
Scheduled Castes and Scheduled Tribes
    (Prevention of Atrocities) Act
    (1989), 15–16, 25, 70, 86, 100,
    106, 159, 170, 309, 343, 385,
    407, 416, 419, 427
    Dalit unrest over dilution of, 106
    Supreme Court of India's decision to
        weaken the provisions of, 36

Scheduled Caste Special Component Plan, 63
Scheduled Tribes (STs), 16, 130n1, 134, 221, 270, 326, 343, 394, 418
programmes for the upliftment of, 309
reservation policy for, 232
as *sarkari damad*, 397
welfare of, 63
SC–ST Teachers Front, 174
secular citizenship, idea of, 245
self-esteem, 268
self-identity, 2, 10
self-mobilization of caste groups, 168
self-respect marriages, 252
Self-Respect Movement, 2, 8, 13, 59–60, 72, 134, 252, 276, 288, 358
sense of self, 397
separate electorates, 86–87, 201–3, 235, 369–70, 375, 387
separation of powers, principle of, 378
sevadar castes, 105
sevakarya (social service), 273
Shaadi.com, 296
Shah, Amit, 100–01, 103
*shakha*s, 53
Shakti Kendra, 101
Sharma, B. D., 425
Sharma, Neeru, 46, 48
Sharma, Smriti, 415
Shastri, Bhola Paswan, 398
Shekhawat doctrine, 103
Shepherd, Ilaiah, 224
Shinde, Rashi, 294
Shiv Sena, 240–41
short-video platforms, 294
Shudras, 317, 319, 324
Siddharth, Jyotsna, 297

Siddique, Zahra, 418
Siddiqui, Naseemuddin, 67
Sikh ideology, 198
silent revolution, 78
Simon Commission (1927), 375
Singh, Charan, 404
Singh, Hukum, 399
Singh, I. P., 47
Singh, Manmohan, 443
Singh, Nirmal, 48
Singh, Pritam, 46
Singh, Rajnath, 273
Singh, Santosh K., 49
Singh, V. P., 404
Singh, Yogendra, 197
Sinha, Anubhav, 136
Sivagnanam, Sujatha, 248
slave trade, transatlantic, 336n2
Snack, 294
snowballing, technique of, 131n9
Social Attitudes Survey, India (SARI), 328
social capital, 304
Dalit identity as, 309–11
process of formation of, 310
social change, 49, 194, 197, 206, 220, 258, 303, 309, 312, 347
social citizenship, 341
social coalitions, 174, 349
social consciousness, 307
social democracy, 140, 142
social deprivation, self-awareness of, 205
social discrimination, 235
social engineering, 31, 37, 270
BJP's strategy, 38, 96–97, 102
social identity, caste-based, 440
social inequalities, 214, 257
social isolation, 317
socialist revolution, 196

social justice, 2, 51, 70, 125, 160, 179, 215, 244, 252, 256, 306, 349, 419
  Bahujan struggle for, 121
  caste-based, 103
  politics of, 99, 103, 242
social justice committee, formation of, 399
socially marginalized groups, 244
socially marginalized people, politics of, 234
social media, 133, 161
  Black Lives Matter campaign, 292
  political mobilization on, 291–94
  transformative power of, 291
social mobility, beneficiaries of, 273
social order, of Hindu society, 407
social reforms, for annihilation of castes, 217
social revolution, class as a universal agent for, 219
social torture, 252
social welfare, 63
sociocultural–political consciousness, 8
Socio-Economic and Caste Census (SECC), 181n21
Socio-Economic Caste Census (2011), 102
socio-economic development, 79
socio-economic matrix, 213
socio-economic mobility, 99, 106, 305
  among Dalits, 302
socio-economic progress, indicators of, 12
socio-economic well-being, 316
sociopolitical empowerment, 13
socio-religious reforms, 216
Sooryavansham (1999), 136
Soundarajan, Tamilisai, 251
Southborough Commission (1919), 375

Spearman correlation rank, 421
Special Area Incentive Package, 62
Special Component Plan (SCP) (1979), 309
special development packages, 311
Sridharan, Eswaran, 249
Srinivas, M. N., 308
Stalin, M. K., 250
standards of living, 343
'Stand-up India' scheme, 39
  to promote entrepreneurship among Dalits, 158, 160
state bureaucracy, 85
subaltern Hindutva, phenomenon of, 61, 98
sub-caste identity, 69
sub-castes, in India, 293
Subramanian, Ajantha, 290
Subramanian, Narendra, 259
Suheldev, Maharaja, 103
suicides, cases of, 16, 169–70, 286. See also Dalit suicides, incidence of
  in India, 433
  socio-demographic factors influencing, 433–34
Sunday Times, 296
Supreme Court of India, 172
Surya, Tejasvi, 102, 108n9
suvarnas (upper castes), 202. See also savarnas

Tadvi, Payal, 16
Tamil-linguistic nationalism, 89, 248
Tamil nationalism, 89, 254, 257
Tanwar, Ashok, 156
tech industry, 291
Telangana Mass and Social Organisations (T-MASS), 224
Telangana Rashtra Samithi (TRS), 29
Telegu Desam Party (TDP), 29

Teltumbde, Anand, 210, 255
Telugu cinema, 8
thakara plant (*Senna tora*), 319
Thakur, Arvind Kumar, 291
Thakur, Karpoori, 399
The Chamcha Age (1982), 202–03
The Discreet Charm of the Savarnas
    (2020), 138, 144–45
The Hindu, 142, 288
The Narrow Corridor (2019), 348
The Pioneer, 153
Third Front, 240
Third Round Table Conference (1932),
    London, 235
Third World countries, 222
Thirumavalavan, Thol., 247–48, 250,
    252–53, 256
    arrest for a speech on Hindu temples,
        251
    criticism of Gandhi's views on
        Hinduism, 251
Thompson, E. P., 222
Thorat report, 443
TikTok, 294
Times of India, 47, 345
transfer of power, 50, 78
Trehan, Prerna, 49
tribal communities, 394
tribal stigma, 397
Truly Madly, 296
trust-deficit syndrome, in Dalit politics,
    242, 243–45
tumbi, 120
"twice-born" Hindus, 135
Twitter, 288

Ujjwala scheme, 5
Una cow-vigilantism incident, in
    Gujarat (2016), 70
Una Dalit Atyachar Samiti, 3

Una flogging case (2016), 157
underrepresentation of Dalits, in
    businesses, 347
unfreedom, politics of, 102
unified payments interface (UPI), 39
unique identification number (UID),
    18*n*1
United Progressive Alliance (UPA), 29,
    62, 240
United Spectrum of Hindu Votes
    (USHV), 97, 101
universal adult franchise, 376, 406
Uniyal, B. N., 153
Unlawful Activities (Prevention) Act
    (UAPA) (1967), 255
untouchability
    and caste-based discrimination, 420
    practice of, 18, 316, 375, 396, 406,
        414
        by rural households belonging to a
            higher caste, 420
    as source of stigmatization of castes,
        396
    stigma of, 396, 404, 406–7
        consequences of, 396–98
    survey declarations on, 420
    Untouchability Offence Act (1955),
        15
    victims of, 420, 423
UP Anti-Terrorism Act (2007), 66
upliftment of Dalits, 340
upper-backward classes, 398
upper-caste Hindus, gross enrolment
    ratio of, 325
upper castes (UCs), 173, 288, 305, 308
    caste-based protests of, 177
        Dalit protests *versus*, 177
    domination of, 210
    protest against, 7
    harassment of, 155

hegemonic consciousness, 135
non-reservation related protests, 177
reservation-related demands, 176
resource advantage, 177
*savarna*s, 105, 318, 328
voters, 203
upper-caste violence, Dalit resistance to,
424–26
ur (caste settlements), 92*n*17
urban development, 63
urban employment markets, 417
Uttar Pradesh (UP) legislative assembly,
376, 404
findings for, 385–86
Uttar Pradesh Mukhyamantri
Mahamaya Garib Aarthik Madad
Yojana, 63

Vajpayee, Atal Bihari, 68
Vajpayee government, 153
fall of, 154
Valmikis, 270
value added tax (VAT), 74*n*4
Vanchit Bahujan Aghadi (VBA), 3
Dalit politics, 241
under the leadership of Prakash
Ambedkar, 240
vote share in the 2019 Lok Sabha
elections, 240–41
Vanchit castes, 241
Vanchit, idea of, 237, 240–42, 245
Vanchit Vani (newspaper), 161
Vani, B. P., 417
vamsa (clan name), 97
Varnashrama Dharma, 256
varna system, 9
Veeramani, Krishnasamy, 253
Velivada.org, 161
Vemula, Rohith, 16, 36, 70, 106, 169,
286, 440

Venkatraman, Shriram, 295
Verma, Rahul, 5, 71
Vicziany, Maria, 86
Viduthalai Chiruthaigal Katchi (VCK),
6, 11–12, 79, 85, 90*n*2, 247,
249–50, 256
alignment with the DMK, 255
approach towards the OBCs, 256
Conference on Land Rights (17 June
2007), 92*n*19
embrace of Tamil Nationalism, 257
emergence of, 240
engagement with Ambedkar, Periyar,
and Marx, 258
entry into party politics, 257
Hindu card, 255
ideological challenge to Hindutva, 257
as the ideological heir of Periyar,
252–54
nouveau riche, 91*n*13
opposition to RSS, 247
as political heavy-weight in Tamil
Nadu, 248–49
portrayal as a Periyarist party, 253
protests against caste atrocities and
national policies, 255
slogan of uprooting Hindutva, 247
virality, right to, 294–96
vote banks, 89, 271
vote shares, for independent candidates,
362
vote swings, constituency-level, 32
voting patterns, among Dalits, 26–30
in the 2009 Lok Sabha elections, 26,
28
in the 2014 Lok Sabha elections, 26, 28
in the 2019 Lok Sabha elections, 29
shift towards Aam Aadmi Party
(AAP), 27
Vrindavan convention (2017), 271

Washington Post, 153
Wasnik, Mukul, 156
welfare schemes, 100–02
West Bengal
    constitutional rights of Dalits in, 51
    Dalit political leadership in, 53
    Dalit politics in, 50–55
    Namasudras of, 52
    party-society of, 51
    political life of, 50
    rehabilitation of all Dalit migrants
        from East Bengal in, 50
    rise of BJP in, 4, 53
    upper-caste leadership in, 50
WhatsApp, 291
white collar jobs, 213
worker–peasant party, 218
working class
    consciousness, 223

making of, 223
organizations, 212
strike in the textile mills, 218
Wright, Erik Olin, 214
Wyatt, Andrew, 249

Yadav, Akhilesh, 395, 399
    Rath Yatra by, 402
Yadav, Mulayam Singh, 30, 395,
    399
yagna (ritual sacrifice), 97
Yechury, Sitaram, 250
Yengde, Suraj, 135–36
YouTube, 286–87, 289
Yuvajana Shramika Rythu (YSR)
    Congress Party, 28–29

zaat-biradari (kinship cluster), 193
Ziegfeld, Adam, 362